Franklin D. Roosevelt and Foreign Affairs

VOLUME II: MARCH 1934–AUGUST 1935

Roosevelt in Washington. February 1935.

Franklin D. Roosevelt and Foreign Affairs

VOLUME II: MARCH 1934–AUGUST 1935

Edited by Edgar B. Nixon

Franklin D. Roosevelt Library

HYDE PARK, NEW YORK

The Belknap Press of Harvard University Press

Cambridge, Massachusetts   1969

Franklin D. Roosevelt and Foreign Affairs, an annotated collection of documents, will ultimately cover all of Roosevelt's terms as President. The first three volumes, being published simultaneously in 1969, cover the first term, 1933 to 1937. The documents are drawn from the Roosevelt papers in the Franklin D. Roosevelt Library, Hyde Park, New York.

Editorial Method

Annotation of the text is confined to identification of persons and explanation of events mentioned; there is no attempt to provide a narrative of the events of the period. It is assumed that users of the volumes will be familiar with the general history of the years covered. However, every effort has been made to explain in the notes obscure or incomplete references. Significant items not printed are cited to source and briefly described. Cross references to related documents "above" and "below" are provided, and running heads give dates of documents on the page for easy location of cross references. Enclosures are printed directly below a document, and when not reprinted their presence or absence in the Roosevelt papers is noted.

Texts are reproduced verbatim except that obvious typist's errors were corrected. Where letters are handwritten all eccentricities of spelling and punctuation are retained. Crossed-out words are printed with a line through them and words substituted for the crossed-out words are in italics. All parenthetical words in the press conference transcripts are by the reporter unless otherwise noted. Uniform style is used in rendering headings, salutations, closes, and signatures. Annotations on the document are reproduced, with a descriptive symbol (explained in the list following) and indication, when possible, of authorship. Marguerite LeHand, private secretary to President Roosevelt, is the LeHand who appears frequently on such notations. When it is apparent that a letter or other document was drafted for the President's signature, either the name of the drafter or that of the department in which it originated is indicated. Explanatory words inserted in the text by the editor appear in italics in brackets.

The different kinds of texts of President Roosevelt's speeches and messages to Congress are indicated in the notes. They may be drafts, the final copy or reading copy, the press release of the final copy, the stenographic transcript, or in the case of speeches a recording of the radio broadcast. The broadcast recording is used as the text when available and differences between this and other texts are noted.

The citation in brackets at the end of each document gives the particular section of the White House files in which the document is located, the subfile, and a descriptive symbol. These designations are explained in the list of abbreviations below. (The Roosevelt Library has in large part retained the White House filing system.) The documents printed are from the Roosevelt papers in the Library (the White House papers) or, in the case of one or two items, Group 14, Roosevelt family papers, or from their collections acquired by the Library. Of the latter, several items are from the papers of R. Walton Moore, Assistant Secretary of State and Counselor to the State Department, 1933–1937. Other collections in the Library from which a few items have been selected for publication are the papers of Louis McHenry Howe, President Roosevelt's personal secretary until his death in 1936, and the papers of Rear Admiral Wilson Brown, Naval Aide to President Roosevelt.

The index to the first three volumes is at the end of Volume III.

Abbreviations

File division

OF: Official File
PPF: President's Personal File
PSF: President's Secretary's File
RL Recordings: Roosevelt Library Recordings

Descriptive symbol

A: autograph, not signed
AS: autograph, signed
CT: carbon typescript, not signed
CTS: carbon typescript, signed
M: mimeographed
T: typescript, ribbon copy, not signed
TS: typescript, ribbon copy, signed

Contents

Franklin D. Roosevelt and Foreign Affairs

VOLUME II: MARCH 1934–AUGUST 1935

Roosevelt to the Congress, March 2, 1934

To the Congress: I am requesting the Congress to authorize the Executive to enter into executive commercial agreements with foreign nations; and in pursuance thereof within carefully guarded limits to modify existing duties and import restrictions in such a way as will benefit American agriculture and industry.

This action seems opportune and necessary at this time for several reasons.

First, world trade has declined with startling rapidity. Measured in terms of the volume of goods in 1933, it has been reduced to approximately 70 per cent of its 1929 volume; measured in terms of dollars, it has fallen to 35 per cent. The drop in the foreign trade of the United States has been even sharper. Our exports in 1933 were but 52 per cent of the 1929 volume, and 32 per cent of the 1929 value.

This has meant idle hands, still machines, ships tied to their docks, despairing farm households, and hungry industrial families. It has made infinitely more difficult the planning for economic readjustment in which the government is now engaged.

You and I know that the world does not stand still; that trade movements and relations once interrupted can with the utmost difficulty be restored; that even in tranquil and prosperous times there is a constant shifting of trade channels.

How much greater, how much more violent is the shifting in these times of change and of stress is clear from the record of current history. Every Nation must at all times be in a position quickly to adjust its taxes and tariffs to meet sudden changes and avoid severe fluctuations in both its exports and its imports.

You and I know, too, that it is important that the country possess within its borders a necessary diversity and balance to maintain a rounded national life, that it must sustain activities vital to national defense and that such interests cannot be sacrificed for passing advantage. Equally clear is the fact that a full and permanent domestic recovery depends in part upon a revived and strengthened international trade and that American exports cannot be permanently increased without a corresponding increase in imports.

Second, other governments are to an ever-increasing extent winning their share of international trade by negotiated reciprocal trade agreements. If American agricultural and industrial interests are to retain their deserved place in this trade, the American Government must be in a position to bargain for that place with other governments by rapid and decisive negotiation based upon a carefully considered program, and to grant with discernment corresponding opportunities in the American market for foreign products supplementary to our own.

If the American Government is not in a position to make fair offers for fair opportunities, its trade will be superseded. If it is not in a position at a given moment rapidly to alter the terms on which it is willing to deal with other countries, it cannot adequately protect its trade against discriminations and against bargains injurious to its interests. Furthermore a promise to which prompt effect cannot be given is not an inducement which can pass current at par in commercial negotiations.

For this reason, any smaller degree of authority in the hands of the Executive would be ineffective. The executive branches of virtually all other important trading countries already possess some such power.

I would emphasize that quick results are not to be expected. The successful building up of trade without injury to American producers depends upon a cautious and gradual evolution of plans.

The disposition of other countries to grant an improved place to American products should be carefully sounded and considered; upon the attitude of each must somewhat depend our future course of action. With countries which are unwilling to abandon purely restrictive national programs, or to make concessions towards the reestablishment of international trade, no headway will be possible.

The exercise of the authority which I propose must be carefully weighed in the light of the latest information so as to give assurance that no sound and important American interest will be injuriously disturbed. The adjustment of our foreign trade relations must rest on the premise of undertaking to benefit and not to injure such interests. In a time of difficulty and unemployment such as this, the highest consideration of the position of the different branches of American production is required.

From the policy of reciprocal negotiation which is in prospect, I hope in time that definite gains will result to American agriculture and industry.

Important branches of our agriculture, such as cotton, tobacco, hog products, rice, cereal and fruit-raising, and those branches of American industry whose mass production methods have led the world, will find expanded opportunities and productive capacity in foreign markets, and will thereby be spared in part, at least, the heartbreaking readjustments that must be necessary if the shrinkage of American foreign commerce remains permanent.

A resumption of international trade cannot but improve the general situation of other countries, and thus increase their purchasing power. Let us well remember that this in turn spells increased opportunity for American sales.

Legislation such as this is an essential step in the program of national economic recovery which the Congress has elaborated during the past year. It is part of an emergency program necessitated by the economic crisis through which we are passing. It should provide that the trade agreements shall be terminable within a period not to exceed three years; a shorter period probably would not suffice for putting the program into effect. In its execution, the Executive must, of course, pay due heed to the requirements of other branches of our recovery program, such as the National Industrial Recovery Act.

I hope for early action. The many immediate situations in the field of international trade that today await our attention can thus be met effectively and with the least possible delay.

The White House
March 2, 1934[1]

[White House Press Releases:M]

[1] Assistant Secretary of State Francis B. Sayre's name appears on the draft of this message (Speech File), as do the initials of Herbert Feis, economic adviser to the State Department. Roosevelt made a number of changes in the language and paragraphing of the message; paragraphs five and six were added in the White House but whether by the President is not clear. The message is also printed in *Public Papers,* III, 113–116, with a note on the operation of the Trade Agreements Act from 1934 to 1936.

Press Conference, Executive Offices of the White House, March 2, 1934, 4:07 P.M.

[*Excerpt*] Q: Is there anything you can tell us about the mission of Mr. Norman Davis to London?

The President: Norman hasn't any mission to London. He is going over on some private business, purely as a lawyer, as I understand it.

He has got no messages, no work to do. I think he is going to Sweden. Is he going to London?

Q: He is in London now.

The President: I suppose he is on his way to Sweden.

Q: I understand there are dispatches from London indicating that we are submitting some sort of formula regarding armaments.

The President: Norman Davis is going over purely and solely in a private capacity. He is not on the Government pay roll and he won't have anything to do with the Government work until and unless there is a meeting in Geneva, and Lord knows when that will be.[1]

Q: We understand a communication has been sent to the British Government concerning disarmament.[2] Can you tell us anything about that?

The President: There was one went off a couple of weeks ago. I think it is going to be given out this afternoon by the State Department at the request of various people.

Q: It was not a special message sent by you?

The President: No. There is nothing in it that in any way changes the attitude. It shows polite and real interest in the progress—any progress that they can make over there in the European political situation, with the hope that it will bring things around to the point where we can again discuss world disarmament.

Q: That will be given out by the State Department?

The President: There or here?

Mr. Early: Immediately following your Conference, by the State Department.

The President: There is no story in it because it is merely a reiteration of what we have said half a dozen times before.

Q: Does that go over your signature?

The President: no.

Q: Can you tell us whose signature?

The President: I don't know. I think I saw it at the time; it is one of the regular State Department dispatches.[3]

Q: Wasn't it a reply to the British memo sent to us about that time?

The President: That I do not know. I do not know that they sent a memo.

Q: They presented one to us. It was the regular British note, which was sent around to all the powers about a week ago.

The President: Yes?

Q: The belief had been, until the bill was made public up on the

Hill, that you were asking emergency powers to last three years. The bill that Senator Harrison[4] gave us this afternoon indicates that these agreements are terminable within three years but that they may be renewed for any number of years in addition to that.[5]

The President: I don't think it makes any difference one way or the other.

Q: Some persons recommended the adoption of a permanent tariff policy?

The President: You will see the word "emergency" very distinctly in the Message.

Q: I was speaking about the bill.

The President: I do not care what the bill is so long as I get the authority. If they make it a three-year authority, that is perfectly all right.

Q: You expect to terminate the authority within three years?

The President: It is an emergency power, distinctly asked for as that. The agreements can only be made over a period of three years. Congress can terminate them at that time, if they want. In other words, it is a purely academic discussion. The intent is quite clear . . .

Q: Sir, is your debt Message any nearer? Any time soon?

The President: You are right, it is nearer. (Laughter)

Q: Is it coming any time soon?

The President: I do not think as a matter of fact that there is anything much more in prospect of sending up to Congress except minor matters. Pretty nearly everything is completed with today's action except the war debts and we are nearer that.

[President's Press Conferences:T]

[1] Davis had reported to Roosevelt on November 14 following his return from Geneva, and had seen the President on two occasions thereafter, on January 18 and February 19 (PPF 1-0). Roosevelt's mention of Davis' private business in Sweden refers to his representation of the American creditors of the bankrupt Kreuger and Toll Company. However, Hull had informed Hugh Wilson (in Geneva) that Davis was only on leave of absence and that he was ready to take charge of the United States delegation if conditions warranted (Feb. 20, 1934, *Foreign Relations, 1934*, I, 23–24).

[2] Memorandum, State Department to the British Embassy, Feb. 19, 1934, printed in *Foreign Relations, 1934*, I, 22–23.

[3] Sent in a cable from Lindsay to Simon, Feb. 19, 1934 (*British Documents, 1919–1939*, VI, 443–444).

[4] Senator Byron Patton (Pat) Harrison.

[5] The Reciprocal Trade Agreements bill, H.R. 8687, introduced as an amendment to the Tariff Act of 1930 by Robert L. Doughton on March 16, 1934 (*Cong. Rec.*, vol. 78, p. 4718), was approved June 12, 1934, as an amendment to the Tariff Act of 1930.

Lincoln MacVeagh, Minister to Greece, to Roosevelt

Athens, March 2, 1934

Personal

Dear Franklin: It occurs to me that the following may interest you in connection with your vast program of reconstruction in the United States.

Greece is a small country. Economic experiments here have not the importance of those at home, but just because the country is so small the time-element does not figure so largely and results can be tabulated with comparative promptness. From the American point of view, therefore, the experience of Greece which I am about to discuss may appear as a kind of laboratory experiment, but one which has some bearings upon our larger problems.

We have had in Greece for the past year an example of a country operating almost completely under the principles of a planned economy. The plans and their coordination are of course simpler than with us, but the principle remains the same. Economic and financial enterprise has been subjected to governmental regulation to a degree which has been described by the Bank of Athens as "detrimental to the principle of the freedom of commerce." Yet, on the whole, increased prosperity and national satisfaction have been the result.

By governmental action resulting in the reestablishment of confidence, the flight of capital from the country has in great part been arrested, and with certain vital exceptions, the importation of foreign articles has been subjected to a vigorous control under a quota system. Clearing agreements, obviating the use of currency in foreign commercial transactions, have been concluded with nearly all the countries regularly and largely trading with Greece. In addition, the great impulsion to domestic manufacture resulting from restrictions on imports has been controlled by a law which prohibits the introduction into the country of machines and industrial tools except under special permission from the Ministry of National Economy. Exports, as well as imports, are now carefully supervised and the production of wheat, which has never been sufficient for the needs of the nation, has been fostered even to the point of a guarantee by the government to purchase any and all stocks remaining on the cultivators' hands. The payment of commercial debts to foreigners, both in foreign exchange and in drachmas, has been drastically regulated, and the sums paid on the foreign governmental debts skilfully reduced to a minimum consonant with the preservation of a national credit-standing at least as high as that of most European States. Altogether, the government has worked swiftly and tirelessly in a coordinated effort to strengthen the economic life within the country; to guide, as well as foster, home manufactures; to diminish as far as safety allows the out-flow of exchange; and to bring price levels to a parity with those of the world at large. This last aim should, if realized, eventually make possible the full resumption of payments on the foreign and internal debt, with the consequent renewal of the normal flow of capital.

What has been the result of such interference by the State with the course of free, individualistic competition? The gold reserves of the Bank of Greece have increased to a remarkable degree. Foreign commercial debts have been in large part liquidated. Maritime tonnage laid up has decreased by more than 50%. Average quotations on stocks and bonds have risen considerably and price levels on domestic products have been maintained as against falling prices on imported articles. In addition, owing only partly to meteorological conditions, the wheat crop has taken a great step forward and promises this year to maintain its progress.

The operation of a planned economy such as Greece has never known has thus, beyond any question of doubt, proved itself a material success in one short year. But what of its political and social effects? Greece is in many ways a more individualistic country than the United States. Every man here sincerely thinks himself at least as good as his neighbor. Politics veer and change with the wind. But all signs point to the present policy of national economy being more truly national than any policy in Greek statecraft that I have heard of. No party is shooting at it. Its benefits are too obvious even for the marksmen of the café-table. Looked at from a social angle, therefore, it may be regarded as a national unifier, and for the political party which put it into effect a tremendous advan-tage.

Leaving aside possible dangers from other aspects of the situation here, which have largely to do with Greece's political history and are emo-tionally involved, I believe that the more recent experience of Greece demonstrates pretty clearly the efficacy of a planned economy in difficult times, and its acceptability to people of democratic tendencies. In spite of the fact that our problems are vaster, this may seem to you, as it does to me, good news.[1]

Sincerely yours,

Lincoln MacVeagh

[PPF 1192:TS]

[1] Answered April 19, 1934, below.

Henry L. Roosevelt, Acting Secretary of the Navy, to Roosevelt

Washington, 2 March 1934

My dear Mr. President: I have just received from the United States Naval Attaché at Tokyo a report dated 11 January 1934, dealing with Japanese preparations for the next conference on limitation of armaments.

I feel that you will be interested in the contents of this report, consequently I am forwarding it herewith.

Sincerely yours,

H. L. Roosevelt

[PSF:London Naval Conference:TS]

[*Enclosure*] Report No. 6, Japan, January 11, 1934

Japanese Preparation for Next Conference on Limitation of Armaments

The Japanese Government has formed a new group to study Japan's position and policy at the next naval conference, this being part of the government's policy in preparation for the so-called crisis of 1936 which is expected in Japan's international relations.

The new group will be known as the disarmament investigation study committee and is the outgrowth of a series of meetings which have been held by representatives of the Foreign, War and Navy Ministers. Mr. Shigenori Togo, director of the American and European affairs Bureau of the Foreign Office and formerly attached to the Japanese Embassy in Washington is chairman of the committee. Section chiefs from all three ministries will compose the committee with the addition of Navy Captains and Army Colonels who are experts on the technical aspects of Japan's disarmament problems.

The Committee will collect material and data covering all possible measures to be adopted at the forthcoming conference. The draft of these will be submitted to examination to a group of Ministers, Vice Ministers and bureau chiefs. The idea being, according to the press, to prepare for any conceivable measure which may be proposed by the other Powers. Technical preparations are expected to be completed by October this year.

Nothing definite has actually been adopted to date, but, according to reports, the following basic principles probably will be decided upon:

1. The scope of the coming conference must be restricted to naval questions, such as naval tonnage, maintenance of coastal defenses and maintenance of naval bases. Under no circumstances whatever must other questions relating to the Far East or political issues of the Orient or elsewhere in the world be brought up for discussion.

2. Japan may or may not make proposals to the other Powers concerned regarding preliminary negotiations. However, Japan will make no proposal regarding the date of the conference, place to be held or other matters of procedure.

3. Japan will insist upon the right to participate in any preliminary negotiations. In case other nations hold such preliminary negotiations without the participation of Japan at which plans are made for submitting them later to Japan for approval, Japan will refuse to attend the conference.

The latest report is that the Navy Department authorities charged with making preparations for the 1935 naval disarmament conference are planning to complete a general outline of a new disarmament proposal to be submitted at the 1935 parley.

The agenda of the Disarmament Measures Study Commission mentioned above is given as follows:

1. How shall Japan dispose of the qualitative and quantitative disarmament proposal, aiming chiefly to achieve reduction of aggressive weapons which was submitted at Geneva in December, 1932?

2. Should Japan notify the Powers concerned at the end of 1934 of her desire to cancel the Washington Naval Limitation Treaty?

3. What are the international situations in America and Europe since the Manchurian incident and the conditions in those countries as regards military and naval armament?

4. Should Japan propose calling a preliminary conference in the spirit of disarmament within this year and prior to the 1935 parley?

5. The preparation of a new naval disarmament plan to be submitted to the 1935 parley.

6. The advisability of discussing at the 1935 parley the questions of non-recognition of Manchukuo by the Powers and the proposed return of the mandated islands in the South Seas to the League as side issues of the disarmament conference.

7. Establishment of a new policy for a Pacific defense limitation pact.

The report continues that the naval officials will study the above problems with caution with a view to drafting a new disarmament plan based on the spirit of equality in armament right by giving up the present pact, which in their opinion, injures the feeling of security as regards national defense. The new plan is intended to be completed by March for submission to a tripartite conference of the Foreign Office, Navy and War office officials.

The opinion is being expressed in naval circles that should the Powers reject Japan's new proposal based on the desire to promote world peace, stick to the existing naval ratio and attempt to extend the present pact, the Navy would not mind the break-up of the conference and the armament race that would follow it. Japan, it is added, has the strong conviction that the country can defend itself by adopting an economical free naval armament and is, therefore, agreed that the failure the country suffered at the London Naval Conference shall not be repeated.

Lately there has been a report that both the United States and England are considering an extension of the naval treaties for one or two years in view of the recent failure to come to any agreement at Geneva. The unofficial spokesman of the Japanese Navy Department has stated that the Japanese will be unable to agree to this due to Japan's well known position in regard to these treaties.

The above are largely newspaper reports, but as they have been published repeatedly by practically all papers the Naval Attaché believes they can be taken as being reliable. There is no question but that the Japanese Navy is now in a high state of efficiency and very confident. They believe they can get what appropriations are necessary to build the number and type of ships they require and that the Japanese navy yards and private plants are fully capable of turning out first class ships. That they can build good ships and in numbers is correct, but it is a question how long the increasingly mounting budgets for the Army and Navy with ever increasing taxes can be borne. The concensus of opinion of students of the situation here, in which the Naval Attaché agrees, is that the best answer to Japan's military preparations is to build up our own Navy to full treaty strength as rapidly as possible. An immediate statement and continued propaganda bearing on our intention to replace capital ships, increase our air force and replace overage ships as they become due for replacement and a statement that in case of an upward revision of Japan's treaty ratio is demanded the United States must take steps to build bases in Guam and the Philippines would be the best and only way to cause naval authorities here to stop and ponder over the question of a "free building policy." The Naval Attaché believes that the great pace with which Japan is attempting, and succeeding, to build up her Army and Navy is not with the idea of an immediate war in mind, but to have sufficient armed forces to back up her diplomacy in 1935–36 when she feels she will have the whole world against her as regards withdrawal from the League, the mandated islands, the renewal of the Washington and London treaties, and the situation in the Far East in general.

The Naval Attaché also believes that in case the next naval conference fails to reach an agreement, the Japanese will begin at once a regular systematic, though perhaps modest program of submarines, torpedo boats, destroyers, small cruisers and aircraft, in other words ships of comparatively small cost, in order to complete her defensive armaments and make her position in the Far East as secure as possible at as small a cost as possible. These types, which comprise the second replenishment program, are greatly favored by the Japanese naval authorities.[1]

[PSF:London Naval Conference:T]

[1] An attached memorandum, Hull to Roosevelt, March 13, 1934, reads: "I have read the attached report with much interest."

Roosevelt to Marvin H. McIntyre, Assistant Secretary to the President

Washington [March 5, 1934]

M. H. McIntyre: Thank Mr. Stone—greatly interested. Ask him to send at our request copies of it[1] to the following:

Senator Robinson
Senator Harrison
Congressman Byrns
Congressman Doughton
Congressman Buchanan

F.D.R.

[PPF 5684:CT]

[1] The President here referred to a draft report of recommendations of the Committee on Commercial Policy of the Foreign Policy Association sent by the Association's Washington representative, William T. Stone, to McIntyre in a letter of Feb. 26, 1934

(OF 5684). This 5,000-word report urged that the tariff be revised "so as to make it a truly national instrument for the general welfare rather than for sectional or special privilege." It supported the principle of tariff bargaining through reciprocity and recommended that the President "should be given the power to change the tariff, fix certain quotas, and conclude and put into effect reciprocity agreements." This report was printed as *Recommendations of the Committee on Commercial Policy . . . March, 1934* (New York: Foreign Policy Association, and Boston: World Peace Foundation, 1934). McIntyre wrote to Stone who replied March 6 (PPF 5684) that copies had been sent to the persons mentioned and also to members of the House Ways and Means Committee.

Stephen T. Early, Assistant Secretary to the President, to Cordell Hull, Secretary of State

Washington, March 5, 1934

Memorandum for the Secretary of State: This has come to me through an intermediary—a newspaper man—who said that he came at the request of the German Ambassador.[1]

I was advised that the Ambassador was deeply concerned that the Mayor of New York, former Governor Alfred E. Smith, Professor Raymond Moley, William Green, Rabbi Wise and Senator Tydings, etc. were to participate as speakers in a program against Hitlerism.

Confidentially, I was told that the Ambassador thought that this might lead to his recall; that the President should use his good offices to intercede with the speakers named and at least ask them not to make their remarks personal as to Hitler himself.

I was further informed that the Ambassador already has discussed this with the Secretary of State.

Obviously the President can do nothing in the way of interceding with any of these gentlemen and if he made any personal move and the news leaked out it would give the affair headlines in the newspapers which it would not otherwise get.

Stephen Early

[OF 198-A:TS]

[1] The note here referred to is printed below. Nothing is known of its authorship.

[*Enclosure*]

I beg to draw your attention to the enclosed clipping from the New York *World-Telegram* of February 27/34 which in my estimation is a direct violation of the ethics prevalent among nations having Diplomatic relations with each other.[1]

As an American Citizen (by birth) I wish to be recorded against such a procedure as trying the German Nation or its Chancellor on any question, in the United States.

This is not a question of liking or disliking Herr Hitler, or of being in favour or opposed to the present attitude of Germany on the Jewish question, but one of common international decency and international courtesy.

[OF 198-A:T]

[1] An advertisement of an anti-Nazi mass meeting, "The Case of Civilization Against Hitlerism," under auspices of the American Jewish Congress in cooperation with the American Federation of Labor, to be held in Madison Square Garden on March 1, 1934.

James Clement Dunn, Special Assistant to the Secretary of State, to Stephen T. Early, Assistant Secretary to the President

Washington, March 6, 1934

My dear Mr. Early: The Secretary has asked me to hand you the attached memorandum in reply to your memorandum to him of March fifth,[1] regarding the meeting to be held in New York on March seventh, in which certain speakers are to participate in a program considering the acts of the Hitler Government in Germany.

Sincerely yours,

James Clement Dunn

[OF 198-A:TS]

[1] Early to Hull, March 5, 1934, above.

[*Enclosure*] James Clement Dunn to Stephen T. Early

[Washington] March 6, 1934

Memorandum for Mr. Early: With reference to your memorandum of March 5, 1934, regarding the proposed mock trial of the Hitler

Government to be held in Madison Square Garden on March 7, the German Ambassador has, on several occasions, discussed this matter with the Secretary of State.

An investigation of the possible responsibility of this Government to interpose in this matter was made. The precedents indicated that the Department of State has never recognized any duty to suppress public utterances regarded as hostile to friendly States.

When, on March 2, during a conversation, the German Ambassador again referred to the question of the proposed mock trial, Mr. Hull told him that the participants were acting as individuals and not in any sense as representing the Federal Government; that they were not under the slightest control of the Federal Government with respect to the proposed trial; that no legal authority could be found that would enable the Federal Government to instruct or order the participants to refrain from entering upon such a mock trial; that a study of the law books had been made in order to ascertain the complete international law relating to this sort of situation; and that no law had been discovered which clothed the Federal Government with any legal authority to compel the abandonment of the proposed mock trial.

Mr. Hull agrees with you as to the effect of any intercession in this matter, should it receive publicity.

[OF 198-A:T]

Norman H. Davis, Chairman, American Delegation, London Naval Conference, to Roosevelt

London, England, March 6, 1934

My dear Mr. President: I wrote you today on the naval matter[1] but, in addition to that I think you may be interested in the political situation here which, of course, has a bearing on what may happen.

MacDonald and Simon have both had a rather hard time of late and there has been a particularly strong attack against Simon. He volunteered the information to me Sunday, however, that everything has been straightened out and that there will be no changes in the Cabinet before next Fall. In spite of that there are those who believe that MacDonald may be forced to make some changes.

There seem to be two particularly strong trends of public opinion.

One is that the Government must stop standing pat and do something vigorous to cope with the present situation. What you have been doing in America is having a very great influence on the masses of people. A leading Tory member of Parliament told me that the majority of his constituents are saying that the Government should follow your example.

The other trend is in favor of disarmament and peace. The growing opinion seems to be that there can be no peace without a real disarmament agreement and that without this Great Britain will inevitably be drawn into another European war and that, therefore, the wiser and safer course is to make every effort to secure an agreement providing for strict supervision and even, if necessary to insure respect for the Disarmament Treaty, to agree to impose an economic blockade against a nation violating the treaty.

They seem to be getting entirely away from the idea of treaties of guarantee or mutual assistance. There is also a growing realization on the part of the most thoughtful people here that, while Europe offers the principal difficulty just now in the way of disarmament, it is essentially a world problem and should be treated as such, and that England should not go into a treaty that is essentially European.

The Dominions are more concerned about peace and disarmament in the Far East than in Europe and for that reason, as well as the British concern over the effect of the Japanese activities, they feel that the only hope of solution lies through a world treatment of the problem and through British and American cooperation.

With best wishes, I am, Faithfully yours,

Norman H. Davis

P.S. I am satisfied that Simon does not hate the United States. In fact, as one man told me, who knows him very intimately and in whom I have absolute confidence, Simon does not hate anything and one of his faults is that he does not hate some things that he ought to hate. He is merely expedient.[2]

[PSF:London Naval Conference:TS]

[1] Davis said the British were disturbed over Japanese activities and were anxious to reach an agreement with the United States because of "the salutary effect" this might have on Japan (*Foreign Relations, 1934*, I, 222–230).

[2] See Bingham to Roosevelt, March 8, 1934, below.

Press Conference, Executive Offices of the White House, March 7, 1934, 10:55 A.M.

[*Excerpt*] Q: The House Ways and Means Committee is holding hearings on the free ports. I think it is understood you were in favor of it?

The President: I did not know they had any legislation up there at all. I have always been interested in the possibility of free ports, but nothing specific. It is a perfectly fine idea and they do have free ports in certain parts of the world that work very, very well.

Q: Do you think it would help our foreign trade?

The President: Yes. Where they have free ports it seems to work out very well. It encourages trade.[1]

Q: Mr. President, the mayors of the Great Lakes cities are coming in tomorrow about St. Lawrence.[2] Anything you can tell us?

The President: I understand they are coming here to endorse it.

Q: We thought they were going to put the heat on. (Laughter)

The President: That would not be a bad idea either (Laughter) . . .

Q: The Inter-American Highway, do you favor its extension beyond Panama down to Buenos Aires?

The President: No. The general thought is that if we can get all the Central American Republics to go along with the building of it, then the South American Republics can take it up of their own accord. Eventually, if we can link North America and South America, it would be a great achievement.

[President's Press Conferences:T]

[1] See Roosevelt to Celler, March 9, 1934, below.
[2] The mayors were at the White House at 11:45 A.M. the next day. The appointments list identifies only three: Daniel W. Hoan of Milwaukee, Frank Couzens of Detroit, and Harry L. Davis of Cleveland (PPF 1-0).

Robert W. Bingham, Ambassador to Great Britain, to Roosevelt

[London] March 8, 1934

Dear Mr. President: Since Norman Davis has written you fully about the meeting with the Prime Minister,[1] it is unnecessary for me to go further with that, beyond saying that I fully concur with his conclusions on this subject.

I am enclosing a recent article from the *Daily Telegraph,* which, in my judgment, is the best one which has yet appeared in a British newspaper, and also an article in the *Times* by Willmott Lewis, which is the first one of its type he has written. These two indicate the change in the general attitude here towards the situation in our country.[2]

I had an appointment with Sir John Simon at his office in the House of Commons on last Monday, at 3:45.[3] When I arrived I was told by one of his secretaries that he was on the floor of the House, but would probably be free in a half an hour or possibly longer. I then asked him to say to Sir John when he saw him that if he would be good enough to communicate with my secretary that I would arrange to see him at some other time, and started to leave. The result was rather interesting, as the secretary urged me to wait only long enough for him to fetch Sir John from the House, and he left hurriedly and in a few moments Sir John appeared. I took up two routine matters with him very briefly, and then told him that I was interested in discussing some phases of the naval situation with him, whereupon he stated that he would like to have Anthony Eden in, and he came in almost immediately. He then told me that the Prime Minister had told him of his meeting with us on Friday, and that the P.M. was preparing a memorandum covering the meeting, a part of which he had seen.

I told him we were naturally interested in the British attitude towards the probable demand by the Japanese for naval parity, and he said that he thought this was a matter which concerned us more than it did the British. I told him, with all due respect for his opinion on the subject, that it was not shared by any man, woman or child in the United States. From that point his attitude changed, and, while proceeding with due legal caution, he made it quite obvious that the British are disturbed over the situation, and are eager to cooperate with us, but as usual, of course, on their own terms; that is to say, that we are to seek their cooperation as a favor to us. He did not say this, and was suave and courteous, as he always is. They are nervous and anxious. He himself nearly lost his scalp recently,[4] but it is generally thought that there will be no changes in the Cabinet before next Autumn. I believe the government is eager to cooperate with us, but eager to avoid irritating the Japanese until they finish the great system of fortifications they are building at Singapore. I may say I do not think Sir John personally has an attitude of hostility towards our country.

I have thought over this a great deal and feel sure I am right about it. However, he is not only a lawyer, but an English barrister, accustomed to having things prepared and laid in his lap with instructions how to proceed. Hence, he is not an executive, and is always inclined to fall back on legal hairsplitting, and excessively timid about assuming any kind of responsibility for action. I think the foundation has been laid with the Prime Minister and Sir John, and that the next move is up to them, and that they will make it. I believe our strategy should be to stand pat until they come back to us, although it may take some time for them to make up their minds.[5]

With kindest regards, Very sincerely,

Robert W. Bingham

[PSF:London Naval Conference:TS]

[1] See Davis to Roosevelt, March 6, 1934, above.
[2] Clippings from the *Daily Telegraph* of March 3, and from the London *Times* of March 5, 1934; the articles were friendly reviews of Roosevelt's accomplishments in his first year in office.
[3] March 4.
[4] Bingham here presumably referred to criticism of Simon's conduct of foreign affairs and a recent report that he was to return to the Home Office, with Eden to handle Foreign Office affairs on the continent (New York *Times,* Feb. 25, 1934, p. 22).
[5] See letter following.

Robert W. Bingham, Ambassador to Great Britain, to Roosevelt

[London] March 8, 1934

Dear Mr. President: Since writing to you this morning,[1] I attended a luncheon given by our retiring Naval attaché, Capt. Arthur L. Bristol, and was seated next to the First Lord of the Admiralty, Sir Bolton Eyres-Monsell. Almost immediately he said to me that he thought our general situation, particularly our Japanese situation, made it highly desirable for both countries to cooperate in dealing with the whole naval situation, and that we could handle the Japanese situation satisfactorily if we handled it together. I told him that I agreed with him and thought there was every reason why we should act together in our common interest. He said that their situation required a number of fast, light cruisers in order to protect their commerce, and I told him that I quite understood that, and, furthermore, told him that our situation required ships large enough to make long journeys and come home, because we did not have the facilities for re-fitting and re-fueling which the British had, and he said that he understood that perfectly. At the end of the conversation I told him that I thought we ought to be able to carry out our naval programs along the lines best suited to our own countries, without suspicion, competition or hostility, with which he expressed himself as heartily agreeing.

I mention this as supplementary to the information already sent you and to show the attitude of mind which I believe now exists.[2]

Sincerely yours,

Robert W. Bingham

[PSF:London Naval Conference:TS]

[1] See preceding letter.

[2] This and the preceding letter were sent by Roosevelt to Phillips who returned them with a note of March 21, 1934 (PSF: London Naval Conference). Phillips said that Bingham confirmed his and Hull's guess that although the British were disturbed over the naval situation and were eager to cooperate with the United States, for the moment they appeared to prefer to cooperate on their own terms. He believed, however, that they were slowly changing their position.

Senator Key Pittman of Nevada to Roosevelt

[Washington] 8 March 1934

22 Doubtful Democrats

Fletcher, Florida
Thomas, Oklahoma
Russell, Georgia
McGill, Kansas
Hatch, New Mexico
Stephens, Mississippi
Trammell, Florida
Neely, West Virginia
Reynolds, North Carolina
Tydings, Maryland
Coolidge, Massachusetts
Bankhead, Alabama
Connally, Texas   *Sheppard is OK*[1]
Smith, South Carolina
Lonergan, Connecticut
McCarran, Nevada
Murphy, Iowa

Bailey, North Carolina
George, Georgia
Adams, Colorado (*Rolling Mill of Colo. Fuel & Iron*)
Caraway, Arkansas
Gore, Oklahoma

7 Doubtful Republicans

Carey, Wyoming
Hatfield, West Virginia
Steiwer, Oregon
Couzens, Michigan
McNary, Oregon
Walcott, Connecticut   *Fred—Hoover's plan—*
Gibson, Vermont—*an anti-power man—*[2]

[*Notation*:A:FDR] Get Key on the reservations   Ask those members of
For. Rel. Com. to come to see me.[3]
  We have 42 outside of these lists

These are	42
Dem.	22
Rep.	7
	71
Against	25
	96

[PSF:St. Lawrence Waterway:T]

---

[1] Morris Sheppard of Texas. This and the following italicized notations opposite the names, and the notation at the end, are in Roosevelt's hand. The list referred to the impending vote in the Senate on the St. Lawrence Waterway Treaty with Canada.

[2] This list is unaddressed and was brought by Pittman to the White House (see Pittman to Howe, March 10, 1934, below). In the same file is a memorandum from Kannee to McIntyre, March 9, 1934, giving the content of a telephone call from Under Secretary of State Phillips. Referring to the probability of the defeat of the treaty resolution, Phillips said: "The Sec. (Hull) brought the matter up in Cabinet today with the Pres. and made the suggestion that he get hold of some of the Sens. pretty quickly; that there is a real need for action, but I couldn't make out whether the President intends to take any vitalizing action, so to speak." He added that both he and Hull were worried and that the Secretary thought the President should call in a number of the Democratic leaders to see what could be done.

[3] No appointment is noted in the White House appointments list but it is probable that a conference was held March 9 or 10 (Friday or Saturday). The treaty came up for vote on March 14 and was defeated by a vote of 42 nays to 46 ayes, a two-thirds affirmative vote being needed for ratification (*Cong. Rec.,* vol. 78, pp. 4469–4475).

Press Conference, Executive Offices of the White House, March 9, 1934, 4:08 P.M.

[*Excerpt*] Q: Can you tell us anything about your conversation with Sumner Welles?

The President: Oh, that was about starting a Cuban bank. That is all ready to be signed this afternoon, the Executive Order . . .

Q: In connection with the Cuban bank, has it not been definitely decided to extend $10,000,000 of credit for silver purchases?

The President: No, the bank, as organized, will have $250,000 in common stock and two and a half million dollars in preferred stock. Of course that can always, at any time later, be amended but that is the way it will be organized.

Q: And the purpose of the bank, Mr. President, is to finance trade?

The President: The immediate purpose of the bank is to make it possible for Cuba to obtain silver currency, of which there is a shortage.

Q: How much will Cuba take at the beginning, sir?

The President: I do not know.

Q: To whom will this stock be sold, the RFC?

The President: Yes . . .

Q: In connection with the Cuban bank, can we understand that the credit granted will be granted to American exporters of silver?

The President: I have no idea what the latest details are. I think it is a straight transaction with the Cuban Government, but I am not sure.

Q: Will it involve a cash loan to the Cuban Government?

The President: No, it is a banking transaction . . .[1]

Q: I understand Ray Stevens has withdrawn from the Foreign Bondholders' Protective Council and there are charges that the Council has been doing business with some of the issuing houses of the Latin American securities, something which you warned against. Is there any chance, under these conditions, that you will revive Section II?

The President: Ray Stevens was in bad need of a holiday, which he had not had since his return from Siam.[2] As I understand it, he got out temporarily in order to be entirely free during the balance of the winter and, as I understand it, he hoped to be able to go back in the spring sometime. What the details are, I do not know.

Q: There is no plan to revoke under Section II?

The President: No.

Q: There have been several reports lately that despite the promises made by Litvinov, when you recognized the Soviet Government, the Communists have continued their propaganda in the United States?

The President: I have not heard anything about it at all. Have you any reports, specific ones?

Q: Quite a few.

The President: Ask the State Department; I haven't any . . .

Q: How about the group on St. Lawrence?

The President: They left a three-page full and complete endorsement, which they say came from practically every city in the whole Great Lakes area, in favor of the St. Lawrence Treaty. I sent them up to the Hill.

[President's Press Conferences:T]

[1] See press conference of Feb. 28, 1934, above.
[2] Stevens had been adviser on foreign affairs to the Siamese government.

Roosevelt to Representative Emanuel Celler of New York

[Washington] March 9, 1934

Dear Mannie: Thank you for your letter of March sixth enclosing a copy of your Free Port Bill and a copy of the previous hearings held on similar bills.[1] I am glad to have these available.

Very sincerely yours,

[OF 614-A:CT]

[1] Celler asked for Roosevelt's support of H.R. 3657 to provide for foreign trade zones (OF 614-A). He said that the bill would supplement the President's policy of fostering foreign commerce, that it had been approved by maritime associations and chambers of commerce, and that both the Commerce Department and the Tariff Commission favored it. Celler had introduced the bill the year before but it had only recently been reported following hearings: *Foreign Trade Zones, Hearings Before Subcommittee, 73d Cong., 2d Sess., on H.R. 3657, to Provide for Establishment, Operation and Maintenance of Foreign Trade Zones . . . Mar. 6 and 7, 1934* (Washington, 1934). The bill finally enacted was another, similar one, H.R. 9322, introduced by Celler April 25, 1934. This bill was passed after attacks in the House by Republican congressmen who said it followed the Democratic program of favoring foreign producers (*Cong. Rec.,* vol. 78, pp. 7376, 9762–9773, 9774–9780). It was approved June 18, 1934 (48 *Stat.* 998).

Senator Key Pittman of Nevada to Louis M. Howe, Personal Secretary to the President

Washington, D.C., March 10, 1934

My dear Colonel: The following are the Senators who are polled by the newspaper men as against the treaty: Adams, Austin, Bailey, Clark, Coolidge, Copeland, Davis, Dickinson, Dieterich, Goldsborough, Hale, Hastings, Hébert, Kean, Keyes, King, Lewis, Long, McCarran, McNary, Metcalf, Overton, Patterson, Reed, Reynolds, Steiwer, Thomas (of Oklahoma), Townsend, Tydings, Wagner, Walsh, and White.

Thirty-three votes can defeat the ratification of the treaty. It is apparent, therefore, that we must not only reduce the list of those against it, but we must hold all of the doubtful Senators.

I have already given you a list of the doubtful Senators.[1] This list may include some of those who were polled by the press as against the treaty.

In addition to this list, both of the Virginia Senators are supposed to be opposed to the treaty.

I am also certain that at the present time the following additional Senators will vote against the treaty: Barbour, of New Jersey, Hatfield, of West Virginia, Lonergan of Connecticut, Smith of South Carolina, and Walcott of Connecticut.

It is apparent, therefore, what little chance there is for ratifying the treaty. It will be essential, therefore, for the last named Senators to either be induced to vote for the treaty, or not to vote at all. It will also be necessary for safety sake to induce, if possible, Adams, King, Reynolds, Thomas (of Oklahoma) and Bailey to vote for the treaty, or not to vote at all.

May I call your attention to the fact that La Follette, Vandenberg and myself have carried the whole burden of this fight so far. We have done the best we could, but we have not had sufficient support upon the floor of the Senate to indicate seriously that it was an Administration measure, in spite of the President's very strong message.

I think it would greatly help the situation if Senator Robinson would make a twenty-minute speech on Tuesday at the time when the debate will be limited to one speech each for Senators and not to exceed twenty minutes. I realize that Senator Robinson's time has been all consumed in the performance of his duties as Leader, which he has excellently performed, and therefore that he has had no opportunity to study this

23

treaty. I will, however, be pleased to furnish him with the data for a twenty-minute speech.

I consider this matter of vast importance, and I think that the President should give it precedence over every other matter. I may say that in the event we are defeated in the ratification of the treaty, in my opinion it would be useless to return the treaty to the Senate at this session.

I hope you will convey to the President my opinion with regard to this matter, in addition to the other matters that I verbally submitted to you today.[2]

With best wishes, I am, Sincerely,

Key Pittman

[PSF:St. Lawrence Waterway:TS]

[1] March 8, 1934, above.

[2] At his March 14 press conference, Roosevelt was asked to comment on the impending defeat of the St. Lawrence Treaty. He said that he was confident that the waterway would eventually be built, either by Canada alone or by Canada and the United States jointly. He added: "The thing is going through; perhaps not today but the St. Lawrence Seaway is going to be built just as sure as God made little apples. The only difference is that I would like to see it done by joint action of two neighboring Nations. If we don't go along, Canada has a perfect right to build an all-Canadian seaway and discriminate against us, if it so desires" (*Public Papers*, III, 145–148). See Early to Williams, March 25, 1934, below.

Roosevelt to C. W. Linscheid, President, Export Managers Club, New York

[Washington] March 12, 1934

My dear Mr. Linscheid: Such meetings as yours give heartening evidence of the will of American business to cooperate in the solution of the problems of world trade. Promoting a mutually advantageous exchange of goods between the United States and other nations is a vital part of our recovery program and as you are aware it is a matter to which I am giving particular and immediate attention. The joint efforts of your Government and of the progressive businessmen of America will enable us to attain our objective in restoring American foreign trade.[1]

Very sincerely yours,

[*Notation*:T] Sent special delivery
[PPF 1225:CT]

[1] This letter was drafted by Secretary of Commerce Roper. Linscheid first asked that the President speak to the Export Managers Club by telephone and Early told him that this was impossible. Linscheid then asked for a "brief message of encouragement on the foreign trade situation" (Linscheid to Early, Feb. 21, March 2, 1934; Early to Linscheid, Feb. 27, 1934, PPF 1225). The Export Managers Club was made up of several hundred export executives of American manufacturing companies. Linscheid thanked Roosevelt in a letter of March 19, 1934 (PPF 1225). He said that although the meeting was devoted to export problems the members generally felt that two-way international trade was what was required to restore national prosperity.

Josephus Daniels, Ambassador to Mexico, to Roosevelt

Mexico, D.F., March 12, 1934

Dear Franklin: Mr. Ralph W. Morrison, who has known Mexico for many years, and is interested in doing everything possible to strengthen friendly relations and promote peace, was here last week.[1] He told of the suggestion he made to you when he was at the White House a short time ago. I think the idea he presented would bear good fruit.

Returning from Cuenervaca where he had a long and satisfactory talk with Gen. Calles, who greatly admires the course you have pursued, Mr. Morrison told me that within a few days Gen. Calles would send me a formal invitation to a luncheon, breakfast or dinner at a date to be fixed by me shortly before I leave for Washington. At that meal I would express my appreciation of the welcome extended me by Mexicans and my interest in the policies in Mexico which are in keeping with the New Deal in the United States. I would then read a letter which Mr. Morrison says you would write to Gen. Calles, sending it to me to be presented on that occasion.

I am enclosing an outline of a suggested letter which Mr. Morrison agrees with me would be fitting and helpful if it meets your approval.

Please be good enough to wire "Satisfactory" if you approve or words to that effect, and mail the letter to me.[2]

Faithfully yours

Josephus Daniels

[PPF 86:AS]

[1] Morrison, a retired cotton merchant and banker of San Antonio, Texas, was one of the delegates to the 1933 London Economic Conference.

[2] Roosevelt telegraphed Daniels March 22, 1934 (PPF 86): "Entirely satisfactory. Am mailing letter. All well here. Affectionate regards to you both." See letter to General Plutarco Elías Calles, same date, below.

R. Walton Moore, Assistant Secretary of State, to Roosevelt

Washington, March 12, 1934

Dear Mr. President: The Johnson bill will be considered tomorrow morning by the House Committee on Foreign Affairs, to which it was transferred from the Judiciary Committee. Mr. McReynolds, Chairman of the former Committee, has suggested that the bill should be explained by Senator Johnson, with whom I have talked this afternoon, and who will appear and be careful not to unnecessarily quote you. Mr. McReynolds does not desire the presence of any representative of the State Department, except our legal adviser,[1] who will be available if needed to explain the two minor amendments, one permitting the purchase or sale of obligations that may possibly be issued in adjustment of existing debts, and the other permitting the sale or purchase of obligations issued by a debtor country to any agency created or controlled by our Government, as for instance the first Export-Import Bank. I will assume that we should be guided by Mr. McReynolds' judgment, since he knows your attitude and all that occurred in the Senate, unless you notify me to appear before the Committee and explicitly state that you wish the bill enacted.[2]

Yours very sincerely,

R. Walton Moore

[OF 212:TS]

[1] Green H. Hackworth.

[2] Correspondence in the Moore papers ("Johnson Bill") further explains the Administration's role in getting the kind of bill it wanted. On February 28 Johnson had asked Moore's help in getting his bill out of the House Judiciary Committee. Moore replied February 1 that he thought the bill would come up soon and asked Johnson if he wanted to explain the legislation to the committee. On March 7 Moore informed Johnson that the bill had been moved to the House Foreign Affairs Committee, and on March 9 he sent him a copy of Senate Document 123, *Indebtedness of Foreign Governments to the United States as of Jan. 4, 1934* (Washington, 1934). On March 10 Moore asked Hackworth (in a memorandum of that date) to appear at the House hearing on March 13. He said Johnson understood that the President did not wish to be quoted, and that McReynolds (chairman of the House Foreign Affairs Committee and co-sponsor of the bill) knew of the Administration's attitude. He added: "Thus I have complied with my promise to Senator Johnson, made some time ago, to make an effort to bring about consideration of the bill in the House . . . What I have done is in accordance with the general wish of the President, as indicated to me."

British Ambassador Lindsay was concerned over the language of the bill as it was reported by the House Committee and had asked Phillips what Roosevelt's attitude toward the bill was (Phillips to Moore, March 20, 1934). Moore replied to Phillips on March 21: "While it is a fact that the President favors the legislation, that was not stated in the Senate, nor was it stated in the hearing before the House Committee, nor does it seem probable that there will be any need to state it when the bill, as now expected, is put upon its passage in the House under suspension of the rules on April 2nd."

The bill was passed by the House on April 4 and approved by the President on April 13, 1934 (*Cong. Rec.*, vol. 78, pp. 6048–6057, 6550; 48 *Stat.* 574). Asked at his April 13 press conference whether the Johnson Act would apply to countries making token payments on their war debts or other obligations, Roosevelt said: "I had better talk to the Secretary of State before answering that question; I don't know" (President's Press Conferences). Asked who would administer the act, he said he supposed that its administration would be shared by the Federal Trade Commission, the Federal Reserve, and the State Department.

Chancellor Adolf Hitler to Roosevelt

[Berlin, March 14, 1934][1]

Aide Memoire

The Chancellor of the Reich begs Ambassador Dodd to be good enough to transmit his greetings to President Roosevelt and at the same time to state that he sincerely congratulates President Roosevelt for his heroic efforts in the interests of the American people. The President's successful battle against economic distress is being followed by the entire German people with interest and admiration. The Chancellor is in accord with the President in the view that the virtue of duty, readiness for sacrifice, and discipline should dominate the entire people. These moral demands which the President places before every individual citizen of the United States, are also the quintessence of the German state philosophy which finds its expression in the slogan "The Public Weal Transcends the Interests of the Individual."

[OF 198:T]

[1] This date is derived from Foreign minister von Neurath's cable to the German consul general in New York sending the note; in this he said: "Please communicate the following orally, accompanied by a short note, to Ambassador Dodd, who will be arriving there shortly on the *Manhattan*" (*German Documents*, II, 611). Dodd sailed from Hamburg on March 14 and arrived in New York on March 23; his *Diary* entry for the latter date (p. 93) reads: "At Quarantine. Dr. Karl Werkmeister, acting German Consul General in New York, came to me with a letter from Chancellor Hitler to President Roosevelt. Werkmeister was merely finishing the interview I had with Hitler on March 7th." In this interview Dodd asked Hitler if he wished to send a message to President Roosevelt; the Chancellor said he wished to think it over (memorandum by Dodd, undated, in *Foreign Relations, 1934*, II, 218–221). In this memorandum, Dodd states that Hitler in

the March 7 interview "agreed heartily" to Roosevelt's proposal that no nation should cross another's boundaries. Hans Dieckhoff, of the German Foreign Office, in a memorandum of March 12, 1934 (*German Documents*, II, 597), said that Dodd had proposed a message from Hitler to Roosevelt, and had said that "it would represent something quite substantial if the Reich Chancellor were to let President Roosevelt know that he approved his proposal (whoever crosses the border of a state with armed force is an aggressor)." Dieckhoff added: "With respect to this message . . . Mr. Dodd seemed to be chiefly concerned in general with the question of disarmament and security, [and] not with economic questions."

Dodd delivered Hitler's message to Hull on March 24. The message was presumably typed in the Consul General's office from the cable mentioned at the head of this note. The message is in German, and, though Dodd refers to it as a "letter" (above), it is in the form of the State Department translation here printed: headed simply "Aide Memoire," undated and unsigned. Hull sent the note and the translation to Roosevelt under cover of a note of March 24 (OF 198). The translation printed in *German Documents*, II, 611, is a bit more felicitous. Neither Hitler's message nor Roosevelt's reply was released to the press; for the reply, see Phillips to Roosevelt, March 26, 1934, below.

Press Conference, Executive Offices of the White House, March 16, 1934, 4:10 P.M.

[*Excerpt*] Q: Mr. President, the hearings before the Senate Interstate Commerce Committee developed that the main opposition to the Dill Communications bill was the going beyond the bare recommendation which you made for transfer of existing authority. Would you care to express your attitude on that?

The President: I do not know. I have not read the bill. In what way does it go beyond?

Q: Providing for effective regulation of rates, interlocking directorates and intercompany transactions.[1]

The President: Not having read the bill, I cannot talk about it intelligently. The only thing I talked with—who was it put in the bill, Sam Rayburn—the only thing I talked with him about was the general thought that we ought to provide for control of communications between this country and other countries by any company which is foreign owned, that that ought to be an American controlled company. In other words, I only talked about the principle and I do not know what the actual details of the bill are.

Q: The president of the I. T. & T. (International Telephone and Telegraph Company) said $9^{35}/_{100}$ per cent of the stock was foreign owned.

The President: Only 9 per cent?

Q: Just about.

The President: Then the company would not have any trouble. It means 100 per cent control.

Q: Twenty per cent foreign is the limit.

The President: I will have to tell you this off the record: The general thought on that was this; that there is a tendency on the part of foreign companies which are either Government controlled or quasi Government controlled, like the British Communications, Ltd., which is actually privately owned but the policy of it is dictated by the British Government, to interfere in our communications with foreign countries and it is our thought to prevent such interference. Well, one simple example is the feeling we have had that the dissemination of news by the Havas Agency in South America has been, as practised, very distinctly anti-United States. There is no particular secret about that. I have complained to the Havas people about it and of course the Havas Company is subsidized by the French Government. We won't be able to get United States, American news, and especially press news out of this country in such a way that foreign newspapers will get proper news.

Q: Did you complain to the Havas news agency?

The President: Entirely unofficially. I did not do it myself.

Q: Is that in the dissemination of news from the United States through South America?

The President: Yes.

Q: Is this on the record?

The President: On, no. I think you had better treat that off the record, this last part about foreign news agencies, because that is a thing that concerns all of us rather than the general public in this stage of the game.

[President's Press Conferences:T]

---

[1] S. 2910, "To provide for the regulation of interstate and foreign communications by wire or radio," abolished the Federal Radio Commission and in its stead set up the Federal Communications Commission. It was introduced by Senator Dill on Feb. 27, 1934, and referred to the Committee on Interstate Commerce. Back of the bill was the desire to give authority to the government to prevent the setting up in the United States of foreign-controlled broadcasting studios. Hearings were held: *Hearings, 73d Cong., 2d sess., on S. 2910 . . . Mar. 9, 10, 13–15, 1934* (Washington, 1934), and in consequence a new bill (S. 3285) was introduced by Dill on April 4, 1934. S. 3285 contained a number of changes in language designed to give the government more authority, among other things, to permit it more readily to determine the actual interests controlling radio stations (*Cong. Rec.,* vol. 78, pp. 3275, 5952). S. 3285 was approved June 19, 1934 (48 *Stat.* 1064).

Roosevelt to General Plutarco Elías Calles, Mexico City

[Washington] March 22, 1934

My dear General Calles: I am requesting my old friend and colleague, Ambassador Josephus Daniels, upon the eve of his departure for a short stay in Washington, to convey to you my cordial greetings and felicitations upon the peace and growing prosperity of Mexico in these difficult days—a happy condition to which you have made large contribution.

It has gratified me during the year I have been in office to acquaint myself, through official sources and otherwise, with the progress your country has made and is making along the lines of social reform leading to social justice and the education and welfare of the Mexican people.

Hoping to have the pleasure of seeing you in Washington during my Administration, I am[1]

Very sincerely yours,

[PPF 86 :CT]

[1]Drafted by Daniels.

Press Conference, Executive Offices of the White House, March 23, 1934, 4:08 P.M.

[*Excerpt*] Q: The French, in a note sent to Great Britain and made public today, declared that the willingness of other powers to consult in case of treaty violations is not sufficient guarantee of their security and they must have guarantees of effective action, particularly by groups of nations.[1] That is a bit further than we are prepared to go?

The President: What do they want?

Q: They want Great Britain to come to their aid if Germany violates any of the treaties, but they do not specify Great Britain, they say the community of nations should come to their aid.

The President: Of course we cannot change what we said last year.[2]

Q: And that still stands?

The President: Yes.

Q: While we are on foreign affairs, we have a report that Ambassador Dodd arrives in New York today. Any significance in his return?

The President: No. He wrote me about a month ago and said it would be a good thing to get a little holiday and, at the same time, to report and tell us the situation.[3] I did not know he was landing today . . .

Q: Have you signed the Vinson Bill yet?

The President: No, it has not come down. It does not come down until tomorrow. If I do sign it and if I have time and do not get taken up too much with automobiles and things like that, I will file with it a memorandum for your information. Perhaps you had better not break the story at all and make this off the record. It will be a memorandum which will point out the distinction between an appropriation and an authorization. It is time that the public was informed of the difference. It is not the fault of the press, because we have all used a word that we understand, but the reading public does not understand when they read a story in the newspaper that Congress has authorized the building of 102 new ships. The public assumes that they are going to start building those 102 new ships right away. So I have to point out in a memorandum that this bill is really, in its essentials, nothing more than a resolution that it is still the policy of the United States to build up to the London Naval Treaty limits and, having passed that resolution, it depends on the action of future Congresses as to whether the ships will be actually started or not. I have to do that because I have had so many appeals from pacifist organizations which do not understand it.[4]

[President's Press Conferences:T]

[1] The French note of March 17, 1934, appeared in the New York *Times* of March 24, 1934, p. 6; for the original text see *British Documents, 1919–1939*, VI, 556–560. This note was in reply to the British disarmament proposal of Jan. 29, 1934. The French found the British proposal unacceptable and Wilson (U.S. delegate in Geneva) gave credence to reports that the French now wished to give the Conference "a correct juridicial funeral." Once this was done, they would discuss a "status quo limitation treaty" (memorandum by Phillips, March 19, 1934; Wilson to Hull, March 23, 1934, *Foreign Relations, 1934*, I, 33, 34).

[2] Davis' statement of May 23, 1933, at the Disarmament Conference, that the United States would take part in any general consultation that might be called in consequence of a breach of the Pact of Paris and would "refrain from any action and . . . withold protection from its citizens if engaged in activities which would tend to defeat the collective effort" decided upon (*Foreign Relations, 1933*, I, 166–168).

[3] No letter of this description has been found.

[4] The Vinson bill, H.R. 6604, was approved March 27, 1934 (48 *Stat.* 503). Roosevelt's statement on signing it is in *Public Papers*, III, 172.

Roosevelt to George N. Peek, Special Adviser to the President on Foreign Trade

[Washington] March 23, 1934

Dear Mr. Peek: Pursuant to Executive Order No. 6651, of March 23, 1934, establishing the Office of Special Adviser to the President on Foreign Trade, I have appointed you the Special Adviser, at a salary of $12,000 per annum, subject to the provisions of section 2, title II, of the act of March 20, 1933 (Public, No. 2, 73rd Congress), effective at once.[1]

Sincerely yours,

[OF 971:CT]

---

[1] The executive order is printed in *Public Papers,* III, 158–160. Drafts of this order and correspondence concerning it are with the letter to Peek here printed. Also in this file (OF 971) is a "Memorandum of Suggestions Concerning Duties of President of Export-Import Banks and Foreign Trade Adviser," prepared by Assistant Secretary of State Sayre. It is not dated but bears the filing date of April 5, 1934. Peek's duties were to collect information on foreign trade and to keep the President informed of developments. He was also authorized to carry on negotiations with persons, corporations and other agencies "interested in obtaining assistance from the Federal Government through financing transactions, barter transactions, or other forms of Governmental participation authorized by law." Such proposed transactions were to be brought before the appropriate government agency.

Peek had drawn up the original draft of the executive order (sometime before March 2), and a later draft "worked out in conjunction with the Departments of State and Commerce and . . . approved by the Secretary of State and the Secretary of Commerce" (Peek to Roosevelt, March 23, 1934, OF 971). For some reason he did not formally accept the post until April 14, 1934, according to his letter of that date to Roosevelt (OF 971). Of Peek's appointment Hull said, "If Mr. Roosevelt had hit me between the eyes with a sledge hammer he could not have stunned me more than by this appointment. . . . His efforts, and those of his associates, aided at times by the President, came perilously near supplanting my whole set of international economic policies . . ." (*Memoirs,* I, 370).

Stephen T. Early, Assistant Secretary to the President, to James T. Williams, Jr., Washington

[Washington] March 25, 1934

Dear Mr. Williams: Just a word of explanation as to the delay and to dissipate any thought you may have had as to whether I had forgotten your inquiry of March seventeenth.[1]

I have taken the request to the President twice but have not been able to get a definite answer. The automobile strike negotiations of the past five days helped add to the congestion and the confusion. That was disposed of last night and today new chores arose and caused routine to be sidetracked. As you know, the President will leave for Florida tomorrow.

I can tell you that the President has not reached any definite decision on future action in relationship to the St. Lawrence Treaty. Personally, I do not expect him to take up this subject again until some time after his return from Florida.

I have noticed publication of the editorial suggested in the telegram. Hence I wonder whether you want me to follow up on the inquiry or whether the appearance of the editorial has disposed of the question.

With kindest regards, Very sincerely,

[OF 846:CT]

[1] In a note to Early of March 17, 1934 (OF 846), Williams, an editor of the Hearst newspapers, enclosed a telegram of the same date he had received from Hearst through the latter's secretary, J. Willicombe, in Los Angeles. Hearst urged that the sectional opposition to the St. Lawrence Waterway Treaty be removed by a program that would include a fuller development of inland coast canals "and possibly some western project like Columbia River." He said he would like to advocate this editorially. Willicombe, who signed the telegram, added: "The above was dictated by chief who asks that you kindly see President about it to learn if he is inclined to approve it. There is no use shooting editorials unless project would meet with Administration's approval." Early placed the correspondence before the President who said he would let Hearst know as soon as possible (Early to Roosevelt, March 17, 1934, OF 846). Hearst had lunch with Roosevelt at the White House on May 24; what was discussed is not indicated in the correspondence about the appointment but since it was arranged through Williams the St. Lawrence Waterway Treaty was probably brought up (McIntyre to Hearst, May 16, 1934, and accompanying memoranda, OF 846).

Roosevelt to George H. Dern, Secretary of War

[Washington] March 26, 1934

Confidential

My dear Mr. Secretary: I enclose a copy of a letter which I have just received from the Secretary of State which speaks for itself.[1] I too am concerned over the situation in Panama. I suggest that you detail an officer to confer with a representative of the State Department and a representative of the Navy Department in order to advise us as to whether all practicable measures are being taken and, if not, to make such recommendations as may appear to fit the immediate needs.

If you and the Secretary of State and the Secretary of the Navy will confer on this in a preliminary way, I shall be grateful.[2]

Very sincerely yours,

[OF 197:CT]

[1] March 22, 1934 (OF 197), reporting that an unusual number of Japanese nationals had recently appeared in Panama; some were known "to be closely connected with the Japanese Government," and some had been expelled from the Philippines in 1910 as spies. The War Department had also received information of extensive Japanese espionage in Panama.

[2] A like letter was sent to the Secretary of the Navy (Roosevelt to Swanson, March 26, 1934, OF 197).

Roosevelt to Cordell Hull, Secretary of State

[Washington] March 26, 1934

Memorandum for Secretary of State: Will you ask Dodd whether he thinks I should send a personal message back to Hitler when he returns to Berlin and if so, to try to prepare one for me![1]

F.D.R.

[OF 198:CT]

[1] See letter following.

William Phillips, Under Secretary of State, to Roosevelt

Washington, March 26, 1934

Dear Mr. President: I enclose a draft reply to Chancellor Hitler on which I should be very glad to have your comments. The message from the Chancellor is also enclosed in case you do not have it before you.[1] We should like to have your corrections or your approval, if possible, before you leave Washington tomorrow.[2]

Faithfully yours,

William Phillips

[*Notation*:AS] OK. But show to Dodd first   FDR
[*Notation*:AS] Approved by Ambassador Dodd   WP[3]
[OF 198:TS]

  [1] March 14, 1934, above.
  [2] Roosevelt left Washington at 5 P.M. the next day for a vacation aboard the *Nourmahal,* Vincent Astor's yacht. In a note from Kannee to Forster of March 27, filed with the letter here printed, Kannee said that Phillips had been asking about the message to Hitler, and that the President said he had approved it as drafted. Forster added the following to Kannee's note: "Phoned Mr. Phillips. He said he had rec'd the President's O.K. O.K."
  [3] Dodd, home on leave, was on duty in the State Department at this time (*Diary,* p. 93).

[*Enclosure*] Roosevelt to Hitler [draft]

The President of the United States desires to thank the Chancellor of the German Reich for his message to him, conveyed by Ambassador Dodd. The President appreciates the Chancellor's words of congratulation, yet feels that they apply not to him personally but to the American people who have freely and gladly made heroic efforts in the interest of recovery. In reciprocating the Chancellor's cordial greetings, the President wishes to express the hope, in which he is joined by the people of the United States, that Germany's ~~attempts~~ *efforts*[1] toward economic restoration may be entirely successful and so contribute to that universal recovery from which all alike will benefit.

[*Notation*:A:FDR] Corrected
[OF 198:T]

  [1] This revision is not in Roosevelt's hand but was no doubt made at his direction. Thus revised the note was sent to Hitler in a note from our Embassy, March 29, 1934, printed in *German Documents,* II, 690. Dodd states that Hull was "a little puzzled about an answer to be given by the President to Hitler's code message—publicity might follow" (*Diary,* p. 93). This reference to the document as a "code message" is not further explained.

Cordell Hull, Secretary of State, to Roosevelt

Washington, March 26, 1934

My dear Mr. President: March 13 the German Ambassador informed me orally that his Government was unable to make the payment of about

127,000,000 Reichsmarks (payable in dollars at the current rate of exchange and therefore equal to about $50,000,000) due March 31 under the Debt Agreement of June 23, 1930, and the Hoover Moratorium Agreement of May 26, 1932. He stated he desired to find ways of arranging some adjustment which would have the effect of postponing payment and added that the entire debt would have to be readjusted but that this would not be taken up until a little later.

The payments due include 20,400,000 Reichsmarks semi-annual principal instalment on mixed claims; 102,000,000 Reichsmarks representing five semi-annual instalments on mixed claims which have been postponed to March 31 under the option granted Germany in the debt agreement and can be postponed no longer; 2,550,000 Reichsmarks interest for the past six months on these postponed instalments; 627,125 Reichsmarks interest for the last six months on postponed army cost instalments; and 1,529,049.45 Reichsmarks semi-annual instalment due on account of army costs under the moratorium agreement of 1932.

No reply has been made to the Ambassador and no further proposal received from him but the suggestion having been brought up in informal discussions between an officer of the Embassy and officers of this Department that if unable to pay the principal, Germany could at least pay and continue to pay interest on arrears (this would be 4,706,000 Reichsmarks including the moratorium payment, or 3,177,000 Reichsmarks without it), the Embassy asked Berlin and was told that Germany could not pay more in dollars than $500,000. The Embassy also brought in a memorandum regarding the condition of the Reichsbank which on March 15 had reserves of gold and foreign exchange totaling only 274,000,000 Reichsmarks (about $109,000,000 at current exchange).

I should add to complete the picture that except for postponements permissible under the existing agreements Germany has made all payments due until September 30, 1933, when it deposited to the order of the United States Treasury in the Reichsbank the sum of about 4,000,000 Reichsmarks due that day, defaulting on its obligation to transfer this sum into dollars. It has used its option to postpone army cost payments since the end of the Hoover moratorium including the payment due March 31, 1934, and can postpone one more payment on this account under its option.

As of September 30, 1933, the Treasury accounts carried mixed claims awards in favor of private American claimants against Germany, of $55,000,000; German claims in the amount of $115,000,000; and awards in favor of the United States Government in the amount of $79,000,000 (the Government awards under the schedule of priorities established in the Settlement of War Claims Act cannot be paid until American and German private claims have been paid in full, with interest). Of the original $292,700,000 costs of the United States Army of Occupation $181,900,000 remained unpaid.

You may remember that efforts have been made by private claimants to work out a settlement whereby the time of payment of private claims could be materially reduced, Germany assuming the liability to pay its own nationals in Reichsmarks and permitting the dollars already held in this country for account of German nationals, either in the Treasury or with the Alien Property Custodian, to be used for payment of American claimants with a further contribution by Germany to the American claimants, suggested at one time as $15,000,000.

While I have not made any direct response to Ambassador Luther, I instructed our Embassy at Berlin March 24 to leave an Aide Memoire at the Foreign Office, referring to his démarche, calling attention to recent remarks of Doctor Schacht regarding German private debts and asking a statement affirming that Germany recognizes the obligation to pay debts to the full capacity of payment of the debtor and will do everything in its power to see that this obligation is faithfully carried out. I enclose copy of this telegram.

The Treasury holds about $5,000,000 cash and the Alien Property Custodian has about $15,000,000 which may serve as partial security for the payment of mixed claims awards to Americans. German default will raise the question whether congressional action to insure that no part of these funds or of any other funds in the hands of the Alien Property Custodian be disbursed to German claimants is necessary and should be recommended. Such action will probably be immediately proposed in Congress unless the Administration moves first or announces that it is unnecessary.

I am informed by Secretary Morgenthau that the position of the Treasury is that the minimum which the United States should accept is the amount due as interest on account of army costs and mixed claims. This amounts to 3,177,000 Reichsmarks or about $1,250,000.

May I have your instructions as to the attitude to be taken toward the German Ambassador in respect of the payments due March 31. Shall we indicate that we expect to receive at least the interest payments? If Germany should agree to this, could we agree not to withhold all payments to German nationals, as above, or in some other way meet the German desire not to incur the odium of unilateral failure to pay the principal sum due?

Faithfully yours,

Cordell Hull

[OF 198:TS]

[*Enclosure*] Cordell Hull to William E. Dodd, Ambassador to Germany

[Washington] March 24, 1934

[*Telegram*] Urgent 35   Please call at the Foreign Office and after appropriate discussion leave an Aide Memoire on the following lines:

"March 13 the German Ambassador calling on the Secretary of State referred to payments due by Germany March 31, 1934, under the Debt agreement of April 23, 1930, and the Hoover postponement agreement of May 26, 1932. He stated that his Government was unable to make this payment amounting to some 127,000,000 Reichsmarks when due and he desired to find ways of arriving at some adjustment which would have the effect of postponing payment. He added that the entire debt due from his Government to ours would have to be readjusted but that this matter need not be taken up until a little later.

"It appears that in this as in other debts payable by foreign governments to the United States under agreements authorized by act of Congress, there is no power in the executive branch of the American Government to agree to the postponement of payments due thereunder except as stated in the agreement.

"The payments due March 31, 1934, differ in part from strictly intergovernmental debts in that some 125,000,000 Reichsmarks out of 127,000,000 Reichsmarks thereof are payable by Germany in respect of awards of an international tribunal in favor of American claimants against Germany. The disposition of these payments is regulated by an act of Congress establishing a deposit fund and a scheme of priorities which would permit payments to some German interests while American private claimants remain unsatisfied. The Congress has appropriated and paid considerable amounts into this deposit fund and it now contains substantial balances. In the circumstances it is probable that the Congress would take immediate cognizance of this situation.

"Consideration of the attitude to be taken toward the German Ambassador's request for postponement of the maturities of March 31 is rendered more difficult by the effect on public opinion of reports from Germany of agitation against the foreign debts of Germany and Germans such as the recent remarks of the President of the Reichsbank of which extensive excerpts were telegraphed verbatim to the American press. Doctor Schacht is quoted as saying:

In the well-known Layton report on the 1931 Basle conference,[1] you can read for yourselves that 10,300,000,000 marks of these commercial loans never found their way into German business but were used directly for effecting reparation payments. Yet these 10,300,000,000 marks of debts still live on in a commercial shape.

When you add the interest we have paid on that amount since 1924, when you take into consideration further that our debts abroad now total only 15,000,000,000 marks, you can see that Germany's total present foreign debt corresponds exactly with its political origin, whereas all indebtedness which has been used not for reparations but for German industry has been paid back in full.

"This in connection with other expressions from Germany is immediately and inevitably interpreted by public opinion in the United States to imply that all that Germany owes privately was really for political account and should therefore be written down if not entirely wiped out.

"Without desiring to enter into discussion of the German debt situation on the basis of remarks of the kind quoted, it is felt that the German Government should not be left in ignorance of the unfortunate impression created on American public opinion. In considering what position it can take toward the maturities of March 31, 1934, my Government desires to call attention to the difficulty of the creditor taking any action to mitigate the unilateral nature of failure to pay money owed by the German Government when high-ranking German authorities are describing the debts of all German borrowers, whether national, municipal or corporate who have borrowed abroad since the war as 'political' debts with some implication that they should not be met.

"In the circumstances my Government requests some explicit reassuring statement of the German Government affirming its recognition of the obligation that debts be paid up to the full capacity of payment of the debtor and as to the intention of the German Government to do everything in its power to see that this obligation is faithfully carried out."

Hull

[OF 198:M]

[1] Sir Walter Thomas Layton drafted the report of the special advisory committee on reparations headed by Albert H. Wiggin, chairman of the Chase National Bank. Layton was editor of the *Economist*.

Roosevelt to Cordell Hull, Secretary of State

[Washington] March 27, 1934

Personal

Memorandum for the Secretary of State: I am dictating this just before leaving.[1]

In regard to the problem of German payments, what do you think of suggesting to the German Ambassador:

(a) That we expect to receive at least the interest payments from them.

(b) That we will make payments to German Nationals in proportion to the German payments to us, holding the balance of our payments to German Nationals in escrow for further conversations.

For example, if Germany pays us 4% interest, we would pay 4% on the amounts due from us to German Nationals.

I am inclined to suggest that for the next week or so we be rather stiff in our attitude toward Dr. Luther and Dr. Schacht.

F.D.R.

[OF 198:CT]

[1] For his Caribbean cruise on the *Nourmahal*.

Roosevelt to Senator Burton K. Wheeler of Montana

[Washington] March 27, 1934

My dear Senator Wheeler: I have considered your letter of March 12, 1934, signed jointly with Senator Hayden suggesting that the taxes on imports contained in the Revenue Act of 1932, which will expire June 30, 1935, might advantageously be extended beyond that date to give increased trading power in tariff bargaining negotiations.[1]

I am inclined to feel that just now would not be the most appropriate time to take action which might be construed as increasing barriers with a view to bargaining negotiations. We should object to others doing this. For this reason it would seem wise to defer bringing up this matter at the present time, since there will be ample opportunity before these provisions expire.

Needless to say, your forethought in bringing this matter to my attention is appreciated.

I am sending a similar letter to Senator Hayden.[2]

Sincerely yours,

[OF 962:CT]

[1] Wheeler and Hayden said (OF 962) they had been responsible for the amendment to the 1932 Revenue Act that had added four cents per pound to the import tax on copper. They claimed that unless the tax was continued beyond its expiration date of June 30, 1935, many copper mines would have to close and urged that the tax be extended before the President's authority (under the NIRA act) expired on June 16, 1934.

[2] This letter was drafted by Hull. In his covering letter to Roosevelt, March 26, 1934 (OF 962), he made this comment on the Hayden-Wheeler proposal:

"I feel that this suggestion is a strong reason against its adoption. The history of reciprocity negotiations shows that one of the greatest dangers to their success as an instrument for promoting international trade lies in the tendency of governments to raise barriers prior to negotiations with the expectation of bargaining them away—with the result that, even if they are in fact bargained away, there may be no net gain in the matter of barrier removal. In our own negotiations we propose to watch for and combat this evil. We shall wish to be in a position to insist that, where a country has raised its tariff so recently as to indicate such motive, negotiations with the United States must be on the basis of the duties in force before the duties were enacted. In order that we may consistently so insist, I urge that no step be taken that might be construed as action on our part comparable to the 'padding' of rates which we shall oppose when engaged in by others."

J. V. A. MacMurray, Minister to Estonia, Latvia, and Lithuania, to Roosevelt

Riga, Latvia, March 27, 1934

My dear Mr. President: You will perhaps recall having asked that I should write you, when I had become somewhat familiar with my new post here, my impressions of the activities and the influence of Hitlerism in this region of the Eastern Baltic. A mere summary statement in general terms is easy enough to give: In each of the three countries to which I am accredited (Latvia, Estonia and Lithuania), a Nazi movement has been more or less surreptitiously undertaken among the resident minority of German extraction; in each, the disclosure of this movement has aroused general popular as well as governmental opposition, and has resulted in repressive measures; and in each, it may be said to have failed to become a political force of any potential influence for the purposes it has in view.

Such a summary and over-simplified statement would, however, be misleading in that it would ignore the very real, though somewhat intangible, indirect influences of the Nazi movement upon the complex political attitudes, both external and domestic, of the peoples of this corner of Europe. These three little nations, often grouped together for convenience under the name of "the Balticum," do indeed have much in common; they are all peasant republics, whose peoples have for the first time since the XIII Century attained their aspirations of nationhood after centuries of subjection; they are hemmed in by three vastly larger and stronger neighbors—Germany, Poland and the Soviet Union; their political independence has itself cut them off from any economic hinterland, and they are situated almost at a dead-end of the European trade routes; they have virtually no wealth or economic opportunities other than their fields and forests; and since they have nothing to offer which is not produced in abundance by most of their neighbors, their economic existence may almost literally be said to depend upon their sales of lumber, pork and dairy products to England, primarily, and to Germany, secondarily.

Despite these similarities in their general situation, there are differences of race, of language, of historical tradition, and of cultural and religious background, which sharply distinguish the three peoples, and differentiate their views and their characteristic responses to political influences. While the Lithuanians and the Letts are fairly closely related branches of the same Indo-European stock, and speak similar languages derived directly from the Sanskrit, the Estonians are of an Asiatic stock and speak a language wholly unrelated to that of any other people in Europe except the Finns and the Magyars. Yet this kinship between the Letts and the Lithuanians seems to make them no more alike in temperament, or in instinctive social and political reactions, than the greater community of historical experience has made the Letts and the Estonians. For while Latvia and Estonia have been about seven centuries (including the recent period when they were politically incorporated in the Russian Empire) been dominated by the German Baltic barons mostly descended from the conquering Teutonic Orders, Lithuania has similarly been under the domination of Polish landlords. The culture of the Germans in Latvia and Estonia seems clearly to have been far higher, but more aloof from the people, who were indeed scarcely more than serfs in their ancestral lands, regarding their Balt masters with sullen hatred, but in greater or less degree absorbing their basic concepts of life and culture; whereas the more easy-going Polish nobles seem not to have created such a sharp cleavage between themselves and the people of Lithuania, nor aroused such bitterness of feeling, even though they contributed very little cultural influence. Out of such divergent influences, the minds and tempers of the three peoples developed striking differences. The Letts are a somewhat dour people, distrustful of themselves and of others, self-conscious and reticent and passive, and prone to stand on the defensive stubbornly though rather timidly: the Estonians, though equally hard-boiled in seeking their own interests, have nevertheless a blitheness and openheartedness and freedom from self-consciousness which gives them a far more positive intellectual and moral force: and the Lithuanians, thinking of themselves always as the race that (for a very short period, it is true, and very long ago) were masters of Eastern Europe, are full of a sense of superiority, yearn to appear like a Great Power, and carry things with a high hand and with a bit of playboy bluster. Perhaps one accredited to several countries should not even let himself be conscious of any differences in his esteem for them; but it seems to me that in order to understand the current developments of affairs in the Balticum, one must recognize that the Estonians have more of the qualities of leadership, and that the Letts are likely to be grudging followers, whereas the Lithuanians will be forever trying to start a parade of their own in the hope that the others will fall in.

Such are, indeed, roughly the parts which the three countries are taking with regard to the project of a Baltic Union for the protection of their common economic and political interests. They are all, in varying degrees, preoccupied with the necessity of some such understanding among themselves (and with Finland included) in view of their consciousness of their individual weakness and exposed position among the powerful and discordant nations that hem them in on the shore of the Baltic. And it is Germany that they particularly fear. Although watchfully on guard against the Soviet Union, they seem at the moment to have less apprehension than one might expect that Russia will in the foreseeable future take the aggressive against them. The same is true of the attitude of Estonia and Latvia towards Poland; and although Lithuania has of recent years been violently and rather melodramatically at odds with Poland because of her seizure of Vilna, I am inclined to believe that this quarrel involves no deep or permanent antipathy or fear of Poland on the part of the Lithuanians. But all three peoples remember that one of the incidents of the confusion that followed the close of the war on the Eastern Front was that their territories were overrun by German irregular forces got together at the instance of the dispossessed Baltic barons for the purpose of gaining for the Fatherland these outposts of *Deutschthum*. And the reiteration, by Hitler and his followers, of the doctrine of Germany's destiny lying to the eastward has given these peoples a sense of insecurity. In the case of Estonia and Latvia, that fear is the more vivid and terrifying because of their centuries of enslavement to German Balt landlords and their realization that absorption by Germany would mean for them not merely the loss of technical sovereignty as independent nations but a restoration of the nationalized baronial estates and the reestablishment of a system in which they would again be hewers of wood and drawers of water for their old oppressors. In the case of Lithuania, there has been no such particular antipathy and fear prompted by the experience of their own past; but direct contiguity to Germany, with the tendencies to friction intensified by the anomalous situation of Memel which the Versailles Treaty established as an apple of discord between the two countries, has given the Lithuanians occasion to feel conscious of their danger. All three nations are in a nervous mood, predisposed to "jumpy" reactions against any manifestation of an attempt to extend German influence among them.

Such manifestations of Nazi activity followed substantially the same lines in Latvia and in Estonia. Among the more ardent elements of the Balts, who have been wholly or substantially dispossessed of their estates, and who, while not German citizens, think of themselves always as the bearers of German culture, there spread an enthusiasm for the new Nazi spirit which they felt had regenerated what they call their Motherland. A comparatively small number of them, in each country, organized themselves into Nazi groups which may or may not have been formally affiliated (that point does not seem to have been definitely established in either case) with the official organization in Germany; and they began a somewhat vague and cautious propaganda for the Nazi cause among their fellow Balts. These activities led, under the circumstances, to veritable explosions of popular feeling: and the Governments investigated the organizations, declared them illegal, and deported such resident German citizens as were involved. No other result could be expected; it is doubtful whether the more sober-minded members of the Balt communities are not themselves relieved to have an end put to an agitation that could only serve to embitter relations and jeopardize such cultural privileges as the national minorities enjoy in both countries; and the suppression of the local Nazi movement does not appear to have created in either case any strain on relations with Germany.

In Lithuania, there are virtually no Germans except in Memel; and Nazi activity has manifested itself only in connection with the struggle for economic and cultural supremacy in that uneasy District. The Statute enacted by the League of Nations gave a considerable degree of autonomy to the Memel District, in which Germans predominate; and most of the municipal office-holders, judges, and teachers in the schools have been Germans. It would seem that the Germans, conscious of their cultural superiority to the Lithuanians, and presuming upon the safeguarding of their position by the Statute, have been scarcely conciliatory towards the officials or the people of the country under whose sovereignty they have been put; and the Lithuanians have yielded to the temptation to assert their authority against what seemed to them a contemptous challenge. It was in connection with this struggle for dominance in the Memel District that the Lithuanian authorities uncovered a local Nazi organization which did not indeed seem to enjoy much support from the home party organization or widespread approval on the part of compatriots in Memel, but which of course tended to rationalize in Lithuanian minds the rather harsh measures which they have been taking against the German civil employees in the District. Whatever the legal merits of the case ostensibly at issue, it seems difficult to avoid the feeling that the Lithuanians have been imprudent in forcing such a situation with a powerful and not very complaisant neighbor—that they have made a nervous error of judgment in assuming that the assertion of their authority in the relatively unimportant port of Memel would in any degree tend to assure them against the danger of German aggression.

The case of Memel illustrates the way in which the menace implied in Hitlerism, or attributed to it, not only intrudes into the consideration of particular problems, but conditions the political thinking and the emotional responses of those who feel that they have reason to be afraid of Germany. It tends to create, in their relations with other peoples, a suspicious and irritable mood, a disposition to make much out of small matters, and to carry a chip on the shoulder and resort to an aggressive attitude in going out to meet any real or fancied injury to their rights or affront to their dignity.

And the same nationalistic temper exhibits itself, in the internal life of these states, in the form of a kind of Fascism which, curiously enough, is largely modeled upon the German Nazi type whose threatened influence has called it into being. It involves, to begin with, a hardening of feeling towards the minority racial elements in their populations—an intolerance that leads to the curtailment of the fairly liberal régime of cultural independence hitherto prevailing, and to indulgence in the sort of self-assertion that prescribes, for example, that letters cannot be delivered unless addressed only in the language of the country. This type of Fascism furthermore predisposes these peoples to a changed attitude towards the functions of government. The Lithuanian Government has for some years been an out-and-out dictatorship; Estonia has recently remodeled its constitution in the direction of making it a more authoritarian state; and Latvia is now considering similar constitutional changes, with every probability of their eventual acceptance. There are doubtless other contributory causes for this drift away from the purely democratic form of government with which these three new countries began their existence—such reasons as the economic crisis, and their own political inexperience, which led them to break up into such a multiplicity of factions as deprived their governments of all stability and coherence of action. But it seems to me that the present tendency is in large measure the result of a feeling that the peril of the times requires concentration of authority, and that the form in which they conceive that result is influenced by the awe with which they regard the Nazi organization as embodying the concentration of German national power that they fear and want to emulate.

The real influence of Hitlerism in the Balticum, therefore, lies in its indirect effects in stimulating, among these peoples, a form of nationalism which finds expression in a somewhat overwrought and touchy temper in international matters, and, in their domestic politics, in a tendency to be less liberal towards their national minorities, and a reaction away from democracy towards a rather narrow authoritarian concept of the state.

With warmest regards and good wishes, I remain, Mr. President, with great respect, Yours, very sincerely,

J. V. A. MacMurray[1]

[OF 909:TS]

[1] Answered April 18, 1934, below.

William C. Bullitt, Ambassador to the Union of Soviet Socialist Republics, to Roosevelt

Moscow, Easter Day [April 1] 1934

Personal and Confidential

My dear Mr. President: I have not burdened you with letters because I know you get too many from ambassadors. But I wish so much that I could talk with you tonight that I am seizing the excuse of a couple of matters that cannot go into despatches to the Department in order to give myself the sensation that I am not utterly cut off from you . . .[1]

Second—Madame Litvinov is very anxious to have their seventeen year old son visit America this summer. If he should visit Troyanovsky, would you invite him to lunch or dine at the White House—or better still, could you drop me a line saying that if he should come over you would be glad to have him overnight as your guest? Litvinov would appreciate this more than a dozen large concessions, and, as we do not intend to concede anything to him officially, such an invitation might pull a lot of chestnuts out of the fire for us.

Moscow has turned out to be just as disagreeable as I anticipated. The honeymoon atmosphere had evaporated completely before I arrived.

As Wiley[2] says, "The Japanese have let us down badly." The Russians are convinced that Japan will not attack this spring or summer and, as they no longer feel that they need our immediate help, their underlying hostility to all capitalist countries now shows through the veneer of intimate friendship. We shall have to deal with them according to Claudel's formula of the donkey, the carrot, and the club.

In addition to the "misunderstanding" about the extra interest on credits, there have been similar "misunderstandings" about the property on which we expect to build our Embassy, the obtaining of paper roubles, the payment of consular fees in paper roubles, repairs to the Embassy residence, and apartments in the office building. The only effective way of dealing with this general attitude, I believe, is to maintain the friendliest possible personal relations with the Russians but to let them know clearly that if they are unwilling to move forward and take the carrot they will receive the club on the behind. For example, the next time I discuss the payment of debts and claims with Litvinov, I shall allow him to derive the impression that if the Soviet Union does not wish to use the credits of the Import-Export Bank the Japanese Government will be eager to use the facilities of the Bank to finance large purchases from certain American heavy industries.

The bright spot in the murky sky is the Embassy staff. The men I selected in Washington have turned out to be both able and filled with the finest spirit. We have had to have secretaries of Embassy and clerks answering the front door bell and carrying furniture, and they have done so as a matter of course without complaint. I am delighted with every man on the staff.

But I am a bit homesick. It is a new sensation for me and it arises from a very happy thing. In many years I have not had the sensation that I had a home, but in this past year you and Mrs. Roosevelt and Miss LeHand have made me feel that I was a member of the family, and the thing I miss so much is the afternoons and evenings with you in the White House. I am much too fond of you all.

Take good care of yourself. Good luck, and the Lord be with you! Yours always,

William C. Bullitt

[*Notation*:A:FDR] File
[PSF:Russia:TS]

[1] Omitted are several paragraphs in which Bullitt asked the President to grant a pardon to a man convicted of subversive activities in World War I.
[2] John C. Wiley, counselor of embassy.

Conference of Roosevelt with House Democratic Leaders, at the White House, April 15, 1934, 8:30 P.M.

Confidential

[*Excerpt*] The President discussed Silver. Among other things, he said: "I am in favor of bi-metallism or, if you will, a fused metallic standard. We are ready to go ahead with the American nations to see if we can get an international agreement for a bi-metallic or fused metallic standard. If we can do that, it is the first step toward a world currency on a bi-metallic base." The discussion covered an international unit of exchange. The President later explained the situation in relation to China. He finished the discussion with this statement: "Personally, I am in favor of a fused standard. I am absolutely opposed to any silver legislation at this session."[1]

[OF 419:T]

[1] The memorandum from which this is taken is a summary of a discussion of Roosevelt's proposed legislative program; his remarks, for the most part, are given in the first person. (There is no indication of authorship but it does not appear to have been typed in the White House.) Those present included Speaker Henry T. Rainey, Majority Leader Joseph W. Byrns, Majority Whip Arthur H. Greenwood, Caucus Leader Clarence F. Lea, and the heads of the principal committees (New York *Times,* April 16, 1934, p. 1). No report was given out on what had been discussed; however, when Rainey was asked if silver legislation had been mentioned, he replied that it had been: "All I can say about that is that the President said he was as much for silver as I am" (*ibid.*).

Robert Underwood Johnson, Secretary, American Academy of Arts and Letters, to Roosevelt

New York, April 16, 1934

Dear Mr. President: The American Academy of Arts and Letters, for which I spoke before the Senate Committee on Foreign Relations on the 28th of March, in advocacy of the Copyright Treaty, is deeply gratified by your action in sending the Treaty to the Senate, and also for the cordial support of it by the Department of State as manifested at the same hearing by Mr. Wallace McClure.[1] Also, at that time, Dr. Raney[2] of the University of Chicago, presented a petition in favor of the Treaty and the Cutting Bill from fourteen Presidents of leading American Universities. The Cutting Bill is in the nature of an enabling act, and may not be necessary if the Treaty is ratified.

A few days ago, the Copyright Committee of the New York Bar Association, after consideration of the text of both Treaty and Bill, endorsed the former, and, in principle, the latter, reserving however so far as the Bill is concerned, some details of legal nature which no doubt can be readily adjusted. If the Bill is necessary, it will have great prestige from the approval of the Treaty, and we are very desirous that no time shall be lost in the matter, for time and again we have experienced the dangers of copyright measures becoming entangled in the legislation of a waning Congress.

Your signature to the Treaty would proclaim to the world in most memorable fashion that we are standing for the highest conception of literary rights, and would thus relieve us of the disgrace of tolerating piracy as we now do in the case of English authors by excluding them from the security of our law unless they manufacture a second edition in this country. While they have suffered under this onerous condition, we have been obtaining rights on the Continent by publication in

English. Only by the removal of this condition can we obtain the immense benefit of entering the Berne Copyright Union which would give us immediately and automatically the security of the 53 countries composing the Union.

If we ratify quickly, we will get the credit of at least doing a just, if not a generous act; if we haggle and delay, we shall be thought to yield only to the possibility of English retaliation, which would involve another aspect of commercial warfare.

Every author in America, living or dead, has regarded this as a moral question, and of course, it is so regarded abroad.

Therefore, on behalf of the American Academy of Arts and Letters, the most distinguished body of its kind in the country, and of the nine surviving members of the Council of the original 37 of the American Copyright League of 1890-1891, which led in the reform of that era, I respectfully invoke your commanding influence in representing to the Senate the desirability of ratifying at the earliest possible moment this long delayed, honorable and necessary international agreement. I beg to call your attention to the enclosed editorial from the New York *Times*,[3] which I think presents clearly the merits of the Treaty and the Bill.

I have the honor to remain, Mr. President, Most respectfully yours,

Robert Underwood Johnson

[*Notation*:A:LeHand] Secretary of State   Preparation of reply[4]
[PPF 1442:TS]

[1] Assistant chief of the Treaty Division.
[2] M. L. Raney, director of libraries, University of Chicago.
[3] Issue of April 1, 1934.
[4] April 25, 1934, below.

Press Conference, Executive Offices of the White House, April 18, 1934, 10:52 A.M.

[*Excerpt*] Q: Mr. President, do you care to discuss the condition in Japan yesterday in which it stated that the Japanese Government made objection to foreign loans?[1]

The President: I have not talked to the State Department at all. I do not think they have heard anything.

Q: How about the debt Message to the Congress?

The President: Yes, yes, we are three days nearer . . .

Q: Have you any comment on Britain's very splendid financial condition and her action in not taking any cognizance of debt payments to us in her new budget?

The President: No; wait until the debt Message.

Q: In that connection, have you had an opportunity to discuss with the Secretary of State the Johnson Bill and its attitude toward token payments?

The President: No.

Q: Do you care to offer any comment on the silver legislation? There seem to be several bills and some anxiety.

The President: The less comment I make at this particular moment, the better.

[President's Press Conferences:T]

---

[1] On April 17, 1934, the chief of the bureau of information and intelligence of the Japanese Foreign Office issued a statement on the Japanese position on the giving of assistance to China by other countries. The statement declared that Japan would oppose any attempt by China to get the help of any other country in resisting Japan, even if this were in the guise of financial or technical assistance. Furnishing war planes and air fields and sending military advisers would be opposed (Grew to Hull, April 20, 1934, *Foreign Relations, Japan, 1931–1941*, I, 223–225). The statement was hastily labeled "unofficial" by the Japanese Foreign Office but it aroused much concern: see memorandum by Phillips, April 24, 1934 (*ibid.*, pp. 225–227). Hull sent a strong protest to Tokyo on April 28 and protested the statement at an interview with the Japanese ambassador on May 19 (*ibid.*, pp. 231–232, 233–236).

Roosevelt to Grenville T. Emmet, Minister to The Netherlands

[Washington] April 18, 1934

Personal

Dear Grenville: It is mighty good to get your nice letter of March twenty-fourth[1] and I am so glad that your reception was so cordial, even though it came at the difficult moment of the Queen Mother's death.

I hope you and Pauline are comfortably settled. Give Pauline my love and tell her that I shall expect to talk to her in Dutch the next time I see her.

I have had a fine two weeks holiday on Vincent's boat.[2] The Congress may still give us a good deal of trouble, but I hope they will go home in a month.

Keep me in touch with developments.

As ever yours,

[PPF 372:CT]

[1] Emmet's letter had to do mostly with his reception by Queen Wilhelmina (PSF: Netherlands). Emmet had been a member of Roosevelt's old law firm of Emmet, Marvin and Roosevelt (at this time Emmet, Marvin and Marvin). He had hoped for an appointment to Rome and had refused one to Hungary. He then asked to be named to Berlin or Vienna or, failing that, to Budapest or Constantinople (Emmet to Roosevelt, April 14, 28, June 5, 1933; Phillips to Roosevelt, Aug. 16, Dec. 4, 1933, PPF 372).

[2] Astor's *Nourmahal*, in the Caribbean, from March 27 to April 12.

Roosevelt to John V. A. MacMurray, Minister to Estonia, Latvia, and Lithuania, Riga

[Washington] April 18, 1934

My dear John: That is an extraordinarily interesting letter of yours and I am glad to have such an excellent picture of the three countries.[1] I often wonder what can be the future of European civilization if racial isolation maintains itself through the centuries. I much wish that I could visit your three countries.

Things are going well on the whole at home and we hope that Congress will go home in about a month. I suppose that this summer you will have a chance to run over to Stockholm and to go to Moscow.

Very sincerely yours,

[OF 909:CT]

[1] March 27, 1934, above.

Roosevelt to Lincoln MacVeagh, Minister to Greece, Athens

[Washington] April 19, 1934

Dear Lincoln: Yours of March second[1] is most interesting and I am delighted to know that Greece seems to be getting on so well through what might be called a planned economy.

You must be glad to be rid of that old man of the sea, Mr. Insull. I do hope all goes well with you.

I am just back from a two weeks' trip on the *Nourmahal.*[2]

As ever yours,

[PPF 1192:CT]

[1] Above.
[2] Answered May 9, 1934, below.

William Phillips, Under Secretary of State, to Louis M. Howe, Personal Secretary to the President

Washington, April 20, 1934

Dear Mr. Howe: Just before his departure today, the Secretary of State asked that there be sent, for the President's perusal, the memorandum here attached.

This memorandum was prepared in connection with anticipation, on the basis of hints which have been coming steadily from Japan during recent weeks, that the Japanese Government is contemplating approaching this Government with some "proposal" or "proposals." In it there are an estimate of the present situation from point of view of the general problem of Japanese-American relations, suggestions with regard to what might be the official attitude and procedure here, and a listing, with comments, of several "proposals" of which it is conceived that the Japanese may contemplate laying before us one or more.

May I request that you bring this matter to the President's attention.[1]

Yours sincerely,

William Phillips

[PSF:Japan:TS]

[1] The Japanese proposals were handed to Hull in the form of a memorandum on May 16, 1934, by Ambassador Saito who described them as his "private thoughts." As matters stood, Saito said, the United States suspected Japan of aggressive designs on the Asiatic continent. Japan, on the other hand, suspected that the United States was trying to prevent Japan from pursuing her national aim: the establishment of peace and order in the Far East. Neither was true and both sides should make a joint declaration that each reposed full confidence in the sincerity of the other's motives (*Foreign Relations, Japan, 1931–1941,* I, 232–233).

Hull's memorandum on first receiving Saito's proposal, dated May 16, 1934, and his memorandum of a meeting with Saito devoted to the same subject on May 29, 1934, are printed in *Foreign Relations, 1934,* III, 650–653, 653–661. Hull did not believe that a joint proposal would have the effect desired; the peace of the Pacific would be assured only when all countries there concerned made it their policy to abide by article II of the Pact of Paris. In a note to Roosevelt of June 9, 1934 (*ibid.,* pp. 661–662), Hull said Saito might not accept as final the State Department's rejection of the idea of a joint declaration and might appeal to the President; he urged that he be given no encouragement. See also Hull's *Memoirs,* I, 281, 285.

[*Enclosure*] Stanley K. Hornbeck, Chief, Division of Far Eastern Affairs, to Cordell Hull, Secretary of State

April 5, 1934

Strictly Confidential

Problem of Japanese-American Relations: Considerations Relating to the Immediate Future; Estimate of Policy and Suggestions of Strategy

A

I. The real problems of Japanese-American relations arise out of and revolve around facts and factors in the Far East. They have very little to do with facts and factors on this side of the Pacific Ocean. (Note: The question of Japanese immigration into the United States may be regarded as a special exception; but it is a problem the solution of which calls for changes within the United States before the Department of State can to advantage take any position in reference thereto in the field of external relations.)

There are two things that stand in the way of Japan's progress under the concept of a "manifest destiny": (1) the political concepts and principles of policy of certain other countries; and (2) the actual or potential military and economic power of certain other countries (Note: Treaty provisions, past, present or future, should not be regarded as constituting serious obstacles to action by Japan along the line of political—and probably territorial—expansion in Asia).

II. What the Japanese especially desire at the present moment is relief from any apprehension of possible action of restraint or coercion (sooner or later) by or from the United States and/or Great Britain. If Japan could be sure that the United States and Great Britain would stand completely aside, Japan could (and probably would) rapidly proceed with new steps in a program intended ultimately to establish Japan's authority not only in Manchuria and Mongolia but in certain portions of China and of Siberia.

Hence, Japan's diplomatic efforts are being directed toward bringing about the adoption by the American and the British Governments of policies of surrender or abandonment, with regard to interests, both actual and potential, in those adjacent regions, especially in China. They seek, if possible, that such abandonment be consummated in fact; but that, if it cannot be brought about in fact, it nevertheless be brought about in appearance. Contributory thereto and in connection therewith, they desire that there shall be such developments in the field of comparative naval strength that Japan shall become invulnerable in the Pacific Ocean north of Singapore and west of Hawaii.

III. At the present moment the group in control in Japan is endeavoring to arrive at a decision with regard to the next active steps forward to be taken by Japan. They apparently have excluded (for the time being at least) from consideration the idea of war with the United States. They apparently do not feel prepared to begin a war with Russia. Their thoughts seem to be directed toward possible taking of further steps in relation to China, steps which would especially affect Mongolia and North China. In connection with their consideration of this matter, the question of the actual or possible attitude of the United States and of Great Britain is of importance to them. They therefore are assiduously attempting to discover what is and what may be the present thought of the highest officials in the United States and in Great Britain; and, while making that attempt, (a) to bring about on the part of those officials an attitude as far as possible favorable toward Japan, of indifference or disfavor toward China, and of willingness to overlook or to countenance further use of force by Japan toward coercion of China, and (b) to elicit any action or statement that may indicate or may be used to suggest (in diplomatic connections or in publicity) that such is the attitude of those officials.

IV. In general, the United States and Great Britain are committed along with many other powers to the ideal of world peace. These two powers along with many others believe in the principle of naval disarmament. But the Japanese nation cares little about world peace and is utterly skeptical with regard to disarmament—except as agreements to disarm may make it possible to bring about relative increases in Japan's armed strength.

In their approach to any of the so-called "problems" or "issues" in relations between Japan and the United States, Japan's spokesmen make it a point to rely heavily upon the fact that the American Government and people are imbued with a certain emotional idealism and are enamoured of certain idealistic concepts with regard to international relations. They endeavor to induce the American Government to make to the Japanese Government real concessions desired by Japan, in connection with Japan's Asia policy, in return for nominal adherence by Japan to idealistic objectives to which the United States is committed in connection with world problems. Regularly, the Japanese ask for concessions in fact by this country as the price of concessions in principle (or to principle) by Japan.

V. It is the view of the writer that the United States has no "Far Eastern policy" as a thing separate from and different from our foreign policy in general. We have a world policy (i.e., a general "foreign policy"). That policy, in its application in and with relation to the Far East (especially in relation to China), has had certain particular manifestations; to those manifestations there have been attached certain labels (such as "the Hay doctrine," "the open door policy," etc.); but these supposedly special policies are in fact special only in name. Often, a mere detail of action in our conducting of our relations with the Far East has acquired the reputation of a special item of policy, whereas in fact the action in question is merely a matter of strategy or tactics in application of a general principle which, given a similar situation, we would (or do) apply in any other part of the world. To illustrate; the concept of the "open door" has been and is applied in determining our attitude and that of other countries toward problems elsewhere (especially in Africa) similar, *mutatis mutandis,* to those which are met with and dealt with in connection with China. Also illustrative, the concept of "non-recognition" (resorted to and declared by the American Government in 1915 with regard to developments in China, in 1921 with regard to developments in Siberia, and in 1932 with regard to developments in Manchuria) is a concept which has its roots in Occidental (and particularly American) thought with regard to the value of regulation of international relations by treaties and the necessity, in connection therewith, of respect for treaties. The idea was and is one which could be made use of in regard to situations in any other part of the world and by any countries which might choose to make use of it. We have in fact made use of it with regard to a situation in South America. The League of Nations in fact saw fit to make use of it, as did we, in relation to the situation in Manchuria. It could be used by any or by all the powers in relation to any and every situation where unlawful means are about to be, are being, or have been resorted to toward attainment of unlawful ends. Its potential application is general and not restricted to the Far East.

VI. The Japanese Government has intimated recently that it intends to make to us some suggestions for action which would improve relations between Japan and the United States. The Japanese press and various Japanese spokesmen have given some indication of various possible proposals which the Japanese Government is alleged to be considering. Among these are: a proposal for a bilateral non-aggression pact; a proposal that the United States amend its immigration act; a proposal that the United States "recognize Manchukuo"; a proposal that naval ratios be discussed in advance of the holding of a naval conference, with a view to there being arrived at an understanding that the naval ratios shall be revised upward in Japan's favor. The most outspoken of Japan's public men not in office at the present moment and not in military service, Mr. Matsuoka, has recently stated that the United States must stop "bullying" Japan, that the United States must give recognition (and assent) to Japan's "Monroe Doctrine for Asia," that the United States must cease to be especially friendly toward China and toward Russia, that the United States must admit the right of Japan to naval parity, etc.

It may well be doubted whether the Japanese Government will formally put forward proposals on any of these lines; and still more whether, if it puts forward any of these proposals, it will do so with the expectation of their being given a favorable response. The strategy which the Japanese Government is apparently employing is that of unofficial or informal suggestions by prominent Japanese (in or out of office), inspired statements in the press, *ballons d'essai* of one type and another, various types of "hands across the sea gestures," etc., intended to implant certain ideas in the minds of officials and of the public abroad and to elicit indications of official thought (and intent) and of public opinion abroad, especially in the United States and in Great Britain.

B

VII. The question then for us is: (1) What, in the presence of the Japanese effort to mold opinion and to elicit expressions of official thought in this country, should be the attitude of the American Government and (2) what should be our procedure.

It is believed that there is no need for any revision of American policy in regard to the Far East or for any change of position with regard to any feature of the general "set-up" which now prevails in the Far Eastern situation. Our policy is one which has evolved in the course of a century and a half of contact with the Far East wherein our effort has been to promote and safeguard by lawful (and peaceful) means interests which have grown and which exist there legitimately. In general, our policy is just what the history of our efforts shows it to have been, that of seeking to maintain for the United States and American nationals and interests, by peaceful means, rights which are theirs under the general principles of international law and/or the express provisions of treaties. This policy does not envisage and is not directed toward any acquisition by the United States of territory or of local political responsibilities in the Far East; and it does not seek to obtain for the United States or for American nationals and interests any special or exclusive rights, titles or privileges. It neither contemplates nor involves any use of armed force on our part for any purpose other than that of clear-cut protection—where local authorities are unable to afford protection—of life (and in connection therewith, of property). It calls for no taking of sides as between other nations which may engage in conflicts (with or without armed hostilities) there. Above all, it involves no intention or thought on our part of employing arms for the purpose of enforcing our views or of advancing any interest which we have or may have in or with relation to that part of the world. (Note: This, however, is one of those things which, well understood among ourselves and among thoughtful, well-informed and disinterested observers in many places, should not be officially and formally affirmed either in public or in conversation with officials of other governments, especially those of governments most directly and most vitally concerned in the Far East,—for official and formal affirmation of such a position would tend to encourage disregard of our views and indifference to our interests on the part of other governments inclined to such courses.)

Any changes for which there may develop need in our policy, our strategy, and/or our tactics, can and should be made quietly, without announcement, and without abruptness; and without commitment to any other (one) power.

VIII. With regard to attitude, it is believed that our intention should be to "stand pat." We should be good "listeners," but in regard to any suggestion that any move—especially one involving a concession or "change" of any sort on our part—is called for or is in order, we should make no admission or affirmation until we have had time and opportunity to scrutinize the suggestion and the contentions made in support of it.

We have certain clear rights and obligations in the Far East with regard to: (1) American citizens and interests there, (2) countries, governments and peoples there, and (3) other countries with which we have in common certain rights and obligations there and elsewhere. Our position and that of American citizens and interests in the Far East rests for the most part upon provisions of treaties. The question of any move or any statement which we might be asked to make should be carefully thought over from point of view of our existing legal commitments and our moral responsibilities in connection with other (all other) countries and with reference to the effect which such move or statement would have on the interests and rights both of this country and of other countries and on the general situation.

There is no reason why we should especially "favor" any country in the Far East or why we should discriminate to the advantage or disadvantage of any. We should have constantly in mind our rights and obligations under the Pact of Paris; the same, under the Washington Conference treaties; the same, under our treaties with China and under our treaties with Japan. Unless and until any one of several or all of those treaties are altered, we should scrutinize with utmost care any suggestion that we take a new step or make a new statement in definition or declaration of our policy.

IX. With regard to procedure, it is believed that, confronted with newspaper stories or inquiries and/or suggestions unofficial and informal in character, we should proceed on the principle of "saying nothing," i.e., of avoiding, so far as possible, the giving of any indication of concern or of active interest. We should state that the subject is not under consideration and that we do not wish to discuss it. To such inquiries or suggestions made orally or in writing (as distinguished from print), there should be made acknowledgment with thanks but with avoidance of discussion or of disclosure of reaction, favorable or unfavorable. Confronted with inquiries or suggestions made from official sources and through official agencies, we should make our tactics those of delay—in order that we may have opportunity to subject the subject matter to scrutiny before giving any indication of attitude or intent. With no commitment (except in certain cases: see *infra*), we should ask for time and should then as soon as possible study both the substance and the phraseology of the inquiry or request and decide whether to reply promptly or at leisure and in what sense and by what method. From beginning to end, we should keep in mind the thought that the ultimate objective of the Japanese is to promote and facilitate the attainment by Japan of a paramount and dominating position in the Far East and that their immediate objective is to discover what is our present attitude and probable future attitude and intent.

X. With regard to particular proposals which may be made: (Note: In connection with each and every one of the possible proposals listed *infra*, it is believed that at the time when the proposal is made, care should be taken to avoid making any casual statement which might imply or from which the Japanese might infer that we are eager to act or that we are predisposed to view with favor the particular project submitted.)

(1) If confronted with a proposal that there be concluded between Japan and the United States a (bilateral) non-aggression pact, we should indicate at the outset that we doubt whether it will be possible for us to discuss seriously such a project. We should, however, before making any reply, examine the phraseology in which the proposal is made. Our reply, though made promptly, might need to be phrased carefully. (Note: In the light of previous consideration of possibilities in connection with such a possible proposal, it is believed that there is no need in the present connection to go into a discussion of the merits or demerits of the idea of a Japan-United States non-aggression pact. Moreover, it is believed that there is little likelihood that the Japanese will present such a proposal.)

(2) If confronted with a proposal that there be concluded between Japan and the United States a treaty of arbitration or conciliation, it might be pointed out that there has been under consideration by the two Governments for several years past a draft of such a treaty. We have been perfectly willing to conclude with Japan an arbitration (or conciliation) treaty on the model of treaties of that character which we have in effect with other powers. It is our understanding that the Japanese have made no reply to the most recent communication which we made to them on that subject. It might be stated that we would be glad to hear what is the Japanese Government's view with regard to the draft outstanding. It should be requested that, for the time being, the proposal be given no publicity.

(3) If confronted with a proposal that the United States recognize "Manchukuo," officials of the American Government might well immediately point out that consideration of the question of recognition of "Manchukuo" requires consideration in particular of two sets of facts: first, the facts in relation to and in the light of the identic notes addressed by the American Government to the Japanese and the Chinese Governments on January 7, 1932, and the action taken by the League of Nations; second, the facts with regard to the characteristics and the qualifications of "Manchukuo" itself as a political entity. It is believed

that nothing should be said which might warrant an inference by the proposers that this proposal would be given serious consideration. It might be stated, however, that we feel that discussion of that question, whether in private or in public is, the general situation being what it is, inopportune.

It is believed that recognition of "Manchukuo" would be inconsistent with and contrary to the spirit and the substance of the notes above referred to; that unless and until States members of the League of Nations shall have recognized "Manchukuo," recognition of "Manchukuo" by the United States would be a betrayal by us of States with which we have associated ourselves in connection with the "non-recognition" principle; that recognition by us of "Manchukuo" would contribute little or nothing of advantage toward a permanent solution or settlement of "Far Eastern problems" or toward the improvement of relations between the United States and Japan; that it would gain for us little or nothing in the way of material advantages; and that it would amount to a technical affirmation by us that there exists a sovereign political entity where there does not in fact exist such an entity. It may or may not be true that "'Manchukuo' has come to stay"; the permanence or impermanence of the present set-up and the present political régime in Manchuria depends upon a great many factors in the future, some involving developments within Manchuria, some involving developments in Japan and in China, and some involving developments in relations between and among Japan, Russia, China, and other powers. Whatever the future may have in store, "Manchukuo" exists today by virtue of the presence in Manchuria of approximately 100,000 Japanese soldiers; it is by no means a sovereign or an independent political entity. There is no urgent reason why any foreign country should be in a hurry to recognize "Manchukuo." There is no great advantage either political or commercial that can accrue to any country in consequence of an early recognition of "Manchukuo." Neither the United States nor any other country is actively putting any obstacles in the way of the evolution of "Manchukuo." There is no reason, either legal or moral or of expediency, why any country other than Japan should exert itself toward making conclusively effective the severance of Manchuria from China. Recognition of "Manchukuo" by the United States would of course be pleasing to Japan; but it would be displeasing to China. We have taken no steps against "Manchukuo"; there are no reasons why we should take any steps in its favor. We declared, in the notes referred to above, that we do not intend to recognize situations brought about by certain processes.

When we made that declaration "Manchukuo" had not come into existence. Our position with regard to "Manchukuo" has been and is negative. Recognition by us of "Manchukuo," if and when, would require a positive act on our part. Withholding of recognition involves taking no action: it requires mere standing still, with neither action nor statement. We should give no serious consideration to any suggestion that we recognize "Manchukuo" until such suggestion is supported by and can be viewed against a background of facts making it clear that there has been a substantial change in the situation and that weighty considerations render it essential and imperative that we move in that direction.

There is no need whatever for haste on the part of any country to take any step with regard to "Manchukuo." On the basis of recent indications, it would seem that Japan is now bringing great diplomatic pressure to bear in China toward some action in the direction of recognition by the Chinese; if this does not work out, it may happen that the Japanese will before long bring to bear against China additional armed pressure. If recognition of "Manchukuo" is to come at any time from one of the great powers, the United States can well afford not to have taken that step until after the taking of it by some other major power. A war between Japan and Russia—which is by no means impossible in the comparatively near future—would either destroy "Manchukuo" or put the question of "Manchukuo" into eclipse. Even if there were no "non-recognition" notes and "resolutions," the world, and especially the United States, may well afford to take with regard to the question of the recognition of "Manchukuo" an attitude of "wait and see."

It therefore is believed that we should politely decline to discuss any proposal which the Japanese might make calling for recognition by the American Government of "Manchukuo."

(4) If confronted with a proposal which would call for some action by the American Government in regard to the question of Japanese immigration into this country, we should at once state, for purposes of record and guidance, that, as the Japanese Government well knows, this question is one with regard to which no conclusive action can be taken in this country by the executive branch of the Government without action first by the legislative branch; and we should state that, pending scrutiny of the proposal, we believe that it would be well to give no publicity to the fact that it has been submitted. We should then examine the proposal on its merits.

It is believed that no proposal could be submitted of such ingenious character as to warrant the taking toward it by the Administration, at this time, of a favorable position. The organized opposition in California to any alteration of the existing provision of our Immigration Act in relation to this matter has taken the position that it will fight any proposal to reopen this question; it stands on the principle that the present situation is satisfactory to it and that any alteration of the existing law would necessarily alter the situation and therefore be unacceptable to it. This opposition is strongly entrenched and has shown itself amply prepared to meet with counter-attacks any attack upon its position. The Congressional delegations of California and of Oregon have gone on record as being unanimously opposed to any attempt to alter the law. The Administration has indicated that it does not intend to bring up this question. The bringing forward by the Administration of any proposal in this connection would bring upon the Administration a vigorous attack; and in the course of that attack many bitter words with regard to Japan would be spoken. It is utterly unlikely that any measure which might now be introduced into Congress toward altering the law would meet with success there. The net result of making this subject one of official discussion and consideration would be to create a new increment of criticism of the Administration and to inject new and inflammatory irritants into the situation as between the United States and Japan.

It therefore is believed that we would need to prepare a very carefully phrased reply the substance of which would be that in our opinion the present is not an opportune time to attempt to do anything with regard to the Japanese immigration question.

(5) If confronted with a proposal that the American Government should give the Japanese Government an assurance that we will, if and when the naval conference meets, assent to a revision in Japan's favor of the naval ratios, we should say that we will take the matter under consideration, and that we believe that, in this instance also, pending consideration, no publicity should be given to the fact that a proposal has been made.

We should then examine the proposal. It is believed, however, that we should expect that we will not be able to make a favorable reply. In this connection it is believed that we should place the question of our national security above all other considerations. We should not let our devotion to the cause of peace, coupled with our desire to see measures of disarmament achieved, lead us into commitments the result of which would be a proportionate strengthening of Japan's naval armament and weakening of ours.

Of course the security of this country would be best ensured if arrangements could be affected which would ensure the peace of the whole world. But such a situation will be arrived at only when all countries wish and are determined that there shall be peace, or when, being in a majority, those countries which wish peace are willing to pool their forces and efforts in order to coerce (toward maintenance of peace) those that regard other considerations as more important than those of peace. The attainment of either of these alternatives still lies far in the future. The nations are still under the necessity of providing in substantial measure each for its own security. China has been attacked and invaded by Japan in consequence of the two facts that, on the one hand, Japan is willing to use force, and, on the other hand, China was not and is not able to defend herself or to induce other powers to come to her defense. Russia would probably have been attacked by Japan before now were it not that the Russians have armed themselves to such an extent that the Japanese hesitate to make the attack. Had the United States been less adequately prepared to defend itself, it attacked by Japan, we would have had, in 1932, either to have kept silent on the subject of peace or, probably, to have sustained an attack at the hands of Japan's armed forces.

The naval ratios as they now stand were designed, it is believed, on the principle of making it possible, on the one hand, for each of the powers concerned adequately to safeguard its own interests, on a defensive basis, and of making it impossible, on the other hand, for any one of the powers, provided that each and all built up to and maintained its allotment of naval equipment, to indulge in aggression against one or more of the others. Assuming that the technical calculations have been sound, the existing ratios are the correct ratios for the purpose of maintaining the equilibrium thus sought. The situation has not changed, as regards the rightful interests of the various powers concerned, separately and collectively, from the point of view of problems of self-protection (as distinguished from possible contemplated programs of aggression), since these ratios were worked out and agreed upon. It would therefore seem that any alteration of the ratios in favor, upward, of any one power, would tend toward an upset of the equilibrium and would impair the principle on which the powers have proceeded in the formulating and concluding of naval limitation agreements.

It therefore is believed that, although we might admit need for making readjustments in detail within the ratios, we should hold and adhere to the view that, insofar as any agreement to which we would be parties is concerned, the ratios themselves must continue to stand. It is believed that this should be our fixed position in relation to the agenda of any naval conference contemplated or held. The President has intimated recently, in his statement on the Vinson Act, that such is our idea and hope.[1] We should be prepared to let it be known, when the situation has sufficiently unfolded, and to say in a carefully prepared statement, that such is our position. (Before the moment for so doing arrives, some other government may or may not have disclosed its similar position.) Thereafter we could await evidence of desire and intention on the part of other powers. But, no matter what appeared or failed to appear, we should make the continuance of the existing ratios the fixed point from which, to which and around which any and all further consideration by the American Government of the question of a naval conference and (if and when such conference is held) of agenda and action thereat must proceed.

If an attitude and procedure by us in the sense above suggested should result in there being held next year no conference, we could, it is believed, view that development with equanimity. We would not be subjected because of it to any military attack or formidable diplomatic assault. There is perceived no reason why we should discuss or think of entering into any agreement by and under the provisions of which Japan would, with our assent, become relatively stronger and we become relatively weaker in naval armament, and it is believed that no step that we might take would contribute more effectively than would such a step toward rendering real, in the long run, likelihood of an attack by Japan upon this country.

Our reply to the Japanese in connection with any such proposal should, therefore, be in the negative.

(6) If confronted with a proposal that there be an exchange between the United States and Japan of diplomatic communications comparable in character to the Lansing-Ishii exchange of notes (of 1917), it is believed that reference should at once be made to the fact that letters expressive of good will and amicable intent have recently been exchanged between Japan's Minister for Foreign Affairs and the Secretary of State of the United States, and it should be intimated that we feel that those communications are sufficiently indicative of the good will which prevails officially and reciprocally between the two Governments and be pointed out that there appear in them express statements to the

effect that it is not the intention of either country to initiate resort to measures of force in its relations with the other (or with others). It should then be stated that we will take the proposal under consideration but that we do not at the moment perceive that there is any need of such action; and it should be requested that the proposal be not given publicity.

It is believed that we should expect to give an unfavorable reply. In the light of the history of the Lansing-Ishii exchange of notes, there is little if any warrant for an assumption that the conclusion of another exchange of comparable communications would serve any useful purpose from the point of view of the best interests of the United States or toward any general improvement of the situation in the Far East. In the course of the drafting of the Lansing-Ishii notes every possible effort was made by the Japanese to gain a commitment from the American Government to principles and affirmations inconsistent with the general principles of American foreign policy. After the notes were exchanged the Japanese immediately circulated in the Far East a translation so shaded as to serve their purposes and to make us appear to have affirmed that we had declined to affirm. Any such exchange which might now be so wrought as to be acceptable to the Japanese would be one the contents of which would be such as, in phraseology or in interpretation, would be calculated to limit our freedom of action and to enable Japan to go further afield, with our assent, real or inferred, in pursuance of her policy of making her influence paramount in Eastern Asia. What Japan most wants of us is that we should adopt with regard to what may happen as she goes ahead with her program an attitude of "hands off." While it may be well for us to watch our step with regard to any actual interference, and though we may not wish or may not be able to object effectively to developments which we do not view with approval, tacit acquiescence is one thing and definite assent in advance is quite another thing. There is perceived no need, in the present situation, for any spectacular action for the purpose of resolving a crisis between Japan and the United States (there being no crisis) and no reason why there should be taken a step which would tend at once to tie our hands, to increase Japan's self-confidence, to alarm and alienate the Chinese, to render the Soviet Union suspicious and uneasy, to have a disturbing rather than a reassuring effect as regards the whole situation in the Far East, and, incidentally, to subject the Administration in this country to a new increment of criticism from many quarters.

There are outstanding between Japan and the United States exchanges of notes and treaties the provisions of which cover the question of the "open door," the "integrity of China," cooperation, consultation, and peace. It is not perceived that any new exchange of communications could bring to bear any principles and provisions which are not already contained in one or more of these. If those principles and provisions are not effective by virtue of the existing agreements, would they be made so by the conclusion of new agreements? If we think of revising them, whether in the direction of limitation or of amplification, we should keep in mind the fact that most of them are multilateral and may not appropriately be amended by the conclusion of agreements between the United States and Japan only. Some of them, moreover, are agreements which, while complete within themselves, were concluded in the light of and with definite and conscious relation to the provisions of other agreements; for instance, the Washington Conference treaties, resolutions, etc. We should not lightly and without ample consideration enter into any new commitment, between ourselves and one other country only, which in fact or by implication would involve in any respect a departure by us from the principles and provisions of such existing agreements to which this country is a party.

In this connection, as in others, the soundest course for us to pursue would probably be found to be that of doing nothing. It therefore is believed that we should expect to prepare a carefully phrased statement making reply in the negative.

(7) If confronted with a proposal for a reciprocity agreement with regard to trade and tariffs, and if with that only, we should take considerable satisfaction in the fact that something has been proposed which we can at least consider seriously. To even such a proposal, however, we should need to give careful scrutiny before making any commitment. There are doubtless in the trade between the United States and Japan commodities with regard to which, being imports into this country, we could agree to some tariff concessions, and there are some with regard to which, being imports into Japan, the Japanese could agree to some tariff concessions. There is room here for some bargaining and agreements. (Note: However, with regard to certain commodities in relation to which certain suggestions have already been reported to have been made by Japanese officials, namely, silk and cotton, it would be necessary for us to study the matter closely before committing ourselves; for instance, a proposal that we guarantee that there shall be no duties or restrictions on imports of Japanese silk into this country in return for a similar agreement with regard to Japan in relation to imports there of cotton from this country.)

It would probably be safe for us to say to the Japanese at the outset that we believe that it would be possible to make some sort of reciprocal agreement with regard to some matters of trade but that we will need time to look into the subject.

(8) If confronted with any proposal with regard to the Japanese Mandated Islands, it is believed that we should at the outset make no comment, but that we should expect after examination of the proposal to take the position that this question should be addressed by the Japanese in first instance to all (or the most important) of the powers most concerned by virtue of action which took place in connection with the creation and conferring of the mandate.

(9) If confronted with a proposal for American-Japanese cooperation in relation to a program of "assistance to China," it is believed that we should be prepared to suggest that, inasmuch as the League of Nations has already given itself considerable concern in relation to that question, and inasmuch as the powers party to the Nine-Power Treaty with regard to China are especially concerned, that proposal should be addressed in first instance either to the League of Nations or to a conference of the principally interested powers.

(10) If confronted with a proposal for revision or modification of one or more of the Washington treaties, and/or for a conference of the powers parties thereto, it is believed that we should expect to say that we will examine the proposal but that, in case, upon examination, we find ourselves favorable thereto, we would in all probability also find ourselves inclined to suggest to the proposers that the proposal be submitted to others of the powers most concerned and that we would expect to ask that we be informed, before we ourselves make any definite commitment, with regard to the reaction of those other powers to it. We could then proceed to examine the proposal on its merits.

XI. It is possible that the Japanese may conceive some proposal of a type with regard to which we have not, in what appears above, taken into consideration the possibility. However, the survey made in connection with preparing what appears above leads to and supports the conclusion that there is little indeed that needs to be done and little that can safely be done by the American Government by way of special and definite action of a formal character toward "improving" the situation in the relations between Japan and the United States. The trouble, insofar as there is trouble, between these countries is not something that has been artificially brought about or that arises out of artificial measures or that can be resolved by artificial measures. The situation is one which would exist and be much what it is if there were no treaties and which would not be very greatly altered if the number of agreements were doubled or trebled. The two countries are outstandingly the two great powers on the Pacific Ocean: both are youthful and vigorous; both are growing and neither has reached the peak of its development; in the matter of various fundamental concepts the two nations differ and in the matter of natural endowment the two countries are unequal; there is bound to be competition between them, and in the course of that competition there will continue to be differences of opinion with regard to what is right, what is fair, what is just, what is expedient, and so forth, etc.

Whenever there is talk of "doing something" to improve the relations between these two countries, suggestions are put forward which are in substance suggestions that concessions or gifts be made by the United States. Now as a matter of fact the United States has taken nothing from Japan and owes nothing to Japan. The one concession which we might on the basis of some allegation of moral obligation make to the Japanese would be something in the field of immigration. That, however, is at present out of the question. No other concessions that we might make—with the exception of concessions made on a basis of give-and-take in connection with a "reciprocity agreement" for the regulation of commerce—could be made without impairing in some manner our existing legal and/or moral obligations to some country or countries other than Japan. All of which brings us back to the point that there is little indeed that we can appropriately and safely do in the field of commitments toward special signalizing of cordiality of relations between Japan and this country.

The thesis that there is extraordinary "tension" between the United States and Japan has repeatedly been advanced and is almost invariably over-emphasized. There have been, it is true, periods in which there has been reason for apprehension lest by one process or another there might be brought on armed conflict between the two countries. It should be taken into account, however, that the American Government has at no time threatened Japan or made minatory gestures in Japan's direction. Even at the time when two years ago the American Government was remonstrating vigorously against acts of aggression in which Japan was indulging in Manchuria and at Shanghai, the American Government at no time threatened to take or suggested that this country might take forceful action of a military type; on the contrary, the President of the United States expressly declared that we would not use force, not even the force of economic measures of coercion. All of the threatening at that time, as in earlier periods, came from the Japanese side. Although it may be possible for Japanese leaders to believe or to say to their people that the American Navy constitutes a standing threat to Japan, it is scarcely conceivable that they can convince any large number of intelligent and sober-minded people elsewhere that the United States has any intention to make an armed assault upon Japan or that we would engage in war with Japan in consequence of any developments other than those of an actual attack by the Japanese upon the United States. No one outside of Japan and China any longer believes that the United States would make war on Japan for the purpose of maintaining the principles of the Open Door and of territorial integrity in connection with and in relation to China.

There is not in fact the "tension" between the two countries which some people imagine and which more people talk loosely about. We do not need to enter into new and special commitments for the purpose of and as the only means for allaying an exacerbation of the situation which exacerbation does not exist.

The problem of avoiding trouble between and of maintaining and improving good relations between Japan and the United States is a problem of continuing and continuous sympathetic, patient, thoughtful and skillful day-to-day diplomatic action. The less we are hampered in connection with that by the presence of fancifully conceived and fancily phrased special agreements or commitments, themselves in turn susceptible of misinterpretation and misrepresentation, the more readily can we deal with actual difficulties which arise—deal with them when they arise—out of contacts between the peoples of the two countries and out of the conduct by the governments of each of relations with the other and with the remaining countries of the world. With a situation unfolding and changing as rapidly as is the situation in the Far East, the strategy and tactics of every government concerned must necessarily be in no small measure opportunistic. That situation is full of uncertainties and in it there are many variable and varying factors. The concluding of special arrangements between pairs of countries involved (arrangements such as the Anglo-Japanese alliance, the Lansing-Ishii notes, several other sets of such notes which Japan exchanged with other countries, the secret agreements which Japan concluded with each of four European powers in 1917 for disposal at the Peace Conference of former German territory in the Far East, etc., etc.) cannot really improve the situation and may readily add to the confusion inherent in it. There are already in existence a sufficient number of agreements, containing a sufficient number of provisions of principle and of procedure, to contribute all that can usefully be applied toward a general regulation of the situation. On and with these we should rest. Our attention, our time and our effort should be devoted not to the concluding of—and after conclusion to contention over—more agreements; they should be devoted rather to handling, with all of the intelligence and common sense that, animated by the "good neighbor" principle, we may be able to bring to bear, those problems of or relating to the Far East which are inevitably and rightfully of concern to us.

[PSF:Japan:T]

[1]March 27, 1934, printed in *Public Papers,* III, 172.

Norman H. Davis, Chairman, American Delegation, London Naval Conference, to Roosevelt

New York, April 23, 1934

My dear Mr. President: I did not write you from London giving an account of the last talks with the British on the naval matter because these only took place the last few days before I sailed and I expected to arrive by the time a letter would arrive. I tried to reach you by telephone Friday night and also Saturday morning to tell you how the naval matter stands but you were engaged and unable to talk to me at the time.

As a result of the talks in London I feel that there is not going to be any particular difficulty with the British over the technical naval questions themselves.

With regard to the contemplated informal negotiations preparatory to the Naval Conference, Secretary Hull cabled me, as you are probably aware, that it was deemed wiser to adopt as a procedure the alternative indicated in my letter to you of March 6th.[1] We accordingly directed our conversations to that end, with the result that the British came to the conclusion, subject to the approval of the Cabinet, that it would be better for them to openly invite us to sit down and talk over naval matters with them, and that, in order to avoid arousing Japanese suspicions, an invitation should be issued to the Japanese at the same time to join in the negotiations which, however, would be so arranged that our conversations would begin at least a week ahead of those in which we would both join with the Japanese. Just before I left they told me that it might take a week or two to take up this question with the Cabinet but that they would send word through Bingham as soon as possible and arrange the details, if this were satisfactory to the United States government.

There are some interesting side lights and certain important aspects about this whole situation which I will be glad to discuss with you at your convenience.

As ever, Faithfully yours,

Norman H. Davis

P.S. I am enclosing a memorandum of the last conversation we had which sums up the discussions and tentative conclusions.[2]

[PSF:London Naval Conference:TS]

[1] Above.

[2] Davis and Hull talked with Roosevelt on the morning of April 27 (PPF 1-0). Asked about the meeting at his press conference later that day, the President refused to comment, saying Davis was coming back the next day for lunch (President's Press Conferences).

[*Enclosure*] Memorandum of Conversation Between Mr. Craigie, Admiral Little, Ambassador Bingham, and Mr. Norman Davis at Claridges Hotel, London, April 12, 1934

Mr. Craigie of the Foreign Office[1] and Admiral Little[2] came to my room at 4:30 P.M. today for an informal talk with Ambassador Bingham and myself, as had previously been arranged. It was understood at the outset that the talk was to be exploratory in nature, in advance of possible future arrangements for discussions and negotiations preparatory to the Naval Conference in 1935. It was explained that neither Mr. Bingham nor myself were authorized to make any agreements with regard to this but that, since I was sailing for home, it would be helpful to have all the information possible with regard to the attitude of the British Government on the various questions involved and of the Admiralty with regard to the more technical naval questions.

It was the concensus of opinion that, as to policy, there were two principal questions to be dealt with by the two governments; first, the time and the manner of instituting informal negotiations and, second, of determining what their respective attitudes would be with regard to the Japanese claim for parity or an increased ratio. Among the questions to be dealt with in the contemplated discussions would be the differences of opinion as between the two respective navies with regard to tonnage and future types of vessels, particularly battleships and cruisers, and also whether or not the United States and England should agree to renew the Treaty on the basis of parity between them in case of a failure on the part of Japan to renew on conditions which would be acceptable.

Mr. Craigie said that with regard to arranging for the informal negotiations it was important for Japan not to get the idea that we were combining against them, but that since it was desirable that we should clear up certain questions before taking up negotiations with Japan, the British Government might communicate with the United States and Japan at the same time, stating in effect that it was deemed desirable to have discussions preparatory to the Conference in 1935 and inviting them to send representatives to London for this purpose; and that it might then be arranged for the conversations with the United States to begin some days in advance, which would be easy to do without arousing any suspicion because of the greater length of time that Japan would require to get representatives here. He said he thought they should at the same time notify France and Italy so that they would be prepared later on to join in conversations. He also said that while they might arrange to have the conversations in Washington if we preferred, he thought it was better to have them in London because it would make it easier to deal with France and Italy. He said, however, that this was a question which the government would have to pass upon, but he assumed the Cabinet would reach a decision on it within a week and that they would then inform Ambassador Bingham so that he could get word to Washington, perhaps by the time I arrive, so that the United States Government could then make its decision.

With regard to the Japanese claim for parity or an increased ratio Admiral Little said that, from the naval standpoint, they would be opposed to any increase in the Japanese ratio; that he did not see how Japan could justify such a claim; that the Washington treaties were negotiated on the basis of security and that since the navies of England and the United States have much more territory to protect in a defensive way, whereas Japan has only a very limited area, from a defensive

73

standpoint the Japanese were already on a parity. Craigie said that, while the British Government had not made any formal decision with regard to this, he felt that nothing had happened since the treaties establishing the ratios which would justify any increase for the Japanese and that he felt that, while Japan would at first make such demands, they would finally give in provided we do not ask for any reduction in the present treaty level since the Japanese contend that a nation with an inferior ratio is weakened more relatively by a reduction than a nation with a larger ratio. We asked Admiral Little if he agreed to that and he said he thought there was nothing in it and that, as a matter of fact, if the British navy were reduced he thought it would be put relatively more at a disadvantage for an operation in the Far East than Japan.

After considerable discussion it was the concensus of opinion that it would be desirable as soon as possible for the British and American governments to determine definitely whether or not they would stand together in opposition to any Japanese increase and that it would, perhaps, be advisable for each one to let the Japanese know what its attitude was, even, if possible, before the informal negotiations began so as to prevent the Japanese from going any further on a false scent.

I then told Admiral Little that, while I had neither the authority nor the technical knowledge to discuss the differences in point of view between our two navies with regard to certain types of vessels, etc., as to which we were all, however, more or less conversant, it would be helpful to know what the present attitude of the British Admiralty is and what they have in mind as to a future treaty, if he would feel disposed to give me such information. He said that he would be glad to do so.

He said, with regard to battleships, that there was a well-known and he thought now better understood difference; that, as we knew, the British Admiralty would prefer battleships of 25,000 tons equipped with 12 inch guns; that their reason for such preference was largely a question of economy and a belief that if all battleships in the future were reduced to this each would be relatively as well off. He said, however, that because of our lack of bases we, of course, felt the need of battleships of greater tonnage, but that, if the calibre of guns should be reduced to 12 inches, he doubted if we would want battleships of more than 25,000 tons. I told him I was under the impression that our navy had doubts as to the practicability of a 12 inch gun as compared to a 14 inch gun and that I seriously doubted if they would agree to a 12 inch gun. I said I had understood that Japan had objected to reducing the calibre of guns of battleships below 14 inches and Craigie and Admiral Little said that was true.

We then discussed the possibility of a compromise on 30,000 ton battleships with 14 inch guns. Admiral Little said that even for a 14 inch gun battleship they would prefer 28,000 or 28,500 tons but that perhaps they would, if necessary, consent to a 30,000 ton battleship with 14 inch guns. I told him I did not know just how our navy would feel about this.

I then asked Admiral Little what their views were with regard to cruisers and said that the note that the British Government had sent regarding our 10,000 ton 6 inch cruisers had been quite a surprise and had been hard to understand in view of the fact that one of the chief conditions of the United States at the London Naval Conference was for the right to such cruisers and a limited number of 8 inch gun cruisers, all of which was provided for under the Treaty. Craigie then said that the note was sent in the most friendly spirit; that while there was no question of our right to do this the British Government, which was most desirous of keeping cruisers down to 7,000 tons had finally consented to a Treaty for six years duration in the hope that during that period we would not see fit to build the new type which was authorized under the Treaty. We intimated that there was no ground upon which to base such an expectation, which he admitted to be the case. I furthermore said that, while I understood that it had been the definite policy of our navy to build such types, none had been launched previously because there had been no appropriation, but that, after all, Japan was the first one to lay down a new type of 8,500 ton cruiser, which they had done considerably before we had, and I asked if they had protested to the Japanese. Admiral Little said that it was only considerably after the laying down of these cruisers by the Japanese, that they learned about it and that, in fact, it was just about the time that we began to lay down ours. Craigie then said that perhaps they should have communicated with the Japanese but that they thought it was more important to reach an understanding with us and had therefore communicated with us at once in the hope that we might be able to reconsider before we had gone too far. Admiral Little then said that, realizing the very definite views and insistence of the American navy with regard to cruisers up to 10,000 tons, he thought the British Admiralty would agree to a continuance of the provisions in the present Treaty provided that the same principle that had been applicable to 8 inch gun cruisers should be extended to 6 inch gun cruisers. In asking him to explain just what he meant he said that he thought that, in addition to the global tonnage, some limit should be fixed upon the number of 10,000 ton 6 inch cruisers. In other words, that while they would not object to such cruisers, if we should have the right to put all of our permitted cruiser tonnage into 10,000 ton vessels they would find it difficult to keep to the smaller cruisers; that what they need above all are numbers whereas we are more interested in tonnage.

Craigie then remarked that they were also interested in economy and that it cost less to build smaller cruisers. I told him that I had understood it would cost less to put all of the allowed tonnage in larger vessels, to which Admiral Little agreed.

As regards destroyers, Admiral Little said that if it were not possible to get France to limit her submarines to 75,000 tons the British would probably have to insist upon the right to a larger tonnage in destroyers. I asked him if it would not be a little difficult to insist upon this since they have not kept fully up to the destroyer allowance that is now permitted. He intimated that that was so and indicated that perhaps they would not be insistent upon that.

As to submarines Craigie and Little both said that they hoped to get a reduction and, of course, abolition of submarines but that they did not see much chance of this.

With regard to air-craft carriers, Admiral Little said that they would favor limiting the size of air-craft carriers in the future to that which both navies are now building. There was then some discussion as to a possible reduction.

I remarked that my own personal view was that, aside from practical considerations, it might have a bad effect on public opinion of the world if no reduction whatever were provided for under a new treaty; that from a naval standpoint it would seem to me wise and desirable to agree upon a reasonable, practical, long-term program which would involve some economies as well as certain reductions and a more scientific rounding out of navies. Admiral Little agreed with this view. He said that the British navy was in favor of reduction but by tonnage rather than by numbers, whereas, under the Hoover proposal, we had advocated a reduction in tonnage through a reduction in numbers and not in the size of vessels. He indicated that public opinion would likely be unfavorable to the building of any more such expensive battleships as those of the present type and that if we could possibly agree upon a reduction in tonnage and calibre of guns it would make a tremendous difference in the ultimate cost of maintaining the navies and be more apt to ensure public support. He and Craigie both said however that they did not see how they could possibly agree to reduce the number of battleships for the future and that a proposal to that effect would make it much more difficult to get the Japanese to agree to a renewal without an increase in their ratio.

Craigie said that it was, furthermore, difficult to reduce the number of battleships without raising real complications with regard to the Japanese ratio because it was not possible to cut a battleship in two. He remarked that when Admiral Hepburn[3] and Admiral Bellairs[4] were discussing this question over a year ago some consideration was given to allowing the United States to have fourteen battleships of say 30,000 tons and the British fifteen of 25,000 tons but that this would raise difficulties with the British as regards Japan.

There was then some discussion as to the desirability of a naval agreement in any event between our two countries which, it was suggested, would provide for maintaining parity but also for raising or lowering the level depending upon what the other naval powers might do.

In concluding the conversation Craigie and Admiral Little both said they had been glad to have this talk, which they thought would be most helpful; that they were most desirous of reaching an agreement with us; that there was more reason than ever why we should cooperate in the most friendly way and that there seemed to be more than ever a better understanding as to the points of view of the respective navies and a desire to reconcile them in a fair and practicable way.

Mr. Craigie in saying goodbye, stated that he thought it was of the utmost importance that we act quickly with regard to the proposed negotiations and he asked how soon I could come back to London and I told him that I would probably be back for the meeting of the General Commission in Geneva. He said he thought it would be advisable to have the meetings even before the 23rd. I told him that so far as I was concerned it would be very difficult to go home and get back a week ahead of the Geneva meeting. It was then suggested that we might arrange to have the meetings begin in Geneva at that time.[5]

NHD

[PSF:London Naval Conference:TS]

[1] Sir Robert Leslie Craigie, assistant under secretary of state. From 1937 to 1941 he was ambassador to Japan.
[2] Sir Charles J. C. Little, Lord Commissioner of the Admiralty.

[3] Arthur J. Hepburn, member of the U.S. naval staff at the 1927, 1930, and 1932 conferences on the limitation of armaments.

[4] Roger M. Bellairs, British representative on League of Nations Permanent Advisory Commission, 1932–1939.

[5] Following consultations with Roosevelt and Hull, Davis cabled Ambassador Bingham on April 28 that the procedure proposed in their conversation of April 12 (above) "would be acceptable here." If the British Cabinet considered it desirable that the naval talks should begin in three or four weeks, he wished to be informed as soon as possible (*Foreign Relations, 1934,* I, 232). Bingham replied on May 2 that the Cabinet had not yet reached a decision. He also said that an important section of British official position had now reached very definite views on the Japanese problem: that until the menace of Japanese policy was more pressing than it was, the British would oppose any appearance of American-British cooperation vis-à-vis Japan "as allegedly would strengthen the hands of the militarists in Japan and weaken the civilian element which is reportedly recovering political strength" (*ibid.,* pp. 232–233).

Robert W. Bingham, Ambassador to Great Britain, to Roosevelt

[London] April 23, 1934

My dear Mr. President: Norman Davis has reported to you in writing, and doubtless also verbally, the conferences with the Prime Minister on March 2nd,[1] and with Admiral Little and Mr. Craigie on April 12th.[2] In addition, I have discussed the naval situation twice with Sir John Simon, first on March 5th and second on April 20th. In view of the Japanese statement on China, while I had an appointment with him on a routine matter, after disposing of that I told him that I had seen his statement in the House of Commons the day before to the effect that he had nothing to say on the Japanese matter because he had not seen the text of the statement.[3] He told me he had now seen the full statement from the British Ambassador to Tokio and read it to me. He then said he considered the situation very grave indeed, and that undoubtedly great pressure would be brought upon the British government by British financial interests, if the Japanese attempted to carry out their plan. More then ever he hoped for cooperation between our government and the British government in handling the whole Japanese situation. The new development has increased his interest greatly on the whole problem. I told him I had no instructions from our government on this subject, and spoke my personal views only on this later phase, but that I agreed with him that the situation was grave, and that cooperation between our governments was desirable. At a favorable opportunity, I discussed the subject of the coming naval conference with Sir Bolton Eyres-

Monsell, First Lord of the Admiralty, and found him fully alive to the situation and very frank in stating that he thought cooperation between our governments in dealing with the Japanese was essential. Later the subject came up with the Admiral of the Fleet, Sir Roger Keyes, now retired, and a member of Parliament, but very influential in naval circles, who expressed the same opinion emphatically.

I dined recently with the Ray Athertons, and after dinner had a very interesting talk with Lord Hailsham. He said that neither this, nor any other British government, could give the French any guaranty of military support in advance, and that, in his opinion, this meant that any disarmament agreement of value was impossible. He said that he thought that economic sanctions might prove of great value in preventing war, but that his government could not undertake them without the support of the United States, and that they were proceeding on the theory that any such support was unobtainable.

He said that if the British government prevented the sale to belligerents of munitions, war material and the necessities of life without similar action by the United States, such action would not only be futile, but no British government could afford to attempt it. I told him I thought it desirable at least to explore this subject, without assuming in advance that some form of cooperation between the two governments was impossible. He also expressed himself as being in full sympathy with the effort to bring about cooperation between the British and ourselves in dealing with the naval program.

At his own suggestion, the Prince of Wales came to the Embassy, and, while I merely touched upon the naval situation with him, he made a statement which I want to give to you. He said he was convinced that there must be a change in conditions here, and a correction of social injustices among the English people, which would relieve poverty and distress; that this must come and that it would come either wisely, constructively and conservatively, which would save the country, or it would come violently, which would destroy it. I told him that this was the basis on which you were proceeding, and were succeeding in the United States. He said that he was just coming to that, and that he thought what England most needed was just the type of leadership which you were giving to the United States.

I want to tell you now my opinion on the debt situation for what it may be worth. As things stand now, I believe it is probable that the British will work satisfactorily with us in connection with the naval conference. The recent menacing and dangerous statement by the Japanese as to the relations with China has made this cooperation the more probable. If Congress had adjourned by the middle of this month, consideration of the debt question might be on a different basis. I understand now that it is not likely to adjourn before the middle of May, if then. At any rate, very little time will be left before June 15th. I hope you may consider it wise and practicable, despite the Johnson bill, to accept another token payment on the 15th of June, so that six months will be left in which the British may prepare for the next payment on such terms as you deem proper. I do not mean to convey that I think there is anything in the situation which entitles them to this further consideration, but I want to deprive them of any opportunity to claim that they were not given ample notice. From my position here I cannot, of course, see the situation in the full and complete light and from all of its angles, as you see it, but I feel I must give you my opinion, based on the facts as I see them.

The British are deeply concerned over the situation, both in Europe and in the Far East. They realize they are in no position to repel an attack from the air. They believe all hope for disarmament is gone, and I am convinced that all thoughtful people here believe that the only hope for peace in the world lies in cooperation between the British and ourselves, and that they eagerly desire it. They want peace as earnestly and sincerely as we want it, and we are in a better position to deal with them now than in all the long period since I have known them. We are in a good position to treat with them, so far as it may be advantageous to us. For these reasons, I believe to precipitate the debt question in the short time remaining before the 15th of June, would make it much more difficult to deal with them, and would give them the opportunity for complaint on account of the shortness of time, of which I should like to see them deprived.

Moreover, I fully agree with the view you suggested to me of a settlement of this difficult question along the lines you mentioned. In the long run I believe a reasonable concession would strengthen our efforts for peace and make for our advantage as well as theirs. I have accepted an invitation from Sir Robert Vansittart to lunch with him at his country place on Sunday. He said he wanted to talk to me privately and alone on the Japanese situation.

On Thursday, my wife and I are dining and spending the night at Windsor Castle.

I shall write you by next Tuesday's pouch about my interview with Sir Robert and also tell you what happens at Windsor Castle.[4]

Sir Roger Keyes asked me to express his warm regards to you. With every good wish for you and yours, Sincerely yours,

Robert W. Bingham

[PSF:London Naval Conference:TS]

[1] See Davis to Roosevelt, March 6, 1934, in *Foreign Relations, 1934*, I, 222–230.
[2] April 23, 1934, above.
[3] See n. 1 of April 18 press conference, above.
[4] See Bingham to Roosevelt, May 1, 1934, below.

Roosevelt to Robert Underwood Johnson, Secretary, American Academy of Arts and Letters, New York

[Washington] April 25, 1934

My dear Mr. Johnson: This is to acknowledge and to express appreciation for your letter of April 16, 1934,[1] in which you advocate the ratification of the convention for the protection of literary and artistic works, which I sent to the Senate requesting advice and consent to adherence thereto on the part of the United States, on February 19 of the present year.[2]

Needless to say, I fully concur in your sentiments and assure you that it would be most pleasing to me if, early in my administration, I should be empowered to make the United States a party to this convention.[3]

Sincerely yours,

[PPF 1442:CT]

[1] Above.
[2] *Cong. Rec.*, vol. 78, p. 2768. The copyright convention was referred to the Senate Committee on Foreign Relations. On Feb. 24, 1934, Hull wrote to Pittman, chairman of the committee, enclosing a note from the British ambassador of Dec. 20, 1933. The note reviewed the grievances of the British government against the American treatment of British books under existing copyright laws and indicated that these complaints would be met by adoption by the United States of the pending convention (Thorvald Solberg, *The Present International Copyright Situation; Threats of Reprisal*, Washington, 1934, p. 8).
[3] Johnson asked permission to make the letter public and Roosevelt consented (Johnson to Roosevelt, May 2; Early to LeHand, May 3; Early to Johnson, May 7, 1934, PPF 1442). In Early's note to LeHand, he pointed out that such permission was not ordinarily given and asked if the President had "any personal interest." Roosevelt's "OK" appears in two places on this note, once underlined. See Roosevelt to Pittman, April 30, 1934, below.

Cordell Hull, Secretary of State, to Roosevelt

[Washington] April 26, 1934

Strictly Confidential

Memorandum for the President: I attach for your information a memorandum of an interesting conversation which Mr. Phillips had with the British Ambassador this afternoon.

C.H.

[PSF:Great Britain:T]

[*Enclosure*] William Phillips, Under Secretary of State, to Cordell Hull

Memorandum of Conversation with the British Ambassador, April 26, 1934

The British Ambassador called this afternoon and, with reference to the attitude of his government to the Far Eastern situation, said that they were opposed to any concerted action. They believed that each power should state its own views.

Sir Ronald then went on to say that he was prepared to read to me the instructions which had been sent to the British Ambassador in Tokyo and which he understood were delivered yesterday, as follows:

The Japanese statement[1] is of such a nature that we cannot leave it without comment. The Ambassador was told "to point out that the Nine Power Treaty guarantees equal rights to its signatories and Japan is a signatory. His Majesty's Government of course must continue to enjoy all the rights in China which are common to all the signatories or which are otherwise proper, except in so far as they are restricted by special agreements or in so far as Japan has special rights recognized by other powers and not shared by them.

"It is the aim of His Majesty's Government to avoid all the dangers to the peace and integrity to China on which the statement purports to be based. We could not admit Japan's right to decide alone whether anything such as technical or financial assistance promotes such a danger. Under the Nine Power Treaty Japan has the right to call attention to any action which may appear to her inimical to her interests and this provides Japan with safeguards. We assume that the statement is not meant to abridge the common rights of other powers or to infringe Japan's treaty obligations."

82

I thanked Sir Ronald for this communication and asked whether it was the intention of his government to give publicity to it. He said that in all probability the substance of these instructions would be given to Parliament; that since nothing had been given today presumably there would be no publicity until Monday when Parliament again meets. He was very anxious that we should keep him advised of any step which we might make; he was leaving for New York tomorrow not to return until Tuesday; but in his absence Mr. Osborne would be glad to communicate any message to him.

William Phillips

[PSF:Great Britain:T]

[1] The Japanese statement of April 17 objecting to foreign loans to China.

Roosevelt to James Truslow Adams, London

[Washington] April 30, 1934

My dear Mr. Adams: Many thanks for your note.[1] I hope much that the Copyright Treaty will go through. I am speaking to Senator Pittman about it.

Very sincerely yours,

[OF 699:CT]

[1] April 20, 1934 (OF 699); Adams referred to an appointment with Roosevelt that the latter had been unable to keep because of the prolongation of his Florida trip. Adams said he had heard from Robert Underwood Johnson that the Copyright Treaty had a good chance of being approved: "I hope with all my heart that this treaty may pass both for our own sakes, and for those of English authors. Owing to the generous way in which England has treated American authors as contrasted with the way in which my own country has treated English authors, I should be delighted if this stigma upon our honesty and good faith could at last be removed." See below.

Roosevelt to Senator Key Pittman of Nevada

[Washington] April 30, 1934

Dear Key: Could you let me know what is the status of the Copyright Treaty?[1]

F.D.R.

[OF 699:CT]

[1] No reply has been found; however, Pittman talked with Roosevelt at the White House on May 3 (PPF 1-0). See Pittman to McIntyre, June 12, 1934, below.

Robert W. Bingham, Ambassador to Great Britain, to Roosevelt

[London] May 1, 1934

My dear Mr. President: In my last letter to you[1] I told you I would write you about the conference I expected to have with Sir Robert Vansittart on Sunday, April 29th, but that engagement has been postponed until Sunday, May 6th, as the Vansittarts were invited for that week-end to Windsor Castle.

My wife and I went there on Thursday, the 26th. After dinner I had about an hour alone with the King. He spoke of the coming Naval Conference and of the situation produced by the recent statement by the Japanese.[2] He said that his government had had a satisfactory treaty arrangement with the Japanese, which had been abrogated because the British believed that we wished them to do so; that he thought our interests were similar, if not identical, in the Pacific, and that he hoped that we would be able to cooperate in maintaining trade and maintaining peace. I assured him that we shared this hope.

He then said that he had received a charming letter from you,[3] containing a number of envelopes addressed to you by his subjects in the various parts of the Empire, which were very amusing indeed; that he was grateful for this letter and especially for the fact that you had said you thought it would be possible to work out a settlement of the debt question; that this was the only real difficulty and trouble between our countries now. Without attempting to discuss the details of the creation of the debt, and without attempting to discuss the obligation on the part of the British, the King said that he felt that the British people were entirely unable to pay this great sum of money in money, and that they were prevented from payments in goods and services; that if some settlement of this question could be made which the British could take care of, it would remove the only serious difficulty existing between us and make practicable a measure of cooperation which otherwise would be difficult to bring about. He assured me he did not mean to bring it up in any official way, but only referred to it because of his gratification at your reference to it in your letter to him. I told him I was not authorized in any way to discuss this subject officially, and personally I considered it a question requiring the exercise of supreme statesmanship, which would understand the great difficulties and complexities inherent in the situation on both sides, and that certainly the British must realize the difficulties with which we were confronted. He assured me that he realized this situation himself and agreed with what I had said.

He asked me a number of questions about the progress we had made in restoring confidence and prosperity to the country, and expressed himself as being delighted at the report I gave him. He asked, with great interest, about your health, and asked me to present his cordial regards to you.

With kindest regards, Sincerely yours,

Robert W. Bingham

[PSF:Great Britain:TS]

[1] April 23, 1934, above.
[2] See *ibid.*
[3] Nov. 5, 1933, printed in *Personal Letters, 1928–1945,* I, 370–371.

Press Conference, Executive Offices of the White House, May 4, 1934, 4:10 P.M.

[*Excerpt*] Q: Do you expect to sign the sugar bill today or tomorrow?

The President: Probably not until Monday. There again there will be some kind of a statement which has to cover a great many things, Puerto Rico and Hawaii, Cuba, the Philippines, et cetera.[1]

Q: Have you given any thought to asking the Congress for authority to accept some payments from the debtor nations on June fifteenth at your own discretion?

The President: No.

Q: In connection with the silver conference tomorrow[2]—that is my old subject—there are reports in Wall Street of a lot of buying of silver and there is some speculation that that might be done by the Government?

The President: I would probably tell you if I knew anything about it but I don't, one way or the other.

Q: Your intention to send a debt Message to Congress this late in the session, does that mean you will not ask for Congressional action on the war debts?

The President: You are about two weeks ahead of time on that.[3]

[President's Press Conferences:T]

[1] The act approved May 9, 1934 (48 *Stat.* 670), brought sugar beets and sugar cane under provisions of the Agricultural Adjustment Act and set quotas for producers in continental United States and in Hawaii, Puerto Rico, the Philippines, the Virgin Islands, and Cuba. The President discussed the act in a news release issued May 9; in a note to the text as printed in *Public Papers,* III, 219–222, he said that one of the principal objectives was "to arrest the decline in Cuban sugar imports to the United States so as to increase the Cuban market for American exports of other products to Cuba."

[2] This conference was held on the presidential train on Saturday morning, May 5, while Roosevelt was en route to New York to attend the funeral of former Treasury Secretary Woodin, who had died May 3. Pittman, Shipstead, Wheeler, and Thomas (Okla.) were among the leaders of the silver bloc present; also on the train were Treasury Secretary Morgenthau and his general counsel, Herman Oliphant, Eugene R. Black of the Federal Reserve Board, Jesse H. Jones, head of the Reconstruction Finance Corporation, and Vice-President Garner. The silver group urged adoption of Senator Thomas' measure: nationalization of silver at a coinage ratio of 30 per cent silver to 70 per cent gold, silver to be bought at not more than 50 cents an ounce, and authorization to the President to make international agreements on silver (New York *Times,* May 6, 1934, p. 1). The President was reported as being sympathetic to the 30 per cent silver ratio but preferred discretionary authority so far as the nationalization of silver was concerned. He was represented as being favorable to a silver aid program on the ground that an increase in the world price of the metal would increase Japanese manufacturing costs and lessen the inroads Japanese competition was making in certain American markets (*ibid.*) The next day, however, Senator Wheeler denied that the President had made any kind of commitment to the silver group (New York *Times,* May 7, 1934, p. 1).

[3] See message of June 1, 1934, below.

Edward W. Schramm, Editor, *Lutheran Standard,* to Roosevelt

Columbus, Ohio, May 4, 1934

Dear Mr. President: You are of course well aware of the fact that the Lutheran Church has never been a political Church. It has always conceived its proper contribution to the State to be the training of consecrated Christian citizens. Cognizance of the Lutheran position on this subject was taken by the Honorable Theodore R. Roosevelt, [*sic*] who, when President, expressed himself as being glad to note that the Lutheran Church stood so firmly for the separation of Church and State, "because that is one of the fundamental articles of the Constitution of the United States."

The Lutheran Church is of course aware that its political philosophy is not shared by all the Christian Communions in our land. While content ordinarily to permit other church bodies to carry on whatever political activity they may deem wise, both the Christian conscience and the patriotic urge of American Lutheran citizens compel them to speak out when they read in the public press of the proposed recognition on the part of our Government of the Vatican State. I refer specifically to a copyrighted release, with the date-line: "Rome, April 14," that was reprinted in the Columbus *Dispatch* in its issue of April 15. This release begins:

The "preparation" by President Franklin D. Roosevelt of a favorable public opinion now appears to be considered at the Vatican as the only obstacle remaining in the way of a resumption of diplomatic relations between the United States and the Holy See.

Concerning this endeavor to "prepare" public opinion for the recognition of the Holy See I have considered it my duty to write editorially in the *Lutheran Standard*, official English organ of the American Lutheran Church. Editorial comment on the situation has also appeared in *Lutheran Youth*, the Sunday school paper of our body, and in the *Lutheran Witness*, official English organ of the Evangelical Lutheran Synod of Missouri, Ohio, and other States, with headquarters in St. Louis, Mo. I am confident, Mr. President, that the convictions expressed in these official publications are the convictions of the entire Lutheran Church (4,228,268 baptized membership) and, indeed of all American Protestantism. Corroboration of this statement could be gotten from Dr. Ralph H. Long, executive director of the National Lutheran Council, a body which has frequently represented the entire Lutheran Church of America before the Government. The headquarters of the National Lutheran Council are at 39 East 35th St., New York City.

I am taking the liberty of sending you under separate cover a marked copy of the *Lutheran Standard*, in which editorial comment on the matter under discussion is made.[1] I have received for publication in the *Lutheran*

Standard an open letter to the President of the United States in which the reasons of the Lutheran Church for protesting against the proposed recognition of the Vatican are set forth in some detail. I purpose publishing that letter in our issue for June 2 and shall send you a copy prior to the mailing of the issue to our subscribers. In this issue (for June 2) I should like to add further editorial comment on the matter and for that reason would be happy to receive from you a statement that would throw any further light on the newspaper dispatches which have been published. As you will observe in the editorial in our issue for May 12, we have no desire to foment unnecessary or unseemly strife. An official statement from you to the effect that there is no possibility of the recognition of the Vatican State materializing will of course enable me to write an editorial of a far different nature than the absence of such an official statement will necessitate.

I respectfully await your further advice, Very sincerely yours,

Edward W. Schramm

P.S. To make sure that you receive a copy of the editorial that has already appeared I am not only sending a marked copy of the issue, but attaching to this letter a clipping of the editorial.[2]

[OF 76-B:TS]

[1] The issue of May 12, 1934.

[2] Early sent this letter to the State Department for a draft reply. Phillips sent back a draft, commenting that the letter was similar to a great many that the State Department had received (Phillips to Early, May 16, 1934, OF 76-B). Early wrote Schramm, May 16, 1934 (OF 76-B), that the question of the recognition of the Vatican by the United States had not arisen, and that the newspaper article was "entirely without foundation of fact." Schramm wrote again May 26 (OF 76-B), saying that Early's letter had reached him after Schramm's "Open Letter to the President" had been set in type but that he had been able to publish Early's letter with it.

Robert W. Bingham, Ambassador to Great Britain, to Roosevelt

London, May 8, 1934

Dear Mr. President: I am enclosing a copy of a telegram I sent to the Department of State on May 2nd for Norman Davis in reply to a message from him. I have marked the section which I particularly want you to note.[1]

I spent some time in the country on Sunday with Sir Robert Vansittart, the most able Under-Secretary of State for Foreign Affairs. Insofar as he went I am certain he was sincere in what he said, but one always has to form an opinion in such situations as much by what is not said as by what is actually said. This interview convinces me that I had sensed correctly the change in the British attitude since the latest Japanese outbreak, as expressed in the enclosed telegram. Up to the time when the Japanese Foreign Office spokesman made his first statement I am satisfied that the British intended to go along with us in preparation for the coming Naval Conference as far as they could without giving offence to the Japanese. Now I am convinced that unless conditions should change meanwhile, they expect to cooperate with us ultimately, but they are not willing to adopt any Anglo-American policy that might be interpreted as coercion in Japan and solidify the control of the militaristic element.

Sir Robert said he thought the danger now was in Europe, and from Germany; that the Germans were not only arming generally, but in particular were building a large number of heavy bombing planes; that the French know this, and it was this knowledge which caused them to decline to go further with the British and ourselves on disarmament and produced their last Note to the British practically ending disarmament proceedings.[2] I gathered from what he said that for the present the British considered that the Russian and Chinese (and obviously the United States) attitude in the Far Eastern situation would deter Japan from taking any immediate action. However, he realized that the Japanese had never abandoned for a moment their twenty-one demands they served on the Chinese in 1915, and he had no doubt they would not only put these demands in force but add others in the event of the outbreak of war in Europe.

Meanwhile he saw no immediate danger in the Far Eastern situation and believed any disturbance there was unlikely until and unless Germany precipitated war in Europe.

The only deduction, in my opinion, to be drawn from his statement was that the British Government has made up its mind to run no risk, so far as the Far Eastern question is concerned, at this time and to concentrate all of its efforts upon trying to keep peace in Europe. He said he was going to Geneva, but that he thought that nothing could be accomplished there. That the Germans were training their children from the age of two years up, for war; were teaching them from babies that they were mentally and physically superior to other peoples, and that their mission was to conquer and control the world, giving the world the benefit of control by the noble and superior Germans.

In conclusion he added that British public opinion had advanced or developed to the point that it would approve stronger forms of sanction with regard to France in view of the German menace.

In my opinion we should leave the preliminary discussions of the coming Naval Conference where they now lie and make no further effort at this time to press the British to go ahead with them until they voluntarily re-open the subject with us after the Cabinet Council which has this particular situation in review has completed its labors. I am advised that it is impossible to determine how early such a decision may be reached.[3]

With kindest regards, Very sincerely yours,

Robert W. Bingham

[PSF:Great Britain:TS]

[1] Davis, in a cable of April 28, 1934, asked what the British wished to do with respect to the beginning of informal naval conversations. Bingham replied May 2 that the Cabinet had not yet concluded their discussions; also, that an important section of British official position was now opposed to such overt Anglo-American cooperation as would strengthen the hands of the Japanese militarists. This group would rather give up the idea of a later conference than "to force Japan into a ratio agreement that would arouse national resentment there" (*Foreign Relations, 1934*, I, 232, 232–233). It was this part of his dispatch that Davis had marked for the President's special notice.
[2] The note of March 19, 1934 (*British Documents, 1919–1939*, VI, 556–560); see press conference of March 23, 1934, above.
[3] See Davis to Roosevelt, June 4, 1934, below.

R. Walton Moore, Assistant Secretary of State, to Roosevelt

Washington, May 8, 1934

My dear Mr. President: After I saw you yesterday,[1] Mr. Troyanovsky came in. He objects to the Soviet being classed by the Attorney General as a defaulting nation and inclines to make a public statement of his reasons. I urged that to go into the newspapers further would tend to complicate the situation without any advantage to either country. I further impressed him with the fact that the opinion places the Soviet in even better position than before because it sanctions ordinary commercial transactions as not being within the purview of the Johnson Act.

I told him that we are advised that Litvinoff has said that he has spoken his last word, whereupon he stated Litvinoff has cabled him that Bullitt has made a similar remark. Then he authorized me to inform Bullitt that Litvinoff will be very glad to resume the negotiations, and I have wired Bullitt accordingly.[2] Troyanovsky went away in excellent good humor.

Yours very sincerely,

R. Walton Moore

[PSF:Russia:TS]

[1] At the White House, from 12:30 to 1 P.M. (PPF 1-0).
[2] Hull to Bullitt, May 7, 1934, in *Foreign Relations, The Soviet Union, 1933-1939*, p. 90.

Press Conference, Executive Offices of the White House, May 9, 1934, 10:43 A.M.

[*Excerpt*] Q: Can you tell us whether you consider now that the debtor nations can escape the penalties of the Johnson Act?

The President: You are going to anticipate that famous Message going to the Congress. It is nearer now than last week.[1]

Q: Will an explanation of that be contained in the Message?

The President: Maybe; I do not know.

Q: Can you give us any clarification on the debt Message at all?

The President: No, because all these stories being written—I do not know where they come from. I believe that the position of this Government is what it has been all along. There has been no change—

Q: Mr. President—

The President: —no applications made by any other nations or revisions . . .

Q: As I understand it, if they do not ask for a revision of war debts, we are not offering any?

The President: The position is exactly the same. In other words, for over a year and three months we have said very definitely that if a person owes money and feels he cannot pay it, it is up to him to go to his creditor and tell him the story.

Q: That means no negotiations with England at all?

The President: None.

Q: Didn't Britain come and tell us the story last November?

The President: Yes, came and told us the story and made a suggestion as to terms, which was not satisfactory.

Q: Have they come back again?

The President: No.

Q: You say the position of the Government has not changed. Doesn't the Johnson Act change it as regards partial payments?

The President: No.

Q: It raises the question, can we still accept the partial payments and declare they are not in default?

The President: That question came up last year just about this time. I took the position at that time, under all the circumstances, that I personally did not consider it in default. Then they came back last November and we canvassed the situation as of that time and again thought it over very, very carefully, and decided again that from my own personal point of view it did not constitute a default. Now, the question has not come up in regard to the general payment yet.

Q: You do not wish to say anything regarding—

The President: That would be prognostication without facts . . .

Q: They are drawing a bill up on the Hill providing for the nationalization of silver—a 25% ratio.

The President: I think, for background, the easiest way to put it is this: that on the question of increased metallic reserves of silver, there is nothing new in that. That is an old, old thing. We have had much larger silver metallic reserves in a great many other periods of history. We had them during the McKinley Administration, the T. R. Administration, and it is only in comparatively recent years that the silver metallic reserve has been brought down as low as it is now, around 12% at the present time.

As you know, last year we talked in London about trying to get all the nations to increase the ratio of their silver metallic reserves to gold. There is nothing new and startling in it in any way. Half of the world, after all, is on silver, so that part of the story is not exactly new in any way.

The only thing that is new is the canvassing that we are doing as to the desirability or the necessity of giving to me or the Treasury Department the same authority to take over silver stocks in this country that we already have and have carried out in the case of gold stocks. The difference really would be that in taking over the silver stocks we would take over only the silver bullion stocks. In other words, we would not put the silver coins out of general circulation. People would still be allowed to hold them for circulation but not for hoarding purposes.

Q: Have you the power to do that under the existing Thomas Act?

The President: We don't think so. We don't think we have the right to commandeer silver in the same way we did to commandeer gold.

Q: On the war debt, I understood you to say that the Johnson Bill does not change the Government's position. Does that mean that the question will be decided on its own merits each time?

The President: Yes . . .

Q: You say the question of token payments will be decided on their own merits. Does that mean if the debtor nation should offer a substantial payment we might except them from default?

The President: You cannot answer that categorically because it would depend entirely on the circumstances when they arose and they have not arisen . . .

Q: On the silver, are you considering anything beyond the possible acceptance of authorizations with respect to silver? Is there any talk of mandatory legislation in any form?

The President: No.

Q: That was given out generally in some circles on the Hill?

The President: Now, wait a minute, you get to a very fine distinction. In that second thing, we did mention and we did discuss yesterday the possibility of Congress either stating an ultimate objective or a national policy as a declaration of the Congress. Now, of course, in a sense a declaration of the Congress is mandatory but if the method and time of carrying it out is not put down in the bill, that part of it is permissive. So you get two factors right away.

Q: That is the point I was thinking of.

The President: In other words, what I was talking about yesterday is both mandatory and permissive. The policy becomes a mandatory policy but the method of carrying it out remains permissive.

Q: Nationalization would be mandatory, would it not?

The President: No.

Q: It would give you authority?

The President: Yes.

Q: And so far as that goes, that would be acceptable to you?

The President: I am still studying it. I have not said that yet; you nearly had me.

Q: Has Russia made any offer to us?

The President: No; nothing has come in at all.

Q: They are supposed to have offered, I think, one hundred million dollars?

The President: No.

[President's Press Conferences:T]

[1] June 1, 1934, below.

Roosevelt to William C. Bullitt, Ambassador to the Union of Soviet Socialist Republics, Moscow

[Washington] May 9, 1934

Dear Bill: Reginald Leaycraft, who sends me the enclosed, is a distant cousin of mine; was at school with me and is an awfully nice fellow.[1] He is going to Russia on business but I do not know anything of the details or the merits of said business!

I get a lot of chuckles out of the scraps that you and Litvinov have. Keep up the good work![2]

As ever yours,

[PSF:Russia:CT]

[1] Leaycraft, a member of the Long Island branch of the Roosevelts, was in Groton School with Roosevelt.
[2] Answered June 14, 1934, below.

Lincoln MacVeagh, Minister to Greece, to Roosevelt

Athens, May 9, 1934

Personal and Confidential

Dear Franklin: Here is another report from Athens, for you to read if and when you have a moment for it.

It was a great surprise and pleasure to receive your note of April 19th.[1] How do you manage not only to keep us all in mind, but to keep in touch as you do, when you have such a vast number of things always on your hands?

I was indeed glad to get rid of Insull, and in case you may be interested, I will complete the story as I began it to you last fall.

I felt, even after the second extradition hearings had been decided against us, that the Foreign Office here was really on our side. Though this belief was not shared by many skeptical persons in Athens, I simply could not believe that M. Maximos,[2] the Foreign Minister, had been misleading me all the time. So the very next day after the extraordinary decision which I sent you was handed down, I went privately to see him. I told him that I had no instructions, but that as a friend of his, and of Greece, I wanted to lay before him my fears in regard to the Insull matter. I told him that the reaction to the decision in America would be wide-spread and unfavorable to Greece. Indeed, I said Greece would probably get the widest publicity she had ever received and all of it would be bad. M. Maximos agreed with me and asked what I would propose. Whereupon I said that a man who was likely to cause such serious embarrassment to a country might well be classed as an undesirable alien, subject to expulsion under a certain Greek law, which I quoted. He agreed again, but warned me that it would be very difficult to effect such an expulsion in Insull's case, because the Greek Courts had twice declared him an innocent person, and the Government would fear the inevitable criticism that it was not upholding its judiciary. I countered this by pointing out that no reflection on the courts would be involved, since the reason for the proposed action would be one of policy rather than jurisprudence. Later, this same attitude was actually taken by the Council of State, to which Insull appealed, but from the date of this conversation M. Maximos worked with a will, and with great astuteness, to put Insull out of Greece against the determined opposition of several members of the Cabinet, and the spineless indecision of a temporizing Premier. His method was simple, but of necessity slow. He would force the Premier to agree that Insull be expelled, and then announce the fact to me and to the press before the Opposition got in its counter-offensive and switched the Premier around. Thus he repeatedly put the government on record as determined to expel the fugitive, and all that the friends of Insull could do was to secure repeated delays. Finally the State Department, which had all this time wisely kept its hands off, insisting that any decision in the matter must be taken by the Greeks themselves, asked to know when Greece intended to put into effect the assurances so many times given the American Minister, and that did the trick. Insull saw the writing on the wall, and fled.

If our Department of State had not taken the attitude it did, and anything but unofficial pressure had been exerted, the touchy Greek character would certainly have prevented our ever getting Insull out.

We never bullied or threatened, and so far as "commercial reprisals" were concerned, we increased the Greek liquor quota at this time five hundred percent! I myself was particularly careful never to appear to push or demand. I indeed supplied much material to the political opposition wherewith to interpellate the Government, but arranged matters so that my part was not known. Similarly in communicating with the Government, it was all unofficial "in the interests of Greece which I had so much at heart." Thus I can report to you truly that in the entire course of this long-drawn out and delicate affair, there arose not the slightest unpleasantness in official relations to hamper the usefulness of this Legation in aiding and protecting American interests. In fact, I feel that we are now better friends than ever.

I know that there is little in the news that escapes you, so I will explain what may have puzzled you, namely, why Insull fled, and why the Greeks brought him back and let him go again. He fled because he wanted to go out his own way, secretly, to escape notice, and not to go, as the Greeks were sending him, publicly on the Orient Express, where his movements could be followed. The Greeks brought him back because the Minister of Marine, an old fire-eater called "the Mad Admiral," insisted that no man could sneak out of the Piraeus under his nose and get away with it. Finally, the Greeks did not care how Insull went out, as long as he went, and went properly; so when they had checked up on him, they let him go out as he wished, on his expensive freighter.

When he fell into the hands of Turkey he fell into the hands of a dictator, and might as well have landed up in Italy. But where could he go? Only in Greece were the conditions really favorable to him, with his two court decisions and the muddy political waters in which to fish. I pinch myself sometimes to make sure I am not dreaming, and I shudder when I think what might have happened had the man been even half-way human and given a modicum of the money he spent on his camp-followers to the needy and the sick. The Greeks love a benefactor, and Insull missed the best trick of all by not becoming one. As it was, he got a lot of sympathy.

The Insull case is a small thing, and only interesting because so much of it has no parallel. More important in this region have been the diplomatic developments having to do with the Balkan Pact. When I last wrote you about it the Pact was a thing of the future. But it was drawn up very shortly after, initialled in Belgrade and signed in Athens. Briefly, it represents a consecration in this part of the world of France's policy of non-revisionism, and a virtual extension and reinforcement of the Little Entente. It draws an iron ring around Germany's old ally, Bulgaria. It ties Greece and Turkey into the Central and Western European tangle, and, as Veniselos[3] has not failed to note, removes Greece from her natural Mediterranean grouping with Italy, if indeed it does not actually commit Greece to fight Italy should the latter move against Yugoslavia through Albania. The immediate reasons which led Greece into the Pact have largely to do with her fears of the Slavic peoples on her Northern frontier, and that she is determined to put teeth into it is evidenced by the mission she has just sent to Ankara, consisting of the Minister of War, the Chief of Staff, and a high official of the Foreign Office. The four Powers signatory to the Pact are now reported as planning to adopt a common standard of military equipment including guns and ammunition, so as to simplify supply problems in case of war. The Pact has indeed the support of the strong local Balkans-for-the-Balkans sentiment, but it is essentially an extension of the great French armed camp in Eastern Europe down into the Aegean and across the Dardanelles, for whatever this may mean in the ultimate line-up of European forces. Thus, while it would certainly be a guarantee of Peace in the Balkans if the Balkans only were involved, its implications outside the Balkans make the Pact really another step in the progressive enlargement of the theatre of possible war.

With best wishes always, I am, Devotedly yours,

Linclon MacVeagh[4]

[PSF:Greece:TS]

[1] Above.
[2] Spiros Maximos.
[3] Eleutherios Venizelos.
[4] See Roosevelt to Hull and Phillips, May 24, 1934, below.

Press Conference, Executive Offices of the White House, May 11, 1934, 4:15 P.M.

[*Excerpt*] Q: Mr. President, we understand that the State Department has been notifying the representatives of the debtor nations that their governments will not be exempt from the penalties of the Johnson Act if they continue to make token payments. The State Department refuses to say anything officially. Can you tell us whether that is so?

The President: I think you will have to get it from the State Department. I hate to cross wires.

Q: Is it not conceivable that if the debtor nations where to offer us a substantial payment, considerably higher than the token payment—

The President: That is the same question that Stevie[1] asked the day before yesterday. In other words, exactly what I said the other day, that I cannot give an answer to any specious case until I know the case.

Q: What puzzles us is whether or not you are going to hold them liable to the Johnson Act unless they make full payments or whether you might be willing to find some means of getting around the Johnson Act if they made substantial payments along the lines of their capacity or desire to pay.

The President: There you are running into the same thing. We cannot say anything about these things until some nation makes a proposition.

Q: Then that is still an open matter?[2]

The President: Yes.

Q: Has any nation asked new negotiations?

The President: I do not think so.

Q: The British today seemed to express the feeling that if you could call a general debt settlement conference, they would appreciate it very much. How does the Administration feel about that?

The President: Just what we felt for a year and two months; exactly the same thing. In other words, no such thing as a general debt conference. Each nation is a debtor and talks with its creditor.

There has been a general effort to—this has to be off the record—there has been a general effort, ever since I have been here, ever since I was elected in November, 1932, to gang me, this is off the record, into saying that we would have a general conference. I said, "No, we will talk anything over with any individual debtor at any time." We have not changed that position.

Q: May we point out that our position in dealing with them individually still remains unchanged?

The President: Yes.

Q: How far off is our debt Message?

The President: Well, I should think I ought to be able to get it in inside of the next ten days. In other words, what I am planning for is to get it up the week after next, the early part of the week.[3]

[President's Press Conferences:T]

[1] F. M. Stephenson of the Associated Press.
[2] See Phillips to Roosevelt, May 17, 1934, below.
[3] See Roosevelt to the Congress, June 1, 1934, below.

René Léon to Roosevelt

New York, May 11th, 1934

Dear Mr. President: The Japanese situation looms so prominently, and in a fashion which is so puzzling to thinking men, that I wonder why so many fail to appreciate the extent of our control over Japan.

The Yen which, incidentally, is the most cleverly managed currency in the world today, constitutes the greatest threat to the economy of Occidental nations because it furnishes the basis for costs of production which are so low as to defy all competition based on Western living standards. And yet careful examination of Japanese trade relations with the United States supports the view that we hold control of the Japanese situation:

One of Japan's principal export commodities is silk whose chief market is the United States; another is cotton fabrics. Unless Japan sells silk to the United States she cannot create the credits wherewith to buy American cotton; yet if world demand for cotton piece goods is not supplied by Japanese spinners, someone else will spin American cotton and meet this world demand.

Assuming that we were to impose a prohibitive tariff on Japanese silk imports into this country, the net effects would be as follows: Internally we would impose a hardship on our local silk industry, which would be partly compensated by an expansion of the silk substitute industries such as rayon, celanese, etc. Externally Japanese purchasing power for American cotton would contract to the detriment of the Osaka cotton spinners. These spinners would lose their trade to the Manchester mills who, in turn, would be the ones to purchase the American staple. Hence, it is through our silk imports that we hold the key to the Japanese problem.

It has always been my contention that the most effective weapons in defense of a nation's economy are not forged by munition factories, but by Central Banks through the rate of exchange, and by governments by way of tariffs.[1]

I am, dear Mr. President, Faithfully yours,

René Léon

[*Notation*:A:LeHand] Mac   to thank him
[OF 197-A:TS]

---

[1] Léon wrote again to Roosevelt on May 16, enclosing a study of the British Empire quota system as it operated against Japan. The letter and study were sent at Roosevelt's

direction to Morgenthau, who was asked to talk it over with the Interdepartmental Commercial Policy Committee (McIntyre to Morgenthau, May 22, 1934, OF 197-A). Apparently neither the letter nor the study was returned to the White House. Léon was a securities and exchange expert with an office at 40 Wall Street who wrote frequently to Roosevelt on financial matters. In January 1934 it was reported that he was being considered for the post of economic adviser to the Secretary of the Treasury (New York *Times,* Jan. 12, 1934, p. 1).

Roosevelt to Cordell Hull, Secretary of State

Washington, May 14, 1934

Memorandum from the President for the Secretary of State: This longhand letter is interesting because it is from an American—uncle of my friend George Briggs—who lives on a mountain in Switzerland and surveys the world as a whole.[1] He prides himself on his detachment from everything except books and occasional visitors.

[*Notation*:AS] Return to President.   Very interesting—Hull.
[PPF 402:T]

[1] Sinclair Kennedy to Briggs, April 22, 1934, enclosed in Briggs to Roosevelt, May 4, 1934 (PPF 402). Kennedy's letter commented at length on political conditions in France, Germany, Italy, and Spain and on terroristic acts of the Nazis and Fascists.

Roosevelt to William C. Bullitt, Ambassador to the Union of Soviet Socialist Republics, Moscow

[Washington] May 14, 1934

Dear Bill: I am heartbroken about the Hawaiian trip but a decision had to be made now on account of the cruiser and also in order to make other preparations.

I was ganged! Your dear old Far Eastern Division, plus the Assistant Secretaries, the Under Secretary and the Secretary, felt that if you came I would have to have Grew and Johnson also, in order apparently to accord equal importance to Russia, Japan and China. That being decided by them, they felt that a gathering of this kind would be almost a Far Eastern Pacific conference and would create such a stir that there might be real discussion and speculation at a time when they want to avoid just that.

With much reluctance I yielded, though I am not in a happy frame of mind about it and still believe that you and I could have had our little party in Hawaii without bringing on a World War! However, there is one consolation—the foregoing of the Hawaiian trip gives you a much better excuse to run back here this fall.

After this wild-eyed Congress goes home I will be able to pay more attention to dispatches and you might also write me the real low-down on what happens at your parties with the Russian foreign office at 3 a.m.

We all miss you much. Take care of yourself.[1]

As ever yours,

[PSF:Russia:CT]

[1] Answered June 14, 1934, below.

Roosevelt to Cordell Hull, Secretary of State

[Washington] May 15, 1934

My dear Mr. Secretary: Before Bullitt's departure, I told him that I wished him to meet me in Hawaii on July 12th and asked him to visit Japan and China and study the political situation in those countries as well as the Soviet Union before embarking for Hawaii.

Will you please issue orders to Bullitt to meet me in Hawaii, proceeding via Japan and China by whatever route he may choose? He should also be instructed to return to his post by way of Vladivostok, with freedom to stop in Japan or China on his return journey if he should consider it advisable.[1]

Yours very sincerely,

[PSF:Russia:CT]

[1] Roosevelt again changed his mind about Bullitt's joining him; sometime between May 15 and 18 Hull cabled him that the President thought it inadvisable for him to come to Hawaii (Bullitt to Roosevelt, May 18, 1934, PSF:Russia). In the letter cited Bullitt wrote that he was deeply sorry that he would not see Roosevelt; that together they might have been able to arrive at a method of settlement of "this Russian business."

Judge Philip James McCook, New York State Supreme Court, to Roosevelt

New York County Court House, New York, N.Y., May 15, 1934

Dear Mr. President: A combination of attendance at a school performance of "Iolanthe" and the news that a British brother had referred to us as "defaulting creditors," was just too much for me one morning recently, when I woke before the family, so I rose and penned the enclosed.

My first thought was to give the readers of the "New Yorker" a good time. Then I fancied I might by doing that go counter to national policies, and so have decided to surrender my responsibilities to you. The effusion is yours: I abandon all my rights. If it does not assist your diplomatic endeavors and at the same time save England from doing something foolish, I trust it will at least lighten the cares of state a bit.

With regards to you and Mrs. Roosevelt, from Mrs. McCook and myself, I am, Sincerely yours,

Philip James McCook

[PPF 1591:AS]

[*Enclosure*] "Defaulting Creditor" log

(With apologies to Gilbert)

1. When Britain really paid her debts
    In Queen Victoria's time,
    The Parliament made no pretense
    A promise of one hundred cents
    Was only worth a dime.
    Oh, English credit was a craze
    In good Victoria's solvent days.

2. When Britain's back was to the wall,
    (As history will tell)
    The Treasury, throughout the war,
    Liked Yankees in particular
    And did itself quite well.
    Yes, "hands across" was just the phrase
    In Royal George's anxious days.

3. And if the present Parliament
    Its policy would halt
    Of searching ocean, earth and sky
    To find one little reason why
    'Tis British to default,
    The Government the wind might raise
    As in Victoria's honest days.[1]

[PPF 1591:AS]

---

[1] An attached note reads: "The President wants this poem for the Cabinet Meeting." See Roosevelt to McCook, May 22, 1934, below.

Ernest H. Wilkins, President, Oberlin College, to Roosevelt

Oberlin, Ohio, May 15, 1934

Dear President Roosevelt: I have the honor to transmit to you herewith a letter signed by several men and women who share with me the responsibilities of college presidency.

. We are tremendously concerned for the well-being of the tens of thousands of young men and women to whom we stand *in loco parentis*; and on their behalf we venture to set before you certain convictions as to steps which should be taken before they should be asked to participate in the last and tragic resort of war.

I have had the letter printed primarily for your own greater convenience. If by any chance you should wish additional copies, I should be delighted to provide them.

I enclose for your information a copy of the covering letter sent out with the draft of the general letter; also a copy of the explanatory statement therein referred to.[1]

With great admiration for your leadership, and with the profound hope that you may lead also toward an International New Deal,

Very sincerely yours,

Ernest H. Wilkins

[*Notation*:A:LeHand] Mac   to prepare reply
[PPF 1616:TS]

---

[1] Not printed.

[*Enclosure*] W. D. Agnew, President, Woman's College of Alabama, Montgomery, and Others, to Roosevelt

Oberlin, Ohio, May 15, 1934

To the President of the United States: At a time when rumors and prophecies of war in Europe and the Far East are being voiced continually in the press and by public speakers, we, the undersigned presidents of American colleges and universities, respectfully request your careful consideration of the following statements. We submit them to you not because they represent our views alone, but because we believe they represent the opinion of many thousands of college men and women throughout the United States—administrators, teachers, alumni and students.

We turn to you with the more confidence because our country has already renounced war as an instrument of national policy and because we have learned to expect from you a keen interest in human welfare, and courage to tackle the hardest problems.

We believe that the outbreak of war in Europe or Asia must sooner or later involve the United States, unless the government of this country is willing to take extraordinary steps to prevent it. Under modern conditions, even nations which strongly desire to remain neutral may all too easily be drawn into war—through interference with neutral commerce, seizure of neutral ships, confiscation of neutral property, inadequate protection of the lives of neutrals, injury to national pride, instigation by those who hope for private profit, or in any one of many other ways.

We know, and those who sit in college class rooms know, far more about the nature of war and its causes and consequences than did college men and women of twenty years ago. We believe that another war, in itself and in its consequences, would be a terrible disaster for the United States.

We believe the time for action against war is the immediate present, before the obvious world trend toward war reaches its end in the actual outbreak of hostilities, and while we and the other major countries of the world are still at peace. We ask therefore that you urge upon the Congress of the United States, at the earliest possible moment, the passage of legislation intended to keep this country clear, so far as is humanly possible, of all circumstances and forces that draw nations into war. If it should seem to you possible to prolong the present session of the Congress until such action should be taken, we believe that you and the members of the Congress would win thereby a vast volume of gratitude, and would be taking a step of permanent world-wide significance. If you should regard the pressure for early adjournment as irresistible, we would ask you to consider the possibility of calling the Congress together in special session as soon as might seem to you possible, to undertake consideration of such a program as is here suggested.

We suggest that immediate legislation should include the following acts:

1. An act empowering and requiring the President of the United States to declare a complete embargo upon trade between this country and any belligerent nation in the event of hostilities in any part of the world.

2. An act forbidding the flotation in the United States of bonds of belligerent governments, and of all private lending by American nationals to belligerent countries or their citizens.

3. An act empowering and requiring the President of the United States, in the event that the United States becomes involved in war, to take immediate control and operation of all business establishments in this country, industrial or otherwise, engaged in the manufacture, transportation, and/or sale of materials of every description used in the prosecution of war—such control and operation to continue for some reasonable period after the close of the war, and to be paid for at a reasonable rate of interest not greater than say 6% on the value of capital plant and equipment at the time of acquisition, or the average earnings of each such establishment during say the preceding five years, whichever is lower.

4. An act prohibiting the use of the armed forces of the United States either for the collection of debts owed to Americans by foreign nationals or their governments, or for the protection of American property owned abroad.

We recognize the fact that the taking of such steps would involve serious costs and sacrifices; but we submit that no costs or sacrifices incurred through them in the interests of peace are likely to approach those which would be caused by war.

We believe that protection to American lives and property by means other than the force of arms requires the following actions, which we ask that you urge upon Congress at your earliest opportunity:

5. The immediate adherence of the United States to the World Court without reservations unacceptable to the Court; and thereafter the submission to the Court of any dispute with another nation which seems likely to result in war, and the acceptance of decisions handed down by the Court.

6. The early submission to the League of Nations of conditions under which the United States would be willing to take full membership in the League, and the offer of complete cooperation with the League while action upon these conditions is pending.

7. In the event of an overt act against our government or its nationals, or of any other threat of hostilities against us, an immediate request for full membership in the League of Nations without conditions unacceptable to the League.

We believe that permanent peace is not possible without a further act, which we urge you to recommend to Congress not later than the next session.

8. An act prohibiting the manufacture, purchase or sale of firearms, and of ammunition of every description, within the United States, or in foreign trade between the United States and other countries, except by the federal government of the United States or under license and complete control by the federal government.

We desire to express our belief that unless our government has made complete use of every available agency for peace and taken every possible step to prevent the coming of war it has no moral right to ask of the youth of America the sacrifice, in war, of themselves, their opportunities for the future, and the companionship of the men and women of their generation whom they hold dear, or to subject them and their children to a renewal of the post-war conditions which have so impoverished and degraded the only life they have known.

It is our judgment that support and aid in the conduct of a war cannot rightly be asked unless every effort possible to human ingenuity has been made to prevent such war.

Very respectfully yours,

W. D. Agnew[1]

[PPF 1616:Printed]

[1] Also signing were almost two hundred other heads of colleges and universities. See reply of June 5, 1934, below.

Press Conference, Executive Offices of the White House, May 16, 1934, 10:40 A.M.

[*Excerpt*] Q: Is Ambassador Davis taking over any suggestion from you in connection with the disarmament situation?

The President: No. I can say no to that but there is no particular reason why you should not know that Norman Davis has been writing a speech. In other words, he has been writing a statement to make and we are going over it at the present time. I cannot tell you what it contains because that will have to wait until he gets to Geneva.

Q: It is a safe assumption that it outlines our policy?

The President: Yes.

Q: Does it propose any new schemes or plans?

The President: Wait a minute—I will be giving it away . . .[1]

Q: Mr. President, in connection with the disarmament, can you tell us anything yet about the Naval Conference for next year?

The President: There hasn't been a single thing done on that yet . . .

Q: Anything on the Soviet trade credit situation? The Soviet Ambassador talked to you about it.

The President: No, that is still in negotiation here and in Moscow.

Q: In connection with the debts, various dispatches state that the French may be considering sending over a debt mission to us. Have we heard anything officially?

The President: No.

Q: Have any of the nations made overtures for relief on debts?

The President: Not so far as I know. I have not talked with the State Department since the day before yesterday so it is subject to check with them.

Q: On the silver, anything on that subject as far as this Conference is concerned?

The President: No, I have not heard a word from the group. I think they saw Secretary Morgenthau day before yesterday. I have not talked with any of them.

Q: There has been some talk that an international conference may be called on silver.

The President: No; have not even got to the discussion stage of that.

Q: Have you any message planned to go to Congress in the near future besides that war debt Message and the one on cocoanut oil?

The President: I do not think so. Yes, I have got another one but I cannot tell you about it yet. I will tell you what it relates to: I might just as well tell you the subject of it—I might not send it—but it relates to munitions makers. That is all I can tell you.[2]

Q: Mr. President, the announcement that we are going to make a new statement at Geneva undoubtedly is going to arouse widespread interest in Europe.

The President: I don't think they may have any interest in it at all.

Q: They may have new hope.

Q: Will this Message you have just mentioned be concerned at all with the report of the War Policies Commission, or the recommendations?

The President: What is the War Policies Commission?

Q: A commission interested in the advisability or possibility of an amendment to the Constitution—war without profit—[3]

The President: I have not thought about that at all. It is germane but it is not tied in with that particular report.

Q: I mentioned that because there was a resolution on munitions makers in it.

The President: Yes, and then there is the Nye Resolution that went through.[4]

Q: Will it have any connection with the Nye Resolution?

The President: You will have to read it.

Q: In connection with the disarmament, will it be a safe guess that it is a restatement of our policy rather than a new statement?

The President: I guess it would not.

Q: You are receiving the Belgian Mission today?

The President: Yes.

Q: Do you expect to take up any international subjects with them?

The President: No, I do not think so. It is just a formal party.

[President's Press Conferences:T]

[1] Davis held a last conference with Roosevelt on May 15 and sailed for Europe on May 19. The statement here referred to was made at a meeting of the general commission of the Disarmament Conference on May 29, 1934 (printed in *Foreign Relations, 1934,* I, 79–83). The speech contained a general review of United States policy, beginning with Hoover's proposal of June 1932 for a percentage cut in all types of armaments. Davis said the President had authorized him to say that the United States was willing to "negotiate a universal pact of nonaggression and to join with other nations in conferring on international problems" arising out of any treaties to which it was a party.

[2] See message to the Senate of May 18, 1934, below.

[3] The War Policies Commission was created by joint resolution of June 27, 1930, "to promote peace and to equalize the burdens and to minimize the profits of war" (46 *Stat.* 825). The Commission, composed of representatives of the Senate, House, and Cabinet, prepared a report that was submitted by President Hoover to the Congress on March 7, 1932 (*Cong. Rec.,* vol. 75, pp. 5340, 5418). The report recommended that with the declaration of a state of war, taxes on all individuals and corporations should be levied at a rate of 95 per cent on all income in excess of the previous three-year average (*Report of the War Policies Commission Created by Public Resolution 98,* 72d Cong., 1st sess., House Doc. 163, Washington, 1932).

[4] S.R. 206, to investigate the arms and munitions industry, was introduced March 12, 1934, and passed April 12, 1934 (*Cong. Rec.,* vol. 78, pp. 4228, 4229, 6485).

Carrie Chapman Catt, Honorary Chairman, National Committee on the Cause and Cure of War, to Roosevelt

New Rochelle, N.Y., May 16, 1934

My dear Mr. President: The Executive Section of the National Committee on the Cause and Cure of War at its meeting held yesterday instructed me to write you. All members of this Committee had observed that the League of Nations had called upon this country and a few others to cooperate in the effort to stop the war between Bolivia and Paraguay. We noticed, also, that the Commission recently returned from South America reported that both parties to the war were amply supplied with up to date armaments, largely secured from the United States and from England.

Possibly they are sufficiently supplied to carry on the war for some time, but we hope you may find a way to cut off further shipments of armaments to those countries and that some new appeal may be discovered to which they may give consideration. I understand that both countries are near exhaustion.

Mr. President, the people in this country, in general, are feeling great sympathy and appreciation for the many tasks you are called upon to perform and never, in my long life, have I heard so many people say that they were praying for the President.

Sincerely yours,

Carrie Chapman Catt

[*Notation*:A:FDR] Mc   To prep reply for me[1]
[OF 338-C:TS]

[1] June 6, 1934, below.

William Phillips, Under Secretary of State, to Roosevelt

Washington, May 17, 1934

My dear Mr. President: Inasmuch as you are going to receive the British Ambassador this afternoon, it occurs to me that you might be interested to glance through a memorandum of conversation which I had with him on May 11th.[1] Sir Ronald's question as to whether full satisfaction of the June 15th payment would clear the British Government from the stigma of default (in view of the fact that Great Britain is in arrears on past payments) has been put up to the Attorney General and we are still awaiting his reply.[2]

Faithfully yours,

William Phillips

[PSF:Great Britain:TS]

[1] *Foreign Relations, 1934,* I, 535–536.
[2] The Attorney General informed Secretary Hull on May 18, 1934, that "if a government which made a token payment under the circumstances stated in my opinion of May 5 should pay the full amount of the installment next due on its indebtedness, it would not be in default" (38 *Op. Atty. Gen.* 581, as quoted in *Foreign Relations, 1934,* I, 540). For the opinion of May 5, see 37 *Op. Atty. Gen.* 506. A memorandum by Phillips on Ambassador Lindsay's meeting with the President is printed in *Foreign Relations, 1934,* I, 541; Lindsay reported this interview in his dispatch to Simon of May 18, 1934 (*British Documents, 1919–1939,* VI, 926–929).

Senator Key Pittman of Nevada to Marvin H. McIntyre, Assistant Secretary to the President

United States Senate [May 18, 1934][1]

For Mr. M. H. McIntyre, Assistant Secretary to the President: I return herewith the proposed message of the President relative to Arms and Munitions of War.[2]

The message seems excellent and complete.

The Convention for the Supervision of the International Trade in Arms and Munitions and in Implements of War, signed at Geneva, Switzerland, June 17, 1925, has been delayed in the Committee pending an understanding between the State Department and the Committee relative to a reservation as to the coming into effect of the Convention. That understanding has been arrived at, and the Convention will be reported in today. There will, in my opinion, be no difficulty in ratifying the Convention.

Key Pittman

[Speech File:TS]

[1] A supplied and approximate date.
[2] Printed below.

Roosevelt to the Senate, May 18, 1934

To the Senate of the United States: I have been gratified to learn that, pursuant to a Resolution of the Senate, a Committee has been appointed to investigate the problems incident to the private manufacture of arms and munitions of war and the international traffic therein. I earnestly recommend that this Committee receive the generous support of the Senate in order that it may be enabled to pursue the investigation with which it is charged with a degree of thoroughness commensurate with the high importance of the questions at issue. The Executive Departments of the Government will be charged to cooperate with the Committee to the fullest extent in furnishing it with any information in their possession which it may desire to receive, and their views upon the adequacy or inadequacy of existing legislation and of the treaties to which the United States is a party for the regulation and control of the manufacture of and traffic in arms.

The private and uncontrolled manufacture of arms and munitions and the traffic therein has become a serious source of international discord and strife. It is not possible, however, effectively to control such an evil by the isolated action of any one country. The enlightened opinion of the world has long realized that this is a field in which international action is necessary. The negotiation of the Convention for the Supervision of the International Trade in Arms and Ammunition and in Implements of War, signed at Geneva, June 17, 1925, was an important step in the right direction. That Convention is still before the Senate. I hope that the Senate may find it possible to give its advice and consent to its ratification. The ratification of that Convention by this Government, which has been too long delayed, would be a concrete indication of the willingness of the American people to make their contribution toward the suppression of abuses which may have disastrous results for the entire world if they are permitted to continue unchecked.

It is my earnest hope that the representatives of the nations who will reassemble at Geneva on May 29 will be able to agree upon a Convention containing provisions for the supervision and control of the traffic in arms much more far reaching than those which were embodied in the Convention of 1925. Some suitable international organization must and will take such action. The peoples of many countries are being taxed to the point of poverty and starvation in order to enable governments to engage in a mad race in armament which, if permitted to continue, may well result in war. This grave menace to the peace of the world

is due in no small measure to the uncontrolled activities of the manufacturers and merchants of engines of destruction, and it must be met by
the concerted action of the peoples of all nations.[1]

Franklin D. Roosevelt

[*Notation*:A] To Bachman special committee investigation of arms &
munitions. Nye[2]

[Speech File:TS:Microfilm]

---

[1] This message was drafted by Joseph C. Green of the Division of Western European
Affairs; two identical copies of the draft are present (Speech File). Of three changes
(in an unidentified hand) one only is significant: the substitution in the next to the
last sentence of the message of the phrase "may well result in war" for "will inevitably
result in war." The draft message was sent to Pittman (see above) and to Hull; presumably Hull was asked to approve the change mentioned. The text here printed is that
of the message sent to the Senate (microfilm of the original in the National Archives).
It was read in the Senate on May 18, 1934, and referred to the Special Committee
on Investigation of the Munitions Industry. It was ratified June 15, 1934, with a
reservation concerning Persia's sovereignty over the Persian Gulf (*Cong. Rec.,* vol. 78,
pp. 9095, 11601). The convention is printed *ibid.,* pp. 11589–11601. The reservation
created difficulties; see Roosevelt to Hull, Aug. 15, 1934, below.

[2] Senator Nathan L. Bachman, presiding over the Senate when the message was read,
was on the Senate Committee to Audit and Control the Contingent Expenses of the
Senate. Following the reading of the message, Vandenberg said that he hoped the
committee would seriously consider increasing the appropriation for the munitions
investigation beyond the $15,000 allotted (*Cong. Rec.,* vol. 78, p. 9095).

Press Conference, Executive Offices of the White House, May 18, 1934, 4:25 P.M.

[*Excerpt*] Q: On the Munitions Message today, any background on
that?

The President: No, except that we want to do everything that we
possibly can on that.

Q: Does it apply to Paraguay and Bolivia?

The President: That is a different thing. I cannot talk to you about
that yet, except off the record, because here is the story: It only came
up just within the past twenty-four hours. We would very much like
to stop the shipment of any munitions to either Paraguay or Bolivia
but we have treaties with them that go back to 1856 or something like
that and to put a resolution through the Senate that would forbid the
export would be in violation of those treaties.

You see, they are inland countries and those treaties were made on the basis of their being inland countries and therefore it would not be sufficient for the nations around them to say, "We won't allow shipments to go in," because we have treaties with them that allow goods through by the Rio Plata. The Secretary of State is consulting at the present time—that is the reason we have to keep it off the record for the moment—with Key Pittman or the Chairman of the Foreign Affairs Committee in the House, and discussing with them the possibility of a resolution which will authorize me to stop the sale of any munitions destined for them within the United States. In a sense it is getting around those old treaties but we do not want to act in a way that would be definitely violative of those treaties. We want to accomplish the same end and the language is being worked out now.

Q: The Senator pointed out this treaty this afternoon.

The President: On the Chaco thing, don't say anything yet because Cordell will probably tell you when he has talked with Key Pittman.

Q: Does the 1925 treaty set up the treaty as you desire, that is to stop the sale by the licensing clause?

The President: Not if it is in contravention of existing treaties.

Q: But if you get the resolution, you can use it in stopping the sale?

The President: Stop the licensing because it is going out of the country—I think so. It is so long since I have looked at it . . .

Q: To turn back to the Chaco for a moment, stories have already been printed that the United States will stop the sale of American war supplies. Is there any objection to saying such plans are going forward?

The President: If you do it in very general terms. I don't want to have anything said that would anticipate the conversation between Cordell Hull and the two Chairmen . . .

Q: London reports that the British Ambassador's visit yesterday was to ascertain or make certain the status of a token payment on the fifteenth.

The President: That is very interesting.

Q: Anything about your talk with the British Ambassador?

The President: No, I cannot comment at all.

[President's Press Conferences:T]

Roosevelt to Jesse Isador Straus, Ambassador to France

[Washington] May 18, 1934

Dear Jesse: You are entirely right about the serious hardships of our government servants abroad.[1] The only answer I can give you at the present time is the enclosed letter from Bill Phillips.[2] I wish I could add something to it, but the matter is in the lap of the Congress and we are doing everything humanly possible to correct the situation.[3]

Very sincerely yours,

[OF 67:CT]

[1] Roosevelt refers to Straus's telegram to Hull and Phillips of May 8, 1934, and his letter to Roosevelt of the same date (OF 67). Straus urged immediate adjustment of pay of Foreign Service personnel. He said that there was great suffering through inability of employees to pay rents and, in the case of small salaried clerks, to provide sufficient food and clothing for themselves and families.

[2] Phillips to Roosevelt, May 16, 1934 (OF 67), covering Straus to Hull and Phillips, May 8, 1934, cited above. Phillips said the question of providing relief for loss by exchange to Foreign Service officers was of "tremendous concern" to the State Department. "The appropriation is in the legislative bill and has been agreed to by the Conferees of the Senate and House but they are in disagreement over a small item affecting Senate employees and seem at the moment to be at a deadlock." The funds referred to were made available by Sec. 5 of the Legislative Branch Appropriation Act of 1935, approved May 30, 1934 (48 *Stat.* 817).

[3] Drafted in the State Department. Straus expressed his thanks in his reply of May 31, 1934 (OF 280). He said he had asked for home leave for the summer and hoped to be able to see the President in July or August.

Roosevelt to Fred B. Smith, Chairman, Executive Committee, World Alliance for International Friendship Through the Churches, New York

[Washington] May 21, 1934

My dear Mr. Smith: I know of no better way to make clear my attitude on the points discussed by us today[1] than to reiterate statements I have made from time to time. I adhere to these now with the same degree of earnestness and conviction as that which marked their first utterance.

For example, in my address of May seventh, 1933,[2] I said:

Hand in hand with the domestic situation which, of course, is our first concern, is the world situation, and I want to emphasize to you that the domestic situation is inevitably and deeply tied in with the conditions in all of the other nations of the world. In other words, we can get, in all probability, a fair measure of prosperity return in the United States, but it will not be permanent unless we get a return to prosperity all over the world.

In the conferences which we have held and are holding with the leaders of other nations, we are seeking four great objectives. First, a general reduction of armaments and through this the removal of the fear of invasion and armed attack, and, at the same time, a reduction in armament costs, in order to help in the balancing of government budgets and the reduction of taxation. Secondly, a cutting down of the trade barriers, in order to re-start the flow of exchange of crops and goods between nations. Third, the setting up of a stabilization of currencies, in order that trade can make contracts ahead. Fourth, the reestablishment of friendly relations and greater confidence between all nations.

Our foreign visitors these past three weeks have responded to these purposes in a very helpful way. All of the Nations have suffered alike in this great depression. They have all reached the conclusion that each can best be helped by the common action of all. It is in this spirit that our visitors have met with us and discussed our common problems. The international conference that lies before us must succeed. The future of the world demands it and we have each of us pledged ourselves to the best joint efforts to this end.

It is pertinent also to recall a quotation from the address I delivered almost eight months later before the Woodrow Wilson Foundation[3] and I take this opportunity to say again:

I believe that I express the views of my countrymen when I state that the old policies, alliances, combinations and balances of power have proved themselves inadequate for the preservation of world peace. The League of Nations, encouraging as it does the extension of non-aggression pacts, of reduction of armament agreements, is a prop in the world peace structure. It is but an extension of the challenge of Woodrow Wilson for us to propose in this newer generation that from now on war by governments shall be changed to peace by peoples.

In this connection, it is fitting that I cite a brief extract from the message I sent to the Sovereigns and Presidents of the Nations represented in the World Economic and Disarmament Conferences.[4] At that time, I said:

The happiness, the prosperity, and the very lives of the men, women and children who inhabit the whole world are bound up in the decisions which their governments will make in the near future. The improvement of social conditions, the preservation of individual human rights, and the furtherance of social justice are dependent upon these decisions.

In conclusion, because it touches upon the final point mentioned in our conversation, I quote from the address of last December before the Federal Council of Churches of Christ in America.[5] In the last two paragraphs of my remarks on that occasion, I said:

115

From the bottom of my heart I believe that this beloved country of ours is entering upon a time of great gain. That gain can well include a greater material prosperity if we take care that it is a prosperity for a hundred and twenty million human beings and not a prosperity for the top of the pyramid alone. It can be a prosperity socially controlled for the common good. It can be a prosperity built on spiritual and social values rather than on special privilege and special power.

Toward that new definition of prosperity the churches and the governments, while wholly separate in their functioning, can work hand in hand. Government can ask the churches to stress in their teaching the ideals of social justice, while at the same time government guarantees to the churches—Gentile and Jew—the right to worship God in their own way. The churches, while they remain wholly free from even the suggestion of interference in government, can at the same time teach their millions of followers that they have the right to demand of the government of their own choosing, the maintenance and furtherance of "a more abundant life." State and church are rightly united in a common aim. With the help of God, we are on the road toward it.

Very sincerely yours,

[PPF 1627:CT]

[1] Smith was at the White House from 11 to 11:15 A.M. (PPF 1-0). In a letter to McIntyre of May 14, 1934 (PPF 1627), he referred to previous correspondence concerning an appointment and said that Nancy Cook and Mary Dreier were interested in what he wished to tell the President as a churchman. (Miss Cook, close friend of Mrs. Roosevelt, was on the New York State Democratic Committee; Miss Dreier, long prominent in women's trade union, and anti-war causes, was a member of the Regional Labor Board in New York.) On May 16, 1934, Miss Cook wrote to Miss LeHand (PPF 1627) that before Roosevelt went south he had told her he would see Smith.

[2] Printed in, *Public Papers,* II, 160–168.

[3] Dec. 28, 1933, above.

[4] May 16, 1933, above.

[5] Dec. 6, 1933, *Public Papers,* II, 517–520.

Roosevelt to the Congress, May 22, 1934

To the Congress of the United States: On January 11, 1934, I recommended to the Congress legislation which was promptly enacted under the title, "The Gold Reserve Act of 1934." [1] This Act vested in the United States Government the custody and control of our stocks of gold as a reserve for our paper currency and as a medium of settling international balances. It set up a stabilization fund for the control of foreign exchange in the interests of our people, and certain amendments were added to facilitate the acquisition of silver.

As stated in my message to the Congress, this legislation was recommended as a step in improving our financial and monetary system. Its enactment has laid a foundation on which we are organizing a currency system that will be both sound and adequate. It is a long step forward, but only a step.

As a part of the larger objective, some things have been clear. One is that we should move forward as rapidly as conditions permit in broadening the metallic base of our monetary system and in stabilizing the purchasing and debt paying power of our money on a more equitable level. Another is that we should not neglect the value of an increased use of silver in improving our monetary system. Since 1929 that has been obvious.

Some measures for making a greater use of silver in the public interest are appropriate for independent action by us. On others, international cooperation should be sought.

Of the former class is that of increasing the proportion of silver in the abundant metallic reserves back of our paper currency. This policy was initiated by the Proclamation of December 21, 1933, bringing our current domestic production of silver into the Treasury, as well as placing this nation among the first to carry out the agreement on silver which we sought and secured at the London Conference. We have since acquired other silver in the interest of stabilization of foreign exchange and the development of a broader metallic base for our currency. We seek to remedy a maladjustment of our currency.

In further aid of this policy, it would be helpful to have legislation broadening the authority for the further acquisition and monetary use of silver.

I, therefore, recommend legislation at the present session declaring it to be the policy of the United States to increase the amount of silver in our monetary stocks with the ultimate objective of having and maintaining one-fourth of their monetary value in silver and three-fourths in gold.

The Executive Authority should be authorized and directed to make the purchases of silver necessary to attain this ultimate objective.

The authority to purchase present accumulations of silver in this country should be limited to purchases at not in excess of 50 cents per ounce.

The Executive Authority should be enabled, should circumstances require, to take over present surpluses of silver in this country not required for industrial uses on payment of just compensation, and to regulate imports, exports and other dealings in monetary silver.

There should be a tax of at least 50 per cent on the profits accruing from dealing in silver.

We can proceed with this program of increasing our store of silver for use as a part of the metallic reserves for our paper currency without seriously disturbing adjustments in world trade. However, because of the great world supply of silver and its use in varying forms by the world's population, concerted action by all nations, or at least a large group of nations, is necessary if a permanent measure of value, including both gold and silver, is eventually to be made a world standard. To arrive at that point, we must seek every possibility for world agreement, although it may turn out that this nation will ultimately have to take such independent action on this phase of the matter as its interests require.

The success of the London Conference in consummating an international agreement on silver, which has now been ratified by all the governments concerned, makes such further agreement worth seeking. The ebb and flow of values in almost all parts of the world have created many points of pressure for readjustments of internal and international standards. At no time since the efforts of this nation to secure international agreement on silver began in 1878 have conditions been more favorable for making progress along this line.

Accordingly, I have begun to confer with some of our neighbors in regard to the use of both silver and gold, preferably on a coordinated basis, as a standard of monetary value. Such an agreement would constitute an important step forward toward a monetary unit of value more equitable and stable in its purchasing and debt paying power.[2]

Franklin D. Roosevelt

THE WHITE HOUSE, May 22, 1934.
[*Notation*:A] V.P.   Read 5-22-34   Table.   Print
[Speech File:TS:Microfilm]

---

[1] Approved Jan. 30, 1934 (48 *Stat.* 337).

[2] This text is from a microfilm copy of the original in the National Archives. A typed draft of this message is present (Speech File); this contains a number of revisions in Roosevelt's hand. The message is also printed in *Public Papers,* III, 253–255. Following reading of the message in the Senate, Pittman introduced the Administration's silver purchase bill, S. 3658; for the text as introduced and as immediately modified, see *Cong. Rec.,* vol. 78, pp. 9211–9212. The bill passed was the House version, introduced by Martin Dies, following some compromises with the Senate. For the debate, see *ibid.,* pp. 9975–9982, 9983–10033, 10124–10130. The act was approved June 19, 1934 (48 *Stat.* 1178).

Roosevelt to Fred I. Kent, New York

[Washington] May 22, 1934

Personal

My dear Mr. Kent: Many thanks for yours of the fifteenth in regard to debts.[1] There is, of course, a lot in what you say but, unfortunately, when one comes down to figures our European friends talk such ridiculous sums that no self-respecting Congress and, for that matter, no self-respecting President, could go on with the discussion.

Perhaps your price level theory of 1930 has definite merit now—as a matter of fact, price level and exchange are in favor of the European nations at this time.

I have the utmost sympathy for the European nations but there are other factors to consider. Remember, for example, that the definite agreement with France, entered into many years after the close of the war, included in it payment by France for the war materials which our Army left in France. These war materials were figured at way below cost. Up to the present time France, under the general agreement, has not even yet paid us for the war materials—a large part of which incidentally the French Government sold to corporations and private individuals at a price higher than they agreed to pay us.

It is things like this, plus for example the offer of Great Britain last fall to pay us $460,000,000 in full settlement of a debt which over a period of years amounts to $8,000,000,000, that make the Congress of the United States and, incidentally, a great majority of their constituents (to put it mildly) somewhat put out.

Very sincerely yours,

[PPF 744:CT]

---

[1] Kent (who had been chairman of the Allied Debt Committee of the National Foreign Trade Council and a member of the Inter-Allied Debt Settlement Committee) made the point that our loans to the Allies had been made in lieu of supplying men and that this should be considered in our demands for repayment. He described a proposal he had made in 1930 to the Commerce and Marine Commission of the American Bankers Association, of which he was chairman, that this country "accept payments against the Allied Debts, reduced by the percentage that the commodity price index was below some certain fixed figures, such as the index for 1926 . . . and that if the commodity price level went above the one selected . . . payments be increased until such time as amounts, that might not have been remitted by the allies during the period of low commodity prices, had been made up" (PPF 744).

Roosevelt to Judge Philip J. McCook, New York State Supreme Court, New York

[Washington] May 22, 1934

Dear Phil McCook: That little poem is a joy and I am taking the liberty of reading it confidentially at the next cabinet meeting.[1]

You are absolutely right about ten cents on the dollar. In my old horse trading days that kind of an offer used to bring the conversation to an end!

Always sincerely,

[PPF 1591:CT]

[1] See McCook to Roosevelt, May 15, 1934, above.

George N. Peek, Special Adviser to the President on Foreign Trade, to Roosevelt

Washington, May 23, 1934

Dear Mr. President: Pursuant to our conversations, I have caused certain studies to be made with respect to foreign trade problems. In the course of these studies we have set up a tentative international balance sheet to see what the present situation is with respect to our foreign business and to attempt to ascertain from the records some reasons for the prevailing conditions.

The figures in the attached exhibits show that the trend in our international trade has been cumulatively disadvantageous to us. In our international commercial relations we have not utilized the simple device of a balance sheet to discover whether we have been doing business at a profit or at a loss. As you have stated a number of times, our exports and our imports of goods and services must balance. During the periods covered by the figures these exports and imports have been grossly out of balance; nevertheless, we have pointed with pride to our "favorable balance of trade."

We have no adequate national bookkeeping system for our foreign financial relations. The statistical bases for the balance of payments estimates since 1922 are the figures published annually by the Department of Commerce. For earlier years extensive use was made of the studies by the Harvard University Committee of Economic Research which compiled estimates for a number of years, ending with 1921. The basic data are unsatisfactory in some respects and in some instances represent estimates, but they serve to indicate the necessity for developing exact balance sheets between this country and each of the countries with which we are now dealing, or with which we propose to deal.

From these data we have assembled the figures covering the years from 1896 to 1933, inclusive, in order to show the commercial and financial trends of this country with the rest of the world. Thus assembled, they indicate that in this 38-year period—

We sold to the world goods in the amount of $121,250,000,000

We bought from the world goods in the amount of 84,604,000,000

Thereby placing the world in debt to us for goods in the amount of 36,646,000,000

Thus, the value of our imports of goods is, on the face of these figures, less than 70 percent of our exports.

As against this export excess we must in fairness deduct the amounts which our tourists spent abroad, and which our immigrants, charitable organizations, and others sent abroad 19,429,000,000

leaving an apparently favorable balance of 17,217,000,000

Services rendered by us to the world such as shipping and freight services, together with interest and dividend payments on our foreign investments, interest and principal payments on war debts, miscellaneous and other items, placed the world in debt to us for an additional. 26,461,000,000

making a total owed to us of 43,678,000,000

Services rendered to us by the world such as shipping and freight services, together with our interest and dividend payments on foreigners' investments in the United States, miscellaneous and other items, in the amount of $18,938,000,000
together with net gold imports of 2,095,000,000
reduced the world debt to us by. 21,033,000,000

resulting in a net increase during the 38-year period in the debt owing to us amounting to 22,645,000,000

This increase in debt is represented by foreign securities and other investments in foreign countries bought by United States citizens, net

$14,398,000,000, and war loans advanced by the United States Government, $10,304,000,000, making a total of $24,702,000,000. From these figures must be deducted United States securities and other investments made by foreigners in the United States, net $2,057,000,000, resulting in the above net increase in debt of $22,645,000,000. Our national assets will be diminished by the amount of this debt which is not paid. (These figures represent net capital movement, and should be added to the estimated $2,500,000,000, which foreigners had invested in the United States in 1896, and the estimated $500,000,000 which we had invested in foreign countries in that year, to reflect the approximate present position.)

For the purpose of better comparison, and in order that the account for the war period may be set off by itself because of its special features, the accounts have been set up for four separate periods within the total period of 38 years covered by these studies. The first period is from 1896 to 1914, during which a relatively satisfactory state of commercial intercourse existed throughout the world; the second from 1915 to 1922, in which our trade with the world was distorted by the World War; the third from 1923 to 1929, during which the foundations for present conditions in world trade were laid; and the fourth from 1930 to 1933.

I invite your attention to certain outstanding items of each of these periods, namely:

Period 1896–1914

1. The value of the goods we exported exceeded by the sum of $8,853,000,000 the goods we imported.

2. Our tourists and immigrants spent or sent abroad funds to the extent of $6,080,000,000.

3. Our own foreign investments increased from $500,000,000 at the beginning of the period to $1,500,000,000 at the end of the period.

4. At the beginning of the period foreign investments in the United States amounted to $2,500,000,000, and at the end of the period they had increased to the new high of $4,500,000,000.

Period 1915–22

1. The value of the goods we exported exceeded by the sum of $21,186,000,000 the goods we imported.

2. Our tourists and immigrants spent or sent abroad funds to the extent of $3,500,000,000.

3. Our own foreign investments (private) increased by $6,779,000,000 during this period, and we acquired obligations of foreign governments (the "war debts") in the sum of $10,304,000,000.

4. At the beginning of the period foreign investments in the United States amounted to $4,500,000,000, and at the end of the period these were reduced to about $2,250,000,000.

Period 1923–29

1. The value of the goods we exported exceeded by the sum of $4,976,000,000 the goods we imported.

2. Our tourists and immigrants spent or sent abroad funds to the extent of $7,021,000,000.

3. We took new foreign investments to a grand total of $7,140,000,000.

4. During the period foreign investments in the United States increased by the sum of $4,568,000,000.

Period 1930–33

1. The value of the goods we exported exceeded by the sum of $1,631,000,000 the goods we imported.

2. Our tourists and immigrants spent or sent abroad funds to the extent of $2,828,000,000.

3. Our investments abroad were decreased by the net sum of $521,000,000.

4. Foreign investments in the United States were decreased by the net sum of $2,289,000,000.

I am transmitting with this letter certain summary sheets for the periods discussed and a recapitulation, in detail, for the entire period. During these preliminary studies I have become convinced that a change is necessary in our approach to foreign trade activities and their relation to our domestic problems. We must develop complete balance sheets between this country and each of the countries with which we are now dealing or with which we propose to deal. Certain information necessary in preparing these new balance sheets is not now available to the Government—I have particular reference to capital movements. To understand the past and to prepare for the future we must get the facts.[1]

Faithfully yours,

George N. Peek

[OF 971:TS]

[1] Roosevelt replied June 12, 1934: "Your letter of May 23d and the figures you have presented are of tremendous interest to me and I am sure will be to others. I suggest that you make them public." No copy of this reply has been found in the Roosevelt papers; this is quoted from *Letter to the President on Foreign Trade from George N. Peek, Special*

Adviser to the President on Foreign Trade (Washington, 1934), a pamphlet in which is printed the May 23 letter and the President's reply. Peek conferred with Roosevelt on May 24, June 8, and June 12 (PPF 1-0), and apparently at one of these meetings the President suggested that Peek discuss the May 23 letter with the Secretaries of State, Treasury, and Commerce (Peek to Howe, June 30, 1934, OF 971).

This letter was supplemented by the letter to Howe just cited; in this Peek described the principal steps taken or proposed in the field of foreign trade. "Balance sheets" were to be prepared by the Commerce Department to show the state of trade between the United States and each of the countries with which it was proposing to deal. The Executive Committee on Foreign Policy was preparing "a complete report for the coordination of foreign trade research by commodities and countries" for treaty bargaining. With respect to the new reciprocal trade agreements, Peek urged that the emphasis be on commerce and trade. Diplomatic considerations could not be ignored but the new proposed agreements were not treaties in a formal sense but "business arrangements." He feared that the importance of this fact had not yet been fully realized. The Reciprocal Trade Agreements Act was signed June 12, 1934; Fite, in *George N. Peek,* p. 275, says Roosevelt had not at this time decided whether Peek or Hull should administer the act.

Roosevelt to Cordell Hull, Secretary of State, and William Phillips, Under Secretary of State

Washington, May 24, 1934

Memorandum for the Secretary of State and the Under Secretary of State: This is an interesting story of the Insull case in Greece. After you have read it will you return it for my files?[1]

FDR

[*Notation*:AS] Interesting—Thanks   Hull
[PSF:Greece:TS]

[1] MacVeagh to Roosevelt, May 9, 1934, above.

Sumner Welles, Assistant Secretary of State, to Roosevelt

Washington, May 24, 1934

My dear Mr. President: In my conversation with you yesterday regarding the projected treaty with Cuba,[1] you raised the two following points:

(1) Whether Article II of the new treaty should contain a clause referring to the acts of the Second Military Occupation of Cuba in addition to the provision contained in Article II as now drafted covering the acts of the First Military Occupation; and

124

(2) Whether the Navy Department had given special consideration to the possibility of retaining the use of the waters of Bahia Honda for refueling or provisioning purposes in time of war between the United States and a non-American power.

Upon consulting the legal advisers of this Department, I am advised that upon the termination of the Second Military Occupation the acts of that Occupation were validated by an exchange of notes between this Government and the Government of Cuba. Furthermore, this Government maintains that the Second Military Occupation was undertaken in accordance with the right of intervention granted us in the Treaty of 1903, and that, consequently, all acts of the American authorities during the Second Occupation were carried out by contractual right and therefore are not open to question. This, of course, is not the case in so far as acts of the First Occupation are concerned.

With regard to the second point mentioned, I had, this morning, a conference with Admiral Standley,[2] who advised me that the Navy Department had given full consideration to this matter and that, in the judgment of the Navy Department, the rights we now possess at Guantanamo, as well as the facilities afforded in Puerto Rico, the Virgin Islands, and continental ports, are so ample from the military standpoint as to make it unnecessary for us to consider utilizing the waters of Bahia Honda for the purposes mentioned.

Consequently, in view of the authorization you gave me yesterday, we are having prepared the final draft of the proposed treaty, in the form you approved, for signature during the early part of next week.[3]

Believe me, Faithfully yours,

Sumner Welles

[OF 159:TS]

[1] At 11 A.M.
[2] William H. Standley, Chief of Naval Operations.
[3] Sent to the Senate on May 29, 1934.

Mary E. Woolley, President, Mount Holyoke College, to Roosevelt

South Hadley, Massachusetts, May 31, 1934

My dear Mr. President: May I express my deep gratitude for the way in which you have helped the international cause this week? The authorization of Mr. Davis's speech at Geneva;[1] your attitude toward the Platt Amendment;[2] and the transferring of the administration of Porto Rico to the Department of the Interior,[3] are long steps forward.[4]

Very sincerely yours,

Mary E. Woolley

[PPF 537:TS]

[1] Of May 29, 1934; see press conference of May 16, 1934, above.
[2] See Roosevelt to the Senate, May 29, 1934, *Public Papers,* III, 270–271.
[3] From the War Department, on May 29, 1934.
[4] Answered June 6, 1934, below.

Roosevelt to the Congress, June 1, 1934

To the Congress of the United States:[1] In my address to the Congress January 3 I stated that I expected to report later in regard to debts owed the Government and people of this country by the governments and people of other countries. There has been no formal communication on the subject from the Executive since President Hoover's message of December 19, 1932.[2]

The developments are well-known, having been announced to the press as they occurred. Correspondence with debtor governments has been made public promptly and is available in the Annual Report of the Secretary of the Treasury. It is, however, timely to review the situation.

Payments on the indebtedness of foreign governments to the United States which fell due in the fiscal year ended June 30, 1932, were postponed on the proposal of President Hoover announced June 20, 1931, and authorized by the Joint Resolution of Congress approved December 23, 1931.[3] Yugoslavia alone suspended payment while rejecting President Hoover's offer of postponement.

In the six months of July to December, 1932, which followed the end of the Hoover moratorium year, payments of $125,000,000 from twelve governments fell due. Requests to postpone the payments due December 15, 1932, were received from Great Britain, France, Belgium, Czechoslovakia, Estonia, Latvia, Lithuania and Poland. The replies made on behalf of President Hoover through the Department of State declined these requests, generally stating that it was not in the power of the Executive to grant them, and expressing a willingness to cooperate with the debtor government in surveying the entire situation. After such correspondence, Czechoslovakia, Finland, Great Britain, Italy, Latvia and Lithuania met their contractual obligations, while Belgium, Estonia, France and Poland made no payment.

In a note of December 11, 1932, after the United States had declined to sanction postponement of the payment due December 15, the British Government, in announcing its decision to make payment of the amount due on December 15, made the following important statements:

> For reasons which have already been placed on record His Majesty's Government are convinced that the system of intergovernmental payments in respect of the War Debts as it existed prior to Mr. Hoover's initiative on June 20th, 1931, cannot be revived without disaster. Since it is agreed that the whole subject should be re-examined between the United States and the United Kingdom this fundamental point need not be further stressed here.
>
> In the view of His Majesty's Government therefore the payment to be made on December 15th is not to be regarded as a resumption of the annual payments contemplated by the existing agreement. It is made because there has not been time for discussion with regard to that agreement to take place and because the United States Government have stated that in their opinion such a payment would greatly increase the prospects of a satisfactory approach to the whole question.
>
> His Majesty's Government propose accordingly to treat the payment on December 15th as a capital payment of which account should be taken in any final settlement and they are making arrangements to effect this payment in gold as being in the circumstances the least prejudicial of the methods open to them.
>
> This procedure must obviously be exceptional and abnormal and His Majesty's Government desire to urge upon the United States Government the importance of an early exchange of views with the object of concluding the proposed discussion before June 15th next in order to obviate a general breakdown of the existing intergovernmental agreements.[4]

The Secretary of State, Mr. Stimson, replied to this note on the same day[5] that acceptance by the Secretary of the Treasury of funds tendered in payment of the December 15 installment cannot constitute approval of or agreement to any condition or declaration of policy inconsistent with the terms of the agreement inasmuch as the Executive has no power to amend or to alter those terms either directly or by implied commitment.[6]

No payment was made by France December 15, 1932, as the French Chamber of Deputies by a vote on the morning of December 14 refused authorization to make the payment. The resolution voted by the French Chamber at that time invited the French Government to convoke as soon as possible, in agreement with Great Britain and other debtors, a general conference for the purpose of adjusting all international obligations and putting an end to all international transfers for which there is no compensating transaction. The resolution stated that the Chamber, despite legal and economic considerations, would have authorized settlement had the United States been willing to agree in advance to the convening of the conference for these purposes.

This resolution of the French Chamber is to be read in relation with the public statements of policy made by President Hoover and by myself on November 23, 1932. President Hoover said, "The United States Government from the beginning has taken the position that it would deal with each of the debtor governments separately, as separate and distinct circumstances surrounded each case. Both in the making of the loans and in the subsequent settlements with the different debtors, this policy has been rigidly made clear to every foreign government concerned."[7] I said:

I find myself in complete accord with the four principles discussed in the conference between the President and myself yesterday and set forth in a statement which the President has issued today.

These debts were actual loans made under the distinct understanding and with the intention that they would be repaid.

In dealing with the debts each government has been and is to be considered individually, and all dealings with each government are independent of dealings with any other debtor government. In no case should we deal with the debtor governments collectively.

Debt settlements made in each case take into consideration the capacity to pay of the individual debtor nations.

The indebtedness of the various European nations to our Government has no relation whatsoever to reparations payments made or owned to them.[8]

Of the $125,000,000 due and payable December 15, 1932, the Treasury received $98,750,000 of which $95,550,000 was the British payment made subsequent to the above correspondence, and the other $3,000,000 represented payments by five other debtor nations. The amounts due from Belgium, Estonia, France, Hungary and Poland which were not received amounted to $25,000,000, of which $19,260,000 was due and payable by France.

In my statement issued November 23, 1932, I had said:

I firmly believe in the principle that an individual debtor should at all times have access to the creditor; that he should have opportunity to lay facts and representations before the creditor and that the creditor always should give

courteous, sympathetic and thoughtful consideration to such facts and representations.

This is a rule essential to the preservation of the ordinary relationships of
life. It is a basic obligation of civilization. It applies to nations as well as to
individuals.

The principle calls for a free access by the debtor to the creditor. Each case
should be considered in the light of the conditions and necessities peculiar to
the case of each nation concerned.[9]

On January 20, 1933, President Hoover and I agreed upon the following statement:

The British Government has asked for a discussion of the debts.

The incoming administration will be glad to receive their representative early
in March for this purpose. It is, of course, necessary to discuss at the same time
the world economic problems in which the United States and Great Britain
are mutually interested and therefore that representatives should also be sent
to discuss ways and means for improving the world situation.[10]

On March 4, 1933, the situation with regard to the indebtedness of
other governments to the United States was, in brief, as follows:

France—[11] The French Parliament had refused to permit payment of
$19,261,432.50 interest due on the $3,863,650,000 bonds of France owned
by the United States;

Great Britain—With respect to the British bonded debt held by the
Treasury in the principal amount of $4,368,000,000, Great Britain in
meeting a due payment of $30,000,000 principal and $65,550,000 interest
had stated that the payment was not to be regarded as a resumption
of the annual payments contemplated under the funding agreement of
June 19, 1923, but was to be treated, so far as the British Government
was concerned, as a capital payment of which account should be taken
in any final settlement;

Italy—With respect to the $2,004,900,000 principal amount of bonds
of the Italian Government held by the United States Treasury, the
Italian Government had paid the sum of $1,245,437 interest due Decem-
ber 15, 1932; but in doing so it referred to a resolution of the Grand
Council of Fascism, adopted December 5, 1932, in which "a radical
solution of the 'sponging of the slate' type was declared to be necessary
for the world's economic recovery";

Czechoslovakia in making a payment of $1,500,000 principal due Decem-
ber 15, 1932, on its debt of $165,000,000 had stated that "this payment
constitutes in the utmost self-denial of the Czechoslovak people their

final effort to meet the obligation under such extremely unfavorable circumstances";

Belgium had declined to pay $2,125,000 interest due December 15, 1932, on its bonds of $400,680,000 held by the Treasury of the United States and in doing so had recited circumstances which it stated "prevent it from resuming, on December 15, the payments which were suspended by virtue of the agreements made in July, 1931," adding, "Belgium is still disposed to collaborate fully in seeking a general settlement of intergovernmental debts and of the other problems arising from the depression";

Poland had not paid the $232,000 principal and $3,070,980 interest due December 15, 1932, on its bonds in the principal amount of $206,057,000 held by the Treasury of the United States.

Of the nine other governments whose bonds are held by the Treasury of the United States, *Estonia* and *Hungary* had not met payments due December 15, 1932;

Austria is availing itself of a contractual right to postpone payments;

Greece was making only partial payments on its foreign bonded indebtedness, including that held by the United States;

Yugoslavia had declined to sign any Hoover moratorium agreement and had stopped paying;

No payment by *Rumania* had fallen due since the close of the Hoover moratorium;

Finland, Latvia, and *Lithuania* were current in their payments.

Although I had informal discussions concerning the British debt with the British Ambassador even before March 4, 1933, and in April there was further discussion of the subject with the Prime Minister of Great Britain and between experts of the two governments, it was not possible to reach definitive conclusions. On June 13 the British Government gave notice that in the then existing circumstances it was not prepared to make the payment due June 15, 1933, but would make an immediate payment of $10,000,000 as an acknowledgment of the debt pending a final settlement.[12] To this notice reply was made by the Acting Secretary of State, pointing out that it is not within the discretion of the President to reduce or cancel the existing debt owed to the United States nor to alter the schedule of debt payments contained in the existing settlement.[13] At the same time I took occasion to announce that in view of the representations of the British Government, the accompanying acknowledgment of the debt itself, and the payment made, I had no personal hesitation in saying that I would not characterize the resultant situation as a default. In view of the suggestion of the expressed desire of the British Government to make representations concerning the debt, I suggested that such representations be made in Washington as soon as convenient.[14]

The Agricultural Adjustment Act, approved May 12, 1933, had authorized the President for a period of six months from that date to accept silver in payment of instalments due from any foreign government, such silver to be accepted at not to exceed a price of fifty cents an ounce. In the payments due June 15, 1933, the Governments of Great Britain, Czechoslovakia, Finland, Italy, Lithuania and Rumania took advantage of this offer.

On June 15, 1933, payments of about $144,000,000 were due from foreign governments, the larger amounts being about $76,000,000 from Great Britain, almost $41,000,000 from France and $13,500,000 from Italy. The amounts actually paid into the Treasury were $11,374,000 of which $10,000,000 was paid by Great Britain and $1,000,000 by Italy. Communications were received from most of the debtor governments asking a discussion of the debt question with the United States Government.

In October, 1933, representatives of the British Government arrived in Washington and conferred for some weeks with representatives of this Government. These discussions made clear the existing difficulties and the discussions were adjourned.[15]

The British Government then stated that it continued to acknowledge the debt without prejudicing its right again to present the matter of readjustment and that it would express this acknowledgment tangibly by a payment of $7,500,000 on December 15.[16] In announcing this I stated that in view of the representations, of the payment, and of the impossibility of accepting at that time any of the proposals for a readjustment of the debt,[17] I had no personal hesitation in saying that I should not regard the British Government as in default.[18]

On December 15, 1933, there was due and payable by foreign governments on their debt funding agreements and Hoover moratorium agreements a total of about $153,000,000. The payments actually received were slightly less than $9,000,000, including $7,500,000 paid by Great Britain, $1,000,000 by Italy, and about $230,000 by Finland.

At the present time Finland remains the only foreign government which has met all payments on its indebtedness to the United States punctually and in full.

It is a simple fact that this matter of the repayment of debts contracted to the United States during and after the World War has gravely complicated our trade and financial relationships with the borrowing Nations for many years.

These obligations furnished vital means for the successful conclusion of a war which involved the national existence of the borrowers, and later for a quicker restoration of their normal life after the war ended.

The money loaned by the United States Government was in turn borrowed by the United States Government from the people of the United States, and our Government in the absence of payment from foreign Governments is compelled to raise the shortage by general taxation of its own people in order to pay off the original liberty bonds and the later refunding bonds.

It is for these reasons that the American people have felt that their debtors were called upon to make a determined effort to discharge these obligations. The American people would not be disposed to place an impossible burden upon their debtors, but are nevertheless in a just position to ask that substantial sacrifices be made to meet these debts.

We shall continue to expect the debtors on their part to show full understanding of the American attitude on this debt question. The people of the debtor nations will also bear in mind the fact that the American people are certain to be swayed by the use which debtor countries make of their available resources,—whether such resources would be applied for the purposes of recovery as well as for reasonable payment on the debt owed to the citizens of the United States,[19] or for purposes of unproductive nationalistic expenditure or like purposes.

In presenting this report to you, I suggest that, in view of all existing circumstances no legislation at this session of the Congress is either necessary or advisable.

I can only repeat that I have made it clear to the debtor Nations again and again that "the indebtedness to our Government has no relation whatsoever to reparations payments made or owed to them" and that each individual Nation has full and free opportunity individually to discuss its problem with the United States.

We are using every means to persuade each debtor nation as to the sacredness of the obligation and also to assure them of our willingness, if they should so request, to discuss frankly and fully the special circumstances relating to means and method of payment.

Recognizing that the final power lies with the Congress, I shall keep the Congress informed from time to time and make such new recommendations as may later seem advisable.[20]

Franklin D. Roosevelt

THE WHITE HOUSE, June 1, 1934
[White House Press Releases:M]

[1] This message was drafted in the State Department (Early to Roosevelt, May 31, 1934, OF 212). The draft (Speech File) is in two parts, the first part concludes with the sentence (below), "*Finland, Latvia,* and *Lithuania* were current in their payments." This first part was drafted in the Office of the Economic Adviser and bears the initials of Frederick Livesey, assistant economic adviser. There is no indication of the authorship of the second part; possibly Phillips drafted it. Roosevelt made some changes in the State Department draft and the more important of these are noted below.

[2] Printed in Wm. Starr Myers, *The State Papers and Other Public Writings of Herbert Hoover* (Garden City: Doubleday, 1934), II, 547–554.

[3] 47 *Stat.* 3.

[4] *Foreign Relations, 1932,* I, 776–778 (quoted here only in part).

[5] *Ibid.,* pp. 778–779.

[6] In the draft, this paragraph concluded with the following sentence, which Roosevelt crossed out: "Mr. Stimson added that our future course as pointed out in the correspondence was clear and referred to a previous statement that the President of the United States was prepared, through whatever agency may seem appropriate, in cooperation with the British Government, to survey the entire situation (in which the debt of the British Government to the United States necessarily plays a part) and to consider what means may be taken to bring about the restoration of stable currencies and exchange, the revival of trade and the recovery of prices."

[7] *State Papers of Herbert Hoover,* II, 487–493.

[8] Myers and Newton, *Hoover Administration,* pp. 287–288.

[9] *Ibid.*

[10] New York *Times,* Jan. 21, 1933, p. 1.

[11] Italics, here and below, indicate underscoring in original.

[12] Lindsay to Phillips, June 13, 1933, in *Foreign Relations, 1933,* I, 839–840.

[13] Phillips to Lindsay, June 14, 1933, *ibid.,* p. 842.

[14] *Public Papers,* II, 242–244.

[15] The draft reads: "These discussions made clear the difficulty if not impossibility of determining the amounts of international payments practicable over any considerable period of time and it was agreed that the discussions should be adjourned until the world situation became more clarified."

[16] Lindsay to Hull, Nov. 6, 1933, in *Foreign Relations, 1933,* I, 844.

[17] The draft has: "and of the impossibility of passing finally and justly at this time upon the request for a readjustment of the debt."

[18] Press release, Nov. 7, 1933, *Foreign Relations, 1933,* I, 845–846.

[19] The State Department submitted two alternate statements here; the one rejected by Roosevelt reads: "whether such resources would be applied to relief from taxation in the debtor countries and to the reasonable payments on the debt owed to the citizens of the United States" (Speech File). In Early's memorandum to Roosevelt cited above, Early called attention to the two proposed drafts of this sentence: "Bill Phillips prefers the one in which the word 'recovery' is used. He thinks the reference to 'recovery' rather than to 'relief from taxation' is to be preferred. His reason is that it is altogether possible for the taxation reference to be interpreted abroad as meaning that the Governments

may reduce taxes and satisfy their people who undoubtedly prefer reduced taxes to debt payments to the United States. Then too, it is suggested that people of the United States who have little present prospect of tax reduction for their benefit would react unfavorably to the suggestion that taxes be lowered by European Governments for their peoples."

The New York *Times* Washington dispatch of June 2, 1934 (p. 1) reported that diplomats were puzzled over the passage, and that some of them wondered whether the President was introducing a new eligibility test for debt revision.

[20] Roosevelt signed the message on the evening of May 31 in Hyde Park where he had gone after reviewing the fleet earlier in the day from the *Indianapolis* off New York harbor. It was read in the Senate and House on June 1, 1934 (*Cong. Rec.,* vol. 78, pp. 10190–10192, 10244–10246). It is also printed in *Public Papers,* III, 275–283. British Ambassador Lindsay sent a summary to Simon on June 1, 1934, and in a later cable of the same day informed him that the message did not require any revision of the British note on debts that they had been drafting (*British Documents, 1919–1939,* VI, 938–939). For this note, dated June 27, 1934, see State Department, *Press Releases,* June 30, 1934, pp. 435–436.

Norman H. Davis, Chairman, American Delegation, Disarmament Conference, to Roosevelt

Geneva, June 4, 1934

My dear Mr. President: As I shall be going to London for the naval conversations about the time you receive this letter, I wish to raise certain points about which I will want your guidance and instructions.

As I have cabled to the Secretary,[1] it is my opinion that we must be careful not to be jockeyed into a position of conducting, for an indefinite period, only bilateral discussions because this gives the British too much of a chance to act as broker between the Japanese and ourselves. This role is an old one which they have learned to play very well. I think, however, that we will be able to deal with this when the time comes.

I understand the Japanese first want to discuss the time and the place for the 1935 Conference. I think it better for us to take the position that this would be putting the cart before the horse because it is essential that we first ascertain whether it is possible to agree upon certain fundamentals and thus have a reasonable assurance of the successful outcome of the Conference.

Assuming that we reach the stage of fixing the place and time for the Conference, it is well to bear in mind the following considerations. The two naval conferences which resulted in a treaty were held in Washington and London and the Japanese will, therefore, no doubt make a strong effort to have the next one in Tokyo. We will be unable to reach an agreement unless the Japanese reduce their present pretentions and give in on the question of ratio, and it would undoubtedly be easier for them to give in in Tokyo than elsewhere because, if the Conference is held there, they would have every incentive to make it a success, and would be better able to get their public opinion to accept the concessions necessary to bring about agreement. Furthermore, it would have a tendency to bring the Japanese mind more into contact with the Western world and probably curb the present trend of going so entirely oriental.

If, however, we should be willing to concede to the Japanese this point of the place for the Conference, we must make it really count for something and should play it accordingly, keeping it absolutely secret until the proper moment.

There are, of course, reasons why we would naturally prefer to have the Conference in Washington, but, since in the Japanese mind there is the feeling that they were out-traded in Washington, I am inclined to think they would agree to this only under pressure.

On the other hand, if the developments should be such as to require a more complete naval agreement, including all the powers concerned, to be tied into a general disarmament program, it would mean that, besides England, Japan, France, Italy and ourselves, Germany, Sweden, Holland, Spain, Turkey, Jugoslavia and Russia should be invited to attend the Conference, in which case Tokyo might be out of the question. It might be deemed necessary, in view of such a large conference, to hold it in Geneva where there would be the machinery of the League for handling the technical side of the work.

There are some over here who have suggested that it would be well to have the Naval Conference in Rome, on the theory that this would help bring Italy and France into the next treaty and would give Mussolini some sugar.

The French want it in Paris but that seems to me to be out of the question because the French press would be almost sure to kill it.

While I think the British are still feeling their way, as they are disturbed over the political trend in Europe, and while there are certain Tories who would favor a closer affiliation with Japan, I am satisfied that the British Government and the Dominions, as well as their people, would never be willing to go so far in that direction as to interfere in any fundamental way with a closer cooperation with us, particularly with regard to naval matters.

One thing that disturbs me is that, until there is some solution of the Japanese position on the Chinese mainland, there is not a very sound basis for a real solution of our political relations with Japan which, after all, affect the naval situation. The most logical solution would be an agreement between China and Japan. I think that the Japanese would, as a last resort, agree to renew the Treaty substantially as it is, without any modifications in the ratio, provided the British and ourselves would enter into a pact of non-aggression with them. On the other hand, I do not see how we could well do that so long as they continue to penetrate China and do things in flagrant violation of treaties which we have already signed with them. They simply can not have it both ways. I also doubt the wisdom of our entering into limited treaties of non-aggression. I think that the constructive way to do this would be as a supplement to the Kellogg-Briand Pact and a General Disarmament Convention.[2]

With warmest regards, I am, As ever, Sincerely yours,

Norman H. Davis

[PSF:Geneva Disarmament Conference:TS]

[1] June 2, 1934 (*Foreign Relations, 1934,* I, 245–246).
[2] The policy decided upon by Roosevelt and Hull was to keep the preliminary talks (which began June 18) on the ambassadorial level; the object was to allay Japanese suspicions that the Americans and British were aiming at a separate arrangement. Davis was not at first convinced of the wisdom of this tactic and was persuaded only after Hull and Roosevelt had talked with him at length on June 14 by telephone (Davis to Hull, June 12, 1934, and the dispatches following, *ibid.,* pp. 247–254). See Hull to Davis, June 26, 1934, below.

Norman H. Davis, Chairman, American Delegation, Disarmament Conference, to Roosevelt

Geneva, June 4, 1934

My dear Mr. President: It is not possible as yet to tell where we are going to end up in our disarmament efforts. I think, however, that I have given in my cables to the Department of State, a fairly clear account of the situation and the various currents and counter-currents.[1]

The crux of the problem is to get Germany back into the negotiations, which I now feel is possible provided we can agree upon a means of doing so which would not be humiliating to Germany and provided that France and England can be brought into agreement as to what concessions will be made to Germany and what limitations will be placed upon her.

It has taken some days to get at the bottom of the Anglo-French tension that has developed. I am now satisfied, however, that it is primarily due to the British refusal to make an out-and-out alliance with France. Eden told me very confidentially last night that they had practically told the French a few weeks ago that they would be willing to guarantee the execution of a disarmament agreement provided there were a real program for disarmament, although the actual disarmament might not begin for several years, and that he thought this was the only way short of war to keep German rearmament within reasonably safe limits. He said that the French then said that they would not agree to any disarmament short of an Anglo-French alliance, which the British refused.[2]

As a result of that the French pride was hurt and they proceeded to run to cover in the direction of a combination between Russia, France, the Little Entente, Poland and the Balkan states, with the idea that if Germany could be induced to come in it could be made into an Eastern Locarno, but if not it would be a combination against Germany. I still believe that their principal idea was that they would thus bring indirect pressure on England to change her mind and form an Anglo-French alliance.

I am afraid, however, that France is playing too much into the hands of Litvinoff, who knows so well what he wants and how to go about getting it that he is going to lead them into all sorts of trouble. The net effect of such an arrangement, if it is effected, would be that France and her allies will protect Russia in the rear in case of trouble with Japan and that Russia could never render any assistance to France against Germany because the moment she should do so she would expose herself to an attack from Japan. However, while Litvinoff is terribly bitter towards the Germans and greatly mistrusts them, for which he has real justification, and while he therefore is not interested in getting Germany back to the Conference now, at least until he gets what he wants from France while she is so scared, he does want peace. He has asked me to lunch with him today and I will find out some more then.

Dodd writes me from Berlin, and I am also informed through other channels, that the Germans would like very much to find a graceful way to return to a participation in the negotiations. One German has just told me that they would like to have me come to Berlin to help find a way, which I told him I could not do, or to have the United States request Germany to return to the Conference.

However, the situation seems to be shaping itself to where they may all ask us to use our good offices to get Germany back and to reconcile the differences between England, France and Germany which have been reduced and crystallized in the French note of January 1, to Germany,[3] the British Memorandum of January 29,[4] and the German note of April 16, to the British.[5] While the situation is difficult and dangerous it is not yet by any means hopeless. While it would seem impossible to get an actual agreement just now there is a possibility of agreeing upon a basis of negotiation which would make it possible to get an agreement in September or October.[6]

With warm regards I am, as ever, Sincerely yours,

Norman H. Davis

[PSF:Geneva Disarmament Conference:TS]

[1] See *Foreign Relations, 1934,* I, 83–88, 94–101.

[2] See Eden to Simon, May 15, 1934, in *British Documents,* VI, 702–704.

[3] Refusing Germany's demand for rearmament (*ibid.,* pp. 238–243).

[4] Printed, under date of Jan. 25, 1934, *ibid.,* pp. 314–324.

[5] Accepting, with certain modifications, the British proposal of Jan. 29, 1934. This note is printed as an annotated draft in *German Documents,* II, 742–743.

[6] The Conference adjourned June 11 without adopting a convention. See Henderson to Roosevelt, July 18, 1934, below.

Roosevelt to Ernest H. Wilkins, President, Oberlin College, Oberlin, Ohio

[Washington, June 5, 1934]

My dear Doctor Wilkins: I desire to acknowledge herewith the receipt of your letter of May 15,[1] with which you enclosed a communication signed by yourself and a number of fellow college presidents, urging upon me an eight point program for the preservation of peace.

I have given your letter and its enclosure my careful and sympathetic attention and, while I prefer not to enter at this time upon a discussion of the individual suggestions, I may say that I am in hearty accord with the objective which inspires your statement. I share with you the wish that our country not only avoid being drawn into another war, but that it also contribute its full share toward the preservation of world peace. This Administration has already initiated a number of steps designed to give practical application to this policy, the most recent among which have been the negotiation of a new treaty with Cuba, placing our relations with that nation on a new footing of equality and friendship, and the establishment of an embargo against the sale of munitions of war to Bolivia and Paraguay, with the aim of putting an end to their useless and sanguinary conflict. The cooperation I have had from the Congress in putting these and similar measures into effect bears witness to its will to collaborate fully in solving the world problems which face us and is a symbol of the unity of purpose of our whole people.

Sincerely yours,

[*Notation*:A] RWM[2]
[PPF 1616:CT]

[1] Above.
[2] R. Walton Moore, Assistant Secretary of State, and presumably drafter of this letter.

William Phillips, Under Secretary of State, to Roosevelt

Washington, June 5, 1934

Dear Mr. President: It occurs to me that it may be of interest to you to glance through some excerpts of despatches and private letters written by Mr. Messersmith shortly before he left Berlin for his new post.[1]

I am enclosing a memorandum from the Office of the Economic Adviser with regard to direct trade interchanges with the German Government at the present time. I feel that the substance of this memorandum is of sufficient importance to suggest that you may find it well worth while to glance through it.

Mr. Messersmith is definitely of the opinion that the Hitler regime is in far more serious straits than is generally realized and, as he puts it:

There are only two ways out which the Germans can see. The one is by negotiation of very favorable agreements with the major suppliers of raw materials, and the other through the getting of credits.

With respect to the first way out, Germany has already concluded a considerable number of agreements with her imports; but these do not assure her of the major supplies of raw materials which she needs and do not open to her for her exports the major markets which she needs desperately . . .[2] I think they still believe that we are so eager to find an outlet for our agricultural surplus and that agricultural interests can exert such a pressure on our Government, that an agreement very favorable to them would be made by us.

The second way out would be through credits . . . and I rather think that the Government will place its main reliance in that. Schacht wants a credit from us for the purpose of propping up a regime which is daily by its acts and by those of a Party, which it is frankly proclaimed is the State, discriminating against American imports and American interests in Germany guaranteed by treaty and international practice. He wants a credit from us to help a regime which, by its own acts, is destroying its capacity to repay.

Quotations from a still later letter:

The acuteness of the export and the raw material question has done more than any other single factor to bring a realization of the dangers to the regime. The intelligent foreign observers here who in December felt that the regime might last are now, so far as I can see, a unit in believing that it cannot continue for more than five or six months at the most. I talked last evening with the best informed of the American correspondents here and the one who has wide and close contact with the highest leaders of the Party, and he was very direct in his statement that they would be finished in five or six months, unless help comes to the regime from the outside which will prop its falling prestige in the country and which will provide the raw materials which they have to have. I have information showing that business men in various parts of the country who have been rendering lip service to the present regime for various reasons are now being more outspoken and have lost all confidence. . . . Schacht can hardly agree to pay anything, because if he does, it is practically certain that he can't pay anyway. If he did agree to pay and if they could pay, I am sure the agreement wouldn't be of any use, for the secondary people in control here are not going to permit any exchange to be used for interest payments. Their only hope is to try to force us into some agreement by which they pay nothing and the bankers promise to use their influence to get credits for raw materials and to add credit or bilateral agreements through which Germany will pay for raw materials with exports of finished goods. I realize thoroughly that we want an outlet for raw materials and that Germany is potentially one of our best customers for such materials; but I am convinced that anything that we do now, directly or indirectly, will be of no real help to us and will merely aid to maintain a regime which is beginning to totter, and that the only hope for Europe, and for us all, is that this regime does fall so that it may be replaced by a Government with which we can deal in the ordinary way. . . . As I see it, we have nothing to lose and everything to gain by a policy of waiting.

Faithfully yours,

William Phillips

[PSF:Germany:TS]

---

[1] George S. Messersmith was consul general in Berlin from 1930 to 1934; after an appointment as minister to Uruguay was canceled, he was sent to Vienna as minister.
[2] All the ellipses here are as in the original letter.

[*Enclosure*] Herbert Feis, Economic Adviser,
to William Phillips

June 4, 1934

Memorandum

Economic considerations regarding the desirability of entering into direct trade interchanges with the German Government at the present time.

(1) The elements of recent German commercial policy (of which the chief factors have been quotas often established on arbitrary bases, the creation of state monopolies for import, treaties giving arbitrary and sometimes discriminatory rights to import, and restrictions on exchanges) have deprived our most-favored-nation treaty with Germany of effectiveness. The German Government refused an invitation extended by this Government some months ago to mutually define most-favored-nation rights.

(2) In regard to the commodity most often mentioned, lard, the German Government has (a) created a monopoly for dealing in all fats, which monopoly strives to develop home supplies to the utmost, regardless of price, and (b) in treaties signed with other countries has given these other countries quotas for lard import more favorable than those allotted to the United States (this is measured by reference to previous trade). Thus, if we were given an increased opportunity for lard export, it would merely be restoring a part of the trade opportunities we are entitled to under the treaty.

(3) If the German Government finds that by harsh and discriminatory curtailment of shipments of American goods, it can secure as a consequence special concessions in the American market, it is almost certain that existing curtailment will be maintained and possibly extended with the German Government asking for special market opportunities or special credits.

(4) If we deal with the German Government on this basis, it is quite possible that other European countries will feel that Germany has gained an advantage and will seek to impose the same conditions for continuation of American trade. In short, dealing with Germany on this basis might open the way to having much of our trade deliberately shut off and then only having it restored for special and directly compensating concessions. The European countries which consider their trade balances with us to be unfavorable are likely to believe that much more can be gained this way than by merely entering into ordinary reciprocal treaties with us.

(5) It would be difficult to promise an expansion of the American market for any substantial quantity of German goods—(a) because so many of Germany's goods are competitive with American products, and (b) because of the widespread boycott on German goods in this country.

(6) Failing the ability to quickly increase the market for German goods, we would be likely to be called upon to extend credit to the German Government. As bearing on that it may be remembered (a) there would be a great number of prior claims on the resources of the German Government, so that all German Government paper would have a very dubious credit standing; (b) Germany has defaulted on the payment of most of the long term government securities held in this country.

(7) The formulation of any special trade agreement with the German Government at the present time, even though the scope of the agreement is small, is not apt to increase the friendliness in economic matters of those European countries which are at present opposed to German policies.

(8) It is probable that the German Government's interest in the transaction is not so much a calculation that its trade situation would be greatly eased thereby as (a) the knowledge that any special arrangement of this type with the American Government would enhance the prestige of the Hitler Government, (b) perhaps form the beginning of a credit arrangement, and (c) create a generally advantageous bargaining position *vis-à-vis* the United States, divested of treaty obligations.

(9) It may be added, in conclusion, that over a period of time, even as short as six months, it would be difficult, if not impossible, for Germany to get along without a large part of the raw materials now purchased from the United States.

[PSF:Germany:T]

Henry S. Hooker to Marguerite LeHand, Personal Secretary to the President

New York, June 5, 1934

Dear Missy: I have just received an interesting letter from our friend Myron Taylor touching on various matters—a talk he had with Mussolini, one with Ruprecht of Bavaria re Germany, and some comments on the steel situation—and I thought the President would like to read it. It may interest the President to know that Prince Ruprecht was Commander of the German troops in front of our Division when the President spent part of the day with us at Molliens au Bois in the summer of 1918.

You will note that Myron and Mussolini are having their pictures painted by Frank Salisbury, and Myron, who is President of the New York Geneological and Historical Society, would like the President to have Salisbury do a picture of him for the Society next fall. If the President regards this idea favorably, let me know, and I will tell Myron.

Just throw Myron's letter away when the President is through with it.
Best as ever,

H.S.H.[1]

[OF 116-S:TS]

---

[1] Henry S. Hooker (1879–1964) had been a member of Roosevelt's old law firm, Marvin, Hooker & Roosevelt from 1910 to 1918 and was a close friend of the family.

[*Enclosure*] Myron Taylor to Henry S. Hooker

115 Via Boccaccio, Florence

Dear Harry: We spent last week in Rome on Academy matters—and incidentally had 30 minutes with Il Duce—who enquired about the President and matters financial in America. I will give you a more intimate account when we are together again. Anabel & I also had an audience with the Pope—which was quite inspiring—marked by its simplicity—and his Holiness' earnestness. I was reprimanded later for not calling upon His Majesty the King—but I had no thought of pursuing Royalty—both the audiences mentioned having been unsolicited, one at the immediate request of Il Duce's Admiralty Cabinet officer—the other at the request of Cardinal Hayes.

Prince Rupprecht of Bavaria, a former acquaintance spent two hours with us yesterday—walking about—and discussing German conditions. Some here have hopes of his taking a leading part when Hitler fails—as many think he must.

Queen Helene of Roumania and her Greek sisters are lunching here tomorrow. We have known them several years—and I must say I have a tremendous admiration for the Queen who has stood for decency and regularity of domestic life in a marvelous way. Besides she is very charming.

Frank Salisbury has just arrived here from London to do a picture for the Steel Corporation to remind future generations of my existence and it has now been arranged he is to paint Il Duce in Rome. I wish the President would let him do a portrait for N.Y. Geneological & Historical Society (of which you may know I am President). Salisbury would come over in the fall to do it I am sure.

Apart from a temperature of about 100 which troubled me for a week before we went to Rome I am in good condition as is Anabel.

I trust you are in equally good form. My tennis is improving as I trounced my English army friend who is here, this morning 6-2,6-1.

So much for the "news behind the news" and best regards from both—

Faithfully

Myron

I am in constant touch with our problems at home both by telephone & otherwise. Our business is much better. Our committee is now working with Genl J. on revision of Code. MCT

[OF 116-S:AS]

Press Conference, Executive Offices of the White House, June 6, 1934, 10:45 A.M.

[*Excerpt*] Q: Mr. President, with reference to that report you sent up the day before yesterday, concerning the survey of the drainage areas of the United States, I notice the one dealing with the Great Lakes presupposes the building of the St. Lawrence Seaway.[1] Anything you can tell us about that? Are they going to negotiate a new treaty or anything of that sort during recess?

The President: All I can tell you is off the record on the St. Lawrence. It has got to be off the record because I have not done anything on it. During the course of the summer probably I will be in touch with the Canadian Government and also with our own people in the Senate here and see what we can do. The only thing we have to bear in mind, very firmly, is that we haven't by any means abandoned the St. Lawrence Seaway. We are going ahead with it but as to the time and method, as to whether there will be any amendments to the Treaty, I cannot say, because I have not taken it up . . .

Q: I understand you have been conferring with some of the Naval officers about the forthcoming talks in London.[2] Can you give us any intimation of what the attitude of the United States will be?

The President: The only thing is that some officers are going over very shortly for preliminary conversations. That is all. We won't have any announcement to make at all as to what the policy is. It will probably come out of London, not here.

Q: Who is going over?

The President: Admiral Leahy[3]—ask the State Department if there is any reason why the personnel, as to who is going over, should not be—

Q: It has been made public.

Q: Are we going to have any platform?

The President: No, just conversations.

[President's Press Conferences:T]

[1] See Roosevelt's message to Congress of June 4, 1934, in *Public Papers,* III, 283–284, submitting a number of reports on the Interior Department study, *Development of the Rivers of the United States* (Washington, 1934).

[2] Admiral William H. Standley, Chief of Naval Operations, and Admiral Richard H. Leigh, adviser to the American delegation at the forthcoming London naval conversations, were at the White House the day before (PPF 1-0).

[3] Rear Admiral William D. Leahy, at this time chief of the Bureau of Navigation.

Roosevelt to Carrie Chapman Catt, Honorary Chairman, National Committee on the Cause and Cure of War, New York

[Washington, June 6, 1934]

My dear Mrs. Catt: I thank you for your letter of May 16, 1934, conveying the view of the Executive Section of the National Committee on the Cause and Cure of War, that this Government should join with the League of Nations and other Governments in cutting off further shipments of armaments to Bolivia and Paraguay.[1]

I heartily share your hopes that the war between the two countries may be promptly ended. On May 18, as you are doubtless aware from a reading of the press, a joint resolution to prohibit the sale of arms and munitions of war in the United States under certain conditions, was submitted to the Congress. This resolution has received the unanimous approval of both Houses of Congress. In pursuance thereof, I have issued a proclamation prohibiting the sale of arms or munitions of war in the United States, to the countries involved in the Chaco conflict.[2]

In view of your interest in this subject, I take pleasure in transmitting herewith, for your information, a copy of the joint resolution in question, as well as a copy of the proclamation giving it effect.[3]

Sincerely yours,

[OF 338-C:CT]

[1] Above.
[2] The proclamation, printed in *Public Papers,* III, 268–269, quotes the resolution.
[3] This letter was drafted in the Department of State.

Roosevelt to Mary E. Woolley, President, Mount Holyoke College, South Hadley, Massachusetts

[Washington] June 6, 1934

Dear Miss Woolley: Many thanks for that nice note of yours of May thirty-first.[1] I think we are getting somewhere in spite of the attitude of Europe!

Always sincerely,

[PPF 537:CT]

[1] Above.

Roosevelt to Irving Fisher, Yale University, New Haven, Connecticut

[Washington] June 8, 1934

My dear Professor Fisher: Many thanks for the short statement. I shall be glad to have the digests of the three books and will take them on my cruise with me.[1]

My general thought is that our economic problems necessarily differ greatly from those of almost all European countries. For the same reason that British financial problems could only be compared with ours if Canada, Australia, and South Africa were tacked onto England and Scotland!

Very sincerely yours,

[PPF 431:CT]

[1] The "short statement" was enclosed in Fisher's letter to Roosevelt of June 4, 1934 (PPF 431). Prepared by Fisher as a newspaper release and entitled, "Is the New Deal a Consistent Whole?", the statement was a digest of three books: Erik Kjellstrom's *Managed Money; the Experience of Sweden* (New York: Columbia, 1934); Douglas Copland's *Australia in the World Crisis* (Cambridge, Eng.: University Press, 1934); and *Economic Reconstruction; Report of the Columbia University Commission* (New York: Columbia, 1934). Fisher said that the three studies supported Roosevelt's monetary policy but not his policy of restricting production. He said he would also send him digests of the separate books.

William Phillips, Under Secretary of State, to Roosevelt

Washington, June 11, 1934

Dear Mr. President: In view of its importance, would you be so good as to glance through the enclosed draft note to the British Government, which I should like to have ready for the Secretary's signature tomorrow morning? We have smoothed it somewhat since this morning and have added the suggestions which you made to me.

Faithfully yours,

William Phillips

Perhaps its tone is a bit too severe?

[*Notation*:AS] No—OK   FDR
[*Notation*:AS] Final draft to British Embassy 6-12-34 H.F.[1]
[OF 48:TS]

[1] Herbert Feis, economic adviser to the State Department, and presumably drafter of the enclosure.

[Enclosure] Cordell Hull, Secretary of State, to Ronald Lindsay, British Ambassador

Draft No. 10. Rough Draft.[1]

Excellency: The observations contained in your note of June 4, 1934, concerning the indebtedness of His Majesty's Government to the United States have been studied with close attention.

This Government is sensible of the elements of the situation set forth by His Majesty's Government, the heavy war expenditures undertaken in its own behalf and in behalf of its Allies, the burden of taxation that has been borne by the British people, and the transfer difficulties that under certain circumstances may arise in the foreign exchanges. With certain observations, however, and the inferences drawn therefrom, I regret that the American Government is unable to concur and in three instances it feels that, for the purpose of record, it should make its own attitude clear.

First, His Majesty's Government states in effect that, unless payments were made in full in the sum of $262,000,000 as set forth in the communication from the United States Treasury dated May 25, 1934, the United Kingdom would fall within the effects of the recent legislation mentioned in paragraph seven of your note, so that the payment of this amount is regarded as the only alternative to suspension of all payment. The Attorney General has advised me that, in his opinion, the debtor governments which, under the ruling of his Office of May 5, 1934, are not at present considered in default because of partial payments made on earlier instalments, would have to pay only the amount of the instalment due June 15, 1934,—for Great Britain $85,670,765.05—in order to remain outside the scope of the Act.

Second, in regard to the record cited by the British Government of its loans to its Allies and the fact that His Majesty's Government has given up great sums due to it under those loan contracts, this Government must emphasize the complete independence between the aforementioned transactions and the debt contracted by His Majesty's Government to this Government. The British Government undertook to borrow under its own name and on its own credit standing, and repayment was not made contingent upon the fate of debts due to the British Government.

Third, this Government notes with disappointment the declaration of His Majesty's Government that "while suspending further payments until it becomes possible to discuss an ultimate settlement of intergovernmental war debts with a reasonable prospect of agreement, they have no intention of repudiating their obligations, and will be prepared to enter upon further discussion of the subject at any time when, in the opinion of the President, such discussion would be likely to produce results of value."

In effect, this Government reads the declaration of His Majesty's Government to mean that it will fail to meet any further payments on the debt due to the United States as evidenced by the settlement of June 19, 1923, until this Government shall first scale down this debt to an unascertained sum to which His Majesty's Government might be willing to accede. This declaration appears to represent insistence by His Majesty's Government that before it makes any payment whatsoever it must be assured of a settlement satisfactory to it and not necessarily in accordance with any accepted standards of payment or readjustment of the amounts due. The only indications before this Government of the extent to which His Majesty's Government has proposed to meet its obligations are the small fractions of the sums due mentioned by His Majesty's Representative in the course of the discussions in the spring and autumn of last year referred to in your note of June 4. Adhering to the opinion so often expressed by the United States Government a situation of this kind necessarily calls for the initiation of proposals by the debtor and not by the creditor.

Should His Majesty's Government wish to put forward proposals for the resumption of payments, this Government would be glad to entertain and discuss them informally. For instance, no proposal has ever been presented to this Government looking towards payments in kind to an extent that might be found mutually practicable and agreeable. Any proposals of this or a similar character which promise mutual benefit will be carefully considered for eventual submission to the American Congress.

In conclusion, may I refer to the statement made by the President in his message to the Congress on June 1: "The American people would not be disposed to place an impossible burden upon their debtors, but are nevertheless in a just position to ask that substantial sacrifices be made to meet these debts."[2]

[OF 48:T]

[1] No change was made in this "rough draft" and it was sent, under date of June 12, 1934, by Lindsay to Simon in a dispatch of the same date (*British Documents,* VI, 942–944).

[2] See Roosevelt's message to the Congress of June 1, 1934, above.

Statement by Roosevelt on the Signing of the Reciprocal Trade Agreements Act

[Washington, June 12, 1934]

The President gave out the following statement on the signing of the Tariff Bill at 9:15 tonight.

The adoption by Congress of the policy of expanding the markets of products of the United States by negotiated agreements reciprocally affording market opportunities for the products of other countries is an act of broad wisdom. The unprecedented shrinkage of world trade has been an important element in the present world condition. This step should help to reverse the trend and thereby to assist recovery. The use of the granted powers will require care to assure that each agreement makes a real contribution to recovery. Wise reciprocity between countries, each having regard to its own best interests, will be needed. Years have been spent in building barriers against mutual trade which have effectively impaired not only the foreign but also the domestic commerce of all countries. The restoration of healthier trade by the removal of mutual impediments will require time and patience but progress should be sure from the beginning and should accelerate.[1]

[Speech File:T]

[1] This is the typed original of the press release; the first sentence is in Roosevelt's hand. He first began it: "The President and the Secy of State gave out . . . ," then crossed out "Secy of State." For the act, see 48 *Stat.* 943.

Senator Key Pittman of Nevada to Marvin H. McIntyre, Assistant Secretary to the President

Washington, D.C., June 12, 1934

Memorandum for Mr. M. H. McIntyre, Assistant Secretary to the President: Your memorandum of June 9th, sent to me on behalf of the President, enclosing communications from Professor M. L. Raney, Director of the University Libraries, University of Chicago, in the matter of the hearings on the Copyright Bill (S. 1928) and the Copyright convention pending before our committee, has been examined by me.[1]

Professor Raney's letter to the Honorable Cordell Hull, dated 15th, which is enclosed with your memorandum, was submitted by Professor

Raney to our committee and has been published in the records of the hearings.[2]

Professor Raney received every courtesy and was given every consideration that was possible in the circumstances.

Further hearings were demanded on the Copyright convention, and therefore a subcommittee was appointed to conduct such hearings. The subcommittee is still conducting these hearings.

There are many questions that are being intensely controverted.[3]

Key Pittman
Chairman, Committee on Foreign Relations

[OF 699:T]

[1] No copy of McIntyre's memorandum is present. Pittman returned the enclosures and they are filed with the letter here printed. Raney, in his letter to Roosevelt of June 5, 1934 (OF 699), urged ratification of the Copyright Treaty and said that it was clear that the Foreign Relations Committee would take no action during the session without "a clear-cut word" from him. He enclosed a typed copy of his remarks before the Foreign Relations Committee hearings of March 28, 1934; in this he represented twenty-two learned societies, or virtually all those of national scope.

[2] *Hearing, 73d Cong., 2d session, on S. 1928, to enable the United States to enter the International Copyright Union, Mar. 28, 1934* (Washington, 1934). Signing with Raney were the presidents of a number of American universities, including California, Chicago, Johns Hopkins, and Harvard.

[3] Congress adjourned June 18 but those urging ratification hoped until the last minute for a favorable report and vote. On June 16 Robert Underwood Johnson wired the President on behalf of the American Academy of Arts and Letters and asked that he sign the convention with the quill pen used by President Harrison to sign the Copyright Act of 1891 (OF 699). See Roosevelt to Solberg, June 25, 1934, below.

Press Conference, Executive Offices of the White House, June 13, 1934, 10:55 A.M.

[*Excerpt*] The President: I do not believe there is any news today at all.

Q: Tell us about the 22 billions.

The President: You have this. This is George Peek's story, given out on foreign trade.[1] I do not know whether you are familiar with it but apparently it is the first time it has ever been done. This is something already given out by George Peek's office so I suppose you are all familiar with it. It is what might be called a preliminary estimate and subject of further studies, but it is the first thing of its kind that has been attempted, showing the total of American exports and imports from 1896 down and through 1933. In other words, it is a thirty-seven or thirty-eight year period.

I suppose most people have the idea that during that period, because we had an apparently favorable export balance, that this country has made a lot of money out of its foreign trade. Well, these figures that George Peek's office has been working out, which have been at least partly checked by the Department of Commerce, rather disprove the theory that the United States makes a lot of money out of its so-called favorable balance. You will have to read the letter to me to get the details of it. The rough figures are that during this whole period we sold to the world goods to the amount of 121 billions—that is billions, don't make it millions—and we bought from the world goods valued at 84 billions, so there is an apparently favorable balance to the United States of 36 billion dollars, which means that, in another way of putting it, our imports were only seventy per cent of our exports.

But, as against that apparently favorable balance of 36 billions, George Peek says that we ought, in fairness, to deduct the amount that good Americans spent on their trips to Paris, in other words the tourist money, which amounts to 19 billions, so with that deduction it leaves an apparently favorable trade balance of only 17 billion dollars.

Then, you have two other amounts that you have to take into consideration: First, the services rendered by us to the world in shipping and freight services, interest and dividend payments, interest and principal payments of various debts, etc., which add to the amount owed us 26 billions, making a total owed us of 46 billions. Of course, if you do that, you have to charge off the other side of the picture and deduct the services rendered to us by the world shipping and trade services, interest and dividend payments on all foreigners' investments in the United States, things of that kind, and net gold imports, which would reduce the world debt of 43 billions by 21 billions, which would show that during this 38-year period the net amount owed to the United States is about 22 billion dollars.

And then, Peek makes the point that that 22 billion dollars, which is the net profit—the easiest way of putting it—the net profit of all of our foreign dealings, that that 22 billion dollars has not been paid us, that we have only got evidences of indebtedness, so that if those evidences of indebtedness are paid, then we will be 22 billion dollars better off for this 38-year period.

Now, of course, that is a very interesting thing and I suppose all of you people who know more of these things than I do will be able to write some fascinating stories; then you will turn it over to the headline man and he will do some more editing. However, it is a fine subject to go into because, as far as I know, this is the first time there has ever been what might be called a serious attempt to estimate these figures and perhaps a lot of people will dispute them.

Q: Does it mean that the world welshes on their debts?

The President: Oh, no.

Q: How do they owe us 22 billion dollars?

The President: Well, they have not paid us the favorable balance of trade in cash.

Q: What are the evidences of indebtedness?

The President: I will have to study it some more before I answer that question. Well, there are balances that various American firms have in Europe, which they cannot bring back here. The whole foreign exchange situation is involved in that. Then there are notes of foreign corporations, bonds of municipalities, their notes and bonds of all kinds of foreign corporations that are held here, not only by investors but by companies. If the General Electric (for example) sells a lot of equipment to some private concern in Italy, it takes notes of that private concern over a period of years, part cash and part notes. In other words, it is all the various mercantile type of debts.

Q: A good part of that is liquid short-term stuff?

The President: Yes.

Q: Is it true that the whole 22 million dollars, none of it has been paid in cash?

The President: 22 billions. That is the net part that has not been paid in cash. In other words, all the rest has been paid, just the same as we paid for what we bought.

Q: Is it true that goods and services of foreign countries must be accepted by us if this country is to be paid off?

The President: That, of course, is much too definite a statement because goods and services are one form of payment, only one form. Just the same way as the reply the Secretary of State made.[2] For example, there are large headlines in the papers which would give the average layman who reads those papers—it is the headline fellow's fault, not yours—the idea that we had definitely made an offer to Great Britain that they could pay all their debt by sending us goods. That is what the layman gets from reading that type of headline in the morning papers. If you will read Hull's reply carefully, you will see that that kind of headline was unjustified.[3]

Q: In that connection, the London dispatches state that the British are a little puzzled by what we mean. Do we mean we would be willing to open our markets here sufficiently to permit them to accumulate dollar balances here?

The President: We would be willing to discuss that with them as they had suggested on several previous occasions, in order to avoid the obstacle they raised, which was the payment in cash. We would be entirely willing to go along and talk about what they had suggested, which was partial payment in kind, but very partial. Obviously, you cannot transfer the whole—what did they agree to pay us, 350 or 400 million dollars? Of course that could not be paid in kind.

Q: Isn't it a safe guess we are not going to open our markets to permit them to accumulate dollar balances here?

The President: That is a perfectly impossible question to answer. You cannot answer yes or no unless you start beating your wife. In other words, suppose we had agreed to take some tin. I just take that out of the air because I saw it in the paper this morning. Suppose we agree to take a certain amount of tin which we do not produce, does that open the markets in this country or not?

You can't write a definitive story on any of this stuff; that is the real answer. I could not if I tried.

Q: Isn't the main purpose of this note to keep the debt question open?

The President: No, the main purpose is to answer the British note.

Q: Coming back to the Peek Report for a moment, he says in his report that the figures show that the international trade has been cumulatively disadvantageous to us and he says we have to make a new approach. Has he made any definite suggestions to you as to what the new approach might be?

The President: No. As I say, this is the first time these figures have been worked up. Then, too, he divides them into a series of periods which are quite interesting: 1896 to 1914; 1914 to 1922, which is really the war period; 1923 to 1929, which is really the madness period; and 1930 to 1933, which is what might be called the reconstruction period.

Q: What, if any, moral might be drawn from the figures?

The President: None, absolutely none. That is exactly what I am trying to drive home, that nobody is trying to point any moral or do anything more about it except to give out these figures for people to think about and get interested in.

Q: What effect on your policy in negotiating reciprocal trade agreements will that report have?

The President: I have not any idea, any more than you have.[4]

[President's Press Conferences:T]

[1] See Peek to Roosevelt, May 23, 1934, above.
[2] Hull to Lindsay, printed as an enclosure in Phillips to Roosevelt, June 11, 1934, above.
[3] The New York *Times* page one article of June 13 on the note was captioned: "Hull Proposes to Britain Debt Payments in Goods; Lays Basis for Negotiation."
[4] See Peek to Roosevelt, Aug. 30, 1934, below.

William C. Bullitt, Ambassador to the Union of Soviet Socialist Republics, to Roosevelt

Moscow, June 14, 1934

Dear Mr. President: A courier has just brought your letters of May 9, 14, and 21.[1] I am deeply grateful to you for your letter about the Hawaiian trip.[2] I really miss seeing you and hearing the sound of your voice.

You may be sure that if there should be another 3 A.M. party in the Kremlin I will write you privately. I got word from the Kremlin a few days ago that Stalin had chided his intimates for not seeing more of me. They replied that the lack of such parties had been my fault and not theirs. They have all entertained me lavishly and as yet I have not been able to have one of them in the house. That sort of party requires at least one door that can be closed and kept closed, and I still have the privacy of the information clerk in the Grand Central Station.

Within two weeks, however, I expect to have the Chancery out of my house and the dozen boys who are boarding here safely in the Mokhovaya building. Moreover, I hope to have a dining room table and some living room furniture. I shall then try to make up for lost time.

I will do everything I can, of course, to help your cousin Leaycraft.[3]

Fair winds and a smooth sea to you both for your Hawaiian trip and thereafter.

Yours affectionately,

Bill

[PSF:Russia:TS]

[1] The May 21 letter is not present; the others are printed above.
[2] May 14, above.
[3] See Roosevelt's letter of May 9, above.

Press Conference, Executive Offices of the White House, June 15, 1934, 4:10 P.M.

[*Excerpt*] Q: Inasmuch as it is debt pay day, can I induce you to comment on the generosity of the debtors?

The President: No.

Q: Can you tell us anything about your plans for the summer other than—

The President: I suppose you would like to know, Fred.[1] Well, the only thing that is definite is that the actual date of departure is indefinite. In other words, I do not know what day we are going to push off. I might put it off three or four days to give me a little bit more time to go up to New London and then come back here for three or four days just to clear up odds and ends and then push off from Annapolis instead of New York. But the date is on a moveable basis, some time, we hope, between the twenty-sixth of June and the fourth of July. That is as near as I can give it.

Q: Have you given any thought to touching at any ports?

The President: Yes, I hope very much to be able to go to Cartagena, Colombia, and pay a call on the President of the Republic of the United States of Colombia. It is about fifty miles—less than that, about forty miles out of the way of the straight course from St. Croix to Panama, so all it would involve would be spending one extra day and go in there if the President of Colombia comes down to Cartagena. We would spend the day together and that would be the first time that any American President has ever visited any nation in South America during his term of office.

Q: What is the occasion of this official visit?

The President: What?

Q: What is the occasion of the visit to Colombia?

The President: Just to say, "How do you do?" It is on the way.

Q: Any celebration?

The President: No, we get there on the Fourth of July if we leave on the twenty-sixth.

Q: Would that involve landing on their soil?

The President: Oh, yes; there would be nothing new in that.

Q: I thought they might come out to your boat.

The President: I am going to lunch with the President of Panama. That has been done on many occasions.

Q: Mr. President, I am not sure whether there is a map out there in the Press Room. Do you mind spelling the name?

The President: Well, anglicized it is C-a-r-t-a-*g*-e-n-a and it takes you quite a while to practise the pronunciation of the "g" . . .[2]

Q: Mr. President, on this German moratorium business, Germany complains that she has not been permitted to pay in goods on these obligations. In view of the fact that we have more or less invited partial payment of war debts in goods, would it not be possible for Germany to come here with goods for payment on these other debts?

The President: I don't know. In other words, we have not considered it one way or the other at all. They have never offered to pay in goods, have they?

Q: No, sir; not that I know of.

[President's Press Conferences:T]

---

[1] Frederick Essary of the Baltimore *Sun.*

[2] Roosevelt first mentioned his plan to visit the Caribbean and the West Coast at his Jan. 19, 1934, press conference. By June 6 he had settled on a vacation schedule that called for departure from New York on June 26; stops at Cap Haitien, Cartagena, Balboa, Panama, and Cocos Island; and then northwest across the Pacific to Hawaii (Roosevelt to Vernou and Brown, June 6, 1934, OF 200). The trip actually began July 1, when the President boarded the *Houston* at Annapolis.

Cordell Hull, Secretary of State, to Roosevelt

Washington, June 16, 1934

Dear Mr. President: I enclose for your information copy of a telegram which I am sending to Ambassador Dodd in Berlin, regarding the recent debt action taken by Germany.[1]

During the negotiations between representatives of the American bondholders and the German officials over the past few weeks at Berlin, we have made suitable representations on various occasions in support of the rights of our nationals and especially in the matter of any possible discrimination against them. This I did again in conversation with the German Ambassador here, both some days ago and as late as yesterday.

Faithfully yours,

Cordell Hull

[PSF:Germany:Dodd:TS]

---

[1] June 16, 1934 (*Foreign Relations, 1934,* II, 364–365), instructing Dodd to protest the German action on the American loans.

Roosevelt to Harry Bergson, Boston

[Washington] June 18, 1934

Dear Harry: Many thanks for your note. As you say there is real difficulty in the use of the word "default." We have the right now to ask for bonds from the debtor governments. The trouble is they would not pay the interest on the bonds any more than they would the interest due to the United States.[1]

I am awfully sorry that I cannot get to the reunion to give the crowd my best.[2]

As ever yours,

[PPF 1669:CT]

[1] Bergson, in his letter of June 14, 1934 (PPF 1669), said that use of the terms "repudiation" and "default" in the negotiations with the British over the debt strained the temper of both parties and did not advance matters. "I think all sensible people concede that the war debts cannot be collected in full, and that the totals due must be scaled down. Why not let the foreign governments offer the defaulted State bonds as an offset against our claims?"

[2] Bergson had hoped to see Roosevelt at their Harvard class reunion at Nahant, Mass., on June 19.

Roosevelt to Cordell Hull, Secretary of State

Washington, June 18, 1934

Memorandum for the Secretary of State: Please let me know before we appoint our representatives to examine claims with the Turkish Republic. I have just signed a Joint Resolution for $90,000 for this.[1]

F. D. R.

[Notation:AS] For response see the Attached—Hull[2]
[OF 86:CT]

[1] Approved June 18, 1934 (48 *Stat.* 1018).

[2] The "attached" is a memorandum from Green H. Hackworth, legal adviser to the State Department, to Hull, June 20, 1934, reporting that two commissioners had already been designated, Fred K. Nielsen and Julian E. Gillespie. The latter was commercial attaché at Istanbul and was serving as commissioner without compensation. Hackworth reported that very little progress had been made in the work; he therefore recommended that no new appointment (to take Gillespie's place) be made for the time being.

Roosevelt to Senator Gerald P. Nye of North Dakota

[Washington] June 18, 1934

My dear Senator: Thanks for yours of June fourteenth in regard to disarmament information.[1] I am asking the Secretary of State to make available to your committee a résumé of the difficulties we have had in regard to the Chaco problem and also the status of the Geneva Disarmament Conference. I suggest that you call on the State Department when you are ready.

Very sincerely yours,

[OF 404–A:CT]

[1] Nye referred (OF 404–A) to the President's half-hour meeting on June 6 with the Senate committee appointed to investigate the munitions industry. He said that the President had suggested that the committee might avail itself of certain correspondence he had had with Norman Davis on the subject of disarmament "and the part which the United States stood ready to play in promoting any degree of disarmament." Nye asked that this correspondence be sent to him.

Press Conference, Executive Offices of the White House, June 19, 1934, 10:50 A.M.

[*Excerpt*] Q: The British and the French Governments have threatened to impound some of the trade profits on credits affected by the debt moratorium. Is there any action along that line that we can take?

The President: I do not know. If I said, "Yes," you would probably say we were going to do it. I have not the faintest idea on it but three days ago I asked the Secretary of State whether legislation was necessary before Congress went home and he said no, that the legislation was not necessary because the control over the foreign exchange in last year's bill seems sufficiently broad to cover it if we wanted to do it.[1] I have no idea what the State Department feels about what we should do. You had better check up there. We have the power to do it.

[President's Press Conferences:T]

[1] The act approved March 9, 1934 (48 *Stat.* 1).

Roosevelt to Thorvald Solberg, Washington

Washington, June 25, 1934

My dear Mr. Solberg: Your letter of June 4, in which you so carefully set forth arguments in favor of the adherence by the United States to the Convention for the Protection of Literary and Artistic Works, as revised at Rome in 1928, has been given attentive consideration.[1] I sincerely regret that action by the Senate at the session of Congress which has just closed proved to be impracticable.

I want to assure you that I desire whole-heartedly the adherence of the United States to this Treaty and also that, during the interval before the assembling of the next Congress, such preparatory steps as may be practicable will be taken with a view to obtaining, after the new Congress convenes, prompt and favorable action.[2]

Sincerely yours,

(signed) Franklin D. Roosevelt

[OF 699:T]

[1] Solberg (OF 699) said that failure of the United States to remove the existing discrimination against British authors—the requirement that they manufacture their books in the United States in order to secure copyright protection—would ultimately result in the British imposing a similar condition. This, he said, would be catastrophic. Opposition to ratification came from motion-picture producers and exhibitors, periodical publishers, and radio broadcasters who were unwilling to bargain individually with foreign authors. He urged prompt ratification of the treaty, with consideration of further copyright legislation to follow. Roosevelt's reply was drafted in the State Department; Assistant Secretary of State R. Walton Moore urged that the President sign the letter in view of Solberg's "long service to the Government, and his careful work in favor of this Convention" (Moore to McIntyre, June 21, 1934, OF 699).

[2] See Roosevelt to Solberg, March 11, 1935, below.

Cordell Hull, Secretary of State, to Norman Davis, Chairman, American Delegation, London Naval Conference

[Washington] June 26, 1934, 9 p.m.

From the President for Davis

Quote   Tell the Prime Minister confidentially from me that it is still my thought that the difficult situation of modern civilization throughout the world demands for the social and economic good of human beings a reduction in armaments and not an increase; that I am well aware of the pressure exercised by Navy Departments and Admiralties; that, nevertheless, I hope those in high authority in government will work with me for a new naval treaty calling for a reduction in navies and to that end I have suggested a renewal of the Washington and London treaties for at least ten years on a basis of a 20% reduction to be accomplished during that ten year period.

I am not going into technicalities of tonnage or classes or guns at this time, because these can be solved if the naval nations agree on the big basic principle. Unquote.

The President says that the Prime Minister may communicate this message to the Cabinet, if he so desires, but he requests that no (repeat no) publicity be given to it at the present stage.[1]

Hull

[PSF:London Naval Conference:T]

[1] This cablegram was occasioned by the impasse created by the wide divergence of the American and British proposals, the Americans urging a total treaty tonnage reduction in all classes except aircraft carriers of 20 per cent, and the British holding out for varying reductions in some classes but for increases in cruiser tonnage (*Foreign Relations, 1934,* I, 262ff). See reply, from Ambassador Bingham, below.

Robert W. Bingham, Ambassador to Great Britain, to Cordell Hull, Secretary of State

London, June 29, 1934, 4 P.M.

[*Telegram*] Personal and confidential for the Secretary: The Prime Minister requests that the following personal and confidential message be telegraphed to President.

To the President from the Prime Minister. Many thanks for message, sentiment of which I fully reciprocate.[1] British problem, however, has to be brought down to reality. We do not envisage increases except in certain directions in definite relation to international needs, while in other directions we urge reductions, for example, in a cut of perhaps twenty per cent in the size of capital ships and in size and numbers of submarines. European maritime nations enormously increasing naval power. Far East armaments also increasing our risks. Therefore either stand-still or reductions depends solely on conditions. Should be delighted to reduce ten, twenty, or thirty per cent if risks were reduced in similar proportion. It is not a question of desire but of realistic need.

We have explained in great confidence our obligations and risks to American representatives and hope that mutual examination and understanding will lead

161

to an agreement on how to face the situation, remembering that a thorough understanding between us will enable us within bounds of our separate possibilities to maintain complete cooperation, because I firmly believe that that is an essential condition of the maintenance of sanity and peace in the world.

Regret profoundly that my eye sight compels me to leave at once for three months rest. We are all delighted to have your charming mother with us.[2]

Bingham

[PSF:London Naval Conference:T]

[1] Above.
[2] Mrs. Roosevelt had arrived in England on June 24. She was MacDonald's luncheon guest on June 25 and on the next day she was received by King George and Queen Mary (New York *Times*, June 26, p. 9; June 27, 1934, p. 1).

Cordell Hull, Secretary of State, to Roosevelt

Washington, June 29, 1934

My dear Mr. President: I submit herewith for your consideration and, if you approve, your signature, a draft of a Proclamation designed to place this Government in a position to supervise and control the exportation of arms and munitions of war from the United States to Cuba, with a view to enabling the Cuban Government to maintain peace and tranquility in that country.

I respectfully invite your attention to Article II of the Convention between the United States and Cuba to Suppress Smuggling, signed at Habana March 11, 1926, which reads in part as follows:

The High Contracting Parties agree that clearance of shipments of merchandise by water, air, or land, from any of the ports of either country to a port of entry of the other country, shall be denied when such shipment comprises articles the importation of which is prohibited or restricted in the country to which such shipment is destined, unless in this last case there has been a compliance with the requisites demanded by the laws of both countries.

The laws of Cuba restrict the importation of arms and munitions of all kinds by requiring an import permit for each shipment.

There would not appear to be any legal means by which this Government can effectively carry out its treaty obligations with respect to the traffic in arms and munitions between the United States and Cuba, unless a Proclamation is issued pursuant to the Joint Resolution of Congress of January 31, 1922.

The Cuban Government, through its Ambassador in Washington, has expressed to this Government its approval of this action.

I feel that, in conformity with our policy of the good neighbor, we should proceed accordingly.

The action which I recommend is by no means novel or unprecedented, as is indicated by the following table of Proclamations which have been issued by your predecessors, pursuant to the Joint Resolution of Congress of January 31, 1922, and the similar Joint Resolution of March 14, 1912, which it superseded:

Brazil:	Proclamation October 22, 1930. Revoked March 2, 1931.
China:	Proclamation March 4, 1922. Still in effect.
Cuba:	Proclamation May 2, 1924. Revoked August 29, 1924.
Honduras:	Proclamation March 22, 1924. Still in effect.
Mexico:	Proclamation March 14, 1912. Revoked February 3, 1914.
	Proclamation October 19, 1915. Revoked January 31, 1922.
	Proclamation January 7, 1924. Revoked July 18, 1929.
Nicaragua:	Proclamation September 15, 1926. Still in effect.

If this Proclamation meets with your approval, I shall, as soon as it is promulgated, issue regulations prescribing that shipments of arms and munitions to Cuba shall be limited to those for which a license has been issued by the Department of State and that such licenses shall not be issued except upon the request of the Cuban Ambassador in Washington.[1]

I am, my dear Mr. President, Faithfully yours,

Cordell Hull

[OF 159:TS]

[1] The enclosed proclamation was issued under date of June 29, 1934; it is printed in *Public Papers,* III, 319–320.

Roosevelt to Representative Numa F. Montet of Louisiana

[Washington] June 30, 1934

My dear Mr. Montet: This is in reply to your letter of June 14, 1934, in reference to the negotiation of a commercial treaty with Cuba.[1]

In my message to the Congress of February 8, 1934, I said:

Furthermore, in the negotiation for a new treaty between the United States and Cuba to replace the existing Commercial Convention, which negotiations are to be resumed immediately, favorable consideration will be given to an increase in the existing preferential on Cuban sugars, to an extent compatible with the joint interests of the two countries.

Administration of the Costigan-Jones Act of May 9, 1934, is creating a number of unusual market factors in sugar. I refer especially to the imposition of a processing tax and the establishment of quotas. It is not yet clear at this time, pending the first period of operation of the Act, to what extent it will be in the public interest and in the interest of Cuba to widen the preferential on Cuban sugars. The problem will require most careful consideration of the Department of State and other interested governmental departments.

May I draw your attention, however, to entirely new forms of protection to domestic growers of sugarcane and sugar beets which now exist as the result of the enactment of the Costigan-Jones Act. Hitherto when the price of sugar declined in the world markets, the income of farmers growing sugarcane or sugar beets in the United States declined despite tariff protection.

Under the Costigan-Jones Act, growers of cane or beets receive benefit payments which will supplement the prices paid growers by the processors.

Furthermore, the Secretary of Agriculture will establish quotas for the full duty countries under the provisions of the Costigan-Jones Act and as you know quotas have already been established for the domestic and insular sugar producing areas and Cuba. The price of sugar in the United States will, therefore, be determined by the balance established between the aggregate supplies under the quota arrangements and the demands of consumers. With all the sugar producing areas which supply the United States market on a quota basis, the tariff preferential on Cuban sugars has much less significance than formerly.

Very sincerely yours,

[OF 241:CT]

[1] Montet wrote (OF 241) that domestic producers of sugar had in the past been disappointed because Cuban producers had failed to take advantage of their tariff differential. He asked that some provision be inserted in the proposed commercial treaty with Cuba "whereby the Cubans must accept and use the tariff preference given them, or lose it. In other words, the Cuban preferential should be available to the Cubans only to the extent to which they are willing to accept the benefits." Montet's letter bears this inscription, in Roosevelt's hand: "Sec. Agric. to prep reply for my sig.   FDR."

Roosevelt to H. Milton Colvin, Federal Emergency Relief Administration, Washington

U.S.S. *Houston,* July 9, 1934

Dear Dr. Colvin: I have been greatly interested in reading your address at Earlham College.[1]

I am now on a trip which will, I hope, strengthen the doctrine of "The Good Neighbor."[2]

Very sincerely yours,

[PPF 1680:CT]

[1] "President Roosevelt's Policy of 'The Good Neighbor' in Latin American Relationships." Colvin, counsel for the Federal Emergency Relief Administration and an authority on international law, had sent Roosevelt a copy of his speech in a letter of June 30, 1934 (PPF 1680).

[2] Roosevelt had sailed from Annapolis on July 1 for his Pacific cruise. At this time he was en route from St. Croix to Cartagena (PPF 1-0).

John F. Montgomery, Minister to Hungary, to Roosevelt

Budapest, July 13, 1934

Dear Mr. President: I have the honor to report that I have been impressed since my arrival in Hungary by the fact that in spite of several years of depression, during which Hungary has been struggling for its economic existence, there is a stable government and an absence of unrest such as has been so prevalent in other parts of Europe.

"Justice for Hungary" through the revision of the Treaty of Trianon is the country's watchword, and one need be in Hungary but a few hours to realize that the whole nation is in mourning for its lost territories. This being so, it is easy to understand that the eight million inhabitants of this agricultural country instinctively draw close to those who sympathize with them in their plight and hold aloof from those who do not. For those neighboring countries which were given Hungarian territory after the war, i.e. Czechoslovakia, Yugoslavia and Rumania, there is openly manifested bitterness. Hence Hungary's friends are Italy and Germany, while her enemies are the members of the Little Entente and France. A small piece of territory was given to Austria, but the matter is seldom mentioned now, and the two countries are on friendly terms and harmonizing their interests daily.

Next to revision comes the question of the restoration of a monarch. The Government maintains that this question is not timely. It repudiates the idea of a dual monarch and affirms that if Hungary ever has a king he must be a Hungarian king only and one who has nothing in common with any other country. The question is not active at the moment.

Concerning disarmament, it is only necessary to say that Hungary has been and is in agreement with Germany because of their common interest arising out of the peace treaties. The triumph of Hitlerism in Germany and the advent to power of the National Socialists were important events to Hungary especially, as a stable government there removed the threat of Communism.

Austria's present struggle for self-preservation obviously interests Hungary greatly. Hungarians hope that she will succeed without their country being drawn into any embarrassing situation.

Although Hungarians have long considered the Prussians a ruthless and brutal people, they were aghast at the extreme measures taken by Hitler recently against members of his own party. His hypocritical proclamation and the massacre that followed has sickened and disgusted the Hungarian people. Those in the Government, while publicly asserting that he has strengthened his position, privately say without hesitation that he is finished and that Germany as a nation is in a precarious position both economically and politically.

For the first time since I have been here I detect a distinct uneasiness over political conditions in Europe. What happens in Germany is a matter of great importance to Hungary and the Danubian States. Germany is their most important market, and any economic deterioration there will greatly affect them all.

Politically, Germany has been a great asset to Hungary during the last year. The Hungarians have had great hopes that Italy and Germany would form an alliance which would include Austria, Poland and Hungary and isolate the Little Entente from France. That the Little Entente had been aware of the political and economic dangers of the situation, is quite apparent. The recent meeting between Mussolini and Hitler seemed the beginning of negotiations which would ultimately result in an alliance. This would now seem improbable. While Hungary has been able to show a certain independence with regard to Italy during the last year, because of German advances and Italy's political needs, the situation in Germany may force Hungary again to become a satellite of Italy. Instead of being sought by two Great Powers, Hungary fears she will be hanging on the skirts of one unless, by some miracle, Germany conquers her extremist tendencies, makes her peace with the world and betters her economic condition.

In their present discouraged frame of mind, Hungarians are inclined to be despondent. They believe that Hitler will in future be only a name with the Reichswehr in the saddle, and they fear what will follow. If the economic situation becomes worse they see Communism not far away.

Whatever benefit Austria may obtain from the present conditions is offset, it is believed, by the gains Socialists are making there, for if Germany becomes Communistic, Austria, and later Hungary, will be in grave danger.

In the meanwhile the relations between Hungary and the Little Entente remain as strained as ever, and have not been improved by the recent anti-revision speeches of Barthou in Rumania, which naturally aroused great resentment in Hungary, nor by Hungary's ceaseless revisionist activities.

While political conditions in Europe have been strained for some time, the uncertainty regarding Germany has intensified the situation by reviving the threat of Communism. Possibly the situation will become so bad that the Great European Powers will be forced to agree on a common program to save themselves. Nothing, however, that has happened in the past could encourage anyone to believe that they will; everything has been done too late. If France had granted Brüning one half of what she has been willing to give Hitler, there would have been no Hitler. Europe never seems to realize that it is all tied up in one sack, and that it must be saved as a whole if the individual States are to save themselves. A combination of Powers unless all are included only serves to make matters worse and increase the probability of war. At present there seems little to encourage the belief that the near future will bring anything but trouble to the European people and the world. Possibly I am too pessimistic; I sincerely hope that I am.[1]

I am, my dear Mr. President, Respectfully yours,

John F. Montgomery

[OF 507:TS]

[1] Montgomery also sent a brief personal note (of the same date) in which he noted that the President had asked him to report on political conditions as observed from his station. Roosevelt replied Aug. 29, 1934, below.

Arthur Henderson, President, Disarmament Conference, to Roosevelt

London, July 18th, 1934

Dear Mr. President: I have been anxious for some time past to write to you on the position and prospects of the Disarmament Conference.[1] This temptation has never been as great as now, and I must confess that I yield to it with an undoubted pleasure.

You are fully aware how this great venture has from the start been hampered by a series of unfortunate events not calculated to enhance that feeling of mutual confidence and security which is essential for any serious measure of reduction and limitation of armaments. But I need not, towards the end of the third year of the Conference, attempt a review of all its vicissitudes. It will be sufficient for all practical purposes to say a word or two about the last meeting of the General Commission and the Bureau.

The position of the Conference was at that moment critical. We were all conscious of being faced with perhaps our last chance of reconciling the demand for security made by a great number of delegations with the claim of Germany for equality of rights, accepted conditionally in December 1932 by certain other great Powers, and later on supported by a larger number of delegations to the Conference.

I am aware that, in making this statement, I may seem to resign myself to a gradual modification of the original purpose of the Conference, which was convened to secure a reduction and limitation of armaments. I need hardly say that two-and-a-half years of strenuous effort in an assembly of sixty-four nations have convinced me that in this imperfect world a very high price may have to be paid for even a moderate success in disarmament. It is indeed hard for those who believe in promoting peace by disarmament to be obliged to accept a less ambitious programme of peace through security, accompanied perhaps by only a tentative first effort toward disarmament. The statesmen meeting in Geneva—and the President of the Conference with them—had, however, to weigh the advantages and disadvantages of a convention embodying very little reduction against no convention at all. A sense of the appalling consequences of choosing the latter alternative drove us all finally, in despair of a better achievement, to content ourselves with aiming at a first convention providing a moderate reduction and limitation of armaments, accompanied by such agreements on security as might be obtained without prejudice to the fundamental principles embodied in the Covenant of the League of Nations, under whose auspices this Conference was convened.

Incidentally, it was unanimously recognised by the Conference that even this measure of success could not be attained without Germany's participation in our proceedings, more especially as the return of that country to Geneva would imply that a solution had been found for the difficult problem of equality of rights. When, therefore, the Conference made an effort to agree, in a formal resolution, on the necessity of Germany returning to the Conference, it was expressing a general desire to secure a convention which would introduce a system of international regulation in the field of armaments, where so far, if we except the questions covered by the Washington and London Naval Treaties, unlimited freedom has hitherto existed.

I must emphasize that this compromise between the two tendencies, security and equality, was achieved largely because the United States, not being committed to either of them, were in a position to act as a mediating influence between the delegations concerned and made good use of the opportunity thus afforded them of helping to bring the parties to agreement.

The recent conversations which have taken place in London constitute a first step towards giving effect to the undertakings accepted on June 8th 1934 by those participating in the Conference.[2] Mr. Davis has no doubt informed you in detail of these London negotiations.[3] In my opinion they have considerably facilitated Germany's return to the Conference, since, if the regional agreements contemplated by certain Powers materialise, the Protocol of December 11th 1932,[4] providing for the grant of equality to Germany in a régime of general security, will have received as satisfactory an application as is possible in present circumstances.

I am therefore not without hope of still securing a convention providing for a reduction and limitation of armaments, such reduction and limitation constituting an integral part of the Protocol to which I have just referred.

The Bureau of the Conference will meet again early in September, probably during the second week, and important decisions will have to be taken in the light of the situation then obtaining. If the regional agreements have by that time proved acceptable in principle to those chiefly concerned, we should look forward to Germany's return with a certain optimism. In this event we may reasonably hope that a convention will be obtained. It should baffle neither our patience nor the ingenuity of the experts to give legal form to the technical decisions reached by the Conference in the last two-and-a-half years.

But past experience has taught me not to underestimate the difficulties which may be awaiting the Conference and I venture to hope that, despite the important tasks claiming your attention at home, you will continue to show in our work here that active interest which has so heartened us in the past. I would in particular refer to the message which you addressed in May of last year to the heads of States urging upon them the elimination of offensive weapons as an ultimate object of the Conference,[5] and to the communication which you recently addressed to Congress on the subject of the trade in and manufacture of arms.[6] In consequence of that communication the appropriate Committee was able, as a preliminary step, to prepare a series of draft Articles which I have submitted to the General Commission and which in my view offer a more hopeful method of approach to that very difficult problem.

Before closing, I would express the hope that we may before Christmas secure a disarmament convention which will profoundly affect national and international affairs for years to come. It will be a source of encouragement to me in facing these supreme issues to recall that the United States Delegation to the Conference has, throughout its proceedings, supported with energy the cause of disarmament and has shown itself ever ready to make its contribution to the general system of security and peace.

I am, dear Mr. President, Yours faithfully,

Arthur Henderson[7]

[PPF 1727:TS]

[1] The Conference had adjourned June 11, 1934.

[2] The "undertakings" were embodied in a resolution adopted by the Conference on June 8, 1934, directing the bureau of its general commission to seek the return of Germany to the Conference, and directing the continuation of the work of the committee on air forces (bombardment) and that of the committee on manufacture of and trade in arms. The bureau was directed to have as complete a convention as possible in draft by the time the general commission convened (*Foreign Relations, 1934*, I, 113–114).

[3] See the section, "American Sponsorship of a Treaty on the Manufacture of and Traffic in Arms, June 15–December 31, 1934," *ibid.*, pp. 120–216.

[4] *Ibid., 1932*, I, 527–528.

[5] Roosevelt to Heads of Nations, May 16, 1933, above.

[6] May 18, 1934, *Public Papers*, II, 239–240.

[7] Printed also in *Foreign Relations, 1934*, 136–138. This letter is reprinted here to provide a convenient review of the history of the Conference. Roosevelt's reply of August 14, in which he expressed his hope for the successful outcome of the work of the Conference, is printed *ibid.*, p. 141. This printing does not contain the President's postscript: "I do hope you will come over here some day and see me" (PPF 1727).

William C. Bullitt, Ambassador to the Union of Soviet Socialist Republics, to Roosevelt

Moscow, August 5, 1934

My dear Mr. President: I hope you had as good a time in Hawaii as we expected to have. I regretted not seeing you every day of your trip.

Jean Monnet,[1] one of my closest French friends, who has just spent six months advising the Chinese Government on financial reorganization, passed through Moscow a few days ago and gave me a creatively intimate picture of China and Japan. He is definitely of the opinion that the Japanese can be handled in such a way as to settle Eastern questions by peaceful means and I should like to spend a couple of weeks in China and Japan trying to verify his observations.

When our Hawaiian meeting was "spurlos versenkt," you suggested that you would want me to come back this autumn. If you still want to see me you might order me to report in Washington for a conference about December 1 and to come by way of the East. I could leave Vladivostok about October 15 and be in Washington by December 1st with the latest Far Eastern and Russian information. Do let me know soon how you feel about such a trip as I shall not make any plans to leave here until I know your personal wishes.

I have not been able to get anywhere with Litvinov and, while maintaining very cordial personal relations with him, have tried to build a backfire in the Kremlin by way of Voroshilov[2] and Karakhan.[3]

As a means to develop close relations with Voroshilov I imported a lot of polo equipment and have taught the Red Army Cavalry to play the game. We play every other day on a broad plain. The game at the outset had a number of unusual features not provided at Meadowbrook. All the ponies were sixteen-hand stallions who savaged each other and the riders whenever they came to close quarters, and on the first day a Mongolian soldier with an undeveloped genius for the game carried the ball in a bee-line three miles cross country before he could be stopped! The polo has brought not only myself but our military men into the closest relations with the Red Army leaders and has been most useful.

As you know, I have also started baseball here and that has helped to bring us into intimate relations with the Moscow Soviet.

We have had dozens of indications lately that Stalin, Voroshilov and Molotov are most anxious to develop really friendly relations with us and I think the most important thing I can do at the moment is to get my feeble Russian into shape to have conversations with them about various matters without the aid of an interpreter. I got word from the Kremlin the other day that all the leaders of the Government, including Stalin, would be glad to see a great deal more of me than they have been seeing and in the end I think we shall be able to beat down Litvinov's resistance. I do not expect any immediate results, however, as Litvinov is about to leave Moscow for a two months' holiday and Stalin is leaving for a cure in the Caucasus.

Do you know that our pet courier service has been stopped and also that the Comptroller General has snarled in scarlet tape the payment of Moscow salaries in gold and that we are all rapidly going bankrupt? I have had no explanation from the Department with regard to stopping the courier service which is, of course, absolutely essential to this mission. I am sending my own couriers now to Berlin but our funds are too limited to keep this up long. The exchange equalization is also vital for us here and I should be most grateful if you would give the Comptroller General a graceful but swift kick.

I am really too eager to see you all. The summer here has been delightful with plenty of polo, baseball, tennis and swimming in the late afternoons but the sun is already beginning to leave us and Washington is beginning to look more alluring than ever.

My very best wishes to Mrs. Roosevelt and Miss LeHand, and the hope that I may see you all soon.[4]

Yours permanently,

William C. Bullitt

[PSF:Russia:TS]

[1] French diplomat; for a time first Deputy Secretary General of the League of Nations.
[2] Kliment E. Voroshilov, People's Commissar for Defense.
[3] Lev M. Karakhan, Vice-Commissar of Foreign Affairs.
[4] Answered Aug. 29, 1934 (*Personal Letters, 1928–1945*, I, 416–417). Roosevelt said that he had not seen Ambassador Troyanovsky since Bullitt had returned to his post, "but everybody likes him at the State Department and I am very certain terms could be arranged if he had a more free hand."

Lincoln MacVeagh, Minister to Greece, to Roosevelt

Athens, Greece, August 6, 1934

Dear Franklin: Although you are far away, farther indeed than usual, seeing to American interests in the Pacific where our policy is so important, I feel that the time may come when you will think again of this part of the world, and so I shall write of what I see here at present for what it may be worth.

Europe seems more and more clearly to be divided into two armed or arming camps—the French and the German—and this fact is perhaps nowhere more apparent than in this Balkan region where international intrigue habitually blooms in all its luxuriance. During the winter and spring, most of the Balkan nations joined the French groupment, causing considerable excitement here and much speculation. In Greece, the Balkan Pact was severely criticized by the local Opposition. The attitude of both England and Italy towards Near Eastern problems was then uncertain. But the events of the summer brought about a decided change. The French entente with Russia greatly strengthened those who saw security in the French camp, and the skillful manoeuvrings of M. Barthou[1] in relation to his proposed "Eastern Locarno" did perhaps as much, in its way, to the same effect. Then the murder of Dollfuss and the bringing of England and Italy, particularly Italy, into sharp conflict with Nazi ambitions, has put what seems like the quietus on the critics of the policy of the Greek Government in throwing in its lot with the French. It has shown how definitely the other great European powers are opposed to Germany's first serious attempt to upset the *status quo*. Revisionist Italy has had troops concentrated on the border, ready to move to the defense of Austrian independence, and the British Minister here told me, only the other day, that after the murder of Dollfuss he expected nothing less than the concentration of the English Mediterranean fleet, part of which now lies in the harbor of Athens. There is now undoubtedly a general feeling here that Greece has taken her proper place in the balance of power which everyone believes is the only guarantee of peace. There are no pacifists in the Balkans.

While the international ferment is now less active than hitherto in this region, there is some uneasiness felt over Germany's political course of action now that Hindenburg's steadying hand is removed. Herr Goering's recent visit here, during which he made a considerable show of his Prussian personality, has done little to allay this feeling. The Greek Foreign Minister told me after his last visit to Geneva, that he did not expect war in Europe except as the result of the action of some madman. Mussolini recently took a very dangerous step in sending his fleet unannounced into the harbor of Durazzo.[2] The immediate cause was apparently of no great importance, but the consequences might have entailed a general conflagration. Mussolini, however, controls even his wildest actions. He sees and foresees and there is a general impression that he has method in his madness. But this cannot yet be said of Hitler. Indeed,

I have no doubt that M. Maximos's remark reflects the attitude of his Turkish, Roumanian and Yugoslavian colleagues, as well as his own, and refers chiefly to the German Chancellor. Certainly the nations of the Near East can now be regarded as fearing more than anything else, some inflammatory action on Germany's part. The vexed Macedonian problem is still with us. But a determined effort is being made by the new Bulgarian government to deal firmly with this dangerous question. Furthermore Greece has shown the strength of her good will toward Turkey by acquiescing gracefully in the expulsion of more Greeks from Istanbul, and there seems to be nothing to fear at present at the Bosphorus, Saloniki, the Dodecanese or Albania—the chief danger spots of this region. All eyes are on the West.

Internally, the general economic condition of Greece continues to improve, at the same time, I am sorry to say, that American trade here continues to encounter increasing difficulties. This latter fact is, however, largely our own fault. Our trade is guaranteed by a *modus vivendi* defined in an exchange of letters under date of 1924. According to this old agreement, we should receive the usual most-favored-nation treatment. But much has happened since 1924; new men are in power here and new policies are being followed at the dictates of new conditions. Thus the new policy of restricting imports and rigidly controlling the export of foreign exchange has fathered a host of regulatory acts which fit in nicely with the provisions of special commercial treaties concluded with other nations, but which make it necessary to secure continual exceptions to preserve the simplest American rights. To prevent such acts from creating actual discrimination against our trade, this Legation has been in constant, and usually successful, conflict with the Greek authorities. Unfortunately, however, as I have pointed out repeatedly to the Department of State, the Legation's attention is called, in the nature of things, only to the most important cases, and hundreds of small ones never come to its notice at all, while they go to swell immeasurably the balance against us. I have, therefore, been working my hardest, both with the Department and the Greek Government, to get our position rectified. To the Greek Government, aside from the individual cases in which I have been called upon to protest, I have pointed out that our balance of trade is now so favorable to Greece that restrictions on our imports cannot economically be justified. I have won here a partial victory, in so far as bids for Government contracts will now be accepted from American firms without the restrictions hitherto enforced. The British, whose trade balance is not so clearly favorable, have not yet won such a concession. But in private business there is still the need of constant official protest against discrimination, and our trade is being discouraged and our customers disheartened, by all sorts of regulations which countries having recent trade agreements with Greece do not have to contend with. My despatches on this subject to the Department of State therefore always end on the same note, like the speeches of Cato.[3] The Greeks, into whose country we now pour some $25,000,000 more per annum than we get out of it, should, I believe, be made to face the loss of some of this or play the game. A commercial treaty with them was on the cards some time ago but was dropped. I believe the idea should be revived, and that the men who are now handling Greek affairs should no longer be merely called to book from time to time on the basis of letters exchanged in 1924, but should be made to undertake and carry out such explicit arrangements in regard to our trade as we feel to be consonant with the fact that America does more than any other nation today to keep the Greek people alive. I do not mean to imply that there is anything anti-American in the Greek attitude. On the contrary, I think we are rather specially liked, if not by all the ruling or upper class at least by the nation at large, and we get along famously, all things considered. But so long as other nations actively foster their trade while we only protect ours, they can be expected to get the lion's share. I am therefore hoping to see us snap into the game more vigorously. The reports from this Legation for the past year, both mine to the Department of State and those of the Commercial Attaché to the Department of Commerce, amply substantiate all that I have written here, and speak volumes into the bargain.

Recent arrivals from America testify to improving conditions there. You have certainly understood the American people well in getting them to work together to such effect in lifting themselves out of the hole. Here is wishing you health and happiness. You deserve more of both than one man can ever have! Please give my love to Eleanor, and to Smouch[4] when you see him. We hope to have little Eleanor with us next winter. It will be fun to carry on with Smouch through the second generation, and we hope the little girl will not find it too strange over here so far from home.[5]

Affectionately yours,

Lincoln MacVeagh

[PSF:Greece:TS]

[1] Jean Louis Barthou, French Minister of Foreign Affairs. On his efforts to achieve a security pact in eastern Europe, see *Foreign Relations, 1934,* I, 97–98, 107–109, 122–127, and *British Documents,* VI, 686–826.

[2] On June 23, to assert Italy's special interests in Albania.

[3] See MacVeagh's letters on trade matters in *Foreign Relations, 1934*, II, 550–583, and his letter to Roosevelt of Aug. 14, 1934, below.

[4] Hall Roosevelt, brother of Mrs. Franklin D. Roosevelt, and father of Eleanor, mentioned in the next sentence.

[5] Answered Sept. 12, 1934, below.

Roosevelt to Jesse H. Jones, Chairman, Reconstruction Finance Corporation

[Washington, August 9, 1934] [1]

My dear Mr. Jones: In order that there should be no doubt in anyone's mind as to the purpose of the export-import bank which was the subject of my Executive Order of February 2, 1934,[2] I am writing you this letter to say that I wish this bank to concern itself solely with transactions with the Soviet Union and agencies thereof, and I do not wish it to be employed for any other financing whatsoever. If it shall seem desirable to use similar banks for other purposes, I wish such bank or banks to be set up as independent units, and not to be attached to the export-import bank above referred to.

With all good wishes, I am, Yours very sincerely,

[OF 971:CT]

[1] This letter is undated; the date supplied is the filing date.

[2] Printed, with a note on the background and later history of the bank, in *Public Papers*, III, 76–81.

Lincoln MacVeagh, Minister to Greece, to Roosevelt

Athens, Greece, August 14, 1934

Dear Franklin: Just a word to supplement my letter of last week.[1]

I am glad to report that I have just heard from the Chief of the Near Eastern Division of the Department of State[2] as follows:

We fully appreciate the force, in the light of the circumstances you relate, of your suggestion that it would be desirable to seek to replace our present commercial *modus vivendi* with Greece by a new agreement more suited to existing circumstances. It is indeed our hope that under the powers conferred upon the President by the Tariff Reciprocity Act of June 12, 1934, it will become possible and practicable to effect a satisfactory solution of the problems of our trade with Greece through the negotiation of a reciprocal treaty agreement in the not too distant future.

In accordance with the wishes of the Department, I am now formulating suggestions which recommend themselves here as of possible use in the drawing up of a trade agreement with Greece, and in the meantime carrying on as heretofore to meet the individual problems and difficulties affecting our trade with Greece as they are brought to my attention. In this latter connection, I am glad to report that Mr. Murray remarks in the same letter that "a noticeable measure of success is already attending your efforts."

Always devotedly yours,

Lincoln MacVeagh

[PSF:Greece:TS]

[1] Aug. 6, 1934, above.
[2] Wallace Murray.

Press Conference, Executive Offices of the White House, August 15, 1934, 10:50 A.M.

[*Excerpt*] Q: On the Cuban trade agreement, are you going to give that back to the State Department with your approval? Can you tell us when?

The President: It won't come to me for approval.

Q: It will not come to you for approval until it gets to the final form?

The President: This memo is just to keep me in touch.[1]

Q: Have you had time to study the Russian debt situation?

The President: I have not had time to talk about it at all.

Q: Do you expect to go into that?

The President: I suppose so. Of course all of these people are coming in to see me, have come in to see me in the last three days more to bring me up to date than anything else.

Q: Anything from Secretary Hull on the status of the debt?

The President: The general debt situation?

Q: No, Russian?

The President: No, not yet . . .

Q: Mr. President, have you had time to hear anything about the administration of the Jones-Costigan Sugar Bill? There seems to be some difficulty, particularly with Hawaii and Puerto Rico. Hawaii seems to think that as a result of your visit there they are likely to get an increase in their quota.

The President: In the Hawaii case there will be no change in the quota. They are taking in this year about four million dollars more than they took in last year. In the case of Puerto Rico, that came up late yesterday afternoon. We will probably get action on it today.

The only other thing I have heard is the demand from some of the refineries that under the Act the differential on Cuban refined be greatly increased—no, I am wrong on that—that the amount of the differential be greatly decreased so as to allow more sugar to be refined in this country than has been in the past. That comes under the Cuban Treaty.

Q: Anything new on silver?

The President: No, I don't think so. I might just as well tell you a secret on silver. I have had three or four telegrams and four or five people come in to congratulate me on the marvelous timing of the Green Bay speech[2] and the nationalization of silver,[3] that it was within three minutes the two appeared on the Stock Exchange ticker. The actual story was this: If anybody had read the law they would have known exactly what was going to happen two months beforehand. The law provided that we were to go ahead and buy silver with the ultimate objective of getting 25 per cent of silver and 75 per cent of gold as bullion reserves. We started in to carry out that law in good faith and bought a good deal of silver. Before I went away, about a week before, I had a talk with the Secretary of the Treasury and others and it was obvious that if we were going to buy silver on a fairly good scale the price would go up, the world price. Now, the law also says that the silver in this country which is speculatively held, somewhere around 200 to 250 million ounces, can be bought by us at 50 cents an ounce if we are going to take it over. Now, suppose the world price of silver goes to 55 cents an ounce. We would be in the position of offering less than the public market for all of that silver. Therefore, we must make provision to take over the American stocks of silver before silver reaches 50 cents an ounce.

Before I went away I signed all the papers, a complete set of papers, which were to go into effect merely by sending me a radio if I had been on the boat or a telegram if I had been on the train, saying that silver has gone to 49¾ cents an ounce, "Do you authorize your orders going into effect?" All that was done before I left and the price set was 49¾ cents an ounce. Silver struck that the morning of the Green Bay speech. That was the careful timing.

[President's Press Conferences:T]

[1] The "memo" is not further identified. The trade agreement with Cuba was signed Aug. 24, 1934 (49 *Stat.* 3559). For the diplomatic correspondence on the agreement, see *Foreign Relations, 1934,* V, 108–168.

[2] At Green Bay, Wis., Aug. 9, 1934 (*Public Papers,* III, 370–375).

[3] Proclamation 2092 on silver coinage, and executive order 6814, requiring delivery of all silver to the government for coinage, were issued on the same day, Aug. 9, 1934 (*ibid.,* pp. 375–378, 378–381).

Roosevelt to Cordell Hull, Secretary of State

Washington, August 15, 1934

Memorandum for the Secretary of State: I hesitate a little about this. There is no question that Great Britain and other nations have exploited Persia in the past to a disgusting degree—oil, etc. I do not know enough about the Islands and the Gulf to form any final opinion, but I should hesitate to have us get into the position before the world of apparently upholding concessions given to Great Britain and other foreign nations when Persia was completely helpless.

Perhaps we might discuss it a little further.[1]

F.D.R.

[PSF:Disarmament Conference:T]

[1] This memorandum was in reply to Hull's letter of Aug. 15, 1934 (*Foreign Relations, 1934,* I, 476–478). On June 15, 1934, the Senate had approved the Geneva Arms Traffic Convention of 1925, with the following reservation: "Resolved that such adherence to this treaty shall not be construed as denying any right or sovereignty which the Kingdom of Persia may have in or to the Persian Gulf or the waters thereof" (*Cong. Rec.,* vol. 78, p. 11601). This resolution was the result of the activities of the Persian minister who had for some time been objecting to the convention "upon the ground that the Persian Gulf was made a prohibitory or neutral zone, as though it did not belong to Persia" (memorandum by Hull, May 14, 1934, *Foreign Relations, 1934,* I, 451). The reservation threatened to prevent the adoption of the convention by the signatory powers and Hull therefore recommended (in his letter of August 15) that the President return the convention to the Senate for reconsideration. See *ibid.,* pp. 449–488, and Hull to Roosevelt, Sept. 10, 1934, below.

William E. Dodd, Ambassador to Germany, to Roosevelt

Berlin, August 15, 1934

Dear Mr. President: According to your suggestion of May 3rd when you gave me a few minutes of your time,[1] I am summarizing the situation in Europe, with especial reference to Germany:

1. On October 17, I had a long interview with the Chancellor in the presence of the Foreign Minister.[2] When I reminded them of your attitude about crossing borders in a military way, Hitler asserted most positively that he would not allow a German advance across the border even if border enemies had made trouble. I named the French, Austrian and Polish fronts, and he said war might be started by violent S. A. men contrary to his command. That would be the only way.

Now what has happened since? More men are trained, uniformed and armed (perhaps not heavy guns) than in 1914, at least a million and a half; and the funeral all the Ambassadors and Ministers attended at Tannenberg August 7 was one grand military display, contrary to von Hindenburg's known request. Every diplomat with whom I spoke regarded the whole thing as a challenge under cover. And we have plenty of evidence that up to 10 o'clock July 25 the Vienna *Putsch* against Austria was boasted of here and being put over the radio as a great German performance. Only when defeat became known was the tone changed and the radio speaker removed from his post, Habicht of Munich. So, I am sure war was just around the corner, 30,000 Austro-German Nazis waiting near Munich for the signal to march upon Vienna. These men had been maintained for a year on the Austrian border at the expense of the German people. So, it seems to me that war and not peace is the objective, and the Hitler enthusiasts think they can beat Italy and France in a month—nor is high-power aircraft wanting, the Wrights having sold them machines last April.

2. Last March, in another interview, the Chancellor almost swore to me, without witnesses, that he would never again allow German propaganda in the United States.[3] On March 12 or 13, he issued an order that no man must be arrested and held in restraint more than 24 hours without a warrant. This was supposed to be in response to my representations about the harm done in the United States by violent treatment of the Jews here. I explained to you how, on the assumption that these promises would be kept, I managed to prevent a Hitler mock-trial in Chicago and otherwise persuaded American Jews to restrain themselves. But on the 12th of May I read excerpt on the boat from a speech of

Goebbels which declared that "Jews were the syphilis of all European peoples." Of course this aroused all the animosities of the preceding winter, and I was put in the position of having been humbugged, as indeed I was. All the personal protests which I made late in May were without effect, except that the Foreign Office people expressed great sorrow.

I have reviewed these points because I think we can not depend on the promises of the highest authority when we have such facts before us. I am sorry to have to say this of a man who proclaims himself the savior of his country and assumes on occasion the powers of President, the legislature and the supreme court. But you know all this side of the matter: June 30 and July 25![4]

3. One other point: Germany is ceasing as fast as possible the purchase of all raw stuffs from the United States, in some cases in direct violation of treaty obligations. She is mixing wood fibre in her cotton and woolen cloth, and is setting up plants for this purpose at great expense. Schacht acknowledged this today in conversation. He said: "We can not sell you anything but hairpins and knitting needles. How can we pay you anything?" He does not believe in the system, but he says it can not be stopped.

So the South is about to lose its market for 2,000,000 bales of cotton a year, and the Middle West is losing the last remnants of its German market for farm products. The New York bankers have been here of late to negotiate some sort of corporation deals between German business firms and American banks. "It is the only way to check German defaults on short-term loans" by American banks, some $300,000,000 the last time I had the figures; but this means other loans to save the cotton market and perhaps loss of all, including the cotton market itself.

Mr. Perkins of the National City Bank has tried his best to find a way out, and he will see you soon after his return.[5] When he left here I was a little hopeful Schacht and Hitler might give some more promises with security. But since July 24, events look worse, not better. I have written Perkins my doubting attitude via British pouch. It all looks bad. I do not see any solution so long as present policy continues here. English and French have made barter arrangements. What Sayre and Peek can do, I cannot see. I am inclined again to look at the League of Nations when Russia is admitted. The "encirclement" may include Holland before long. Perhaps you can see a way out.[6]

Yours sincerely,

William E. Dodd

[PPF 1043:TS]

---

[1] From 12:15 to 12:55 P.M., a more generous allotment of time than most visitors received.

[2] Von Neurath; see Dodd, *Diary,* pp. 48–50.

[3] March 7, 1934 (*ibid.,* pp. 88–91).

[4] The Roehm and Dollfuss killings.

[5] James H. Perkins, chairman of the board of the National City Bank, had been in Germany with other American bankers in an attempt to prevent the complete default by Germany of short-term loans held by banks in the United States.

[6] Answered Aug. 25, 1934, below.

Grenville T. Emmet, Minister to The Netherlands, to Roosevelt

The Hague, Netherlands, August 17, 1934

Dear Mr. President: I hope very much that you had a good trip to Honolulu and were able to get some rest from the stress and strain that you must constantly be under. I am afraid that the calamity of the drought in America did not make it any easier for you on your return.

Since I last wrote you[1] a good deal has happened in Europe and we have, of course, followed closely the Disarmament Conference, the German situation, the Austrian situation, and the Japanese-Dutch negotiations in Dutch India. I had the pleasure of a visit from Richard Washburn Child the latter part of June, just before he left for America, and he may have told you something about our life here, as he and Mrs. Child came out to see us several times.

I have had one or two interviews with Dr. Colijn, the Prime Minister, and took occasion to give him the personal messages of good will from you.[2] He is a sagacious, wise statesman, with a delightful personality, and always seems glad to see me and to hear as much as he can about you. I sent a lengthy despatch to the Department after my first visit to Dr. Colijn, which I won't repeat to you here as it is too long,[3] but I remember the last day I saw you in Washington,[4] you spoke about Japan and Japanese activities in the Pacific as affecting not only ourselves, but the Netherlands and I thought you might be interested in hearing Dr. Colijn's views. He felt that Japan, as at present governed, was a distinct menace to the security of China, British India, the Philippines, Dutch India and Australia, and that eventually it would strike out to dominate them all. The time when this would take place could not be determined but would depend upon a proper stage setting.

He had great respect for Japanese sagacity in determining the right moment to act. At the present moment he thought that Great Britain's determination to remain free of entangling European alliances and maintaining her freedom of action in the Pacific was the greatest deterrent to Japan's ambitions and he rejoiced that Great Britain was pursuing such a policy. Japan, he thought, feared Great Britain's interference and her policy was to attempt to involve the British in continental affairs so that her hands might be tied. He was glad that at Geneva the British had opposed the French position, which would have involved them in some sort of guarantee of French security.

Dr. Colijn had no doubt but that the ultimate objective of the Japanese, though they might move slowly, would be the complete domination of China, British India, Dutch India, the Philippines, and eventually Australia. Her geographic position is such that she could move slowly in that direction with almost certain success. She probably would not strike, however, until the world is busy with other things. He compared Japan to the Roman Catholic Church—patient and resolute, willing to wait and to gain its objective without fighting, feeling pretty sure that in the long run most of what it is after will fall into its lap.

Concerning the Conference at Batavia between the Dutch East Indian officials and the Japanese, he said that the Netherlands Government was frankly worried by the great economic inroads made by Japan in the Indies and that the Colonial delegates intended at the present Conference to place restrictions on the importation of Japanese goods.

Turning to the Philippines, he expressed the opinion that once we withdrew entirely from the Islands, government would disintegrate there and it would only be a question of years before the waiting Japanese would assume control. He hoped that we would not stand by and see such a thing happen.

I am struck with the intelligence of the Dutch press, which is free and uncontrolled. There are five or six excellent daily newspapers with first class reporters and editorial writers, who are not afraid to say what they think and whose articles carry considerable weight,—very different from the press of Italy, Germany and France.

Things are going very well with us. We have taken a delightful country place called "Clingendaal," with beautiful grounds about it and, although it is an estate of several hundred acres, only five or six minutes from the Chancery. Pauline has entirely recovered from her distressing illness of last year. She is entirely her old self again and has made many friends in Government and diplomatic circles. She is doing her part admirably. All three children are with us and we have had a delightful summer. We had hoped to induce your mother to make us a visit but her time was too limited.

I hope that you are well and have not come back to too strenuous a life after your trip to Hawaii. Apart from the drought, which seems to be a real calamity, it must be gratifying to you to see steady improvement in conditions in America and to feel that the people are behind you even more than they were last year.

Pauline sends her affectionate regards to you and Eleanor, in which I join. I am going to try to come home for a short visit in December and will look forward to seeing you then.

With best wishes, believe me to be, As ever, Faithfully yours,

Grenville T. Emmet

P.S. I am enclosing two pictures of "Clingendaal" which I thought might interest you and Eleanor.[5]

[PPF 372:TS]

[1] March 24, 1934 (PSF:Netherlands), written shortly after his arrival at his post.
[2] Presumably oral; no written messages have been found.
[3] Not printed in *Foreign Relations;* Emmet's correspondence with the Department in 1934 dealt with reciprocal trade agreements and a proposal for a reciprocal air navigation treaty (*ibid., 1934,* II, pp. 627–641).
[4] Emmet had tea with the President on Oct. 23, 1933 (McIntyre to Emmet, Oct. 20, 1933, PPF 372); no later appointment is noted (PPF 1-0).
[5] Present. See Roosevelt's reply of Sept. 6, 1934, below.

Roosevelt to Representative Walter Nesbit, Belleville, Illinois

[Washington] August 22, 1934

My dear Mr. Nesbit: Many thanks for letting me see that letter from the National Association of Manufacturers and your very excellent reply.[1] I had a practical illustration the other day when a manufacturer demanded that I give advance notice of every possible proposal relating to every possible commodity which might be discussed in the pending negotiations for a reciprocity tariff agreement with Brazil. I asked him whether his company purchased anything from Brazil or sold anything to Brazil and he said No. He was just trying to muddy the waters—like so many of them.

Very sincerely yours,

P.S. I am returning the enclosures.

[PPF 1057:CT]

---

[1] In Nesbit's covering letter of August 15 (PPF 1057), he said that he thought Roosevelt might like to know "what some of the boys were up to" during the latter's absence from Washington.

Press Conference, Executive Offices of the White House, August 24, 1934

[*Excerpt*] The President: . . . There is only one other thing, for the benefit of the Hearst papers, and there may be others which may copy the idea. I horrified the Secretary of Agriculture coming back on the train,[1] by suddenly announcing out of a clear blue sky, that I was very glad that he had said what he did about the theory, the economic theory of foreign ships carrying some American goods. If you will read his letter, it is a rather interesting thing, and shows why it is necessary to always give the whole story instead of part of the story.[2] Representative Bland wrote him a letter in June and he answered it about July fifteenth, and in effect he said that while there were many considerations, such as national defense, etc., in regard to our Merchant Marine, one should also at the same time consider certain other things, which were not always considered. And in effect what he said was absolutely true from the point of view of economics. One reason why American manufacturers and American farmers can't sell more goods to other countries is because other countries can't buy. It is obvious if they could pay they could buy more. If other countries were able to pay a portion of that cost in the form of services, they could buy more American goods. There is apparently no question that if every time our American exports were carried on foreign ships foreigners could buy more American exports. But that is only one side. Hearst papers take notice. There are other factors to which the Secretary of Agriculture referred. He didn't outline them but they are very simple. There are three other factors they forgot to counterbalance against the facts he mentioned. One is the fact that from the point of view of national defense we obviously need a certain number of American merchantmen which could be used for national defense in time of war. That's perfectly clear. Number two, in the event of a war in which we were not a party, let us say, a general European war or a Far Eastern War, foreign shipping might be finally eliminated because of that war and then we would have no bottoms to carry our American goods and we would be out of luck. So that is another case of the necessity for having American ships. And there is a third factor: We know that when we didn't have American ships on certain runs in certain lanes of world trade, foreign ships and foreign shipowners have had an unfortunate tendency in getting together and squeezing American exporters on rates. In other words, in having control of the ships and using it against American trade, and in favor of their own trade, you have a third insurance factor that makes it necessary for us to have an American Merchant Marine, and all the Secretary of Agriculture did was to call attention to the obvious economic factor on the other side of the insurance question; that the more we make it impossible for foreign ships to carry some of our goods, the more difficult it makes it for them to buy our goods. There is the whole story, not just a part of it. And if the whole story is written the answers are perfectly obvious.

[President's Press Conferences:T]

[1] From the funeral of Speaker of the House Henry T. Rainey, in Carrollton, Ill., on August 22; the President left Washington August 21 and returned August 23, Secretary Wallace accompanying him on the return trip.

[2] Rep. Schuyler O. Bland of Virginia, chairman of the House Merchant Marine Committee, had made public a letter he had received from Wallace on shipping subsidies; most of the letter is published in the New York *Times* of Aug. 19, 1934, p. 16. Wallace's view was that shipping subsidies might well be reduced because shipping services performed by foreign countries were an important source of dollar exchange used by them in buying United States agricultural products.

Roosevelt to William E. Dodd, Ambassador to Germany, Berlin

[Washington] August 25, 1934

My dear Dodd: I am glad indeed to have your letter[1] even though your situation cannot exactly be called a rosy one. It confirms my fear that the drift in Germany, and perhaps in other countries in Europe, is definitely downward and that something must break within the next six months or a year.

Harry Hopkins is back today and he is equally pessimistic. So was George Harrison of the Federal Reserve Bank.[2]

I am on the whole fairly well satisfied with our own progress. We are under bitter political attack and will be until after election. You will have read of the formation of the American Liberty League by Shouse,[3] Al Smith, James W. Wadsworth, Irenee Du Pont and John W. Davis. It has already been nicknamed the "suicide club."

I hope to see Perkins when I go to Hyde Park.[4] I too am downhearted about Europe but I watch for any ray of hope or opening to give me an opportunity to lend a helping hand. There is nothing in sight at present.

Take care of yourself and keep on letting me have an occasional line.

As ever yours,

[PPF 1043:CT]

[1] Aug. 15, 1934, above.
[2] Hopkins, who had been investigating housing and unemployment insurance in Europe, returned August 23. Harrison, who had attended meetings of the World Bank, returned July 23.
[3] Jouett Shouse.
[4] James H. Perkins of the National City Bank. Roosevelt was in Hyde Park from August 26 to September 25 (PPF 1-0).

R. Walton Moore, Assistant Secretary of State, to Roosevelt

Washington, August 27, 1934

Dear Mr. President: Complying with the request you made last Saturday afternoon, I am handing you herewith the original of Mr. Charles Warren's paper on neutrality, along with my summary of his suggestions, which need not be returned, since I have had copies of the Warren paper made and placed in the hands of officials of this Department who are charged with the duty of studying the subject.[1]

Yours very sincerely,

R. Walton Moore

[OF 1561:TS]

[1] Moore was at the White House on August 25. The Warren memorandum, some 65,000 words in length, is present. About the same material, in different form, was published by Warren in three articles: "Troubles of a Neutral" and "Safeguards to Neutrality" in *Foreign Affairs*, XII (April 1934), 377–394; XIV (January 1936), 199–215; and "Prepare for Neutrality" in *The Yale Review*, XXIV (March 1935), 467–478.

[*Enclosure*] Summary, by R. Walton Moore, of a Memorandum on Neutrality by Charles Warren[1]

August 21, 1934

Neutrality

This is written after some consideration of the memorandum of Mr. Charles Warren, and is intended in the main as a summary of his discussion.

Mr. Warren suggests the necessity of legislation to which reference is made under the headings that follow:

1. He is of opinion that existing legislation authorizing control of the radio and probably the telegraph and cable lines is inadequate and should be strengthened.

2. He suggests that it should be considered whether existing legislation is entirely adequate to prevent our ports from becoming or being used as a base of supplies for warships of a belligerent on the high seas, and in that connection he recommends further legislation, if existing legislation is inadequate, authorizing the President to require heavy bonds from shippers conditioned against the delivery of cargoes to warships of a belligerent; and also the desirability of legislation authorizing the President to deny further clearance to any ship entering our ports after having delivered such cargoes. He points to the procedure and regulations adopted by several of the Latin American countries and particularly Chile.

3. There is an elaborate statement as to the proposed embargo on arms and munitions. He apparently favors the enactment of very comprehensive legislation vesting authority in the President to impose such an embargo.

4. In his opinion, legislation should be enacted limiting the right of Americans to travel on merchant ships of belligerents, by authorizing the President to enable the State Department to determine whether or not passports should be issued in specific cases, and also empowering the President to withhold clearance from any merchant or passenger ship of a belligerent having on board an American passenger, and also giving the President authority to prohibit a merchant ship of a belligerent from carrying passengers, if any of its cargo shall consist of arms and munitions.

5. He recommends the enactment of legislation authorizing the President to prevent entrance into our ports of an armed merchant ship

of a belligerent, or to permit its entrance only on condition that it may be treated in the same manner as a belligerent warship or a naval supply ship.

6. He seems to advocate legislation giving complete control by permissive legislation of ships owned, chartered or requisitioned by a belligerent for the transport of supplies.

7. He is of opinion that there should be legislation authorizing the President to refuse entrance to our ports or territorial waters of any submarine, of course including merchant submarines, during time of peace or during time of war, and to refuse clearance to any such submarine that may have entered our ports, with the right to use the army and navy to enforce the prohibition.

8. He believes that there should be legislation authorizing the President of the United States to refuse entrance to or clearance from our ports of the merchant ships of any belligerent nation which permits the use of neutral flags on such ships.

9. He believes that there should be legislation authorizing the President to prohibit any type of aircraft, whether military, naval or commercial, of a belligerent from entering or landing in our ports or upon our territory.

10. Mr. Warren does not mention the possible expediency of legislation suggested by Professor Borchard[2] to penalize the enlistment in the army of a belligerent of an American citizen residing abroad, and also to penalize the direct or indirect negotiation of a public loan in the United States by a belligerent.

Much of the legislation recommended by Mr. Warren, Professor Borchard and others is above specified.

In Part II of his Memorandum, Mr. Warren discusses the violation variously of neutral rights and offers many suggestions.

He mentions the extent to which Great Britain and Germany in the last war undertook to close trade routes to neutrals by planting mines and otherwise and, as I understand, he suggests that at the very outset of any future war the United States should endeavor to have an agreement on that point with the belligerents in default of which it should resort to methods of retaliation, which, however, it would seem might involve the United States in the war.

As I understand, he also suggests a prompt agreement, if possible, relative to the limits of war zones or areas and as to that matter makes a similar suggestion.

Furthermore, he mentions the possibility of protecting our merchant vessels from seizure by either license or assurance systems guaranteeing the character of the cargoes, and again refers to the possible expediency of retaliation in the event the safety of our ships is menaced.

While Mr. Warren has distinctly in mind the failure of our Government to bring about any understanding with the belligerents at the outset of the last war respecting the questions just mentioned, he apparently doubts whether that would have resulted in safeguarding our rights as neutrals. That doubt brings him to the submission of what he outlines as "A Proposed New System or Policy" which he speaks of as "requiring entire readjustment and the revision of our views as to neutral trade in time of war, but placing such trade on a basis more consonant with public sentiment against war and war profits than such trade has heretofore been." In this connection, he recognizes the increasing number of products supplied to a belligerent that are practically as effective as arms and munitions in enabling it to carry on war. Accordingly, he advises a course which would call for legislation of some character looking to the strict curtailment by the adoption on a pre-war quota basis or otherwise of export trade to a belligerent. This policy would, by tending to discourage war profiteering, greatly minimize the risk of the United States being drawn into a conflict. Mr. Warren says that it would practically be the following announcement to such of our citizens as may be engaged in the production of a given commodity:

The United States will allow you to trade in that article to the same extent as you normally did before the war, but further trade is not to be allowed; nor is your government going to run the risk of becoming involved in a war simply that you, some of its citizens, may have an opportunity to indulge in an unusual trade and to make excessive profits by reason of the existence of a war to which the United States is not a party.

Under a heading entitled "United States Policy as to Belligerent Aircraft and Neutral Trade" Mr. Warren emphasizes his view already expressed as to the new conditions that demand consideration and legislative action.

Under another heading entitled "United States Policy as to Prize Court Procedure," he says, "Consideration of the diplomatic correspondence would lead one to the belief that this is a subject which might be settled by negotiation and agreement at the outset of a future war." He evidently believes that touching this and other questions involving violation of neutral rights an international agreement prior to any future war is hardly to be expected.

Under another heading entitled "United States Policy as to Search and Detention of the Mails," Mr. Warren says,

Careful study of the correspondence of France and England makes it evident that this subject of interference with the mails is one which should be taken up with belligerent countries at the very outset of the war; and some agreement as a *modus vivendi* should be arrived at. It should not be allowed to be presented by diplomatic exchange of notes after action violative of American rights has taken place. With our past experience we know what England and France would try again to do with respect to the mails. We should at the outset prevent this either by agreement, if one can be obtained, or by the use of retaliatory measures.

We should consider whether legislation is needed to permit the President to negotiate such agreements at the outset of a future war as those suggested by Mr. Warren, and also what are the "retaliatory measures" he would suggest.

Under another heading entitled "United States Policy as to Removal of Persons from Neutral Ships," Mr. Warren again urges the importance of a prompt agreement between the United States and belligerents before war progresses to such a point as to make an agreement impossible.

Under a final heading entitled "American Policy as to the Black List," Mr. Warren points to the abuses that occurred during the last war and to retaliatory measures that may be taken to prevent or reduce the extent of such abuses in a future war.[3]

[OF 1561:T]

[1] This title has been supplied.

[2] Edwin M. Borchard, professor of law at Yale University Law School, had been asked by Moore to outline his ideas on neutrality legislation; he did so in a letter to Moore of Jan. 31, 1934 (Moore Papers). He recommended enactment of legislation to: (1) prohibit shipment of munitions of war to all belligerents in a war in which the United States was neutral; (2) prohibit the raising of public loans in the United States on behalf of belligerents; (3) prohibit enlistment of American citizens abroad; (4) prohibit the entrance into American harbors of armed merchantmen; (5) prohibit (at the President's discretion) travel of Americans on the merchant ships of belligerents; (6) prohibit (at the President's discretion) shipment of American cargoes on the merchant ships of belligerents; and (7) prohibit the furnishing of supplies to belligerent ships at sea. Borchard also said the use of armed convoys should be considered if the United States insisted on the right to trade with belligerent powers. By these methods, Borchard believed, the United States should be able to "fortify the rights of neutrals, enable it to remain out of coming foreign wars, and render a service to all mankind interested in practical rather than verbal peace."

[3] See Roosevelt to Hull, Sept. 25, 1934, below.

Roosevelt to John F. Montgomery, Minister to Hungary, Budapest

[Washington] August 29, 1934

My dear Mr. Minister: I am glad to have your interesting letter.[1] You are not the only one of our representatives who takes a somewhat pessimistic view. I, too, am much concerned, for at the present I see no answer. You are right in saying that Europe never seems to realize that it is all tied up in one sack and that it must be saved as a whole if the individual states are to save themselves. We Americans can realize the European situation if we were to draw a parallel to it within our own continental limits—state against state, section against section.

I shall hope to see you when you get over here in October.[2]

Very sincerely yours,

[OF 507:CT]

[1] July 13, 1934, above.
[2] An attached note, Roosevelt to Under Secretary of State Phillips, Aug. 29, 1934, reads: "Will you make an appointment for him when he gets here in October?" Montgomery saw Roosevelt on October 4.

Richard Washburn Child to Roosevelt

New York, August 30, 1934

My dear Mr. President: When I returned from Europe on the mission which your letter to the State Department inspired[1] I was told by your secretaries that you would not be able to talk with me.[2] This was an unusual decision in spite of the press of business. I did not ask for that assignment.

When after the campaign I had conscientiously as a Republican enlisted for the purpose of urging Republicans who constitute the American majority to elect you, you asked me if there were anything I wanted. I was asked that same question by three other Presidents, and my answer has always been the same, to wit: "Only what you wish of me to give of service that no other available person can give."

You spoke of Russia. Thank God that you did not ask me to serve you there. Your appointment of another without notification to me caused me embarrassment, which loyalty in me would never have caused you.

To-day any spirit of loyalty I may have is certainly connected with no more request for favor than I have ever made, except when I suggested that I might serve you in Ireland after the death of McDowell—that loyalty is somewhat put into confusion.

Of much that you have approved, I as an American citizen, disapprove. As you know, I disapprove of many of your advisers. I disapprove of your unintentional effect of splitting this country into a right and a left, even as much as I disapprove of the conservatives' move to do so. No country has ever split that way and survived with solvency.

I approve your dash, your courage, your love of humanity.

Some of your entourage could never be endorsed by you openly—nor their acts.

I have written you often—I have no replies. I do not know whether you receive my letters. I do not know how much you are—like many foreign and domestic administrators I have known—kept from knowledge.

I do not expect you to read this letter—

Not now—

Some day—

I am ready to help you, but not by any loss of self-respect.[3]

Faithfully yours,

Richard Washburn Child

[PPF 1760:TS]

[1] Roosevelt to Phillips, Feb. 21, 1934, above.

[2] Child apparently sent no written reports during his trip. On June 26 his law firm telegraphed McIntyre that he was arriving the next day and asked for an appointment for him before Roosevelt left for the West Coast (PPF 1760). No acknowledgment of this telegram has been found.

[3] Answered Sept. 4, 1934, below.

George N. Peek, Special Adviser to the President on Foreign Trade, to Roosevelt

[Washington] August 30th, 1934

Dear Mr. President: Supplementing my letter of May 23, 1934[1] containing analysis of our foreign trade for the 38 year period 1896–1933, I submit explanation of the form in which the increase in net debt was evidenced by international investments, or loan transactions.

The gross investments by the U.S. in foreign securities, loans to foreign governments (including war debts) and other investments during the 38 year period aggregated $36,875,000,000
As against this sum there was repurchased, redeemed, and allowed as commissions, discounts, etc. the following:

Repurchases.................. $4,466,000,000
Redemptions 6,517,000,000
Commissions and discounts....... 1,190,000,000

an aggregate of 12,173,000,000
resulting in a net increase during the 38 year period in U.S. loans and investments in foreign countries of... 24,702,000,000
During the 38 year period the world bought from us, U.S. securities, etc. gross amounting to $11,076,000,000
During the period we bought or redeemed U.S. securities, etc. held in foreign countries 9,019,000,000
resulting in a net increase during the 38 year period in foreigners' investments in the U.S. of............ 2,057,000,000
which amount deducted from the net increase in the U.S. loans and investments in foreign countries, makes up the net increase in debt for the 38 year period mentioned in my report of May 23, 1934 of $22,645,000,000

Submitted in this connection are three exhibits in which the security and loan transactions summarized above are divided into the same periods as the foreign trade transactions were in my report of May 23, 1934.

Period 1896–1914

1. Our own foreign investments increased from $500,000,000 at the beginning of the period to $1,500,000,000 at end of the period.
2. At the beginning of the period foreign investments in the United States amounted to 2,500,000,000
and at the end of the period they had increased to.. 4,500,000,000
3. Our net debtor position with the world was increased by $1,000,000,000 to.................... 3,000,000,000

Period 1915–1922

1. During the war period our investments in foreign countries increased in the amount of $6,779,000,000; and we acquired obligations of foreign governments (the "war debts") in the sum of $10,304,000,000, a total of $17,083,000,000.

2. On the other hand foreign investments in the United States were decreased during this war period in the amount of $2,222,000,000.

3. At the end of the period our investments in foreign countries were increased to $18,583,000,000, while foreigners' investments in the United States were decreased to $2,278,000,000. Thus the increase in the indebtedness of the world to us transformed us into a net creditor at the end of the period in the amount of $16,305,000,000

Period 1923–1929

1. During this period, U.S. investments in foreign countries or the amount which foreigners borrowed from the United States, totaled . . . . $ 7,140,000,000 whereas at the same time, foreigners increased their investments in the U.S. by $4,568,000,000 to 6,846,000,000

2. Our total investments in foreign countries increased to $25,723,000,000 and we were a net creditor at the end of the period in the amount of 18,877,000,000

3. Our foreign investments at the end of this period included $1,617,000,000 of short-term investments, while foreigners had $3,037,000,000 of short-term investments in the United States more than half of which represented demand deposits by foreigners in U.S. banks. We were thus a net debtor nation on short-term investments in the amount of. 1,420,000,000

Period 1930–1933

1. Our investments abroad were decreased by the net sum of 521,000,000

2. Foreign investments in the United States were decreased by the net sum of . . . . 2,289,000,000 due to reduction in short-term investments and demand deposits by foreigners in U.S. banks, which was made possible by net debtor position of the U.S. on short-term investments.

3. At the end of the period our investments in foreign countries totaled $25,202,000,000, or $23,702,000,000 more than in 1914.

4. At the end of the period foreign investments in the United States totaled $4,557,000,000, or an amount practically equal to that of 1914.

As stated in my letter of May 23, 1934, "we have no adequate national bookkeeping system for our foreign financial relations." I would like to add that we have no adequate knowledge of our investments in foreign countries or of foreigners' investments in the United States. An inventory is necessary for a complete understanding of our international investments.

We are undertaking to develop balance sheets between this country and each of the countries with which we are dealing or with which we propose to deal. As indicated, certain information necessary in preparing these balance sheets is not now available to the Government. In years past we have gone to great trouble and expense in recording and regulating the flow of emigration and immigration. The time has arrived when, as a nation, we must pay equal attention to the migration of capital and its relation to our foreign trade.[2]

Faithfully yours,

George N. Peek

[OF 971:TS]

[1] Above.

[2] With this letter Peek enclosed three memoranda: one on the international financial situation before and during the depression; one on the balance of international payments; and one recommending a foreign trade program. This last proposed creation of an agency directly responsible to the President to encourage and control foreign trade; its object would be "to secure the fullest possible recognition of the difference between the commercial and business aspects of foreign trade and the diplomatic and political aspects." He suggested as an interim arrangement that someone on the President's immediate staff review all foreign trade matters. This procedure would ensure some coordination and would give the President needed information.

The letter here printed and its enclosures were sent by Peek on Aug. 31, 1934, enclosed in a folder. On the folder appears this note in Roosevelt's hand: "Brazil—Tell Welles any 3 cornered transaction must be in *goods*, for *goods*, for *goods* & not goods vs. foreign exchange vs. goods—" A few weeks later Roosevelt repeated his instructions. In a note to Welles of Sept. 25, 1934 (OF 11), he said: "In working on the preliminary agreement, I hope you will in every way possible consider any three-cornered transactions in the light of goods vs. goods, rather than in terms of goods vs. foreign exchange vs. goods."

Certain minor changes were made in the text of the letter here printed before it was released. The changes were made at the request of the Treasury Department (Early to Roosevelt, Sept. 17, 1934, OF 971). The release of the letter to the press was discussed by Peek and the President at Hyde Park on September 3 (Early to McIntyre, Sept. 5, 1934, OF 971). Early referred to it as "hot stuff" and proposed that it be released

September 10; Morgenthau, however, asked that publication be held up until September 17, "because of Treasury refinancing" (Early to Roosevelt and McIntyre, Sept. 7, 1934, OF 971). It was finally made public on September 18; see the New York *Times* of Sept. 19, 1934, p. 1.

Possibly inspired by the Peek report was a statement by Hull opposing the export-import balance system urged by Peek. At a press conference on Sept. 17, 1934, Hull, during a discussion of a possible reciprocal trade agreement with Germany, said he took no stock in the "narrow quid-pro-quo policy of balancing trade between every two nations that have trade transactions with each other." Hull favored "triangular trade," "whereby one nation might buy from another more than it sold, balancing this by selling to a third nation more than it bought from it (New York *Times,* Sept. 18, 1934, p. 33). In his *Memoirs* (I, 371), Hull says that throughout the summer of 1934 he and his associates in the State Department "spent much time contesting Peek's theories." See Peek to Roosevelt, Nov. 12, 1934, below.

William Phillips, Under Secretary of State, to Roosevelt

Washington, August 30, 1934

Dear Mr. President: In accordance with your request, I am sending you enclosed a brief memorandum containing a number of "war debt solutions" which have been lying in the files of this Department. There are, of course, many other solutions which have been suggested, but the ones enumerated in the enclosed memorandum seem to us the more worthy of consideration.

If you would like us to explore any of them further, please do not hesitate to let me know.

In this connection, it occurs to me that you might be interested to have before you a report of a conversation between Ambassador Bullitt and M. Georges Bonnet, which Bullitt sends us under date of July 14th.

Faithfully yours,

William Phillips

[PSF:War Debts:TS]

[*Enclosure 1*] William C. Bullitt, Ambassador to the Union of Soviet Socialist Republics, to Cordell Hull, Secretary of State

Moscow, July 14, 1934

Subject: Report of conversation between Ambassador Bullitt and Monsieur Georges Bonnet.

Sir: I have the honor to report, as of possible interest to the Department, a conversation which I had yesterday with Monsieur Georges Bonnet, former French Finance Minister.

It will be recalled that M. Bonnet, as French Finance Minister, was chairman of the French Delegation to the World Monetary and Economic Conference of 1933 at London. In view of the fact that M. Bonnet at that time had been rancorous in his opposition to the policy of the American Government and that I had been obliged personally to have several most acrimonious conversations with him, I did not anticipate a pleasurable meeting; but M. Bonnet appeared to be a much chastened individual and displayed great cordiality.

M. Bonnet gave me what he said was a full account of a conversation with the British Chancellor of the Exchequer, Mr. Neville Chamberlain, on the final day of the Conference. He said that Chamberlain had invited him to have a formal conference on the subject of war debts, that Chamberlain had said that he was confident that he could settle the British debt to America for ten percent of its face value, that if he should do so he would at once demand of France a settlement of the French debt to Great Britain of sufficient amount to cover all Great Britain's payments to the United States. Bonnet replied (so he said) that he doubted greatly that the Congress of the United States would ever accept a ten percent settlement from Great Britain, that if Great Britain should be able to make such a settlement France would at once make a similar settlement with the United States, that France would not agree to pay England sums which England might pay to America, that the British Government at Lausanne had made promises to the French Government that it would make no demand for payment of France's debt to Great Britain. Chamberlain replied (so Bonnet said) that the situation had been changed by the failure of Great Britain to obtain a settlement with the United States and that Great Britain considered her claims against France still valid. Bonnet replied that he could not engage his government in any way but speaking *à titre personelle* he could say that he might advise a payment to England which would bear the same proportion to the whole French obligation to Great Britain as any payment made to the United States might bear to the whole French obligation to the United States.

In discussing the present British policy with regard to stabilization Bonnet said that recently he had received full information as to the British point of view, that Chamberlain still insisted that the British would do nothing whatsoever to stabilize the pound until a debt settlement with the United States had been made. He said that to his certain knowledge Chamberlain had always been in favor of default and that Chamberlain had said to him several times that he considered refusal to stabilize the pound the best method of forcing America to accept a ten percent settlement of the British debt. Bonnet asserted that the British were still most anxious to have the debts settled and that the French were also, and asked me if I felt that the British default had seriously injured the prestige of Great Britain in the United States. I replied that I believed it had relieved certain persons of the idea that Great Britain's sense of honor extended to matters in which her interests were involved.

M. Bonnet informed me of certain facts with regard to French Financial Attachés which are doubtless known to the Department. He told me that M. Monique was to be withdrawn from Washington and made Financial Attaché at London, that M. Ruef, French Financial Attaché in London, was to be given a prominent position in the financial administration in Paris.

In conclusion, M. Bonnet said that the idea of revaluing the franc was gaining headway in Paris and that he personally would have no objection to a devaluation provided it were accomplished by a single act, but that he remained unalterably opposed to subjecting France to a floating currency.

M. Bonnet is about to tour the southern areas of the Soviet Union and then visit Constantinople.

Respectfully yours,

William C. Bullitt

[PSF:War Debts:T]

[*Enclosure 2*] Frederick Livesey, Assistant Economic Adviser, State Department, to William Phillips, Under Secretary of State

August 23, 1934

War Debt Solutions

Proposals for solving the war debt problem generally present, singly or in combination, the following bases:

(1) Rearrangement of annuities and reduction or elimination of interest.

(2) Lump sum settlement.

(3) Deliveries in kind.

(4) Interposition of financial machinery to facilitate payment through commercial credits.

I. Rearrangement of Annuities. The present debt settlements are in the form of annuities, generally 62 in number, providing for the repayment with interest of a principal amount established at the date of the agreement (generally between 1923 and 1926). The principal so established included amounts representing unpaid interest from the date the debt was originally incurred. Retroactive application of all payments to principal account would permit the establishment of a new principal amount now owed which, if permitted to be paid without interest by a series of annuities, would greatly decrease the outstanding debt obligation and, in most cases, the amount of the current scheduled annuities. In the case of some countries with ascending annuities (France and Italy) rearrangements on this basis into uniform annuities would not greatly reduce the present scale of payments for the next few years.

II. Lump Sum Payment. A natural way of disposing of a long series of annuities is to settle the obligation by a lump sum payment approximating the present value of the annuities at some agreed on rate of interest, but with some concession by the creditor in view of the advantage of cash over the hazards of future annuities. In view of the size of the necessary lump sum payments and the impossibility of transferring them without upsetting the foreign exchange market, such a settlement would normally depend largely on the public sale of securities of the debtor for dollars in the United States. The absorptive capacity of the American investment market for the securities of the debtor government would be a limiting factor.

III. Deliveries in Kind. Inasmuch as war debt payments have been alleged to involve transfer difficulty rather than budgetary impossibility, many suggestions have been made that the right be given the United States Government to draw upon the debtors for payments in kind. In so far as such suggestions would merely mean that transactions that will take place anyway should be paid for by special arrangement between governments rather than through the normal operation of the exchange markets, they would leave the transfer question unchanged. However, suggestions have been made for transactions out of the ordinary, such as the provision by the debtors of raw materials to be held in stock in the United States against war or other emergencies, and plans for stimulating additional tourist travel of Americans in debtor countries with special arrangements of a clearing nature to assure that these additional payments were made available in dollars to the United States Treasury.

IV. Interposition of Special Credit Machinery. Many suggestions have been made that the debtors pay in their own currency into a fund in the Bank for International Settlements for temporary investment or manipulation by the Bank and eventual transfer to the United States in dollars. It is assumed that the funds could thus be used to great advantage in improving world economic conditions and that this in turn would facilitate the gradual transfer to the United States.

Combinations. Most schemes advanced combine two or more of the above bases, apparently because proposals dealing with payments in kind or banking manipulations seem difficult to advance as a definite solution assuring payment by Europe of a series of 50 annuities averaging about $400,000,000 dollars each. Many of the best-sponsored suggestions are those, generally vague, which would provide for the establishment of an international financial fund in the Bank for International Settlements to be manipulated by the Bank as trustee with ultimate transfer to the United States.

One or two relatively recent suggestions may be mentioned:

Shepard Morgan Proposal. Mr. Morgan proposes that we accept from our great debtors (this would probably be Great Britain, France, Italy and Belgium) marketable bonds representing 10 percent of our total claim against them, that all our debtors should be required to pay into the Bank for International Settlements sums up to the amount of two years scheduled payments, that these deposits be re-lent to the debtor governments by investment in their short-dated negotiable treasury bills, and that the United States be authorized to draw on the deposit of a given country only when for three successive months (or in total for one calendar year) the balance of merchandise trade between that country and the United States becomes adverse to the United States. When such withdrawals have taken place the debtor country shall restore the deposit to the original level. Based on 1933 trade figures, this would mean that we could continue to collect from eight small countries representing generally our relief debtors (Austria, Czechoslovakia, Greece, Hungary, Finland, Latvia, Lithuania, Yugoslavia) while the principal allied powers, debtors in respect of pre-Armistice obligations, would pay 10 percent of their present indebtedness and accept a contingent obligation to resume payments to the United States during periods when their normal balance of trade with the United States may be reversed, as by war purchases by the United States. This suggestion is probably relatively close to British ideas. A fuller statement is attached.[1]

International Currency Proposals. In addition to suggestions that debt payments be used to establish an international fund in the Bank for International Settlements to be used to facilitate trade by investment in commercial credits or to be used as a currency stabilization fund, suggestions have been received that the Bank for International Settlements invest such a fund in gold, silver, eligible commercial paper and secured obligations purchased in the open market (or, according to one proposal, in gold, silver, copper, platinum, tungsten, manganese and tin) and shall issue its own currency notes secured on these investments. If such notes could be made legal tender at least for the payment of debts expressed to be payable therein, the notes might circulate as an international currency. Provision would have to be made as to the metals and national currencies in which the international notes would be redeemable. Presumably they would not be made redeemable until several years after the initiation of the scheme.

F. Livesey

[PSF:War Debts:TS]

[1] Not printed. The statement is an eight-page single-spaced typed document entitled, "Shepard Morgan Debt Suggestion. Abbreviated from letter of July 25, 1934." Morgan, vice-president of the Chase National Bank, pointed out the artificial conditions of commerce that gave rise to the war debts (exportation of goods to Europe unbalanced by a like exchange), and proposed a scheme of repayment based on special contingencies: a future war or a future disaster (such as successive crop failures) when the United States would draw on its European reserve of credit. A third part of the plan was an arrangement whereby payments would be made by a debtor country only when "the balance of merchandise trade between that country and the United States [became] adverse to the United States."

Jesse Isidor Straus, Ambassador to France, to Roosevelt

Paris, August 30, 1934

Personal

Dear Mr. President: Monsieur Etienne Flandin, Minister of Public Works in the present French Cabinet, has gone to Canada for the Cartier celebrations and will, I am informed, visit the United States. Flandin, shortly before his departure, told Mr. Marriner,[1] Counselor of Embassy, that while he hoped sincerely for the opportunity of a talk with you, as he would have no official capacity whatever in the United States (his mission being only to Canada), he would not wish to obtrude and did not intend to go to Washington, but if you should be at Hyde Park he hoped there might be some informal way of seeing you.[2]

I suppose this all means that he would like an intimation from you to the French Chargé d'Affaires that a visit would be agreeable.

Flandin is extremely ambitious and very influential with the Extreme Right. You will recall that he was Minister of Finance in the Laval Government at the time of the Hoover moratorium, and was at that time and has remained ever since extremely intransigent on the subject of any debt payments by France to the United States.

If you should receive him, I make bold to make the suggestion that if you have an opportunity, you impress upon him the unfavorable impression that has been created by some of the inimical steps that France has taken against our products. I have, as occasion offered in private conversations with members of the Government, mentioned, among other things, failure on the part of the French Government to ratify the Double Taxation Treaty, signed by M. Tardieu and Ambassador Edge in April 1932, and which our Senate promptly ratified;[3] discriminations against various of our products such as that contained in the unequal application of the import turnover tax on copper and other goods; difficulty relative to obtaining modus vivendi tariff rates on rice and other items, etc.; inimical treatment of American films.

I mentioned to you when last I saw you that I was glad to learn that the policy of your Administration would be to negotiate a commercial treaty with France later than negotiations with various other countries. I said to you that I believed that France should be put in the vocative, and that in order to receive the proper treatment we would have to show some teeth. That France is slightly worried already is evidenced by the enclosed memorandum made by Mr. Harold L. Williamson, Second Secretary of Embassy, after a conversation with M. de la Baume of the Foreign Office.[4] France is, as you are aware, a trading nation that wants a quid pro quo for everything.

I trust that you have had some rest while at Hyde Park and remain, with kindest regards,

Very sincerely yours,

Jesse Isidor Straus

[OF 280:TS]

[1] James T. Marriner.
[2] See press conference of Sept. 7, 1934, below.
[3] The object of this treaty was to do away with certain double taxes, chief example

of which was one levied by France on earnings of French subsidiaries of American firms and corporations and also on the earnings of the parent companies. The treaty was signed in Paris April 27, 1932, and approved by the Senate on June 15, 1932 (*Cong. Rec.*, vol. 75, pp. 13007–13009).

[4] Present.

William C. Bullitt, Ambassador to the Union of Soviet Socialist Republics, to Marguerite LeHand, Private Secretary to the President

Moscow, September 1, 1934

Dear Miss LeHand: I enclose a letter to the President from that admirable old gentleman with one leg, Philippe Bunau-Varilla, who put through the Panama Canal.[1] As you know, the old gentleman still carries a good deal of weight in France and a great deal of influence with the press since he and his brother own the *Matin,* and his letter to the President ought to receive as prompt attention as possible.

Incidentally, Bunau-Varilla's idea is not half bad—the old man is no fool. In case the President does not have time to read either the letter or the pamphlet the gist of both is this:

(1) In view of the situation in the Far East it is essential that the security of the Panama Canal should be absolute.

(2) The Panama Canal may be destroyed by the Japanese in case of war or may be temporarily put out of commission by an earthquake.

(3) The Canal can be made absolutely secure only by eliminating locks and making it a sea level project.

In the pamphlet Bunau-Varilla demonstrates, at least to his own satisfaction, that this is entirely practicable; and in his letter to me he suggests that the orders to American heavy industry for machinery necessary to complete the transformation might give a highly desirable fillip to that branch of our national economy.

When I came back from my trip to the Ukraine I found Miss Davidson[2] had already arrived in Moscow. She lunched with me the next day and we sent you a joint telegram which I hope you received. I was really sorry to hear that you had had such an unsatisfactory trip and even more so to hear that you had been ill. Take care of yourself.

Bill

[OF 25-I:TS]

[1] Bunau-Varilla was chief engineer of de Lesseps' canal company. After collapse of the project, he secured President Theodore Roosevelt's support for the Panama route, and, as first Panamanian minister to the United States, negotiated the Hay-Bunau-Varilla Treaty of 1903. He was author of a number of publications on the Canal; the pamphlet mentioned below is *The Strait of Panama: The New and Necessary Form of the Panama Canal* (Paris, 1924 [?]). His letter is adequately summarized by Bullitt; see Roosevelt's reply, Sept. 25, 1934, below.

[2] Not identified.

Roosevelt to Richard Washburn Child, New York

[Washington] September 4, 1934

Dear Dick: I am a little surprised by your letter[1] because, first, I did not know that you had asked to see me, and, secondly, because you got back from your very excellent trip when I was in the throes of a closing Congress.

Some day I hope that you will come to see me, as I should much like to have your thoughts on a number of matters—as for instance, the pending European situation which does not seem to grow easier with the passage of time.

I am telling Mr. McIntyre to be sure to let me know if you want to talk with me and to arrange a time.

Always sincerely,

[PPF 1760:CT]

[1] Aug. 30, 1934, above.

Hugh Gibson, Ambassador to Brazil, to Roosevelt

Rio de Janeiro, September 4, 1934

Dear Mr. President: When I left Washington it was with a special injunction to report directly to you on anything I thought you ought to know. Here is an item which may be of use.

Dr. Oswaldo Aranha, the newly appointed Brazilian Ambassador, will arrive in Washington shortly after this note. He is today probably the most influential man in Brazil, and so far as can be foreseen, will be the next President, either at the end of this administration, or perhaps sooner in the event of an earlier upset.

205

He has unusual intelligence and a readiness to learn. He is keenly interested in what is going on in the United States and entirely sympathetic. This is not a matter of words because, since I have been here, he has gone to great lengths to get fair treatment for American interests, which have been in for some heavy sledding; and if he tells you how friendly he feels toward us you will want to bear in mind that it is justified by his own past performances.

So far as I can judge, he is the initiator of the present definite movement in Brazil to draw away from Europe and throw Brazil's lot in with the United States. He has done this on realistic grounds, which is the best assurance that he will stand hitched.

He is responsive to friendliness and kind words, and knowing this, I am sure that you will with little effort be able to consolidate a friendship which will pay big dividends for us in the future.[1]

Respectfully yours,

Hugh Gibson

[OF 405:TS]

[1] Answered Sept. 20, 1934, below.

Roosevelt to Grenville T. Emmet, Minister to The Netherlands, The Hague

Hyde Park, N.Y., September 6, 1934

Dear Grenville: That is a grand letter of yours[1] and I am so happy that Pauline is all well again and that you have had the children with you this summer. What a delightful place your country house must be.

I will wait until December to discuss the Pacific matters and, in the meantime, I hope you can impress the Dutch government with the importance of frankness between us in regard to important problems like this.

We are at Hyde Park for a few weeks and I will return to Washington about the twenty-fifth of this month.

As ever yours,

[PPF 372:CT]

[1] Aug. 17, 1934, above.

Press Conference, President's Study, Hyde Park, September 7, 1934, 4:15 P.M.

[*Excerpt*] The President: . . . I had Monsieur Flandin, Minister of Public Works, he and his wife and daughter came in to lunch,[1] and we talked about everything relating to the United States and France except public works.

Q: Did you talk about the debt?

The President: No—this has got to be off the record—we spent most of the lunch hour talking about Germany.

Q: What is the situation there?

The President: Off the record, the French are not very happy.

Q: Are they worried?

The President: Oh, yes.

Q: Why?

The President: What they are afraid of—we will have to keep this entirely off the record; you know I cannot talk foreign affairs about so-called friendly nations. The situation—all those fellows that have been coming back—really what they are afraid of in Germany is that the German economic situation is breaking down. In fact, as it is they have no gold, no foreign exchange, they cannot buy materials on the outside. What are they going to do to keep the factories going? They are turning out synthetic rubber, gasoline, synthetic cattle and horse fodder— perfectly amazing—and employing all those people to turn out synthetic substitutes for everything.

He says that a thing like that cannot go on, that you cannot use synthetic rubber and synthetic food for everybody and that it is bound to break down of its own weight. The question is, when?

Then, they are afraid in France that when the thing does get to the point of closing down their factories, with already a very large unemployment list, then one of two things will happen: Either they will have chaos inside of Germany, with all of these fellows fighting among themselves—we got one report the other day from Dodd describing how Hitler's Secret Service was being followed by Goebbel's Secret Service, which was being followed by Reichswehr's Secret Service, which was being followed by the Gestapo, all of them following each other around— or else that the leaders over there, to retain their power, will start to march on something, to walk across the border. I suppose the easiest way would be to toss a coin to see which border they will have to walk across to retain the present regime in power and the whole of Europe is scared pink of something like that.

Q: How can they get the money to buy the bullets to shoot at people?

The President: Of course the French say they have an awful lot of it on hand. The French are convinced. They say big guns are the easiest thing in the world. When you are casting a stern tubing for a ship, for the shaft tubing, it is almost exactly the same process as casting the tube of a gun, of a 14-inch gun. It is exactly the same thing. You cast two and put one over in the corner. The French are convinced that they have all the small artillery, the 75's and the 155's, according to the French, and the French—this did not take place today so don't think it is Flandin—the French are perfectly sure that the Germans have more machine guns than the French Army. And they are also perfectly sure that they have as many airplanes available as France has.

Another lovely story is that the school children—this is one of the silly ones, but it may be true; we do know that every factory worker in Germany works with a gas mask in a bag above his bench and every once in a while a whistle blows twice and everybody puts on his gas mask. I tell you the silly things because we get them all the time and only a few get printed.

The school children in Germany are now going through an educational process. They have a box of matches and the head of the match is impregnated with the particular smell of the poisonous gases used in the World War. They gather around in the classroom and the children light a match and that is gas No. 3. They train them in knowing those different smells. It sounds crazy but we know there is a lot of that stuff going on. There are seven different smells and you have on the gas mask seven different slides, each one against a different type of gas.

Then there is the story of the professor of foreign languages at Bryn Mawr, who went over there last fall and visited a German professor in Stuttgart. She went to his house—she had stayed with him before. His family and workmen were working down in the basement. She said, "What is all this work that is going on?" "I am carrying out the orders of the Government. I am putting a bomb proof in the cellar. We are all doing it." She said, "What are you doing it for?" "We get a remission of half year's taxes if we prepare against airplane attack. They are doing it in France." She said, "They are doing it in France?" "Oh, yes; the papers say so. The English are doing it and they are doing it in the United States along the whole Atlantic Seaboard."

She said, "I have not been home for two months but I am sure I have not seen it." "You do not know. We know. Our Government tells us."

Now, there is a professor who swallows the whole thing, hook, line and sinker.

And then the little boy came down at night to say his prayers, his age eight or nine years, and he kneeled down at his mother's knee and said his prayers and ended up in good German, like a good German boy, and he said, "Dear God, please permit it that I shall die with a French bullet in my heart."

You get that sort of thing and that is what has got the French scared when ninety per cent of the German people are thinking and talking that way. If I were a Frenchman, I would be scared too. There are only 40 million Frenchmen and there are 70 million Germans.

Q: When is this war going to start?

The President: I said last winter on that that as long as they are talking war in Europe there won't be a war.

Q: They might talk themselves into one, don't you think?

The President: They are all saying there won't be a war.

Q: Isn't Italy going to collapse?

The President: No; they have $240,000,000 of gold left.

Q: It is decreasing, though.

The President: Oh, yes. Those things aren't so hot.

Q: Pretty bad in France?

The President: Harry Hopkins talked to you about Italy?[2]

Q: I wasn't there.

Q: He did.

The President: He thought Italy was much worse off than any of the stories we have been getting would indicate because he said out in the country the average family did not have enough money for spaghetti. I said, "What do they do?" He said, "I think most of them are using wheat chaff which they boil into soup."

Q: How much did the French Minister say about France's unemployment, economically?

The President: He said they were not as well off as last year but still not serious. I think he said something like three or four hundred thousand. Of course, the French are very conservative. They do not put a man down as unemployed unless he really is, and we do.

Q: Do those reports coming to you indicate there is a general slight recession in world business, that is, abroad as well as at home in the last month or two?

The President: Oh, undoubtedly, of course. England, we know, is off and I do not know whether Italy and Germany have gone off but they are coming to an end of their resources, which is just about as serious. They have not got any foreign exchange to buy their raw materials with and, of course, France is a little off from last year, but not as much off as they were in the last three or four months. Our foreign trade is the only one that has gone up. We have gone up pretty well on foreign trade.

Q: And imports reduced?

The President: Imports reduced but exports up.

[President's Press Conferences:T]

[1] On September 7; Senator McAdoo of California was also a guest (PPF 1-0).
[2] Hopkins had returned from Europe on August 23 (PPF 1-0).

William C. Bullitt, Ambassador to the Union of Soviet Socialist Republics, to Roosevelt

Moscow, September 8, 1934

Dear Mr. President: I was delighted to get your letter of August 14, and even more to get that cable.[1] Thank God I shall see you all again before Christmas.

I am sorry that the State Department was not able to get anywhere with Troyanovsky. I hoped that a discussion of specific trade deals might lead to a settlement.[2]

The answer, I think, is that the Russians have had so much success lately that they are feeling exceedingly cocky. The harvest, which at one time looked catastrophic, was so revived by continuous rains that it will be good, and the Russians are convinced that if the Eastern Locarno should fail, France and Czechoslovakia will at once enter an alliance with the Soviet Union. The Government, therefore, feels that its back will be protected by France from attacks by either Poland or Germany in case Japan should decide to go after the maritime provinces.

Furthermore, the Government believes that Japan will not attack either this autumn or next spring and that by next summer the Red Army in the Far East will be so strong that Japan will not dare to attack.

The maintenance of really friendly and intimate relations with us, therefore, seems to the Russians much less important than it did when Litvinov was in Washington. If a Japanese attack should again seem likely, or if we should begin to develop any sort of a real understanding with Japan, it would not take the Soviet Government very long to discover that our demands with regard to debts and claims were most reasonable.

I cannot tell you how glad I shall be to see you.

This place is fun but I often wish I were with you in Washington. Good luck till we meet and a large embrace to the entire White House.

Yours permanently,

Bill

[PSF:Russia:TS]

[1] The letter is published in *Personal Letters, 1928–1945*, I, 411; Roosevelt said that he had had no conversations on the Russian debt question but expected to before he left for Hyde Park on August 24. No copy of the cable has been found.

[2] Troyanovsky had returned to Russia on October 3. For the 1934 correspondence between Hull and Bullitt and Hull and Wiley (chargé) on the efforts to arrive at a settlement of Russian debts and claims against Russia, see *Foreign Relations, The Soviet Union, 1933–1939*, pp. 63–165.

Dave H. Morris, Ambassador to Belgium, to Roosevelt

Clingendaal, den Haag, Sept. 9, 1934

Personal

My dear Franklin: I am spending Sunday with your delightful Minister here in his enchanting home. Congratulations all around. He and Mrs. Emmet are the right people in the right place, and all is well! Indeed very well.

Of course we think and talk of you. Our hope is to be helpful in solving some of your problems in the cases where you want our cooperation. We sincerely trust you will call on us. Both the countries to which you have acredited us need trade agreements under your new powers, and if you confine them to a few items at first, later ones can be added readily from time to time. But those wretched "debts" are at the bottom of so much trouble that until they are eliminated the future is not bright.

Does it not seem as if all countries needed a lot of education on that point? And are you not really the only person in U.S.A. to whom our people will listen? So, by the middle of November, if the time then seems propitious, do consider explaining the situation as you know well how to do. (Remember that Will Rogers said you could explain banking so that even the Bankers understood it.)

Please let me thank you for the time you gave me on Aug. 10th to tell me so many things of interest. It was more than kind and I am very grateful for your generous hospitality.

Sept. 13. Before I left Bar Harbor in August, I saw Gov. Brann. He seemed a bit worried. "Uncle Henry" said all hands were to help. Apparently a good job was done in the whole State of Maine and I hope you are well pleased.[1]

I am enclosing some stamps, new and otherwise, which may be of interest.

Finances dont look very cheerful here or in Germany, but the predicted "blow-up" seems to be regularly postponed for worse times.

May I sign myself

Affecly yrs

Dave H. Morris

[PSF:Belgium:AS]

[1] Louis J. Brann had just been re-elected governor of Maine by a large majority. "Uncle Henry" refers to Henry Morgenthau, Sr., former ambassador to Turkey, who had spoken in behalf of the Democratic ticket at a campaign rally in Augusta on August 17 (New York *Times,* Aug. 18, 1934, p. 15).

Roosevelt to Stephen T. Early, Assistant Secretary to the President

[Hyde Park] September 10, 1934

Memo for S.T.E.: Will you tell the Staff that the State Department envelopes must come to me unopened?[1]

F.D.R.

[OF 20:CT]

[1] With this note is a copy of a telegram from Early to Rudolph Forster in the White House, Sept. 10, 1934, asking that he inform all White House staff members, "including Col. Howe's office," of this request.

Cordell Hull, Secretary of State, to Roosevelt

Washington, September 10, 1934

My dear Mr. President: you will recall that in connection with the question of the ratification of the Geneva Arms Convention you suggested to Mr. Phillips the inclusion in the ratification proclamation of a statement interpreting the Senate reservation regarding the Persian Gulf,[1] and that recently I showed you a draft of such a statement.[2] We have continued to give this matter most earnest consideration and we have now come definitely to the conclusion that such a method of procedure would not accomplish the end which you have in mind, that is, the entrance of the Convention into force at an early date.

Immediately upon the adoption of the Senate reservation we got in touch with the Governments chiefly concerned and with important officials at Geneva and endeavored to smooth the way for the acceptance of the reservation by the interested Powers. We made the strongest possible representations to that end. Our efforts in this direction were, however, fruitless. The French Government, as depositary of the Convention, made clear that it would be necessary to circularize the reservation for acceptance by the thirty-seven signatory Powers and possibly by eleven other Powers to whom the Convention was open for adherence. The mere mechanical details of obtaining the acceptance of those Powers would require many months and we have no assurance, of course, that the reservation would be favorably received by all of the Powers. Some of them, indeed, might be inspired to make new reservations of their own, thus further complicating the situation.

The British Government likewise has explained its misgivings to our Ambassador at London and on two occasions has instructed its representative at Washington to point out to the Department that the terms of the reservation gave ground for serious concern and raised the fear of further complications in Anglo-Persian relations. Under the circumstances it is most unlikely that Great Britain, in view of its vital interests in the Persian Gulf, would ever accept the reservation; and without the participation of Great Britain the Convention would remain a dead letter.

Moreover, the situation as described above would not be altered by the inclusion in the ratification proclamation of such an interpretive statement as you proposed, for such a statement would in no way affect the Senate reservation nor would it obviate the necessity of obtaining the acceptance of the reservation by the numerous signatory Powers and by those to whom it is open for adherence. It seems clear therefore that, with or without an interpretive statement, we cannot hope to bring the Convention into force as long as the reservation stands.

I should also mention that the whole question of the revision of the 1925 Convention, including that section to which the Persian Government takes exception, is now before the appropriate sub-committee of the Disarmament Conference which is expected to make its recommendations to the full committee in the near future. It seems undesirable for us to inject ourselves into the matter while it is thus under active consideration.

As of general interest in connection with this whole question and particularly as indicative of the attitude of the Persian Government in the matter, I enclose a copy of a despatch recounting a conversation between the Persian Minister for Foreign Affairs and Mr. Hornibrook, our Minister at Teheran.[3]

In view of all the circumstances, I feel confident that a decision to hold the matter in abeyance could not be interpreted as showing any lack of respect for the Senate on your part. Accordingly, bearing in mind all the aspects of the case, from the point of view of our international relations and otherwise, I am reluctantly forced to the conclusion that I have no alternative but to recommend that the Convention be not ratified with the present reservation regarding the Persian Gulf.

I understand that Judge Moore hopes to have an opportunity of seeing you at Hyde park within the next few days and I have asked him to hold himself in readiness to furnish you with any further information which you may desire on this subject.[4]

Faithfully yours,

Cordell Hull

[PSF:Iran:TS]

[1] See Roosevelt to Hull, Aug. 15, 1934, above.

[2] Printed in *Foreign Relations, 1934,* I, 481. The draft statement was to the effect that the reservation was not "to be construed as implying that the United States of America has any intention of expressing any opinion, or becoming involved in any controversy in regard to the sovereignty of the waters of the Persian Gulf."

[3] William H. Hornibrook; his dispatch of Aug. 15, 1934, is printed *ibid.,* 474–476.

[4] With this letter is a draft message from the President to the Senate resubmitting the convention without the Persian Gulf reservation; accompanying this is a memorandum in his hand of Sept. 14, 1934: "C.H. O.K. to hold in abeyance & return to Congress in January. FDR." In the meantime the British indicated their objection to the reservation, largely because of disputes over the ownership of property in Bahrein. Assistant Secretary of State Moore talked with Roosevelt about the convention on September 13, according to his memorandum of September 14 (Moore Papers). Moore said the President told him he would not sign the convention until December, when he would have an opportunity to talk with Senator Pittman about it. Moore also said that the President seemed much interested in the convention but did not believe the reservation "necessary or expedient." See also Roosevelt to Pittman, Feb. 4, 1935, below.

Press Conference, Hyde Park, September 12, 1934, 10:30 A.M.

[*Excerpt*] Q: What is the Rome conference?

The President: It is the International Agricultural Institute.

Mr. McIntyre: The Institute of Agriculture.

The President: That is the International Institute of Agriculture and it is an organization that was started a great many years ago by some very famous American.

Q: Lubin.[1]

The President: By a man named Lubin, who was one of our great experts on agriculture about thirty-five or thirty years ago, wasn't it, Ernest?

Mr. Lindley: I think so.

The President: It antedated the League of Nations by years and years. It was the first effort in the world to have a central organization which would be fact-finding and interchange information of all kinds on some particular thing. On agriculture, they undertook to find out what the crop production would be, et cetera, and Lubin started this thing and I think it was after his death that the thing sort of began to die and the Italian Government got interested and kept it going. It is only in the past year, since I started the Wheat Conference and the general interchange of information on world surpluses that the thing seems to have taken a new lease on life. Also, we did not subscribe to it for years and I got through an appropriation of $50,000 a year ago so we are now members in good standing and we are sending Tugwell over there. We are sending, also, MacMurray,[2] who is our Minister to one of the Baltic States down there, and he is the American delegate to the Wheat Conference, and also Bingham is a member of the Wheat Conference. Tugwell is going to London to keep in touch with the wheat situation, and then, with Bingham and MacMurray he is going down to Rome. We are very much interested in the success of the Institute.[3]

Q: Will there be any new efforts for world wheat control?

The President: Well, it is going on.

[President's Press Conferences:T]

[1] David Lubin; see Roosevelt to Pittman, May 24, 1933, n. 1, above.

[2] John V. A. MacMurray, minister to Latvia, Estonia, and Lithuania.

[3] The Institute opened Oct. 22, 1934, with Tugwell as head of the American delegation.

Roosevelt to Lincoln MacVeagh, Minister to Greece, Athens

Hyde Park, N.Y., September 12, 1934

Dear Lincoln: Many thanks for that fine letter.[1] I am glad that if the European bombs explode you will probably be safe from the earlier fragments.

I do hope we can go ahead with a new commercial treaty or reciprocal agreement with Greece, and I am taking it up with the State Department.

We are very happy that little Eleanor[2] is to be with you. Hall continues dynamic and is thrilled by the swiftly moving panorama over here. You are doing a grand job.

As ever yours,

[PPF 1192:CT]

[1] Aug. 6, 1934, above.
[2] Daughter of Hall Roosevelt, brother of Mrs. Franklin D. Roosevelt.

Roosevelt to Cordell Hull, Secretary of State

Hyde Park, N.Y., September 13, 1934

Memorandum for the Secretary of State: For your information. I saw Monsieur Flandin the other day.[1]

F.D.R.

[OF 280:CT]

[1] At lunch at Hyde Park on Friday, September 7, with Mme. Flandin and Senator McAdoo of California (PPF 1-0). McAdoo had recently returned from Europe; see Bowers to Roosevelt, Sept. 19, 1934, below.

Cordell Hull, Secretary of State, to Roosevelt

Washington, September 18, 1934

My dear Mr. President: I enclose herewith copy of a telegram from Ambassador Grew in Japan reporting that Hirota had told him yesterday that Japan had definitely decided to give notice before December 31, 1934, to terminate the Washington Naval Treaty.[1]

I have sent a paraphrase of this to Norman Davis and another to the Secretary of the Navy emphasizing its strictly confidential nature and the importance of preventing any leak from American sources before the negotiations scheduled to be held in London in mid-October.

Faithfully yours,

Cordell Hull

[PSF:London Naval Conference:TS]

[1] Grew's telegram of Sept. 18, 1934, is published (in paraphrase) in *Foreign Relations, Japan, 1931–1941,* I, 253–254.

Claude G. Bowers, Ambassador to Spain, to Roosevelt

Madrid, September 19, 1934

Personal and Confidential

Dear Mr. President: When I was at San Sebastian taking a short vacation McAdoo came down from Paris and spent four days with me.[1] I notice that on his return he called upon you[2] and you may need no report on his present outlook and plans. However, on the theory that he may not have talked frankly, it may not be amiss to give you my impressions. He was on the whole quite favorable but his critical faculty, which is well known, was as active as usual. Naturally he could have done some things better. But he was on the war path about the debts and says that this winter he proposes to make a speech or two upon them. I found him almost as bitter against the British as against the French, and he talked a bit wildly about inviting Britain to turn over to us her western world possessions and even implied that in his speech he may talk about Canada. He was especially critical in reference to the removal of the naval base from Halifax to Bermuda where he says powerful fortifications are being built. "Any other country in the world under similar circumstances," he said, "would stiffly interrogate London as to its intentions." I thought you ought to know.

The atmosphere for negotiations with Spain is ideal and Spain actually is giving us more concessions than she has given any other country just now. The Government here is enormously pleased with our agree-

217

ment to get together.[3] The announcement of the negotiations was made here yesterday in accordance with an agreement in Washington. In the afternoon Pita Romero called me on the phone with a request to see me and I saw him at seven. He was much distressed by news just received that three shipments of olives, one to New York, one to New Orleans and one to Chicago had been held up on orders of our Agricultural Department on a sanitary ground with which I am familiar. The thing came up once before and apparently was settled. It merely is a new stiffer rule than has been enforced previously and I quite agree with Romero that it is most unfortunate that the Agricultural Department should select this particular moment for its action. I assume, as has happened before, the Agricultural Department acted without informing the State Department of its intention. I hope that pending the negotiations it can be persuaded that it should consult the State Department before taking steps that cannot but complicate our negotiations in Washington.

Politically, things are interesting here. The Cortes meets on October 1st. I understand that Gil Robles of the Catholic party will force a political debate and withdraw his confidence from the Samper Ministry. It will fall, and it will have no mourners. Samper[4] has both the features and the brain of a frog. It is the plan to then place Lerreux[5] back in with a Ministry composed mostly of members of Robles party and the Agrarians—the reactionaries. Just what will happen then is on the lap of the gods.

Lerreux is old and many think in his dotage. The Lefts pretend to believe he has sold out the Republic for the job. He has lots of charm, and has been a clever politician, but his reputation has not been good for many years. He would make an excellent subject for a satirical biographer not prone to look too closely at the gossip used for source purposes. One story which appears to be true is that he made a tour of South America some years ago raising money for "the republican movement in Spain." He raised the money, returned and bought himself a palace in Madrid.

Another amusing story, said to be true is this: A prominent physician here wrote an article in the newspapers charging him with some financial dishonesty. Lerreux with pen and ink wrote a denial addressed to the doctor, saying that now he hoped the physician would make a correction. The doctor replied that he had not mistaken the fact, that he had documentary proof and would publish it also if Lerreux insisted. Then he added: "I note by your handwriting that you are suffering from a certain disease and are in serious need of immediate medical treatment. I would advise you to consult a doctor." To which Lerreux replied: "You are quite right about my physical condition. Will you take my case?"

The physician took the case!

Congratulations on your comment on the Liberty League.[6] "Short horse soon curried." And on the results in Maine. Amazing! Also on Hoover's attacks. That man has no friends or a friend would whisper to him that he has none—if you will excuse an Irish bull. Newspaper men who write me, and some who are here fresh from America, tell me that your health is almost indecently good. I had Clark Howells with me two days and enjoyed him.[7]

Sincerely,

Claude G. Bowers

[PPF 730:TS]

[1] McAdoo sailed for Europe on August 4 and returned on September 4 (New York *Times*, Aug. 5, p. 15; Sept. 5, 1934, p. 3).

[2] For lunch at Hyde Park on Sept. 7, 1934 (PPF 1-0).

[3] An agreement to begin negotiations for a reciprocal trade agreement, arrived at by an exchange of notes on Sept. 6, 1934 (*Foreign Relations, 1934*, II, 706, 707).

[4] Ricardo Samper Ibáñez.

[5] Alejandro Lerroux. Bowers' eccentric spelling has been followed throughout.

[6] At his press conference Roosevelt said the Liberty League paid little attention to the obligation of the government to help the unemployed, to aid people in keeping their homes, to provide education, and to protect the individual against those who sought to enrich themselves at the expense of others. The remark was reported in the New York *Times* of Aug. 25, 1934 (p. 1) and presumably was what Bowers here referred to.

[7] Answered Oct. 6, 1934, below.

Stephen Duggan, Director, Institute of International Education, Inc., to Roosevelt

New York City, September 19, 1934

My dear Mr. President: I have recently returned from a nine months' visit to Europe, paying special attention to such dictatorship countries as Germany and Russia. I saw Messrs. Dodd and Bullitt and several of our consuls-general.[1] Moreover, I had many conversations with both official and non-official persons of influence in the different countries. When I wrote to you from Stuttgart you answered to the effect that upon my return you would like me to give you my observations and conclusions, particularly about Germany and Russia.[2] If you still wish me to do so, I shall be glad to await your convenience. If you are too busy, simply say so.

Sincerely yours,

Stephen Duggan

[*Notation*:A:LeHand] Mac   Give him a date to come down to Wash. sometime in October   FDR[3]

[PPF 1404:TS]

[1] See Dodd, *Diary,* for March 12, 1934, p. 92.
[2] March 9 and 26, 1934 (PPF 1404).
[3] Duggan saw the President on October 4 (PPF 1-0).

Roosevelt to Hugh Gibson, Ambassador to Brazil, Rio de Janeiro

Hyde Park, N.Y., September 20, 1934

Dear Hugh: I am delighted to know about Doctor Aranha and I am looking forward to receiving him when I get back to Washington.[1]

I hope all goes well with you both.

Always sincerely,

[OF 405:CT]

[1] See Gibson's letter of Sept. 4, 1934, above.

Roosevelt to Matthew Woll, Vice-President, American Federation of Labor, New York

Hyde Park, N.Y., September 24, 1934

Personal

Dear Matt Woll: This is only a letter to "kid" you! I saw the other day that you had said that the Cuban Trade Agreement was of no benefit whatever to American labor, but only to "international bankers and to owners of sugar and tobacco lands."

I have received the following extracts from reports of the American Commercial Attaché at Havana:

During the six actual working days from noon, September 1, until midnight, September 9, 18,797 short tons of American products arrived in Habana for entry into the country. This tonnage is one of the highest on record and is due almost entirely to the favorable tariff changes on American products included in the Reciprocal Trade Agreement which became effective on September 3. It is important to remember that this tonnage does not include the large stocks of American merchandise in Cuban warehouses ready for entry through the customs on September 3.

The tonnage of 18,797 was brought into Cuba by 24 American-owned steamships. The merchandise consisted of 5,329 short tons of coal, hog lard, edible and inedible oils, wheat flour, meats, potatoes, canned fruits and vegetables, canned fish, fruits, feedstuffs, salt, cotton goods, dry goods, rayon fabrics, iron and steel products, chemicals, pharmaceutical preparations, cosmetics, toothbrushes, paper, cardboard, paints, hardware, electrical equipment, automobiles, automobile tires, bricks, bottles, agricultural implements, machinery, specialties, glassware, refrigerators, motion picture films, cigarettes, radios, leather, office equipment, toys, canvas rubber footwear, tanned hides, lumber and petroleum products.

It is expected that approximately 4,000,000 pounds of hog lard will be imported into Cuba during the month of September. Since total imports of this product during 1933 amounted to only 9,873,000 pounds, a monthly average of approximately 822,750 pounds, the effect of the trade agreement in increasing lard importations is apparent.[1]

Do not get yourself out on a limb like that again!
Very sincerely yours,

[OF 66:CT]

[1] This information was sent to Roosevelt by Welles in a letter of Sept. 19, 1934 (OF 66). Welles said he had given the figures to the press "in view of recent speeches by some of our Republican friends and notably one made the day before yesterday by Matthew Woll, in which the latter said that the Cuban Trade Agreement was of no benefit whatever to American labor, but only to 'international bankers, and to owners of sugar and tobacco lands.'" The trade agreement with Cuba had become effective Sept. 3, 1934.

Roosevelt to Philippe Bunau-Varilla, Paris

Hyde Park, N.Y., September 25, 1934

Dear Colonel: I am delighted to have your letter with its interesting pamphlet which Ambassador Bullitt has forwarded to me,[1] and even if you and I do not live to see the day, I am confident that somebody will take up the sea level possibility in the future.

If there is any chance of your coming over here this winter I hope you will be sure to let me know.

Very sincerely yours,

[OF 25-I:CT]

[1] Sept. 1, 1934, above.

Roosevelt to Cordell Hull, Secretary of State

Hyde Park, N.Y., September 25, 1934

Memorandum for the Secretary of State: This matter of neutral rights is of such importance that I wish you and Phillips and Judge Moore would discuss the whole subject and let me know if you think I should recommend legislation to the coming session of Congress.

F.D.R.

[*Notation*:T] Memorandum from State Department, 8/21/34, on memorandum of Charles Warren, relative to Neutrality.[1]

[OF 1561:CT]

[1] See Moore to Roosevelt, Aug. 27, 1934, above.

Roosevelt to Nicholas Murray Butler, President, Columbia University, New York

[Washington] September 26, 1934

Personal

Dear Doctor Butler: I fear I agree with that important personage in Europe.[1] I am making it very clear that the United States definitely seeks additional Naval reductions and at the least a renewal of existing treaties. Equally definitely we must oppose any increases by any powers. At least this policy is clearly understood by everybody.

Nevertheless, I am concerned, especially because I am not certain of the cooperation which we *ought* to get from our friends the British.

You and I will continue to preach peace and to live up to our preachings, but I sometimes think that we are sowing seed in exceedingly rocky gound—at least for the moment.

Always sincerely,

[PPF 445:CT]

[1] Writing to Roosevelt Sept. 25, 1934 (PPF 445), Butler quoted from a letter he had just received from "a most important personage in Europe": "I am not very happy about the way the Naval discussions are going. If they are properly handled they create a great opportunity, but if they are bungled there will be the devil to pay." The "important personage" is not identified; however, Butler was at this time corresponding with John Buchan, Baron Tweedsmuir (later Governor General of Canada), concerning his visit to the United States to dedicate the Harkness Library at Columbia.

Press Conference, Executive Offices of the White House, September 28, 1934, 4:15 P.M.

[*Excerpt*] Q: Mr. President, have you taken up with anyone yet the note from China protesting our monetary policy?[1]

The President: I am going to see Secretary Morgenthau and Secretary Hull about it in the course of the next two or three days.

Q: We understand the communication which the Chinese Government has sent us complains that our silver policy is having a detrimental effect on the internal economic situation there. That is, it is making it more difficult for them to send their silver abroad. Was that anticipated by us?

The President: By Congress?

Q: Yes.

The President: I do not know. I have not seen the note yet.

Q: I thought the general impression prevailed here that it would be helpful to rather than hurt China?[2]

The President: There are three different schools of thought and they are probably all wrong. In other words, it is one of those things where one man's guess is as good as another . . .

Q: Have you seen Norman Davis on naval disarmament yet?

The President: I talked with him yesterday and he is coming—I do not know if he is coming back today or next—he is coming down next Tuesday or Wednesday for a final talk before he goes abroad. He is sailing on the eighth or tenth on the *Manhattan*.[3]

Q: Is it pretty well worked out now?

The President: Oh, yes.

Q: Can you tell us anything about the general aspects?

The President: Again, in this Naval Conference, we will pursue exactly the same methods we pursued heretofore when Davis first went over to the other side. There won't be any announcement from here of any kind and any announcement will be made by the American delegation over there—it is not really a delegation—the American conferees—because this is not the conference itself. It is merely a perfunctory and informal meeting of the conferees of the three powers.

Q: Any statement contemplated this far in advance? It will depend on what the conferees have to say?

The President: Everybody has the say.

Q: Will it be announced here as to who the conferees are to be?

The President: Yes.

Q: Will that be ready this week end?

The President: Probably not until next Wednesday.

[President's Press Conferences:T]

[1] Passage of the Silver Purchase Act of June 19, 1934 (48 *Stat.* 1178), and the fixing of the price of silver at fifty cents an ounce on Aug. 9, 1934 (*Public Papers,* III, 378–381), accelerated the flow of silver from China and brought protests from Finance Minister H. H. Kung. In Kung's note to Hull of September 24, 1934, here referred to, Kung said that a further material silver price increase would cause serious injury to China (*Foreign Relations, 1934,* III, 442–443).

[2] The silver bloc's argument had been that higher silver prices would enhance China's purchasing power.

[3] Davis was at the White House on October 4 and sailed for Europe on October 10.

Roosevelt to Cordell Hull, Secretary of State, Henry A. Wallace, Secretary of Agriculture, and Daniel C. Roper, Secretary of Commerce

Washington, October 1, 1934

Personal & Confidential

Memorandum . . . Professor Rogers of Yale has completed his mission for the Treasury Department to China and the Far East, and is making his final report.[1]

I suggest that as he has returned to his duties at Yale, you and the officers of your Department should not show him any further dispatches or consult him without first taking the matter up with me.

F.D.R.

[PPF 3038:CT]

[1] James Harvey Rogers, the Yale economist, had informed Morgenthau from Shanghai on April 21 that any considerable rise in silver prices would further depress agricultural prices in China and would have serious political effects (*Foreign Relations, 1934*, III, 432). His report was not made public.

Press Conference, Executive Offices of the White House, October 5, 1934, 4:15 P.M.

[*Excerpt*] Q: As a result of your conversations with Ambassador Davis are you at all optimistic as to any possibility of achieving disarmament?

The President: That was close to an "if" question. (Laughter)

Q: I wonder if we will concentrate on limitation rather than actual disarmament.

The President: I don't think you had better concentrate on anything. In other words, as I have said before—this part has to be off the record—we are very, very sincere in hoping that we are going to get a new Naval treaty next year. The more that is said by Government officials and the more that is said by the Press at this time, the more difficult, frankly, it becomes for these conferees—I suppose they should be called "conversationalists" rather than conferees—the more difficult it becomes for them to come to an agreement. That is why I am trying to say nothing about it and I hope very much that you good people won't do too much guessing or stating that our delegation is going to do this or that. What we are trying to do is to get an agreement and the less we talk about it, the more chance we have to encourage a reduction in Naval armaments.

It is not much of a secret that we are seeking to carry out the language of the Washington Treaty, the preamble of the London Treaty that has the whereas clauses in it that state as the objective of all of these conferences a progressive reduction in Naval armaments as being a very great contribution to modern civilization. I think it is worth noting that the Washington Treaty of 1922 was the very first voluntary step that nations took towards limitation or reduction of armaments. Previous steps such

225

as the Versailles Treaty could not properly be called a voluntary step. The disarmament of the Versailles Treaty was felt to be imposed by a number of the nations concerned.

What we are trying to do is to carry out the spirit of the previous conferences and seek a continuation of progressive reduction. I don't think it is possible to go any further than that without making it difficult, more difficult for the British delegates, the Japanese delegates and the American delegates—they are not delegates, that is the wrong word to use—to sit in a friendly way around the table and get somewhere. Of course things are not in the least bit helped—this is off the record entirely—by the kind of statement that was made by our old friend Billy Mitchell the other day at that hearing.[1] Billy Mitchell would be a much more useful person to this country if he would not talk that way.

Q: Do you not personally think that we would have to give a little way on such things as our existing ratios if we hope to get the Japs to agree to anything?

The President: That is entirely speculative.

Q: We are not taking an adamant stand on that?

The President: I think the only way you can put it, the only thing I can say that is truthful, is that we are trying to carry out the objectives and purposes we have been seeking since 1922. I cannot go any further than that . . .

Q: Referring to the TVA again, is there any intention of divorcing the power venture of the St. Lawrence Treaty from navigation in order to get the treaty through at the coming Session?

The President: No.

Q: The treaty will be submitted in the same form?

The President: It ties together. I will have to make the rest of the answer off the record because we haven't, as far as I know, said anything to Canada about it at the present time. It is possible we might talk with Canada about certain rather minor modifications of the treaty as it was submitted last year to the Senate but the general principle will remain. You will remember the one question raised about American workmen on the American operation of the project. That is a thing that can be cleared up very easily. I have said that before so you can make it background.

Q: The Chicago diversion is a point there; have you considered that matter?

The President: Yes. I have considered it quite finally some time ago . . .

Q: Is there anything you can say as to how this country might mitigate the effects of its silver program on China?

The President: I cannot talk about that. The Secretary of State has talked to the Chinese Minister. What the status of those conversations is I don't know.[2]

[President's Press Conferences:T]

[1] General William A. Mitchell, former assistant chief of the Army Air Corps, had testified on October 2 before the Federal Aviation Commission against a War Department proposal to reorganize the Air Corps. He said Air Corps planes were so antiquated that the United States was vulnerable to air attack by Japan (New York *Times*, Oct. 3, 1934, p. 4). In 1925 General Mitchell had been convicted of insubordination by court-martial for expressing similar views of the state of the nation's air defenses.

[2] Hull's memorandum of his talk with Dr. Sze on October 2 is printed in *Foreign Relations, 1934,* III, 443–445. Hull rejected as impracticable Finance Minister Kung's proposal of Sept. 24, 1934 (*ibid.,* pp. 442–443), that China exchange gold for United States silver and adopt a gold standard. To Sze's proposal that the United States restrict for a time its silver purchases to silver produced within the United States, Hull replied that this would be barred by the Silver Purchase Act. Roosevelt, Morgenthau, and Hull had met at the White House on October 1 and had discussed means of making required silver purchases without disrupting China's economy (New York *Times,* Oct. 2, 1934, p. 38).

On October 15, the Chinese government placed a tax on silver exports but reserved the right to export silver through the Central Bank of China without duty. Bernard Baruch told Roosevelt that this move was exactly what he and the President had concluded would follow when they had "discussed" the silver situation (memorandum by Baruch, Oct. 15, 1934, PPF 1820). It is not known when this discussion took place but in the memorandum Baruch said that they had agreed that after the United States had bought about 10 per cent (presumably of the available world supply), the other nations would suggest a world agreement: "If this country could acquire about two billion ounces of silver together with its seven billion gold dollars, we would be in a position to work out an international agreement affecting money, tariffs or related subjects, in our own time and manner."

Roosevelt to Norman H. Davis, New York

[Washington] October 5, 1934

My dear Mr. Davis: In asking you to return to London to continue and expand the conversations begun last June preparatory to the Naval Conference in 1935, I am fully aware of the gravity of the problems before you and your British and Japanese colleagues. The object of next year's Conference is "to frame a new Treaty to replace and carry out the purposes of the present Treaty." The purposes themselves are "to prevent the dangers and to reduce the burdens inherent in competitive armament" and "to carry forward the work begun by the Washington Naval Conference and to facilitate progressive realization of general limitation and reduction of armament."

The Washington Naval Conference of 1922 brought to the world the first important voluntary agreement for limitation and reduction of armament. It stands out as a mile-stone in civilization.

It was supplemented by the London Naval Treaty of 1930, which recognized the underlying thought that the good work begun should be progressive—in other words, that further limitation and reduction should be sought.

Today the United States adheres to that goal. That must be our first consideration.

The Washington and London Conferences were not mere mathematical formulae. The limitations fixed on the relative Naval Forces were based on the comparative defensive needs of the Powers concerned; they did not involve the sacrifice of any vital interests on the part of their participants; they left the relative security of the great Naval Powers unimpaired.

The abandonment of these Treaties would throw the principle of relative security wholly out of balance; it would result in competitive Naval building, the consequence of which no one can foretell.

I ask you, therefore, at the first opportunity to propose to the British and Japanese a substantial proportional reduction in the present Naval levels. I suggest a total tonnage reduction of twenty per cent below existing Treaty tonnage. If it is not possible to agree on this percentage, please seek from the British and Japanese a lesser reduction—fifteen per cent or ten per cent or five per cent. The United States must adhere to the high purpose of progressive reduction. It will be a heartening thing to the people of the world if you and your colleagues can attain this end.

Only if all else fails should you seek to secure agreement providing for the maintenance and extension of existing Treaties over as long a period as possible.

I am compelled to make one other point clear. I cannot approve, nor would I be willing to submit to the Senate of the United States any new Treaty calling for larger Navies. Governments impelled by common sense and the good of humanity ought to seek Treaties reducing armaments; they have no right to seek Treaties increasing armaments.

Excessive armaments are in themselves conducive to those fears and suspicions which breed war. Competition in armament is a still greater menace. The world would rightly reproach Great Britain, Japan and the United States if we moved against the current of progressive thought.

We three Nations, the principal Naval Powers, have nothing to fear from one another. We cannot escape our responsibilities, joint and several, for world peace and recovery.

I am convinced that if the basic principle of continued naval limitation with progressive reduction can be adhered to this year and next, the technicalities of ship tonnage, of ship classes, of gun calibers and of other weapons, can be solved by friendly conference. I earnestly hope that France and Italy, which are full parties to the Washington Treaty, will see their way to participate fully in our efforts to achieve further naval limitation and reduction.

The important matter to keep constantly before your eyes is the principle of reduction—the maintenance of one of the greatest achievements of friendly relations between Nations.[1]

Sincerely yours,

[PSF:London Naval Conference:CT]

[1] Davis submitted a draft letter of instruction to himself in a note to Roosevelt of Oct. 1, 1934 (with the letter here printed). Davis said his draft was along the lines they had discussed, presumably on September 27 when he and Hull were at the White House (PPF 1-0). Davis also said it might require some polishing but he was sending it along so the President could read it before they met on October 3. On that day Davis, Hull, and Admiral Standley, chief naval representative of the American delegation, were at the White House from 3 to 3:30 P.M. (PPF 1-0). The President used but a few sentences from Davis' draft in his own draft (also present), and the letter as sent was further extensively revised. The next to last sentence, "I earnestly hope . . .," was at the last minute suggested by Davis and inserted by Hull. Hull asked Roosevelt's approval in a note to him of Oct. 5, 1934 (PSF:London Naval Conference); this note bears the notation, in the President's hand: "OK FDR." The letter as here printed is quoted in Hull's dispatch to Bingham of Nov. 30, 1934 (*Foreign Relations, Japan, 1931–1941,* I, 281–284).

Roosevelt to Allen W. Dulles, New York

[Washington, October 5, 1934]

Dear Allen: Norman Davis informed you of my desire and hope to get you to go to London with him in a technical advisory capacity during the preparatory naval conversations. He has shown me your telegram to the effect that in view of your present professional obligations and of some of the difficulties and complications which have arisen with regard to your going to London you prefer that consideration of this matter be dropped. While I regret very much that circumstances have been such as to lead to this conclusion, I fully appreciate the spirit that has animated you and I hope very much that the Government may be able later on to avail itself again of your services which have in the past been so satisfactory and valuable.[1]

Very sincerely yours,

[OF 29:CT]

[1] This letter was drafted by Norman Davis. Dulles replied Oct. 19, 1934 (OF 29), that it was a "real satisfaction" to know that his services in the past had been considered of some value and that his motives for not wishing to go to London were understood.

Roosevelt to Claude G. Bowers, Ambassador to Spain, Madrid

[Washington] October 6, 1934

Dear Claude: It is fine to get yours of September nineteenth.[1] I have seen McAdoo since his return and I do hope that he will try to keep both feet on the ground during the next session. If he would only play with the team it would be best for him, as well as for the team.

I envy you Spain. I wish I could get on a cruiser next summer and visit you and North Africa and Egypt and Greece. The trouble is that I would have to go to Italy and France and England too and that would be a useless performance.

I am delighted with everything I hear about your stewardship. Keep up the good work.

As ever yours,

[PPF 730:CT]

[1] Above.

Roosevelt to Cordell Hull, Secretary of State

Washington, October 8, 1934

Private and confidential memorandum for the Secretary of State: Do you think it would be a terrible thing to send this man as Minister either to Ireland or Albania?

I really think we should help Ickes.[1]

[OF 20:T]

[1] This memorandum refers to one of the aides of Secretary Ickes with whom Ickes was not getting along.

Nicholas Murray Butler, President, Columbia University, to Roosevelt

New York City, October 9, 1934

My dear Mr. President: At a time like this I do not wish to trouble you unduly with my reflections and suggestions, but I am so much concerned at what seems to me the increasing dangers of the world situation that I wish to put before you a suggestion upon which I have reflected long and earnestly, and which I have discussed with some of the leading personalities in Europe. These men have uniformly thought well of it. It is this:

The surest and most certain path to the assurance of international peace is that the Governments of the United States and of the British Commonwealth of Nations should quickly unite in this declaration:

We reaffirm the solemn obligation which we took upon ourselves seven years ago when we ratified the Pact of Paris, under the terms of which we renounced war as an instrument of our national policy. Should any other power signatory to that Pact violate it for any reason whatsoever, we shall have no relations with that power while its act of violation continues. We appeal to every other power signatory to the Pact of Paris to join us in this declaration.

It is my considered judgment that if this be done, public confidence will be restored throughout the world, international trade will begin to be rebuilt and the problem of disarmament will solve itself in due time to our reasonable satisfaction.[1]

With highest regard and every good wish, I am, Sincerely yours,

Nicholas Murray Butler

[PPF 445:TS]

[1] Answered Oct. 16, 1934, below.

Roosevelt to Chester C. Davis, Administrator, Agricultural Adjustment Administration

[Washington] October 10, 1934

Personal and Confidential

Dear Chester: Do you think perhaps you could strengthen the Foreign Trade Division or whatever you call it? I am very anxious to get expeditious work on all Foreign Trade suggestions.

I am enclosing for your eyes only the memorandum which I asked George Peek to give me after he told me about what he considers a somewhat long delay.[1]

Very sincerely yours,

[OF 1-K:CT]

[1] Peek's memorandum apparently was not returned by Davis. A letter from Davis to Roosevelt, Oct. 26, 1934 (OF 971), possibly relates to the letter here printed. In this Davis suggested that before the Export-Import Bank referred proposed projects to the Agricultural Adjustment Administration for review and approval, the projects should be "subjected to a careful economic analysis and report." He described in detail the work done on a recent project having to do with a proposed exchange of American cotton for Italian silk that had finally been disapproved by his agency.

Breckinridge Long, Ambassador to Italy, to Roosevelt

Rome, October 12, 1934

My dear Chief: Italian economic policy is operating against the interests of the United States. A week ago I finished and sent in the report on their imports, exports, and trade policies. The week before I sent in a resumé of the situation, which was not very encouraging in tone.[1] I address you now because I think it is a matter of high policy. I would delay taking up the subject until my return, but I have had to postpone my departure once and it looks as if I would have to postpone it again. The assassinations at Marseilles have unsettled conditions here to such an extent that I will not be able to tell until the eve of my intended departure whether I ought to leave.[2] Consequently I am writing you directly in order to present to you and to those whom you may consult in connection with it the rather serious aspects of the loss of export trade to Italy.

The principal export crop from America to Italy is cotton. It forms 60% of the total of Italian purchases from the United States.

Their trade balance is so heavy against them as far as we are concerned and their supply of gold so small that they have been forced to take drastic measures to restrict purchases. Naturally their principal objective is toward their largest item of trade—cotton.

The Italians have bent every scientific effort to find a substitute for cotton. They have discovered and are making in quantities a material which is reported to be so similar to cotton that the eye has difficulty in detecting it at comparatively short range. Whether it will serve the purpose or not remains to be seen.

In addition to that they are extending the planting of cotton in their East African colonies. They will probably raise there a cotton similar to the Egyptian cotton, which is not as serviceable for some purposes as our cotton and consequently may not prevent their purchases of our cotton. But it may serve to cut down considerable quantities of purchases from us.

However, if they have found a substitute which is passably as good for many purposes as American cotton, it is certain to make an enormous difference in their purchases.

They used to buy enormous quantities of wheat from us. Now they buy practically none, largely for the reason that they have stimulated the production of wheat in Italy to an extent which makes them 80% self-supporting.

They are following the same line of policy as regards cotton, and I am very fearful that next year will see an enormous falling off in their purchases of cotton from America. From confidential sources I have been advised that the principal cause for the loss of gold in Italy has been the purchase of cotton futures. For some reason unknown to me they have determined that the time is ripe to purchase large quantities of American cotton for future use and have transferred gold to effect the purchase. The next statement of the Bank of Italy, which will be due five days from now, will report a period which is already closed and which, according to my information, will show a distinct further loss in gold, and my information is that that loss too is accounted for by purchases of cotton futures.

If they have bought so much cotton for future delivery, they will not be buying it next year. They will be very apt to place an embargo upon cotton and to use the supplies which they have already purchased to mix with the substitute which they think they have discovered and to run them along with the produce of their East African colonies and eliminate the largest item on their adverse balance of trade with America. I am afraid it is a real danger. If it should happen, it will affect enormously the price of cotton and the situation of our southern planters to say nothing of its general effect upon the efforts we are making at recovery.

I am sending our Commercial Attaché on a mission leaving Rome this afternoon and to be gone about a week with the hope and expectation that he will be able to get samples of this substitute and certain specimens of cloth which they have made from it. The process of course is guarded very carefully and the fact that they have such a thing is more or less of a state secret. But the bits of information which I have been able to pick up leads me to believe definitely that they have discovered something which to their minds is partially satisfactory as a substitute.

Taking it all in all and considering the economic consequences of the Hoover tariff law—as regards not only Italy but all of the European countries and its unfortunate effect upon us and its large contribution as a factor to the development of the crisis—considering that it makes it increasingly difficult for all of these countries to sell their agricultural products in America such as olive oil and lemons and various other things—considering also the fact that the diminution of the gold content of the dollar added 40% to that tariff as far as the exports from these countries are concerned—considering all this and the entire picture and the real probability that Italy will take some definite stand in connection with her cotton imports, I am venturing to call to your attention as a matter of high policy the question as to whether it would be worth while to make a beau geste to Italy now by reducing to an appreciable extent the tariff in America on certain goods coming from Italy, for instance, such as olive oil, lemons, and cheese.

I make the suggestion for this very substantial reason: If Italy has arrived at a method of making cloth without the use of a large percentage of American cotton, it will mean that she not only will not buy American cotton next year but that she will continue the policy not to buy American cotton—so that we will have lost permanently one of our very best customers for one of our very greatest products.

Whether a beau geste would stop it is another matter. We cannot be supplicants to Italy in matters of trade. They apparently are disinclined to bargain with us. Whether the reduction of tariff on some of their most important products would change their frame of mind to the point of view of inducing them to continue their purchases of cotton is debatable. But I see no alternative except just to sit complacently by and watch the thing develop. This I would not like to recommend, because I am afraid it will develop adversely to our interests. I am really very much concerned over the prospect, and so I bring it most seriously to your attention.

I am not following the orthodox method of submitting this in the form of a despatch to the Department of State for the reasons which I have intimated above. Moreover I feel that if a gesture is to be made, it ought to be done quickly before they realize that we know that they have in contemplation a step which would be so antagonistic to our interests. If there is a beau geste, it ought to be done quickly. Otherwise it would not be a beau geste.

With apologies for the length of this for which my only excuse is the importance I attach to it, I am, as always,

Sincerely and affectionately,

Breckinridge Long[3]

[OF 447:TS]

[1] The resumé is printed in *Foreign Relations, 1934,* II, 589–593; see also related correspondence, *ibid.,* pp. 584–589, 593–597.

[2] King Alexander of Yugoslavia and French Foreign Minister Louis Barthou were assassinated in Marseilles on October 9. The French had hoped to effect a reconciliation between Yugoslavia and Italy and to concert the policies of the three countries. Long sailed from Naples on October 30 (New York *Times,* Oct. 31, 1934, p. 22).

[3] Answered Oct. 25, 1934, below.

Roosevelt to Robert E. Wood, President, Sears, Roebuck and Company, Chicago

[Washington] October 15, 1934

Dear General Wood: Many thanks for your note.[1] Things depend, of course, a good deal on the actions of foreign nations in the next few months.

I hope to see you when you next come to Washington.

Very sincerely yours,

[PPF 1365:CT]

[1] In his letter of Oct. 11, 1934 (PPF 1365), Wood said that he had never lost faith in the money policy stated by Roosevelt at the time of the London Economic Conference; he felt that the devaluation of the dollar and the rise in the price of gold to $35 was largely responsible for the progress made toward recovery. He urged Roosevelt to raise the price to the limit permitted, $41, and to announce at the time that there would be no further devaluation unless the action of foreign nations forced it.

Roosevelt to Nicholas Murray Butler, President, Columbia University, New York

[Washington, October 16, 1934]

My dear President Butler: I have received with appreciation your letter of October 9,[1] in which you suggest that if the Governments of the United States and of the British Commonwealth of Nations should unite in a solemn declaration re-affirming the obligations they assumed under the Pact of Paris and announcing a policy of abstaining from all relations with any Powers that violated the Pact during such time as its act of violation continued, it would constitute an immediate and constructive step in the direction of peace. I shall give your thought careful consideration and I shall likewise ask the Secretary of State to undertake a detailed study. Meanwhile, I wish to express to you my very real thanks for your helpful suggestion and remain,

Sincerely yours,

WE:PM:VAS[2]
[PPF 445:CT]

[1] Above.
[2] Drafted by J. Pierrepont Moffat, chief of the Division of Western European Affairs of the State Department.

Press Conference, Executive Offices of the White House, October 17, 1934, 10:30 A.M.

[*Excerpt*] Q: Mr. President, there was a story appeared in the paper this morning that a letter has been delivered to the State Department and also to you, requesting the recall of Ambassador Daniels in Mexico because of a speech he made down there last July?[1]

The President: What has he done?

Q: He is supposed to have endorsed the Mexican policy of closing the churches and—

The President: No, I never heard of it. It sounds fishy to me. You had better ask the State Department . . .

Q: Can you tell us anything with respect to relaxation of foreign exchange restrictions?

The President: What kind of foreign exchange restrictions?

Q: That is general relaxation of the general restrictions which confine the purchase of exchange to commercial transactions and tourists.

The President: Is the Montreal silver market interested? (Laughter)

Q: There have been stories—I think the U.P. carried the story.

[President's Press Conferences:T]

[1] No such letter has been found in the Roosevelt papers. A speech made by Daniels on July 27, 1934, was interpreted as endorsing the Mexican government's program for the removal of the Church from all educational activities. The only mention of this matter in the New York *Times* (Oct. 18, 1934, p. 20) was that the protests of Catholic organizations in the United States had caused Phillips to secure a statement from Daniels over the telephone; in his statement Daniels denied having referred to the issue.

Norman H. Davis, Chairman, American Delegation, London Naval Conference, to Roosevelt

London, October 23, 1934

Dear Mr. President: Enclosed you will find a cartoon by Low, which I am sure you will find amusing.[1] I am also enclosing the leading editorial in the *Times* today, on the naval conversations.[2] This was evidently inspired by the British Government and shows the tack they are taking at present. We can not tell, however, for some days yet just which way the wind is blowing.

Simon told me that he would be quite surprised if the Japanese seriously intended to denounce the Washington Treaty and that he did not believe they would do so unless they were unable to get at least a face saving agreement for a renewal of the existing Treaties.

So far we have had only perfunctory exchanges of visits with the Japanese, but we will probably get down to business with them tomorrow, after which we can tell better whether they will be satisfied with minor changes or whether they are determined to alter fundamentals. If it is the latter then it is not a naval question but a purely political one which will confront us. I hope that we will know within a few days.

With warm personal regards, I am, Faithfully yours,

Norman H. Davis

[PSF:London Naval Conference:TS]

[1] The cartoon by David Low, from the London *Evening Standard* of Oct. 22, 1934, shows three very fat admirals labeled "Jap Parity," "British Demands," and "U.S. Demands" about to embark in a diminutive dinghy named "Fat Hopes."

[2] The editorial said, in part, that, "It would be folly for any Government to take up a completely rigid attitude at the outset of these conversations since all three are sincerely desirous of reaching a limitation agreement; and it may be supposed that the British Government will not be likely to insist too strongly on the form of the ratio so long as in practice relative programmes suitable to the defence needs of each country can be arranged and maintained for a period of years."

Robert P. Skinner, Ambassador to Turkey, to Roosevelt

Istanbul, Turkey, October 23, 1934

Personal and Confidential

Dear Mr. President: Almost the last remark you made to me when I saw you in Washington one year ago, or thereabouts, was to ask that I write you privately my impressions of the Gazi, Mustapha Kemal. I have put off doing so from day to day, knowing that you had many more important things to read, but as my esteemed predecessor has now told me that he intends writing another book, one that is to be in the Plutarchian style, drawing a parallel between you and the Gazi, it seems high time that I break my silence. I can think of no one in a prominent station in the whole world so little like yourself as Mustapha Kemal, and if I were writing the book instead of my friend Sherrill, instead of drawing a parallel I should draw my lines at right angles, as the only meeting point is in the fact that both are presidents.[1]

That is not to say that Mustapha Kemal is not a remarkable man —anyone who runs a considerable country successfully for eleven years, and at the same time wastes his physical resources as he does, is, in more ways than one, a remarkable man. There are as many stories afloat about him as there used to be about President Coolidge, some true, some apocryphal—and very few indeed Sunday school stories!

When the Shah of Persia visited Ankara, on two nights in succession, and after long days spent in reviewing troops and what-not, the Gazi went into poker games that lasted from midnight until nine o'clock the next morning on one occasion, and ten o'clock on another, and the one man who emerged from these games fresh and well disposed was our President.

To illustrate his almost uncanny hold upon the people, who try to anticipate his lightest wishes, let me mention that when he came to Istanbul this summer, he liked going with his cronies to the Park Hotel to watch the dancing and the attractive girls. One evening, having heard the muezzin in a near-by minaret call the faithful to prayer, he made some not too complimentary remarks about muezzins, minarets, and prayer. That was all. The next time he appeared at the Park Hotel, which was within a few days, the offending minaret had disappeared. His worshippers had had it demolished. It was a very nice minaret.

There is much honesty in his make-up. When I came out here everybody was reading the *Grey Wolf* (a biography of the Gazi),[2] and as its circulation was then prohibited we kept it carefully out of sight. It gives the Gazi credit for many things, and it also tells of his relations with women in the plainest language. It got to the Gazi that there was such a book, and that its circulation had been forbidden, so he procured a copy and had its contents made known to him. Then he called in the proper people and said: "Why have you excluded the book?" "Because it is extremely scandalous, Excellency." "Nonsense," said he, "Does it not say that I am a great man?" "Yes, Excellency." "A great patriot?" "Yes, Excellency." "A winner of battles?" "Yes, Excellency." "That I created the Turkish State?" "Yes, Excellency." "Well, where is the harm in letting the people read all that?" "True, Excellency, but there is much about women." "What of it? These things simply prove that I possess all the qualities of a real Turk." "True, Excellency." "What I did, I did. The book tells the truth. It gives me much credit. Your prohibition is idiotic."

I like the following which indicates that this singular, crude, brilliant at times, ruthless man possesses also a heart. A certain politician who at one time had been close to the Gazi died last winter when I was in Ankara. It was said of him that he had told the Gazi a good many unpleasant truths, in consequence of which their relations had become somewhat strained and they no longer saw each other. A secretary at the presidency knew that this politician had fallen desperately ill, but did not mention the matter to his chief until the poor man was actually dead. Mustapha Kemal inquired: "You knew that———was very low?" "Yes, Excellency." "And you failed to tell me?" "Yes, Excellency. I knew that your relations were not as good as they had been, and I thought it best not to disturb Your Excellency." "Fool. You should have told me at once when you knew that he was about to die. That man and I have been friends. Had I known that he was going to die I should have gone to him at once and I should have held out my hand and have assured him of my affection. Now it is too late."

The particular secretary referred to soon left the presidency.

Nowadays the Gazi takes little exercise, no doubt drinks much more than is good for him, and enjoys hearty food. Probably one day he will pay the penalty of his indiscretions, but today he can work harder and longer than any of his associates, and his appearance indicates an excellent state of health.

But all of the foregoing is by way of leading up to what occurs to me as the great achievement of this man who, born and bred under the Sultans, a witness to the rise of dictatorships in Europe, who might have said: "I am the State, and after me the deluge," yet who decided to found a Republic. Unquestionably the Turkish people, ignorant, poor, illiterate, are not today qualified to operate a democratic state according to our notions; unquestionably today the strong-arm government of Mustapha Kemal is the kind of government that can keep order and get things done; but the Gazi, as I try to read his conceptions, has looked out into the future when he himself shall have passed on, and he has made up his mind while he possesses power to lift up his people, if it can be done, to such a point that it will be possible for them to take over the liberal institutions which he has founded and to continue the orderly administration that he has organized. Therefore, today, every act of government follows the constitutional rule. Let us admit that these acts are practically dictated from the top; nevertheless, the mere carrying on of parliamentary procedure, the mere repetition of a variety of constitutional practices, forges habits not easily shaken off, and in the long run may render possible the full realization of the plan. At least so it looks today. When we take into account the cheap and ill thought-out attacks on democracy now rather popular in Europe (but less so since the executions in Germany) is it not remarkable that it remained for Turkey to say to the world: "We have lived under a dictatorship for a thousand years, we know more about dictatorships than any country in the world. It was an autocratic system that brought ruin to Turkey. We have now resolved to prepare ourselves to live as a republic as more likely to give us peace and happiness than any other known system of government." And they are making quite a success of it.

I must apologize, Mr. President, for venturing to take up your time. I am always, very respectfully and

Sincerely yours,

Robert B. Skinner[3]

[PSF:State:TS]

[1] Skinner refers to Charles H. Sherrill, ambassador to Turkey from 1932 to 1933; see Mussolini to Roosevelt, April 24, 1933, above, n. 1.

[2] Harold C. Armstrong, *Gray Wolf, Mustafa Kemal: an Intimate Study of a Dictator* (New York: Minton, Balch, 1933).

[3] Roosevelt replied Nov. 28, 1934, that he would like to see Sherrill's book (*Personal Letters, 1928–1945*, I, 436).

Press Conference, Executive Offices of the White House, October 24, 1934, 10:45 A.M.

[*Excerpt*] Q: They told us that this equality demand is a take-it-or-leave-it proposition with them, that if they do not get it at London they will go home and get what they want.[1] Any position—

The President: I have not had any dispatches from the other side from Norman Davis. I do not think they have had any meetings, the American delegation, except that one courtesy call on Sir John Simon.[2] So far as I know, that is the only thing that our people have done.

Q: I think there is a meeting with the Japs today.[3]

The President: Is there? . . .

Q: Ambassador Bingham in London made a speech yesterday in which he said that stabilization between the United States and Great Britain would be a great thing.[4] Would you say anything on that?

The President: The only thing I can tell you is off the record because I did not know anything about it until I read the *Times*. Mac called me up at midnight and told me there was a *Times* report. If I have any connection with it, the thing will be that the President repudiates the Ambassador, or something like that. I know absolutely nothing about it.

Q: Does that mean you are going to repudiate? (Laughter)

The President: No, but if I dignified it by comment in any way, if I even said out loud that I did not know anything about it, somebody would say that I repudiated the Ambassador.

[President's Press Conferences:T]

[1] The Japanese demand for equality in naval armament ratios. This is the first mention of the topic in this press conference transcript; the immediately preceding discussion was on the coming Pennsylvania election.

[2] See Davis to Hull, Oct. 19, 1934, in *Foreign Relations, 1934,* I, 311–312.

[3] Reported by Davis in his dispatch to Hull of Oct. 24, 1934 (*Foreign Relations, Japan, 1931–1941,* I, 254–256).

[4] Bingham spoke at the Edinburgh Philosophical Institute on October 23; he was quoted as urging stabilization of the pound and dollar, with the concurrence of the other nations if possible, but the United States and Britain together, in any event. The New York *Times* correspondent, writing from Edinburgh, said that "in some quarters" it was believed that Bingham would not have made this statement if it had not first been approved by the White House, and noted that George L. Harrison, governor of the Federal Reserve Bank of New York, had been visiting the White House more frequently than usual since his recent return from Europe (New York *Times*, Oct. 24, 1934, pp. 1, 3). Harrison had talked with the President on October 5, 16, and 23 (PPF 1-0).

Roosevelt to Breckinridge Long, Ambassador to Italy, Rome

[Washington] October 25, 1934

Dear Breck: That is an extraordinarily interesting letter of yours[1] and the other day I had a further dispatch to the Secretary of State in regard to cotton. I want to see the cloth when it comes. My chief question is whether these new fangled processes can be stopped or curtailed by any beau geste. At this moment of writing I am a pessimist but I may feel better tomorrow morning.

I look forward to seeing you very soon. Do arrange to stay here a couple of months and get a real holiday.[2]

Always sincerely,

[OF 447:CT]

[1] Oct. 12, 1934, above.
[2] An attached note reads: "Letter from Ambassador Long sent to the Secretary of State for his information. G.G.T." (Grace Tully).

Josephus Daniels, Ambassador to Mexico, to Roosevelt

Mexico, October 26, 1934

Personal

Dear Franklin: The submission by the Mexican Congress of an amendment to Article Three of the Constitution, to be voted on by the States, has created a situation here which has had reverberations in the United States and has accentuated divisions here. It provides that "primary education shall be obligatory and will be imparted gratuitously by the State." It outlaws all church schools, provides for granting the right of licensed private schools, subject to the provision that they must impart "socialistic education" as prescribed by the State. The article declares that "the education imparted by the State shall be socialistic, and furthermore will exclude all religious doctrine and combat fanaticism and prejudice, and toward this end the school will organize its teachings and activities so as to imbue in the young a rational and exact concept of the universe and social life." There is also a provision which declares that "religious corporations, ministers of the cults, societies exclusively or preferably devoted to educational activities, and associations or societies directly or indirectly connected with the propaganda of a religious creed, may not in any manner participate in the activities of primary, secondary or normal schools, nor furnish them financial assistance."

There is much resentment, particularly among Catholics, toward the ban upon schools conducted by religious organizations, and it has manifested itself in protest parades, in strikes by children in schools, the closing of some schools, and, according to General Calles, in organized opposition by priests, amounting in his opinion to "sedition." Undoubtedly the rift is deep and something of a crisis exists. A South American diplomat told me last week that he feared the worst, for the opposition to "socialistic education" is resolved to prevent its being carried out in the schools. He is a strong Catholic and his view may be colored by his earnest belief in the attitude of his church associates. The government authorities recognize the opposition.

The present agitation, beginning with the introduction of the Amendment to Article Three, demanding no instruction that is not "socialistic," is mainly responsible for the criticism of my address made to Americans attending the Seminar last July. In that address I quoted this remark in an address by General Calles: "We must enter and take possession of the mind of childhood, the mind of youth," and I also commended the Mexicans for encouraging universal public education. I had not seen General Calles' entire address, only the extract I quoted. It seems that in another part of the address General Calles used terms that were very critical of church education, which I had not seen. There was no criticism of my approval of public education, only of my having quoted with approval one portion of the address in which in another portion General Calles used expressions which offended Catholics. At that time Article Three had not been introduced. It was only when the amendment to this Article was introduced, approved by Calles and Cárdenas and unanimously ratified by the Mexican Congress, that the storm of opposition broke. Naturally the closing of church schools and the expulsion of some priests aroused Catholics in Mexico and in the United States. It was then, misunderstanding my address, that some Catholics at home criticized me . . .[1]

I have never discussed religion or socialistic education with any of the high Government officials. General Calles once told Ambassador Morrow that he did not wish the American Ambassador to take up with him anything concerning the policy of Mexico touching religion. From all appearances that seems to be the policy of his successors, and I have not volunteered to discuss any action relating to religion or the amendment to Article Three, and no official has so much as touched upon these controversial matters in my many interviews.

This letter is much too long, but I thought it well to send you such information as would throw light upon a situation here which baffles full understanding.[2]

Faithfully yours,

Josephus Daniels

[PSF:Mexico:TS]

[1] Omitted are several pages on the historical background of the Mexican religious controversy.

[2] Roosevelt discussed this letter with Under Secretary of State Phillips on Nov. 2, 1934 (Phillips to McIntyre, Nov. 2, 1934, PSF:Mexico). No reply has been found; see Daniels to Roosevelt, Nov. 6, 1934, below.

Sumner Welles, Assistant Secretary of State, to Marvin H. McIntyre, Assistant Secretary to the President

Washington, October 26, 1934

Dear Marvin: As I was leaving, the President promised me that he would read the so-called Brazilian memorandum tonight and I am enclosing herewith a revised and, I think improved version of the draft which he has. I will appreciate it if you would give him this copy as a substitute for the one now on his desk. I may say that the draft as it now stands has been approved by the Secretary of State himself.

We have been delayed almost two and a half weeks in the negotiations for a trade agreement which we commenced with the Brazilian Ambassador, since I did not want to go ahead until I was perfectly sure that the proposals contained in this memorandum which we intend giving the Brazilian Ambassador met with the specific approval of the President himself. I will appreciate it if you will let me have the President's views at the earliest possible moment.

Believe me, Yours very sincerely,

Sumner Welles

[OF 11:TS]

[*Enclosure*] Memorandum by Sumner Welles on U.S.-Brazilian Trade Relations[1]

Memorandum

The current trends in commercial policy throughout the world present peculiar difficulties for countries such as the United States and Brazil which customarily have large favorable merchandise balances of trade. Through quota restrictions, governmental trading monopolies, import licensing, exchange control, clearing and compensation agreements, a large section of the world is moving more and more toward a close regulation and control of foreign trade. Under these tendencies, the principle of equality is rapidly being superseded by preferential treatment and special advantages.

In particular, clearing and compensation agreements tend toward the bilateral balancing of trade and the destruction of the surplus exports of countries normally having favorable balances. They tend to reduce the volume of triangular trade, and have thus contributed to the disastrous decline in total world trade. Moreover, they tend to divert purchases from the best markets and to force the import of goods which are less urgently required, or altogether unnecessary. This diversion of trade from its established channels tends to engender international ill-will, and has profoundly disturbed international economic relations.

Under these circumstances the Government of the United States would welcome the cooperation of the Brazilian government in an effort to check the present tendency toward such agreements.

The Government of the United States proposes as a basis for discussion with the Brazilian Government, first, that there be written into the trade agreement, clauses reciprocally safeguarding the interests of the nationals and commerce of the two countries in so far as they may be affected by the operation of any exchange control system, and all arrangements involving the provision of exchange; and, second, that upon the conclusion of the trade agreement, the two Governments join in a declaration of policy with respect to clearing, compensation, and other special agreements.

With respect to the clauses regarding the operation of exchange control to be written into the trade agreement, this Government suggests provisions to the following effect: That the customs concessions and other benefits provided for in the agreement are reciprocally granted on the understanding that steps will be taken to insure that such concessions and benefits will not be nullified by discriminations, inequalities, or inequities in either country against the nationals or trade of the other in connection with the operation of any exchange control system or of any arrangement involving the provision of exchange; and that in order to formulate the necessary measures to insure the effectiveness of the preceding provision and to review the operation of this section of the trade agreement, representatives of the two Governments shall meet immediately on conclusion of the trade agreement and quarterly thereafter, the Governments agreeing to make available to each other all pertinent records and information.

With respect to the joint declaration referred to above, it is suggested that the Governments of the United States and Brazil set forth therein their intention to bend their best efforts to direct their commercial policies in such a way as to discourage the multiplication of clearing, compensation and other special agreements.

This Government recognizes that the policy reflected in these two proposals is distinctly divergent from the policies recently pursued by many important trading countries, which in many cases are endeavoring to force upon countries with which they have an unfavorable balance of trade provisions for offsetting purchases, which require that all or part of the exchange proceeding from their imports be used for reciprocal purchases within their territories. It recognizes further that the line of action proposed may involve some sacrifice of immediate interest. From the standpoint of this country, the curtailment of imports into Brazil from the United States, as a result of the limited amounts of foreign exchange allotted for the purchase of American goods, and the long delays in payment now being suffered by those who sell goods in Brazil, are regarded by many American exporters as particularly onerous, in view of the circumstance that American imports of Brazilian products, principally coffee, create a volume of dollar exchange far in excess of the amount required to pay in full all obligations due to American interests. American holders of Brazilian bonds upon which service has been reduced or suspended altogether, have vigorously asserted similar views. Naturally enough, therefore, the Government of the United States has explored fully the possibility of proposing a clearing agreement which would ensure prompt and full payment for all merchandise shipped to Brazil and for the service of Brazilian debts held by Americans. There can be no doubt that such an agreement would be of immediate advantage to American exporters and bondholders whose interests are preponderantly in Brazil.

246

Nevertheless, realization of the inherent defects of the system of clearing and compensation agreements as a long-run policy has caused the Government of the United States to decline to adopt such a policy, as long as there is any other solution of safeguarding the interests of the United States such as that embodied in the proposal presented in the fourth paragraph of this memorandum.

If satisfactory progress toward such a solution should prove to be impossible, the United States, in order to secure itself against inequality of treatment, might be compelled to seek arrangements whereby exchange created by the sale of products in the United States would be applied to the purchase of American goods and to the service of debts owed to Americans. This it does not wish to do.

By refraining from such arrangements in connection with Brazilian-American trade, and in their relations with other countries, the Governments of the United States and Brazil may help to check the present tendency toward such agreements. A joint declaration to this effect would, it is hoped, help to reverse the present trend of international commercial policy by furnishing an example of international agreement, between two of the most important countries on this hemisphere, on a policy which looks toward the progressive removal of the existing network of restrictions on international commerce—a policy consistent not only with the best long-run economic interests of the parties to the agreement themselves, but also of those of the whole world.

This Government would ask the Brazilian Government to give most sympathetic consideration to the judgments expressed above and to the two proposals which have been submitted. It wishes to proceed with the negotiation of a commercial agreement with Brazil with all expedition possible.[2]

[OF 11:T]

[1] This title has been supplied.
[2] An attached note, Tully to McIntyre, Oct. 29, 1934, reads: "Take this up with Peek the first thing in the morning and let the President hear from Peek this afternoon." Peek returned the memorandum to McIntyre the same day, with a letter (OF 11). He said he had expressed his objections to the State Department policy proposed at a meeting of the Executive Committee on Commercial Policy of October 19 and in a letter to Assistant Secretary of State Sayre of the same date, a copy of which he enclosed. He asked to see the President before the latter acted on the memorandum. To Sayre, Peek wrote that he opposed the State Department's proposed policy of trying to do away with quota restrictions, exchange controls, clearing and compensation agreements, and other special arrangements. Many nations used these devices and each case should be considered on its merits. The position of the United States was different from that

of other nations because we had a favorable balance of trade. To make such a policy declaration as the memorandum proposed might prove embarrassing later. He thought these matters should be considered in advance of a general trade agreement or at least at the time, and not after the event.

On November 12, Peek attended a conference with the President, Wallace, Chester Davis, Jesse Jones, Francis Sayre, and others involved in the cotton section of the Brazilian negotiations (PPF 1-0). There is no information on what was decided at this meeting but presumably Peek was given a hearing for his views; a letter from him to Roosevelt of November 14 (OF 971) referred to the latter's request at the conference for data in support of Peek's stand that it was impossible "to negotiate trade agreements contemplating the mutually advantageous exchange of goods upon a reciprocal basis and at the same time adhere to the unconditional most-favored-nation policy of the last twelve years." This argument was supplementary to those he advanced in his letter to the President of Nov. 12, 1934, and its enclosure, below.

Roosevelt to Cordell Hull, Secretary of State, Pinehurst, North Carolina

[Washington] October 29, 1934

Dear Cordell: I enclose suggestions made by Sumner Welles for Diplomatic transfers. Apparently our present Minister to Colombia does not wish to be transferred to Panama—cannot stand it in Colombia any longer—and I think he might go on the waiting list.[1]

You might be thinking these over. I am merely transmitting them to you and have no personal thoughts on the subject.

I do hope you are getting a real rest. Things seem to be fairly quiet except that the Japanese negotiations are not proceeding well.

I trust you and Mrs. Hull will be able to accompany us November fifteenth. I go first to Harrodsburg, Kentucky, for a few hours and if you do not want to go there you could join the party at the Norris Dam at 2 P.M. on the sixteenth.[2]

Faithfully and affectionately,

[OF 20:CT]

[1] Sheldon Whitehouse, a career Foreign Service officer, resigned as minister to Colombia in December 1934 (Whitehouse to Roosevelt, Nov. 19, 1934, OF 729).

[2] On November 15, 16, and 17 Roosevelt visited Wilson, Wheeler, and Norris Dams, going from there to Warm Springs. Hull apparently did not accept this invitation.

Press Conference, Executive Offices of the White House, October 31, 1934, 10:40 A.M.

[*Excerpt*] Q: Can you make any comment on the present status of the naval discussion?

The President: No, I will have to refer you to London.

Q: Have you read the interview given by Ambassador Saito here yesterday?

The President: No, I just read the headlines.[1]

Q: Can you tell us anything about your visit with Stimson?

The President: As you know, he is a very, very old friend of mine and I have not seen him since he went abroad. He came in and we talked about general world conditions, people he had seen on the other side. There was nothing specific. There was no object to it, just to say, "How do" to him again. He comes to lunch with me every few months . . .[2]

Q: Can you tell us about your talk yesterday with Secretary Morgenthau and the gentlemen from the State Department?[3]

The President: The State Department was just talking about reciprocity and trade agreements—nothing specific.

Q: Did you discuss the most favored nation—

The President: No, it was not mentioned; it did not come out at all.

[President's Press Conferences:T]

[1] Saito had just returned to Washington after conferences in Tokyo. At his October 30 news conference, he said that the Japanese wanted eventual equality in naval tonnage with the United States and Great Britain; that the Japanese people regarded the ratio principle as a stigma, and that if the limitation effort failed, they would support their government in the naval race that would ensue. Future reductions in naval strength would have to be on a basis of equality (New York *Times,* Oct. 31, 1934, p. 6).

[2] Stimson had lunched with Roosevelt on the previous day (PPF 1-0).

[3] Jacob Viner, special assistant to the Secretary of the Treasury; Assistant Secretary of the Navy Henry L. Roosevelt; Assistant Secretary of State Wilbur J. Carr; and Assistant Secretary of State Francis B. Sayre (PPF 1-0).

Roosevelt to Senator Frederick Hale of Maine

[Washington] October 31, 1934

My dear Senator Hale: I have your letter of October 16, 1934, enclosing a letter which you had received from Mr. F. N. Beal, of Beal and Toothaker, of Phillips, Maine, protesting against any reduction in the duty on matches in the contemplated trade agreement with Sweden.[1]

I am glad to have your comments in support of Mr. Beal's statements, and I assure you that they have been given careful attention.

Mr. Beal states that the Swedish Match Company, through the Swedish Minister in Washington, has asked for a fifty percent reduction in the duty on matches under the Trade Agreements Act. Similar reports have lately come to the attention of those in charge of the trade agreements program, and I wish to take this occasion to state that negotiations with Sweden have not yet advanced beyond the initiatory stage and nothing has been finally determined regarding either the requests of the two governments or the contents of the proposed agreement.

On September 10, 1934, public notice was given of intention to negotiate a foreign trade agreement with the Government of Sweden. It is understood that American match producers have availed themselves of the opportunity to present pertinent information, together with their views regarding this proposed agreement, in accordance with the regulations prescribed by the Committee for Reciprocity Information. A copy of these regulations is enclosed for your information. By ruling of this Committee, all written statements relating to the agreement with Sweden were required to be submitted not later than October 29, 1934. Oral presentation of views by representatives of the match interests and others whose applications therefore have been approved are scheduled to be heard November 5, 1934.[2]

Very sincerely yours,

[OF 61-M:CT]

[1] Both letters are present; Beal's is dated Oct. 13, 1934. Beal and Toothaker were lumbermen. Beal said it was ridiculous for Sweden to ask for a tariff reduction under a reciprocal act "when there can be nothing reciprocal in regard to matches on the part of the Swedish Trust, whose monopoly contracts in twenty-four countries act as complete embargoes against our matches and whose control of the industry in Sweden prevents our exporting a single match to that country. Rather should they be told to remove these monopoly embargoes against our matches before they can even appear in good standing before any of our government agencies considering reciprocal treaties."

[2] Drafted in the State Department.

Norman H. Davis, Chairman, American Delegation to the London Naval Conference, to Roosevelt

London, England, October 31, 1934

My dear Mr. President: As I indicated in cables yesterday to the Department, the Japanese here have definitely confirmed the decision of their government to denounce the Washington Treaty by the end of December.[1]

In a long talk alone on Saturday with Matsudaira,[2] with whom I went to play golf, and with whom I can talk very frankly, he told me that he deeply regretted that his government had felt compelled to make this decision, but that there was now no chance of changing it as they were already definitely committed at home to such a course. I gathered the impression that he had hoped to be able to change the decision but had been unable to do so.

He said he had wished not to complicate the situation by injecting this difficult question; that their desire in the present conversations was to bring about an understanding of their own situation, to avoid arousing ill feeling and suspicion, to try to establish a new basis for future limitation and at least to avoid, in so far as possible, any ill effects from the denunciation, because they have no desire nor intention nor, in fact, the ability to engage in a naval race.

I told him their recent campaign of publicity, about which I recently spoke to him would indicate that they were staging a run-out, or at least that they were not concerned about stirring up ill feeling. He said this publicity had been most ill advised and that after I spoke to him he had sent a very long cable to Tokio, which he was satisfied would result in preventing a repetition of such tactics. He intimated that this was done by the military authorities who had practically gotten out of hand.

I told him it seemed to me that the hostility of Japanese people to the Naval Treaties and to the inferior ratio, which they look upon as a stigma, was due to a misunderstanding and to a failure to explain to them that equal naval ratios do not necessarily give equal security and that, in fact, the 5-3 ratio, together with other collateral agreements, established relative equality in security. He said that was true but that the real cause of the hostility in Japan to the naval ratio originated in their resentment at the Immigration Act of our Congress, which they considered to be a deliberate effort to brand them as an inferior race, and which they feel is reflected in the inferior naval ratio.

I told him that he must realize they were raising issues and making proposals which, if adhered to, would make agreement impossible and that I would appreciate it if he would tell me what their real objective is and where he thinks this will all lead. He intimated that they realized they could not get agreement on their proposals but that they hoped it might be possible to agree upon a modus vivendi which would prevent a naval race and any ill consequences, and which would enable us, with time and patience, to find a mutually satisfactory basis of agreement and cooperation. I asked him if he could envisage any possible new arrangement that would be mutually satisfactory, to take the place even temporarily of the existing treaties. He said that personally he was unable to do so but presumed that Tokio was working on this.

In substance he said that, regrettable as it was to him, he felt that the government had been forced to the conclusion that it was better to get rid of treaties which had caused such national resentment; but that there was no desire to alter the status of the political agreements and bases upon which the present treaties rested. He indicated that, in effect, they would like to reach a diplomatic understanding which would avoid a naval race and prevent any effort on the part of anyone to alter the real status established by those treaties.

It is certainly difficult to know just how to deal most effectively and wisely with the problems that confront us. The situation as I see it, insofar as it concerns the Japanese, is substantially as follows. Public opinion, and particularly the militarists in Japan, never fully approved the Washington Treaty of 1922 which they felt to be a curb on legitimate Japanese aspirations. The subsequent resentment over our Immigration Act helped put the militarists in control. The political element being unable to withstand the pressure of public opinion backed by the militarists, and even perhaps being more or less at heart in sympathy with their feelings, and with their ambitions, have been forced against their desire and better judgment, to surrender at least to the extent of agreeing to denounce the Washington Naval Treaty. It is possible, however, that the wiser political leaders, who feel compelled to acquiesce in this course, will endeavor to avoid any serious international repercussions and will seek to curb the power of the militarists by allowing them to destroy themselves.

The latter possible objective is indicated by the fact that the navy has been put in charge of difficult and highly complicated political negotiations, for which their experience and temperament do not fit them. The wiser Japanese statesmen may perhaps think that by denouncing a treaty which has become an embodiment of international resentment, public opinion will calm down and that, after the realization comes that Japan has gained nothing and perhaps lost much by such action, it will be possible to put the militarists where they belong and then to take steps to repair the mistake that has been made.

The objective of the Japanese militarists is, of course, to get the United

States and Great Britain to tie their hands, while that of the political leaders is to avoid ill feeling and real harm but at the same time to beat down Chinese resistance. Neither element wants trouble with either the British or ourselves.

It seems to me that, under the circumstances, our chief objective should be to have infinite patience and to apply the brakes so gradually as to avoid creating a state of mind that will tend to increase a tension that might lead to war and, with that in view, to cooperate insofar as possible, with the British in standing for the principles and policies upon which the naval treaties were based. If England and the United States should take a common stand along that line, coupled with a joint statement that, "having for thirteen years experienced the benefits of naval limitation and the equilibrium established thereby, it shall be their policy to adhere to the principle of naval equality as between themselves; and that they will avoid in every possible way the destruction of any existing peace machinery." In this way not only could they make a very strong appeal for peace but their statement could be so worded as to imply that no nation which earnestly desires peace can afford to be the cause of destroying any of the machinery for peace.

I am not sure that the British would be prepared now to do this without an agreement with us that would in effect be an alliance, but they know that we will not enter into an alliance. They are, however, just as opposed to the Japanese demands as we are but they are more inclined to give and take than we are and there is a slight possibility that they might possibly be in favor of agreeing to what would be in effect some increase in the Japanese ratio. I casually told Simon, whom I saw at luncheon today, that I hoped they would not be tempted to make such a mistake and he was rather emphatic in his assurance that they would not do so.

I still do not believe that the small, but rather powerful element, that favors some kind of an agreement with Japan will not prevail [*sic*].

So far as the British are concerned, they have behaved with us as satisfactorily as could be expected under the circumstances. All we can do at present is to try to be as patient and as wise as possible, not to do or say anything to further inflame public opinion in Japan but, at the same time, to avoid giving the impression that our rights and interests can be violated with impunity.

MacDonald and Simon expressed themselves firmly of the belief that if we will be patient but fair and firm with the Japanese, and ask them constantly to consider the consequences of their refusal to continue to cooperate on the basis of the existing treaties, they will begin to change their point of view.[3]

With warmest personal regards, I am, Faithfully yours,

Norman H. Davis

[PSF:London Naval Conference:TS]

[1] See Davis' two dispatches of Oct. 29, 1934, in *Foreign Relations, 1934,* I, 317–318, 318–321.
[2] Tsuneo Matsudaira, Japanese ambassador to Great Britain.
[3] Answered Nov. 9, 1934, below.

William Phillips, Under Secretary of State, to Roosevelt

Washington, October 31, 1934

My dear Mr. President: You know how much the State Department and all other branches of the Government dealing with the international economic and financial interests of this country have been concerned with the development of the special types of intergovernmental agreements known as "clearing" and "compensation" agreements. In my judgment, these new types of agreements increase the difficulties of reviving international trade, and accentuate the discriminations as between the treatment accorded different countries. The employment of such agreements, for example, has led to a situation in which other foreign investors in Germany are still receiving payment while American investors are not. The Department, in cooperation with other branches of the Government, has been exerting itself to arrest this type of agreement while also giving the fullest consideration to what changes in our own methods of trade may be required adequately to safeguard American interests in the event that employment of the other type of agreement extends still further.

The League of Nations, as a result of a resolution of the Assembly and action taken by the Council, has created a special Committee to study these agreements and to report on their causes and consequences. This special Committee is made up of five representatives chosen from the Economic Committee of the League and five from the Financial Committee of the League. This joint Committee is in turn asking for the collaboration of other governments, and an invitation to collaborate is in the hands of the Department.

In view of the American interest in this matter, I strongly recommend that we designate a representative to serve with this Committee and to present the American point of view. I have consulted with the Treasury, the Tariff Commission and other branches of the Government and all agreed that Mr. Oscar B. Ryder, a member of the Tariff Commission, could undertake this assignment admirably. If the proposed action is agreeable to you, would you kindly indicate your approval?

Faithfully yours,

William Phillips

[*Notation*:AS] W.P. OK   FDR
[OF 184:TS]

Roosevelt to James A. Farrell, Chairman, National Foreign Trade Council, New York

Washington, November 1, 1934

[*Telegram*] It gives me pleasure to send cordial greetings to those assembled at the World Trade Dinner of the National Foreign Trade Council which has done much valuable work in the promotion of our foreign commerce. It is an appropriate time to give thought to the subject of world trade since it has fallen in the past few years from a flourishing state to a very low level. The causes of the decline are various, but among the most serious of them are the unnecessary and artificial barriers which hamper the healthy interchange of commodities. As you are aware this Government has given zealous attention to the problem and under authority of the Trade Agreements Act is seeking to make arrangements with other countries designed to improve existing conditions. Our object is to secure concerted action to untangle the network of existing restrictions. Just as the sudden falling off in world trade reacted disastrously on the domestic economy of all countries, so revival of world trade should have a favorable influence on domestic recovery everywhere. We are seeking to rehabilitate international commerce in a way that will benefit not a single nation but all nations, not a group of nations but the whole world. Swift communications have made us all near neighbors. They should also make us good neighbors.[1]

Franklin D. Roosevelt

[PPF 1908:T]

[1] The draft of this message, prepared in the State Department, bears a number of revisions in Roosevelt's hand. Secretary of State Hull was to have addressed the meeting (held at the Commodore Hotel) but illness prevented him, and his address was read by Assistant Secretary of State Francis B. Sayre. Both the President's telegram and Hull's speech were printed in the New York *Times* of Nov. 2, 1934, p. 4. Hull's speech was a plea for the principles of reciprocal trade.

Press Conference, Executive Offices of the White House, November 2, 1934, 4:10 P.M.

[*Excerpt*] Q: Mr. President, what, if any, recourse is left to us if any one of the signatories to the Nine-Power Pact completely disregards the obligations under it?

The President: Say it again.

Q: What, if any, recourse is left to us, if any one of the signatories to the Nine-Power Pact completely disregards the obligations under it?

The President: I will get out my library on that subject. I think there have been twelve volumes written on it so far.

Q: You haven't given any thought to it yet?

The President: No . . .

Q: Now that you have seen Davis' report on the London conference, can we induce you to tell us whether—or at least comment on it?

The President: Which report?

Q: The report you had on your desk last Wednesday?[1]

The President: There have been six or eight since then. That is entirely out of date.

Q: Anything you can tell us?

The President: Nothing we can say except that we are still hoping for a favorable outcome.

[President's Press Conferences:T]

[1] No report was mentioned during the October 31 press conference (above); possibly Davis' two dispatches to Hull of Oct. 29, 1934, are meant (*Foreign Relations, 1934*, I, 317–318, 318–321).

Roosevelt to Sumner Welles, Assistant Secretary of State

[Washington] November 5, 1934

Memo for Assistant Secretary Welles: I think it is important that before any further reciprocal trade agreements are made, you should check with Dr. Gruening, Director of the Division of Territories and Island Possessions in the Department of the Interior. I am particularly anxious that we should not do anything which would seriously hurt our difficult task in Puerto Rico, Virgin Islands and Hawaii.[1]

F.D.R.

[OF 20:CT]

[1] On October 31 Roosevelt had conferred for nearly two hours with Gruening, Assistant Secretary of Interior Oscar Chapman, and Governor Blanton Winship of Puerto Rico (PPF 1-0).

Josephus Daniels, Ambassador to Mexico, to Roosevelt

Mexico, November 6, 1934

Personal

Dear Franklin: With relation to the criticisms made by certain Catholic papers and organizations about my speech to the members of the Seminar, composed of Americans who were here in July, I had a letter today from Hon. Ernest Gruening,[1] who was here at the time, in which Mr. Gruening said:

I noted with surprise that you had been made the target of a barrage—apparently carefully timed—because of your alleged support of attacks on the Catholic Church. I was even more surprised when I realized from reading the newspaper accounts that the basis for this charge was contained in the words of greeting which you addressed to the Seminar last July. I had the good fortune and the pleasure to be present on this occasion, and if you should desire it (should the need arise), I should be most happy to testify that nothing seemed more remote from the purport and obvious purpose of that address than the intent with which you were charged. Not that I think you will need any such assistance, but should you do so, I should be most happy to serve.

By today's pouch I am forwarding to the State Department a despatch containing the substance of recent informal talks with Dr. Puig, Minister for Foreign Affairs, and with General Calles, head of the National

Revolutionary Party, who is credited with leadership in the proposed amendment to the Constitution introduced recently in Congress, calling for "socialistic education." As these interviews throw light upon a delicate situation, I thought you would be interested in reading them.[2]

With warm regards, Faithfully yours,

Josephus Daniels

[PSF:Mexico:TS]

[1] Gruening, an editor with a special interest in Latin-American affairs (in 1933 he accompanied the United States delegation to the Montevideo Conference as a general adviser), had recently been appointed chief of the Division of Territories and Island Possessions. He was elected senator from Alaska in 1959.

[2] Daniels' dispatch of Nov. 5, 1934, reporting his conversation with General Calles of Nov. 2, 1934, with a memorandum of the conversation by W. W. Schott, the Embassy interpreter, Nov. 2, 1934, is present (PSF:Mexico); the other is not.

Norman H. Davis, Chairman, American Delegation, London Naval Conference, to Roosevelt

London, November 6, 1934

Dear Mr. President: The net result of the naval conversations and manoeuvers to date is about as follows:

The British, preoccupied as they are with the European situation, had hoped to avoid or postpone coming to grips with the issues raised by the Japanese. They had evidently hoped also that we might take the initiative, or show more inclination than we have heretofore, to enter into some agreement with them that would make them feel justified in taking a firm stand against the Japanese demands for a change in the present status. They have, however, been practically forced by the nature of the Japanese proposals and the public manner of their presentation, to take a definite stand.

When we got here there was a sentiment in certain quarters in favor of making some kind of a deal with Japan as the best means of keeping Japan in bounds, and also a feeling that Great Britain might, at any rate, play the role of mediator. However, the Japanese proposals, made public by Yamamoto,[1] have been looked upon as so unreasonable and unjustifiable as to force the British government to take a definite stand and to realize that it could not honestly or usefully act as mediator. Furthermore, the idea of a separate deal with Japan has diminished, not because of any increase in friendly sentiment towards the United States, but because of doubt of the Japanese themselves as suddenly augmented by the recent action of the Japanese with regard to oil in Manchukuo.[2] The only argument the government members still favoring some sort of a rapproachement with Japan can offer is the belief that, after Japan has obtained this indefensible position for treaty abrogation, she will be disposed, if not pushed too hard, to agree to a naval compromise which England can accept.

There is a strong element in Parliament that does not favor any deal with the United States and it is this same group that is advocating some gesture towards Japan. I am persuaded, however, that the major influence in the Cabinet is definitely opposed to any deal with Japan that would be misinterpreted by the United States and that, after all, might not be lived up to by Japan. This hostility in Parliament towards the United States is one of soreness, which began during the Economic Conference and which has reached full expression as a result of the Johnson Resolution, which they look upon as a deliberate slap by the Administration to Great Britain, which was at least paying something, as a worse defaulter than France which had paid nothing on the debt.

While the British still wish to be as conciliatory as possible with Japan, and avoid an absolute impasse, it is still my belief that, whenever they feel the situation demands the choice between standing with us on basic principles or of trying to conciliate Japan in such a way as to alienate us, they will choose the former.

The British press have for the past few days been reflecting this attitude very definitely. I am enclosing an article by Garvin in Sunday's *Observer*, which I understand has attracted considerable attention, and more especially an article by Sir Walter Layton in the *Economist* of the 3rd.[3]

Unless there is some new move it is difficult to see how we can now proceed much further with the conversations. The Japanese are now telling their press that, having presented their views fully to both of us, they will not make another move for the present and that the next move is up to the British.

Since the Japanese now find that they can not get agreement for fundamental alterations in the Washington Treaty, and since they have gone so far in their proposals as to make it difficult, if not impossible, to recede from their position, they may decide at the forthcoming meeting of the Cabinet, in consultation with the Emperor, to give, without further delay, notice of the termination of the Washington

Treaty. Under the terms of that Treaty, their notice would be given officially to our Government and within one year thereafter the five Powers parties to the Treaty must meet in conference. This would change the basis and purpose of a conference in 1935, from that now contemplated. Instead of a conference to be held under the London Treaty to negotiate a renewal thereof, it would be necessary to meet under the provisions of the Washington Treaty. I feel, therefore, that you should have in mind that, with the denunciation of the Washington Treaty by Japan, you may have to decide, under the terms of the Washington Treaty, to summon a conference for next year.

It is possible that, once Japan has given notice of termination of the Washington Treaty, her public opinion will calm down; and when she sees that the other four powers, parties to the Washington Treaty, are in favor of its continuance, Japan might be able and willing to accept a face saving formula for the maintenance of the present basis of naval limitation. At any rate, I think we should give some consideration to the advisability of inviting the other three powers, parties to the Washington Treaty, to confer with a view of determining whether the four remaining parties to the Washington Treaty should not continue to abide by its terms and to receive its benefits, with some elastic provision to be operative in case Japan, once outside the Treaty, starts to increase its navy.

The Japanese proposal for a fundamental change in the basis of the Washington and London Treaties, is due, of course, to a fundamental change in their foreign policy. The Japanese government that signed the treaty in 1922 had a peace policy, whereas the predominant element in Japan today has a war policy. In 1922 they were prepared to cooperate with other powers with interests in the Pacific and in China. Today they want to act independently and in disregard of the treaty rights and interests of other powers. The whole crux of the problem, therefore, will be whether Japan can be induced to cooperate for the promotion of peace, or whether she will go alone in the opposite direction.

There is a strong element in England today who feel that, if Japan is not coerced she will ultimately come back to a more sane attitude towards international relations. The more balanced minds in the British Cabinet still entertain some hope that, if no attempt is made to single out Japan for denunciation but, rather, a world program is pursued, from which she has voluntarily withdrawn, she will return at a later date of her own free will.

As indicated in my previous letter, I think it most important for us not to say or do anything to inflame Japanese public opinion, and particularly not to make any threats. I also think it desirable that we stress the question of cooperation and peace, and that the press begin to sound the note that, if Japan's intentions are peaceful, it is impossible to understand why she would wish to destroy a substantial peace machinery which was set up under the Washington Treaty, and which has proven to be beneficial to all and detrimental to none.

With warmest personal regards, I am, Faithfully yours,

Norman H. Davis

P.S. In spite of the present soreness of a certain group of Tories in Parliament, and their resentment over the Johnson Resolution, I am satisfied that even that group would not favor, in case of a show down, departing from what has become a cardinal policy of Great Britain, namely to cooperate as closely as possible with us, or at least to do nothing that would definitely alienate us.[4]

[PSF:London Naval Conference:TS]

[1] Rear Admiral Isoroku Yamamoto, technical adviser to the Japanese ambassador to Great Britain at the London Naval Conference.

[2] Establishment of a Japanese oil monopoly there.

[3] In a long article, "Sea-Power and World Policy," in the Sunday *Observer* of Nov. 4, 1934, J. L. Garvin said that the United Kingdom and the United States would no doubt have to alter their present naval arrangements as between each other; in the present matter, however, Anglo-American understanding had to be "the firm principle, the unswerving aim, and the impregnable foundation of British policy." Britain and America might in future be divided on minor matters but never on the subject of sea security. Layton in his article said that public opinion in Britain was convinced that "cordial friendship and mutual confidence" between the two English-speaking countries should be one of the cardinal points in British policy.

[4] Cf. Davis to Hull, Nov. 6, 1934, in *Foreign Relations, 1934,* I, 325–326, and see Roosevelt to Davis, Nov. 9, 1934, below.

Roosevelt to Admiral J. M. Reeves, Commander-in-Chief, United States Fleet, U.S.S. *New Mexico,* San Pedro, California

[Washington] November 8, 1934

Private and Confidential

Dear Admiral: It is good to get your letter from the Canal Zone and I am glad to know that the cruise has been so successful.[1] I hope that when the Canal Zone authorities replace those electric lights which were carried away by the *Lexington* and *Saratoga* they will put them a few feet further back!

I am taking up the subject of protected anchorages right away and I hope that we can get something in the budget to start the work.

I like your plans for the winter and for the summer operations.

Be sure to come to see me when you get to Washington early in December.[2] Several matters have come up since you left which you might be thinking about. First, there are reports to the League of Nations that Japan is fortifying the Mandated Islands. Second, there are reports that Japan is seeking new types of vessels, supposedly along the line of the German pocket battleship. Third, I saw the U.S.S. *Farragut* at the Washington Navy Yard and I think she is quite a success in spite of the fact that we have built no destroyers for fourteen years. The Department feels that we have too many gadgets on board her. Her Commanding Officer reports her an excellent sea boat, capable of sustained high speed in fairly rough weather. I think one of her sister ships has gone into commission on the Pacific Coast.

In regard to the international situation, the newspapers give fairly accurate accounts of the London Conference developments. Frankly, I gravely doubt a successful outcome but Admiral Standley and Mr. Davis seem to be succeeding in getting the British in line with us. I do not anticipate any serious developments in the Pacific in the near future, though the oil storage situation in Japan proper and the oil marketing situation in Manchukuo, together with similar possible incidents in China, might bring matters to a disagreeable situation.

The news from Europe is still disquieting and I should feel more pessimistic if I did not realize that it has amounted to a day to day problem for many months past.

I fully appreciate the need for personnel though I cannot decide on final numbers to be asked for until early in December. I think we shall get a minimum of eighty-eight thousand, and I am wondering if we cannot use more of the Marines in the manning of secondary batteries, especially on smaller ships. In the absence of any immediate prospect of Expeditionary Forces, I do not think it is necessary to keep as many Marine units ashore as we have at the present time.

I get back to Washington about December fifth and will see you shortly thereafter.

Very sincerely yours,

[OF 1818:CT]

<hr />

[1] Oct. 27, 1934 (OF 1818). Reeves described recent fleet maneuvers and recommended improvement of the Atlantic and Pacific anchorages of the Canal.
[2] Reeves saw the President for almost an hour on December 12 (PPF 1-0).

Roosevelt to Norman H. Davis, Chairman, American Delegation, London Naval Conference

[Washington] November 9, 1934

Private and Confidential

Dear Norman: I find yours of October thirty-first on my return from Hyde Park after election.[1] Your golf game with Matsudaira must have been exceptionally interesting. The latest news by cable seems no more encouraging.

I hope you will keep two definite considerations always in mind. First, that Simon and a few other Tories must be constantly impressed with the simple fact that if Great Britain is even suspected of preferring to play with Japan to playing with us, I shall be compelled, in the interest of American security, to approach public sentiment in Canada, Australia, New Zealand and South Africa in a definite effort to make these Dominions understand clearly that their future security is linked with us in the United States. You will best know how to inject this thought into the minds of Simon, Chamberlain, Baldwin and MacDonald in the most diplomatic way.

The second point is that I get increasing information that Japan cannot stand the cost of a Naval race.[2]

By the way, that continued reference to the Immigration Act is, in my judgment, nothing more or less than a smoke screen—whether it be laid by Japanese militarists or by Japanese Ambassadors.

If the worst comes to the worst and Japan in effect walks out on the three party conference, I am inclined to go along with your thought at the bottom of Page 5, that England and the United States should join in a statement. As a matter of practical fact, in such a case we could easily agree with the British by some form of dovetailing categories so that they would have more light cruisers and we more battleship strength or something along that line.

It is unthinkable that the British would go along with even a slight Japanese increase. It would mean a further increase five years from now. You will remember that 1930 did give Japan an increase over 1922.

I am glad you are patient. I would be much out of place in such a conference![3]

Always sincerely,

[PSF:London Naval Conference:CT]

---

[1] Above.

2 Under Secretary of State Phillips was shown this letter before it was sent; he told the President it should be sent "just as it is" (Phillips to Roosevelt, Nov. 9, 1934, PSF: London Naval Conference). He added: "It may be that the situation will develop in London next week which will make it desirable to telegraph him the text, as the letter cannot arrive for another ten days. I do not, however, recommend that course at present because we must assume that the British decipher everything that we send by code. With regard to your second point, Stanley Hornbeck has always expressed the views that the Japanese have means at their disposal to stand the cost of a naval race over a considerable period of time, but we need a good deal more information on this point before we can be certain." Phillips enclosed a telegram from Davis, "just received," and commented: "You will see that the British have put up a new proposition to the Japanese." The Davis telegram to Hull here referred to is printed in *Foreign Relations, 1934*, I, 326. Davis reported that the British had offered the Japanese "a formula recognizing the equality of status of the contracting powers." This would satisfy Japanese prestige but by mutual agreement the nations would agree not to build up to the limits permitted by "equality of status." See Roosevelt to Hull, Nov. 14, 1934, below.

3 Answered Nov. 27, 1934, below.

Press Conference, Executive Offices of the White House, November 9, 1934, 4:15 P.M.

[*Excerpt*] Q: The Great Lakes-St. Lawrence Tidewater Association seems to indicate that there has been some change in the St. Lawrence Treaty since the last session. Has there been any change in that up to date?

The President: I suppose there is no particular—that sort of puts me in a hole because I do not know whether I want to answer that on the record or for background. Suppose you put it this way: I think it is perfectly all right because, naturally, I do not want to step on anybody's toes. When Under Secretary Phillips was in Ottawa, he spoke informally with the Prime Minister in regard to one or two small changes which he hoped that we could discuss. That is, really, as far as it has got.[1]

Q: Do you recall what the Prime Minister said, Mr. President?

The President: What?

Q: Do you recall what the Prime Minister said, Mr. President?

The President: Well, he has taken it under advisement.

Q: Did you hear of Buchanan's hope of a short session in the Seventy-fourth Congress?[2]

The President: I always do.

Q: Could you tell us whether those one or two small changes had reference to Lake Michigan?

The President: I can give you this as background, simply repeating what I have said so often to the Chicago papers. They might just as well get it through their heads once and for all and then you won't have to ask questions again. Under common law, if I am a property owner on a stream, I can use the water of that stream for drinking purposes, for feeding cattle, for running a mill wheel, but I have got to put that water back into the stream.

Now, that is common law and if it is the common law between two people that our civilization is founded on, it is certainly common law between nations. The United States has not the right and never will have the right to divert water from one watershed into another watershed to the detriment of somebody that lives downstream. Furthermore, the Supreme Court has said that it would not be reasonable to divert more than the amount provided for by treaty. And, number three, the Army states in absolutely categorical terms that that amount of water is sufficient for navigation from Lake Michigan out to the Mississippi. They might just as well get that through their heads in Chicago; they have enough water and they won't get any more water . . .

Q: Can you tell us anything about a naval pact in London?

The President: I will have to tell you this off the record. After I read this morning's papers, I got a bit worried and I called up Bill Phillips and I said, "What is the news from London?" He said, "None," and told me that up to an hour ago there hadn't been anything from Norman Davis, not a thing.

Q: What were you worried about?

The President: It looked quite serious. One or two of the dispatches had it that the British and Japs got into a jam. This is off the record because I haven't any news.

Q: There is a report around town that the present Minister to Norway may be replaced.

The President: That is a report around town. It had not got here until you mentioned it.

[President's Press Conferences:T]

[1] In addition to the Tidewater Association, Senator Robert M. La Follette, Jr., of Wisconsin, and Frank P. Walsh, chairman of the New York State Power Commission, had been active in keeping the St. Lawrence Waterway issue before the public. La Follette had written to Roosevelt Aug. 29, 1934 (PPF 1792), to call attention to the speeches made by Walsh in the Michigan-Minnesota-Wisconsin area in which he had drawn the issue "clearly against opposing interests and demonstrated the equal importance and the national benefit of St. Lawrence power and navigation." La Follette concluded: "I am convinced prompt action in the negotiations with Canada and energetic efforts to make public sentiment effective in the score of states directly interested in St. Lawrence power and navigation will help to insure action in January and strengthen the policy of public development of our water resources all along the line."

[2] Rep. James P. Buchanan of Texas.

William Phillips, Acting Secretary of State, to Roosevelt

Washington, November 9, 1934

My dear Mr. President: I have consistently followed the practice of submitting for your approval the names of all persons to represent the United States at international congresses or conferences. It may be that in certain cases this procedure places an undue burden on your time. A large portion of the international meetings in which this Government participates are of a technical, scientific or humanitarian nature where the delegations are made up wholly or in part of persons already in the employ of the Government.

With a view of saving your time and expediting business I venture to suggest the following modification of the practice now observed:

That you authorize the Secretary of State or the Acting Secretary to designate persons to represent the United States at international meetings when all of the following circumstances are evident:

1. The person in question is already in the Government's employ;

2. The congress or conference is not of a political character but purely technical, scientific or humanitarian;

3. The person to be appointed has been recommended by the head of his Department or other agency of the Government;

4. That the attendance at the conference of the person named will involve no additional expense to the Government.

I should be glad to know if this meets with your approval.

Faithfully yours,

William Phillips

[*Notation*:AS] W.P. I would rather continue present practice as it keeps me "au courant"! FDR

[OF 20:TS]

Marvin H. McIntyre, Assistant Secretary to the President, to L. N. Rosenbaum, New York

[Washington] November 10, 1934

My dear Mr. Rosenbaum: I have your letter of October twenty-sixth concerning the financing of American-Soviet trade and related matters, and have taken due note of your view that the financing of such trade, by this Government apparently, should be made possible irrespective of the progress of the present negotiations between this Government and the Soviet Government concerning outstanding questions of debts and claims.[1]

In this connection, I desire to draw your attention to the fact that the policy of the Government in this matter is set forth in the following resolution which was adopted by the Board of Trustees of the Export-Import Bank of Washington and was read by Mr. McReynolds in the House of Representatives during the debate on the Johnson Act (printed in the *Congressional Record* of April 4, 1934, Seventy-third Congress, Second Session, page 6192):

It is the sense of the board of trustees of this Corporation that no actual credit transactions with the Soviet Government shall be undertaken unless and until that government shall submit to the President of the United States an acceptable agreement respecting the payment of the Russian indebtedness to the government of the United States and its nationals.

I have not been informed of any change in the policy above described and in Secretary Hull's absence from the city I am unable to get in touch with him with regard to the matter. However, I shall refer your letter to his Department in order that it may be brought to his attention upon his return.[2]

Sincerely yours,

M. H. McIntyre

[OF 614-A:CT]

[1] Rosenbaum said he had recently talked with Hull who had told him that he saw no reason why the Russian credits could not be financed "irrespective of the negotiations for the debt settlement" (OF 614-A).
[2] Drafted in the office of Assistant Secretary of State Sayre.

George N. Peek, Special Adviser to the President on Foreign Trade, to Roosevelt

Washington, November 12, 1934

My dear Mr. President: Information developed at the hearings of the Reciprocity Information Committee, in various Country Committees and elsewhere in connection with trade agreements being currently negotiated has indicated to me the immediate advisability of revising our unconditional M.F.N. policy in the light of the general domestic and world situation, and with particular reference to our internal recovery program. The essential incompatibility of the unconditional most-favored-nation interpretation with a policy of reciprocal trade agreements was pointed out in the Tariff Commission report of 1919[1] and has again become apparent in the current trade negotiations. Furthermore, it seems plain that an automatic generalization of tariff concessions made by us may in many instances jeopardize the legitimate interests of American production for the American market.

Up to 1922 the traditional course of the United States was that of seeking equal treatment abroad through employment of the conditional M.F.N. policy. The results of changing that policy and of adopting the unconditional M.F.N. interpretation, which was in effect a measure of unilateral economic disarmament, have not been encouraging from the standpoint of American foreign trade. Foreign nations instead of following our example have continued and intensified restrictive measures such as high tariffs, administrative restrictions, quota systems, exchange controls, and special exclusive trade agreements from the benefits of which the United States has been barred. Figures published in the New York *Times* of July 15, 1934, to which I referred in my letter to Secretary Hull of September 22nd (copy enclosed), indicate that the greatest gains have been made in international trade by those countries which have resorted to the employment of special trade agreements, and that these gains have been made largely at the expense of the United States.[2] The exigencies of American domestic economy and of foreign markets alike appear to me to call for a revision of the unconditional M.F.N. policy of the past twelve years, if foreign trade is to be properly related to and to play its proper part in our national recovery.

The example of England is particularly enlightening and is well reflected in the following statement made by Walter Runciman, President of the British Board of Trade, speaking for the British Government in reply to a question in the House of Commons, on March 15, 1933:

In negotiating, both sides must make concessions. I want to make it clear that if any nation sits back in the hope that we will enter into negotiations with another Power and that they will be able to achieve most-favored-nation treatment without consideration coming from them, they will come to a deadlock. If they gain any advantage from us, they must be reciprocal in their action. They must be ready to make concessions similar to ours and to those of other countries. Unless they do that, we cannot agree to most-favored-nation treatment being retained as a permanent element in the conditions which control their traffic and ours. If it is used against us in any instance we will drop it at once, and we will be ready to enter into individual relationships without regard to most-favored-nation treatment in such cases as I have in mind. I hope those who are now doing so, after discussing it with us, will bear in mind, therefore, the fact that while this system plays such a large part in the commercial life of this country, we are not so firmly wedded to it that we can allow it to be used to our disadvantage.

While conditions in England may differ considerably from those in the United States, in this respect at least I think we might do well to profit by her example.

This would appear entirely possible under the Reciprocal Tariff Act of 1934, which, in its declaration of policy, states as its purpose:

. . . expanding foreign markets for the products of the United States . . . by regulating the admission of foreign goods into the United States in accordance with the characteristics and needs of various branches of American production so that foreign markets will be made available to those branches of American production which require and are capable of developing such outlets by affording corresponding market opportunities for foreign products in the United States . . . .[3]

While the Act provides for the generalization of tariff reductions to all foreign countries, it makes the exception

That the President may suspend the application to articles the growth, produce, or manufacture of any country because of its discriminatory treatment of American commerce or because of other acts or policies which in his opinion tend to defeat the purposes set forth in this section . . . .

This exception would appear to permit suspension in the case not only of nations which have been discriminating against the United States in the usual sense but also, under its more general provision, of (a) nations which have violated their most-favored-nation commitments to us through the negotiation of special agreements from which we are excluded, (b) nations whose exchange restrictions have the effect of crippling American foreign trade, (c) nations which have not satisfactorily regulated their debts with us, including war debts, and (d) nations which fail to reciprocate for tariff favors received as a result of our trade agreements with other nations, as all these practices have the effect of defeating the purposes set forth in the Act. With respect to such categories of nations the Act does not appear to be mandatory on the subject of generalization and we should be prepared to take the fullest possible advantage of this proviso of the Act to insure the negotiation of agreements beneficial to the United States. The inadvisability of concluding any reciprocal trade agreements until this all important question of conditional or unconditional M.F.N. policy is determined seems to me to be clearly indicated.

I am taking the liberty of advancing these views in the thought that in the final analysis the general national interest, particularly the demands of our internal economy, must determine our foreign policy whether it be in its commercial and financial or in its diplomatic and political aspects.[4]

I have not been able to discuss this particular question recently with Secretary Hull due to his absence but shall, of course, be glad to do so should you so desire.

Faithfully yours,

George N. Peek

[OF 971:TS]

[1] *Annual Report* (Washington, 1919).
[2] "Foreign Trade Up in Britain in June," II, 11.
[3] Ellipsis marks here and below are in the original.
[4] Peek had not hesitated to press his ideas on foreign trade outside as well as within the government. Aside from his criticism of the unconditional most-favored-nation policy, he proposed the use of bilateral agreements to establish "equality" of imports and exports, and the use of exchange controls to correct discrimination against the United States. Two speeches he made at this time are especially important: one before the Export Managers Club of Chicago on October 17, and another before the National Foreign Trade Convention in New York on November 2. (They are reported in the New York *Times* of Oct. 18, 1934, p. 16, and in the issue of Nov. 3, 1934, p. 16.)

[*Enclosure*] George N. Peek to Cordell Hull

[Washington] September 22, 1934

Dear Mr. Hull: I have received and read with the closest interest your letter of September 15, regarding the question of proceeding without delay to the negotiation of clearing agreements where desirable and possible.[1] I note that you are of the opinion that amelioration of the difficulties now being experienced by Americans trading with countries exercising exchange controls is to be found in the application of diplomatic pressure and the negotiation of general trade agreements rather than in the establishment of clearing agreements with such countries.

While not wishing to ignore the valuable results which may be achieved by diplomatic pressure, it is clear that in the nature of things, this cannot always hope to be uniformly successful, as trade, including international trade, is dominated by economic and financial pressures rather than those of sentiments of good or ill will. Moreover, the negotiation of trade agreements is a process that must necessarily involve a considerable space of time, and while such agreements will undoubtedly lead to a gradual improvement of the difficulties to which I have referred, our exporters will in the meantime lie under the disadvantage of having to choose between taking a chance on ultimate payment for the goods they sell to "exchange restriction" countries or of surrendering their markets in those countries to other nations having exchange agreements with the countries in question.

With reference to the specific points you mention, I would say:

(1) It was not my intention to propose a general system of clearing agreements to cover the entire field of our foreign trade, but merely to recommend that where our trade encounters exchange restrictions, an effort be made to meet the situation through the negotiation of clearing agreements where this might be possible and desirable.

(2) It is clearly a case where each "exchange restriction" country must be treated as an individual problem and in this respect my position is analogous to that taken by President Roosevelt on November 24, 1932,[2] prior to his inauguration, regarding reconsideration of war debts, when he stated:

> The principle calls for free access by the debtor to the creditor. Each case should be considered in the light of the conditions and necessities peculiar to the case of each nation concerned. . . . In dealing with the debts each government has been and is to be considered individually, and all dealings with each government are independent of dealings with any other debtor government. In no case should we deal with the debtor governments collectively. As to the application of this principle to foreign trade I note with satisfaction that you and I appear to be in accord.

(3) Obviously clearing agreements would involve administrative problems, but I cannot regard these as insuperable. The necessity of employing clearing agreements or other controls is a distasteful one, but in view of conditions prevailing in the world today, it is one which must be faced if we are to maintain or expand our foreign trade with countries where exchange restrictions are in force. Parenthetically I might observe that recent figures published in the New York *Times* of July 15, 1934, would appear to indicate that the greatest gains in international trade have been

made by those countries which have resorted to the employment of special trade agreements and clearing agreements, and that these gains have been made largely at the expense of the United States.[3] While I am not prepared to vouch for the specific figures, they appear to me substantially accurate and are to my mind of great significance.

(4) It is not my contention that clearing agreements will necessarily develop trade. They do, however, provide what is of prime importance, namely a method of insuring payment for what goods we do ship to "exchange restriction" countries, and they may thus operate to preserve a foothold in markets which might otherwise be lost to American exports.

It does not appear that any one single formula exists whereby our problems of foreign trade may be solved. There are, however, various methods whereby the problem may be approached and the choice of method or methods must, as I have indicated above, depend upon the individual country concerned.

As you pointed out in your article in the New York *Times* of September 15, foreign trade, to be profitable, must be based on a balanced trade, which means essentially the exchange of goods for goods:[4] mere expansion of American exports, unless based on this principle can no more profit us now than it did during the preceding twenty years. To profit we must be paid in one way or another for what we sell, and one way to insure that would appear to be through the negotiation of clearing agreements in the case of countries whose exchange restrictions at present operate to our disadvantage. I would even be prepared to recommend that a satisfactory solution of the question of blocked exchanges be made a prerequisite to the negotiation of any general trade agreement with an "exchange restriction" country.

I recognize fully that the responsibility for negotiating commercial and other agreements is lodged with you, and in bringing to your attention certain obstacles to American foreign trade which have been impressed upon me by American exporters and others, I have merely sought to express my point of view for whatever consideration you might care to give it.[5]

Sincerely yours,

George N. Peek

[OF 971:CT]

[1] Not found in the Roosevelt papers.
[2] The statement of Nov. 23, 1932, is meant. This statement is printed in Myers and

Newton, *The Hoover Administration,* pp. 287–288; and in the New York *Times,* Nov. 24, 1932, p. 1.

[3] There is an article in the New York *Times* of this date ("Britain Maintains New Trade Gains," p. 21) but it does not contain any "recent figures." Presumably Peek meant the article cited in the covering letter.

[4] Hull's signed article (on p. 1) was a statement of the argument for reciprocal trade. He said that the Trade Agreements Act was based on precedents going back to the Wilson Administration; its purpose was to prevent another foreign trade debacle such as had been caused by the combination of high tariffs and foreign loans.

[5] See Roosevelt to Hull, Nov. 19, 1934, below.

Roosevelt to Cordell Hull, Secretary of State

Washington, November 14, 1934, 6 P.M.

Confidential

Memorandum . . . : I have just read Norman Davis' No. 32 of November 13th—10 P.M.[1] It seems that matters may come to a head shortly requiring us to take a position as a result of Japanese intention to denounce the Treaty in December.

I think it might be a good idea to telegraph Davis that in the event the conferences break up he should consider:

(a) Giving out my original letter of instructions to him[2] and Admiral Standley.

(b) Seeking at least a gentleman's agreement from the Japanese and the British that they will lay down no ships over and above the numbers provided in existing Washington and London Treaties until after the actual expiration date of those Treaties.

(c) To obtain from them some kind of definite agreement that after the Washington and London Treaties completely terminate none of the three nations will lay down any ship without formal notice to the other nations—this to apply to any and all vessels of more than five hundred tons and to all submarines of any tonnage.

I am suggesting this with the belief that full publicity of construction will be conducive to some future limitation and also that it will perhaps make unnecessary the expenditures of large sums for Naval Intelligence purposes.[3]

F.D.R.

[PSF:London Naval Conference:CT]

[1] Printed in *Foreign Relations, 1934,* I, 328–331. Davis reported that the British had hoped to get the Japanese to accept a revamped version of the Washington Treaty, "with

some face-saving formula," but it was now plain that the Japanese would not accept this. Japan was determined not to continue naval limitation on present principles.

[2] Oct. 5, 1934, above.

[3] Also printed *ibid.*, pp. 333–334.

Roosevelt to Cordell Hull, Secretary of State

Washington, November 19, 1934

Private and Confidential

Memorandum . . . : Like most problems with which you and I have been connected during many years, there are two sides to the argument.

In pure theory you and I think alike but every once in a while we have to modify principle to meet a hard and disagreeable fact! Witness the Japanese avalanche of cotton goods into the Philippines during the past six months.

I am inclined to think that if you and George Peek, who represents the very hard-headed practical angle of trade, could spend a couple of hours some evening together talking over this problem of the most-favored-nation clauses, it would be very helpful in many ways.[1]

F.D.R.

[OF 20:CT]

[1] Hull regarded this memorandum as a proposal that he abandon his program and let Peek take the economic leadership (*Memoirs*, I, 372). See Kannee's memorandum of Nov. 23, 1934, below.

R. Walton Moore, Assistant Secretary of State, to Roosevelt

Washington, November 20, 1934

Dear Mr. President: You may perhaps find of some interest the enclosures, which please do not go to the trouble of having returned to me.

Dr. Dodd's letter presents a rather dark picture of what is going on in Germany. His proposed historical address points out, as he is much in the habit of doing, what a hard task it has been from ancient times until now to assure the mass of the people a fair measure of the good things of life.[1]

In accordance with your suggestion, I have talked at some length with Mr. Steinhardt and shall have some further talk with Mr. Long and am discussing with the Foreign Personnel Board methods that may be employed for improving our Service abroad.[2]

With great respect and warm best wishes for you always, I am, Yours very sincerely,

R. Walton Moore

[PSF:Germany:TS]

[1] "The Emergence of the First Social Order in the United States," delivered by Dodd as his presidential address at the December 1934 meeting of the American Historical Association; printed in *American Historical Review*, XL (Jan. 1935), 217–231.

[2] Laurence Steinhardt, minister to Sweden, and Breckinridge Long, ambassador to Italy, were at this time in the United States on leave. Moore was on the board of the Foreign Service Officers Training School.

[*Enclosure*] William E. Dodd, Ambassador to Germany, to R. Walton Moore

Berlin, November 5, 1934

Dear Judge Moore: We are sending with this pouch a special report (despatch No. 1417, October 26) which has to do with the general military and militaristic situation here.[1] I thought that I might summarize a little of my own observations so that you might speak to the Secretary about it and perhaps save some of his time.

On October 26 I had a conversation with Dr. Schacht.[2] He raised the point once more of treaty negotiations. I said to him: you know the drift of public opinion in the United States still runs strong; and now we have a church issue here which is already bringing further critical, if not hostile, reactions at home. I might say that a number of people, both Americans and Germans, have expressed this view to me personally. Schacht at once said that he realized what a great blunder was being made in the church matter, that he and von Neurath had on several occasions urged upon the Chancellor a more rational policy. He then turned to me and said: "I want to make an appointment with the Chancellor for you to speak with him. He is so completely surrounded by *Partei* people that I think you ought to tell him very frankly what outside opinion is. It might have good effect." I replied that I could not intermeddle in German domestic affairs, but Schacht showed considerable uneasiness. I mention this to you because it shows so clearly the attitude of a great minority in Germany. The majority, however, is, as I judge, entirely committed to the philosophy of complete German unity in every direction and of war as soon as that unity is attained, war primarily against France.

The next day my son and I drove by way of Wittenberg, Leipzig and Nuremberg to Constance, and on Sunday and Monday returned through Stuttgart, Erfurt, Bitterfeld and Leipzig to Berlin. We observed things as closely as we could, and had conversations at several points. In almost every city or town there was marching, either of Hitler Jugend or of SS and SA men in uniform. In Bayreuth, marching and singing kept me awake nearly all the night.

A year ago I had driven over a part of this area, and most of the smokestacks showed that nothing was being done. This time almost every smokestack showed great activity, especially in Bitterfeld, Nuremberg, Stuttgart and Erfurt. These are not the great industrial centers, but from everything I could learn there is great preparation for war. Just what they manufacture in these districts I cannot say, but the activity seemed as great as it was in Chicago in 1928/29. We have learned from Consular reports that in some places they are making poison gas and explosives in great quantities. The Consul in Dresden reported November 1st 1,000 airplanes in that district.

The following conversation at Hechingen on Sunday, October 28, illustrates what the public thinks is going on. We had luncheon at a hotel there, and on the wall next to my table was a poster which I asked the hotel-keeper to give me a copy of. You will see from this map just what lies behind the intensive military preparation. While we were eating, at least 2,000 Hitler Jugend marched past the hotel door. They were singing the usual songs, one of which starts "Siegreich wollen wir Frankreich schlagen." This song was formerly forbidden. It is now heard everywhere, at least I have reports that it is sung here in Berlin when the troops are marching. When the hotel man handed me the picture, I said: "Are all of you learning to fly, as Göring suggests?" He replied: "A very great many. We have twenty expert flyers in this town (9,000 population), and they have registered 2,000 flyers in Stuttgart (capital, as you know, of Württemberg)." I said to him: "Well, that would make a good many flyers for the whole of Germany." He replied: "Yes, all the big business men want war, and the little men are opposed. I don't know what will happen." This man did not know who I was, as nobody else knew during the whole trip, but he showed his natural reactions and was not a little concerned. I merely mention this as illustrative of the feeling that is frequently reflected in conversations but which is never indicated in any public manner. It is fairly certain that nearly all the population is being held under the strictest control, and as I said above, the object is to put France out of business.

The result of all this, if allowed to go through, will of course mean annexations and predominance of the whole of Europe. I am not saying this is certain, only all the contemporary evidence points that way. I need hardly take more of your time.

Sincerely yours,

William E. Dodd

[PSF:Germany:TS]

[1] Not present.

[2] In his *Diary* (p. 180), Dodd reported his conversation with Schacht as having taken place on October 25.

Claude G. Bowers, Ambassador to Spain, to Roosevelt

Madrid, November 21, 1934

Dear Mr. President: Some time ago you asked me to send to you any discussion appearing in Spanish papers regarding the policies of the Administration. There have been references to these policies, sifted through France, but no discussions until very recently when the *Libertad* began a series of articles which are sympathetic and more understanding than usual here. One I have had translated.[1] We are temporarily crippled in the office or I would have had all put into English. The *Libertad* was once owned by the notorious Juan March who passed it on to Alba,[2] president of the Cortes, and it is now owned by the group that supports the robustly democratic and republican party of Barrios,[3] former premier. I am sending a full set to the State Department.

How does it feel to smash all records in an election? One must go back to the Administration of Jefferson to find anything like it in our history. It attracted great attention here. I was amazed two days after the result was known to have a letter of congratulations from Count de Romanones, the old periodic prime minister of the King who ushered him in to kingship and then advised him to get out—a brilliant old man devoted to the monarchist principle, but more the type of English than Spanish monarchist, who boasts to me that he is "the only liberal left in Spain." The night of that day I was at a small dinner with Fernando de los Rios, academically a socialist, former Minister of State,— the sort of man who in America would be a Democrat, and with Madariaga. Both were much excited about the elections.

De los Rios was positively exuberant, rubbing his hands together and exclaiming, "Well we had a set back here but we have won in the United States and England." Madariaga was infinitely pleased. He has come to be almost an admirer of the United States after a long grouch due to our failure to enter the League. Yesterday I saw Herbette[4] the French Ambassador who was clearly astounded at the results.

The effect appears to have been good in the U.S., convincing the "wise and the good" that they may as well adjust themselves to the sentiment of a new nation; it unquestionably is good in Europe. It is strange but true that correspondents in the United States of European papers are either anti-Democratic or anti-American and reading the papers here one would gather that the tide was running clamorously against you. Most of the news published here comes via France and that invariably is hostile to the United States. Then distinguished relics of the old dead social and economic system, having wealth and heading great corporations, come to Europe and conduct a whispering campaign against your policies. The result has been that the average American here has had an erronious[5] impression of public sentiment at home. On one or two occasions when some rich visitor from home, with a superiority complex, has been a bit nasty before the American Luncheon club I have smashed all precedent in good manners by replying with a meat ax. So the result has changed opinion here also, and I suspect, throughout Europe.

The defeat of Reed[6] has created the greatest sensation, since he was the ablest of the critics and backed with a normal majority of unholy size and by the money of the U.S. Steel, the Penn. R. R. and the Mellons. Two days before the election I had a letter from Joe Guffy and it made me heart sick to find him confident. I was sure he would get up the morning after the election completely crushed in spirit. But what a fine thing to find Pennsylvania back in the Democratic column! It was always there in the days of Jefferson and in the days of Jackson and now it is back home.

We are still under military law here. The truth is that there is a reaction against the extreme Rights now in power and I doubt if they could stand an election. By maintaining a "state of war" the Government is able to prevent the opposition from discussing the use of Moors and the Foreign Legion in Asturia where the "atrocities" of the revolutionists can hardly approach that of the others. During the centuries when the Moors overran and dominated Spain there was one spot they never could touch—Asturia. That has been a proud boast for centuries. And now these same Moors have been there shooting Spaniards and forced in there under the protective gun fire of Government warships. The reaction is bound to be bad.

Meanwhile they have Azana, the one great man produced by the republic, imprisoned with no charge that can stand.[7] It is admitted now that he was bitterly against an armed revolt and that he fought hard to prevent Companys[8] from venturing on his seperation movement in Barcelona. But the Church hates him because he seperated church and state and began preparations for a public school system; and the monarchists hate him because he is the ablest man in Spain, and against them; and the high men in the army hate him because he reorganized the army brilliantly and cut 30,000 sons, brothers and sweethearts of the nobility from the list of officers when in many units there were many times more officers than men. Though once provisional President of the Republic and three years prime minister, they have had him in a miserable tiny second class cabin on a boat, with Bello,[9] who rendered distinguished service to education here by his books, and who is now an old man in the last stages of consumption. There has been some reaction against this too.

Lerreux[10] and Rocha,[11] the new Minister of State, are both exceedingly friendly to me and I have no complaint on that score. Whatever government may be in it will want the commercial treaty.

I was closer to the happenings in the Revolution I think than any other person in the corps, so much so that the British came over each day to get the news, and Sir George Grahame[12] twice came over and sat on my terrace and read me his despatch to London to check up on his news. It was due in a measure to the American correspondents here and to the very partiality of some of them. Carney[13] of the *Times* is almost a "professional Catholic," and utterly unfair for the Rights; Jay Allen of the Chicago *News* is a parlor sociolist and utterly unfair to the Rights; and Rex Smith of the A.P. is rampant for the extreme Rights because Gil Robles paper, *El Debate,* is the only one in Madrid that takes the A.P. service. Ziffern[14] of the United Press is just a ~~fair~~ newspaper man looking for actual news. So is Gervosi of the Hearst paper. Each of these called me constantly on every development during the Revolution so I was never without reports for more than fifteen minutes. By ballancing Carney and Smith against Allen, and checking up with Ziffern and Capt.

Rock of the telephone company I was able to get the truth. Allen, intimate with the sociolist leaders, was very valuable since through him I knew what was going to happen before it happened. He was so good I had to get him out of jail—merely by calling the Foreign Office on the telephone—and within an hour. It may be useful to know which of the correspondents have their prejudices and partialities so as to make allowances on their articles.

But I started out merely to sending you the clippings.[15]

With warm personal regards, Sincerely,

Claude G. Bowers

[PSF:Spain:TS]

[1] "A Managed Economy for All," from *La Libertad* of Nov. 13, 1934. The author (not named) saw the National Industrial Recovery Act as the basis of a managed economy that was the opposite of fascism in that is was "founded on the will of the majority and on the general good." Several other clippings from the same newspaper were enclosed.

[2] Santiago Alba.

[3] Diego Martínez Barrio.

[4] Jean Herbette.

[5] Bowers typed his own letters when writing to Roosevelt; as has been previously noted, his spelling was erratic.

[6] Joseph Guffey had defeated David Reed in the November election for senator from Pennsylvania.

[7] Manuel Azaña y Díaz was president of the Republic from 1936 to 1939.

[8] Luis Companys y Jover.

[9] Luis Bello.

[10] Alejandro Lerroux García, Prime Minister.

[11] José Juan Roca.

[12] British ambassador to Spain.

[13] William P. Carney.

[14] Lester Ziffern.

[15] Answered Dec. 3, 1934, below.

Cordell Hull, Secretary of State, to Roosevelt

Washington, November 21, 1934

My dear Mr. President: Referring to your verbal request for an expression by the Department of its opinion as to the need of an American Merchant Marine:

Of recent years, our Federal legislation has aimed at the promotion of coastwise or domestic shipping, as well as foreign. As this Department, however, is primarily interested in the latter field, our opinion is confined to this aspect of the question.

The Administration is committed to a program of increasing our foreign trade, not only as a recovery measure but as a part of a permanent economic policy for the country. The State Department, as one of the agencies employed in forwarding this program, is now engaged in negotiating trade agreements with other nations, in the hope and expectation that from these will flow an increased volume of such trade. No program can succeed without the means of moving the goods to market. The means are ships. In the matter of ships, this country has the choice of having an adequate supply of its own or of relying, to the extent of the deficiency, upon the vessels of other countries. What constitutes an adequate supply necessarily requires, at the time of a decision on this point, a rather arbitrary measuring rod. I have been informed, however, that in the field of world shipping, our own position today is markedly inferior to that of 1920.

Experience from the beginning of the nation has conclusively demonstrated, and it has been the opinion of many of our statesmen since 1789, that to rely unduly on foreign ships exposes us to grave peril. In the event of a real war, such as the last one, the supply is liable to immediate withdrawal, and this might be true whether or not we were engaged in it. Again, at any time it could be reduced or manipulated for purely economic reasons. Then too, in the present savage struggle for markets in which we are competing with the goods of nations whose ships we patronize, it is believed that we are distinctly subject to handicaps in the form of rate discriminations.

On the other hand, having an adequate merchant marine of our own would measurably relieve us from exposure to such hazards and, in addition, would enable us to more successfully compete in foreign markets and thus to reap the fruits which we hope will grow from the trade agreements.

It is our opinion, therefore, that this country should proceed to reestablish itself in a competitively sound position in merchant overseas shipping, and in accordance with a thoroughly coordinated shipping and commercial policy.[1]

Faithfully yours,

Cordell Hull

[OF 99:TS]

[1] In a message to Congress of March 4, 1935 (*Public Papers,* IV, 90–92), Roosevelt recommended abandonment of the system of disguised government subsidies (low-interest loans to shipbuilders and mail contracts to shipping firms) in favor of outright

subsidies. He also recommended the transfer of the Shipping Board Bureau of the Commerce Department to the Interstate Commerce Commission. The measure subsequently introduced (S. 2582 by Copeland on April 15 and H.R. 8555 by Bland on June 19, 1935) provided for a maritime authority and for continuance of mail subsidies. The idea that a strong merchant marine was an arm of national policy (both in peace as well as war) was vigorously supported but the mail subsidy feature was widely attacked in both House and Senate (*Cong. Rec.,* vol. 79, pp. 5616, 9740; vol. 80, pp. 9885–9889, 9899–9902, 10568–10576). Roosevelt, at his April 17, 1936, press conference, said that the Copeland bill as orginally introduced had not met his request; at his May 22 press conference he said, however, that he would not urge any particular measure. The bill as finally passed was a compromise: it did away with the old mail contracts, created the United States Maritime Commission to administer a shipbuilding program under which the government paid up to 50 per cent of the costs, and it limited profits and salaries. It was approved June 29, 1936 (49 *Stat.* 1985).

Press Conference, President's Cottage, Warm Springs, November 23, 1934, 2:17 P.M.

[*Excerpt*] The President: Now, first of all, have you any questions before we talk about other things off the record?

Q: Are you encouraged by the outlook for foreign trade?

The President: Oh; I think it is generally picking up. All the figures show that it is picking up. If you want, I will talk to you for a minute off the record on foreign trade because there has been such a lot of perfect nonsense. As a perfect example, take cotton. We are down in the cotton country now and it is something we use all the time. There are definite efforts being made by—what is the name of that firm in Atlanta? Anderson Clayton—that type of business man, who is a dealer in buying and selling cotton—mind you, this is off the record, every bit of it—there is a real effort being made by the dealers in cotton to maintain the total volume of cotton. In other words, if they get a fifteen million bale crop to sell, they obviously, as commission men, make more money than if they only sell ten million bales of cotton. It is a little like the stock market operations. If you have an average of fifteen million shares a day, you can support three hundred brokerage firms, but if you only have an average of five hundred thousand shares a day, you cannot support as many brokerage firms. Obviously, they want more and more shares dealt in on the Stock Exchange. Obviously, firms like Anderson Clayton like to see fifteen or twenty million bale crops because it is money in their pockets. Now, those people are spreading the rumor that our cotton exports are falling off for the reason that the price is so much above the world price that other countries cannot buy our cotton. Therefore, they are in favor of cheaper cotton.

Their general—I won't say "theory," because they know better—their general effort is to sell the idea to the public that if we have six-cent cotton European countries would buy a good deal more of our cotton. Of course, that is about 98% nonsense. There is about 2% truth. If we do have cheaper cotton, probably we would sell a little more, but only a little more.[1]

Why is the export sale of American cotton decreasing? There are two very simple reasons: The first is that on the other side they are going more and more to substitutes. If you can get that thing out of the State Department when you get home, there is no reason why you should not have a story about it. Breck Long sent home about a month ago a very interesting story from Italy showing that Italy, with government help, had been experimenting on a new cloth made out of 10% cotton and 90% wood fibre.[2] This year they manufactured out of that substitute cotton cloth about two million kilos, which is a lot of cotton. It is roughly about five million pounds of this new cloth. It is a process akin to the rayon process. They take the wood fibre with 10% of cotton and stick it into the rayon process and then they take it out after about half hour through the rayon process and put it into a new process of their own. Probably Italy will be able to get the cost of that new cloth down sufficiently in the course of the next year or two so that they will buy very little of our cotton. Today, Italy takes about a million bales a year. Assuming that this new cloth is a success, it means they will take only one hundred thousand bales instead of a million.

Now, that is only one country that would be doing it. But why is Italy doing it? For all sorts of reasons, the first being that Italy has no exchange with which to buy cotton. She hasn't any money to send out of Italy. Obviously, she wants to keep her money home.

The same thing applies to Germany. Hitler is wearing today a suit made of 90% fibre and 10% cotton. It is a damn good-looking suit and he points it out with pride to every American that comes.

The most important reason for these substitutes is lack of exchange, because all of those countries have been importing more than they have been exporting and therefore they haven't the money to buy goods on the outside.

Then, there is another reason, and that is that a very large number of nations today who have been buying British cotton cloth and American cotton cloth and so forth, also Czechoslovakian cloth, have now started their own factories. Take Brazil, for example. After the war, in 1920 or 1921, Brazil imported all of its cotton goods. Today Brazil is making somewhere around 55 or 60% of its cotton goods. They are making their own shoes in Brazil for the first time.

Of course, while they are establishing their factories, it means we will be exporting a good deal of machinery, but once that new machinery is set up in Brazil and the Argentine, or any other country, as soon as that is set up and they have begun manufacturing, they will buy less and less of our own goods.

Now, what we are trying to do is to offset that by trying to get special agreements with different countries which are essentially on a barter basis. The thing has only been going for a few months and it is helping in the sense that it is preventing the situation from getting worse.

I don't think we can look forward to a vast volume of foreign trade, exports or imports, but at least, through these agreements, we can keep the situation from getting any worse, and on some special lines we may be able to add a little here, there and some other place. Of course the total will amount to a great deal, but, so long as the other nations are headed for a self-sufficiency program, we are not likely to go back to the old figures unless there is an entire change of feeling all over the world.

Now, let us take it from another point of view. That was on manufactured goods. On foodstuffs, the European nations have almost all, up to quite recently, except Hungary or the Balkans, been importers of foodstuffs. Now, as you know, there has been an intensive drive all over Europe and England to raise their own foodstuffs. Why? There are lots of reasons. In the first place, they don't want to export the capital. In the second place, they want to be self-sufficient in case of war. They don't want to be caught as Germany was caught in 1914. The German population nearly starved to death. Of course, all that means less demand for our food crops.

It is not our fault. It is not because of our high prices. Not a bit. It is entirely because those nations have a definite policy to become self-sufficient, both in agriculture and industry. We are just up against it and we are doing the best we can to save what is left. I think that is the easiest way to explain the general foreign trade situation . . .

Q: Do you think that European countries can be self-sustaining and self-sufficient?

The President: Well, of course it depends a little bit on the country. I will give you two examples: Austria and England cannot grow enough foodstuffs to maintain their population. Without any question, I think that is true. There are forty million people in England, which is more than the acreage will support. It is the same way in Austria. On the other hand, countries like Hungary produce more than sufficient to support their population. But they have practically no manufactures. Taking Europe as a whole, they can come pretty close to being self-sustaining. With the surplus of wheat in the Balkan States you would come very close to making up for the deficiencies of wheat in England and Austria and certain parts of Germany.

Q: Where are we going to export our surplus then?

The President: This is still off the record. That brings up a thing which is going to appear this Winter. George Peek believes in the old McNary-Haugen Bill and many other people do. It, in effect, would say to the cotton growers and to the wheat farmers of the country, "Go ahead and waste—go ahead and plant all the wheat you want and we will fix a price for the domestic consumption. We will fix a price for the portion of your crop consumed in this country."

Let us say, in the case of cotton, it will run to fifteen million bales with unrestricted growing. We can use nine million bales in this country. They would be paid a fixed price for the nine million bales. We would pick some figure and pay them that much for the nine million bales. The other six-fifteenths we will take and dump on the rest of the world. That is the McNary-Haugen theory and, as I said, George Peek still believes in it.

Now, of course, that brings up the difficulty of saying to the other nations, "We are going to dump these six million bales of cotton on you at any old figure." You see the implications? It is a little risky to say that to the rest of the world. They may put up barriers against it.

Q: It means, then, intensifying the crop production program?

The President: It means carrying it along on a definite, orderly procedure. In other words, the first year we plowed under 25% of the crop in 1933. The next year, this year, we restricted it by 40%. This coming year we will restrict it by 25%. Probably that will be enough.

Q: Can we write that?

The President: No, you cannot write that. It has to come out of Washington. The following year, we cannot tell. If our exports fall off, we may have to go back to 40%, and eventually we may have to cut the unlimited acreage down to 50%. But probably not. Probably the domestic consumption in this country will be sufficient to take care of 60% of a fifteen million bale crop, as far as you can tell for a number of years ahead. You take this State and any other cotton-growing state, and if they get twelve or fifteen cents a pound for a 60% crop, they are pretty well off financially. All you have to do is to see the South today compared to what it was two years ago. It seems to work from the standpoint of economics.

[President's Press Conferences:T]

[1] The President recurred to this topic in his press conference of Dec. 4, 1934, when he said that American exports of cotton had diminished even when cotton sold for $5\frac{1}{2}$ cents a pound. "Yet, in spite of that surplus of cotton and that price, foreign production of cotton in India, Brazil and other places was increasing. Therefore, cheap cotton not only means starvation for the cotton grower but it does not in any way guarantee increased exports or the stopping of a foreign growth of cotton. I think that is the thing that ought to be emphasized and emphasized and emphasized."
[2] Oct. 12, 1934, above.

Roosevelt to Representative Anthony J. Griffin of New York

Warm Springs, Ga., November 23, 1934

Dear Tony: You are right about inflammatory statements which stir up friendly nations. It is almost impossible to prevent them. Even the New York *Times* has been often guilty.[1]

As ever yours,

[PPF 1995:CT]

[1] Griffin wrote Nov. 19, 1934 (PPF 1995), enclosing a picture from the New York *Daily News,* showing the cordial reception of Babe Ruth in Tokyo. He thought this better evidence of the sentiment of the Japanese than biased editorials, such as one in the same issue, in which it was said: "Japan would welcome the chance to start a fight with us as soon as our defenses became weak enough to make it a good gamble."

Roosevelt to Robert M. Hutchins, President, The University of Chicago

Warm Springs, Ga., November 23, 1934

My dear Hutchins: That is an intensely interesting report of the Committee on International Economic Relations and I hope it will be read by the Interdepartmental Foreign Trade Committee.[1]

Always sincerely,

[PPF 1834:CT]

[1] *International Economic Relations. Report of the Commission of Inquiry into National Policy in International Economic Relations* (Minneapolis: Univ. of Minnesota, 1934), sent by Hutchins with a letter of Nov. 19, 1934 (PPF 1834). Hutchins said that he was not suggesting that the President read the "formidable document" but thought he might be interested in looking at the recommendations that appeared on pages 5 to 11. Among other things, these proposed a fuller exchange of goods and services among nations; continued cooperation with the League of Nations and adherence to the World Court; repeal of the Johnson Act; immediate settlement of the war debts; tariff reduction; and free exportation of gold for settlement of international obligations.

Henry M. Kannee, Assistant to Marvin H. McIntyre, to McIntyre

Washington, 11/23 [1934]

Sec. Sayre 'phoned abt 4:45. After dictating the message below he said: "What Sec. Hull wanted me to say was this: That we would not be bothering the President on this, as we are following his orders as given in a former memorandum, except for the actions of Mr. Peek and the Sec. (Hull) thought it would be much better to send this in and ask the President's approval before the drafts are handed to the Braz. Ambassador tomorrow morning."[1]

On Oct. 30, 1934 a carefully prepared memorandum was handed to the Brazilian Ambassador setting forth the suggestion of the U.S. as to the basis for the trade agreement to be entered into between Brazil and the U.S.

This memorandum had been the subject of discussion between the State Dept. and organizations represented by the trade agreement committee on the one hand and Mr. George N. Peek on the other.

As the result of discussion between Mr. Peek, Mr. Welles and Mr. Sayre, a final agreement was reached as to this memorandum. The President approved it and it was accordingly handed to the Brazilian Ambassador.

The Brazilian Ambassador now states that he believes that his Govt. is favorably disposed towards going forward along the lines indicated by this memorandum but that before giving a definite reply he wishes to submit to his Govt. a definite text in order to indicate with precision what the U.S. Govt. has in mind. The acceptance of the U.S. proposal will mean the rejection of proposals now being made to Brazil by the German Govt. The Brazilian Govt. has therefore declined to make any commitment to the German Govt. until a decision is reached with respect to the U.S. A German delegation empowered to negotiate with the Brazilian Govt. left Rio when this became known to them and will return to Rio in about ten days. The Brazilian Ambassador therefore says that time is of the essence and that the chances of the Braz. Govt. accepting the American proposal will be very greatly increased if the American proposal can be put before the Braz. Govt. at once.

The draft has therefore been prepared of a proposed trade agreement between Brazil and the U.S., including a joint declaration of policy to be given out by the two Govts. upon the signing of the agreement. These drafts have been prepared in accordance with the suggestions contained in the memorandum handed the Braz. Amb. on Oct. 30th and approved by the President.

These draft texts have been worked out by the interdepartmental trade agreements committees and have had the approval of these committees.

At the meeting of the Executive Committee on Commercial Policy held this morning, the texts were approved and agreed to unanimously by all present except Mr. George N. Peek, who voted against them all.

Since urgency is great the Sec. State would like to present these drafts to the Braz. Amb. tomorrow morning. As has already been explained to the President, the principle embodied both in the trade and financial clauses of the agreement is that of unconditional most favored nation treatment. The Braz. Govt. and ourselves pledge reciprocity in all matters dealt with in the agreement, that each shall accord the other treatment no less favorable than that given any other country. This means as far as handling of foreign exchange matters go that if Brazil should enter into an arrangement with any country providing better exchange treatment than is now being granted, such improved treatment would have to be accorded to American trade. It leaves liberty of action to Brazil and protects American trade against any form of inequality or discrimination.

The Braz. Amb. has informally stated that his Govt. will be prepared to relinquish all exchange control on future commercial transactions upon the conclusion of the proposed treaty and to take steps within a period of some 12 months to clear up present blocked exchanges provided normal American banking facilities are obtained. It will be our intention upon the conclusion of the proposed trade agreements to request the Braz. Govt. to make simultaneously a declaration in this sense.

As regards trade treatment, the Braz. Govt. would reduce their tariff now applying to exports in the U.S. Naturally we have selected in our request for reduction those commodities that we are in a position to supply to the Braz. Govt. in competition with the outside world.

This general approach is the one prevailing in existing treaties of the U.S. It is also based on the view that the rule of equality of treatment and the leaving in existence of full possibilities for triangular trade operations are necessary in order to maintain the position of American commerce in many countries which now buy much more from us than we buy from them, particularly the chief European trading countries.

The opinion that this is the most favorable general approach to the subject while we continue to gain experience through the application of the powers embodied in the Tariff Act of 1934 is shared by all the Depts. represented in the trade agreements work except that of the Special Adviser on Foreign Trade.

The documents in the case were voted on favorably at this morning's meeting by the representatives of the State, Commerce, Treasury and Agriculture Depts. and by the A.A.A., by the Tariff Commn. and by the N.R.A.

Mr. Sayre expects to have some word tonight or early tomorrow.

K

[OF 11:CT]

Roosevelt to Adolph S. Ochs, Publisher, the New York *Times,* New York

Warm Springs, Ga., November 26, 1934

My dear Mr. Ochs: It is with regret that I find it necessary to write to you in regard to articles by a gentleman for whom I have high regard—Mr. Arthur Krock.

The particular occasion relates to Mr. Krock's article in the *Times* of November twenty-first, which is in effect a personal attack on the Foreign Minister of Great Britain, Sir John Simon.[1]

For your own information I may add that this article was carried in full by many British papers and coming from the New York *Times* was widely believed to be true. Also for your own information only may I add that Mr. Norman Davis and his colleagues were given great concern by this episode and feel that it has done much to hinder a friendly progress of negotiations in London.

One point I would make is that this article by Mr. Krock is so written as to make it appear that the statements of opinion are not his statements of opinion but are those of the State Department and my Administration as a whole. Frankly, I would not care if the opinions expressed were those of Mr. Krock but naturally I must object when the language implies that they are the opinions of the Government.

Finally, I must be frank in telling you that this is not the first occasion on which Mr. Krock has rendered a real disservice. I found it necessary to call his attention to a similar episode last year which seriously affected our national foreign policy.[2] There have been a number of other incidents which I have passed over, and I shall not refer to them further.

It is because the *Times* is so widely accepted because of the general fairness of its news stories that interpretive articles such as Mr. Krock writes are accepted as statements of news facts and it is only because of the splendid standing of the *Times,* not only in this country but abroad, that I am making this the first—literally the first—exception to my general rule of not writing to any Editor of any paper in regard to stories which their people send out from Washington.

I know that you will appreciate the spirit in which I am sending this

289

to you because you have often asked me to be quite frank with you and to call your attention to anything which I think is not wholly fair.[3]

With my warm regards, Faithfully yours,

[PPF 29:CT]

[1] The reference is to Krock's syndicated column of Nov. 20, 1934 (New York *Times*, Nov. 21, 1934, p. 18). He said that the attitude of the American government on the naval dispute, "as gathered from conversations in the administration's inner councils," was that (1) neither the United States nor Japan was bluffing and Japanese denunciation of the Washington Treaty was expected in December; (2) the United States would not consent to parity with Japan; and (3) Japan planned complete domination of all Asia. Great Britain would have to ally herself with the American position, short only of an actual offensive alliance. Against the possibility of a renewal in some form of an Anglo-Japanese alliance was the question of Japan's reliability in keeping agreements. This attitude, "typical of the view in the highest official American circles," had been transmitted to Norman Davis for his guidance. (Cf. Roosevelt to Davis, Oct. 5, 1934, above.) Krock went on to say that Washington would prefer some one other than Simon to handle the naval conversations: "Sir John appears to be, in certain quarters, the target for the administration's growing impatience and increasing fear that the United States and Great Britain may not maintain a firm and united front against the Japanese claims."

[2] Not further identified.

[3] Answered Nov. 30, 1934, below.

Norman H. Davis, Chairman, American Delegation, London Naval Conference, to Roosevelt

London, England, November 27, 1934

Personal and Confidential

Dear Mr. President: I was glad to get your letter of November 9th[1] and to have your suggestions which I shall bear in mind.

I cannot of course tell what turn events may ultimately take, but considering how vague and uncertain the British attitude was when we arrived and what it is today, I am really encouraged. In my opinion the hesitancy of the British in making up their minds what their policy should be vis à vis Japan was due not to duplicity but to a conflict of opinion within the Cabinet, and also to the fact that the problems presented are more serious to them than to us. But as evidenced by the press and by recent talks with MacDonald, Baldwin and Simon, there has been a distinct crystalization of opinion in the direction in which it ought to go.

The small willful group that favored playing with Japan, and who were supported by commercial interests seeking trade advantages, have apparently been losing ground. The wiser and more responsible leaders now seem convinced that a trade with Japan would be too costly and uncertain of fulfillment; that Great Britain cannot rely upon Japan to respect or protect her interests in the Far East and that they would not only be placing themselves at the mercy of Japan but that they would alienate us, and if the Dominions cannot look to Great Britain for protection they will inevitably look to the United States.

I have not intimated to the British that we might under certain eventualities take steps to impress upon the Dominions the fact that their future security is linked to the United States because it seemed unnecessary and I was afraid the Dominions might resent it. I have, however, intimated strongly that Anglo-American cooperation is of more vital importance to the British Empire than to us and that in case of trouble with Japan, Canada as a practical matter would in fact become our hostage.

General Smuts,[2] with whom I became well acquainted at the Paris Peace Conference, came to see me about a week before he made his recent and famous speech on world politics, emphasizing the necessity for the British Empire to cooperate with the United States. We discussed this Far Eastern problem fully and frankly, as a result of which I was quite satisfied with what his attitude would be, which is very important since he is generally recognized as the leading statesman in the British Empire. I was reliably informed that after his speech there was a meeting between Simon and the High Commissioners of Australia, Canada and New Zealand which Smuts attended and which unanimously endorsed the policy he had enunciated in his speech. This was encouraging because Australia, which has a very favorable trade arrangement with Japan now for the disposal of her wool and which she did not want to have upset, had been inclined to favor a conciliatory policy towards Japan.

I have had exceedingly frank talks with MacDonald, Baldwin and Simon within the past few days and I am satisfied that their views with regard to the Japanese proposals and intentions are substantially the same as ours, and that the only real difference is in regard to tactics. That I think we can iron out.

While Simon is not popular and many question his sincerity or courage of conviction, no one questions his ability, and I am counting on his intelligence to make him see the wisdom of cooperating with the United States. While he undoubtedly wants to maintain if possible the most friendly relations with Japan, he thinks we could both restrain Japan and deal more effectively with her through a tri-partite agreement. However, if the choice has to be made between alienating Japan or the United States, his choice I feel sure will be to go with us. He has I am sure dealt as frankly with me as was possible for him in his official position to do, and he has assured me that they now have no agreement whatever with Japan and under no circumstances will they make one to which we are not a party or to which we can object.

Lord Lothian[3] told me in confidence that as a result of a recent frank and full talk with Simon he is now convinced that Simon is in accord with our views. As an evidence of this Simon asked him to lunch with Neville Chamberlain and himself, evidently with the idea that he, Lothian, might help with Chamberlain who has been the leader of that group in the Cabinet that favored conciliating Japan. At the end of the talk Chamberlain told Lord Lothian that he was now convinced Japan could not be trusted, that she was perhaps bluffing and that England and the United States must at the proper time take a common stand and call this bluff. He thought, however, that it was better to avoid a rupture just now for fear that we would drive Japan in desperation to make an alliance with Germany, which he was satisfied was under consideration.

I have reported by cable the substance of my meeting with Mac-Donald and Simon on the 23rd which was reassuring.[4] I stressed the fact that if Great Britain and the United States are to cooperate satisfactorily they must fully understand and trust one another, and that it was therefore vital that there should be no cause for suspicion and no effort on their part to play the role of mediator which would arouse suspicion. To this they assented with apparent sincerity.

I agree with you that Japan is unable to keep up in a naval race. I understand that they have now reached the point where they cannot continue military expenditures through internal loans and that they will soon have to resort to an increase in taxation, which will bring home to the people a realization of where the militarists have been leading them.

In a talk with Matsudaira yesterday, which I have reported by cable, he insisted that we must not give up hope yet for arriving at an agreement. My impression is that he thinks the wiser political element in Japan is getting concerned over possible Japanese isolation and that with the aid of the Emperor they may yet exercise sufficient influence to make it possible to reach a mutually satisfactory basis of agreement. He said that there was no escape from denouncing the Washington Treaty, but that since a conference would have to be called within a year, he thought we should be able now to reach an agreement that would prevent anything from happening in the meantime and to at least lay the basis for subsequent agreement.

My judgment is that after the Japanese have gotten denunciation out of their system and have had some time to think it over and see that they have nothing, the chances of agreement will be better. One thing that disturbs me is that the world is getting terribly tired of conferences and I am inclined to believe that if we could agree with the British in the near future to discontinue the conversations for the present and send the Japanese home empty handed, we might in the meantime reach a tentative understanding with the British as to our respective naval programs and meet again for so-called preparatory conversations with the Japanese and then reach an agreement and perhaps avoid the calling of an actual conference.

Admiral Standley and I have come to the conclusion that since Japan, for political reasons, is determined not to continue legally bound to an inferior ratio, we could preserve the fundamental basis for naval limitation by maintaining all of the provisions of the existing treaties except as to quantity and then the British and ourselves could discourage and most probably prevent any effort to alter the actual ratio by a quantitative increase to offset any increase on the part of Japan. Qualitative limitation of course works in favor of the great powers.

I apologize for such a long letter to such a busy person. It has been difficult even for me at times to be patient, but so long as the wind is blowing in our direction I feel that I cannot afford to lose my patience.

With warmest personal regards and best wishes, I am, Faithfully yours,

Norman H. Davis

P.S. I am enclosing a cartoon that will interest you.[5]

[PSF:London Naval Conference:TS]

[1] Above.
[2] General Jan Smuts (with General Louis Botha) represented the Union of South Africa at the Paris Peace Conference.
[3] Philip H. Kerr, 11th Marquis of Lothian.

[4] *Foreign Relations, 1934*, I, 368–375.

[5] A Low cartoon from the London *Evening Standard* of Nov. 21, 1934, entitled "Rule Japannia," depicting two buxom women personifying the United States and Great Britain balancing each other on a seesaw, while a third woman, identified as Japan, between the other two was saying, "Very nice yes?—so long as honourable foreign ladies continue to sit apart."

Cordell Hull, Secretary of State, to Roosevelt

Washington, November 28, 1934

My dear Mr. President: The Assembly of the League of Nations has adopted a report providing for the peaceful solution of the Chaco dispute.[1] In accordance with the provisions of the report, this Government has received two invitations from the Secretary General of the League of Nations requesting the United States to participate in the deliberations of an Advisory Committee whose seat shall be at Geneva, and likewise to appoint a representative to take part in the duties of a so-called "Neutral Supervisory Commission" to deal with the military aspects involved in the cessation of hostilities between Bolivia and Paraguay and in the taking of measures necessary to provide for the neutrality of a zone which it is proposed shall extend between the military forces of the belligerent nations in the Chaco.

As you will recall, this Government has upon repeated occasions lent its best efforts towards a peaceful settlement of the Chaco dispute. From 1929 until 1933 the United States, with other American republics, through a so-called "Commission of Neutrals" sitting in Washington, endeavored in consultation with the two parties to the dispute to find an agreement acceptable to both Bolivia and Paraguay providing for a peaceful settlement of the controversy. While the League of Nations had taken cognizance of the dispute from its inception, since both Bolivia and Paraguay were members, so long as the so-called Commission of Neutrals in Washington was functioning, the League supported the endeavors of this Commission and it was only upon the rejection of the formula for settlement finally submitted by the Commission that the League in the spring of 1933 adopted a more active policy. In the autumn of 1933 a Commission of the League, composed largely of representatives of the European powers, was dispatched to South America with instructions to seek to bring about a cessation of hostilities and to obtain an agreement on the part of both belligerents to submit the controversy to arbitration. During the course of the Montevideo Conference, as you will recall, the moral support of the American republics represented in the Conference, including that of the United States, was offered this peace agency. The efforts of the League Commission, however, failed, inasmuch as none of the reports or recommendations which they formulated were acceptable to the belligerents. Upon the failure of this phase of League activity, the initiative in July last was taken by the Argentine Government, which requested and obtained the active cooperation and support of the United States and Brazil in seeking to bring about an agreement between Paraguay and Bolivia upon bases formulated by Dr. Saavedra Lamas, the Argentine Foreign Minister, which provided for a peaceful adjudication of the dispute. In September last, owing to the fact that the League Assembly was due to meet and, under the terms of the Covenant, was obligated to take further cognizance of the dispute owing to the demand previously formulated by Bolivia, these negotiations were suspended at the instigation of Argentina and with the acquiescence of Paraguay and Bolivia.

The report now adopted by the Assembly provides primarily for three separate stages in the proposed solution of the dispute:

(1) The creation of a Neutral Supervisory Commission to be composed of representatives of Argentina, Chile, Peru, Uruguay (all members of the League) and of Brazil and the United States, neither one of which is a member of the League, should the latter two states agree to participate. The duties of this Commission are to supervise and facilitate the cessation of hostilities between Bolivia and Paraguay, and to regulate the control of a temporary neutral zone between the military forces of the two countries the width of which shall be fixed by the Commission. The Commission is to assemble at Buenos Aires and to decide where its headquarters shall be. It is authorized to determine its own methods of work and to make its own rules of procedure; and its decisions are to be by a majority vote of the members present. The chair is to be held by all members in rotation and should the votes be equally divided, the chairman is to have a casting vote. It is stated that the creation of the neutral zone is "a measure of a purely military character," and that it is not the intent "to prejudice in any way the settlement of the territorial or frontier questions involved in the present dispute."

(2) There is to be constituted with its seat in Geneva an Advisory Committee composed of the representatives of twenty-three states, including European and Asiatic powers as well as American states, which is constituted "to follow the situation more especially as regards the execution of the Assembly's recommendations for the settlement of the

dispute and to assist the members of the League to concert their action and their attitude among themselves and with non-member states, more particularly as regards the most effective application, the modification, or withdrawal of the prohibiting of the supply of arms." The Committee shall have power "to make any communication, recommendation, or proposal which it considers desirable to the members of the League, the Assembly, or the Council"; it is particularly to "bear in mind the Assembly's desire that the state of breach of obligations (of the Covenant of the League of Nations) to settle disputes by peaceful means shall promptly be brought to an end."

(3) The holding of a conference of representatives of American states to meet at Buenos Aires within one month of the date of cessation of hostilities, for the purpose of conducting negotiations looking to the conclusion of a treaty of peace. This conference would be limited to the American republics and would assemble upon the invitation of the President of the Argentine Republic. Its purpose would be to find within a period of not to exceed two months an agreement between Bolivia and Paraguay based upon the final delimitation of the frontier between the two countries, and upon security and economic clauses. In the event that this conference should not succeed in attaining its objective, the report of the League provides that the two belligerent Governments are bound to call upon the Permanent Court of International Justice to give judgment in accordance with provisions which they shall previously have agreed upon.

Neither Bolivia nor Paraguay have as yet expressed themselves with regard to the report.

Throughout the years that this controversy has continued, and during the period when actual warfare has existed, the finding of a peaceful settlement has repeatedly been hampered by disagreement between the American mediating nations. The present report of the League provides the first occasion upon which all of the American republics (other than Brazil and the United States) have officially agreed upon a formal recommendation for the settlement of the dispute. There has likewise, as you know, existed on the part of certain of the American republics the suspicion that the United States might attempt through its major influence to dictate to the exclusion of other American nations the settlement of the controversy. Because of the special circumstances existing, I fear that were the United States to appear to adopt an attitude of passive opposition and refuse to cooperate, so far as it is able to do so, with the other American republics in this peace effort which has met with their official approval, the blame for the possible failure of the

League efforts, or for the refusal of Bolivia or Paraguay to agree to the terms of the report, would be placed definitely upon the United States and that as a result thereof a very considerable amount of resentment might be created against this Government. While it would unquestionably be desirable that all inter-American disputes be adjusted by purely American peace agencies, the time has not yet come when the necessary machinery is functioning, nor have the peace agencies created by common agreement between the American nations so far acquired sufficient prestige to prove their usefulness at this juncture. On the other hand I am, of course, clear that the United States should not take part in any committee which is constituted to sit in Geneva and which is responsive solely to the necessities and exigencies of the League organization.

For the reasons above expressed, and after very full consideration of the important elements in this situation, I believe that the wisest course for this Government to follow would be to decline the invitation to participate in the Advisory Committee of Geneva, but to indicate its willingness to take part in the conference to be called by the President of Argentina, and in the work of the Neutral Supervisory Commission, provided the American representative on the latter Commission shall be without power to vote or to commit this Government in any way without specific instructions to that effect.

I am attaching herewith for your consideration the text of the two invitations received from the Secretary General of the League of Nations and of the draft replies which I recommend should be sent in reply thereto.[2]

Throughout the course of the past months the Government of Brazil, which is, as I have said above, like ourselves, not a member of the League, has been in close and friendly consultation with this Government regarding all developments in the Chaco dispute. Similar invitations have been extended to Brazil, and before our official replies are sent to Geneva, I desire to consult fully with the Government of Brazil in order that if possible our replies may be of similar tenor.

I shall greatly appreciate your early decision as to the policy here recommended, inasmuch as if our official reply to Geneva is not sent in the near future considerable misunderstanding of our position may ensue and an opportunity may be afforded for misconstruction of the motive for our delay in replying to the invitations of the League.

Faithfully yours,

Cordell Hull

Enclosures:
    From American Consul, Geneva, No. 354, November 24, 10 P.M.
    From American Consul, Geneva, No. 356, November 24, midnight.
    Two draft telegrams to American Consul, Geneva.

[OF 338-C:TS]

[1] This report, adopted Nov. 24, 1934, set up an advisory committee headed by Francisco Castillo Nájera of Mexico (New York *Times,* Nov. 25, 1934, p. 28).

[2] Actually one invitation in two cables from Prentiss B. Gilbert, consul in Geneva, to Hull, sent within two hours of each other late Nov. 24, 1935; the second merely added further information (*Foreign Relations, 1934,* IV, 113, 114). The draft reply was approved by Roosevelt in a note to Hull of Dec. 3, 1934 (below), and was sent by Hull to Gilbert under date of Dec. 6, 1934, printed *ibid.,* p. 125.

Cordell Hull, Secretary of State, to Roosevelt

Washington, November 30, 1934

Dear Mr. President: I beg to call your attention to the fact that the term of office of the Honorable Newton D. Baker as a member of the Premanent Court of Arbitration at The Hague expired June 4, 1934, and it therefore seems desirable for you either to re-designate him or to designate someone else to fill the vacancy.

Our Government, as a party to the Convention under which the Hague Tribunal is constituted, is entitled to select not more than four persons of known competency in international law to constitute the panel from which arbitrators are chosen when such a choice is necessary.

At this time the American members of the panel whose terms have not expired are Messrs. Elihu Root, John Bassett Moore and Manley O. Hudson.

The practice is, after deciding upon an appointee, to inquire whether he is willing to accept, and if so, notify the Secretary General of the Permanent Court of Arbitration, through the American Legation at The Hague, of the appointment.

I am enclosing for your information copy of a letter just received from Mr. Baker to whose attention the matter had not previously been invited.

Yours very sincerely,

Cordell Hull

[OF 245:TS]

[*Enclosure*] Newton D. Baker to Cordell Hull

Cleveland, November 28, 1934

My dear Mr. Secretary: My attention has only now been drawn to the fact that my appointment as member of the Permanent Court of Arbitration either has expired or will shortly expire. The record is that I was appointed first by Mr. Coolidge and later by Mr. Hoover. I have thus had two appointments.

The designation of American members is important only because there is always the possibility of a vacancy in the Permanent Court of International Justice and a request for nominations from the American Panel of the Court of Arbitration. Nevertheless the appointments on the American Panel are a real distinction and I know no lawyer who would not be honored by being so designated. Under these circumstances, and in view of the fact that I have been twice appointed, I am writing to urge you to feel most complete personal and official freedom in the next selection. I should wholly understand the action of the Department if some one else, whose professional and personal qualifications the President desires to recognize, is recommended to him for designation.[1]

Respectfully and cordially yours,

Newton D. Baker

[OF 245:T:Copy]

[1] See Phillips to Roosevelt, Dec. 31, 1934, below.

Adolph S. Ochs, Publisher, The New York *Times*, to Roosevelt, Warm Springs

[New York] November 30, 1934

My dear Mr. President: I am sincerely grateful to you for taking me at my word and frankly calling my attention to a publication in *The Times* which impresses you as "not wholly fair" and misrepresentative of the facts.[1] I appreciate even more that your motive in so doing is based on what you consider the high reputation of *The Times* for fairness and accuracy. These standards I have sought to maintain always. Mr. Krock happened to be here today and I showed him your letter.

You say that the attitude toward the policies of Sir John Simon, as set out in Mr. Krock's article, was not representative of the State Department or of your administration as a whole, was therefore untrue and, in addition, was a hindrance to friendly negotiations then proceeding in London between this Government and the British. Mr. Krock informs me that he based his article on the statement of not one, but several persons who are recognized as reflecting the administration feeling in these matters. I am sure if you would discuss the article with Mr. Krock personally he could enlighten you with respect to other details.

He also informs me that, among the many persons who wrote him in approval of this article as having contributed greatly to the Anglo-American amity that, coincidentally, followed its publication, were persons of whose devotion to accord between the two countries you yourself would be the last to question. These persons, moreover, were in the closest touch with what was proceeding at London. Mr. Krock says, further, that representatives of *The London Times* assured him that the article was most useful, and he was surprised and grieved to hear that—instead of being helpful—it had caused you embarrassment and complications in London. We have a dispatch from the diplomatic correspondent of *The London Times* repeating in effect what Mr. Krock had written in expressing the gratification of the British that Sir John, in Parliament and elsewhere, had made amends.

In the instance of the Sir John Simon article, Mr. Krock tells me that he consulted with persons devoted to you and to the cause of Anglo-American accord, who assured him that the publication would serve the best possible purpose.

I sympathize deeply with the magnitude and burden of your great task, on the success of which the fate of the world depends. I am certain I need not assure you that I should not for a moment tolerate what I thought to be mischievous, malicious or untrue writing in *The New York Times*. It is the fixed policy of *The New York Times* to aid the Government in every way possible, and not willingly to embarrass it, and I believe that Mr. Krock understands and makes every effort to carry out that policy. I do not think that, by and large, the contents of *The New York Times* have been a hindrance to you in your effort to bring prosperity and peace to the American people and to the world. Certainly I should be more than distressed if I thought that they had.

With every good wish, Yours faithfully,

Adolph S. Ochs

[PPF 29:TS]

[1] Nov. 26, 1934, above.

Roosevelt to Claude G. Bowers, Ambassador to Spain, Madrid

Warm Springs, Ga., December 3, 1934

Dear Claude: That is an extraordinarily interesting letter of yours and I am asking Cordell to read it because both he and I continue to be concerned about the stories sent out of the United States by the foreign correspondents, especially the French.[1]

I am, of course, delighted that the Spanish papers are discussing American news with some intelligence. The ravens over here all said we could not do half as well in the election as things actually turned out. Since November sixth they have been talking about the dire disaster which will follow from a top-heavy majority in the Congress. I still continue to be unworried.

You are doing a grand job.

As ever yours,

[PSF:Spain:CT]

[1] Nov. 21, 1934, above. Hull said he had read it "with a great deal of interest" (Hull to Roosevelt, Dec. 24, 1934, PSF:Spain).

Roosevelt to Cordell Hull, Secretary of State

Warm Springs, Ga., December 3, 1934

Memorandum for the Secretary of State: As I have told you over the telephone, I entirely approve the course outlined by you in your letter of November twenty-eighth, in regard to our policy in the matter of the Chaco dispute.[1]

F.D.R.

[OF 338-C:CT]

[1] Above.

Lincoln MacVeagh, Minister to Greece, to Roosevelt

Athens, December 4, 1934

Dear Franklin: Christmas wishes will be crowding in upon you and Eleanor by the thousands but a few more, husky enough to reach you in good condition from the other side of the world, can't do you any harm. We all send them, including little Eleanor, who, I am glad to say, has come through her operation very well, and certainly seems a happier and stronger child than before the acute attack which made it necessary.[1]

I am just now taking a vacation, but my address, as you see, is unchanged. We hope to get back home for a vacation next summer, but in the meantime it seems best to use this past year's leave to do and see things in the immediate neighborhood which we have no time for when we are actually "en poste." This idea, however, seems to be so unheard of that the Greek press has taken it up as news, and everyone seems to have read that the American Minister is devoting his precious leave not to going to Paris but to studying Greece! In enjoying ourselves we flatter our hosts, and thus seem to be killing two birds with one stone.

Last week we sailed over to Smyrna on an American Export boat and spent two days there, driving up country to Bergama—ancient Pergamon—and calling on the Consul and the Governor. With our trip to the Dardanelles last Spring, we have now seen a goodly strip of the Asia Minor coast. Here in Greece we hear a great deal about the new Turkey, whose friendship means so much to this country at present. I have the official view of Turkish progress and achievement pretty well by heart. But though the vigor of the Government and the wealth of the land itself seems undeniable, the human material which the Government has to work with is very disappointing to the observer. A huge effort like that of Mussolini, or of Hitler, is being made to construct a great State on the occidental plan, and the population consists of orientals from whom their religion, the only thing that ever galvanized them into action, is taken away! It is a commonplace to remark on the fact that the immemorial business-men of Turkey have been driven out—the Greeks, the Armenians and the Jews. What I have wanted to see is how the Turks are getting along with only themselves as substitutes. Apparently they have taken to the new bureaucracy like ducks to water. They are a governing race. But now they must do the work of the country as well, and the people's poverty and ignorance are appalling. Taxes are terribly high, and paid because it is the will of those higher up, not because the necessity for them is understood. In Greece every person thinks too much about affairs, so that politics are always in a turmoil. But at least the population as a whole is vitally responsive to ideas. It can be appealed to, as any Western people can be. But, with orientals of the dull psychological type of the Turkish peasantry, to try to make a modern organized State seems very like trying to make bricks without straw. I was much impressed by the peasants I talked with who were refugees from Macedonia. They all longed to get back even to that unhappy region from a country where they can call neither piastres nor souls their own. As I wrote to Smouch[2] the other day, I wonder whether the New Turkey, the product of the Great War, will not easily dissolve away in any new general conflagration. Or perhaps a recrudescence of Mohammedanism, when the present strong-willed rulers disappear, will do the trick. Certainly when we got to the Greek island of Samos, across a narrow strait from Asia Minor, we sensed a great difference at once. It was the difference between a small people of high vitality and a huge depressed population. The vitality of Turkey is concentrated in the head. In Greece it quivers in every limb of every Greek that breathes. Differences like this are not to be observed in the rooms and corridors of Foreign Offices. But they inevitably influence international affairs in the long run. In talking with the island Greeks who are near to her, I find less confidence in Turkey as the Greek rock of defense than is expressed here in Athens. Those long-suffering people doubtless know that by taking a fez off a leopard one does not change his spots. East is East and West is West, and the line still runs where it always has. I am very fond of the upper-class Turks I have met and sympathetic with their problems. But to understand, one must get down to humble realities, and one cannot go about in Turkey without gaining the impression that its future is a huge question-mark.

Meanwhile the international situation in the Near East is very strongly affected by the Greco-Turkish rapprochement, however formal or temporary this may be. The Balkan Entente, of which it is the keystone, was further elaborated, along economic lines, at Ankara this fall. As the Balkan Pact stands for non-revision of the Treaties, Bulgaria still refuses to join, but the idea of Balkan solidarity has received such stimulus that in one way or another Bulgaria may yet find a way to take her place beside the others in a regional groupment embracing the entire peninsula. The League of Nations, too, is very useful in this part of the world. By settling the Rhodope Forest dispute, it has opened the way to the composition of other long-standing difficulties between Greece and Bulgaria, and a nasty argument now going on with Albania over the schooling of the Greek minority is also being referred to Geneva.

Greece, like most other countries, was frightened by the assassination of King Alexander, and is watchfully waiting for the League to conjure the dangers inherent in the tempers of Yugoslavia and Hungary. Actually, and for the time being, M. Barthou's death was of more consequence here, however. He had become the active soul of the system in which Greece placed herself, at least with one foot, when she signed the Balkan Pact with two nations of the Petite Entente. The success of the Germans in Poland, and the impression which this created in Rumania (though Titulesco[3] made a quick recovery) has somewhat shaken the Greek faith. On the other hand, the Russian rapprochement with France, which was the answer to Poland's defection, means much to Greece on account of the importance of Russia to Turkey, and meanwhile she waits to see what Laval[4] can do in Barthou's shoes with Italy. Indeed, Greece is so completely vulnerable from every side that she literally must have friends. The old game of the balance of power is being played all over again in Europe today, and Greece's hesitations and fears supply a watcher in Athens with an almost daily record of how it progresses. When the next war comes, I believe she will do her best to repeat her accidental success of 1917–18, and stay out till it is perfectly clear which band-wagon she ought to jump on. In this sense, her foreign policy at present is perhaps nearer that of England than of any other power. The eventual actions of these two depend on so many variables as to be practically impossible of prediction.

Internally, M. Veniselos almost forced the Government to go to the people a few weeks ago, but his lines gave way, and when seventeen of his senators went over to the other side, the jig was up for the moment. The Popular (Royalist) party is now even more securely in the saddle, and continues to pursue its policy of economic and fiscal retrenchment, and of temporizing on every controversial issue. Our trade with Greece is growing in spite of the difficulties in its path, and I have awakened the Foreign Minister's interest in our new tariff policy, so that the way is prepared for approaching a commercial treaty should our authorities think one desirable at any time. Financially, the Government's position goes on improving, and Greece has lived up to the agreement made last year with her foreign bond-holders to pay a percentage of the interest due. We have shared in these payments, though Greece in principle still maintains that our Refugee Loan of 1929 is really a war-loan, and her position on war-loans remains unchanged.

I hope I have not written too much about what are, naturally, vitally interesting topics to me. Greece is still beautiful, and I need say nothing about that. Senator Joe Robinson, who seemed to enjoy it, can tell you what it's like. Senator Tom Connally, too, drove about with us a bit, and Representative Cochran, a very likeable Republican, from my ancestral State of Pennsylvania.[5] You will have seen a lot in the American papers about the marriage of Princess Marina of Greece to the Duke of Kent. There is some sentiment, or sentimentality, about that here too. But almost fifty per cent of the population of Greece would emphasize to any inquirer that the Princess has no Greek blood and no Greek passport. M. Papanastassiou,[6] Ex-Premier and so-called "Father of the Republic" (Mr. Morgenthau, Senior, knows him well), told me: "the English Prince would have had far better chance of becoming King of Greece if he had not married that Princess," and intimated that he had no chance at all, anyway. Royalist propaganda is noticeably absent. But, of course, Greek politics shift so quickly that it may spring up tomorrow. (One has to qualify every statement or prediction involving Greeks.

The results of the election at home were tremendously encouraging. Smouch ends a letter with the post-script: "These are times!" They certainly seem to be, and I'm glad they are times in which you are the boss.

Affectionately yours,

Lincoln MacVeagh

P.S. Your welcome letter of Christmas and New Year's greetings to the Foreign Service has just arrived, in good time for me to relay it on to everyone.[7]

[PSF:Greece:TS]

[1] Eleanor, daughter of Hall Roosevelt, was visiting the MacVeaghs.
[2] Hall Roosevelt.
[3] Nicolae Titulescu, Rumanian Foreign Minister.
[4] Pierre Laval, French Foreign Minister.
[5] Thomas C. Cochran, who with Robinson and Connally had attended the meeting of the Interparliamentary Union in Istanbul.
[6] Alexander Papanastasiou.
[7] The President sent MacVeagh's letter to Senator Robinson to read; he returned it with the comment that his own information confirmed what MacVeagh had said and that he regarded him as the best qualified man for the post (Robinson to Roosevelt, Jan. 11, 1935, PSF:Greece).

Roosevelt to Henry Morgenthau, Jr., Secretary of the Treasury

Washington, December 6, 1934

Memorandum for the Secretary of the Treasury: The enclosed from Nicholson does not alleviate the question mark in my mind in regard to the Chinese situation.[1]

Please remember that I have a background of a little over a century in Chinese affairs. China during the past hundred years has not changed very much if you think of China as an aggregation of four hundred million people.

By the year 1840 foreign finance had a definite foothold along the coast—Macao, Canton, Foochow, Shanghai, Hankow, etc.—also Hongkong which did not become British until 1841.

The fringe of China, represented by the above foreign influences, has been extended very, very slowly until today the foreign influence in banking extends to many interior places. The four hundred million of people in China have no method of expression in monetary or financial matters. The government of China, because it must use or deal with foreign capital, is obliged to conform with international standards. These standards expressed by the foreign advisors of the Chinese Government—i.e., British, Japanese, French, Dutch and American—represent without question what the banking interests of the world call "unorthodox."

You and I know that during the past twenty months our gain has been due to our decision not to accept orthodox advice.

I have no doubt that your missionary friend[2] will give you a very comprehensive report covering all of the back districts of China.

Remember, nevertheless, that he, like all other missionaries, runs in, for instance, to the European advisors in these same back districts for advice on economic questions just as he does when his life or his missionary property is threatened.

China has been the Mecca of the people whom I have called the "money changers in the Temple." They are still in absolute control. It will take many years and possibly several revolutions to eliminate them because the new China cannot be built up in a day.

I am inclined to believe that the "money changers" are wrong and that it is better to hasten the crisis in China—to compel the Chinese people more and more to stand on their own feet without complete dependence on Japan and Europe—than it is to compromise with a situation which is economically unsound and which compromise will mean the continuation of an unsound position for a generation to come.[3]

F.D.R.

[OF 150:CT]

[1] Martin R. Nicholson was a Treasury agent in China.
[2] Not identified.

[3] An appeal for cooperation from Finance Minister Kung, however, led to an agreement by the United States to a maximum price of 55 cents an ounce for silver except that domestically mined (*Foreign Relations, 1934,* III, 455–457). This agreement was shortly given up because of pressure from the silver bloc; see John M. Blum, *From the Morgenthau Diaries* (Boston: Houghton Mifflin, 1959), I, 206–207.

Roosevelt to William Phillips, Under Secretary of State

Washington, December 6, 1934

Memorandum for the Under Secretary of State: I entirely approve your letter to the Canadian Prime Minister in regard to the British Columbia Trail Smelter case.[1] If the Canadian Government should fail to send a representative to Washington to expedite a settlement of this case—what would you think of our asking the Canadian Government to refer the whole matter to the World Court at the Hague, provided always that we could get not only a hearing but a determination from the World Court within a comparatively short space of time, for example, one year?

My suggestion is based on the thought that if the World Court should give us definite action through a decision, and especially if that decision were favorable, it would do much to improve our chances of joining the World Court itself in a permanent manner.

F.D.R.

[OF 1495:CT]

[1] Sent by Phillips to Roosevelt with a note of Dec. 3, 1934 (OF 1495) and presumably returned to him. The smelter was a large one operated by a Canadian mining company at Trail, British Columbia, across the border from Washington. Fumes from it had destroyed crops, timber and all vegetable growth over more than 50,000 square miles and had seriously affected the health of some 2,000 people (Governor Clarence D. Martin of Washington to Roosevelt, Oct. 8, 1934, OF 1495). Efforts of the State Department to obtain satisfaction from the Canadian government for claims of the American citizens affected, carried on for several years, had been fruitless. In the letter cited, Governor Martin asked that the Canadian government either stop the nuisance or agree to submit the matter to an impartial tribunal. See Roosevelt to Phillips, March 18, 1935, below.

Press Conference, Executive Offices of the White House, December 7, 1934, 4:00 P.M.

[*Excerpt*] Q: I have a new question to ask: There has been pending in the Senate since 1931 a treaty for the preservation of the beauty of

Niagara Falls and within the last year there have been two big slides up there and, really, the people on the Niagara frontier are concerned about it. Canada did ratify the treaty but our Government never did, the Foreign Relations Committee turning it down.[1] I am wondering if anybody did anything about it?

The President: I will have to check on that; I did not know there was a treaty.

Q: The operating companies—there was a provision that the power companies would get 10 per cent more water.

The President: I remember that when I was Governor. Didn't I write a letter opposing it?

Q: I do not know.

The President: I think I did on the ground that if there was any more water to be taken, the power companies should pay for it. As I remember it, they were going to get the additional water for nothing and I think, as Governor of the State of New York, I wrote a letter of opposition to it on that ground.[2]

Q: That would be sound opposition but I wondered, on the larger thing, whether there was anything done on the preservation?

The President: I think something should be done. It is a brand new thought. I think I will take it up. It is a grand question. As I understand it from geologists, the question is whether you can eat your cake and have it—in other words, whether you can have enough water go over the Falls and, at the same time, prevent the crest of the Falls receding year by year. They have been doing it at the rate of several thousand years and, at the present rate, they will be getting back to Lake Erie well after we are dead. It is a question. And another suggestion that was made was that the Falls should be turned on every so often for the benefit of sightseers and then turned off again. But I am glad you told me about it. I will take that up and find out where it is.

Q: Can you tell us for what purpose you are sending Ambassador Gibson to Europe?

The President: Sending whom?

Q: Hugh Gibson.

The President: I am not sending him to Europe. I did not know he was going until he told me he had a small boy over there who was sick. He is over in the mountains and Hugh is going over.

Q: I was just wondering whether you had asked him to go over?

The President: No, he is going over to see his boy; nothing official in it.

Q: Can you tell us whether General MacArthur will be Chief of Staff after the fifteenth?

The President: I cannot.[3]

Q: Can we induce you to comment on the naval negotiations?

The President: No. I think that as things stand you know about as much as I do. You read Norman Davis' speech[4] and Cordell Hull talked to you off the record on it yesterday.[5] I do not think there is any more can be said on it now.

Q: Any background on the situation in the Balkans?

The President: Again, off the record, I did not know anything until I read the first edition of the *Star*. I talked to the Secretary of State and he has been telegraphing to various people of ours in the embassies and legations. We have not heard a word yet. Maybe the wires are down.[6]

[President's Press Conferences:T]

[1] The committee, on Feb. 18, 1931, rejected a proposed treaty that would have permitted diversion of 20,000 cubic feet per second more from the falls in exchange for scenic-preservation safeguards the power companies would have built. The committee favored action that would preserve the beauty of the falls but believed the United States should do the work and should pay for it (New York *Times*, Feb. 19, 1931, p. 11).

[2] Roosevelt to Senator Robert F. Wagner, Feb. 9, 1929, in *Public Papers*, I, 167–171. Roosevelt's objection was not to the method proposed but to the fact that the Niagara Falls Power Company had been paying rental for water from the falls under protest. He endorsed the treaty after the power company agreed to withdraw its protest and agreed to pay rental for the additional water.

[3] General Douglas MacArthur served as chief of staff until Oct. 2, 1935.

[4] In his speech of December 6 before the American correspondents in London, Davis said that the Washington Conference had affirmed the inherent right of every power to equal security but that this did not mean equal armaments. It established an equilibrium that the United States wished to continue; abandonment of equal security would lead to insecurity, international suspicion, and costly competition (*Foreign Relations, Japan, 1931–1941*, 269–271).

[5] At his morning press conference of December 7 (OF 20) Hull said that if Japan denounced the Washington Treaty, the assumption would be that she was ending the conversations. But he added: "Even if denounced today its provisions would remain in force until the end of 1936. An adjournment at the time of denunciation would give two years to the interested nations to realize the situation that would be created by the abandonment of the naval treaties and, we hope, to find ways and means of agreeing to continue an effective cooperation both in the fields of political stability and naval limitation."

[6] Although the President made this statement off the record, it appeared in the Washington *Evening Post* of Dec. 8, 1934, in this form:

"The American Government yesterday called upon its diplomatic representatives in the Balkan states for full information on the expulsion of nearly 30,000 former Hungarians from Yugoslavia. The request for details was made by the State Department at the request of the White House, President Roosevelt disclosed. Explaining to newspaper correspondents that this Government had received little information on the Balkan situation, Mr. Roosevelt added with a smile: 'Perhaps the wires are down.' "

Lyle C. Wilson, manager of the Washington bureau of the United Press Associations, apologized for the publication of the off-the-record statement in a letter to Early of Dec. 8, 1934 (OF 182). He enclosed the clipping cited, and said the story had been written by a man who had had many years experience with the United Press but was not regularly assigned to the White House. He thanked Early for the latter's assurance by telephone that he understood the story had been written in good faith.

Roosevelt to Henry L. Stimson, New York

[Washington] December 8, 1934

Personal

My dear Harry Stimson: I read that delightful article by Ramsay Muir one night at Warm Springs after I had gone to bed.[1] I read it through again the next night. Thank you much for sending it to me. It is a splendid expression of faith.

I am glad to say that Norman Davis seems to be making real progress with our British friends.

Always sincerely,

[PPF 20:CT]

[1] Presumably "Civilization and Liberty," in *Nineteenth Century,* XVI (September 1934), 213–225.

Roosevelt to Michael Francis Doyle, Chairman, American Committee in Geneva, Philadelphia

[Washington] December 10, 1934

My dear Mr. Doyle: Thank you very much for sending me the report on the International Regulation of the Trade in and Manufacture of Arms and Munitions, prepared by Manley O. Hudson for the American Committee in Geneva, at the request of the special committee of the United States Senate to investigate the Munitions Industry.

This is a very interesting report and I am glad to have it.[1]

Very sincerely yours,

[OF 178:CT]

[1] Manley O. Hudson, *Munitions Industry, International Regulation of Trade in and Manufacture of Arms and Ammunition, Report Presented on Sept. 1, 1934, by the American Committee in Geneva to the Special Committee Authorized by the Senate to Investigate the Munitions Industry* . . .

(Washington, 1934), enclosed in Doyle's letter of Nov. 22, 1934 (OF 178). Roosevelt sent the report back to Hull with a note of Dec. 8, 1934 (OF 178): "I have read the enclosed with much interest and am sending it to you for your use."

Press Conference, Executive Offices of the White House, December 12, 1934, 10:30 A.M.

[*Excerpt*] The President: . . . Now, most important of all, I am having a meeting at 2 o'clock today with—you had better take these names down because I haven't any copies—with Secretary Hull, Secretary Morgenthau, Secretary Dern, General MacArthur, Secretary Wallace, Secretary Swanson and Harry Roosevelt, Secretary Perkins, Coordinator Eastman,[1] George Peek and Bernard M. Baruch and General Johnson.

Now I have got you all intrigued. Isn't that a funny combination?

Q: Is it for tea? (Laughter)

The President: It all goes back and is a long story. Those of us who served in the World War know that we got into the war in a great hurry. We had never been in a war on such a scale in our national history and, as a result of it, we muddled through the war and did a lot of things we should not have done.

After the war was over, there was a very large sentiment in the country for so ordering things by law that if we should unfortunately get into another war, we would eliminate some of the very great faults of the World War.

One of the principal students of that particular problem was Mr. Baruch. He and General Johnson worked very hard for a good many years on the possibility of legislation which, in a broad sense, could be legislation to take the profit out of war.

Probably no two people have done more work on that subject than Baruch and Johnson. There were a number of Congressional hearings of various kinds, I don't recall just what they were, but I think both Baruch and Johnson did appear before the Senate and House Committees and the whole subject was pretty thoroughly canvassed. Nothing was ever done about it. There was no legislation passed.

We have decided that the time has come when legislation to take the profit out of war should be enacted. We are meeting this afternoon in order to discuss such legislation. It is with the idea that some time, fairly early in the session, I will be able to send a message to the Congress on this general subject.

Everybody in the country knows what munitions profits and other profits meant during the World War. Not only our country, but the world as a whole, is pretty thoroughly alive to these profits of munitions makers in time of war and in time of peace.

Gerald Nye's investigation has helped very materially in making people conscious of it and there is another reason for doing it now and that is that the world is at peace and there does not seem to be any war that is pending. That is another reason why it is an opportune time to take the subject up.

I imagine that we will discuss the whole range of the subject. In other words, not merely the financial side of it but also the economic side of it, bearing in mind that as a result of the last war, the World War, a good many things happened that, perhaps, headed us for the unfortunate ten-year period that succeeded the war such as overproduction, enormous salaries, enormous personal profits and a complete lack of coordination in our economic system.

Then there is the other phase of it which might be called the personnel phase of it. During the World War we did more than in any other war to mobilize the human beings in the United States, and we did a very good job, on the whole. But, as a result of what might be called "unequal" mobilization—well, for example, the whole bonus question is in good part the result of unequal mobilization of human beings during the war.

So this conference is going to take up both sides of the broad problem of how the United States would run a war if we were to get into one. I regard it as one of the very important things that will be laid before the Congress this winter.

Q: What do you mean by unequal mobilization?

The President: Well, just for a very simple example, the boys in the trenches got paid a dollar a day and the boy who was working in the munitions plant in Bridgeport got perhaps $8 or $10 a day. Naturally, the boy in the trenches, when he came back, asked for an equalization, which was the origin of the bonus.

Q: Does that mean taking the profits out of our own war or taking the profits out of munitions?

The President: That is an entirely different subject and perhaps you had better treat that question as not having been asked, because I don't want to spoil a good story. A little bit later on I do think that I will have something to tell you with respect to the position of the United States as a neutral in the event of war between other nations, but I am not ready for it yet. Treat it as off the record.

Q: Would there be any possibility of this country entertaining conversations with other countries so that other countries might do the same as we do for themselves?

The President: I hadn't thought of that. Perhaps the force of example might be good.

Q: Could we put quotation marks on that, "since the time has come to take the profits out of war"?

The President: Yes.

Q: Would the question of compulsory military training come up in connection with this broad plan you speak of?

The President: Oh, no. No, that won't come up. Steve suggests that because there are a good many new faces, just to reiterate the old rule about quotes and also to say what "background" means and what "off the record" means. Will you explain it to everybody who does not know?

Q: That sentence I gave is okay?

The President: That sentence is all right.

Q: The Nye Committee is running pretty low in funds and there seems to be some discussion—

The President: I thought you said, "fun." (Laughter)

Q: And I was wondering if you have any idea of recommending that their supply of money be added to when Congress opens for a continuation of the inquiry.

The President: No, I never recommend anything with respect to Senatorial Committees.

Q: We could not describe this as preparedness, as discussed before the World War?

The President: No. Really it would be of service if you all would leave out any suggestion of this being a question of preparedness. It is a question of permanent national legislation looking to an event which we hope will never happen, and I am bringing it up because there isn't any cloud on the horizon at the present time.

Q: You have a complete report on this line as a result of the report of the War Planning Commission. Will that serve as a basis?

The President: I don't know that.

Q: They studied it here for about two years and brought out a very exhaustive report.

The President: I have got to confess, off the record, that I never heard of it.[2]

Q: Have you any idea as to how this should be done, whether it should be done through an excess profits tax or—

The President: I have no idea at all. We are having our first talk at two o'clock today.

[President's Press Conferences:T]

---

[1] Joseph B. Eastman was Federal Coordinator of Transportation.
[2] Presumably the War Policies Commission, established in 1930, is meant. See press conference of May 16, 1934, above, n. 3.

George N. Peek, Special Adviser to the President on Foreign Trade, to Roosevelt

Washington, December 12, 1934

My dear Mr. President: Since I saw you with regard to the question of most-favored-nation policy, which I discussed in my letters to you of November 12[1] and 14,[2] I have had two talks with Secretary Hull with regard to foreign trade policy.[3] These talks, while entirely friendly, have revealed a divergence of opinion as to foreign trade policy and methods which leaves the Secretary and myself at what amounts to an impasse in the absence of any final ruling by you as to policy under the Reciprocal Trade Agreements Act of 1934 which placed in you the responsibility for their negotiation.

The questions of policy upon which your decision is needed are two in number:

1. Should we not, in our negotiations with "exchange restriction" countries require a concrete and satisfactory solution of the exchange problem as a prerequisite to the conclusion of a trade agreement?

2. Should we not abandon the unconditional most-favored-nation policy of the last twelve years, and return to the traditional conditional most-favored-nation policy pursued from 1788 to 1922 as more consonant with the intentions of Congress in passing the Reciprocal Trade Agreements Act of 1934, and as better adapted in view of existing world trade conditions to the particular needs of American foreign trade?

A definite ruling from you on these two points would go far to expedite the negotiation of reciprocal trade agreements, and thus obviate the criticism which has begun to appear with regard to the slowness which has attended the negotiation of these agreements.

Faithfully yours,

George N. Peek

[*Notation*:A:LeHand] Mac   Give me this in the morning when Sayre comes—FDR[4]

[OF 971:TS]

[1] Above.

[2] OF 971.

[3] Cf. Hull, *Memoirs,* I, 372.

[4] Sayre's appointment was for December 14 (PPF 1-0). On December 12 Peek met with Roosevelt and got his approval of a cotton barter deal with Germany that he had been negotiating through the Second Export-Import Bank under his authority as special adviser on Foreign Trade (PPF 1-0; Hull, *Memoirs,* I, 373). Both the State Department and the Interdepartmental Trade Agreements Committee had opposed the deal (*ibid.;* "Memorandum on the proposed agreement between the German Cotton Import Company and the Second Export-Import Bank," Dec. 11 [?], 1934, OF 971). The President's approval had been given while Hull was away from Washington; when Hull returned (apparently on December 14, the day of the weekly Cabinet meeting), he protested vigorously and Roosevelt, according to Hull, withdrew his approval (Hull, *Memoirs,* I, 372–374).

Roosevelt's decision may not have been as final as Hull believed for on December 19 he told his press conference (below) that the cotton deal was still in the discussion stage. Roosevelt saw Peek, with the Secretary of State, on January 15, according to the press conference of the next day (below); there is, however, no information on what took place at this meeting. In Peek's annual report for 1934, he referred again to the proposed cotton deal as the only practicable way of retaining the American cotton market in Germany, "considering the peculiar conditions under which Germany feels obliged to operate in her foreign trade" (Peek to Roosevelt, Dec. 31, 1934, OF 971). But in his press conference of February 6, Roosevelt said the German deal was no longer being considered: "Of course, the real answer on that cotton deal is a perfectly simple thing: We were offered 25 per cent in cash and 75 per cent in goods. The great immediate question was, wouldn't those goods have come in under the antidumping clause? If they were goods sold in Germany and other nations at the same price they sold to us, it would be a different thing. But the importers didn't think they could sell that goods [*sic*] except in violation of the antidumping agreement."

Hull says that the President's final disapproval of the German cotton deal marked the end of Peek's effort to make similar arrangements with other countries; with this Peek's biographer agrees (Hull, *Memoirs,* I, 374; Fite, *George N. Peek,* 277).

Norman H. Davis, Chairman, American Delegation, London Naval Conference, to Roosevelt

London, December 14, 1934

Strictly Personal

My dear Mr. President: Although our conversations will soon be terminated and we will be going home (but not, I regret, in time for Christmas) I think it well to give you my thoughts on certain aspects of the situation here.

I fully recognize the logic of the position taken by you and the Secretary, as set forth in the recent telegraphic instructions to me.[1] My one doubt and preoccupation has been with regard to tactics, and I should like to explain this in somewhat greater detail than has been possible in my telegrams.

In particular, I do not favor, and have never proposed that we give Japan anything in the way of an agreement to take home which could be construed as a willingness to consider now, or in the future, an alteration in the existing principles of naval limitation.

I have been proceeding on the theory that it was our policy, and in our interest, to maintain an Anglo-American front as the best means of avoiding trouble with Japan or of minimizing it if it could not be avoided. When we arrived the possibility of such a common front was precarious. While our remaining here, against our judgment as to the best tactics to pursue with Japan, has embarrassed you at home, I cannot but feel that it has been distinctly worth while. It has helped very much to crystallize public opinion in England in our direction. It has also forced the British Government to come to grips with the problem and to agree with us on fundamentals; and it has helped to make them realize that they cannot afford to make a separate agreement with Japan or make an agreement that was unacceptable to us. Moreover, it has enabled us to get assurances to that effect.

In fact, the British have come slowly to realize that, if they are to induce Japan to "play ball" they must make her understand that she will have to play on the same team with both of us, or play alone, and this in turn is having its effect on Japan.

This situation has caused embarrassment to each of the three governments but, frankly, I feel sure that the British, and certainly the Japanese, have had more to worry about because their position has been more vulnerable than ours. The British evidently feel that their position, which was from the outset more difficult in many ways than ours, has been made even more embarrassing by the fact that we are unwilling to join with them in their efforts·to reach a basis for a future agreement which they feel to be of vital importance and, at the same time, they are unwilling to act or take a definite position without us, and have so committed themselves to us.

I hope I have succeeded in getting the British to abandon their strategy of minimizing the significance of denunciation by Japan. Aside from the fact that the British technique is different from ours, they, in contrast to us, are guided more by expediency than by principle.

There are several reasons which make the British hesitate to accept our views as to tactics and make them eager to conciliate Japan, but without conceding fundamentals:

First, the British Government has to take into consideration the fact that there is a strong sentiment among the industrialists here, who have considerable influence here and who favor having England reach some agreement with Japan for a division of trade in China where the Japanese would, in effect, have the northern half and the British the southern. They argue that such an arrangement would be profitable and would at least keep Japan occupied for so many years as to remove the incentive to threaten British interests.

Second, the Government leaders insist that they want cooperation with us more than anything else, but that cooperation, in order to be successful requires day-to-day, close and friendly contact and consultation on matters of common interest.

Third, they have an inordinate fear that if the tactics we propose so estrange Japan as to lead to ultimate trouble, we may not be with them when the trouble comes. For instance, they intimate that under American pressure the League adopted our views with regard to Manchukuo, which forced Japan out of the League; and that, since the action thus taken was not followed by cooperative steps looking to a solution, the situation has become increasingly a source of trouble and embarrassment; and that our active interest in promoting a policy of non-recognition and moral condemnation was followed by a policy of more or less withdrawal from the Far East, including the ultimate withdrawal from the Philippines.

Fourth, the British are most eager to avoid a naval race which they feel they cannot afford and which they feel will be inevitable if the Japanese get away without some arrangement for returning later.

Although admitting that an unsuccessful conference is worse than no conference, the British maintain that it is more dangerous still to allow a situation to get so much out of hand as to make a conference impossible. MacDonald particularly is obsessed with the fear that if the door is now shut tight on Japan and it is not made known to her that she may, if she wishes, re-enter negotiations, not by another door but by the same one, it will be politically impossible for her to knock and ask for re-entrance, and naval limitation will be over. Furthermore, MacDonald, for political reasons, wants above all to prevent the impression that the conversations have resulted in a failure.

Fifth, the British are also becoming more fearful of a German-Japanese alliance and point to the fact that there is an increasing amount of propaganda in the Japanese press in favor of this, with the added suggestion that Germany should be brought into any Naval Conference. They insist, therefore, that if Yamamoto gets away from here without being tied up in some way to return at a fixed date, Japan will inevitably get together with Germany.

To sum up, since the British cannot get a binding agreement from us for cooperation such as they would like, they do not feel like casting Japan entirely aside. Their policy is, first and foremost, to cooperate with us in any event, but, second, to induce Japan as far as possible to cooperate with us both, which they are hopeful of achieving by making Japan realize that, while there is not today a common Anglo-American front, there is a common point of view on fundamentals from which we will not depart.

In my talk with MacDonald yesterday, the substance of which I reported by cable, he impressed me definitely as being suspicious of Japan but, at the same time, most fearful of getting into trouble with Japan. He sang his old song about being fearful of inciting the Japanese jingoes and thus placing the British interests in the Far East under the possibility of attack. He said, for instance, that if the Japanese should try to take Hongkong there was no guaranty of our aid since we could not enter into an alliance which, of course, he understood. I replied that what we should have was a broad basis for cooperation and nothing in the way of a political alliance to which the American government and people would never agree.

Judging entirely by the recent change in the attitude and stand taken by Matsudaira and Yamamoto, Japan is looking for a way to recede from its previous impossible position; but we can tell more about that in the next few days.

I am enclosing an interesting editorial from today's *Manchester Guardian*, which is very significant.[2] Heretofore this influential paper has been rather taking the position that we were unreasonable in not conceding more to Japan. I am now informed that the statement of our position, which I recently made, has considerably influenced their change in attitude.

At any rate, we are planning to sail on the 29th of December.

With warm personal regards and looking forward to seeing you in the near future, I am,

Faithfully yours,

Norman H. Davis[3]

[PSF:London Naval Conference:TS]

[1] The American position at this time was that because the Japanese had announced that they were going to denounce the Washington Treaty, no compromise agreement was possible before denunciation. Further there could be no agreement to seek a basis for future agreement after denunciation: to do so would be accepting the Japanese contention that the present system had to be radically altered. Finally, there could be no agreement to meet in the future unless one of the three powers was willing (later on) to make new proposals (*Foreign Relations, 1934*, I, 350, 388ff).

[2] The editorial stated that the security of the system set up by the Washington Treaty lay in its comprehensiveness; the signators now had to decide what they wished to put in its place. The present direction of Japanese policy might not, after all, be permanent.

[3] See press conference of Dec. 21, 1934, below.

Cordell Hull, Secretary of State, to Roosevelt

Washington, December 14, 1934

Personal and Confidential

My dear Mr. President: With reference to the proposed German cotton deal, which is in the nature of a bartering transaction, it is the function of the State Department to concern itself only in so far as the proposed transaction affects the general trade agreements program which we have undertaken, our commercial policy, and our general foreign relations. The Department only offers such comment and information as may be in the main supplemental to that already possessed by government officials dealing immediately with this proposal, and such as may be deemed of value to the President and other governmental agencies concerned in making a final decision.

Naturally, the State Department must deal with broad policies and broad trade methods rather than with individual projects or individual barter transactions or limited transactions, especially those partaking of a bartering nature. It is the policy of the State Department to maintain the broad general policy and practice, as nearly as possible, of the doctrine of equality of commercial and industrial treatment, and hence, of opposition to its violation by the numerous sorts of discriminations and preferences well known to the public. This doctrine is the corner stone of our present foreign policy and of our reciprocal trade agreement program; it is the basis of our repeated protests to Germany, in particular, against her discriminations against us and the preferences recently granted to other countries and their nationals, with respect both to the payment of debt service and to trade.

If exceptions are made to the most-favored-nation policy of equality, it should be made only in case of emergency and temporary conditions and upon thoroughly considered decisions. This rule should not, of course, minimize the important needs of export markets for our various burdensome agricultural and other surpluses, but instead these needs should at all times be duly considered.

The sole purpose of the present program of reciprocity trade agreements is to provide as rapidly as possible in a broad way for the exportation facilities especially for our more burdensome surpluses, such as cotton, tobacco, lard and other hog products, wheat, automobiles, etc., etc. It is believed that the one most effective way to accomplish this vitally important objective is to maintain and promote a policy of gradually reducing discriminations and preferences and increasing equality of trade and commercial treatment, and that the maintenance of this attitude in the public mind of the world is all-important.

The experience and attitude of the State Department toward Germany since the spring of 1934 has been in brief as follows: When Germany was openly planning and practicing defaults on her $2,000,000,000 of debt due in the United States, she at the same time approached the State Department more than once with a professed proposal to agree on a new trade arrangement. It was not possible at that early stage on account of the tariff situation and certain other conditions, for our Government to take up the matter, even if it had been willing to ignore such discriminations as the wholesale debt default to our nationals while paying nationals of other countries, and also discriminating against our commerce with her. I courteously replied on each occasion expressing the desire of this Government in every feasible manner and as early as feasible to enter upon satisfactory trade arrangements with all countries so disposed, and that Germany in this respect was placed in the same deferred class with England, Canada, and a majority of the nations of the world.

Germany, during the past summer, repeated her trade agreement proposals as stated, but, while paying other countries both her debt and trade balances, she flouted our nationals and declined in any trade conversations that might take place to indicate with the slightest definiteness or detail or method any terms to which she might agree, either to pay our nationals or to cease discriminating against our commerce under our commercial treaty with her.

In the meantime reports constantly came to the Department to the effect that we would in any event be forced to sell Germany our cotton and perhaps some copper, lard, etc. The Department at the same time strongly believed, as it still does, that the reverse was true and that Germany would first be forced to buy at least 500,000 bales of cotton from the United States, and that she could and would pay cash for it, as she was promptly paying cash for immense armament and vitally desirable products.

It was in these circumstances that the State Department, since last spring, has not undertaken either a special or general trade arrangement with Germany, but with the strong belief, as stated, that Germany within a reasonable time would find it necessary to make the purchases from us for cash, the Department has gone forward with its plans to promote a system of reciprocal trade agreements bottomed on equality rather than discrimination. This includes Brazil and numerous other countries with whom conversations some time ago had reached an advanced stage of understanding.

This program and this policy have been constantly thrust in the face of Germany, of Japan, and other countries which seemed bent on preferences and discriminations, especially against us. This broad and consistent course is calculated to avoid giving any country any ground or pretext to discriminate, much less driving it to do so.

It was in the foregoing circumstances that the proposed cotton deal came to the notice of the State Department two or three weeks ago. In view of what has been said above it is not necessary to elaborate further upon the effects of the proposed deal.

Faithfully yours,

Cordell Hull

[PSF:Germany:TS]

[*Enclosure*] Considerations Relative to the Proposed German Cotton Deal—Experts' Views[1]

1. The plan would seriously endanger our trade agreements program.

2. If we enter into a special preferential arrangement of this character, other cotton export countries, like Brazil, will be compelled to seek similar preferential arrangements in the German market. Brazil has already expressed grave concern with regard to this proposal.

3. If German fertilizer is given preferential treatment in our market, such as this plan would provide, Chile would be compelled to dump nitrates in our market. Representations to this effect have already been made by the Chilean Ambassador. Will we be able to apply the anti-dumping law against Chile while admitting German fertilizer at prices below the official reichsmark rate?

4. The plan would discriminate against other gold standard countries and give special preference to German exports to the United States through the sale of reichsmarks at a discount. If we seek and grant preferential treatment, can we seek equality of treatment for our commerce and nationals from other countries?

5. The proposed plan is a device to undo, in part, the devaluation of the dollar.

6. The sale of German marks at a considerable discount is likely to exert a depressional influence on American prices and seriously affect those American industries which would be subjected, under this plan, to sharp German competition.

7. On top of her gross discrimination of American nationals, this deal would make a very good trade bargain for Germany, but with little gain and large risks for the United States.

8. There is no assurance that the suggested 800,000 bales can, under the proposed plan, be sold to Germany, since cotton exporters might not, in fact, be able to get dollar exchange.

9. It should be noted also that even though the plan does not break down, there is no assurance that American cotton exporters will not be forced to sell cotton at a loss.

10. Attention should, moreover, be called to the fact that the United States Government, through the Export-Import Bank, stands to suffer what may amount to substantial losses.

11. If this plan goes through, would the Treasury be able to apply the anti-dumping law to similar deals privately arranged and privately financed?

12. The proposed plan is almost certain to engender extreme resentment among that large section of the American public which is violently opposed to the Hitler regime.

[PSF:Germany:T]

[1] "Experts' Views" was added in longhand, presumably by Hull.

Roosevelt to Claude A. Swanson, Secretary of the Navy

Washington, December 17, 1934

Confidential

Memorandum for the Secretary of the Navy: Will you please discuss with the proper Officers the advisability of immediate studies looking to the development of possible new types of ships on the theory that the Washington and London Treaty restrictions may be entirely removed within the next two years?[1]

If special design studies call for additional appropriations for the Design Bureaus, I would be willing to approve a small appropriation for this.

There has been considerable discussion, of course, in relation to new types, such, for example, as a heavy cruiser type larger than 10,000 tons, a lighter cruiser type, large radius, high speed with scouting plane facilities; a pocket battleship type, larger than the German design but much smaller than existing battleship displacement, new aircraft cruiser types designed to operate with fast cruiser squadrons at distant points.

At the same time I should like to have a study made of the possibility of establishing one or two very large air bases in the Philippines, with a smaller base in Guam, and still smaller bases in the Midway-Hawaiian chain and in the Aleutian chain of Islands.

All above studies should, of course, be treated as highly confidential.

F.D.R.

[OF 18-S:CT]

[1] In a letter to Roosevelt of Nov. 28, 1934 (PSF:National Defense), Swanson noted that the Japanese Cabinet had decided to recommend much greater appropriations for national defense. He enclosed a table showing the relative strength of the United States and Japanese navies in each category as of Dec. 31, 1936, assuming the completion of the current building programs of both countries. Among other things Swanson said that the Navy was greatly in need of ships that were outside the treaty categories, "these being those auxiliaries which must go with the Fleet to care for the logistical requirements."

Press Conference, Executive Offices of the White House, December 19, 1934, 10:35 A.M.

[*Excerpt*] Q: There has been a lot said about the new policy of abandoning the freedom of the seas. Can you tell us something about it?

The President: No; that is newspaper talk.

Q: In that respect, so much has been said about this question of neutrality in the papers. Could you tell us what your objective is?

The President: The objective is neutrality, which has always been difficult to retain in the past. Some of you older people who were here in 1914, 1915 and 1916 and the first few months of 1917 know exactly the difficulty of retaining neutrality . . .

Q: Can you tell us something about the Nicaraguan Canal?

The President: Only that when I was a very small boy, about 1890, my father was very much interested in it and my mother still has in a safe deposit box enough stock in that old Nicaraguan Canal Company to paper a whole room.

Q: You ought to be in favor of it then.

The President: That has gone (Laughter) . . .

Q: Can you tell us whether the reports are correct that the cotton barter deal with Germany has bogged down?

The President: Still in the discussion stage.

Q: Can you tell us whether the State Department has advised you that as it stands now it is in conflict with our most-favored-nation treaty policy?

The President: I could not answer the question because I have a long memo and have not read it yet. I don't know. It is in the basket . . .[1]

Q: Can you tell us anything about the naval situation?

The President: That will have to come from London.

Q: Will you comment on the Japanese Privy Council's action in renouncing the London-Washington Treaty?

The President: We have not been advised of any action.[2]

[President's Press Conferences:T]

[1] Not identified; see Peek's letter of Dec. 12, 1934, above.
[2] Only a small part of this press conference is here printed. In the parts omitted the President discussed, among other things, public power and watered utility stocks, the Home Owners Loan Corporation, and labor troubles in the steel industry and the railroads.

Roosevelt to Marvin H. McIntyre, Assistant Secretary to the President

Washington, December 19, 1934

Memo for Mac: Ask Tariff Commission whether they think this should be referred to them either formally or informally. Suggest you speak to Sayre first about it.[1]

F.D.R.

[OF 61-P:T]

[1] This refers to a letter from Rep. Andrew Edmiston of West Virginia of Dec. 15, 1934 (OF 61-P), urging an increase of the import duty on Japanese glass tableware. He said in part: "I have had this matter up with the State Department, urging a limitation or embargo against Japan, which would not affect any other nation, as Japan is the chief offender. This does not seem to meet with much encouragement in the State Department, but it is becoming so serious in my district that I am appealing to you for aid in this matter." Sayre reported that he had been informed that as soon as the import section (of the Research and Planning Division) of the National Recovery Administration received a complaint in the form required it would "be handled according to the established procedure" (Sayre to McIntyre, Dec. 29, 1934, OF 61-P). McIntyre replied to this effect to Edmiston, Jan. 3, 1935 (OF 61-P).

Roosevelt to Francis P. Garvan, New York

[Washington] December 20, 1934

Dear Francis: Thank you for your very interesting letter and the "Briefs" and "Opinions" which I have set aside for future perusal.

I have noted particularly what you say about statistical data on foreign trade and hope to be able to go into that subject in the near future.[1]

With kindest personal regards and the Season's Greetings.

Very sincerely yours,

[PPF 1985:CT]

[1] Francis P. Garvan (former U.S. alien property custodian, New York lawyer, and prominent in Deomcratic party affairs) had written Dec. 14, 1934 (PPF 1985), enclosing two printed briefs he had prepared on the proposed reciprocal trade treaty with Switzerland. He congratulated Roosevelt on his statement of Dec. 12, 1934, on legislation to equalize wartime profits. He also urged the publication of Peek's findings on foreign trade: "The publication of facts about our foreign trade is by all means the most important part of Peek's work. He is doing very good work on the publication about our trade in goods, but not sufficient work is coming out or being published on the financial relations, which constitute 41% of our international relations." In an accompanying note Roosevelt told McIntyre to send a copy of this paragraph to Peek.

Press Conference, Executive Offices of the White House, December 21, 1934, 4:05 P.M.

[*Excerpt*] Q: Can you tell us anything for background with respect to the naval situation in London?

The President: The only thing I can do would be to talk not for background but off the record on that, and this would have to be off the record because, obviously, there isn't anything that I can say, even as background. We are all very much disappointed that the conference over there—they were not conferences but conversations—did not get any further and we all hope that something will turn up in the course of the next year which will make possible a renewal of the limitation of naval armaments or a new treaty which will continue at an even greater speed the reduction of naval armaments.

I do think this: We should all, as Americans, bear this in mind: That we have done nothing in any way to adopt an antagonistic or hostile attitude. Our whole position has been that every nation is entitled to relative security and we have believed that the two previous treaties did give, in one case three nations and in the other case five nations, relative security which has continued for a good many years, from 1921 down to date. And we wanted a continuance of relative security.

The reason I am speaking especially to the Americans present,[1] and speaking off the record, is that I do want to emphasize that every time that any American talks in belligerent terms, it is merely an invitation to somebody else to speak in more belligerent terms. I have regretted anything said by members of Congress, quite frankly, in regard to what we would do under both circumstances. I regretted reading today that somebody had talked about new naval bases anywhere because, as I say, the more we talk about that, the more we are going to get repercussions from other countries.

I am not speaking about any one particular country. It seems to me that our attitude should be to continue to hope that in the next year or two years, since we have two years, to effectuate something, to get a limitation on naval armaments. In the meantime, we should keep our mouths shut about it no matter what we may have personally thought of in regard to hypothetical conditions. They are too hypothetical to express them out loud at the present time. Everything that the Administration will do will be along that line of trying not to antagonize by thought, word or deed.

I think that is the easiest way of putting it.

Q: Also off the record, is there any reason to believe that with the passage of the year the cause of the present breakdown of negotiations will change?

The President: I hope so. I hope so.

Q: Mr. President, do you think it would do any harm if we were to use for background just that part, that you do hope for a treaty?

The President: All right, Stevie, as a way out. (Mr. Early spoke to the President.)

The President: Steve[2] suggests that we let it be used without attribution to the White House sources of any kind. You use it on your own authority. Is that all right?

Q: In that connection and on the same basis, is there anything to say about the McCarran Act, the excluding feature of the McCarran Act?

The President: I don't think so; that is not one of the pending questions.

Q: It might be a cause of a good deal of feeling?

The President: There again, if you get into the reasons assigned by every nation for some kind of a change, it is an interminable subject.

Q: Also on the same basis, how are we getting along with Great Britain on this? There has been some discussion that our relations are improved as a result of the strain in every direction.

The President: I do not think that any human being could write a story one way or the other. They are always what they have been, friendly.

[President's Press Conferences:T]

[1] The transcript does not indicate what correspondents were present other than F. M. Stephenson of the Associated Press, mentioned later in this transcript as "Stevie."
[2] Stephen T. Early.

Roosevelt to Cordell Hull, Secretary of State

Washington, December 22, 1934

Memorandum for the Secretary of State: Mr. Emmet, our Minister to the Netherlands, has spoken to me about a visit by him to the Dutch East Indies next autumn and tells me he believes the Dutch Government would especially welcome such a trip by him.

If you approve will you arrange it?[1]

F.D.R.

[OF 858:CT]

[1] See Roosevelt to Hull, April 25, 1935, below.

Frederick H. Allen to Roosevelt

Charleston, S.C., December 22, 1934

My dear Mr. President: Referring to my letter to you of December 8th, in which I enclose copies of my letter to the Secretary of State,

Mr. Phillips' reply and my reply to him,[1] I venture to add the following, that I entirely agree with Mr. Phillips' statement, "that Paris would seem to be in every way the most suitable seat for the headquarters of the Académie. It is one of the great centers of the diplomatic activities in which meet the lines of communications between nations in all parts of the world," and he adds "For the purposes of the Académie, Washington would seem to be somewhat out of the main current." This too is true, but it moves nearer and nearer the main current all the time, and in my view the establishment of a branch in Washington would greatly increase the knowledge of foreign affairs among our political people and also tend to awaken their interest in matters of world-wide importance. It is for reasons such as these that the establishment of a branch of the Académie would seem to me worthwhile.

I wonder if you won't agree with me that the average man in our country, and I might add the average politician, does not yet realize our immense power in the world and the really great influence we can have in shaping the destinies of mankind. The way in which all foreign nations regard and study what we are doing here under your leadership, and the attention they pay to any pronouncement of ours regarding foreign policies is a testimonial to our influence and power, it is for reasons such as these that it seemed to me that if a branch of the Académie could be established in Washington, a wider appreciation would be had by our people of our influence in world affairs, through an extension of the knowledge of foreign affairs that would be spread throughout the country, because of the establishment of the Académie in Washington, and because of the presence there from time to time of Prime Ministers, Ministers of Foreign Affairs and other leaders from the different countries of the world who would naturally be only too anxious to take part in the activities of the Académie, of which they are members.[2]

I am with high regard, Very faithfully yours,

Frederick H. Allen

[OF 1107:TS]

[1] Dated respectively Nov. 22, Dec. 3, and Dec. 8, 1934, present, with Allen's letter of December 8, with the letter here printed. To Hull, Allen described his efforts to secure funds for the renovation of the Perry Belmont house in Washington as a home for an American branch of the Académie Diplomatique Internationale. Phillips wrote to him that the State Department had concluded that there was nothing the government could do with propriety in supporting the proposal, and he wondered if the upkeep of the mansion would not be too great a drain on the finances of the Académie.

[2] Answered Dec. 28, 1934, below.

328

Roosevelt to Frederick H. Allen, Charleston, South Carolina

[Washington] December 28, 1934

My dear Fred Allen: I am delighted to have your note of the twenty-second,[1] and I hope you are having a delightful time in the delightful city of Charleston.

My thought about a branch of the Académie in Washington is that it would be entirely proper, provided it were financed by private funds and, therefore, at a very low cost. As a matter of fact, I doubt if it would be necessary to spend more than one thousand or two thousand dollars a year—part time pay of a secretary, postage, etc. Such an organization could meet occasionally in private houses. I fear it would be utterly impossible to finance a building of its own and I think you will agree with me.

Always sincerely,

[OF 1107:CT]

[1] Above.

Roosevelt to Cordell Hull, Secretary of State, and William Phillips, Under Secretary of State

[Washington] December 28, 1934

Memorandum . . . : This is an interesting private note from Warren. Please read and return. I ought to make a fairly definite decision about the St. Lawrence Treaty by January fifth. Can I do it?[1]

F.D.R.

[OF 66:CT]

[1] Warren Robbins, minister to Canada, had written Dec. 18, 1934, that he was "utterly disgusted" that so little had been done on the St. Lawrence Waterway (OF 66). See Hull's reply, Dec. 31, 1934, below.

Roosevelt to H. H. Kung, Minister of Finance, Nanking

[Washington] December 28, 1934

My dear Doctor Kung: Ambassador Bullitt has brought me your very welcome letter[1] and the delicious tea. As you know, my family and I have been brought up on really good Chinese tea, and we are enjoying your gift every afternoon. My Mother is especially pleased, for, as you know, she lived in China with her parents seventy years ago.

I do not need to tell you of my great interest in the problems which you are facing, nor need I assure you of our desire for mutual understanding and help.

I hope that perhaps before I leave office you will come to Washington for a visit. It would be very delightful to see you.[2]

With my sincere regards, Faithfully yours,

[PPF 1178:CT]

[1] Nov. 26, 1934 (PPF 1178). Kung said that in China's uphill struggle towards the goal of "political liberty, social justice and economic prosperity," she had much to learn and profit from the experience and friendship of the United States.

[2] An attached note, Roosevelt to Forster, reads: "Will you ask someone in the State Department if this is O.K.?"

Roosevelt to Cordell Hull, Secretary of State

[Washington] December 29, 1934

Memorandum for the Secretary of State: What has happened in regard to the old proposed Treaty with Canada in regard to the use of additional water at Niagara Falls? I think it was sent to the Senate by President Hoover but died there. Will you speak to me about this when we take up the St. Lawrence Treaty?[1]

F.D.R.

[OF 66:T:Copy]

[1] A convention for the preservation of the scenic beauty of Niagara Falls was signed at Ottawa on Jan. 2, 1929, and was sent to the Senate by President Coolidge on Jan. 21, 1929. The Senate Foreign Relations Committee took no action until Feb. 18, 1931, when it disapproved the treaty (*Cong. Rec.,* vol. 70, p. 1954; New York *Times,* Feb. 19, 1931, p. 11).

Roosevelt to Claude A. Swanson, Secretary of the Navy

Washington, December 31, 1934

Confidential

Memorandum for the Secretary of the Navy: In relation to Navy jurisdiction over these Pacific Islands, I think it is highly advisable that the Navy exercise that jurisdiction in some tangible form at the earliest possible moment. You might consult with the State Department and ask them if the establishment of a small supply base or the fixing up of a landing place would be adequate to sustain sovereignty.[1]

With the Department of Agriculture's cooperation it might be possible to plant certain trees, fruit, grasses, etc., for experimental purposes.

Such Government activities, supported by appropriate signs, might be useful.[2]

F.D.R.

[OF 18-V:CT]

[1] On Dec. 13, 1934, Swanson sent to Roosevelt the draft of an executive order placing Wake, Johnston, and Sand Islands, and Kingman Reef, under the Secretary of the Navy. Sand and Johnston Islands were, however, to be used as game refuges and breeding grounds for native birds under Agriculture Department auspices. Roosevelt signed the order on Dec. 29, 1934 (OF 18-V).

[2] Swanson replied Jan. 2, 1935, suggesting that Admiral Claude C. Bloch, Judge Advocate General of the Navy, handle matters concerning the Pacific islands in liaison with the State Department (OF 18-V). He wrote again on Jan. 7, 1935 (OF 6-V), on the question of acquiring Baker, Howland, and Jarvis islands. Swanson also said that Harold Gatty, an airline executive and former navigator for Wiley Post, had been informed that the Navy Department had no objection to American citizens occupying the islands. He added that it was understood that Gatty's company proposed to "place American citizens on these islands in order that the United States may assert its sovereignty and in the future that Mr. Gatty's Company may be granted a permit to use one or more of these islands for purposes of commercial aviation" (*ibid.*). See Roosevelt to Swanson, May 30, 1935, below.

Cordell Hull, Secretary of State, to Roosevelt

Washington, December 31, 1934

Dear Mr. President: Thank you for letting us see this letter from Robbins.[1] As you know, on December 21st Mr. Phillips discussed with the Canadian Minister a number of slight changes in the St. Lawrence Treaty and handed him copies of these alterations. None of them is particularly important, but in spite of that fact Mr. Herridge did not appear optimistic that the Prime Minister would give his approval of them, nor, in fact, that he would be in a position this winter to press for the ratification of the original treaty by Parliament. Mr. Herridge added, however, that should our Senate approve of the treaty in its amended form, the Prime Minister might find it possible to introduce it in Parliament in its new form, explaining at the same time that the changes which have been made in the original text were wholly insignificant and did not in any way alter the fundamental principles involved. Mr. Herridge felt that this might be an easier approach for the Prime Minister than to approve in advance of the suggested changes. We are awaiting Mr. Herridge's reply in this connection.

Mr. Frank Walsh[2] called at the Department on Saturday and seemed entirely satisfied with the steps which the Department has already taken. Our view is that even though Mr. Bennett cannot guarantee to present the treaty to Parliament in January, it would probably be best for us to secure the Senate's approval at the earliest practical moment.

Accordingly, should you approve, I shall be happy to prepare a brief message for you, asking for a reconsideration of the treaty now before the Senate, and at the same time I would send to Senator Pittman the texts of the various amendments which we are discussing with the Canadian Government.[3]

Faithfully yours,

Cordell Hull

[PSF:Canada:TS]

[1] See Roosevelt to Hull and Phillips, Dec. 28, 1934, above.
[2] Chairman of the New York State Power Authority.
[3] See McIntyre to Roosevelt, Jan. 7, 1935, below.

William Phillips, Under Secretary of State, to Roosevelt

Washington, December 31, 1934

Dear Mr. President: The Secretary asked me to say that he would be entirely satisfied with the appointment of Mr. Newton D. Baker as a member of the Permanent Court of Arbitration at The Hague, should you desire to reappoint him. Would you be so kind as to indicate your wishes in the matter?

Faithfully yours,

William Phillips

[Notation:AS] WP OK FDR
[OF 245:TS]

Roosevelt to Cordell Hull, Secretary of State

Washington, January 2, 1935

Memorandum for the Secretary of State: I am still disturbed about the inadequacy of American news for our Embassies and Legations, especially in Europe. Every returning Ambassador or Minister complains that they have insufficient means of knowing what is going on here. Would you speak to me about it at your convenience?[1]

F.D.R.

[OF 20:CT]

[1] Answered Jan. 29, 1935, below.

Roosevelt to Cordell Hull, Secretary of State

Washington, January 2, 1935

Memorandum for the Secretary of State: Will you look into the question of the adequacy of our Consulates in Northern Africa? I have understood that we have none in the Italian possessions. Are we adequately represented in the French and Spanish possessions?[1]

F.D.R.

[OF 20:CT]

[1] Answered Jan. 9, 1935, below.

Roosevelt to Cordell Hull, Secretary of State

[Washington] January 3, 1935

Memorandum for the Secretary of State: At your convenience, I think a conference between you, Senator Pittman and myself, in regard to the St. Lawrence Treaty and the World Court, would be a good thing. Will you arrange it any day after Friday?

Also, would you be good enough to go ahead with the draft of the St. Lawrence Message, as you suggest?[1]

F.D.R.

[OF 202:CT]

[1] Hull, Pittman, Senator Joseph Robinson, and Assistant Secretary of State Sayre met with the President at the White House on Saturday, January 5 (PPF 1-0). There is nothing in the Roosevelt papers on their talk; however, the New York *Times* of Jan. 6, 1935, p. 1, reported Robinson as saying that he did not expect the President to send a special message, and Pittman was quoted as saying that the World Court treaty would be reported with the Reed amendment.

Roosevelt to the Congress, January 4, 1935

[*Excerpt*] To the Congress of the United States: . . . I cannot with candor tell you that general international relationships outside the borders of the United States are improved. On the surface of things many old jealousies are resurrected, old passions aroused; new strivings for armament and power, in more than one land, rear their ugly heads. I hope that calm counsel and constructive leadership will provide the steadying influence and the time necessary for the coming of new and more practical forms of representative government throughout the world wherein privilege and power will occupy a lesser place and world welfare a greater.

I believe, however, that our own peaceful and neighborly attitude towards other nations is coming to be understood and appreciated. The maintenance of international peace is a matter in which we are deeply and unselfishly concerned. Evidence of our persistent and undeniable desire to prevent armed conflict has recently been more than once afforded.

There is no ground for apprehension that our relations with any nation will be otherwise than peaceful. Nor is there ground for doubt that the people of most nations seek relief from the threat and burden attaching to the false theory that extravagant armament cannot be reduced and limited by international accord.[1]

[Speech File:T]

[1] For the entire text of the 1935 annual message, see *Public Papers,* IV, 15–25. The Roosevelt Library has a draft of the message, extensively edited by the President, the copy he read to the Congress, and a carbon copy of the reading copy with shorthand notes of the changes made during delivery. These changes are numerous but not significant. Following delivery of the message, Roosevelt went over his reading copy and incorporated in it a few of the changes he had made orally at the time of reading. A copy of this revised text was signed by him and sent to the Congress as the official message (Early to LeHand and Tully, Jan. 4, 1935, Speech File). In the excerpt here printed, the final revisions occur in the first paragraph: "outside the borders of the United States" originally read "our borders"; "privilege and power" originally read "privilege"; and "world welfare" originally read "welfare." This excerpt and the text as published in the *Public Papers* follow the official text.

Senator Key Pittman of Nevada to Roosevelt

Washington, D.C., January 4, 1935

My dear Mr. President: Mr. Sayre called upon me yesterday and we discussed a proposed resolution for adherence to the world court. Mr. Sayre takes the position which, he says, is concurred in by the Secretary of State, that the so-called Root Protocol protects the United States against an adverse advisory opinion by the world court, in a matter affecting the interest of the United States, or in a matter in which the United States claims an interest. I deeply regret that I cannot concur in the construction of the so-called Root Protocol advanced by Mr. Sayre and the Secretary of State.

The protocol prepared and submitted by Mr. Root to the conference of distinguished jurists would have granted this protection to the United States.

On the day following the presentation of the Root Protocol, Mr. Hurst[1] offered a substitute. The substitute was adopted. It is this protocol that is now erroneously designated as the Root Protocol.

The only remedy the United States has in the event the court proceeds to render an opinion over the objection of the United States is to withdraw from the court. In my opinion such an act would increase the ill feeling against us by Governments and peoples under Governments who are adherents of the court, and would be a severe blow to the permanency and effectiveness of the court. The great majority of our States are opposed to the entire policy of advisory opinions.

Our Foreign Relations Committee has demonstrated on several occasions its opposition to advisory opinions.

I cannot see why Europe, who apparently desires advisory opinions, objects to excluding the United States from the effect of advisory opinions if we desire to be excluded from such effects. I contend that our platform promised adherence to the court upon the terms of the existing resolution and pending reservations. Whether those pending reservations mean the reservations adopted by the Senate at the time it approved adherence to the world court, or whether it means the reservations now pending before the Senate and its Committee on Foreign Relations is not so material, because the Senate in 1926 adopted unconditionally the five reservations, and the five reservations were adopted by the Committee on Foreign Relations to the pending resolutions prior to the adoption of the plank of the Democratic National Platform.

In a letter addressed to Mr. Philip C. Jessup under date of April 12, 1932, I wrote a complete opinion upon this question, a copy of which I attach. I see no reason to change my opinion with regard to the subject. In view of my commitment on this subject I do not feel that I am qualified to present the Administration's view as fully as it deserves. I, therefore, respectfully urge upon you the desirability of requesting Senator Robinson to take charge of the proceedings looking to adherence on the part of our Government to the world court.

I deeply regret this unfortunate situation as nothing would give me more pleasure than to assist you in bringing about our adherence to the world court. I fear, however, that the failure to yield to the adoption of reservations that some of our leading Senators deem essential to the protection of the interest of the United States will bring about unfortunate results.[2]

With expressions of highest regards and respect, I beg to remain, Sincerely,

Key Pittman

[OF 202:TS]

---

[1] Sir Cecil Hurst, then counsel to the British Foreign Office.
[2] For the background of the World Court controversy, see Sayre to Roosevelt, Jan. 9, 1935, below.

[*Enclosure*] Senator Key Pittman of Nevada to Philip C. Jessup, Secretary, National World Court Committee, New York

Washington, April 12, 1932

My dear Mr. Jessup: I am in receipt of your open letter of April 7th, in which you charge me with introducing my resolution in the Foreign Relations Committee relative to the protocol for the purpose of delay alone. In support of your argument you quibble with regard to immaterial statements and matter contained in my letter to Bishop Jenkins published in the *Congressional Record* on April 4th.[1] You have deliberately refrained from discussing the material reasons set forth in such letter for the introduction of my resolution.

It must be evident to you that the character of advisory opinions to which I referred is not such as those that are authorized in a few of the

State constitutions and providing for certain justices advising State officers "on important questions of law and upon solemn occasions." I am speaking of advisory opinions which seek to decide questions as between individuals before such questions can be submitted to judicial determination upon issue joined.

But whether the distinction I had in mind appeals to you or not, such question is totally immaterial in considering the jurisdiction of the World Court to grant an advisory opinion on a question in which we have or claim an interest without our consent and over our protest. Certainly the United States Senate will not tolerate an advisory opinion on such a question, and I am satisfied that the overwhelming majority of the people of this country sustain the United States Senate in this attitude.

The jurisdiction of the court is determined by the statutes of the court. The statutes of the court do not deny the jurisdiction of the court with regard to a question in which the United States has or claims an interest if such question has not reached the status of a dispute or contention between the United States and some other government.

For instance, the question as to whether or not the United States is violating the favored-nation clause in certain treaties where the United States discriminates against the nationality of a certain race under its immigration laws has not and will not be brought into dispute or contention by the United States Government. Our immigration laws are based on our own private internal policy, which policy we will not discuss with other governments.

The right and necessity for our Government to prevent the acquisition of title to and sovereignty over territory adjacent to the Panama Canal by some powerful government is not in dispute, nor will our Government enter into any dispute with any other government with regard to such right and necessity. That right and necessity is also based upon a national policy which we will not debate or permit to be disturbed.

The court has jurisdiction to entertain a request for an advisory opinion with regard to these matters under the statutes of the court. The only question involved is whether the council or the assembly of the League of Nations, under the protocol, has a right to submit to the court such questions for an advisory opinion. The protocol, in article 5, says: "With a view to insuring that the court shall not, without the consent of the United States, entertain any request for an advisory opinion touching any dispute or question in which the United States has or claims an interest," etc.

Then article 5 proceeds to state how such assurance is guaranteed.

What is the assurance? First, that notice shall be given of the intention to request an advisory opinion; second, that the United States shall have an opportunity to protest against the submission of such request; third, that it shall have the same power in the council and in the assembly in voting for or against the submission of the question that the other members of the council or the assembly possess; fourth, that if the council or the assembly determine to submit such question, notwithstanding the protest of the United States, the United States is at liberty to withdraw its adherence to the court. The only partial aid to such assurance is the provision with regard to the vote of the United States in the matter. If a unanimous vote were required, then the United States would have a veto power.

The report of the protocol [committee] to the tenth ordinary session of the assembly of the League of Nations on September 14, 1929, relative to the interpretation of the protocol, says:

> It also implies that, if a majority is sufficient—as it is when the assembly asks for an opinion—the opposition of the United States, being simply equivalent to the vote of a member of the assembly would count when determining the majority; but if the majority is secured notwithstanding such opposition, the request would go forward and the procedure of the league would follow its course.
>
> The opposition of the United States, in a question in which that country maintains that its interests are involved, obviously can not be negatived or canceled by the ordinary procedure of the assembly. And while the United States had to recognize that the assembly's procedure must follow its course, we for our part had to recognize that the United States must be free to denounce the agreement, to withdraw its accession to the statute, in any matter in which the League's machinery might involve a request for an opinion notwithstanding the opposition of the United States.

It was upon this construction that the protocol was signed by the signatory powers. This construction clearly discloses why the provision for the withdrawal of the United States from the court was included in the protocol. It is evident that the signatories signed the protocol with the understanding that they might adopt the practice of agreeing upon a submission of a request for an advisory opinion upon a majority vote.

So the United States, under the protocol, has no control over the council or the assembly in the submission of a request for an advisory opinion. There is no limitation upon the jurisdiction of the court found in article 5 of the protocol. I have just quoted from and described the contents of the protocol. It is erroneously called the Root protocol. As a matter of fact, it is not the protocol that was prepared and submitted by Mr. Root on behalf of the United States. Let us see what Mr. Root did prepare and submit with regard to the matter. At the first meeting of such committee held on Monday, March 11, 1929, we find the following in the minutes:

Mr. Root's note for a Suggested Redraft of Article 4 of the Protocol of 1926 was then read. The text of the note ran as follows:

"The court shall not, without the consent of the United States, render an advisory opinion touching any dispute to which the United States is a party.

"The court shall not, without the consent of the United States, render an advisory opinion touching any dispute to which the United States is not a party but in which it claims an interest or touching any questions other than a dispute in which the United States claims an interest."

The rest of such proposed protocol by Mr. Root is substantially in the form of the protocol now before the Senate.

Subsequently, Sir Cecil Hurst submitted a substitute.

The minutes of the third meeting of the committee, held on March 12, 1929, set out:

The chairman reminded the members of the committee that Sir Cecil Hurst had submitted the following proposals for redrafting article 4 of the protocol of 1926.

Then follows in the minutes a copy of the protocol as it now appears and which I have hereinbefore quoted from and described.

It is evident from the draft prepared by Mr. Root that he segregated questions submitted for advisory opinions into two classes, namely, those which had reached the status of a dispute between the United States Government and some other government and those questions which had not reached such a status or in which the United States claimed an interest. Immediately following the submisssion of the Hurst protocol as a substitute for the Root protocol the minutes set out a construction of the protocol by M. Raestad, a member of the committee. I quote from the minutes:

M. Raestad thought that the committee could hail as a good omen the Anglo-American collaboration as represented by the Root-Hurst draft. A similar occurrence had taken place in 1926 in connection with the Root-Phillimore draft. If the proposal of Mr. Root were examined, the committee would note that it showed progress on the situation which existed in 1926, in so far as the following three points were concerned:

1. The United States formally abandoned all interest in the question whether unanimity or a mere majority was required when the council or the assembly requested an advisory opinion.

2. The United States would explain its point of view when it claimed that a particular question was of interest to it.

3. In case of disagreement, if the council or the assembly maintained its request for an advisory opinion contrary to the wishes of the United States, the United States would not insist on exercising its right of veto and would withdraw from the permanent court.

In opposition to what had been said on the previous day by Mr. Root, M. Raestad did not think that, on two points at any rate, one of which raised a question of principle, the proposal of Sir Cecil Hurst was an improvement on that submitted by his United States colleague. Mr. Root's proposal was divided into two parts:

1. It covered cases when the United States was a party to a dispute. In this connection there was only one provision—the first—in accordance with which the permanent court would not give an advisory opinion without the consent of the United States.

2. It covered the case in which the United States claimed that it had an interest at stake, though it was not a party to a dispute. All the rest of the Root proposals dealt only with cases of this kind.

This was the construction of the Hurst protocol which is now before the Foreign Relations Committee of the United States Senate, erroneously called the Root protocol, which was made by a member of the Committee of Jurists for the benefit of the whole committee and immediately after the submission of the Hurst protocol.

The chairman of the Committee of Jurists is quoted in the minutes as stating:

According to Mr. Root's proposals, whatever might be the nature of the dispute giving rise to a request for an advisory opinion, the United States reserved to itself the right to prevent any request being made for an opinion or to withdraw. The United States would thus have a right which was more extensive than that embodied in the draft of Sir Cecil Hurst, namely, the right to veto a request for an advisory opinion, whatever might be the size of the minority. If that interpretation were false, he would be delighted, as it would signify that the United States renounced its demand, at least in certain cases, but he did not think this was so.

Again the minutes disclose that M. Politis[2] commented upon the ambiguity of the protocol in the following language:

If unanimity were necessary, the veto of the United States would suffice to prevent the request for an opinion being made. If a majority sufficed, the negative vote of the United States would be inoperative. Such was the thesis, and it gave rise to two objections. It was not known what were the cases which required unanimity or a majority vote, and it was precisely this ambiguity which caused the United States some misgiving. This was a practical objection of great importance, which it was necessary to take into account. . . .

In the light of these practical considerations, therefore, the proposals under examination would not establish actual equality between the United States and the members of the council. The equality provided by Sir Cecil Hurst was theoretical.

I have quoted verbatim from the minutes of the meetings of the Committee of Jurists on the Statute of the Permanent Court of International Justice, which formulated the protocol, and also from the report submitting the protocol to the assembly of the League of Nations. It is clear that the United States is not assured under the protocol, either through the procedure of the council or assembly of the League of Nations, or by the statutes of the court, against the submission to and rendering by the court of advisory opinions touching questions in which the United States has or claims an interest that are not the subject of a dispute or contention between the United States and some other government, and without the consent and against the protest of the United States.

It appears to me, and I think to a majority, if not all, of the Foreign Relations Committee of the Senate that the construction placed on the protocol by Senator Root, and now placed upon the protocol by the Secretary of State, has no support in the record that I have submitted. The fact that the committee has already adopted unanimously a reservation offered by Senator Reed,[3] of Pennsylvania, reasserting that we will only consent to the signing of the protocol by the United States, with the understanding that the court shall not have jurisdiction to entertain a request for an advisory opinion touching any question in which the United States has or claims an interest, discloses not only the fact that the committee does not agree with Mr. Root and the Secretary as to the protection granted the United States under the protocol but desires to commit the other signatory powers to the construction set forth in the Reed reservation.

If the protocol should be signed on behalf of the United States containing the Reed reservation, and any of the signatories should denounce such construction, then the signing of the protocol by the United States would be annulled and we would be where we are now.   Mr. Root and

341

the Secretary of State seem to believe that the other signatory powers agree with their construction of the protocol. If this be true, why not let the State Department correspond by cable with the state departments of the other signatory powers and have them confirm the construction given the protocol by our State Department? Whilst such a confirmation might not legally bind the other governments, it would sufficiently satisfy me, and probably a majority of the committee, to justify us in giving a favorable report upon adherence to the World Court under such confirmation.

I have always been an advocate of adherence to the World Court and am now. I do not believe, and I am sure the Senate of the United States does not believe, that the court should have jurisdiction through an advisory opinion to meddle in the internal affairs of the United States, discuss its policies, and through such action probably arouse international opposition against the United States. It is true that we are given the privilege of withdrawing from the court in such event without "any imputation of unfriendliness or unwillingness to cooperate generally for peace or good will." Those words are meaningless. We have a right to withdraw without them, but there is no doubt in my mind that if we did withdraw, those words would not prevent the arousing of unfriendly relations.

I deplore the practice of having treaties so ambiguously drawn that they may be, possibly in years afterwards, given one construction by one government and another construction by another government. I will not be a party to the approval of any such treaty that not only vitally affects the interests of the United States, but which ambiguity may subsequently be the source of grave disputes between governments.

I am astounded that one of your statesmanship and legal attainments should consider that the reference to what appeared to be the opinion of Mr. Stimson, the Secretary of State, in his report to the President in 1929, whether correctly stated or not, should be material in considering the important questions at issue. It was only referred to to show that there was a difference of opinion between great men. By eliminating reference to them in the resolution I now concede that these two great men have the same opinion.

I have disclosed, however, that members of the committee of jurists who prepared and adopted the protocol held a different opinion with regard to the matter from that held by Mr. Root, Secretary Stimson, and yourself. I have shown that the construction given to the protocol in the report to the assembly of the League of Nations is contrary to the construction given to the protocol by Mr. Root and by Mr. Stimson, and possibly by yourself. I am not so much interested in the individual opinions as to the proper construction of the protocol as I am in the construction to be given to the protocol by the other signatory powers, by the government members of the council and assembly of the League of Nations and by the court.

I attach a copy of my resolution that I have substituted for my original resolution.

Respectfully yours,

(Signed) Key Pittman

[OF 202:T]

---

[1] Pittman, in his letter to the Reverend Thomas Jenkins, Bishop of Nevada, Lovelock, Nevada, March 31, 1932, had stated that his objection to the World Court lay in the fact that it provided for advisory opinions, and that Americans did not tolerate advisory opinions in their courts (*Cong. Rec.*, vol. 75, pp. 7348–7349). Jessup, in his letter of April 7, 1932 (printed in part in the New York *Times* of April 11, 1932, p. 2), had disputed this and had listed a number of states where the laws provided for advisory opinions.

[2] Nicolas Politis, at this time Greek Minister of Foreign Affairs.

[3] Senator James A. Reed.

Cordell Hull, Secretary of State, to Roosevelt

Washington, January 5, 1935

My dear Mr. President: In connection with the notice of Japanese denunciation of the Washington Naval Treaty which we communicated under Article 23 of the Treaty to the other signatories of the Treaty, we have received a note, dated January 2, 1935, from the French Government, transmitted through the French Ambassador here, of which the following is the substance:

The French Government recalls its declaration made at the moment of depositing its ratification of the Washington Treaty to the effect that it considered that the ratios laid down therein did not represent the respective importance of the maritime interests of the Contracting Powers and could not be extended beyond the categories of vessels for which they were expressly provided. The French Government also recalls the intention of the French Parliament that the Treaty should come to an end on December 31, 1936. For these reasons and because of difficulties to which the French Government alleges quantitative limitation has given rise it states that it could not have agreed to a continuation of the Washington Treaty in any case.

The French Government also points out that in a settlement of naval questions now it would be necessary to take into account the naval positions of certain countries not represented at the Washington Conference. It expresses the hope that a substitute arrangement will be made before December 31, 1936, but states that such a new understanding should not be limited to the Five Powers parties to the Washington Treaty. It will make known its views regarding a substitute agreement in more detail later but emphasizes at this time that such an agreement must maintain the principle of qualitative limitation and perhaps strengthen such limitation.

I enclose a translation of the French Government's note.[1]

Faithfully yours,

Cordell Hull

[PSF:France:TS]

[1] Present.

Marvin H. McIntyre, Assistant Secretary to the President, to Roosevelt

Washington, 1-7-35

Memorandum for the President: Frank Sayre brought this over this morning.[1]

It will come up Wednesday at 10 a.m. before the Senate Committee on Foreign Relations.

If the resolution is to be predicated on your recommendation your message should go up this afternoon.

Do you want to talk to Joe Robinson or Sayre about it on the telephone?[2]

M.H.M.

[OF 202:T]

[1] A draft of a message to the Senate recommending that it consent to adherence to certain World Court protocols. With a few minor revisions by Roosevelt, the message was sent to the Senate on Jan. 16, 1935, below.
[2] An attached note, undated, reads: "Mac—tell Frank Sayre no message—FDR."

Cordell Hull, Secretary of State, to Roosevelt

Washington, January 9, 1935

Dear Mr. President: I refer to your memorandum of January 2nd,[1] in which you ask that a study be made of the adequacy of our consular representation in Northern Africa.

Our representation appears to be adequate for purposes of information and for the protection of American interests in the French Zone of Morocco and in the French possessions of Algeria, Tunisia and French Somaliland. Our interests in and near the French possessions are covered by our Diplomatic Agency at Tangier, a Consulate at Casablanca in Morocco, a Consulate General at Algiers, and a Consular Agency at Oran in Algeria. We also maintain a Consulate at Tunis, and a Consular Agency at Djibouti in French Somaliland.

We have no representation in the Spanish Zone of Morocco, but, owing to the immediate proximity of the Diplomatic Agency at Tangier, we have not felt the need of establishing such an office. The lesser Spanish colonies, such as Rio de Oro, do not appear to warrant the opening of a new office.

We have no representatives in the Italian possessions of North Africa. There are two main fields. The first is Libya, the principal town of which is Tripoli. The second area centers about Ethiopia and the two neighboring colonies of Eritrea and Italian Somaliland. It would appear unnecessary to open an office in either of the latter two colonies, since questions arising there can, I am told, be adequately handled from our Legation at Addis Ababa, Ethiopia, from the Consular Agency at Djibouti in French Somaliland, and to a certain extent by our Consul at Aden. I do, however, recommend the opening of a consular office at Tripoli in Libya.

I attach a map, showing the location of our present consular representatives in North Africa. The city of Tripoli, in which we have no representation at present but at which the establishment of a consular office might be warranted, is shown in italics.[2]

Faithfully yours,

Cordell Hull

[*Notation*:AS] Mr Wilson   Mr Hengstler   Please work out an arrangement for Tripoli. WP[3]

[OF 20:TS]

[1] Above.

[2] The map is present. See Roosevelt to Hull, Jan. 15, 1935, below.

[3] Thomas M. Wilson, chief, Division of Foreign Service Personnel; Herbert C. Hengstler, chief, Division of Foreign Service Administration; William Phillips, Under Secretary of State.

Senator Key Pittman of Nevada to Roosevelt

Washington, D.C., January 9, 1935

My dear Mr. President: May I congratulate you upon having Reservation No. 5 with regard to advisory opinions attached to the Root Protocol in the reservation of adherence to the Court which Senator Robinson presented and passed through the Committee today.

As I tried to explain in our conference the other day, the only objection I had to the resolution prepared by Mr. Sayre and submitted to me was that it did not definitely provide that the Court should not entertain a request for advisory opinion affecting our interests over our objection. The resolution was reported out by a vote of fourteen to seven.[1]

The inclusion in the resolution of the preservation of the fifth reservation will greatly reduce opposition in the Senate and limit debate. The entire debate now must be based upon the simple question as to whether it is advisable for us to be a member of the Court.

I am so sorry to know that you have been suffering from a cold, and I hope that your recovery may be rapid. While all departments of the Government are retarded in their activities, even though you are temporarily incapacitated, you must protect your health, as we would be much like a ship without a rudder if your activities were long restrained.[2]

With expressions of highest regard, I am, Sincerely,

Key Pittman

[OF 202:TS]

[1] In favor: Bachman, Black, Bulkley, Capper, Connally, Duffy, Harrison, Pittman, Pope, Robinson, Thomas (Utah), Vandenberg, Van Nuys, Wagner; opposed: Borah, Cutting, Johnson, La Follette, Lewis, Murray, Shipstead.

[2] Answered Jan. 11, 1935, below.

Francis B. Sayre, Assistant Secretary of State, to Roosevelt

Washington, January 9, 1935

My dear Mr. President: Senator Robinson asked me to tell you of the action of the Senate Committee on Foreign Relations this morning with regard to the World Court. Senator Robinson introduced the resolution which I had previously agreed to with him embodying the so-called Reed amendment but without the objectionable Moses reservation and without the two objectionable understandings concerning "special treaties" and concerning the Monroe Doctrine. This resolution was carried just as introduced and Senator Robinson was authorized to report it out as thus carried. I enclose a copy of the resolution.

The Reed amendment is merely a restatement of the Senate Fifth Reservation and of Mr. Root's understanding. I do not feel that its inclusion is in any way injurious and I am confident that its inclusion will remove the ground for much hostility and opposition.

Senator Robinson did a splendid piece of work.

Faithfully yours,

Francis B. Sayre

[OF 202:TS]

[*Enclosure*] Proposed Form of Resolution of Adherence

Whereas the President, under date of December 10, 1930, transmitted to the Senate a communication, accompanied by a letter from the Secretary of State dated November 18, 1929, asking the favorable advice and consent of the Senate to adherence by the United States to the Protocol of date December 16, 1920, of Signature of the Statute for the Permanent Court of International Justice, the Protocol of revision of the Statute of the Permanent Court of International Justice of date September 14, 1929, and the Protocol of Accession of the United States of America to the Protocol of Signature of the Statute of the Permanent Court of International Justice of date September 14, 1929, all of which are set out in the said message of the President dated December 10, 1930:[1] Therefore be it

Resolved (two-thirds of the Senators present concurring), That the Senate advise and consent to the adherence by the United States to the said three Protocols, the one of date December 16, 1920, and the other two each of date September 14, 1929 (without accepting or agreeing to the optional clause for compulsory jurisdiction), with the clear understanding of the United States that the Permanent Court of International Justice shall not, over an objection by the United States, entertain any request for an advisory opinion touching any dispute or question in which the United States has or claims an interest.[2]

[OF 202:T]

[1] President Hoover's message of Dec. 10, 1930, and the other documents here listed are printed in Manley O. Hudson, *The World Court, 1921–1934* (Boston: World Peace Foundation, 1934), respectively, pp. 261, 251–259, 155, 209–215, 249–251. Sayre's draft was accepted by the Senate Foreign Relations Committee and Robinson offered it in the Senate on Jan. 14, 1935. (The second paragraph only appears in the *Congressional Record,* vol. 79, p. 417.) On January 15, Robinson reviewed the history of the various reservations to the 1920 protocol, particularly Reservation No. 5, on which the long-time opponents of American adherence to the Court now took their stand (*Cong. Rec.,* vol. 79, pp. 432–437).

[2] Reservation No. 5 was part of the resolution of adherence to the Court adopted by the Senate on Jan. 27, 1926. The first four reservations were proposed by Secretary of State Charles E. Hughes; the fifth was added in the Senate at the insistence of those opposing adherence (*Cong. Rec.,* vol. 67, pp. 2824–2825; *Senate Report* No. 758, 72d Cong., 1st sess., Washington, 1932; printed in Hudson, *The World Court,* as "Report to the Senate from the Committee on Foreign Relations, June 1, 1932," pp. 277–289). Reservation No. 5 reads: "That the Court shall not render any advisory opinion except publicly after due notice to all states adhering to the Court and to all interested states and after public hearing or opportunity for hearing given to any State concerned; nor shall it, without the consent of the United States, entertain any request for an advisory opinion touching any dispute or question in which the United States has or claims an interest" (Hudson, *The World Court,* p. 227).

This reservation was not acceptable to the Court and the matter rested until 1929 when Secretary of State Frank B. Kellogg intimated to the League that further consultation might prove fruitful (Kellogg to the Secretary General, Feb. 19, 1929, *ibid.,* pp. 239–241). The League thereupon appointed a committee of jurists to consider the matter and the committee formulated a protocol designed to satisfy both parties, the United States Senate and the Court members. This protocol (known as the Root-Hurst protocol after two members of the committee, Elihu Root and Sir Cecil Hurst, at that time counsel to the British Foreign Office) reasserted the claim of the Senate to a veto over all advisory opinions and set up rules for the operation of the veto. Under these rules the United States could stop an advisory-opinion proceeding, either before it came before the Court or after the Court had taken it up. If no agreement could be reached, provision was made for United States withdrawal from the Court (*ibid.,* pp. 242–244).

President Hoover urged ratification of the protocol with the Root reservations in a message to the Senate of Dec. 10, 1931, but no action was taken (*Cong. Rec.,* vol. 75, p. 299). In the 1932 presidential campaign, both party platforms advocated ratification but nothing was done during the first session of the 73d Congress. On Jan. 4, 1934, President Roosevelt and Senate majority leader Robinson conferred and decided against bringing up the Court issue. Robinson said that he and the President had agreed that the situation in Europe was so "complex" that the time was not "opportune" (New York *Times,* Jan. 5, 1934, p. 16). Public interest in the issue was so great, however, that the chairman of the Senate Foreign Relations Committee, Key Pittman, was impelled to make a statement in the *Congressional Record* of March 5, 1934, explaining the inaction of his committee. He said that decision by the committee on the reservations to the protocol would require "considerable consideration" and would result in a long debate, both in the committee and in the Senate. He thought that a majority of the committee was opposed to the reservations as they then stood (*Cong. Rec.,* vol. 78, p. 3675). Finally, on March 23, the committee held hearings and numerous influential persons and groups (among them the American Bar Association) urged ratification. In subsequent hearings, opponents of ratification (led by James A. Reed, George W. Pepper, and J. Reuben Clark) took the position that no deviation from the 1926 reservations should be made because the United States had then made all the concessions it should. On May 30,

1934, the committee voted to postpone consideration until the beginning of the next session (New York *Times,* March 24, p. 1; May 17, p. 1; May 31, 1934, p. 8). See Roosevelt's message to the Senate of Jan. 16, 1935, below.

Roosevelt to Morris Rothenberg, President, Zionist Organization of America, New York

[Washington] January 10, 1935

My dear Mr. Rothenberg: I regret that the inescapable pressure of official business prevents me from accepting the invitation to address the Palestine Conference to be held in Washington the latter part of January.

On many former occasions I have expressed my deep and abiding interest in all that pertains to the development, material and otherwise, of the great conception of creating in Palestine a home of happiness and prosperity for those of the people of the Jewish race who turn to the land of their fathers.

Trusting that the Conference will be marked by the fullest measure of success, I am, Very sincerely yours,[1]

[PPF 601:CT]

[1] Drafted by Under Secretary of State William Phillips.

R. Walton Moore, Assistant Secretary of State, to Roosevelt

Washington, January 10, 1935

Dear Mr. President: A few weeks ago there was referred to me for consideration the alleged importance to our Government of Cocos Island and the Galapagos Islands and I have since given the matter consideration.

While it is not probable that in the near future Japan or any other power will seek to acquire any of these islands which we could doubtless claim to be an infringement of the Monroe Doctrine, nevertheless it would seem that if any proper means of doing so can be found it would be well for our Government to obtain ownership or control of all of the islands.

The suggestion that they might be internationalized or neutralized does not impress me as desirable from our point of view. It would probably mean that our Government would have to pay the entire purchase price and then be subject to the will of other governments.

Assuming it to be important that our Government should be placed in position to fortify the islands as well as to make use of certain of the Galapagos group for aircraft landing fields, sooner or later we should obtain exclusive ownership or control by outright purchase or by a long lease. In answer to the argument that this would stir resentment in Latin America, I have thought if acquisition could be effected under binding agreements that the purchase price should be used in the construction of the proposed Pan American Highway, in which all of the nations south of us are intensely interested, there would be general and enthusiastic approval and Mr. Thomas H. MacDonald, Chief of the Bureau of Public Roads, with whom I have talked very confidentially, is most fully in accord with this view.

I enclose (1) correspondence that has been had with the Navy Department; (2) the data that has been prepared showing the location, condition, et cetera, of the Islands; and (3) as a matter of interest a copy of a treaty negotiated with Ecuador in 1854 but not ratified.[1]

No question appears ever to have been raised as to the ownership of the Galapagos Islands by Ecuador, but it is stated that while Costa Rica has been generally recognized as owning the Cocos Island, Colombia has made some claim to ownership.[2]

Secretary Hull has seen this letter.

Yours very sincerely,

R. Walton Moore

[PSF:State:TS]

[1] Not present.
[2] Answered Feb. 4, 1935, below.

Roosevelt to Manley O. Hudson, Law School of Harvard University, Cambridge, Massachusetts

[Washington] January 11, 1935

My dear Manley Hudson: Many thanks for your note. I know you will be very happy to know that the Senate Committee reported out the World Court by a vote of fourteen to seven. Final action will, however, be pretty close.[1]

Very sincerely yours,

[OF 202:CT]

[1] Hudson had sent his congratulations on Roosevelt's annual message of Jan. 4, 1935, and had expressed his pleasure at hearing that the President proposed to send a special message to Congress on the World Court. He said he had just come from "a swing around the circle" and everywhere he had found great interest in the Court (Jan. 5, 1935, OF 202).

Roosevelt to Senator Key Pittman of Nevada

[Washington] January 11, 1935

Dear Key: Many thanks for your nice note of January ninth.[1] I am delighted about the World Court action.

Don't let Will King tack on an amendment to free the Armenians or drain the Persian Gulf![2]

As ever yours,

P.S. If you think Will King's sense of humor is in good running order, you have my permission to show him this.

[OF 202:CT]

[1] Above.
[2] The reference is to the dispute in the Senate over Senate Resolution 176; see Roosevelt to Pittman, Feb. 4, 1935, below.

George H. Dern, Secretary of War, to Roosevelt

Washington, D.C., January 11, 1935

Dear Mr. President: On December 11 and December 31 I dispatched to the Secretary of State my comments on the proposed treaty with Panama which permanently renounces certain rights secured under the Treaty of 1903. In those two letters the civil factors of the question were discussed. I am dispatching today a letter in which the factors affecting the defense of the Canal in peace and war are covered.

I find both the Governor of the Panama Canal and the General Staff of the War Department seriously concerned with some of the proposed Draft Articles, and wish to ask your consideration of the following:

(1) That in any new treaty with Panama, all rights of sovereignty granted by Article III of the 1903 Treaty be retained. Concessions to Panama in the matter of trade rights should not be granted in specific terms, but should be rather in conformity with the general terms proposed by the Governor of The Panama Canal, that the United States, being earnestly desirous of the prosperity of Panama, will continue to impose restrictions upon residence and business conducted in the Canal Zone. The right of the United States to maintain in the Canal Zone the elements essential to furnish to shipping both "sea stores" and "ships' stores" and to continue the "hold for orders" business is considered essential in our peace-time relations to all nations, and, in addition, the supply functions involved are absolutely necessary as the nucleus of the war-time supply system; in this respect I deem it an essential in the defense of the Canal. I feel, therefore, that trade concessions granted to Panama from time to time to meet just representations of the Panamanian Government should be by Executive Order of the President of the United States.

(2) That the right to be granted to Panama to develop its ports should be so restricted as to prevent their development through foreign concessions which would be inimical to the interests of the United States.

(3) The proposal to abrogate Paragraph 3 of Article 7 of the Treaty of 1903 is considered especially unfortunate. The cities of Panama and Colon lie at the very entrances of the Canal. If the right to intervene is abrogated, there is the implied obligation not to do so. In my opinion, this right is a potent factor in maintaining stability of government in the Panamanian Republic, since those in opposition to the government will know that resort to violence will be promptly met by United States forces. If this safeguard be withdrawn, it is not impossible that we may have to confront a condition at the entrances of the Canal similar to that which existed along our Mexican Border during the Carranza and Huerta governments.

It is believed that the Navy Department would be equally concerned, and it is suggested that the opinion of that Department be obtained on the above subjects.[1]

Respectfully yours,

Geo. H. Dern

[OF 110:TS]

[1] Answered Jan. 21, 1935, below.

Elizabeth Eastman, Chairman, Women's World Court Committee, to Roosevelt

Washington, D.C., Jan. 11, 1935

My dear President Roosevelt: The Women's World Court Committee, made up of the following thirteen national organizations of men and women congratulate you on the service you are doing the cause of world peace by urging ratification of the World Court Protocols.

1. National Board of the Y.W.C.A.
2. National Education Association
3. American Association of University Women
4. American Federation of Teachers
5. Council of Women for Home Missions
6. Girls' Friendly Society of the U.S.A.
7. Medical Women's National Association
8. National Federation of Business and Professional Women's Clubs
9. National Congress of Parents and Teachers
10. National Council of Jewish Women
11. National League of Women Voters
12. National Women's Trade Union League
13. Women's Homeopathic Medical Fraternity

We have made a careful poll of the Senate, interviewing the Senators within the last two weeks, and beg to submit our findings to you with the hope that it will be useful. In nearly every case two women jointly called upon the Senator and the report is based on their accurate report checked by letters received by constituents of the Senators.

We have been working for the World Court since 1923 and are hoping that the goal is now in sight, thanks to your activity.

Respectfully yours,

Elizabeth Eastman

[OF 202-A:TS]

[*Enclosure*] Poll of the Senate on Ratification of the World Court Protocols[1]

Senators Favorable to the World Court

1. Alva B. Adams (Colorado)[2] Favorable
2. Henry F. Ashurst (Arizona) Favorable
3. Warren R. Austin (Vermont) Enthusiastic

4. Nathan L. Bachman (Tennessee) Strongly in favor. Voted right in Foreign Relations Committee.

5. Josiah William Bailey (North Carolina) Favorable

6. John H. Bankhead (Alabama) Favorable. Not committed in regard to reservations, but will follow the Administration.

7. W. Warren Barbour (New Jersey) Enthusiastic. Will do everything possible to aid ratification.

8. Alben W. Barkley (Kentucky) Favorable

9. Hugo L. Black (Alabama) Favorable. Voted right in Committee.

10. Fred H. Brown (New Hampshire) Favorable

11. Robert J. Bulkley (Ohio) Enthusiastic

12. W. J. Bulow (South Dakota) Has always been for it and will vote for it.

13. Senator Burke (Nebraska) Enthusiastic

14. Harry Flood Byrd (Virginia) Enthusiastic

15. James F. Byrnes (South Carolina) Favorable

16. Arthur Capper (Kansas) Always been favorable. Enthusiastic

17. Hattie W. Caraway (Arkansas) Has always said she would follow her late husband's example and vote for it.

18. Bennett Champ Clark (Missouri) Favorable

19. Tom Connally (Texas) Always Favorable

20. Marcus A. Coolidge (Massachusetts) Cordially in favor.

21. Edward P. Costigan (Colorado) Enthusiastic

22. James Couzens (Michigan) Probably favorable

23. James J. Davis (Pennsylvania) Favorable

24. L. J. Dickinson (Iowa) Favorable

25. F. Ryan Duffy (Wisconsin) Favorable

26. Vic Donahey (Ohio) Favorable

27. Duncan U. Fletcher (Florida) Favorable

28. Peter G. Gerry (Rhode Island) Favorable

29. Walter F. George (Georgia) Favorable but absented himself from meeting of Foreign Relations Committee.

30. Ernest W. Gibson (Vermont) Favorable

31. Carter Glass (Virginia) Enthusiastic

32. Joseph Guffey (Pennsylvania) Enthusiastic. Also for League of Nations.

33. Frederick Hale (Maine) Last statement in favor.

34. Pat Harrison (Mississippi) Favorable

35. Daniel O. Hastings (Delaware) Says he will vote for it but thinks it won't do any good, nor will it do any harm.

36. Carl A. Hatch (New Mexico) Favorable
37. Carl Hayden (Arizona) Favorable
38. Henry W. Keyes (New Hampshire) Favorable
39. M. M. Logan (Kentucky) Favorable
40. Augustine Lonergan (Connecticut) Favorable
41. William Gibbs McAdoo (California) Favorable
42. Kenneth D. McKellar (Tennessee) Favorable
43. Charles L. McNary (Oregon) Favorable
44. Senator Maloney (Connecticut) Favorable
45. Jesse H. Metcalf (Rhode Island) Favorable
46. Sherman Minton (Indiana) Favorable
47. Harry A. Moore (New Jersey) Favorable
48. Louis Murphy (Iowa) Favorable
49. M. M. Neely (West Virginia) Favorable
50. Peter Norbeck (South Dakota) Will probably not be on floor to vote, but should be paired favorably.
51. George W. Norris (Nebraska) Is discouraged about the value of any treaties when dealing with a nation like Japan, but will probably vote favorably.
52. Joseph C. O'Mahoney (Wyoming) Favorable
53. Key Pittman (Nevada) Favorable
54. James P. Pope (Idaho) Favorable. Enthusiastic
55. Robert R. Reynolds (North Carolina) Favorable
56. Joseph T. Robinson (Arkansas) Favorable
57. Richard B. Russell, Jr. (Georgia) Favorable
58. Morris Sheppard (Texas) Favorable
59. Ellison D. Smith (South Carolina) Favorable
60. Frederick Steiwer (Oregon) Favorable
61. Elmer Thomas (Oklahoma) Favorable
62. Elbert D. Thomas (Utah) Favorable
63. John G. Townsend, Jr. (Delaware) Favorable
64. Senator Truman (Missouri) Enthusiastic. Also for League of Nations.
65. Arthur H. Vandenberg (Michigan) Favorable, but making a noise about his superfluous reservation.
66. Frederick Van Nuys (Indiana) Enthusiastic
67. Robert F. Wagner (New York) Always Favorable
68. David I. Walsh (Massachusetts) Favorable
69. Wallace H. White, Jr. (Maine) Favorable

Senators Opposed to the World Court

1. Homer T. Bone (Washington) Says he is a believer in democracy, and will have nothing to do with the poisonous European mess. He believes in being kind to people who have the smallpox, such as Mussolini and Hitler, but not in going inside their houses.
2. William E. Borah (Idaho) Says that it will be ratified easily. Is opposed for reasons well-known by all who have heard him speak. Wishes full debate, but will not obstruct a speedy vote.
3. Robert D. Carey (Wyoming) Opposed
4. Bronson Cutting (New Mexico) Voted against it in Committee but may possibly vote for it. Probably opposed.
5. William H. Dieterich (Illinois) Probably opposed
6. Lynn J. Frazier (North Dakota) Always opposed
7. Thomas P. Gore (Oklahoma) Opposed
8. Hiram W. Johnson (California) Opposed but says it will be ratified.
9. Robert M. La Follette, Jr. (Wisconsin) Opposed
10. J. Hamilton Lewis (Illinois) Opposed
11. Huey P. Long (Louisiana) Opposed
12. Patrick McCarran (Nevada) Violently opposed.
13. James E. Murray (Montana) Now opposed but Catholic pressure for World Court and clearer understanding may change him.
14. Gerald P. Nye (North Dakota) Has had a thorough education on the work of the League of Nations since conducting the Munitions investigation, but will probably vote against World Court.
15. John H. Overton (Louisiana) Opposed
16. Thomas D. Schall (Minnesota) Violently opposed.
17. Henrik Shipstead (Minnesota) Violently opposed.
18. Burton K. Wheeler (Montana) Opposed

Senators Uncertain About World Court

1. Theodore Bilbo (Mississippi) Probably favorable
2. Royal S. Copeland (New York) Did vote for it 1926 but nobody sure how he will vote now and he is non-committal.
3. George McGill (Kansas) Never will commit himself about anything. Think he will vote favorably.
4. Park Trammell (Florida) Non-committal now but has always been opposed.
5. George Radcliffe (Maryland) probably favorable.

Senators Not Voting on the World Court

1. Holt
2. Tydings   Tydings could be paired for probably.

[OF 202-A:T]

[1] This main heading has been supplied.

[2] In the original, the names and following comment are arranged in columns. The parentheses have been supplied.

Martin H. Carmody, Supreme Knight, Knights of Columbus, to Roosevelt

New York, Jan. 13, 1935

[*Telegram*] The President: Your Excellency: A committee of five from the Supreme Board of Directors of the Knights of Columbus desires an appointment with you as soon as possible, in order to present a resolution adopted at meeting held at Waldorf-Astoria Hotel, New York, today, concerning conditions affecting the people of Mexico and the policy of the Mexican government in suppressing religion and denying other rights. Please advise me care of Waldorf-Astoria Hotel, New York, when such appointment can be had.[1]

Martin H. Carmody

[OF 28:T]

[1] The resolution is with this telegram. It describes the persecutions said to have been suffered by members of the Roman Catholic Church in Mexico at the hands of the Mexican government, and asked that the United States withdraw recognition unless the evils complained of were ended. The resolution was brought to the White House by D. J. Callahan, treasurer of the Knights of Columbus. The petitioners had asked to talk with the President but instead a meeting was arranged with Hull on January 21 (Callahan to McIntyre, Jan. 18, 1935, OF 28). In the interview Hull maintained his previous position that the United States could not interfere in the domestic affairs of other countries (New York *Times,* Jan. 22, 1935, p. 5). See Carmody to Roosevelt, April 22, 1935, below.

Cordell Hull, Secretary of State, to Roosevelt

[Washington] January 14, 1935

My dear Mr. President: A short time ago when we discussed the subject of Foreign Service it was your view that there are in the Service a number of men who fall below the reasonable and proper standard of efficiency which we have a right to expect. The Foreign Service Personnel Board has been diligently engaged upon an appraisal of the efficiency and value of the members of the Foreign Service and they have informed me that they will shortly be prepared to recommend the separation, for one reason or another, of thirty some officers whose aggregate salaries, in addition to the salaries of those already separated from the Service in the past few months, will amount to approximately $200,000. This will equal the amount by which the Bureau of the Budget, with your approval, reduced the appropriations for salaries of Foreign Service Officers. The action of the Board in recommending these separations is strictly in accord with existing law, is in the interest of a healthy and efficient personnel and I feel certain will have your hearty approval.

I am very much concerned, however, over the loss of morale that is likely to be produced as a result of these separations. Due to the economy legislation we have since the spring of 1932 lost over eighty officers. We are now about to lose perhaps as many as forty more, bringing our Foreign Service officer personnel down from some seven hundred and sixty-two to below six hundred and fifty. I am now speaking of the officers constituting our commissioned corps. I might mention that there is apparently a widespread misapprehension among the general public as to the number of officers in our Foreign Service. The six hundred and fifty officers referred to are the commissioned officers who man some three hundred and fifty consular and diplomatic establishments; for example, in the London Embassy we have six officers, in Paris seven, in Berlin four. In addition there are some thirty-six hundred men and women clerks and minor employees, some recruited here and others abroad. With the exception of the promotions made last summer in the lower classes of the Service, there have been no promotions in class or filling of vacancies created since 1932. These drastic reductions in personnel without the recognition of efficient service through normal advancement in class as the law contemplates will, I fear, have a demoralizing effect upon the most capable men in the Service and produce a condition which it may be difficult to repair.

Then I very much question the wisdom at this time of disordered international relations of further decreasing in number the men who must man our diplomatic and consular offices abroad. We have taken no new men into the Service since 1932. I have not called attention to this question before owing to a desire to contribute our share toward keeping expenses at a minimum. The loss of approximately an additional forty men, however, creates in my mind apprehensions that we may be allowing the numerical strength of our Foreign Service officer personnel to fall lower than can be justified at this time. This view is held by those officers in the Department who have given the Service most careful study and I find it is shared by responsible persons outside the Department who are familiar with the Foreign Service and its problems. It takes time and patience to make a really good Foreign Service officer out of a new recruit and it seems to me that failure to resume taking in new men for training and keeping up the numerical strength of the Service to at least what it is at present may eventually prove embarrassing and expose us to just criticism. If permission to take in new men is granted, I intend to see that stronger and more definite efforts are made than ever before to recruit commissioned personnel of outstanding, vigorous character fully qualified to take care of the Government's interests abroad in a manner suitable to the new and changing conditions now facing us. In the past the economic phases of our foreign relations have been in the background and comparatively few of our officers have been competent technically to appraise the available information. We intend to select and advance those men who show promise of being able to deal with and report intelligently on economic and financial matters.

Of course, it would not be sufficient merely to take in additional men in the lowest class. Through the lack of means of promotion there are already entirely too many of the very good officers in the Service in the lower classes. What I have in mind in proposing the advancement of these men is not to reward them in a dollars and cents way through giving them increased compensation, but to put the best qualified into more responsible positions where they will have greater opportunities for broader and more useful service to their Government. The important thing to do, it seems to me, would be to resume both the advancement of the outstanding men in the several classes and the filling of the resulting vacancies in the lowest class by new men. Unfortunately, the reduction in our appropriation by the Bureau of the Budget makes it impossible to take either of these important steps and if that reduction is allowed to stand no appreciable progress is likely to be made in either direction for the next eighteen months. It is my considered judgment that if we are to try to have a live energetic Foreign Service personnel capable of meeting what I believe to be the need of the present situation it would be distinctly in the public interest if you could see your way clear to restoring all or so much as possible of the $200,000 reduction made in the appropriation for salaries of Foreign Service officers by the transmission to Congress of a supplemental estimate to that effect. This is not only my own judgment but when I and my assistants appeared before the Appropriations Committee of the House the importance of this action was urged repeatedly upon us by members of the Committee, and we received the impression that if you were to recommend the restoration of the amount mentioned, the recommendation would be very sympathetically considered. Of course we declined to discuss and in no way advocated a change in the amount which you recommended to be appropriated, but confined ourselves merely to answering questions of fact propounded by the Committee.

In short, therefore, I am asking for this money not to expand the Foreign Service, but to give me the means, while eliminating the unfit and the misfit, to give our finest officers an opportunity through advancement to more responsible posts to give their country the best that is in them, and, at the same time, to revitalize the Service through the injection of new blood at the bottom. In doing this, I shall have the entire Service overhauled and the records of every officer and employee scrutinized with the greatest care.[1]

Faithfully yours,

Cordell Hull

[OF 67:CT]

[1] Answered Jan. 17, 1935, below.

Roosevelt to Cordell Hull, Secretary of State

Washington, January 15, 1935

Memorandum for the Secretary of State: I agree that we should open a Consular Office in Tripoli.[1] Will you take the necessary steps?

F.D.R.

[OF 20:CT]

[1] See Hull to Roosevelt, Jan. 9, 1935, above.

Roosevelt to Cordell Hull, Secretary of State, and William Phillips, Under Secretary of State

[Washington] January 15, 1935

Confidential

Memorandum for the Secretary of State and the Under Secretary of State: In regard to the St. Lawrence Treaty, will you make another check up with Senators Robinson and Pittman and the others and tell me whether, in your judgment, I should send the Treaty back as soon as the World Court is voted on?[1]

F.D.R.

[OF 156:CT]

[1] See Hickerson to Phillips, Jan. 18, 1935, below.

Representative John P. Higgins of Massachusetts to Roosevelt

Washington, D.C., January 15, 1935

Dear Mr. President: In my letter to you, dated December 19, and which obviously you forwarded to Secretary Hull's office for opinion and answer, I asked you to officially inquire into the present day outrages in Mexico and I submitted precedents established by former Presidents Wilson, Harding and Coolidge, who officially took cognizance of outbreaks and violence in Mexico and sent emissaries to put an end to wholesale murder and unspeakable outrages that were being committed.[1]

Present day conditions in Mexico are even more barbarous than they were in previous years and the "Reign of Terror" is being condoned by Ambassador Daniels, who press dispatches as late as January 6, reveal made a two hour visit to the home of Secretary Garrido Canabal, the leading atheist of Mexico and the man who, admittedly, directs the campaign of terrorism against Catholics in Mexico. Ambassador Daniels' actions, during recent months, in associating with the leaders of this movement, together with his tacit approval of their actions, is an indictment of every principle of honor and decency that America has stood for during the past one hundred and fifty years and warrants his immediate removal.

The consortion of Ambassador Daniels with these infidels and the refusal of Secretary Hull to intervene, as described in his letter addressed to me, dated December 28, in which he says, quote:

"It is not within the province of this government to intervene in the situation in Mexico. The procedure you suggest would be tantamount to an effort to determine the course to be taken by another nation and would almost certainly provoke such resentment as to defeat the purpose you wish to achieve," portrays the picture of despair that faces millions of Americans who, in the name of humanity, look to the leaders of our government to send a word of admonishment and disapproval of these outrages to the Mexican government.

The statement of Secretary Hull is inconsistent with our previous experience in Mexico. Were the decisions of Presidents Wilson, Harding and Coolidge to send emmissaries to Mexico "tantamount," as Mr. Hull describes it, "to an effort to determine the course to be taken by another nation"? None of our former Presidents were invited to send these emmissaries to Mexico.

In view of the fact that Secretary Hull is against intervention in Mexico and the fact that your office does not intend to follow well established precedent in this matter, may I suggest another means of approach to this subject, which does not call for an Act of Congress nor intervention in any form.

Three weeks ago, the Mexican Ambassador to the United States, Fernando Gonzalaz Roa, gave up his post and returned to Mexico. Before the new Ambassador is sent to the United States, diplomatic custom decrees that he must have the approval (persona grata) or disapproval (persona non grata) of the State Department. The approval or disapproval is a sovereign prerogative excercisable for any reason and without obligation to reveal the reason. All that you and Secretary Hull need do, to show how the people of this country feel about the Mexican outrages, is to tell the Mexican government that their new nominee for the post of Ambassador is persona non grata. Our government need give no reason and if other names are submitted follow the same procedure of disapproval until the Mexican officials bring their standards of life up to those maintained by men in other civilized countries.

This method of approach circumvents Secretary Hull's complaint that our action on intervention might be construed "as an effort to determine the course to be taken by another nation." The adoption of this method is no breach of international courtesy nor is it an intervention into the domestic affairs of another nation. Fundamentally, we Americans have a right to choose our associates among nations.

May I suggest again, Mr. President, that you recommend to the State Department that they embrace this latter suggestion pending a decision by Congress on Concurrent Resolution #3 printed under my name in the legislative calendar, which calls for the severance of our relations with Mexico and the immediate withdrawal of Josephus Daniels as Ambassador to Mexico.[2]

Respectfully yours,

John P. Higgins M.C.[3]

[OF 146:TS]

[1] Higgins' letter was not, apparently, returned to the White House; a note on McIntyre's memorandum sending it to Hull, Dec. 26, 1934 (OF 146), reads: "Letter . . . presenting briefly 'the facts concerning the "Reign of Terror" that exists today in Mexico' and requesting that Pres. deny official recognition to the newly elected Mexican government under President Lazaro Cardenas until he has investigated the justice of Mexico's claim for recognition by the U.S. government."

[2] "Proposing the withdrawal of diplomatic recognition of Mexico until such time as the policies and conduct of the said Mexican Government in relation to educational and religious institutions of all creeds and nationalities justify a resumption of relations, and further proposing that Josephus Daniels be immediately relieved as Ambassador to Mexico," introduced Jan. 8, 1935, and referred to the Committee on Foreign Affairs. No further action was taken (*Cong. Rec.*, vol. 79, p. 212). A similar resolution (though not asking for Daniels' recall) was introduced on Jan. 31, 1935, by Senator Borah; this resolution was also referred to committee (*ibid.*, p. 1298). Although Borah's resolution caused a good deal of discussion (he was on the Senate Foreign Relations Committee), the Administration succeeded in keeping it in committee.

[3] Answered Jan. 23, 1935, below.

Roosevelt to the Senate, January 16, 1935

To the Senate: The movement to make international justice practicable and serviceable is not subject to partisan considerations. For years, Republican and Democratic administrations and party platforms alike have advocated a court of justice to which nations might voluntarily bring their disputes for judicial decision.

To give concrete realization to this obviously sound and thoroughly American policy, I hope that at an early date the Senate will advise and consent to the adherence by the United States to the Protocol of Signature of the Statute of the Permanent Court of International Justice, dated December 16, 1920, the Protocol for the Revision of the Statute of the Permanent Court of International Justice, dated September 14, 1929, and the Protocol for the Accession of the United States of America to the Protocol of Signature of the Statute of the Permanent Court of International Justice, dated September 14, 1929, all of which were submitted to the Senate, December 10, 1930.[1]

I urge that the Senate's consent be given in such form as not to defeat or to delay the objective of adherence.

The Sovereignty of the United States will be in no way diminished or jeopardized by such action. At this period in international relationships, when every act is of moment to the future of world peace, the United States has an opportunity once more to throw its weight into the scale in favor of peace.

Franklin D. Roosevelt

THE WHITE HOUSE
January 16, 1935

[White House Press Releases:M]

[1] For citations to the published documents, see Sayre to Roosevelt, Jan. 9, 1935, above, n. 1.

Press Conference, Executive Offices of the White House, January 16, 1935, 10:45 A.M.

[Excerpt] Q: Mr. President, can you tell us the nature of your conversation with Secretary Hull and Mr. Peek yesterday?[1]

The President: I think, for background, there is no reason why they should not say a word or two about that. We started in a year and a half ago on the question of possible international agreements on wheat by which, from year to year, world wheat surpluses would be controlled, with the general thought that it would stabilize prices that the wheat producer actually got.

As you know, we made pretty fair progress with that—we ran up, I think, against one or two snags but, on the whole, there seems to be still a logical plan for international cooperation in one of the major crops.

The same general principle applies to cotton and it is being discussed. It is being discussed in a good many countries at the present time. We have not got to any point of calling an international conference or making requests of this, that or the other nation but we are exploring the possibility of international action to control cotton surpluses—that is, export surpluses—with the idea of making fair prices, prices you can look forward to in the world markets, to the cotton producers all over the world. It is a problem somewhat similar to wheat in the total amount. There are a good many nations growing cotton, darn near as many as are growing wheat. We are very much interested in it and we believe that it is one of those things where we should if possible, in the future, try to get some kind of international agreement.

Q: Have we taken it up with any other nations as yet?

The President: No.

[President's Press Conferences:T]

[1] According to the White House appointments list, Hull, Morgenthau, Wallace, and Oscar Johnston were at the White House from 11:45 to noon, and Peek's appointment was for the following fifteen minutes. Johnston, a cotton marketing specialist, was first vice-president of the Commodity Credit Corporation and manager of the Agricultural Adjustment cotton pool. From Jan. 1 to July 1, 1935, he was an assistant to Morgenthau. Presumably the meeting had to do with the cotton barter deal with Germany that Peek had been urging and Hull had been opposing.

Roosevelt to James M. Baker, Minister to Siam, Bangkok

[Washington] January 16, 1935

My dear Mr. Minister: I am sorry to have a letter from Ray Stevens saying that he is resigning but after he has had a rest I hope to put him on one of the Commissions in Washington.[1]

Incidentally, in writing me he says—"I like your friend Jim Baker. He has sound judgment, courage and high character. He has done excellently here. He is the only Minister since I have been here who really runs his Legation and supervises the Consulate. I have become very fond of him and I think he regrets my decision to leave here more than anyone else."

I think you will like to hear that as much as I do.

I hope you will feel wholly free to write me personally from time to time in regard to developments in Siam—not only Siamese affairs—but also the general effect of Japanese and other foreign policies.[2]

Very sincerely yours,

[OF 694: CT]

[1] Stevens had been for several years adviser on foreign affairs to the Siamese government. Roosevelt later appointed him to the Tariff Commission.

[2] Answered April 10, 1935, below.

Roosevelt to Warren D. Robbins, Minister to Canada, Ottawa

[Washington] January 16, 1935

Dear Warren: As an ancient dabbler in Admiralty law, I distinctly remember the phrase "The Agony of Collision." It is a grand expression which covers not only the well known crisis, such as that of March fourth, but in a very real though minor degree, many lesser episodes which are constantly coming up in government and life, as you know.[1]

I take it there is no further news about the St. Lawrence Treaty. I am watching the Congressional situation here but cannot yet decide.[2]

Love to you both, Affectionately,

[PPF 1012:CT]

[1] Robbins (a cousin of the President) in a letter of January 9 (PPF 1012), compared the emergency with which Roosevelt dealt on assuming the Presidency with that known in British admiralty law as "the agony of collision": "the interval of time between the moment when collision becomes inevitable and the actual time of collision." The interpretation of the law was to the effect that actions not ordinarily permissible would, under such dangerous conditions, be allowed.

[2] See Hickerson to Phillips, Jan. 18, 1935, below.

Roosevelt to Cordell Hull, Secretary of State

Washington, January 17, 1935

Memorandum for the Secretary of State: I have been much interested in your letter of January fourteenth relating to the Foreign Service.[1] I agree with you that we need to resume the advancement of outstanding men in the several classes and the filling of resultant vacancies in the lowest classes.

However, the reduction of the appropriation by the Bureau of the Budget was not intended to be taken out on the career men in the Consular and Diplomatic Services. I am still very confident that the greater part of this reduction can be covered by reducing the staffs in Embassies and Legations especially, and in some cases in Consulates—in other words, the clerical etc. forces.

I have no objection to a slight increase in the appropriation but it should be used for promotions and the filling of the resulting places at the bottom. I still think the reductions can be made lower. A rule compelling everybody in all Embassies and Legations to work eight hours a day—five days a week—would create the kind of a cyclone which would be heard round the world![2]

F.D.R.

[OF 67:CT]

[1] Above.
[2] See Straus to Roosevelt, April 9, 1935, below.

Frederick H. Allen to Roosevelt

Charleston, S.C. January 18, 1935

My dear Mr. President: Knowing as you do more or less of the close relations that I have with many of the European leaders in public affairs, I venture to impose upon you what follows: In your admirable address to Congress[1] you spoke of the agitated conditions existing "outside our borders" and certainly the year 1934 has seen ferments all about the World, and while you say "the maintenance of international peace is a matter in which we are deeply and unselfishly concerned," I do not feel that we are carrying our own weight in the boat in what we are doing to maintain it. You will remember that it was not until 1915 that President Wilson's thoughts began to be concentrated on the desperate situation in Europe and that he then began under Colonel House's inspiration to see if we could make some moves to mitigate or to end it. Up to that time what he calls his single track mind was directed to the betterment of conditions in our own Country. Similarly, you, with much more reason, because of the desperate conditions with which you were faced upon your accession to the Presidency, had to concentrate upon measures to alleviate or better these conditions, but now that under your leadership the Country is rising out of the depths into which it had been plunged, I see that you, like President Wilson, are turning your thoughts outward. In your telegram to the Council of Foreign Relations at the time of the presentation of the British State papers to that body, you said "I hope that in the future our outlook will extend to the frontiers of mankind." That statement of yours induces me to speak of the League of Nations.

I have twice attended meetings in Geneva of the Council and Assembly and as I knew and had many friends there among the leaders such as Briand, Benes and others, I was taken into many of their private conferences, and thus was enabled to see the inner works, so to say, of the Institution that is the League, and of course I was present as well in those that were open to the public, and became convinced that we ought to become at least an associated member of the League as we were an associated power during the war.

On my return to the United States, after my second visit at Geneva, I had a long talk with Senator Walsh of Montana and he agreed with me that if we could become a member of the Council, at least an associated member, that we could secure the best and most intimate knowledge of the economic, financial and political conditions in the different countries of the world and especially of those in Europe, and that with such a seat at the Council table we could exert an unparalleled influence in ironing out the various frictions, doubts and fears that disturb the Nations, but he said that while he would strongly favor such a connection with the League, it would not be worth while to bring up such a proposal before Congress, it would be impossible of enactment. Certainly the year 1934 has seen ferments and disturbances all about the world and not only in Europe. Is not this the moment by a proposal to join the League for you to seize and to place yourself and this Country at the height of leadership for the enforcement of the rules of justice and of right dealing which is the purpose of the League of Nations?

Woodrow Wilson raised the flag of the World War from the region of pacts and agreements over plunder and the redistribution of territories into a crusade for a fair and righteous peace. Certainly no one had ever attained such a pinnacle of approbation and such a moral leadership as greeted him upon his arrival in Europe. I think it will be conceded that at the Peace Conference he failed to carry out his ideals to the full extent. Following the Peace Conference there was certainly a great slump in the moral attitude of this Country, and the return to what President Harding called Normalcy came about. We dissociated ourselves from our partners in the War and because of this we are somewhat responsible for the troubles that since have taken place in Europe in its efforts by various combinations and alliances to maintain peace.

Your unparalleled success in the late elections, with the tremendous majorities in Congress, which are due to the belief that people have in you, has put you in a position of power, such as I think it can truthfully be said no President has ever reached. The late happenings in Europe, the reversal of Mussolini of his previous policies regarding Germany and Hungary which certainly took courage to adopt, and the agreements reached between the French and Italians, if the press reports are correct, with the sympathetic backing of England would seem to mean a chance for a period of calm in that troubled part of the world. The French by land concessions to Italy in Africa, by giving one-half share in the railway from Djibuti to Addis Ababa by agreements in Tunis, seem to have adopted the policy toward Italy that was Bismarck's toward themselves: that is, by turning her interest toward colonial expansion to thus wean her thoughts away from the troubled area of the Danube basin, just as Bismarck hoped that France would forget "revanche" because of her attention to colonial expansion. The failure of the disarmament conference, the attitude of Japan, the somewhat blind situation in Germany, especially as regard to her re-arming (have you seen the speeches of Winston Churchill and Mr. Baldwin regarding this?), the great sums being spent for military preparations in other countries, might seem to make the moment opportune for you again to assume a moral leadership for this Country that dropped from the hands of President Wilson by bringing us into the League as a member of the Council, at least as an associated power, so that we could act with it where our interests are concerned, and certainly peace is perhaps our major interest. Should you make such a proposal, with your infinite skill in the handling of men, a skill which President Wilson did not have, with your great majority in Congress, many of whom know that their election was due to you, I believe you could attain a moral leadership in the World such as Wilson did not enjoy, for he was defeated, and his defeat was due, as I view it, because of some narrow political prejudices which were exemplified by asking, as he did, for the election of a Democratic Congress, when he had been supported in his conduct of the War by men regardless of Party, and the putting of such men as Henry White on the Commission to negotiate peace who was without political influence in the Republican Party, instead of appointing men like Mr. Root or Mr. Taft or some man of political influence. Should you adopt the step proposed it can hardly be doubted that Germany and Japan will withdraw their resignations from the League, and should the League thus become a World wide association, the fears which grip the nations today would certainly be abated and an era of cooperation between the nations of the world would be initiated under your leadersip that would cause you to be blessed by mankind.

You well know my deep personal interest in the success of whatever you undertake, and as I see it, should you bring about what I have suggested, no President that we have ever had would leave behind him a reputation greater than yours. You have, of course, a means of gauging the chance of success for such a proposal that I have no means of estimating. Moreover, with the program you have in view in domestic affairs you may well feel that until your measures are adopted you do not care to set sail upon a program such as I outlined. I do not believe that with the great power that you have, and with your great skill in the handling of your fellow men, that you could be defeated, but even if you were the proposal would be in consonance with the ideals and the proposals that you have made and are making for the good and benefit of the people in our own Country, and would mark you at the height of the moral leadership of mankind. Perhaps you may think I am too much of an idealist in what I have to say, but I would rather fight for ideals than leave them out of my reckoning.

I am, always with my best wishes, very sincerely yours, and I hope you will forgive me for having been so bold as thus to write you.[2]

Frederick H. Allen

[PPF 692:TS]

[1] Jan. 4, 1935, above.
[2] Answered Jan. 23, 1935, below.

John D. Hickerson, Assistant Chief, Division of Western European Affairs, to William Phillips, Under Secretary of State

[Washington] January 18, 1935

Mr. Phillips: Following conversations in the last two days with Senators Robinson, Pittman and LaFollette, I am giving you a revised list of Senators whom the President might effectively influence in the matter of the St. Lawrence Treaty. These comments of course take into account the views of the three Senators mentioned above.

First of all, Senator Robinson believes that it would be helpful for the President to ask the five Democratic Senators who did not vote and who were not paired on the Treaty last year to agree to support the Treaty. They are:

Senator King—Utah
Senator Fletcher—Florida
Senator Trammell—Florida
Senator Thomas—Oklahoma
Senator Caraway—Arkansas

Senator Robinson believes that it ought to be possible to obtain all of these votes including Mrs. Caraway who he explained agreed "to have a bad cold" last year on the date of the vote at the President's request, since she would not promise him to vote for the Treaty.

Among the Senators now in the Senate who voted against this Treaty last time are a group of five who come from States which are not directly affected at all by the development and who ought to be fairly easy to line up. They are:

Senator Connally—Texas
 " Adams—Colorado
 " McGill—Kansas
 " George—Georgia
 " Russell—Georgia

We understand from several sources that Messrs. Adams and McGill are practically ready to vote favorably on the Treaty now and we believe that the President could easily persuade the other three to support him in this matter.

The next five Senators who voted against the Treaty last time but to whom it is believed an appeal might be made by the President with a fair prospect of success. These Senators are:

Senator Lonergan—Connecticut
 " Tydings—Maryland
 " Bailey—North Carolina
 " Reynolds—North Carolina
 " Neely—West Virginia

We received just this morning a tip from a newspaper man to the effect that Reynolds of North Carolina was disappointed that the President had not asked him to vote for the Treaty last year.

Out of the newly elected Democratic Senators who have not definitely declared themselves in respect to the Treaty may be mentioned the following:

Senator Gerry—Rhode Island
 " Moore—New Jersey
 " Truman—Missouri
 " Maloney—Connecticut
 " Radcliffe—Maryland

Senator Truman has I understand practically promised to vote for the Treaty and a word from the President should definitely clinch his vote. Senators Maloney and Radcliffe have indicated that they would like to support the President and vote favorably on the Treaty. We have no information about the attitude of Messrs. Gerry and Moore.

John Hickerson

[PSF:St. Lawrence Waterway:T]

Roosevelt to George H. Dern, Secretary of War

[Washington, January 21, 1935]

My dear Mr. Secretary: With reference to your letter of January 11, 1935,[1] I advise you that I have kept myself informed of the negotiations for new agreements now taking place with Panama; and that the views of the Governor of the Panama Canal and of the General Staff of the War Department, as stated in your letter, will be given careful consideration.

Sincerely yours,

[Notation:A] 1/21/35
[OF 110:CT]

[1] Above.

Press Conference, Executive Offices of the White House, January 23, 1935, 10:35 A.M.

[Excerpt] Q: Mr. President, can we induce you to comment on the Senate Progressives' fight against our entry into the World Court.

The President: There are a number of questions. Perhaps I can say something in the way of background. For example, there has been some discussion of the suggestion that if we go into the Court, that in that event no case could be sent to the Court without a two-thirds prior approval of the Senate. Of course, from the strictly Constitutional point of view, that is a definite limitation of the Constitutional prerogatives of the Executive which cannot be of any effect. Just, for example, I suppose there are fifty cases in our history where the Executive has entered into agreements with other nations for the settlement of pending questions without any reference to the Senate of the United States whatsoever. There are, of course, two distinct Constitutional limitations on the part of the Executive to conduct foreign affairs, but only two. The first limitation relates to appropriations. If a settlement of an international question involves the appropriation of money, of course that would have to be passed on by both Houses of the Congress. If the settlement required a treaty for the future, in that event it would require a two-thirds vote of the Senate. The Constitution very definitely, however, places all other conduct of foreign relations in the Executive and not in the Congress.

Q: Do you accept the Vandenberg reservation?

The President: To tell you the honest truth, I do not even know what it is. Was that the reservation—that is the reservation that Senator Vandenberg described as surplusage?

Q: That is right?

The President: Yes.

Q: Can you accept it then because it would appease his feelings?

The President: I have not read it. I read that he had offered a reservation otherwise described as surplusage.

Q: Any other reservations you propose accepting?

The President: I have not heard of any other at all.[1]

[President's Press Conferences:T]

[1] In the lengthy, acrimonious, and involved debate that followed the President's World Court message of January 16 (above), the strategy of the anti-Court senators was to restore by amendment as many as possible of the reservations offered in 1926. The Vandenberg amendment here mentioned was presented January 14. This amendment declared that adherence by the United States could not be construed to mean a departure from traditional American policy of noninvolvement in the political administration of any foreign state (*Cong. Rec.,* vol. 79, p. 417). This was the same amendment offered to the Senate by the Foreign Relations Committee on Jan. 26, 1926 (*Cong. Rec.,* vol. 67, p. 2762).

On Jan. 17, 1935, Norris introduced another amending resolution (the one discussed first in this press conference), that the adherence of the United States was on the understanding that no dispute to which it was a party would be submitted unless the Senate had approved it by a two-thirds vote (*ibid.,* vol. 79, p. 562). Apparently the Administration decided to accept the Vandenberg amendment as the less objectionable of the two proposals for it was approved on January 24 (*ibid.,* p. 893). The Norris resolution came up for vote on January 25 and was defeated by a vote of 47 to 37 (*ibid.,* p. 977).

The margin appeared too close, however, and the Administration took two steps to stave off defeat. Four doubtful senators, Cutting, Gerry, Walsh, and Donahey, were called to the White House on the morning of January 29. Later that day Senator Thomas (Utah), an Administration supporter, offered the amendment Johnson had originally proposed, that recourse to the Court by the United States and another state could be had only through "general and special treaties concluded between the parties in dispute" (*ibid.,* p. 1124). Robinson said this arrangement was acceptable to the President. But

Johnson was outraged and called attention to the fact that the President had originally said that his own reservation (Johnson's) was unconstitutional and invaded presidential prerogatives. The amendment was adopted but the resolution as amended was lost by a vote of 52 to 36, seven less than the two-thirds majority required (*ibid.,* pp. 1125, 1133, 1140). See Root to Roosevelt, Jan. 28, 1935, below.

Roosevelt to Frederick H. Allen, Charleston, South Carolina

[Washington] January 23, 1935

Dear Fred: That was an extremely interesting letter of yours.[1] I am watching the whole situation as it develops from day to day. There are some other complications which I shall tell you about when next we meet.

As ever yours,

[PPF 692:CT]

[1] Jan. 18, 1935, above.

Roosevelt to Representative John P. Higgins of Massachusetts

[Washington, January 23, 1935]

My dear Mr. Higgins: I have received your letter of January 15, 1935,[1] in which you recommend, as a means of indicating this Government's disapprobation of the religious policies of the Government of Mexico, that it decline to signify its approval of the appointment of an Ambassador from Mexico to replace Dr. Fernando Gonzalez Roa.

In reply I may say that on January 8, 1935, in response to an inquiry from the Mexican Embassy in this capital, the Department of State, having been duly authorized by me, advised the Embassy that the appointment of Dr. Francisco Castillo Nájera as Ambassador of Mexico met with my approval. In the circumstances, even though the action along the lines you propose were otherwise desirable, you will realize that it would be quite impossible for me to give consideration to the suggestion contained in your letter.

With regard to your statements concerning Ambassador Daniels, I desire to point out that the newspaper reports to which you refer appear to have been based upon a distortion of the facts surrounding the Ambassador's visit to Secretary Garrido Canabal. Shortly after the inauguration of the present administration in Mexico, Ambassador Daniels paid courtesy calls on all of the members of the new Cabinet, among them the Secretary of Agriculture. These visits were fully reported by Ambassador Daniels in his despatches to the Department of State, and I can assure you that to interpret his actions otherwise than as the performance of a courteous formality is as unjust as it is unwarranted by the facts.[2]

Sincerely yours,

[OF 146:CT]

[1] Above.
[2] Drafted by the State Department (Hull to Roosevelt, Jan. 22, 1935, OF 146). See Roosevelt to Noll, May 23, 1935, below.

Roosevelt to Oswald Garrison Villard, New York

[Washington] January 23, 1935

Personal

Dear Oswald: Perhaps some day you will come down and talk with me about the problem of the Naval Defense of the continental United States in the Pacific Ocean.

Always sincerely,

Many of the statements in the article are just "not so"![1]

[PPF 2178:CT]

[1] According to an attached note, Villard had written on Jan. 16, 1935 (PPF 2178), enclosing a copy of an article, "Our Navy Madness," from *The Nation* of Jan. 23, 1935, and had protested the plan to hold naval maneuvers in the northern Pacific in the spring of 1935. At the President's direction (according to another accompanying note) the letter and article were sent to Assistant Secretary of the Navy Henry L. Roosevelt. See Hull to Grew, Jan. 21, 1935, *Foreign Relations, 1935*, III, 842ff.

Roosevelt to William Phillips, Under Secretary of State

Washington, January 25, 1935

Memorandum for the Under Secretary of State: As you know, I was elected a member of the Académie Diplomatique Internationale in 1931 or 1932, even before my nomination. This came, I think, at the instance of Mr. Frederick H. Allen.

Mr. Allen has corresponded with me in regard to Mr. Perry Belmont's offer of his house as a home for the Académie. I have taken the position that, as the Académie has no large income, the up-keep and taxes on this house would be prohibitive, and that furthermore I doubt the advisability of the proposal for a number of other reasons.

Obviously we could not get funds from the Congress to maintain the Académie. They are much better off in Paris. You might ask Mr. Allen and Mr. Belmont for their thought in the matter.

This letter to me is evidently an official inquiry and I suppose we must make some reply. Will you take the matter up?

F.D.R.

[*Notation:*T] Letter in French from A. F. Frangulie, Academie[1]
[OF 1107:CT]

[1] An accompanying note, McIntyre to Roosevelt, Jan. 23, 1935, reads: "This did not come through the State Department. Someone brought it in personally. If it requires a reply I will handle it through the State Department." Presumably this was done for Frangulie's letter is not present.

Elihu Root to Roosevelt

[New York] January 28, 1935

Dear Mr. President: I am afraid that the World Court protocol without the Johnson resolution which I understand is an equivalent of the resolution adopted by the Senate in 1926, is up against the same thing that has killed every general arbitration treaty since Cleveland's time.[1] That is that it would deprive the Senate of a power which it values highly. At present no important question can be submitted to arbitration without a treaty having the consent of the Senate. If this protocol is adopted the Court would practically supersede arbitration and probably questions could be submitted to the Court without consent of the Senate. This would not only be a great diminution of Senate power but it would rob the Senators from the States subject to repudiated bond claims of the power to prevent the submission of such claims to adjudication by any administration. Consent to such a thing would probably ruin such senators in their own States. Their fellow senators sympathize with them.

It seems pretty hard to ask senators for such a vote.

I take this liberty because I have studied this particular subject both in and out of the Senate through many arbitration contests.

The Johnson resolution is adapted to remove this obstacle.

With sincere respect and personal regards, I am, Respectfully yours,

Elihu Root[2]

[PPF 2201:TS]

[1] On the Johnson resolution, see press conference of Jan. 23, 1935, above, n. 1.
[2] Answered Feb. 9, 1935 (*Personal Letters, 1928–1945*, I, 451–452). Roosevelt said that when the World Court resolution was taken up early in January, he, Robinson, and Pittman expected defeat by a close margin. They decided, however, "to undertake ratification then rather than to wait until the hurly-burly of the closing days." He added: "In time we shall win the long fight for judicial decision of international problems—but today, quite frankly, the wind everywhere blows against us."

Roosevelt to Cordell Hull, Secretary of State, Daniel C. Roper, Secretary of Commerce, and Frances Perkins, Secretary of Labor

Washington, January 29, 1935

Memorandum for the Secretary of State, the Secretary of Commerce, the Secretary of Labor: Please dig out the old London Convention of 1929—Safety at Sea—and advise me as to whether we should press for ratification by the Senate.

I understand it was held up by the Seamen's Union but, at the same time, if it had been in effect vessels without adequate bulkheads and vessels with a large amount of wood construction would not have been built.

If you do not advise seeking ratification, what kind of legislation should we ask for? I feel the Administration should act one way or another.[1]

F.D.R.

[OF 66:CT]

[1] The convention, signed by the United States May 31, 1929, and at this time before the Senate Foreign Relations Committee, provided that passenger vessels be built with additional protection against flooding or fire, with a bulkheaded steel hull, and with fire bulkheads in the passenger accommodations. Roper's reply to the above memorandum recommended ratification, as did Hull's (Jan. 30, Feb. 5, 1935, OF 66). Secretary of Labor Perkins, however, replying February 12 (OF 66), thought the objection of the Seamen's Union sound. This objection was that enforcement of section 14 of the La

Follette Seamen's Act of 1915 (38 *Stat.* 1170) would be vastly more difficult under the new convention. This section required that all vessels, foreign or domestic, operating in American waters be equipped with certain lifesaving devices. Under the convention the United States government would no longer be able to seek enforcement of section 14 in the courts but would be able only to bring violations to the attention of the consular officer of the country to which the offending vessel belonged.

Roosevelt then asked Hull, Roper, and Perkins to discuss the subject with Senator Pittman and to make a recommendation on the advisability of a special message to Congress (Roosevelt to Hull, Feb. 12, 1935, OF 66). No reply to this memorandum has been found. On February 23, Roosevelt asked Early to find out if Hull and Roper agreed with Miss Perkins' view or if they wished to file additional letters (OF 66). Roper replied Feb. 28, 1935 (OF 66), that he still thought the convention should be ratified; no further comment from the others is present. The matter was brought up at a Cabinet meeting on March 8, 1935, but because of "certain complications" (not explained) it was at that time decided to "shelve the whole thing for the time being" (Wilma L. Meredith, secretary to Early, to Early, March 19, 1935, OF 66). Nevertheless, bills to make effective the convention, H.R. 7040 and S. 2368, were introduced March 26, 1935, and referred to the House Committee on Merchant Marine and Fisheries and to the Senate Committee on Commerce (*Cong. Rec.*, vol. 79, 4418, 4490). Neither was reported.

Cordell Hull, Secretary of State, to Roosevelt

[Washington] January 29, 1935

Dear Mr. President: With reference to your memorandum of January 2nd,[1] concerning the need of supplying our ambassadors and ministers with more current information regarding developments here, and to Mr. Phillips' subsequent conversation with you on the same subject, I have given the matter considerable study and believe that the following suggestions may meet your own views in this regard:

I propose that, with the cooperation of the Navy Department, there be set up in our missions in Berlin, Rome, Paris and Geneva, naval short-wave radio receiving sets manned by naval personnel. There will be prepared every day in the Department a careful digest of current domestic news with special emphasis being laid upon your own utterances and upon the policies and aims of your Administration. This digest would then be radioed by the Navy from Arlington, to be picked up by the short-wave sets installed in our missions abroad. The information would then be spread out from the key points mentioned to other neighboring capitals by the most rapid practicable means. The Far East, with the exception of Tokyo, as well as Central America, are already provided with the necessary radio facilities to handle this information without further additions.

The result of these measures would be that your representatives in the key centers abroad would have a digest of domestic news, including the texts of your own remarks, available to them the same day that they appear in the American press, and other missions would receive the information in a very short time.

The cost of organizing and carrying out this plan, will, as a result of the Navy Department's cooperation in furnishing the necessary short-wave equipment, in assigning naval personnel to operate it, and in caring for the entire transmission of the material sent from the Department, be approximately $17,350 annually, which would not appear excessive when the real need, which you have pointed out, of supplying more news to your representatives abroad, is considered. Under the law, the State Department can and will be glad to make provision for $12,250 of this amount for its own expenses incurred in the matter, and would gladly provide for the remaining five thousand odd dollars to be used for the payment of transportation and subsistence of the naval personnel assigned to our missions abroad if the money were available for this purpose and if the law permitted it to do so. Unfortunately, the law prevents the Department making such expenditures on behalf of naval personnel even if assigned to our missions abroad.

Under these circumstances, if you feel that the measures outlined above will meet the situation you have in mind and in the event that you will request the Secretary of the Navy to follow a precedent already set in previous assignments of naval personnel to our missions at Moscow and Peiping with the understanding that the expenses for subsistence and transportation of such personnel, totalling a little more than $5,000, will be paid by the Navy Department, steps will be taken at once to put this plan into immediate effect.

Faithfully yours,

[OF 20:CT]

[1] Above.

Roosevelt to Cordell Hull, Secretary of State

Washington, January 30, 1935

Memorandum for the Secretary of State: In regard to whale oil:

Why is it necessary to repeal Section 602 of the Revenue Act of 1934? Can we not reduce the tax from twenty-four cents to twelve cents by agreement?

Also, nothing is said in these papers about the American whale oil industry. Is it not a fact that more ships have entered the whaling industry in the past year under the American flag?[1]

F.D.R.

[OF 61-W:CT]

[1] Hull had sent Roosevelt a long memorandum (Jan. 29, 1935, OF 61-W) on the request of the Norwegian government for a repeal of section 602, which imposed a tax of three cents a pound on whale oil in addition to the regular duty of three cents a gallon. Hull pointed out that in consequence of the added tax Norway had been obliged to make barter arrangements with Germany to dispose of her oil and had decided not to buy American fuel oil for her whaling fleet. Hull believed that there was much merit in the Norwegian position, "not to mention actual and imminent damage to our commerce and to our trade agreements program." He asked the President to review the question. Apparently Hull wrote again February 12; a note from Roosevelt to the Secretary of Commerce and the chairman of the Reconstruction Finance Corporation of Feb. 14, 1935 (OF 61-W), referred to a letter from Hull on the whale oil tax and asked for their opinion.

Roosevelt to Patrick H. O'Brien, Detroit

[Washington] January 30, 1935

Personal

My dear Mr. O'Brien: Thank you for your letter.[1] It is true that our Party must do everything humanly possible for our far reaching program of social security, but, at the same time, neither the Party nor the Nation can take the position that because of this we have no interest in furthering the cause of world peace.

Some people do not hesitate deliberately to distort facts and mislead good American citizens. Others, luckily few in number, are willing to see a city burn down just so long as their own houses remain standing in the ruins.

I know you will agree with me.

Very sincerely yours,

[PPF 2226:CT]

[1] O'Brien, former Michigan attorney general, said he had tried to find out the opinion "of a great many people" on the question of American adherence to the World Court (Jan. 26, 1935, PPF 2226). He said he had not come to any decided conclusions on the matter and did not fear our joining the Court with proper reservations. Since, however, the Democratic party under Roosevelt's leadership was trying to carry out a far-reaching program "of social security as well as the organization, correlation, and conservation of our natural resources," he thought it would be best not to inject the Court issue into politics at this time.

Roosevelt to Senator Joseph T. Robinson of Arkansas

[Washington, January 30, 1935]

Dear Joe: Will you be good enough to accept my thanks and convey my personal and unofficial gratitude to your 53 colleagues who voted for adherence to the world court? All of you have kept faith with the Republican and Democratic party platforms. More than that: you have done a service for the cause of peace, and in doing it have shown personal and political courage. As to the 36 gentlemen who voted against the principle of a World Court, I am inclined to think that ~~when~~ if they ever get to Heaven ~~or go the other way whichever it may be~~, they will be doing a lot of apologizing ~~for a good many centuries~~—that is if God is against war—and I think He is.[1]

[OF 202:A:FDR]

[1] Cf. the letter as sent, in *Personal Letters, 1928–1945,* I, 449–450.

William E. Dodd, Ambassador to Germany, to Roosevelt

Round Hill, Va., Jan. 30, 1935

Dear Mr. President: This is to express my congratulations and admiration and to wish you all success in the most difficult task in the world. Much as the Senate's minority defeat of the World Court connection may trouble you, you were entirely right; and the first unfortunate results will be the maintenance of trade barriers and the isolation of England in her effort to prevent war and increasing armaments, already worse than in 1914. I can not see how our country is willing to allow minority control of foreign policy.

However, one has to fight for one's ideals and I admire you for this in every direction. All success attend your heroic effort.[1]

Yours Sincerely,

William E. Dodd

[PPF 1043:AS]

[1] Dodd was so strongly affected by the World Court vote that he considered resigning as ambassador in protest; see his *Diary,* pp. 210–211, 214–215. Roosevelt replied Feb. 2, 1935, below.

Cordell Hull, Secretary of State, to Roosevelt

[Washington] January 30, 1935

My dear Mr. President: I believe that you will be interested in the contents of the attached telegrams in regard to reports that important negotiations are now in progress between China and Japan; also in the memorandum of comment upon the latest received of those telegrams, by the Division of Far Eastern Affairs, a copy of which is attached next hereunder. The situation appears to be somewhat obscure and I am disposed to be guided by the suggestion advanced in the memorandum.

We shall of course continue to follow developments with care and to keep you informed thereof.

Faithfully yours,

Enclosures: (See attached sheet.)
[OF 20:CT]

Enclosures:
Memorandum, January 29, 1935;
From Nanking, telegrams: No. 12, January 25, 5 P.M.;
No. 13, January 26, noon; No. 14, January 26, 1 P.M.; No. 16, January 28, 9 A.M.; No. 18, January 28, 3 P.M.;
To Nanking, telegram: No. 5, January 28, 5 P.M.;
From Peiping, telegram: No. 40, January 28, 1 P.M.;
From Shanghai, paraphrase of telegram No. 42, January 28, 10 A.M.;
From Tokyo, telegram No. 17, January 29, 6 P.M.[1]

[OF 20:T]

---

[1] As indicated in Roosevelt's reply of January 31 (below), the enclosures here listed were returned to Hull. Except for the memorandum and for telegrams 5 and 42, the enclosures are printed in *Foreign Relations, 1935,* III, 18–19, 20, 20–21, 21–22, 22–23, 23–24, 26–27.

Roosevelt to Cordell Hull, Secretary of State

The White House

Washington, January 31, 1935

Memorandum for the Secretary of State: I think our immediate course should be to watch closely all evidence, reports, rumors, etc., and be prepared to ask for official information both from China and Japan, if and when the situation warrants it.

F.D.R.

[*Notation*:T] Returning enclosures.[1]
[OF 20:CT]

[1] This memorandum is in reply to the preceding letter. It is also printed in *Foreign Relations, 1935,* III, p. 34.

Philip C. Jessup, School of Law, Columbia University, to Roosevelt

[New York] January 31, 1935

My dear Mr. President: I venture to write you not only as a private citizen, but also as secretary of the National World Court Committee to express to you the appreciation which all of us feel for your efforts to secure the ratification of the World Court Protocols.

I do not believe that the vote in the Senate represents the judgment of the American people as a whole. I believe that it represents the views of a well organized minority backed by the powerful organization of the Hearst papers.

Senator Robinson conducted a courageous and able fight, but the forces of the opposition were apparently too well organized. I venture to assure you of the conviction of very many people that your stand in such matters will have their continuing support. It is a slow process but we are confident that under your leadership further progress can and will be made along the line of developing an intelligent and forward looking American policy in international affairs.[1]

Respectfully yours,

Philip C. Jessup

[OF 202:TS]

[1] Answered Feb. 2, 1935, below.

James T. Shotwell, Director, Carnegie Endowment for International Peace, to Marvin H. McIntyre, Assistant Secretary to the President

New York City, January 31, 1935

Dear Colonel McIntyre: In these critical days I do not wish to write to the President on any matter, but if you think it well and can find an occasion to convey this message to him, I should be very glad.

I wish to say that the vote last Tuesday raises an issue far more serious than that of our entry into the World Court. It is whether the institution of representative government can stand against the impact of demagogue appeal to the prejudices, such as Father Coughlin has been guilty of in his misleading and almost seditious campaign.[1] I am sorry to think that it puts an added burden upon the shoulders of the President himself, for he is apparently the only person who can effectively combat this subversive and pernicious influence.

In any case, he should be assured that one result of the incident will be to increase the support for him upon the part of the intelligent citizens of the country in all of his efforts to keep the country informed as to the real issues ahead of it.

Sincerely yours,

James T. Shotwell

[*Notation*:A:LeHand] Mac to thank him—[2]
[OF 202-A:TS]

---

[1] The Reverend Charles E. Coughlin's radio speeches against United States entry into the World Court were generally considered to have been responsible for the adverse Senate vote. See especially his address of Jan. 27, 1935, "The Menace of the World Court," in his *A Series of Lectures on Social Justice* (Royal Oak, Michigan: Radio League of the Little Flower, March 1935), pp. 122–136.

[2] McIntyre replied briefly on Feb. 13, 1935 (OF 202-A).

Roosevelt to Claude A. Swanson, Secretary of the Navy

Washington, January 31, 1935

Memorandum for the Secretary of the Navy: I hope that this can be done.[1] Please let me know what I can reply to the Secretary of State.

F.D.R.

[OF 20:CT]

[1] Hull to Roosevelt, Jan. 29, 1935, above.

Press Conference, Executive Offices of the White House, February 1, 1935, 4:15 P.M.

[*Excerpt*] Q: Any comment or background on the Russian debt situation?

The President: No, I think the State Department gave out a statement this morning, didn't they?

Q: They gave out a statement last night but it was not very enlightening.[1]

The President: Didn't the Secretary of State talk to you about it this morning?

Q: Not to any great extent.

The President: Try him again.

Q: Returning to the St. Lawrence, sometime ago you said you were going to submit it to this session of the Congress. Has there been any change in that?

The President: In view of the actual situation, I had better not say anything today . . .

Q: Can you tell us whether Litvinov in his discussions with you relative to recognition made any promise that Russia eventually would settle the debts?

The President: I think you had better get it from State Department statements. That is one thing you have to phrase exactly.

Q: Secretary Hull said he could not remember whether you had said anything or not.

Q: Any preparation for a World Economic Conference?

The President: I have not heard a word about it.

Q: Can we phrase it this way: Was it our understanding that they promised to settle debts?

The President: I think there was a formal statement at the time.

Q: Expressing optimism over the possibility of a quick settlement?

The President: You check back and I think you will find some pretty definite statements on it.[2]

Q: At the State Department yesterday Mr. Hull said it would now be up to the Board of Trustees of the Export-Import Bank to decide whether there was any sense continuing the use of that bank. Can you tell us of any steps taken along that line?

The President: Not that I know of. I imagine the thing will be discussed and it will hinge—that is the first bank, isn't it?

Q: Yes, sir.

The President: As to whether they could find some logical use and reason for continuing on some other lines. I have not talked to them about it at all.

[President's Press Conferences:T]

[1] This statement is printed in *Foreign Relations, The Soviet Union, 1933–1939*, pp. 172–173. Hull said that the United States had offered to accept a greatly reduced sum in settlement of its claims against the Soviet Union, to be paid over a number of years. The United States was also ready to make credits available through the Export-Import Bank to American manufacturers and producers so that they could do business with the Soviet. Such loans would have constituted a revolving fund for continuing Soviet purchases, but in view of the Soviet position the United States could not encourage the hope that an agreement was now possible.

[2] In the published exchanges between Litvinov and Roosevelt of Nov. 16, 1933, Litvinov made certain commitments respecting new claims against the United States and referred to "a final settlement of the claims and counter claims" but no specific promise was publicly made (*Public Papers*, II, 484–487). However, a "gentleman's agreement" was made by Litvinov with the President on Nov. 15, 1933, that the Soviet government would pay a sum of not less than $75,000,000 "in the form of a percentage above the ordinary rate of interest on a loan to be granted to it by the Government of the United States" (*Foreign Relations, The Soviet Union, 1933–1939*, pp. 26–27).

Roosevelt to William E. Dodd, Ambassador to Germany, Round Hill, Virginia

[Washington] February 2, 1935

My dear Dodd: Many thanks for that nice note of yours.[1] We shall go through a period of non-cooperation in everything, I fear, for the next year or two. Walter Lippmann expresses the thing pretty well in this morning's *Herald Tribune*.[2]

Be sure to let me know when you come back.

As ever yours,

[PPF 1043:CT]

[1] Jan. 30, 1935, above.
[2] Lippmann's article, "The Defeat of the World Court," was reprinted in his *Interpretations, 1933–1935* (New York: Macmillan, 1936), pp. 347–350.

Roosevelt to Philip C. Jessup, School of Law, Columbia University, New York

[Washington] February 2, 1935

Personal

Dear Mr. Jessup: Many thanks for your very kind letter.[1] There is no question that at the present time we face a large misinformed public opinion and we can only hope that this will change.

Very sincerely yours,

[OF 202:CT]

[1] Jan. 31, 1935, above.

Breckinridge Long, Ambassador to Italy, to Roosevelt

Rome, February 3, 1935

My dear Chief: A few days after my return I saw Suvich[1] and took up the question of cotton where I had left it off when I left for the United States. I indicated that we might make an arrangement to take cheese and olive oil by reduction of tariff barriers but did not commit myself except in a general way. However, I did say that I had authority from you to proceed. He manifested an immediate interest. Yesterday I saw Mussolini and did the same thing. He asked, "Do you think it really is possible to do something before we have to wait for the tedious steps of trade negotiations and a general agreement?" I replied that I thought it was possible. That you had authorized me to proceed. He said that it would please him very much and that he was very much interested.

In other words, they are anxious and willing to increase the volume of international trade. After I talked to Suvich and before Mussolini I sent a telegram to the Department referring to my telephone conversation with you in New York and to the meeting you had with Cordell, Morgenthau, Wallace, and Oscar Johnston.[2] I have heard nothing from the Department.

Now I find myself in this position—informal but definite instructions from you following a conversation I had with Oscar Johnston but no instructions from the Secretary of State.

I do not want to get wires crossed and I do not want to do anything which does not reflect the coordinate policy of the Government—which I understand you to represent and to express. I assume that you have discussed the matter with Cordell and that he is advised of the matters I have proceeded with here. If you have not done so before the receipt of this letter, will you not be good enough to see that the matter is fully understood or that I be advised to the contrary before I have proceeded too far.

Mussolini and Suvich have indicated that they would be prepared to have a preliminary discussion with me within the next few days, the results of which I will telegraph immediately the conference is held, but I can see that they are very much interested, and as I understand from Johnston that the Italian purchases have fallen off 42% since last year I take it that we are very much interested. I believe that we can find some articles here which are almost if not quite the exclusive productions of Italy so that the most favored nation clause will not be involved, but in case I am not able to find such articles in any quantity or in sufficient quantities to serve as the basis for a quid pro quo I did have in mind, all subject to your approval of course, to suggest to the Italians that they buy more cotton than they did last year as the consideration for our tariff reduction on articles which are not produced exclusively by Italy.

But I am a little concerned about the failure to receive any communication from the Department, and I am conscious that in the hurry of my departure and the hectic arrangements which always precede leaving the United States that I did not have an opportunity to talk to Cordell after I talked to you, but I think he knows me well enough to realize that I would prefer to hear from him—and I am sure you know me well enough to know that I want to do the thing you want done as you want it done.

So please get my wires untangled over there and somehow arrange to let me have instructions through the Department to proceed along the line I have already started and from which it would be very difficult and embarrassing now to withdraw.

On the question of European politics I got from Mussolini yesterday the definite and ineradicable impression that he expects war with Germany within a comparatively short time. He said that he thought they could keep the peace during this year because of the agreement between France and Italy but he was very, very doubtful about the future. He thought Germany was not quite ready. I am satisfied he is looking forward to the certainty of war and is preparing. From other sources since my return I have discovered that the Italian steel mills and factories are busily engaged in the manufacture of all kinds of guns and ammunition—even large cannon. The prospect is not so good. It must come. We have all known it must come. It is only that the day is actually approaching. We must be realists.

Incidentally you might consider giving instructions to somebody that a good equipment for your diplomatic and consular officers in Europe would be gas masks, because when it comes it will come over night and come from the air. There will be no long drawn out mobilization. I am serious about the gas masks.

I am taking the opportunity of Harry Hawes'[3] return to Washington to get this to you by his hand rather than wait for the next pouch.

It was bully to be back in the States and was fine to see you to realize at first hand what great things you are doing there.

Affectionately and respectfully,

Breckinridge Long

[*Notation*:A] 2/19/35 Letter to President drafted by AHH.[4] A-S/T
[OF 233:TS]

---

[1] Fulvio Suvich, Under Secretary of State in the Italian Ministry of Foreign Affairs.

[2] Long's telegram of Feb. 1, 1935, is printed in *Foreign Relations, 1935*, II, 519; the meeting took place on Jan. 15, 1935 (PPF 1-0).

[3] A former senator from Missouri.

[4] Alvin H. Hansen, chief economic analyst in the Division of Trade Agreements in the State Department. See Hull to Roosevelt, Feb. 21, 1935, below.

Roosevelt to R. Walton Moore, Assistant Secretary of State

Washington, February 4, 1935

Private and Confidential

Memorandum for Judge Moore: I hesitate to have the acquisition of Galapagos by the United States discussed even confidentially with the Ecuadorian Government.[1] Such action would undoubtedly become known and, at this time, would create an unfavorable impression.

On the other hand, I wish you would discuss with the Secretary the following:

Approach the Ecuadorian Minister, informally, with the suggestion that because of the extraordinarily interesting flora and fauna of these Islands (unlike any in the world) the Pan American Union should consider the possibility of their being converted from Ecuador sovereignty into a Pan American International Park or wild life area. The Pan American nations could chip in some sum—let us say two or three million dollars—to reimburse Ecuador for the money they have spent there. This amount would more than compensate her! The title would then vest jointly in all the members of the Pan American Union. The Pan American Committee could then maintain the Islands as an International Park—prohibiting all fishing and shooting and all colonization. The Committee would also be responsible for the patrolling of the Islands. The only use to which the Islands could be put, under the agreement, is a commercial air line stopping point—no militarization being allowed. The United States would, of course, bear the major part of the purchase price and the patrol. The total cost would be very small.

Such action would forestall any possibility of sale of, or use by, a hostile power.

In regard to Cocos Island, nothing need be done at this time because it has no Naval or Aviation danger to us under existing development of armaments.[2]

F.D.R.

[PSF:State:CT]

[1] See Moore to Roosevelt, Jan. 10, 1935, above.

[2] Roosevelt visited Cocos Island in October 1935, during his Pacific cruise. Much publicity was given to his visit and Smithsonian Institution specialists brought back numerous specimens of the fish and animal life of the island. See André Roosevelt to Roosevelt, Aug. 6, 1936, below.

Roosevelt to Senator Key Pittman of Nevada

Washington, February 4, 1935

Memorandum for Senator Pittman: Will you be good enough to speak to me about this at your convenience?

F.D.R.

[*Notation*:T] Letter to Secretary McIntyre dated Jan. 31, from the Under Secretary of State enclosing copy of letter to the President from the Secretary of State dated Sept. 10, 1934,[1] asking whether the President has had an opportunity to discuss with Senator Pittman the advisability of the introduction of a Senate resolution requesting that the Geneva Arms Convention of 1925 be returned to the Senate for reconsideration. This in order to secure the removal from the Convention of a reservation regarding the Persian Gulf.

[OF 66:CT]

[1] Above.

Roosevelt to Jeanne Rosat-Sandoz, Le Locle, Switzerland

[Washington] February 4, 1935

My dear Madame Rosat: In case you have not seen this newspaper article, I am sending it to you.[1] I have been especially happy in seeing your photograph seated at the piano. I would have recognized you immediately and the picture reminds me that the only thing you failed in teaching me was the art of playing the piano.

I think it will interest you to know that it has been the very greatest possible help to me to be able to speak French—not only during the war days when I was in France and Belgium, but also here in Washington where I meet so many foreigners and Diplomatists who cannot speak English.

I do wish it were possible for me to see you again. Perhaps when this task is finished we shall all be able to go abroad and visit you at Le Locle.

Mama is very well—eighty years old—and I know she would send you her love if she knew I was writing.[2]

With my warm regards and best wishes, Affectionately,

[PPF 199:CT]

[1] According to an accompanying letter from Constance Drexel to Rudolph Forster, undated, this article was about Madame Sandoz, Roosevelt's childhood governess. Miss Drexel, a journalist who was a friend of the Roosevelts, apparently had given the clipping to the President. See her article, "Unpublished Letters of F.D.R. to his French Governess," in *Parents Magazine* (September 1951), pp. 30–31, 80–84.

[2] Madame Sandoz replied in a letter of March 26, 1935 (PPF 199), expressing pleasure at being remembered by the President.

Roosevelt to Francis B. Sayre, Assistant Secretary of State

Washington, February 4, 1935

Memorandum for Assistant Secretary of State Sayre: What do you think of this suggestion of Oscar Johnston?[1]

F.D.R.

[*Notation*:T] Suggests an act to expand and improve export markets for merchandise and to overcome difficulties affecting the export of merchandise from the U.S. which difficulties are occasioned by reason of changes in the relative values of the currencies of the nations.[2]

[OF 614-A:CT]

[1] Answered Feb. 6, 1935, below.
[2] Johnston's letter was not returned to the White House.

Roosevelt to Henry Wolfson, New York

[Washington] February 4, 1935

Dear Mr. Wolfson: I appreciate the spirit in which your letter is written.[1] There are so many angles to the Russian trade matter that I think if you knew them all you would agree with our procedure, and, at the same time, realize that we hope greatly that an increased trade between the two countries may yet be attained.

Very sincerely yours,

[OF 220-A:CT]

[1] Wolfson, a New York City real estate man, had written Feb. 1, 1935 (OF 220-A), to protest what he regarded as Hull's unnecessarily abrupt announcement of the ending of the negotiations with the Soviet Union on debt settlement. Wolfson thought a more tempered statement would have kept the door open for future discussions.

Senator Key Pittman of Nevada, Chairman, Committee on Foreign Relations, to Roosevelt

Washington, D.C., February 4, 1935

Personal and Urgent

My dear Mr. President: The Vice President informed me this morning that you would be pleased if Senator Robinson and I would express our opinion as to the advisability of your returning the St. Lawrence Waterway Treaty to the Senate for action.

There are two problems involved, namely: (a) Will there be sufficient affirmative votes in the Senate to ratify the treaty? and (b) Would it be advisable, even if there are sufficient votes to ratify, to inject the debate over the treaty into the Senate at the present time?

Let us first consider (a). I have had Mr. Biffle,[1] our pair clerk, make as careful and accurate a poll of the Senate as is possible. The result of such poll is as follows:

Ayes 44
Nays 35
Either not seen or non-commital 15
Not qualified (Being Mr. McKellar and Mr. Holt) 2

Those who have not been seen or refuse to commit themselves are as follows: Messrs: Bilbo, Caraway, Connally, Donahey, Fletcher, Gerry, Guffey, King, Maloney, Minton, Moore, Murray, Thomas (Oklahoma), Schwellenbach and Truman.

My guess as to how these fifteen will vote is as follows:

Yeas: Connally, Donahey, Guffey, Minton, Fletcher, Murray and Thomas (of Oklahoma), and Schwellenbach 8

Nays: Bilbo, Caraway, Gerry, King, Maloney, Moore and Truman 7

If this analysis of the fifteen should be accurate, then the vote would stand: Ayes, 52; Nays, 42.

McKellar will undoubtedly be here and sworn in if the vote does not come too early, and as he voted "aye" last year, it is to be assumed that he would vote "aye" again, which would mean 53 to 42.

If McKellar's vote should be counted with the "ayes," and all of the Senators in the list of fifteen who have not been seen or have not committed themselves should vote "aye," then the result would be 60 "ayes" and 35 "nays."

To win the fight and secure ratification it would appear, therefore, from the present poll that not only would it be necessary to obtain the affirmative votes of the fifteen above referred to, but it would also be necessary to change the votes of four as shown on the poll from "nays" to "yeas." While this is not impossible, it is in my opinion very improbable. I feel at the present time that if the treaty is reported to the Senate it will be defeated.

I trust you will pardon me for briefly discussing (b). As a general proposition, I do not believe that it is good legislative strategy to inject into the Senate international matters that will be the subject of long and intense debate while there is pending or imminent vital domestic legislation. Such a debate arouses some bitterness, tends to divide the Administration's supporters of domestic policies, and stimulates the organization of blocs in support of various independent measures and amendments.

Even if these effects were not experienced, at least such a debate takes up the time of Senators from more pressing work, and diverts their minds and their attention from more vital and pressing objects of legislation.

I will not enlarge upon this personal opinion that I hold because I had the honor, at your invitation, to discuss similar problems in connection with our proposed adherence to the protocols of signature to the Permanent Court of International Justice.

I have the honor to attach a copy of the poll prepared by Mr. Biffle.[2]

With expressions of the highest regard and respect, I beg to remain, Sincerely,

Key Pittman

[OF 66:TS]

[1] Leslie L. Biffle, secretary to the Senate majority.
[2] The poll, on a Senate tally sheet, is summarized by Pittman in his letter.

Cordell Hull, Secretary of State, to Roosevelt

Washington, February 5, 1935

My dear Mr. President: This Government has a request from the Secretary General of the League of Nations that he be informed as to whether the Government of the United States would be prepared to take part in a conference proposed for 1936 in Singapore at which would be represented the authorities who are responsible in Eastern countries for the measures taken to prevent traffic in women, with a view to securing closer cooperation and greater exchange of information between them.

Both the Secretary of War, in view of the Philippine interest, and the Secretary of Labor favor participation by this Government in the proposed conference. I should appreciate learning whether such participation has your approval, so that I may inform the Secretary General of the League.

There are no funds available for defraying the cost of American representation at such a conference. However, the Secretary of War will undertake to ascertain whether the Philippine Government would be willing to bear the expenses in case an official from Manila should be designated as this Government's representative. Failing that, it would be possible for an American Foreign Service officer stationed in or near Singapore to represent this Government at the conference without the need for additional funds.

Faithfully yours,

Cordell Hull

[*Notation*:AS] CH   OK   FDR
[OF 20:TS]

Roosevelt to David M. Edwards, President, Friends University, Wichita, Kansas

[Washington] February 6, 1935

My dear President Edwards: It is impossible for me, without writing you many pages, to go into all of the problems which your letter raises.[1] All I can tell you is that some of the things you have read about are not true and that others are not fairly stated unless connected with other facts.

Perhaps if you will come down to Washington some day I can explain some matters which you are evidently not aware of. It would give me great pleasure to see you.[2]

Very sincerely yours,

[PPF 2191:CT]

[1] Jan. 29, 1935 (PPF 2191). Edwards protested Roosevelt's recommendations to Congress for increased military and naval appropriations and the turning over to the

Navy Department of Wake Island. The island's use for naval purposes would, he thought, further aggravate United States-Japanese relations.

[2] There was no further correspondence with Edwards and presumably he did not accept the President's invitation.

Arthur N. Holcombe, National Central University, Nanking, to Roosevelt

Nanking, China, Feb. 6, 1935

Dear Mr. President: I have not wished to make the accompanying unsolicited letter to you[1] a long one by setting forth in detail the grounds for the findings of fact and statements of opinion contained therein. But there are some observations which I feel justified in communicating to you.

1. The Japanese "powers-that-be" believe that they have a right to do in China what the Manchus and Mongols have done before them. There can be no doubt but that they would like to extend their sway over the whole of China. However, they are uncertain how this might best be done, or whether their people would stand for the expense. This uncertainty concerning ways and means of executing their grand project makes it unlikely that they will proceed further than they have already gone, under existing conditions.

2. Important elements in Japan continue to hold grave misgivings concerning the wisdom of the aggressive policy on the mainland and would like to revert to a more friendly policy both toward China and toward the United States. But even they can not look forward to undoing what has been done in Manchuria, though they hope to take advantage of eventual blunders by the military to recover their former power, and ultimately return to a more pacific policy.

While I am engaged in setting forth my opinions, I should like to touch upon another matter.

1. It is not necessary to adhere to the World Court by means of a treaty. The desired result can be accomplished much more easily and no less efficaciously by means of a joint resolution.

2. May I not add, in view of the interest you showed a year ago in my little book, *The New Party Politics*,[2] that before leaving America I finished a little companion-piece to that book, now about to be published under the title, *Government in a Planned Democracy*?[3] I have asked the publisher, W. W. Norton, New York, to send you a copy through Miss

LeHand, as before. The passages which might interest you most are contained in chapters iv and v, and relate to the organization of national planning.[4]

Respectfully yours,

Arthur N. Holcombe

[PPF 2325:TS]

[1] In this letter, of the same date, Holcombe said he had concluded: (1) that the Japanese would not extend their military occupation of China to points south of the Great Wall not already occupied by them; (2) that, in view of the results of their annexation of Korea, it was unlikely that they would undertake the annexation of Manchuria; (3) that it was undesirable for the United States to attempt a new naval understanding with Japan through a treaty but something might be accomplished by a gentlemen's agreement; and (4) that the United States should give the Chinese some assurance on its future silver policy, which would strengthen the Chinese government. Holcombe, a Harvard political scientist, was at this time teaching at the National Central University in Nanking.
[2] New York: Norton, 1933.
[3] New York: Norton, 1935.
[4] Answered March 18, 1935, below.

Roosevelt to Senator Key Pittman of Nevada

[Washington] February 6, 1935

Dear Key: Thank you for your excellent analysis in your letter of February fourth.[1] I think you are right. Will you tell Joe?[2]

Always sincerely,

[OF 66:CT]

[1] Above.
[2] Joseph T. Robinson (Ark.), Senate majority leader.

Roosevelt to Henry L. Stimson, Washington

[Washington] February 6, 1935

Dear Harry: Thank you for that mighty nice note.[1] It heartens me. You are right that we know the enemy. In normal times the radio and other appeals by them would not have been effective. However, these are not normal times; people are jumpy and very ready to run after strange gods. This is so in every other country as well as our own.

I fear common sense dictates no new method for the time being—but I have an unfortunately long memory and I am not forgetting either our enemies or our objectives.

As ever yours,

[PPF 20:CT]

---

[1] Feb. 2, 1935 (PPF 20), expressing his appreciation for Roosevelt's effort to secure ratification of the World Court protocol: "It is a tragedy that it was not successful and I fear the repercussions around the world will be bad. But perhaps some good in the future may come out of the fact that the opponents of such an honest effort for peace as the World Court are now lined up in full view. Hearst, Huey Long and Father Coughlin are not a very inspiring group, and the fact that such a group can do so much damage may wake up some tepid Americans to the necessity of greater effort on their part."

Francis B. Sayre, Assistant Secretary of State, to Roosevelt

Washington, February 6, 1935

My dear Mr. President: Pursuant to your request[1] for my comments on the proposed modification of anti-dumping legislation suggested by Mr. Oscar Johnston, may I make the following suggestions:

Mr. Johnston's proposed bill provides that merchandise may be imported without regard to foreign market value, provided (1) "That such importations are in connection with or related to or offset by exports of merchandise originating in the United States and made to the nation from which the merchandise involved in the transaction is imported and provided that the aggregate values of the imports are substantially offset by the value of the exports," and provided (2) that the merchandise shall not be imported at a cost price lower than that at which similar merchandise may be imported from any other country.

With the general purpose which Mr. Johnston has in mind, i.e. to increase the amount of imports into this country, particularly from gold standard countries, I am in hearty sympathy. Mr. Johnston is quite right in his basic assumption that our anti-dumping law was not designed to meet the peculiar difficulties which confront gold standard countries at present seeking to import merchandise into the United States.

The first proviso which requires that to secure the benefit of the legislation the importation must be proved to be an offset to exports of American merchandise seems to me unfortunate in so far as it rests upon the policy of bilateral balancing of trade. American commerce is, as you know, peculiarly dependent upon triangular trade, and a policy which would strike at triangular trade by promoting bilateral balancing is open to serious objection. For this reason it would seem to me unfortunate to tie up any waiving of the anti-dumping provisions as a quid pro quo for an approximate bilateral balancing of specific exports against specific imports with any particular country. Such arrangements inevitably involve preferential treatment which we are struggling hard to combat in our general trade relations.

Whether such a proposal would be politically wise is a matter upon which I venture no opinion. The provision that the cost price shall not be lower than that at which similar merchandise may be imported from any other country would invite all countries to dump goods into the United States at the extraordinarily low rates at which Japan can sell them because of her greatly depreciated currency.

It is to be noted that the proposed measure would place importers who are allowed to obtain foreign money at rates below the official rates, on a preferential basis, as against other importers. It would, moreover, particularly favor countries which had, for one reason or another, tied up their foreign trade by artificial restrictions. This might give rise to charges of discriminatory treatment from other countries which could not, because they were pursuing a more liberal commercial policy, easily take advantage of these provisions.

Of course, as you realize, it is a rather serious matter to break down our anti-dumping legislation since such action can scarcely fail to tend in the direction of upsetting price calculations and creating even greater uncertainty than now prevails in foreign trade. A number of us have been giving careful consideration to possible modification of the anti-dumping law but we have not as yet reached any satisfactory solution. A sub-committee of our Commercial Policy Committee is at present trying to reach some solution. The matter is of such immense importance and affects so profoundly our relations with gold standard countries on the one side and the sterling group on the other that its delicacy and importance can hardly be over emphasized.

Faithfully yours,

Francis B. Sayre

P.S. If you should like me to come over to talk this problem over with you I should be only too happy to do so. F.B.S.[2]

[OF 614-A:TS]

[1] Feb. 4, 1935, above.

[2] An attached memorandum, Roosevelt to McIntyre, Feb. 12, 1935, reads: "Tell Frank Sayre to talk it over with Oscar Johnston." McIntyre did so, in a note of Feb. 13, 1935, and Sayre replied February 20 that he had already talked with Johnston, that the question of modifying the anti-dumping laws was being discussed by an interdepartmental committee, and that he had brought Johnston's proposal before this committee. Sayre concluded: "The question is bristling with difficulties and the committee has not as yet reached any satisfactory solution" (OF 614-A). The legislation proposed by Johnston was not introduced.

Norman H. Davis Chairman, American Delegation, London Naval Conference, to Roosevelt

New York, February 7, 1935

Personal

Dear Mr. President: In passing through Washington yesterday on my return from Tennessee, I talked with Joe Robinson and Key Pittman with regard to my meeting with the Foreign Relations Committee of the Senate in Executive session, with a view of explaining the problem that confronts us in dealing with the questions involved in naval limitation. They both seemed to think that, since it is impossible to talk confidentially to the Committee—as anything that might be said would leak out—and since there is still some feeling resulting from the fight over the World Court, it would be better at least to find out first what would be the attitude of Senator Johnson and perhaps Senator Borah. They suggested that, in any event, it would be well for me to have a talk with Senator Johnson first and then, depending upon his attitude, determine whether or not to have a meeting with the full Committee after deciding what we should ask the Committee to do.

I will, therefore, plan to go to Washington some time around the middle of next week and talk to Hiram Johnson, unless you think it is better for you to have him around some time and perhaps have me at the same time so that we can talk to him together.[1]

With warm regards, I am, Faithfully yours,

Norman H. Davis

[OF 29:TS]

[1] An attached note, Roosevelt to McIntyre, Feb. 12, 1935, reads: "Tell Norman to go ahead and talk to Hiram Johnson." On February 12 McIntyre wrote to Davis (OF 29) that the President suggested that he see Johnson without waiting for a White House appointment.

Breckinridge Long, Ambassador to Italy, to Roosevelt

Rome, February 8, 1935

My dear Chief: I will try to give you a picture of the appearance of European politics today—since the Rome conference, the Saar plebiscite, and the London conference.

While I doubt if it is reduced to writing, I get the impression that the Italo-French accord amounts practically to an alliance. This is subject to revision and rectification in my thought, depending upon later developments. But the attitude of the Italians toward the French and the confidence with which they look toward unified action in case of German aggression leads me definitely to the belief that the principal business—as yet undisclosed—of the Mussolini-Laval conversations was to align France and Italy against what they probably expect in the form of German aggression.

They all feel that the Saar plebiscite has acted as a big drink of Schnapps to the Germans and that Hitler will be emboldened now to pursue his Pan Germanic ideas into the fields of former German territories and Austria. They are convinced that Germany is very well equipped for war but not yet prepared to take the offensive or to commit an act which might lead immediately to open warfare. Nevertheless, they seem more confident of their efforts and seem to place great reliance upon the accord with France.

The London conversations seem to have laid the basis for common action against Germany in which England would participate, though it has not been—as far as I can ascertain—in any sense reduced to writing or into the exactness of a definite understanding. However, the growth of air forces in Europe has brought England to the realization that the Channel no longer separates her from the Continent, and as Sir Eric Drummond said to me, and as reported in my recent telegram on the subject, he could not see that a Government could distinguish between one kind of warfare and another and that engagement to participate in one was tantamount to being involved in a general struggle. So that on that basis England seems to be now expected to participate on the side of Italy and France and against a possible aggressive move on the part of Germany. And the Germans are always so "dumb" in their maneuvers that it would be comparatively easy to construe any incident as having been brought about by Germany.

What is striking in the whole thing is that Mussolini appears for the time being to have abandoned his role as mediator. The change of heart probably dates, if it actually exists, to the reaction following the Hitler-Mussolini conversations last summer immediately after which Hitler committed his barbarous activities in Germany and offended the Italian sense of propriety. At any rate, for the time being Mussolini seems to have lined himself definitely against Germany and to have made what amounts to an alliance with France with the probable annexation of military support from England.

But the most remarkable part of it from my point of view is that it is simply a continuation of French Continental policy. Ever since the War France has tried to encircle Germany. She got Poland; she got the Little Entente; she got Russia; and she had the sympathetic activity from time to time of Italy and Austria, but the circle was not closed. However, the object of France was to encircle Germany. The present situation seems to encircle Germany—absolutely. So that it seems to be not a diplomatic victory for Italy but to reflect considerable credit upon the dexterous management by France of both Italy and England.

Now it is all up to Germany. The morning press indicates that Germany's demands will contemplate 3000 airplanes as forming a basis of an air equality. This would simply be indicative of the other demands to be made in the form of other equipment. There is neither hope nor dismay over the prospect of the answer which will eventually come from Germany. They seem to be satisfied that whichever way Germany answers the result will be the same, except that it will insure peace without a war if Germany should honestly join the entente of the three western powers. I doubt, however, if anyone will place any great confidence in Germany's declaration to the effect that she would like to continue on friendly and peaceful terms with her neighbors. She is suspected like a wolf, and her intentions are considered to be about as peaceful as were the acts which history records of Attila.

The important elements, as I see it now, are first, what amounts practically to an Italo-French alliance; second, the signified willingness of England to join; third, the delay attending Germany's announcement of a willingness to consider cooperation; and fourth, the ring that has been drawn around Germany.

The failure of Germany to agree will result in a race for armament, and it is my real belief that the Italians will not start from behind scratch. My information is that their steel factories are working overtime.

Connected with this thought and the probability of preparation for war on a considerable scale is the fact that when the bond issue (lire 2 billion) in Italy was proposed for subscription at the end of November last, it was stated to be one of the objectives to retire five hundred million from circulation and to use the other billion and a half to pay the budgetary deficit. They did pay the budgetary deficit, as appear from the statements of the Bank of Italy, but they did not retire five hundred million from circulation nor any amount from circulation. As a matter of fact, circulation has risen just a little. They explained this by saying that there were certain unforeseen items which had to be cleared up. The net result is that the Treasury got five hundred million lire for some purpose now undisclosed.

It may be that part of it is used for equipment, and it may be part of it is being used to advance the Abyssinian movement. Randolph Harrison, our Third Secretary, has a man servant who is a member of the militia. This man advised him this morning that 300 men and three officers from his own contingent had been drafted to go to Abyssinia and would be paid 25 lire a day instead of the ordinary 10 lire. Enormous supplies of barbed wire, trucks, and all that sort of thing continue to be sent, one big ship load having sailed just recently from Naples, as I was advised by the Consul General there this morning. Of course this will be expensive, and it may be that it will consume the five hundred million lire in question without leaving any for preparation for Germany. And if Mussolini foresees war in Europe, I don't know what he is thinking of in spending so much money in Abyssinia and preparing to engage in warfare there, unless he thinks it would be good training for his men. Nevertheless, the Abyssinian campaign proceeds and the thought of eventual conflict with Germany continues.

In connection with our conversation about a communication to Mussolini on the subject of Abyssinia, may I suggest that the situation seems to have changed a little bit since the time you spoke. Since then there have been Ethiopian aggressions against the French which have been well advertised in the European press and in which it is stated that members of the regular army were mingled with the Nomad tribesmen. And also since then the Italian papers state that the American Minister— or Chargé d'Affaires—has been subjected to some mistreatment and indignity. In addition to that, the League of Nations is apparently not to take up the subject but has referred it back for settlement between Italy and Abyssinia. So that our absence from membership in the League would not serve as a predicate. There would remain only our interest in universal peace—but it does seem a long way outside our bailiwick.

However, you will know what you want to do and whatever you decide in the premises, I will be happy to carry out.

Things have been awfully hectic here since my return. I have hardly had an opportunity to leave my desk, but I hope within the next week I will be able to get a respite.[1]

Affectionately and respectfully,

Breckinridge Long

[PSF:Italy:TS]

[1] Long next wrote to the President on Feb. 15, 1935 (PSF: Italy), on Italy's preparations for the Ethiopian campaign.

Roosevelt to Judge Julian W. Mack, United States Circuit Court, New York

[Washington] February 12, 1935

Dear Judge Mack: Thank you much for your nice letter.[1] I did have an excellent talk with Felix when he got back. I like much to keep in touch with the progress being made in Palestine, and I hope you will always feel free to talk with me about it.

Incidentally, do run in and see me one of these days when you are in Washington. I have not had a chance to talk with you for a long time.

Always sincerely,

[PPF 2211:CT]

[1] Jan. 30, 1935 (PPF 2211), reporting on a conversation he had had with M. Maldwin Fertig on Zionist matters. Mack was at this time president of Palestine Endowment Funds, Inc., and had been president of the American Jewish Congress. Fertig, president of the Metropolitan League of Jewish Communities and counsel to Roosevelt during the latter part of his term as governor (June–December 1932), had recently returned from Palestine and had talked with the President on January 21 (PPF 1-0). He apparently had asked Mack to convey some further information but Mack had told him that in Justice Louis D. Brandeis and Felix Frankfurter the President had the best sources of information on the subject. Fertig talked with Roosevelt again in Hyde Park on September 21 or 22 and at that time the President asked him to arrange a meeting with Fertig, Louis Lipsky, and Cyrus Adler (Fertig to McIntyre, Oct. 28, 1935, OF 4092). Lipsky was at this time editor of the *New Palestine;* Adler was president of the American Jewish Committee. The three Zionist leaders conferred with Roosevelt at the White House on Nov. 13, 1935; Fertig wrote to McIntyre on November 18 (OF 4092), that the interview had received wide and favorable notice in the Jewish press.

Henry A. Wallace, Secretary of Agriculture, to Roosevelt

Washington, D.C., February 12, 1935

Dear Mr. President: The enclosed, which is part of a letter to a big business friend from an old time cotton broker and cotton factor, is rather illuminating concerning the cotton situation and the relationships of the farmers of the cotton South to the foreign users of cotton.[1] We are going to have a real job holding the line firm on this situation, at the same time taking care not to violate certain long run economic forces.

I find that some of my good friends in other departments are anxious to have our cotton policy reversed, and at the appropriate time it may perhaps be worthwhile for you to have a talk with some of them.

Undoubtedly the cotton farmer to some extent has been more or less at the mercy of certain international firms. The problem now would seem to be to handle the situation with a firm hand, but without going so far that these international forces can eventually upset us. These foreign firms, I am convinced, have been quite successful in getting their propaganda into the minds of the economists of all branches of our government, and, of course, part of their presentation is sound.[2]

Respectfully yours,

H. A. Wallace

[OF 258:TS]

[1] The author of the enclosure is not further identified. The writer's opinion was that part of the decline in American cotton exports was owing to the fact that the foreign cotton exchanges were hostile to American interests (Americans were ordinarily barred from membership), and that they were refusing to buy in hope of bringing down the price. If the American surplus could be reduced to a point where the United States could bar cotton shipments to defaulting nations, the export price would go from 14 to 40 cents a pound.

[2] Answered Feb. 15, 1935, below.

Roosevelt to Ray Atherton, Counselor of Embassy, London

[Washington] February 14, 1935

My dear Atherton: Oscar Johnston, who has been with the Agricultural Adjustment Administration, is going over on a semi-official, exploratory mission to talk over the raw cotton situation, informally, from the point of view of the British manufacturers and the Egyptian and Indian cotton growers. Out of this may come some agreement, formal or otherwise, to stabilize the world raw cotton markets. It is at least worth discussing.

I have given Oscar Johnston a personal note to the Prime Minister.[1] I hope you can arrange for him at least to present this note and also that you will arrange for him to see the India office people and whoever it is that runs the Egyptian end of things.

Very sincerely yours,

[PPF 2221:CT]

[1] Below.

Roosevelt to Prime Minister J. Ramsay MacDonald, London

[Washington] February 14, 1935

Personal

My dear Mr. Prime Minister: My good friend, Oscar Johnston, who has been with the Government in the Agricultural Adjustment Administration for the past two years, is visiting London on what may well be described as a semi-official mission. The subject he seeks to explore is the world cotton surplus. This, of course, affects not only your own cotton manufacturers, but it especially affects the growing of cotton in Egypt and India. This whole subject is still in the exploratory stage, but I hope that general agreement can be had on some plan which will more greatly stabilize the world raw cotton situation, even if such stabilization is only in experimental form at the beginning.

I hope you will make it possible for Mr. Johnston to see your people who are in charge of the Egyptian and Indian end of this business.

With my warm regards, Faithfully yours,

[PPF 2221:CT]

Cordell Hull, Secretary of State, to Roosevelt

Washington, February 14, 1935

Personal & Confidential

For the President: Thanks for the pamphlet entitled *The Emergence of the New Economic World*, which is being circulated by one Constantine McGuire and the reputed author of which is Ferdinand Fried[1] in Germany.

In the first place, the German Government permits no person in Germany to write and publish anything on economics except what is pleasing and satisfactory to the Government and its own economic policies. It was therefore under a government which is exercising control over the mind, the utterances, and the publications of all individuals that Fried prepared this data. I have never before heard of Thiesing.[2] I assume that whatever Thiesing may be doing, Fried is working in harmony with the Nazi regime. McGuire is understood always to be jumping from one thing to another. So much for the background, which of course should not detract from any inherent merit of the publication.

The publication seemingly has for its objective some sort of support of the Hitler, Fascist or other economic theories which lead definitely and directly to the unrestricted doctrine of The State. It may be observed that social and economic conditions in Italy and Germany today are steadily becoming worse.

The opposition in this country is even now undertaking to state the issue as per the attached news clipping.[3]

Some of us believe that the one practical alternative is embodied in the comprehensive economic program which at this time is being carried forward by the Administration. The progress, as has been stated to the country from the beginning, will inevitably be very gradual and cover a substantial period of time. It can only be pursued slowly and cautiously as public sentiment at home will support it, and as other important countries join in the simultaneous carrying out of this program.

Two years ago the American people were overwhelmingly in a state of mind to try almost anything in the way of governmental plans or devices or expedients to deal with the horribly dislocated financial and economic conditions. The Anglo-Saxon conceptions, ideals, and training over many centuries, however, are such that they could not be led, at least within any short time, away from the fundamentals of the political, social and economic institutions which they have been taught and which are deeply rooted in their minds and hearts. It is especially true that, whatever may have been the disposition of the American people two years ago to indulge in experiments almost ad libitum, a very marked change has since taken place and is continuing.

I am not underestimating the effects of superficial preachments of vociferous demagogues and chronic agitators who are very conspicuous just now.

C.H.

[PPF 1820:Foreign Trade:TS]

[1] No further reference to this pamphlet has been found; it is possible that it may have been the American edition of the author's *Die Zukunft des Aussenhandels durch innere Marktordnung zur Aussenhandels Freiheit* (Jena, 1934). Fried was the pseudonym of Friederich Zimmermann, a writer on economics; his earlier works included *Das Ende des Kapitalismus* (Jena, 1931), and *Autarkie* (Jena, 1932). McGuire was an economist who had written on the problem of the war debts; one of his books, *Italy's International Economic Position* (New York: Macmillan, 1926), was a Brookings Institution study.

[2] Possibly a reference to something in Roosevelt's note or memorandum to Hull (not present) sending the pamphlet.

[3] The clipping is undated and unidentified; it is apparently a quotation from a speech and reads in part as follows: "Shall we follow a growing number of the nations of Europe down the suicide road to the all-embracing state, or shall we gamble our future on an intelligently modernized capitalism that finds its profit in production for the masses and stabilizes its market by a progressively wider distribution of the national income."

Arthur Sweetser, Director, The Secretariat, League of Nations, to Roosevelt

Geneva, February 14th, 1935

Dear Mr. President: May I, at this rather special moment, send you a personal word of cheer and devotion from Geneva?

Countless friends abroad have followed your international efforts with ever increasing enthusiasm. Great progress has certainly been made in clarifying America's position and bringing her back to the helpful, Good Neighbor policy. The new atmosphere emanating from home has brought increased courage abroad.

But progress is never even. Recently have come two sharply contrasting developments. They cut so deep, from opposite angles, into America's international philosophy as to make me wonder if we are not at a turning point of thought.

The World Court decision was, of course, a deep disappointment. Many extreme statements were reported from the debates; they have given what seems to me a disproportionate picture of America's real views and policies as expressed in the preponderant majority vote. Her friends have been unduly discouraged, her enemies unduly cheered. We must, I fear, anticipate a slowing effect abroad at a moment when active goodwill seems so desirable all around.

On the other hand, America has had a gratifying success at the Labor Office. Her representatives secured their permanent seats, largely, it is fair to recognise, because of the statesmanship and generosity which led others to give up their places for them. The way seems cleared for really effective participation, with the important support of the American Federation of Labor.

At this crossroad in international life, I think it may cheer you to know that there is a vast body of friends in all countries who seek and deserve your stimulating leadership. For my own small part, I intend to continue on in the same work as for the last sixteen years, anxiously wondering how in present circumstances to do it most effectively, but more convinced than ever, as I see armaments costs and other dangers mounting, that it is fundamentally on the right lines.[1]

I have the honour to be, Mr. President, Most respectfully yours,

Arthur Sweetser

[PPF 506:TS]

[1] Answered March 5, 1935, below.

Roosevelt to Henry A. Wallace, Secretary of Agriculture

[Washington] February 15, 1935

Dear Henry: This is an interesting letter.[1] The man is right about the foreign firms but we must remember that the Administration is opposed by the majority of the cotton brokers, warehouse men, railroads and ginners.

I want to talk with you and Chester about this in the near future because I want a campaign of education started—a campaign in which we can call names just as well as the other fellow.[2]

Always sincerely,

[OF 258:CT]

[1] See Wallace to Roosevelt, Feb. 12, 1935, above.
[2] On March 13, 1935, Roosevelt conferred with Wallace and Chester Davis, Agri-

cultural Adjustment Act Administrator, Senator Ellison D. Smith, chairman of the Senate Agriculture and Forestry Committee, Rep. Marvin Jones, chairman of the House Agriculture Committee, and Rep. William A. Bankhead (PPF 1-0).

Cordell Hull, Secretary of State, to Roosevelt

Washington, February 15, 1935

My dear Mr. President: I have read carefully the two letters dealing with the Brazilian exchange situation which you sent me along with your memorandum of February 13, and take occasion to briefly summarize for you the considerations and principles by which the Department has been guided in this matter.[1]

I agree of course with the view expressed in the Hinrichs letter that "an increase in our exports is dependent entirely upon our getting paid for them." It is inescapable, however, that payment for a large volume of American exports such as we seek can only be achieved to the extent that our purchases or investments make available to foreign interests sufficient American funds. No change in the method we may use in our commercial relations and no coercion that we may be able to employ vis-à-vis a few countries will furnish a satisfactory answer to this problem as a whole.

In the Brazilian negotiations the problem facing the Department was to secure from Brazil guarantees regarding the exchange treatment it would accord to American interests, without resorting to a line of action that could be invoked against us by other countries at our serious expense. These minimum guarantees are embodied in the exchange of notes with the Brazilian Government with which you are familiar and include promises of a prompt provision of the exchange necessary to pay for all future purchases of American goods, and the further provision of exchange gradually to pay off the present deferred indebtedness.

To have sought more far-reaching terms then these, might well have embittered our relations with Brazil. Besides it could have been used to justify many of our best customers, including Great Britain, Japan, France, Italy, and Canada, in applying the same principle to our trade since the trade relations between ourselves and these countries are the reverse of those in Brazil. As you know, strong forces of opinion, which are more or less the counterpart of the opinions expressed in the letters in question, have been urging that no payment should be made available for the purchases of goods from the United States or payments of debts due to Americans except out of such exchange as might be directly created by American purchases of their goods. The application of this policy to us would cause extremely heavy losses, the type we are now suffering at the hands of Germany, which is pursuing this policy, discriminatory as it may be.

Even these guarantees were difficult to secure and I regard them as a fairly satisfactory solution of the dilemma. The notes embodying them have not been published and the Counselor of the Brazilian Embassy has expressed to the Department fears regarding the political effect. Second, that no termination of difficulties such as we are meeting in Brazil can be expected unless by proceeding as you are endeavoring to in the trade agreements program, we further open the channels of trade between ourselves and foreign countries. Special pressure to gain exceptional terms in the minor instances where we may do so offers no solution. Those who press them upon us are all to often inadequately informed of all American interests, with the exception of their own.[2]

Faithfully yours,

Cordell Hull

[PSF:State:TS]

[1] Roosevelt's memorandum is not present; the letters (both addressed to Peek and by him sent to McIntyre in a note of Feb. 5, 1934, OF 11) were from A. L. Colebrook, treasurer of the Empire Plow Company of Cleveland, Feb. 1, 1935, and from Oscar Hinrichs, a New York exporter and importer, Feb. 2, 1935. Colebrook asked if something could not be done by the government to expedite payments to American manufacturers from their Brazilian customers where such payments were placed in blocked exchange. Hinrichs said he had been unable to agree with Hull in his effort to arrange reciprocal trade agreements on an extensive scale. In the case of Brazil, a reduction in that country's duties in favor of the United States would mean nothing if payments were held up; a treaty should require a fair allocation of Brazil's available exchange to American exporters.

Peek had been pressing this argument on the President and the State Department. On Feb. 8, 1935, he had sent Roosevelt figures on a proposed agreement on exchange with Brazil; these figures showed that while the United States furnished far more of Brazil's foreign exchange than did the United Kingdom, the latter was favored in Brazil's exchange arrangements. Peek recommended that promulgation of the Brazilian trade agreement be held up until a more favorable exchange arrangement was made. In a letter to Sayre of the same date (OF 971), Peek protested other provisions of the Brazil agreement and urged return to the conditional most-favored-nation policy. On this letter Roosevelt wrote: "Why don't we insist on exercise of our rights & reciprocal advantages under our M.F.N. clauses?" Presumably his comment was addressed to Sayre. The negotiations on reciprocity with Brazil in 1934 and 1935 may be followed in *Foreign Relations, 1934*, IV, 542–602; *1935*, IV, 300–321.

[2] Drafted by Herbert Feis, economic adviser to the State Department.

411

[*Enclosure*] Memorandum for the President—Hull
Feby 15—1935 [1]

Unfair and discriminating methods and trade practices are undoubtedly the greatest menace today to international relationships.

Instead of striving to promote distribution, all the nations of the world are doing their best to prevent it. The theory has been that each country proceeding alone would undertake to restore prosperity within its borders, with no interest in foreign trade beyond scattered or limited bilateral transactions of a bartering or bargaining nature. The forces of self-containment, regimentation and isolation, have during past years been championing this narrow economic course. Triangular, four-cornered and multilateral trading is being correspondingly antagonized and injured. The present program of this country proposes a balanced, liberal commercial policy for the normal restoration of international trade and finance. Reciprocity agreements to the extent that they are purely bilateral are but an initial step in this direction. This full program was adopted unanimously at Montevideo. Under this program every method of gradually readjusting downward trade barriers and obstructions is contemplated. Likewise, every method of bartering or other bilateral trading transactions between individuals or groups, and also with governmental participation when not in direct contravention of a major policy of the government, are also contemplated. It is true that experience teaches that trade confined solely to bargaining or other bilateral transactions to the exclusion of triangular and multilateral commerce, while of apparent, as it may be of immediate, advantage, is in the end more restrictive of international trade than otherwise.

This country could get in the rut with other countries and confine its trade activities solely to the extremely narrow methods and practices of barter and bilateral bargaining transactions, but with the knowledge that during the last year our exports increased 450 million dollars, which is as much as the export increase of all the countries of Europe where several hundred of these narrow barter and bilateral bargaining treaty methods and devices were in operation. This country should propose to other nations a broader program calculated to restore the normal volume of international trade. If other nations, after reasonable time and opportunity, decline to join in support of such liberal program, this country then could only mark time and conduct educational appeals until a more favorable opportunity to rebuild international trade. This is the least we can do however.

Our proposed reciprocity agreements, therefore, should contemplate the fullest measure of elasticity or flexibility, in contrast with the narrow bargaining methods, if their operation is to increase the sum total of international trade. It is in these circumstances that the favored-nation policy is made a chief feature of our present reciprocity program. The observation of this broad rule has the effect to encourage and induce nations at a far earlier stage than otherwise to proceed to eliminate and abandon their more drastic and extreme trade discriminations and practices, thereby liberating commerce to a corresponding extent. We should in any event consistently maintain the fundamentals of the favored-nation doctrine and keep this doctrine alive as our ultimate objective. Naturally, until other nations should get ready to join in this broad movement for trade restoration, we would find it necessary, at least for the time being, to make exceptions or modifications of the unconditional form of this policy. We would find it necessary to restrict the number of commodities in the initial agreement. We might find it necessary also to delay any reciprocity agreement with countries where the disadvantages would outweigh the advantages. In any event, the general objective should be to bring American foreign trade through its present period of emergency by the operation of the most-favored-nation policy. The problem in brief is gradually to remove this country from the field of discriminations in all trade methods and practices to the larger field where these discriminations are by degrees abolished or reduced to a minimum under the operation of the doctrine of equality of commercial rights and treatment as embodied in the favored-nation policy. Every trade arrangement under this program would contemplate an increase of production and trade for the United States and the employment of a larger amount of labor than was previously employed.

The Montevideo economic program is based upon the principle that international trade is both a material and necessary factor in the full and stable domestic business recovery of individual nations. This program, therefore, rests upon the broad economic policy of gradually combining with the existing domestic programs of at least the important nations of the world a suitable program of economic cooperation as they emerge from serious depression conditions. To this end it contemplates the gradual removal or reduction of unreasonable or excessive trade barriers to such moderate level as will permit mutually profitable movements of goods, services, and capital between nations.

In thus readjusting downward such trade barriers, special care and caution would be exercised to avoid unreasonable or excessive imports against a domestic industry functioning efficiently under normal conditions, or to afford shelter on the other hand for price monopolies.

While not overlooking any unilateral action deemed justifiable, this program is to be implemented by two additional methods of carrying it into effect, one of which is the pursuit of a policy of bilateral reciprocity trade agreements, based upon mutual concessions, with as much elasticity as can be agreed upon. This method is only a step in the direction of broader movements and methods of trade development, and contemplates the retention and preservation of the fundamentals of the unconditional favored-nation doctrine, and that therefore there would not be enough exceptions to destroy or discredit this cardinal doctrine of equality of trade rights. The second method designed to restore international commerce contemplates that all important countries shall proceed simultaneously, naturally over a reasonable period of time and in their own way, to bring down the excessive and hurtful trade barriers to an ultimate level dictated by a sane, practical, and moderate tariff and liberal commercial policy. The entire program is bottomed upon the doctrine of gradually substituting equality of trade rights and opportunities for the existing network of discriminations, retaliations, and reprisals, under the effects of which world trade today continues at the lowest depression level.

Every method of restoring commerce would, in brief, be invoked to the extent deemed practicable and desirable, such as the unilateral, the bilateral, the regional, and the multilateral methods. Among the first steps would be to eliminate or reduce those excessive duties and restrictions which retard most severely the normal flow of international trade, such as duties or restrictions which exclude competition entirely or to every practical extent, or which have been in effect for a considerable period of time without resulting in domestic production equal to more than 10% or 15% of the total home consumption, or which apply to notoriously inefficient businesses or industries, or those not justifiable from any business or practical viewpoint, or which apply to a vast range of novelties, specialties, patterns, designs, luxuries, semi-luxuries, articles of materially different qualities, commodities of different use, none of which are directly or seriously competitive.

The Montevideo program also would contemplate such sound loans or investments, especially in stable political and more or less undeveloped countries abroad, such as any hardheaded business man would approve. Experience teaches without qualification that nations with surplus capital and surplus production beyond their ability to consume at home or to sell for cash abroad, have found it profitable to supply other countries with credit and to engage in investments deemed sound from every business standpoint.

[PSF:State:T]

[1] This heading is in Hull's hand.

Josephus Daniels, Ambassador to Mexico, to Roosevelt

Mexico, February 19, 1935

Personal

Dear Franklin: It is gratifying that my suggestion of your holding in abeyance any decision about coming to Mexico until the atmosphere clears meets with your approval.[1] In connection with the expectation of your coming, raised by the information conveyed to President Cárdenas by former-President Rodriguez after his visit to the White House, the Minister for Foreign Affairs requested me to call at the Foreign Office yesterday morning. When I arrived he conveyed a message from President Cárdenas hoping you would honor the country by coming here, and adding that he wished me to ascertain your intention. He will be glad to send you a formal invitation, if it is agreeable.

I am enclosing a copy of my despatch to the State Department, giving the conversation between Mr. Portes Gil and myself.[2] You will observe that I indicated you would probably not make any plans for the summer until you knew when Congress would adjourn, and that nobody would know the date of adjournment until late in the spring or early in the summer. I did this to convey the idea that no early decision need be expected. I hope this meets with your approval.

There is one phase of the matter that has occurred to me. It is that the Government's show of interest at this time may be prompted by the belief that your coming would be helpful to the Government officials. It undoubtedly would, but it might be interpreted as implying that you gave your countenance or acceptance of the policies which have caused controversy in the United States. You know that such interpretation might give excuse for hostile criticism by some of the ardent Catholics who are behind the Borah resolution. By all means I would wish nothing of that sort. If any official is to receive their criticism, let it fall on me.

By this I do not mean to imply that the invitation is prompted by desire of the Government to make capital out of a courtesy visit by the President of the United States. By no means. The President and leaders and the people hold you in high esteem and would at any time hail your visit, independent of any advantage that would come to Mexico or its public officials. Naturally, however, they do not overlook the benefit which such show of friendliness to Mexico would impart to the Cárdenas administration. It is equally true that it might enable critics to say your visit was indicative of your approval of the policies so strongly condemned at home, some of which are most deplorable, both from our point of view and in the long run to the highest interest of Mexico.

Please let me know your decision and what answer I shall make to the Foreign Minister.

Hurrah for the Supreme Court! I telegraphed congratulations to Homer.[3] I would have sent one to each of the other four judges who concurred if I had deemed it proper. I also wanted to send this telegram to McReynolds: "Mene, mene tekal upharsin." Personally I like him but share Wilson's disappointment in him. You know Wilson appointed him because though an Assistant Attorney General he prosecuted the American Tobacco combine, having much to do with convicting it as a violator of the anti-trust laws, and he refused to concur in Wickersham's sham settlement.[4] Wilson thought that made him a Progressive, but since he has been on the Court he has been the most reactionary of the reactionaries. One of these days it may be necessary to take action against the four big tobacco companies which have co-operated to starve the tobacco growers until you forced increased prices through the A.A.A. The people have never benefitted from the so-called dissolution of the trust, though Uncle Sam does get more revenue.

Affectionately yours,

Josephus Daniels

P.S. I am hoping to come home for May if Boss Cordell Hull will give me leave. At that time I will go over the whole situation here and give you the background.[5]

JD

[PSF:Mexico:TS]

[1] Feb. 16, 1935 (PSF:Mexico).

[2] Feb. 18, 1935 (PSF:Mexico).

[3] Daniels refers to the Supreme Court decision of Feb. 18, 1935, upholding the United States in the gold clause cases. "Homer" was Attorney General Homer Cummings.

4 George W. Wickersham, Attorney General under Taft.
5 Answered March 1, 1935 (*Roosevelt and Daniels,* p. 156). The President said he could give no thought to summer plans. Congress would probably be in session into the summer and in any event he would wish to avoid visits and official ceremonies.

Norman H. Davis, Chairman, American Delegation, Geneva Disarmament Conference, to Roosevelt

New York, February 19, 1935

Personal

My dear Mr. President: Enclosed you will please find a memorandum of suggestions for what you might say in your press conference with regard to the action of the British Government on arms and munitions.

Faithfully yours,

Norman H. Davis

[*Notation*:A:FDR] File
[PPF 33:TS]

[*Enclosure*] Suggestions for Press Conference

February 19, 1935

Indicate pleasure at the action of the British Government in appointing a committee of a non-political character to investigate the situation relating to the manufacture and export of arms and munitions and to make recommendations with regard to national and international control.

Point out that this Government favors strict governmental control over all arms and munitions but, recognizing that there is a limit to what one Government acting alone can do to deal with the evils of international traffic in arms, favors an international agreement.

Stress that the interest manifested by the British Government in this important problem, as indicated by the action taken, should contribute greatly to the success of the efforts initiated by us here and at the Disarmament Conference in Geneva. An international agreement on the manufacture and export of arms and munitions will aid greatly in securing a general reduction and limitation of armaments.

[*Notation*:AS:Early] Mr. President: Please don't comment on this, at least until we check. Steve[1]

[PPF 33:T]

[1] No use was made of the memorandum in the press conference of the next day.

Senator Key Pittman of Nevada, Chairman, Senate Committee on Foreign Relations, to Roosevelt

Washington, D.C., February 19, 1935

Personal

My dear Mr. President: I have, time and again, postponed burdening you with the political situation on the Hill. I might be unreasonably uneasy, but I am worried with regard to the situation and feel it my duty to communicate the situation to you as I see it.

There has been a great change in the attitude of Senators since we convened. Patriotism and loyalty seem to have gradually surrendered to expediency and self-interest.

Apparently at the present time we have no such thing as a Democratic organization in the Senate. This demonstration first occurred with regard to the World Court legislation. The matter was quite immaterial by comparison with much more vital matters, and yet the result had its effect and demonstrated the drift.

May I guess at the situation in the Senate at the present time? I will take, for instance, your relief bill. Some of your regular Democratic friends led by Senator Glass while presenting the bill are obviously ridiculing it. McCarran, a Democrat, offers an amendment in the Committee to destroy your work relief by making it mandatory that you should pay prevailing wages. By a great effort this amendment was barely defeated in committee.

Adams offers an amendment, after the first adoption of the McCarran amendment, to reduce the relief funds by $2,000,000,000. McCarran votes for this reduction. Practically all of the Republicans on the Committee vote for both amendments. The meaning of these two votes is a dole and no work relief.

Russell succeeds in passing an interpretative amendment through the Committee. McCarran will offer his amendment as a substitute. What will the vote be? I will simply guess. I have not attempted to make a poll. I should guess that those voting for the amendment will be: Adams,

Austin, Barbour, Black, Bone, Borah, Brown, Bulow, Capper, Carey, Copeland, Costigan, Couzens, Cutting, Davis, Dickinson, Donahey, Duffy, Frazier, Gibson, Hale, Hastings, Hatch, Keyes, La Follette, Lonergan, Long, McCarran, McGill, Metcalf, Neely, Norbeck, Norris, Nye, Overton, Pope, Schall, Schwellenbach, Shipstead, Steiwer, Thomas of Oklahoma, Townsend, Trammell, Vandenberg, Wagner, Walsh and Wheeler.

This means half of the Senate. There are others who may vote for the amendment. You will observe that I have included a number of stand-pat Republicans. I base this estimate on the fact that the stand-pat Republicans have caucused and agreed to vote for the McCarran amendment. Most of these stand-pat Republicans and some of the conservative Democrats led by Senator Glass will vote for the Adams amendment reducing the appropriation by $2,000,000,000. It is obvious that if the McCarran amendment carries and your appropriation is not increased that you will be compelled to abandon your relief work program. This is undoubtedly the hope and the program of the regular Republicans.

The Adams amendment will receive less than a majority of the votes but nearly all of the stand-pat Republican votes. If the McCarran amendment is carried then La Follette will offer an amendment increasing the appropriation from $4,000,000,000 to $10,000,000,000. This amendment, in my opinion, will not receive the support of regular Republicans, but it will receive the vote of the progressive Republicans and a very large portion of the Democratic vote. The fact that the McCarran amendment has been adopted, if it is adopted, will justify an increased appropriation and upon that argument it may carry.

Bonus legislation will be offered in some form as an amendment. Whether or not it will receive a majority will depend entirely upon the vote of the regulars and those who will be actuated entirely by politics.

The old-age pension bill will be offered as an amendment. It will certainly receive at least twenty-seven votes and will receive a majority, in my opinion, if the regulars who are actuated by politics vote for it.

Thomas will offer a silver amendment providing that it shall be mandatory that you shall purchase at least 50,000,000 ounces of silver per month. This will be based upon the allegation that the Treasury Department has not carried out the Silver Act in the spirit in which it was enacted. Whether this will carry will depend very largely upon the strategy of the regular Republicans. They may vote for it upon the same theory that their irreconcilables voted for the Lodge Reservation of the Versailles Treaty.

There will be many other wild amendments offered, and no one can predict what the vote may be. Unless I misjudge the Republicans' strategy, they will vote for all destructive amendments and then vote against the bill.

Let it be understood that I have not attempted to make any poll. I am simply guessing. The guess, however, is based upon my judgment and paints a perfect picture of Democratic disorganization in the Senate.

If any of these amendments are carried what will be the result? Defeat of the bill, either by votes or veto. What will be the result of such action? I don't have to comment upon this. It is the most astounding situation that any loyal Democrat could have imagined.

We are faced with an unscrupulous, regular Republican representation; a progressive Republican membership determined upon going further to the left than you will go; a Democratic representation who have more sympathy for the Republican progressive position than they have for yours. And in the midst of this disloyalty you have a regular Democratic representation that conscientiously believe they are saving you by destroying you.

So far I have only given you a statement of a guess. As nobody seems to be doing anything about it I have taken the liberty to intrude myself in the fight, and as a premise to this apparently complimentary statement I wish to announce immediately that I am actuated by selfish motives. I think if this thing continues there is only one alternative: Election of a communist government or a stand-pat Republican government. In either of these events we would ultimately drift into either communism or military distatorship. I have discussed these matters frankly with a number of tycoons in our Party. It's a serious situation.

Thick-headed business brains, in their ignorant egotism, still believe that the three or four million votes they control can control forty million votes and, therefore, they are opposing you and adding ammunition to the communist movement.

Those elected to Congress in 1932 and 1934 have forgotten that, with few exceptions, they were elected virtually because of your popularity. They now feel you are weakening and, therefore, they are going with the strong. Every dog is for himself and, like wolves, they will eat you up if you fall for a moment by the roadside.

Well, this is just a guess, as I said before. The question is, what are we to do about it? It is apparent that there is no Democratic Party in the United States Senate. We have nearly two-thirds of the Members of the Senate elected and registered as Democrats. What's the matter with the situation and what can we do about it? Well, of course, the fault is that there is a lack of confidence in the success of the Administration. There is cowardice. There is discontent with regard to patronage. There is complaint that the Administration is responsible for lack of Democratic solidarity; that the Democrats win a victory after twelve long years, and the Republicans hold office; that the Congress is not considered a part of the Administration; that they are supposed to pass bills and not be interested in the result of the administration of the acts; that strange and peculiar persons have become advisors; that there is no leadership; that thinking is farmed out; that defeat is inevitable; and every man must take care of himself.

I am stating what I hear on every side. Don't understand that I do not combat these thoughts and theories, for I do. It does no good for Senator Robinson and for me and your numerous other friends to combat these things. There can not be but one leader, and that leader must decide the course of battle and lead it, win or lose.

It is contended that your Cabinet are fighting each other and are actuated more by ambition and selfish motives than by the interest in their Chief; that you have made generals in the conquered army your generals and that these generals, through highly pacific expressions and non-partisan assertions, are pulling into the army those of the defeated columns.

What they are all wondering—and I join them in the wonderment—is, who are loyal and who are not loyal?

You announce a policy of deferment of international efforts until domestic problems are settled, and yet it is contended that some of your departments are more interested in international matters than they are in the solution of our domestic troubles.

You announce a policy of non-intervention, which restores the confidence of the entire Americas, and yet our Administration tolerates suggestions of intervention in the domestic affairs of the Americas.

The world is selfish today. Every government is using every power for its own advantage against every other government, and we nobly sacrifice our own safety by being the only government that attempts to make reciprocity treaties for the benefit of all governments while we only treat with one government under the abandoned theory of the unconditional favored-nation clause and the generalization of treaties. This proposition is so innocently simple that it reflects upon the patriotism of our Administration. I venture to say, and with all due humility, if you are inadvertently induced to issue a proclamation that our bilateral treaties are general and are effective with all nations that it will result in the destruction of our whole foreign trade and place our Administration in an indefensible position.

I again recur to your Fourth of July statement of 1933.[1] The success of our domestic program is of primary importance. No one can guess what the international situation will be in a few months from now.

We know what our domestic situation is now. No one apparently is satisfied with what you have accomplished domestically. The fact that you have saved the banks and the credit of this country, that you have raised the price of commodities, increased the purchasing power, and increased the production of our factories seem to amount to nothing.

The fact remains that the unemployed and those dependent upon the Government support have increased and are now increasing. It is immaterial that you have increased the prosperity of some of the producers and that you have increased the wages of those who have employment, so long as unemployment increases.

I sometimes think we have undertaken too great an accomplishment. Our first duty, as you have said, was to the unemployed, the destitute and the unknown man. We started on that theory. The manufacturer and organized labor organized the Party, each intent on obtaining all of the benefits of improvement to the exclusion and loss of the unemployed.

You have had, and have now, issue with both of these selfish classes. You can not satisfy either of them. You have got to go back to the forgotten man, who is the man who has no opportunity to earn a living.

You are seeking in the present relief bill to avoid a contest over details. The unfortunate thing about the NRA was that it involved so many contests over details looking to the distant future, rather than the present emergency, that it has evolved into a general row.

Thank God, the Supreme Court has held that the issuance and control of money is a necessary and inherent power of sovereignty. I am constantly forced to the conclusion that our chief trouble has been, and is now, that we neglect these things as the inherent power of government.

Banks hold $52,000,000,000 of deposits—in most cases, gratuitously. They lend these deposits to the Government, who pays interest on them, while these banks exist solely by permission of the Government and pay only a small interest upon such deposits.

Well, the question is—if you desire my opinion and it amounts to anything—what is the remedy? In the first place, no one can establish an administrative policy except you. In the second place, no one can speak with authority except you and, therefore, it would seem to devolve upon you to establish policies and to lead such policies.

No one today knows what is the foreign policy of our Government. Are we going to participate in European affairs, or are we going to keep out of them? Are we going to enforce treaties, or are we going to abandon them? Are we going to be innocent lambs and simply generous in our international trade, or are we going to be horse traders? Now, anybody can give away his own horse, but he can't give away the horse of his master.

In our domestic policies are we going to control the finances of this country, or are we going to trust the bankers to control them? Are we going to restrict the expenditure of private capital, or are we going to remove the restriction and encourage private capital to move out? Are we going to have a definite policy of public expenditures, or are we going to leave it to the inspiration of the supposedly intelligent genii of the heads of our various departments? Are we going to attempt to coerce Congress, or to guess as to what Congress will do? Or, are we going to have a distinct understanding in the whole Administration as between the Executive and Legislative branches? These things must be determined—and I again only speak humbly as one of your friends—within the next thirty days.

There is no leadership in the Senate today, and I do not speak critically of Senator Robinson or of your other friends in the Senate. Robinson has been courageous and diplomatic.

I suggested to McIntyre, when I first returned from the West, that you should call every Senator down to see you, particularly the new ones, take them into your confidence, win them to your program—which would have been easy—and make them your confidential supporters. Most of them are brave and loyal men, but they don't know they are in the army. With most of them, each one feels that he is the forgotten man and, therefore, is looking out for his own selfish interests. In the army we must be consolidated, and the army consists of every branch of our Government. You must do what Napoleon did—and what you are so capable of doing—in inspiring loyalty, patriotism, courage and the spirit of self-sacrifice in the most lowly private.

I have written this long letter because I know that your time is too much taken up to give me an interview, which would require several times as long as it will require you to read this letter, if you desire to. I would not bother you in this matter except for its extreme importance to the country and because I know that there is nothing I can do, or anyone else, except yourself.

I want to do my small part in every way, and I know how small it is. I will make any sacrifice for you because I know the sacrifices you are making.

May I beg of you to lay all administrative matters aside until you have your legislative matters straightened out.

Sincerely,

Key Pittman

P.S. I apologize for the many defects in expressions in this letter. It was hastily dictated. I would like to cut out considerable of it, but haven't the time. I know that you will understand and will make allowances. K.P.[2]

[PPF 745:TS]

[1] Pittman apparently referred to Roosevelt's message to the American delegation at the London Economic Conference of July 3, 1933 (above), which appeared in the newspapers on July 4.

[2] In an accompanying note to McIntyre of the same date, Pittman referred to an invitation he had previously received to talk with the President on "the political situation in the Senate." Since the President had not had time to see him he had written this letter; it had been hastily dictated but because it was personal and confidential he knew the President would understand.

Roosevelt to the Senate

The White House, February 21, 1935

To the Senate of the United States: In accordance with the Senate's Resolution of February 15, 1935 (S. Res. 76), I return to the Senate for further action the Convention (Executive H. Sixty-ninth Congress, first session) for the supervision of the international trade in arms and ammunition and in implements of war, signed at Geneva, Switzerland, on June 17, 1925.[1]

Franklin D. Roosevelt

[OF 66:T]

[1] The convention was resubmitted to the Senate on June 6, 1935, this time without the Persian Gulf reservation but with another declaring the convention of no effect with respect to the United States until it had been ratified by Belgium, the British Empire, Czechoslovakia, France, Germany, Italy, Japan, Sweden, and the U.S.S.R. Senator King, author of the original Persian Gulf reservation, then offered another, to the effect that

adherence to the treaty was not to be construed "as expression of any opinion or view of the United States as to the sovereignty or right of any government in the Persian Gulf." Senator Pittman, chairman of the Senate Foreign Relations Committee, opposed this reservation on the ground that the rights of numerous nations, not alone those of Persia, were in question in the Persian Gulf, and the amendment was rejected. The convention was then ratified (*Cong. Rec.,* vol. 79, pp. 1825, 1998, 8783–8796).

Cordell Hull, Secretary of State, to Roosevelt

Washington, February 21, 1935

My dear Mr. President: With respect to the letter from Ambassador Long at Rome dated February 3,[1] I wish to state that I received from Mr. Long on February 1 a cable, in which he stated that he had taken up the matter of the possibility of cotton trade with Suvich. The cable contained no information as to what he had in mind. The State Department had no information about Mr. Long's conversation, before leaving the United States, with Oscar Johnston, Morgenthau, Wallace, and others on the matter of cotton trade.

On February 3, the same day that he wrote his letter to you, Mr. Long sent a cable stating that he had talked with Signor Mussolini and that Signor Mussolini had asked if there were a chance that we could have some agreement on some few articles so as to make some immediate advance in the volume of trade, and that he hoped that some such arrangement might be arrived at in advance of the more general arrangements to follow.[2] Mr. Long said that he had replied that he thought this was possible.

In reply to his cable, I wired that it was not clear what he had specifically in mind.[3] There had been some earlier proposal with respect to raw silk. I pointed out that raw silk was already on the free list, and that if any arrangement carried a definite obligation to purchase raw silk, some agency of the Government would have to buy this silk and distribute it, an arrangement which would obviously present difficulties. I pointed out that a preliminary trade agreement containing a few items could not be made until after public hearings had been held, and that the announcement for such hearings had already been made for March 11, 1935, and that if preliminary arrangements were entered into in advance of such hearings, American protected interests could charge that they had not been heard. I asked Mr. Long to give us an expression of his views as to what might be done under these circumstances, and

425

stated that it would be most helpful if he could secure from Signor Mussolini and his officials any suggestions that they might have.

Mr. Long replied the next day, February 6, 1934,[4] expressing his gratitude for my exposition of the situation. He stated that he had made it clear in his conversations that the American Government was not able to purchase commodities of any kind, and that the purchase of silk was therefore out of the question. He had suggested that they find some other items of Italian origin which might be considered in an arrangement which would protect the market in Italy for American cotton. He stated further that he would now wait until they approached him and then report to us.

I think the foregoing exchange of views between the Ambassador and the Department since his letter of February 3, 1934, to you, has brought us all abreast of the situation and that we are now in a position to give careful consideration to any suggestions which the Italian officials might make. I am enclosing copies of all the telegrams relating to this matter. As these telegrams were transmitted in one of the Department's confidential codes, it would be appreciated if they could be returned to the Department at the President's convenience for appropriate disposition.

Faithfully yours,

Cordell Hull

[PSF:Italy:TS]

[1] Above.
[2] *Foreign Relations, 1935,* II, 520.
[3] Feb. 5, 1935, *ibid.,* pp. 520–522.
[4] *Ibid.,* p. 522.

Breckinridge Long, Ambassador to Italy, to Roosevelt

Rome, February 21, 1935

My dear Chief: I seem to be writing you very frequently these days, but I am confident in the belief that if you could sit here as I do and could come in such close contact with the rumors of war and with the actual preparations to engage in war, that you would feel disposed to write as I do.

There is no doubt in my mind that Europe is headed straight for war. Italy is practically on a war basis today. While it cannot be proven,

I am morally certain that the whole of the class of 1911 has been mobilized. That means in the neighborhood of 250,000 men. In addition to that, there have been specialists in motors, air, and engineering called back to the colors from many classes. In addition to that, it is inferred from the Press account that as many as 70,000 of the Black Shirt Militia is to be added to the rolls. That will mean a total of somewhere between 350,000 and 400,000 men under arms.

A great deal of noise and publicity is attending the embarkation of small quantities of troops from Naples. Nothing is being said of the vast mobilization in Sicily. It is estimated there are 100,000 men mobilized in that part of Sicily from Messina down to Syracuse.

In addition to that, the Supreme Council of the Defense has been in session and has broken all precedent by having made a public announcement in the form of a communiqué giving a summary of the decisions of the Council. It is published on the front page of the morning papers under stream-line headers which read "How the Regime has liberated Fascist Italy from the bands interfering with war"—"The Supreme Council of the Defense has decided the steps indispensable to the Nation because an eventual war-like force has been developed for conditions to insure victory"—etc. etc. It is all accompanied by an editorial headed "Ready for any eventuality."

In continuation of the thought expressed in my last letter to you under date of February 15,[1] I am more and more convinced that these people expect war in Europe during 1936—if not sooner—and that they are ready for it. Their embargo on all imports, which has been announced since I last wrote to you but which I have feared and predicted for six months—just puts into the hands of the Government entire control over all imports. It is a war measure pure and simple. They foresee German objections to the arrangements proposed by England. They foresee the continuation of Germany's preparedness for war. They believe that Germany is not yet ready. They look with some trepidation at the unstable political conditions of France and fear that Flandin may not last another six months.[2] They foresee the possibility of internal conflict in France and that Germany will be free to pursue her aims in Austria, Hungary, Czechoslovakia, and elsewhere with the possible reservation that the waving of a German flag on the French frontier would solidify the nation. They see England committed to air warfare with the inevitable consequence of participation in other forms of military activity against Germany, provided France is attacked and provided France, if it should blow up internally, will give Germany the free hand to the

427

southward and eastward, which would deny the probability of British participation, because it would not be directed against France.

The Italians do not like the air arrangement which England has proposed, because it does not commit England to help Italy in case the latter country has difficulty with Germany. The arrangement only contemplates mutual assistance between France, England, and Germany, or France, Italy, and Germany. So that if France should blow up and Germany started into Austria, Italy would be faced with the problem of stopping her single-handed.

In any event, Italy is preparing for what she thinks is a certain eventuality. While no responsible statesman in Italy will admit it, I am just as certain of it as I am that I am sitting in this chair.

If this develops in Europe within the next twenty months, Japan will start to over-run the East. Russia may have all her attention occupied with Japan, or she may simply throw a sufficient cordon along the mountains east of Baikal in the neighborhood of Chita to hold the Japanese there while she participates in the European show with the expectations that she will later attend to Japan.

That leaves the two Americas out, and I hope with every fervent wish that we can stay out of the devastating show and fulfill our real destiny as trustee for the future of the civilization which we have in America and with which we can subsequently revive the world.

But I think we must contemplate that Europe will be at war within two years. I believe we must take into almost definite consideration that fact in making our plans for the future. Personally I cannot see how it can be escaped. The national traditions, the religious prejudices, the local animosities of all these peoples and the strict discipline of each of the Continental States (except France) over the persons under their respective jurisdictions, render unnecessary the creation of a public spirit. The only alternative is that the people will refuse to fight through some manifestation of social disorder amounting in the last analysis to Bolshevism. It is hard to contemplate the recrudescence of disorder in Italy and in Germany under the present regimes. Nevertheless it is possible. It may not take the form of the theoretical Communism. It may, if it should develop, simply assume the form of opposition to established government and manifest itself in a tense terrorism and anarchy.

So the people may refuse to fight. But unless they do, and unless armies refuse to move to the front, I see no escape from a real cataclysm. While the Italian movement in Abyssinia is not popular with the people, and while there is a lack of enthusiasm and some grumbling and a great deal of criticism—yet the troops go. If they should fail in Abyssinia and have a debacle which would affect the prestige of Mussolini and bring about a change of government in Italy, the general picture would not be changed, except to the extent of Italy's participation on the grand scale.

I am not an optimist about the future of Europe. From where I sit there are only visible preparations for the conflict, which all recognize as being indicative of the future of Europe. All agree that if it should come it would be epoch-marking. The only difference in the opinions which are permitted to be expressed is to the proximity or imminence of the movement.

Very respectfully,

Breckinridge Long

P.S. Since dictating the above I have had at luncheon at my residence and have had a long talk with Margherita Sarfatti, whom you saw in Washington last year and whom you will recognize as a former associate of Mussolini and who still is probably conscious of his mental processes. She agrees in substance with everything I have written above. B.L.[3]

[PSF:Italy:TS]

[1] PSF:Italy; not printed.
[2] Pierre Flandin became Premier in November 1934 and resigned in June 1935.
[3] See Roosevelt to Long, March 9, 1935, below.

William E. Dodd, Ambassador to Germany, to R. Walton Moore, Assistant Secretary of State

Berlin, February 24, 1935

Confidential

Dear Judge Moore: When you see the President, I wish you would say to him that at the request of the Appropriations Committee of the House and the Foreign Affairs Committee of the Senate I went over important questions affecting us. He asked me to report to him, especially what the Foreign Affairs Committee's reactions were. You know I saw the Committee two days after the last interview with the President. Borah seemed to make a point of being absent, but other members of the Committee, including Johnson, were present and remained some time after lunch on February 8. Members of the Committee told me that two Senators who had voted against the World Court were surprised at the outcome, and that they said that they would have changed their votes had they realized what was going to happen and especially what it meant. Senator Johnson started the discussion about historical precedents, and I gave him facts about certain minority attitudes in the past and indicated how unfortunate they had been. That led to discussions of Washington's violation of the Constitution (much against his desire) and also of Lincoln's notable violation and his propaganda work in England. This seemed to surprise Johnson, and when every member of the Committee present heard me say that the vote on the World Court was very unfortunate, that it would seriously affect commercial relations and make it impossible for us to raise the question against violation of our treaties before a court which might not give us compensations but which would give us great moral advantages, Johnson kept silent during the rest of the discussion. Other members, even those who apparently had voted contrarily, seemed a little surprised at my statement that our Government's prestige in Europe would have been raised by about 50 percent. I said this was not due to the importance of our cooperating. It was due to the fact that the situation, especially in Berlin, was such that everybody would attribute the drift towards negotiations and peaceful solutions to the Roosevelt attitude. When the debt question was raised, I cited McGrane's book,[1] especially to Johnson, indicating that our country had repudiated between 1820 and 1850 something like 200 millions of valid obligations and had failed to pay interest on nearly all obligations for a period of ten years. This sort of discussion seemed a little perturbing, and once more Johnson insisted on silence. However, there was no disposition on his part to reassert his former attitude. I had the feeling after the adjournment of the Committee that if the matter had been cleared up before all members of the Committee prior to their vote we should have had a different result.

The Committee on Appropriations asked specifically what I thought about the Bluecher Palais business. I said to them that we had $1,700,000 invested; that I didn't believe we could sell it for more than $500,000; that it would probably be wise to make an appropriation during the next few months for finishing the structure. This I think would enable all the representatives of the Government to have offices under one roof. There are certain disadvantages, I said, but that I didn't see any other way out, and that if the work were undertaken in the next year I thought registered marks might be used in such way as to save a considerable amount of the costs. Merrill has estimated the cost at about $700,000. I added that if I had been called on originally to pass on the matter, I never would have put so much money in the venture. However, I would not like to lose a million dollars and consequently saw no other way out than for the Committee to make the appropriation.

The Chairman and every member present agreed that it seemed to them the best solution, though they suggested that there should be no great display and waste, which of course I agreed to. I left a brief memorandum with Chairman Buchanan, and I wish you would indicate to the President this fact so that he will know about what our attitude is. I understood that the State Department was of the same opinion.[2]

Sincerely yours,

William E. Dodd

[PSF:Germany:TS]

[1] Reginald C. McGrane, *Foreign Bondholders and American State Debts* (New York:Macmillan, 1935).
[2] No covering note from Moore is present.

Roosevelt to Fred M. Dearing, Ambassador to Peru, Lima

Hyde Park, February 25, 1935

Dear Fred: I am delighted to have not only the stamps and that very interesting catalogue, but also your delightful letter which gives me such a clear picture of events and thoughts in your part of the world.[1] The Peruvian problem with the Deputies and with minorities is not wholly different from our present situation in Washington. I much hope that the Leticia problem will adjust itself by the end of the year—I am very certain that the Colombian Government and, I think, the Colombian people wholly approve the settlement.

It is very interesting what you say about Japan—I understand we are being accused of similar feelings in other South and Central American Republics.

The stamps will give me an interesting evening. I am delighted to send the photograph under separate cover. Give my warm regards to Mrs. Dearing. It is good to know that you are both in such fine shape.

Yours sincerely,

[PPF 1210:CT]

[1] Feb. 11, 1935 (PPF 1210), a very long letter in which Dearing discussed the Peruvian political situation, the failure of the Colombian Senate to ratify the Rio de Janeiro protocol for the settlement of the Leticia dispute, and the mounting opposition to Japan's drive to expand her Bolivian markets and sources of supplies of raw materials.

Roosevelt to Arthur Sweetser, Director, The Secretariat, League of Nations, Geneva

[Washington] March 5, 1935

My dear Arthur: It was good of you to write me as you did and I am grateful.[1]

Your letter was most interesting and I was glad to have the benefit of the views you expressed on international policies and recent developments. Aside from this, however, was the thought it brought that my friends in foreign lands should take time out to write of their interest in things at home and to send such expressions of support and cheer.

Very sincerely,

[PPF 506:CT]

[1] Feb. 14, 1935, above.

Press Conference, Executive Offices of the White House, March 6, 1935, 10:55 A.M.

[*Excerpt*] Q: Mr. President, have you any steps in mind to extend our foreign credit on these barter agreements?

The President: Of course we are going right ahead. Each one of these barter agreements takes a long time to work out. I think they have five or six of them now.

Q: I mean the two-country barter agreements, the ones that Peek had in mind?

The President: Well, they practically dovetail into each other. Just to be a little bit more explanatory on that, you take this Belgian agreement as an example: That is, theoretically, a reciprocating agreement. That is to say, we reduce certain of our tariffs in order to give the Belgians a chance to sell something more over here, and they reduce their tariffs in order to give us a chance to export some more to Belgium.

Now, it is experimental in this sense: It is directed primarily at the bilateral situation between Belgium and the United States. At the same time, under the most-favored-nation clauses, other nations—not all other nations, it depends a little bit—certain other nations have the right to take advantage of that lowered tariff. At the same time, in the Belgian agreement there is a clause that says, "If this results in the bringing into this country from other nations—not Belgium—imports which will hurt this country in the larger sense, then, within thirty days, we can stop the agreement." So it does not vary very much from the Peek theory. It comes pretty close to being a bilateral treaty but it does give us a little opening for other countries to see how it will affect them too and depending on the way it works out will determine the future continuation of that particular Belgium-United States agreement.

Q: Of course, under the most-favored-nation clause, the other nations have to give us the same concessions. Do you think Belgium has come in in order to get advantage of this?

The President: It depends a little bit on the clause of the individual nation. I don't think there is one rule that will tell. I think there are some treaties that will let them come in anyway, most of them.

Q: Will you comment on the British announcement of the increase in air force because of the rearming in the United States—the Mac-Donald White Paper announced yesterday?

The President: I have not read of it, have not heard of it. They are increasing their air force because of what we are doing?

Q: They included the United States in the list of countries rearming and thereby necessitating their doing the same.

The President: I would like to check the language. I hope you are not right.

Q: It was broader than an airplane increase; it was a naval increase.[1]

The President: We might have been put in as a matter of politeness, you know.

Q: Can you tell us whether any decision has been reached on the possibility of our participation in any international move to help China?

The President: I do not know. You will have to ask the State Department because I have not heard a word about it for a week, not a word . . .[2]

Q: You said that you had not heard anything on the China situation for a week. May I inquire whether, when it was called to your attention, there was something we might do to help China?

The President: No. There was a big question mark at that time.

Nothing specific at that time at all. The question was, "Is there something all the nations can do to help China?"

Q: You are considering that still?

The President: Yes.

Q: Will you make any comment on the speech of General Johnson two weeks ago as to the foreign developments?[3]

The President: No.

[President's Press Conferences:T]

[1] A general policy statement calling for increases in all land, sea, and air forces was presented to Commons by MacDonald on March 4, 1935. The reporter presumably referred to Charles A. Selden's London dispatch of March 4, appearing in the New York *Times* of March 5, p. 1.

[2] On Feb. 5, 1935, the Chinese government had asked the United States for a loan of $100,000,000 and a credit of like amount against silver to be furnished by China on demand (Sze to Hull, Feb. 5, 1935, *Foreign Relations, 1935,* III, 535). See memorandum by Hornbeck, Feb. 14, 1935, *ibid.,* pp. 535–537.

[3] Hugh S. Johnson's speech of March 4 was a defense of the Administration against the attacks of Huey Long and the Reverend Charles Coughlin; there were in it, however, some references to historical precedents and it is probably the speech here meant (New York *Times,* March 5, 1935, p. 10).

Roosevelt to Charles P. Craig, Great Lakes-St. Lawrence Tidewater Association, Washington

[Washington] March 8, 1935

Dear Mr. Craig: Thank you for your letter of February fourteenth. I have not had an opportunity to reply before this.[1]

I must be quite frank in telling you that, in my judgment, the only way the St. Lawrence can ever be developed in the international sector is by committing ourselves irrevocably to the joint and simultaneous development of navigation and power.

I hope much that you will remember the broadest possible objectives and not be led astray.

I think you should know that there seems fairly conclusive evidence that opponents to the development of the St. Lawrence are using two forms of propaganda—trying to persuade the power people that development could proceed for power alone if this angle could be wholly divorced from the ship canal—and trying to persuade the waterway people that they could get it through if power were divorced from the waterway.

I hope much that your Association will not be deceived by people who want no development at all—either power or waterway.

Very sincerely yours,

[OF 156:CT]

---

[1] Craig wrote (OF 156) that the Tidewater Association accepted the fact that without the "full exercise" of Roosevelt's great prestige ratification of the St. Lawrence Waterway Treaty was impossible; the Association now wished the President's advice on further action. If ratification proved impossible, Craig proposed that the United States, with Canada's cooperation but without the need of a treaty, construct side canals and locks on the American side of the international section. For her part, Canada would undertake to complete for navigation that part of the St. Lawrence Waterway from the international boundary to Montreal.

Roosevelt sent Craig's letter to Frank P. Walsh, chairman of the New York State Power Authority, for comment; Walsh replied (March 6, 1935, OF 156) that Craig's letter was further evidence that opponents of the Waterway were trying to divide its supporters by suggesting alternate ways of improving the international section. These people urged that additional power development could be provided at Niagara Falls under a revival of the 1929 Niagara Falls convention, "where the American development might be expected to continue under the control of the dominant private power interests of the northeast." Walsh urged that "no hospitality whatsoever should be extended to these indirect methods of blocking the St. Lawrence power project. In our opinion it would be most effective if those advocating further power development at Niagara Falls and the development of the St. Lawrence River in the international section solely for navigation were given to understand that our policy, as well as the law itself, commits us irrevocably to the development of the international section of the St. Lawrence River for both navigation and power simultaneously and that the Federal Government and the State of New York will adhere to this policy until the work is accomplished."

Jefferson Caffery, Ambassador to Cuba, to Roosevelt

Habana, March 8, 1935

Dear Mr. President: I have heard that some Chiefs of Mission have been giving you their ideas about the Foreign Service. Therefore, I venture to give you some of my own. I will immodestly say that I can speak with authority, because I believe that in the last twenty-four years (I have been twenty-four years in the Foreign Service) no Chief of Mission, either career or non-career, has done as much for protection and assistance of American interests abroad as I have. I claim that possibly I have helped them in one way or another in a figure running into the hundreds of millions of dollars.

I, personally, know Foreign Service officers who are very efficiently doing their part; that is, rendering efficient service in helping to furnish legitimate protection to the interests of the United States abroad and at the same time cultivating on the part of foreign peoples confidence in the United States Government and people, and good will toward them. The efficiency of a Foreign Service officer is based on three things: intelligence, personality, and prestige. By prestige I mean the respect and esteem in which the officer is held by the officials and people of the country in which he is stationed. An officer is not efficient if he lacks one of these qualities. Intelligence and personality explain themselves, prestige is a bit more elusive: whether we like it or not, this prestige is based in good part on externals; that is, the way the officer and his family live, et cetera. Now this may be all wrong, but it is a hard, cold fact that in the majority of countries other than our own, an officer's mode of living, habits, and associations are subject to keen and not always friendly scrutiny, and things which to us may seem trivial and unimportant weigh heavily in the foreigner's scale of values. I know officers in the Foreign Service now who are simply not making the grade, that is, they are of little use to the missions they serve because their salaries are so small (and they have no independent income) that they cannot get around as much as they should in cities where they are located, or know people there in the manner they should know them. I point this out merely because I believe that fact is being lost sight of (or people are afraid to say so) at this juncture. I can say this all the more freely because I never have had a large personal income myself. I have always known that it behooved me to make the best showing on what I had; otherwise I had much better quit and go home.

I believe that few people in the United States appreciate how much can be done in dollars and cents, and I mean big dollars and cents, by an efficient Chief of Mission; but no matter how efficient the Chief is, unless he has an adequate staff, his own efforts will, obviously, be hampered. (I have a good staff here; have picked them myself and have no complaint, personally, on the score.)

Strangely enough, this is not a plea for larger salaries; salaries at present are high enough. However, I do highly approve of an expansion wherever possible of the present system of rent, heat, light allowances, et cetera. (This, however, is merely by the way.)

The point I want to make is simply this: that nothing is more mistaken than the idea which, I hear, prevails in some quarters that you can get satisfactory results out of Foreign Service officers who work efficiently in the office and then, outside, to all intents and purposes, pass out of circulation. That is nonsense. The value of diplomacy, both in tangible accomplishments and in good will, is very largely a matter of personal contact and human relationships, and results are obtained because of mutual understanding fostered by our officers in their out-of-office association with the citizens of the country wherein they are stationed: were it not for this all-important factor of the human equation, our foreign relations could almost be carried on by note, cable, and telephone from Washington. The Foreign Service officer who cannot or does not do his part outside the office (and most of the really worthwhile work is done outside of the office—by worthwhile work, I mean, on the one hand, direct results in thousands and millions of dollars to American interests and, on the other, results in the way of confidence and good will on the part of foreign peoples) is little good to me. I take this Foreign Service business seriously; I know that a lot can be done to create work and improve business conditions in the United States of America by efficient work abroad; and I believe that an efficient Service is worth saving and fighting for.[1]

Faithfully yours,

Jefferson Caffery

[PPF 2331:TS]

[1] Answered March 20, 1935, below.

Roosevelt to Breckinridge Long, Ambassador to Italy, Rome

[Washington] March 9, 1935

Dear Breck: Those letters of yours are extraordinarily interesting even though they are pessimistic in tone.[1] I fear I must agree with you about the general situation. We, too, are going through a bad case of Huey Long and Father Coughlin influenza—the whole country aching in every bone. It is an internal disease, not external as it seems to be in Europe.

These are without doubt the most hair-trigger times the world has gone through in your lifetime or mine. I do not even exclude June and July, 1914, because at that time there was economic and social stability, with only the loom of a war by Governments in accordance with pre-conceived ideas and prognostications. Today there is not one element alone but three or more.

Keep on writing to me.

Always sincerely,

[PSF:Italy:CT]

[1] Feb. 3, 8, 21, 1935, above.

Roosevelt to Westy Egmont, New York

[Washington] March 11, 1935

My dear Mr. Egmont: I wish to thank you for your letter of March 4, suggesting that I designate you as an observer at the forthcoming British inquiry into the munitions industry and traffic.[1] While I agree with you that full information as to the inquiries in other countries on this problem is essential for the fullest understanding, yet I could not with propriety send anyone to London on the mission you suggested unless specifically invited to do so by the British Government, which has not been the case. Even then I should have to give the question careful study. My understanding is that most of the sessions of the British Royal Commission are to be public and I am asking the State Department to instruct the Embassy in London to forward for the use both of this Government and of the Nye Committee such minutes, records and reports as may be available.

It was a pleasure to have heard from you.[2]

Very sincerely yours,

[OF 1502:T]

[1] Egmont was counsel to the Senate Special Committee Investigating the Munitions Industry and was director of the International Law Research Institute. In his letter (OF 1502) he referred to the Royal Commission recently appointed by the British government to investigate the munitions industry in Britain.

[2] Drafted in the State Department (Hull to Roosevelt, March 9, 1935, OF 1502). Egmont wrote again on March 15, 1935 (OF 1502), to say that he was in touch with the London situation, and added: "Were I privately to convey the mere intimation to a certain member of the Commission that you would designate me upon receipt of an invitation a formal invitation would doubtless be sent in the near future." To this Roosevelt replied March 25, 1935, below.

Roosevelt to Thorvald Solberg, Washington

[Washington] March 11, 1935

My dear Mr. Solberg: I want to thank you for your good letter of February 27, 1935.[1] I fully agree with you that the present opportunity for the United States to participate in the General Copyright Convention is one which involves national right-dealing and that taking advantage of it will advance the cause of justice and good will.

I assure you that, as soon as I have received the necessary authorization, I shall take genuine pleasure in perfecting the adherence of our country to this Convention.[2]

Very sincerely yours,

[OF 699:CT]

[1] Solberg again urged (OF 699) that the copyright convention be ratified without waiting for enabling legislation. He said that the President could make a strong plea for this as a matter of right and justice, and he would have the support of educated public opinion. The reply was drafted in the State Department. Under Secretary of State Phillips, in his letter to McIntyre of March 11 sending the draft (OF 699), said that the Department had been making "a very earnest effort to obtain favorable action upon this treaty," and asked that it be brought to the President's attention. He also asked that the President sign the letter.

[2] See Solberg to Roosevelt, Aug. 12, 1935, below.

Roosevelt to Mrs. Andrew Carnegie, New York

[Washington] March 13, 1935

My dear Mrs. Carnegie: I most sincerely agree with you in regard to the great need of all nations ridding themselves of narrow nationalism, and, as you know, I have made every possible effort in every part of the world to get nations to agree to limitation and reduction of armaments.[1] Those efforts I shall continue.

I hope that you have not been misled by false information in regard to the usual Naval manoeuvers to be held by our ships this summer. Last year they were held in the Atlantic; in 1933 and in 1932 they were held in the Pacific. They are not held in the western part of the Pacific Ocean nor are they held simultaneously with, or in the neighborhood of, any Naval manoeuvers of our Japanese friends. There has been much spreading of completely erroneous propaganda by friends of ours who ought to know better.

Very sincerely yours,

[PPF 2304:CT]

[1] Mrs. Carnegie had written March 10 (PPF 2304) to ask Roosevelt to rescind the order for the summer maneuvers in the northern Pacific because it was "flaunting of our strength before our neighbor in the Pacific." Sherwood Eddy had written to the same effect (Feb. 15, 1935, OF 197). Eddy, for a number of years Y.M.C.A. secretary for Asia, was active in the world peace movement.

Cordell Hull, Secretary of State, to Roosevelt

Washington, March 13, 1935

Dear Mr. President: You may recall that I submitted to you, with my letter dated January 22, 1935,[1] a despatch from Mr. Grew, the American Ambassador to Japan, on the subject: "The Importance of American Naval Preparedness in Connection with the Situation in the Far East."

There are enclosed a copy of a further despatch from Mr. Grew, on the subject: "Urge Toward Expansion in Japan," and a digest thereof.[2] In his previous despatch Mr. Grew urged that the United States "be adequately prepared to meet all eventualities in the Far East."

In his most recent despatch Mr. Grew discusses certain social and economic forces and conditions which apply to the Japanese and give rise to the movement toward economic and political expansion.

Mr. Grew presents the thought that the United States, while preparing itself to meet any eventualities in the Far East, might also assume a sympathetic and cooperative attitude toward Japan based on larger considerations reaching into the future. It is our belief that, since the present Administration came into office, we have endeavored, wherever practicable, to be cooperative toward Japan.

It is believed that perusal of the digest and, if time and opportunity permit, of the despatch itself will be found helpful.

Faithfully yours,

Cordell Hull

(PSF:Japan:TS)

[1] *Foreign Relations, 1935*, III, 821–829.
[2] Both enclosures are present; the dispatch is printed *ibid.*, 843–852.

R. Walton Moore, Assistant Secretary of State, to Roosevelt

Washington, March 13, 1935

Dear Mr. President: Here is another letter from Dr. Dodd written previous to the one I handed you this morning[1] and which you need not return. I can send him a copy of the clipping for his file.

After seeing you I 'phoned Sandlin[2] that you will find an opportunity to talk with him.

Yours very sincerely,

R. Walton Moore

[PSF:Germany:TS]

[1] Feb. 24, 1935, above.
[2] Presumably Representative John N. Sandlin of Louisiana.

[*Enclosure*] William E. Dodd, Ambassador to Germany, to R. Walton Moore

On Board S.S. [*Washington*] Feby 22, 1935

Dear Judge Moore: I am enclosing a clipping which gives a fair estimate of commercial drift in Europe.[1] You see the effects of Nationalism carried to extremes: the United States and Germany in similar economic drifts, especially if we fall further for minority controls of imports and labor returns (30 hr. week). I doubt whether Senators can ever again realize the meaning for the masses of this hypernationalism. If the President could reduce tariffs 5% per year on necessity articles, leaving it high on luxury imports, over a period of five years, recovery for the masses of our people would come faster than from any other move—of course based on similar reductions of barriers in Europe.

We have had another stormy trip, every day but two from New York to Havre.[2] This sort of thing keeps one half ill all the time; but the *Washington* is as convenient for storms as any other vessel though a little slow. My only criticism of management is the instinctive habit of trying to over-speed even on a rough sea—and the over-service of our ships. We do not need two waiters for every table of eight people—400 workers, officers and others, are not necessary to carry 400 passengers. Nor can I understand huge subventions for maintaining ships on the ocean (U.S. Eng. France, Germany and Italy), when all countries block commerce

441

and forbid migration! Think of the *Queen Mary* and similar French ship now building!

But you and I are old-time Americans who can not understand policies based on contradictions—maybe Borah knows how to prove that civilization advances by abandoning all modern communications.

You will have seen that Hitler is negotiating with England and France on possibility of European Air-craft co-operation and that Russia puts down her foot for Eastern Locarno agreement. This will compel Germany to show her hand or hasten her entente with Japan (with Far East trade concessions). I shall try to get at facts and cable Department even before this letter reaches you: one man in Berlin is apt to give a bit of light. But if Germany accepts air co-operation, she is almost certain to veer towards League; if she enters League, with all other great powers around the table, we are sure to pay penalties in two ways: continued European barriers and more aggressive moves in Latin America—not omitting Far East—England getting first advantages and Germany second. You might note items in enclosed clipping.

Here again we are reasoning upon the premises of Woodrow Wilson—hated everywhere in Europe and misunderstood in our country. So I must close. I shall write Mr. Wilson[3] about personnel matter soon as I can make another survey. But I think it would be unwise for us in Berlin if other transfers and reductions of personnel were put into effect before everybody knows that similar changes had been applied in London and Paris.

One thing more: in existing state of things in Europe the idea of holding a conference of American representatives would be unwise. When I drove to Constanz, a story ran over Berlin that I was there to confer with Brünning,[4] former and exiled German chancellor!

William E. Dodd

If you can return clipping for our files?

[PSF:Germany:AS]

[1] From the London *Express* of Feb. 21, 1935, stating that British industrial activity was back to the 1929 level.

[2] Dodd sailed from New York on February 14 after a two months vacation spent at his home in Round Hill, Virginia (*Diary*, p. 216).

[3] Thomas M. Wilson, chief of the Division of Foreign Service Personnel of the State Department.

[4] Heinrich Bruening, leader of the German Center party and chancellor from 1930 to 1932.

Press Conference, Executive Offices of the White House, March 15, 1935, 4 P.M.

[*Excerpt*] Q: Church people are disturbed about naval maneuvers in the Pacific. Do you care to comment on those rumors?

The President: Only off the record. If you want me to talk off the record about this, I'm perfectly willing to do it, just so you will understand what it is about.

It is perfectly true that some of our friends in the Federal Council of Churches, for instance, were disturbed by what amounted to a real misconception, misinformation, about the usual, normal, fleet exercises. Well, just to give you an example of how people can get the wrong slant on things, one of them came down the other day and said that the Japanese and American maneuvers were to be held simultaneously, side by side, within two or three miles of each other and that there might be some untoward incident and that we were going to hold our maneuvers out of the Aleutian Islands this summer. It is that kind of a thing that has our church people disturbed.

As a matter of actual fact, we are doing absolutely, literally nothing more than we have done on many previous occasions. When I was in the Navy Department, I cannot tell you which year it was but it was away back, about 1913 or 1914, along there, we had maneuvers on the Pacific Coast and we worked out the problem of the defense of Alaska and the American mainland. This was not against any individual power. It was just the usual fleet exercises. The defense problem involved a search problem covering, roughly, the Eastern half—less than a half, perhaps 40%—of the Pacific Ocean, running from somewhere in Alaska down to Hawaii and then down south in the general direction of Panama. If you will look at the map, you will find that that sea area is roughly the eastern 40%, not going at all into the western 60% of the Pacific Ocean.

They held maneuvers of that kind some time after the war, some time around 1921 or 1922, they held them again—the fleet was out for three years—in 1931, 1932 and 1933. They were over on this Coast last summer and now they are back on the Pacific Coast.

There has never been any question arise between the Japanese and ourselves in relation to the maneuvers, and there never will. I believe the Japanese Admiralty announced some time after we did, and without any relationship to our announcement, that they were going to hold maneuvers down in the general direction of the Caroline and Marshall Islands—I think there is a distance of about two thousand miles from where the American maneuvers are being held—and their maneuvers are going to be held on a totally different thing. In other words, the whole thing is making a mountain out of a molehill—that is not for publication, but the whole thing is absurd.

Q: Do you mind our using this point about the two thousand miles? The President: Yes, but I would rather you did not use it at all.

[President's Press Conferences:T]

Roosevelt to Cordell Hull, Secretary of State

[Washington] March 15, 1935

Memorandum for the Secretary of State: Referring to your letter of February twelfth relating to whale oil, I enclose a letter from the Secretary of Commerce.[1]

I would be willing to go along with reductions in negotiations with Norway, provided Norway would agree, over a period of say three, four or five years, to employ the small number of persons now engaged in our American whale oil industry, or even if they could not employ all of them perhaps they could employ those who have actually been serving on American ships engaged in this industry. The number of persons involved is not great, but I should like to try out the theory of providing at least temporary employment for those deliberately thrown out of jobs by tariff reductions.[2]

F.D.R.

[OF 123:CT]

[1] Neither letter is present; see Roosevelt to Hull, Jan. 30, 1935, above, n. 1.
[2] See Roosevelt to Wallace, May 14, 1935, below.

Roosevelt to R. E. Blackwell, President, Randolph-Macon College, Ashland, Virginia

[Washington] March 18, 1935

My dear President Blackwell: That is a delightful note of yours.[1] As a matter of fact, your old pupil, the Secretary of the Navy, is not making

his game cock crow where anyone else need hear him. The Naval manoeuvers this year are in exactly the same Pacific area as they were in
previous years—a little matter of two or three thousand miles from the
nearest game cock.

With my warm regards, Very sincerely yours,

[PPF 1561:CT]

[1] Blackwell's letter of March 15, 1935 (PPF 1561), referred to the proposed naval
maneuvers in the Pacific: "Will you not speak to my old pupil, Secretary Swanson?
He used to pay attention to what I said. He may not now, but he will heed you. Will
you not remind him that, when he was a boy, if he carried his game-cock across the
vacant lot separating two barnyards and let him crow, it did not mean peace, especially
if his neighbor had a fighting cock too? Our neighbor has a fighting-cock. Suggest to
him the prudence of having the crowing done nearer our line-fence."

Roosevelt to Arthur N. Holcombe, National Central University, Nanking, China

[Washington] March 18, 1935

My dear Professor Holcombe: I am delighted to have your interesting
letter from Nanking.[1] I do hope that when you come back you will run
down to Washington to see me.

Very sincerely yours,

[PPF 2325:CT]

[1] Feb. 6, 1935, above.

Roosevelt to William Phillips, Under Secretary of State

Washington, March 18, 1935

Memorandum for the Under Secretary of State: In view of the apparent agreement by the interested parties and the Senators of the State
of Washington in regard to the Trail Smelter matter, I approve the
proposed Convention.[1]

F.D.R.

[OF 1495:CT]

[1] This memorandum refers to Phillips' letter of March 15, 1935 (OF 1495), explaining
the status of the negotiations with Canada over the Trail Smelter case (see Roosevelt
to Phillips, Dec. 6, 1934, above). The convention proposed by the Canadian government

provided for payment of $350,000 for damages that had occurred before Jan. 1, 1932, and for determination by an arbitral tribunal of the damages that had occurred thereafter. It also provided that the tribunal should decide what should be done about the smelter. Phillips said that representatives of the American citizens affected were now willing that the convention be concluded and he recommended that it be signed. (A copy is with Phillips' letter.) The convention was proclaimed Aug. 7, 1935 (49 *Stat.* 3245).

Senator Frederick Steiwer of Oregon to Roosevelt

[Washington] March 18, 1935

My dear Mr. President: In presenting certain arguments this morning before the Committee for Reciprocity Information, in connection with the proposed negotiation of a foreign trade agreement with Canada, my attention was drawn again to the system under which Part III of Title III of the Tariff Act of 1930, as amended, is administered.

The representatives of the domestic industries interested in this proposed negotiation presented their views before the Committee for Reciprocity Information. This Committee advised the representatives appearing at the hearing that the information would be transmitted to the appropriate agencies, which, I assume, include the Committee on Foreign Trade Agreements. The net result of this system is that the Canadian Government, seeking to acquire a share of the American domestic market on behalf of the Canadian producers, will deal directly with the American agencies which conduct and control the negotiations, whereas the American producers do not enjoy access to those agencies, but present their cause through an information committee which at the most can act only as an intermediary. Under this system Canadian competitors may have their views presented more effectually than can the Americans.

I make no criticism here and now of the Reciprocal Trade Agreements Act, nor of the effort to negotiate any treaty. Such effort is authorized by an Act of Congress, but I most respectfully suggest that the President consider an improved system which will permit interested Americans immediate access to the agencies which negotiate the foreign trade treaties in order that they may be on a parity with foreign competitors.

It was believed by some members of the Congress that the purpose of Section 4 of Part III, was to provide the American producers a direct means of presenting their views to the President or "to such agency as the President may designate," meaning the agency designated to negotiate the treaty and not a buffer agency set up for the sole purpose of collecting information and then transmitting it to a Committee on Foreign Trade Agreements. The present division of authority between two Committees, one on Reciprocity Information and the other on Foreign Trade Agreements, in my judgment will never be accepted as satisfactory by the American producers.

Permit me to suggest also that the organized American groups be fully informed concerning the commodities which may be affected, and that they be advised of the theories of economic reasoning entertained in the Committee on Foreign Trade Agreements so that the American producers may have opportunity to show that the theories entertained do not justify a reduction in duties. The representatives of American producers, where they can be identified through established associations should be given a reasonable opportunity to comment upon the evidence in the hands of the Committee on Foreign Trade Agreements on the score of its sufficiency to justify a reduction in duty.

I suggest also that the commodities upon which duties are reduced shall be only those included in the lists submitted to the American producers. I am advised that this was not done in negotiating the trade agreement with Belgium.

It is my opinion that unless the procedure is modified, improvident action will be inevitable.[1]

With assurances of esteem, I am, Respectfully yours,

Frederick Steiwer

[OF 614-A:TS]

[1] Answered April 8, 1935, below.

Press Conference, Executive Offices of the White House, March 20, 1935, 10:40 A.M.

[*Excerpt*] Q: Mr. President, are there any new developments in the suggestion for an international loan to China?

The President: No. No further news on it at all from any source, so the Secretary of State said yesterday.[1]

Q: Mr. President, I was wondering if you would care to comment on this German arms situation?

The President: No, I think not. I think we can only properly maintain the general principles of the good neighbor and hope that that American principle will be extended to Europe and will become more and more effectual and contribute to the peaceful solution of problems and, incidentally with it, as a very necessary component part, the reduction of armaments. I don't think anything more than that can be properly said by us at this time.[2]

Q: How is the Disarmament Conference coming now?

The President: I think I can put it this way, that they have made substantial progress on details in Geneva during the past month or six weeks, and I think they have all come to the point where most of the details of the problem of disarmament have been pretty thoroughly discussed so that there is fairly complete knowledge of the details, more so than at any time before. We are just hopeful.

Q: Late dispatches indicate the probability of a British, French, Italian Conference on Lake Maggiore, one of the little towns up there,[3] sometime between now and the end of the week. I wonder if it will be possible for the United States to have an observer at that conference, if invited?

The President: I do not know; we have not heard anything about it

. . .

Q: Have you anything to say about the visit of Senator Nye and his Committee here yesterday?[4]

The President: Nothing more than what Senator Nye said. I think the story is perfectly correct. They had hoped to have legislation or, rather, a report and, I suppose, legislation with it ready by the first of April. That relates only to the eventuality of the United States getting into war—what would be done.

Q: Isn't the status of Mr. Baruch's report the same as it was?[5]

The President: Yes, they made a verbal report on it.

Q: Verbal? Will anything be used by the Nye Committee?

The President: No; it all checks in together.

Q: Does the Nye Committee plan suit you?

The President: What?

Q: Does the Nye Committee plan, as published yesterday, suit your ideas?

The President: Oh, we have not considered it in detail. Of course the objective is a common objective, to take the profits out of war.

Q: A few months ago there was speculation about a change in the policy regarding the freedom of the seas. There has been any amount of stories written about it.

The President: Who started it? Grotius, wasn't it?

Q: Three or four started it.

The President: And it is still raging four centuries later?

Q: Yes.

The President: Right.

Q: In connection with the German situation, is there any possibility of the United States sending a note to Germany in connection with the Treaty of Peace?

The President: No news on that at all . . .

Q: Mr. President, Congressional leaders have undertaken to speak for the Administration and have asserted that—

The President: What is that?

Q: They have asserted that the Administration is opposed, definitely, to the Patman and Vinson Bills and I wondered whether or not that also extended to the Tydings Bill to pay the bonus in baby bonds?

The President: No news on that at all.

Q: Mr. Baruch is scheduled to appear before the Nye Committee next Monday. Are you in a position to say whether he will present the views of the Committee of which he was head?

The President: No; I believe he is testifying as an individual entirely.

[President's Press Conferences:T]

[1] At the White House; Norman Davis was also present (PPF 1-0). See Hull to Roosevelt, April 30, 1935, below.

[2] The question referred to the German government's announcement on March 16 that it would reinstitute conscription. The announcement had aroused speculation in the press on what the United States would do. Following the statement by Hull mentioned above, a United Press report originating in the White House press room stated that the President planned no immediate action and that published reports that he was under strong pressure to take some action were false (U.P. teletype, March 19, 1935, OF 182). (Cf. New York *Times,* March 20, 1935, p. 3.)

Two memoranda (PPF 1820) appear to indicate that Roosevelt had given prior thought to his reply to the reporter's query. A memorandum of March 20, 1935, addressed to Roosevelt, unsigned but undoubtedly from Early, reads: "It is worth making the suggestion to the Press that the somewhat complex cross-currents in Europe might well be viewed in the spirit of reflection rather than in the spirit of dramatization or in the spirit of useless speculation of the type which is generally based on misinformation or lack of knowledge." With this is an undated memorandum in Roosevelt's hand: "U.S. a disinterested friend of peace. Hopes that the good neighbor policy will become more & more a factor in Europe, contributing to the peaceful settlement of internat. problems & to reduction of armaments."

[3] Stresa.

[4] The President and the committee (the Senate Special Committee on Investigation of the Munitions Industry) discussed the proposed legislation: drastic governmental controls in time of war, limitation of incomes and greatly increased income and corporation taxes, closing of commodity exchanges, and nationalization of all essential industries.

449

Roosevelt, according to press reports, was in agreement with the general principles of the program (New York *Times,* March 20, 1935, pp. 1, 9).

[5] Bernard Baruch, chairman of the War Industries Board under President Wilson, had been asked by Roosevelt to head a committee to draft a war profits limitation plan at a White House conference of civil and governmental leaders on Dec. 12, 1934. Baruch had been highly critical of the Nye committee proposals (New York *Times,* Dec. 13, 1934, p. 1). See Hull to Roosevelt, April 11, 1935, below.

Roosevelt to Jefferson Caffery, Ambassador to Cuba, Havana

[Washington] March 20, 1935

Dear Jeff: That is an interesting letter of yours of March eighth,[1] and I agree with you very definitely in regard to the qualifications for Foreign Service officers. Because you so well exemplify the broad qualifications, I know you will realize that the only real complaint is against those in the Service who either (a) know and care mighty little about what is happening in their own country, and (b) those who take very little interest in the opinions and problems of the masses in the countries to which they are accredited.

For example of the first case, one of our very important new agency heads went abroad last summer and saw several of our Counselors and Secretaries and not one of them asked any questions about how our big efforts, such as Relief and NRA and AAA, were working out. They had neither the knowledge nor the desire to learn, and yet if they had known they could have been far more interesting in their contacts with foreigners.

The other example is that of the Counselor who did not know that the country where he was serving happens to be the center of what is known as the Youth Movement in Europe.

The Service is so vastly better than it was twenty years ago that no great changes should take place. I do think, however, that there should be a greater weeding out process, in order to get rid of the types I have mentioned above.

I hope all goes well with you and that I shall see you soon.

Very sincerely yours,

[PPF 2331:CT]

[1] Above.

Roosevelt to Valerie Hadden Riggs, Indian Mountain School, Lakeville, Connecticut

[Washington] March 20, 1935

My dear Mrs. Riggs: I am glad to have your letter and I wish much that the great objective which you and I visualize could be more quickly attained. The real problem, as I have suggested before, is that though ninety per cent of the people of the world really want peace and disarmament, the other ten per cent, headed in the opposite direction, block our efforts.[1]

Very sincerely yours,

[PPF 448:CT]

[1] Mrs. Riggs was the wife of Francis B. Riggs, headmaster of Indian Mountain School in Lakeville. In her letter of March 17 (PPF 448) she urged Roosevelt to take world leadership in carrying out the promises to disarm made to Germany in 1919. She also urged cancellation of the proposed naval maneuvers in the northern Pacific, repeal of the Japanese exclusion act, and entry into the World Court and League of Nations.

Senator James E. Murray of Montana to Roosevelt

[Washington] March 20, 1935

Mr. President: On the evening of February 5th a joint caucus of Senate and House members, interested in the further development of domestic manganese deposits, was held in the Caucus Room of the Senate Office Building to discuss the possible consequences of the proposed cut in the manganese duty under the Trade Agreement between Brazil and the United States.

At this meeting the attached resolution was unanimously adopted.[1] In accordance with the resolution the following committee was duly appointed: Senator James E. Murray, Chairman, Representative James G. Scrugham, Representative Isabella Greenway, Representative John E. Miller, Representative Theodore Christianson.

Plans are now being considered by members of Congress, in cooperation with the Administration, whereby the further development of the domestic manganese industry may be continued without interference with the Brazilian Trade Agreement.

If necessary, resolutions or legislation will be proposed in this Congress to bring about the desired results without conflict with the purposes of the State Department.

It appears that the Brazilian Trade Agreement, when proclaimed, will automatically extend to other Nations the same reduction in the duty on manganese as will apply to Brazil unless such extensions are withheld by the United States at the time of the proclamation. We, therefore, respectfully request that the application of the cut in the manganese duty be withheld from India, Africa, Russia and other manganese-producing countries until this matter can be further considered.

Under the terms of the Brazilian Trade Agreement and the provisions of NRA, we further request that an allotment of tonnage of manganese ore to be imported from Brazil be set forth by the Administration so that importations of manganese ore from Brazil may not render or tend to render ineffective the proper administration of the manganese code and the further employment of labor under such code.[2]

Very respectfully yours,

James E. Murray

[*Notation*:A] State Dept for prep of reply
[OF 948:TS]

[1] The resolution (present) declared that the proposed 50 per cent reduction in the import duty on manganese would not expand the foreign markets of the United States, and was therefore not consistent with the purpose of the Reciprocal Trade Agreements Act; application of the reduction to other nations would ruin the American manganese industry. Individual members of the industry and industry representatives made a determined effort to change the terms of the Brazilian treaty (OF 61-M; OF 948), and their communications received carefully considered replies. For example, a telegram to the President from Francis P. Garvan, a New York attorney representing certain manganese interests, March 1, 1935 (OF 948), was sent to the State Department for draft of reply. Under Secretary of State Phillips, in his note to the President of March 21, 1935, accompanying the draft, wrote: "The brief reply is suggested only after careful thought. It would be inadvisable, in my opinion, to give Mr. Garvan the impression that the domestic manganese producers, by means of a concerted attack, can hope to change the terms of the agreement signed with Brazil on February 2, 1935." The reply merely stated that it would be neither practicable nor desirable to reopen the negotiations with Brazil.

[2] Answered April 16, 1935, below.

Roosevelt to Westy Egmont, Long Island City, New York

[Washington, March 25, 1935][1]

My dear Mr. Egmont: Since receiving your letter of March 15,[2] I have given further careful consideration to your suggestion that I appoint an observer to attend the hearings of the British Royal Commission which is to investigate the munitions industry and the arms traffic. I have come to the conclusion that it would be inadvisable for me to appoint an observer, even if I were specifically invited to do so by the British Government. I suggest, therefore, that you take no steps to bring about the sending of such an invitation.[3]

Very sincerely yours,

(s) Franklin D. Roosevelt

[OF 1502:T]

[1] Date supplied from Hull's note sending the draft.
[2] OF 1502.
[3] On April 11, 1935, Egmont sent the President a preliminary report of a committee formed to study neutrality problems, headed by George W. Kirchwey, a distinguished lawyer and penologist (OF 1516). The report proposed a review and revision of international law with respect to neutrality as distinguished from national policy with respect to neutrality. In a reply of April 29, 1935, McIntyre said that the State Department had been considering such a review for some time. To devote public funds to it would be a duplication of effort and the President could not therefore recommend it (OF 1561).

Robert W. Bingham, Ambassador to Great Britain, to Roosevelt

London, March 26, 1935

Dear Mr. President: You were good enough to suggest that I might write you soon after my return to London regarding the European situation. While I find that the European atmosphere is surcharged, I do not agree with the view which I found was held in some quarters in Washington that Europe is headed for a war in the immediate future. The widespread tension which exists does not now arise out of a well-founded fear of immediate war but out of a realization that Europe is at the parting of the ways: a realization that at the eleventh hour either a substantial advance must be made towards some system of collective security or Europe will once again range herself into two rival armed camps; and there are few who cherish the illusion that the initial preponderance of the non-German group will ultimately avail to prevent a fresh outbreak of war at some future date.

But regardless of the political arrangements, in the last analysis peace depends on economic security. Germany has demanded, and by her recent tactics has in reality attained, political equality in Europe. For the past year or more, by stringent economic and monetary regulations, and by stimulating her heavy industries through rearmament, she has maintained some sort of economic equilibrium. But this is purely temporary. At the end of another year she will have to look towards expanding world markets. About one-third of the German people normally depend upon world trade for their livelihood, and the degree of the standard of living of another third is determined by world trade. Naziism will be forced to seek economic as well as political gains. If they cannot be obtained in the normal way of trade, other expansionist methods will doubtless have to be employed. This may quite probably result in war.

I am more than doubtful whether we could keep out of a great European conflagration. We tried hard once before, with no success. Therefore the question arises as to what we can do in our own interest to aid an appeasement in Europe. Certainly our contribution is not that specious form of "moral leadership" which was the easy answer of the previous Administration to every too difficult problem. The practical substantial benefit which we can confer lies in the progress we make in the United States towards economic recovery. May I repeat my belief that the possibility of war is inextricably joined to world economic recovery and the greatest contribution the United States can make, indeed perhaps the only one, would be the confidence and benefit the world would obtain from a decided economic upturn in North America.

Sincerely yours,

Robert W. Bingham

[PSF:Great Britain:TS]

Stephen T. Early to Marvin H. McIntyre, Assistant Secretary to the President, Miami, Florida

Washington, March 27, 1935

Telegraphic Memorandum to Mr. McIntyre: State Department either daily or when developments are sufficiently important to justify will send a brief digest of foreign affairs to you for transmission in confidential code to the President. The President requested Secretary Hull to keep him in touch in this way. The first report follows:

Western Europe. Ambassador Dodd telegraphed that all points in Anglo-French accord of February 3 were discussed; that Eastern Pact with mutual assistance clause is unacceptable to Germany since this might involve Germany in event of Russo-Japanese war, but that Germany would agree to Pact with non-aggression clause, provided no pact interferes with eventual Austro-German relations or guarantees present Austro-German status; that German officials believe German return to the League is possible on basis of equality provided France withdraws her charges and that League is not used by other countries to coerce Germany; that British sources indicated little hope of material results from conversations.

An aggravating factor in situation is verdict in trial of Nazi plotters at Memel.

Vienna reports that increased pro-Nazi and pro-German wave in Austria is feared as result of Germany's apparently successful rearmament moves. Responsible Austrian Ministers publicly speak of desirability of conscription and of their intention to obtain it by peaceful negotiation.

Rome reports strength of Italian armed forces on April 1 will be at least 928,000 including over 56,000 available for East African service.

Japan's withdrawal from League became effective today.

Eastern Europe. Military trial at Kaunas of 126 Memel Nazis accused of preparing armed uprising to return Memel region to Germany resulted yesterday in death sentence for four, life imprisonment for 2, 35 acquittals and remaining accused sentenced to varying terms of imprisonment. Hull[1]

Steve

[OF 20:TS]

[1] This memorandum is typical of the State Department reports furnished the President daily while on his cruise in Florida waters on the Astor yacht *Nourmahal.* He left Washington on March 25 and returned April 9, 1935.

Edward M. House to Roosevelt

New York, March 29, 1935

Dear Governor: A letter comes from Judge Bingham this morning in which you may be interested.

He seems deeply appreciative of the fact that you told him while he was here that you would appoint him as special representative at the King's Jubilee, provided anyone was named. He then goes on to say that in the present difficult crisis it would be a mistake to have anyone other than the regular Ambassadors at the Capitals in Europe. He says:

I can have private and confidential contacts whereas anyone coming on a special mission, however camouflaged, would necessarily be placed in the glare of world-wide publicity.

And again:

Atherton has sent a wireless saying that Simon wants to see me and Straus as soon as he returns from Berlin on the 27th. Mr. and Mrs. Straus are coming to stay with us at that time. I have asked Simon to lunch with Straus, Atherton and me at the Embassy on the 28th. I have no idea of going to the Foreign Office as a matter of tactics and to avoid the inevitable publicity, but I shall welcome Simon when he comes to me and listen with interest to what he has to say. They are in trouble now and are ready to come down from their high horse and treat with us on a friendly and cooperative basis, but we must give them time and show them we can wait, if necessary, longer than they can. The situation is critical but not hopeless.

I fully agree with his conclusions.

I am delighted that you have had your outing and that you have come back refreshed.

Affectionately yours,

E. M. House

[PPF 222:TS]

Breckinridge Long, Ambassador to Italy, to Roosevelt

Rome, April 5, 1935

My dear Chief: The European political situation is marking time until the meeting at Stresa on the 11th.[1] That meeting does not promise to produce anything conclusive. It will probably develop into a larger subsequent meeting either with or without Germany. That subsequent meeting will probably consider some limitation of armament and/or some kind of a general non-aggression pact.

The limitation of armament question will start badly if each of them send back to the conference their old-time representatives. These men have known each other for years—and sat across the table from each other—have each committed themselves to definite proposals—have each declined to accede to the point of view of the other—have each explained their respective positions—and have each so definitely assumed positions from which they cannot recede without losing face that it will be very difficult for them to get anywhere. What they need in any future discussion of armament amongst European Powers is a New Deal in conferees. If they would each send fresh men, there would be a much better chance for them to get together. As it is now, each of them knows each of the other ones and knows their position—and they are at an impasse.

I do not look for any blow-up, though one can never tell what will happen in case someone should get excited and make a mistake—at least under the circumstances that exist here with a lot of French troops on the border and nearly a million men in Italy under arms and military activity all over the Continent of Europe. Nevertheless, it looks quiet for the time being.

Notwithstanding this weakness, there are some rumblings of a preventive war. It is not heard from the tops of the Government but in the second and third strata of Government officials and from at least one careful and responsible source recently in high position (De Francisci, who has just finished a long service as Minister of Justice). The members of my Embassy have heard them speak furtively and hold out the possibility of an attack on Germany before Germany gets better armed. I discount the probability, but my ears are always close to the ground, and I report for possible reference in the next three or four weeks.

These are truly ticklish days. It is the aftermath of another show which is so appalling. With the social unrest widespread as it is, and with the certain exaggeration of it as the sequel to another war, I can only shudder to think of our social situation a year after another conflict.

Affectionately and respectfully,

Breckinridge Long

[PSF:Italy:TS]

[1] Following announcement by Germany on March 9, 1935, of the creation of a German air force, and on March 16 of the reintroduction of conscription, representatives of Britain, France, and Italy met in Stresa, Italy, from April 11 to 14, to demonstrate a common front. The three governments deprecated Germany's unilateral repudiation at a time when the question of armament limitation was being discussed. They also reaffirmed their position on the need of maintaining the independence of Austria. See *Foreign Relations, 1935*, I, 200–269.

Roosevelt to Senator Frederick Steiwer of Oregon

[Washington, April 8, 1935]

My dear Senator Steiwer: I have given careful consideration to the views expressed in your letter of March 18, 1935,[1] with reference to the procedure which is being followed in carrying out the purposes of the Trade Agreements Act of June 12, 1934.

This procedure has been worked out after most careful consideration of all aspects of the matter. Its effect, I am sure, is not to give Canadian or other foreign interests, through their own governments, better access to the agencies responsible for formulating recommendations concerning proposed trade agreements than is afforded to our own domestic interests. On the contrary, the procedure being followed is designed to provide domestic producers and other American interests an orderly and certain means of bringing their information and views to the attention of these agencies.

A reasonable period of time is given after public notice of intention to negotiate a trade agreement for interested persons to submit written statements to the Committee for Reciprocity Information. Oral statements are received by that committee a week or so later from persons whose applications to present supplementary views orally have been approved. The Committee for Reciprocity Information distributes these written and oral statements to the agencies concerned in carrying out the trade agreements program; namely, the Departments of State, Commerce, and Agriculture, the Treasury Department, the Tariff Commission, the Office of the Special Adviser to the President on Foreign Trade, and the National Recovery Administration. Competent experts and high officers of these agencies study all proposals and views transmitted to them by the Committee for Reciprocity Information and cooperate in formulating specific recommendations on the basis of such information and that available from other sources. In addition to the Trade Agreements Committee, a number of special or technical interdepartmental committees have been set up to facilitate the full consideration of important trade agreement matters.

The Committee for Reciprocity Information is in no sense a "buffer agency." It is a convenient channel through which interested persons may bring their views to the attention of the several governmental agencies actively concerned in formulating recommendations in regard to proposed trade agreements. With reference to your statement concerning the "present division of authority" between the Committee for Reciprocity Information and the Trade Agreements Committee, I may say that no such division of authority exists or can exist since the Committee is only an agency of the trade agreements organization for obtaining the information and views of interested persons. In addition to the above-mentioned channel, that is the Committee for Reciprocity

Information, domestic interests have access to each of the governmental agencies concerned in the trade agreements work.

In regard to your suggestion that organized groups be fully informed concerning the commodities which may be affected, you may be assured that full consideration has been given to the possibility of announcing the products or subjects to be considered in connection with any proposed trade agreement. The conclusion was early reached that such a procedure would be impracticable. At the time public notice is given of intention to negotiate a trade agreement, the Administration itself may not know what products or subjects may come up for consideration. If an all-inclusive list should be announced at the time notice is given, and later on it seemed desirable to consider other products, it would be necessary to announce a supplementary list and provide interested persons an opportunity to present their views to the Committee for Reciprocity Information. Such a procedure, if adopted, probably would so complicate and delay the negotiation of trade agreements as to hinder seriously the carrying out of the purposes of the Act.

Because of this and other considerations, I believe that the present procedure of announcing only the name of the foreign country concerned and making readily available statistical and other information concerning the trade between the United States and that country is quite satisfactory. It seems reasonable to assume that domestic producers, importers, and other American individuals or organized groups should know whether their interests are in fact involved.

With reference to your suggestion that the commodities upon which duties are reduced "shall be only those included in the lists submitted to the American producers" and to your statement that you have been advised that this was not done in negotiating the trade agreement with Belgium, I should like to point out that no such lists are given out. Whoever advised you that such was the case may have been referring to the statistical information concerning the principal items entering into the trade between the United States and the foreign country concerned, which is issued in the form of a press release at the time public notice is given, for the convenience of interested persons and is in no sense a definitive list of the products which may be considered. At the head of every such tabulation of trade statistics is the following statement:

The following table indicating in a general way the nature of the trade between the United States and Belgium has been compiled by the Division of Foreign Trade Statistics of the Department of Commerce. The table shows the principal commodities entering into this trade. More detailed statements of the trade with Belgium will be available shortly at the Division of Foreign Trade Statistics and the District Offices of the Department of Commerce.

The statement quoted above is taken from a Department of State press release of September 4, 1934, a copy of which I enclose, which was issued in connection with the public notice given on that date of intention to negotiate a trade agreement with Belgium.

The purpose of the Trade Agreements Act is to facilitate the restoration of our foreign trade by means of agreements with foreign countries providing for reciprocal reductions of excessive trade barriers. In carrying out this purpose, the trade agreements organization is actuated by a sincere desire to conclude trade agreements which will promote the national interest. By making possible an increased flow of trade, these trade agreements should contribute materially to the relief of unemployment and to the improvement of the general economic situation in this country.

If you would like to study further the trade agreements organization and the procedure which has been adopted in connection with its work, I suggest that you talk with Assistant Secretary of State Sayre or with Dr. Henry F. Grady, Chief of the Trade Agreements Section of the Department of State. They would, I am sure, be glad to have an opportunity to discuss these matters with you.[2]

Sincerely yours,

[Notation:A] 4/8/35
[OF 614-A:CT]

[1] Above.
[2] Drafted in the State Department.

William C. Bullitt, Ambassador to the Union of Soviet Socialist Republics, to Roosevelt

Paris, April 8, 1935

Personal and strictly confidential

Dear Mr. President: You will, I fear, think that your remark that you really wanted me to write to you is going to produce an endless flood of letters when you see this in addition to the pages I wrote you yesterday.[1] I want simply to explain to you developments flowing from that P.P.P.S.

It was indeed Laval who phoned last night and I saw him this morning. I reported at once to Jesse Straus and you will unquestionably have seen the telegram which Jesse dictated as a result of my reports on conversations with Titulescu, Laval and Potemkin.[2]

Laval said that he would reach Moscow on the 25th and would sign the mutual assistance pact on that date or on the 26th. I asked him if he would remain in Moscow for the fetes of the first of May and he said that he would not as the French people would consider that he should not participate in a revolutionary celebration! It is a long way from 1789!

Laval said that the definitive text of the pact was not yet established but that he was working on it. He added that he had had some hesitation about concluding the agreement because, in his opinion, the Soviet Army was essentially a force for keeping down the Russian people and handling internal problems and could not operate effectively outside the Soviet Union. He added that his military advisors, however, believed the Soviet air force had a certain value. He then described the agreement and indicated that France and the Soviet Union in case of aggression against either by another power would convoke the Council of the League of Nations immediately. If the Council should agree unanimously in accordance with paragraph 6 of Article XV of the Covenant of the League, France and the Soviet Union would place all their armed forces at each other's disposal. If the Council should fail to adopt a unanimous report France and the Soviet Union would regain their liberty of action under paragraph 7 of Article XV of the Covenant of the League and would at once place all their armed forces at the disposal of each other. He added that he hoped he could persuade the Italians to make a similar agreement with the Russians and that he hoped to bring into a similar pact the entire Little Entente and the Balkan League. He also said that he was not without hope of bringing in Poland. He added that the mutual assistance pact would, of course, be open to the participation of Germany and went on to say that he himself would continue to make every effort to prevent the conclusion of the mutual assistance agreement between France and the Soviet Union being interpreted in Germany as an act to encircle the Reich. He said he believed personally there would be no genuine peace in Europe until France and Germany had been reconciled and that he would continue to work for good relations between France and Germany.

He then asked me what policy I thought the Russians would follow. (This question seemed to me to be the cause of his insistence on seeing me.) I replied that the Russians would doubtless follow the example of France and attempt to develop close relations with Germany. He said that he thought the agreement would place the Soviet Union in a very favorable position to bargain between France and Germany. I replied that I agreed that Russia would be in the happy position of being able to wait for the offers of the highest bidder.

Laval then said that he was somewhat troubled about his relations with the United States. He said that he had never published his conversations with Hoover at the time of the Moratorium but that Hoover had promised him definitely *not* that the United States would cancel the French debt but that the Moratorium would be extended. He asked me what was the present attitude of the United States towards the debts. I replied that for the first time the debts were beginning to have some value, that so long as they were not paid they would constitute an insurance policy that the American people would not precipitate themselves into a terrible conflict which did not concern them. He laughed and said that he quite understood that point of view, and added that the American people had every reason to remain aloof.

We talked about lots of other things of minor importance and he displayed a really surprising cordiality throughout our conversation.

Potemkin, the Soviet Ambassador in Paris, confirmed today at luncheon all the statements that Laval had made and said in addition that he was discussing with Laval a subsidiary pact which would be adopted shortly after the pact of mutual assistance. Potemkin said that this subsidiary agreement would provide for immediate declaration of war by the Soviet Union and France in the case of flagrant aggression by Germany. He said that there would be no waiting for action by the League Council and that the agreement would be fitted into the language of Article XVI of the League. How that is possible I leave to subtler brains than mine and I do not believe the French will sign any such document. Potemkin said also that after the signature of the mutual assistance agreement by France and the Soviet Union, the Soviet Union would sign immediately a similar mutual assistance agreement with the Czechoslovaks. Both Potemkin and his staff were in a triumphant state of mind. Potemkin told me that Litvinov will arrive in Berlin the same morning I arrive (April 10) and urged me strongly to telephone the Soviet Ambassador and see Litvinov enroute.

My own opinion is that the Soviet Union will be the single great beneficiary of the agreement described above. Neither Germany nor Japan will dare to attack the Soviet Union, and France and Germany will be compelled to begin to bid high for Soviet assistance. A few months after the agreement with France is signed, Litvinov will begin negotiating with the Reichswehr via Voroshilov, and the French within six months will begin to be as worried about the condition of their Soviet alliance as they are now about their Polish alliance.

It is obvious, of course, from all of these maneuvers and counter maneuvers that no one in Europe is any longer thinking of peace but that everyone is thinking furiously about obtaining as many allies as possible for the next war. As each day passes I become more convinced that our only sane policy is to stay just as far as possible outside the mess. In this connection it was interesting at luncheon today at the Soviet Embassy to see the reaction of a large table full of guests which included French cabinet ministers and former ministers. Rosenberg,[3] who is now the Soviet assistant secretary at the League of Nations and was formerly Soviet Chargé d'Affaires in Paris, called across the table to me and said that he felt that the United States should participate actively in the present negotiations and asked me why the United States was remaining so aloof. To a silent table, I delivered a short oration which, if I may say so, was worthy of yourself. At the end of the discourse everyone, including the French cabinet Ministers, said, "You are perfectly right. No one can expect the United States to involve itself in the events which are approaching."

During the course of the luncheon I said to the Soviet Ambassador that of course the mutual assistance agreement with France was just an old fashioned alliance camouflaged by a smear of League of Nations paint for the benefit of the French people. He said, "You are quite right." I then said that I felt the only weak point in the whole project was Austria, that I was informed on good authority that there was a considerable possibility that Austria, not from external pressure but from internal force, would go Nazi this summer and that I could not with a telescope ascertain any legal justification for an invasion of Austria by Italy or anyone else if the people of Austria should desire of their own accord to have a Nazi Government. He replied that he agreed that Austria was the sore and dangerous point and that no scheme but war had yet been proposed that promised to keep Austria out of the hands of the Nazis.

My guess is that Laval's visit to Moscow will be followed by a series of visits of the ministers of the minor powers especially the Little Entente. Titulescu indicated that he would probably visit Moscow in June. ~~and would then sign a mutual assistance pact similar to the French one~~.

I write you all this because from Paris I cannot report to the Department. I have given Jesse a full written account of all the conversations

I have had but I do not know how much finally will reach Washington.

Excuse me if I have burdened you too greatly. Goodnight and the Lord be with you.

Yours permanently,

Bill

[PSF:Russia:TS]

[1] A long letter on, among other things, the future of Franco-Soviet relations and the results of the introduction of conscription in Hungary (PSF:Russia).

[2] Vladimir Potemkin.

[3] Marcel Rosenberg.

Jesse Isidor Straus, Ambassador to France, to Roosevelt

Paris, April 9, 1935

Personal

Dear Mr. President: Despite your many burdens, I feel that I must write you about some of the problems that confront me in the conduct of this mission, and for the correction of which I am convinced appeal must be made to you.

From various sources I get the impression that you are being filled up with stories about the iniquities of the diplomatic service: that it is overstaffed, underworked and overpaid; that the average career man is a tea hound and a lounge lizard.

My two years' experience indicates that at least those with whom I have been associated in this Embassy, and those whom I have had the pleasure of meeting when they passed through Paris, are a lot of serious-minded men who are most attentive to their duties and spare neither time nor thought in their endeavors, sometimes under very trying and difficult conditions, to accomplish, under the direction of the Department of State, the objectives of the service. Long hours mean nothing to them. But there seems to be for some reason or other a degree of unreality on the part of the Department of State as regards appointments in the Foreign Service field.

Thus, I cannot understand the attitude of the Personnel Division of that Department, which, without reference to me, has deprived me during the last two years of two First Secretaries without replacement, and which this morning has notified me that Alan S. Rogers, Third

Secretary, who has been acting as my Private Secretary and who, in the absence of Robert T. Pell, Special Attaché in charge of the European Information Center, is carrying on Pell's work, is ordered to Vienna on Mr. Pell's return. I make no mention of Mr. Keena, the Consul General, who recently at my suggestion was made Commercial Counselor, to whom you so justly gave a well deserved appointment.[1]

In other words, a Chief of Mission appointed by you and on whom falls the responsibility of directing a mission as important as Paris, at this time when careful reporting is essential to the State Department, is, without consultation, deprived of men whose contacts and experience enable them to get information and interpret it, and may receive in their stead, when he receives any, men who can have little knowledge of local conditions, who can have no immediate contacts, and, in one instance at least, that of the Consul General replacing Mr. Keena, no previous service in Europe.

Before I came to Paris I requested of the State Department that no change should be made in the members of my diplomatic staff. I had heard that they were all competent and since my contacts with them I have found them so. We had, when I came here, in addition to myself and the Counselor, four First Secretaries, Messrs. Howell, Scotten, Cochran and Tuck; two Second Secretaries, Messrs. Williamson and MacVeagh; a Third Secretary, Mr. Rogers; and Special Attachés Pell and Dawson. We were well and adequately staffed. At the moment we have two First Secretaries, Messrs. Cochran and Tuck; two Second Secretaries, Messrs. Williamson and Werlich; one Third Secretary, Mr. Rogers; and Mr. Dawson. Mr. Cochran is occupied practically every instant with special financial work for the Departments of State and Treasury, and Mr. Rogers, as I said at the outset of this letter, is to be ordered away. Furthermore, Mr. Pell, who has a specific job, has gone home on leave completely broken in health, largely because of the difficult and arduous work that he has performed without vacation during the past two years. The Department, I know, has assigned to this mission Mr. Robert English, Third Secretary, but he is not arriving until the end of this month.

The impression seems to prevail in a certain bureaucratic circle of the State Department that there should be a minimum staff in missions abroad. It appears to be their belief that every man should be physically active during prescribed hours. A display of physical activity seems to be the gauge of efficiency. Now consultation among the members of the official family of a mission, consultation which is time-consuming but essential properly to lay down policies and give coordinated opinions to the Secretary of State, seems to me of much greater importance than pen-pushing and time-serving. It is my opinion that an Embassy of the importance of Paris should have rather two officers too many than one officer too few. For, although the regulations of the State Department fix the hours, no member of my official family can, under ordinary circumstances, pay attention to these hours and no member ever gives any thought to the length of time that he puts on his work. Most of the information so necessary to all of us is gained outside of office hours. Social contacts and the formation of friendships are of major importance; entertainment of officials, newspaper people, writers, etcetera, is, as you well know, most necessary. And in that connection, the funds provided by the State Department are utterly insufficient for the amount of entertainment that the officers of the Embassy, in the pursuit of their duties are compelled to undertake. In a recent report made at the request of the State Department as to the income received by members of the Foreign Service from the Government in relation to their expenditures, about half the officers of this Embassy spent more than they received. I doubt whether this has ever been brought to your attention.

I have recently heard that there are those who would endeavor to persuade you that a chief of mission can live on his salary. Of course, he can: there are more families living on much less than the salary of an Ambassador than there are spending more. However, certainly at this post, and in many of the other European posts, as I know from conversation with heads of missions, the salary of an Ambassador is not more than one-third sufficient to cover expenditures that are proper, appropriate and practically unavoidable. In comparison with other countries our appropriations for chiefs of mission are beggarly and certainly we, one of the largest countries, should "when in Rome do as the Romans do" and represent our country in accordance with custom and diplomatic usage. I have heard it remarked that entertainment, living in style, putting on side, is undemocratic. Custom, however, has decreed that certain amenities be observed and to me it seems far more undemocratic to restrict, through the appropriation of inadequate funds, the appointment of chiefs of mission to those who are possessed of private means.

However, this last is parenthetical. The main point that I would like to bring to your attention, Mr. President, is that I am being hampered in an attempt to serve the country and you. This Embassy, occupying as it does a new building, headquarters for all Government services in France, presents problems somewhat different from most missions. I was asked by the Secretary of State when I left for France, to study and recommend changes in method and coordination of effort to attain economy and greater efficiency. This I have tried to do, and in attempting to do so have apparently recommended so much and complained so much at failure to adopt my recommendations that I have incurred the displeasure of certain subordinate officers who want to take it out on me and, by withdrawing competent men and reducing my staff, wear out my patience. They are succeeding; that may comfort them, but will not lead to maximum results.

As an instance of the foregoing, the replacement of Mr. Keena is typical. Some two months ago Mr. Keena, who has long been Consul General here and who is a man of great experience with many French contacts and who has a good knowledge of the French language, was, as I said above, given a well deserved promotion by you and appointed Minister to Honduras. At that time I requested that Mr. Coert du Bois, Consul General at Naples, who knows European conditions and has previously been stationed in Paris and who speaks fluent French, be assigned here. Instead, Mr. Clarence E. Gauss, who has spent his entire career in the Far East and knows nothing of European conditions, although he is, I am told, a first class administrator, was assigned without consulting me. The whole situation is utterly incomprehensible to me and most distressing.

I do not wish to burden you longer, but before closing I would like to touch on a subject that may have something to do with my future difficulties. I understand that an effort is being made in the various appointments in the Foreign Service to insist upon experience in both branches of that service. Of this in theory I heartily approve, provided, however, that there is a realization that there is a difference in type, in background, in acquaintanceship with social amenities and customs that must be observed. A good administrative type may be a first class Consul or Vice-Consul, but often he is not at all fitted for a service in which social contacts are essential, whether the envious, devoid of certain characteristics, admit it or not.

Some time ago, I asked Miss LeHand to arrange to have Mr. Marriner, Counselor of Embassy, who sails tomorrow on leave, see you while visiting Washington. At that time I had in mind that you could get direct verbal information from him. It now becomes much more important for Mr. Marriner to see you because he will be able to tell you personally of all the difficulties under which we are here laboring.[2]

With kindest regards, believe me, Very sincerely yours,

Jesse Isidor Straus

[PSF:France:TS]

[1] Leo John Keena was appointed minister to Honduras on Feb. 22, 1935.
[2] See Roosevelt to Hull, April 26, and to Straus, May 9, 1935, below.

Press Conference, Executive Offices of the White House, April 10, 1935, 10:40 A.M.

[*Excerpt*] Q: Can you tell us whether the Treasury will raise its price for silver if the world price goes up above that being paid by the Treasury?

The President: I guess I had better not. I guess you had better ask Henry Morgenthau.

Q: He won't say anything.

The President: I will give you a tip on it. If the price of silver in Montreal, or London, or the New York market goes above $64\frac{1}{2}$ cents, the people who mine the silver will get more than $64\frac{1}{2}$ cents. It does not make much difference whom they sell to. It is the point of view of the silver miner . . .

Q: In view of the critical nature of the European political situation at the present time, do you think the best policy of the United States is to remain on the sidelines?

The President: How old is that? I think you will have to do your own deducing from things happening from day to day . . .

Q: Has Hull discussed with you the neutrality program he has been working on?

The President: Not yet. We are going to talk about it today. He is coming in at three o'clock.

[President's Press Conferences:T]

Roosevelt to Nicholas Murray Butler, Director, Carnegie Endowment for International Peace, New York City

[Washington] April 10, 1935

My dear Dr. Butler: I have been much interested in reading the pamphlet which you were good enough to send me with your note of April third,[1] and want you to know how deeply I appreciate your thoughtfulness.

With kind regards, Very sincerely yours,

[PPF 4826:T]

[1] The pamphlet, *International Conference Held at Chatham House, London, March 5–7, 1935 on Steps to be Taken to Restore Confidence by Promotion of Trade and Reduction of Unemployment* . . . (New York: Carnegie Endowment for International Peace [1935]), contained the recommendations of the Conference and a list of the members. Butler asked Roosevelt to give the recommendations his "earnest personal attention," and added: "The members of the conference had no official responsibility of any kind, and their impressive action represents their own untrammeled and uninstructed sense of what the world needs if recovery is to be hastened in all lands or in any land" (PPF 4826).

James M. Baker, Minister to Siam, to Roosevelt

Bangkok, April 10, 1935

My dear Mr. President: Your letter of January 16th conveying to me Mr. Stevens' commendation of my work in Siam, pleases me very much and I thank you for the same.[1]

Mr. Stevens' resignation here was much regretted by his numerous friends and especially by me. The King conferred upon him the Highest Order of the White Elephant for his distinguished services as Adviser of the Siamese Government. I hope his cruise home and a complete rest for several months will enable him to accept an appointment from you as he is an ardent supporter of yours and your policies.

The abdication of King Prajadhipok became effective March 2nd. The Premier who has complete control of the Assembly, through the State Council, has created a compromise Regency and succeeded in keeping peace and order in Siam. Some of the influential supporters of the King have been retained in their official positions, thus strengthening the forces of the present government. The new government has an ambitious program involving highway construction and better schools, and have increased their budget accordingly. The economic depression here has been severe and the improvement necessarily must be slow.

A word as to Japan. She is alert and engaged in a publicity program extending throughout the Far East. She is making great efforts to extend her trade in Siam, Burmah, the Dutch East Indies and the Philippines. I am glad to see in the press that our Asiatic Fleet is making a friendly visit to Japan.

Again thanking you for your letter and with assurances of my highest regards, believe me to be

Very sincerely yours,

James M. Baker

[PSF:State:TS]

[1] Above.

Cordell Hull, Secretary of State, to Roosevelt

[Washington, April 11, 1935][1]

Memorandum: Cooperation with the Nye Committee. It is my understanding that in your conference with the Nye Committee there was some reference to a further conference between you and the Committee on your return to Washington.[2] I am informed that the Committee will request another conference in the near future. In view of the importance of the questions involved, I respectfully suggest that you may wish to give consideration to the following observations.

There are four phases of the activities of the Nye Committee to which I invite your attention—Neutrality, Taking the Profits Out of War, Control of the Arms Traffic, and the Investigation of Loans Made by the Allied Powers through American Banks in the Period 1914–17.

Neutrality. The Nye Committee had not, before their recent conference with you, contemplated the introduction of legislation modifying our neutrality policy. Something which was said in that conference was interpreted by some of the members of the Committee as a desire on your part that the Committee study that problem and, after a further conference with you, introduce appropriate legislation. In statements given to the press by Senator Nye, the impression was given that at your request the Committee was turning aside from other problems which it had in hand to expedite the preparation of draft legislation on neutrality.[3] A few days later, statements were published to the effect that the Committee was in practical agreement on the type of legislation which should be introduced. Thereupon Senator Pittman called me by telephone and protested in his own name and in that of Senator Borah against what was construed as an attempt of the Executive to charge the Nye Committee with the preparation of legislation on a subject which, under the rules of the Senate, and according to precedent, properly fell within the jurisdiction of the Committee on Foreign Relations. I brought Senator Pittman's observation to the attention of members of the Nye Committee and I am informed that the Committee thereupon decided not to go forward with the preparation of legislation on all phases of our neutrality policy. However, the report which the Committee made to the Senate on April 1 contains the following Article:

IV. The Committee is in substantial agreement on a principle to govern the export of munitions and contraband in case of a major war, and expects to make certain recommendations to the Senate on this subject in the immediate future and for action in the present session of Congress. This is the only phase of the neutrality problem which the Committee considers to be within its jurisdiction.[4]

This phase of the neutrality problem is sufficiently broad to cover most of the important of the questions [*sic*] with which neutrality legislation would be likely to deal. It is my understanding that the Committee at its conference with you will probably present a draft of legislation on this subject, for your approval.

You may wish to refrain from committing yourself to the support of any specific legislation in respect to neutrality at this time. There is apparently great diversity of opinion among your closest advisers as to the proper method of dealing with this subject and certainly great diversity of public opinion. I am informed that the leaders in the Senate are opposed to the raising of any question of foreign policy which would result in acrimonious discussion and in delaying action on necessary domestic legislation. Furthermore, it is contended that in view of the present situation in Europe, discussion of this question at this time would tend to arouse unjustifiable fears of imminent war. The subject is so complicated in respect to domestic law, international law and questions of policy that you may deem it unwise for the Administration to commit itself to the support of any specific program of legislation until the subject has been further studied and until a program can be drawn up on which your advisers are in substantial agreement.

A Committee of the Department has been studying this problem for some time and I am prepared to submit to you, if you so desire, a draft of possible legislative provisions. This draft may be of assistance to you in considering this subject although I am not prepared to advocate this or any other specific program for legislation on this subject at this time.

Legislation to Take the Profits Out of War. I have been informed that from something said in your conference with the Nye Committee, members of the Committee have inferred that you approved the draft of the bill to take the profits out of war which the Committee was then considering. The report which the Committee made to the Senate on April 1, contains the following articles:

II. The Committee is in substantial agreement on a very thorough plan to take the profits out of war and to equalize the economic burden of war, and expects to report on this subject to the Senate legislation on the matter in the immediate future, and for action in the present session of Congress. This relates to the actual period of war only. The presentation of this report and the legislation covers one of the three major obligations imposed upon the Committee.

III. The Committee is emphatically convinced that no bill which contains only general authorizations to the President to fix prices or to commandeer industry or to arrange for priorities and licensing is at all adequate "to equalize the burdens and take the profits out of war."

Article III refers to the McSwain Bill which, in amended form, passed the House on April 9.[5]

There are attached hereto a digest of the Committee's bill and a copy of the text.[6]

The Senate, in setting up the Nye Committee, charged it, among other things, "to review the findings of the War Policies Commission and to recommend . . . specific legislation." The attached bill constitutes the "specific legislation" which the Committee was charged to prepare.

Taking the profits out of war is a difficult thing to accomplish as past experience has demonstrated. It may be doubted whether any means can be found to accomplish it to the extent to which some proponents of the idea appear to believe possible. You may regard it as wise to refrain from committing yourself to support any specific legislation on this subject, until a great deal of further careful study has enabled the Administration to formulate some definite program for dealing with this complicated matter. An attitude of complete neutrality on the part of the Administration may perhaps be particularly desirable at this time when there is so much controversy in Congress between the proponents of rival bills.

Control of the Arms Traffic. Two principal methods have been suggested for dealing with the evils of the international traffic in arms.

The suggestion has been made in various quarters that a Government monopoly of the manufacture of and trade in arms and implements of war is the best method of dealing with the evils which have arisen from the present lack of Governmental supervision and control in that field. From various public statements made by Senator Nye, it would appear that this is the solution which he favors. The Committee has not, however, committed itself to this program and there appears to be reason to hope that it may be willing to support a program in accord with the policy of the Administration. In your discussion with Mr. Phillips and Mr. Green of our telegram of May 28, 1934, to Norman Davis, you decided, wisely I believe, that although the elimination of all private manufacture of arms and munitions might be admirable as an ultimate objective, it is not feasible at this time.[7]

Since the negotiations of the Arms Traffic Convention of 1925, this Government has consistently followed the policy of attempting to establish, by international agreement, a system of supervision and control of the international traffic in arms based upon export and import licenses and full publicity. Under your administration, we have proceeded one step further and have attempted to establish by international agreement a similar system of licenses and publicity for the manufacture of arms.

Although this Government has been foremost during the last two years in efforts to obtain an international agreement along the lines I have indicated, we have lagged behind almost all the other civilized nations of the world in our domestic legislation. The Nye Committee asked Mr. Green of the Department to prepare a draft of legislation following the principles embodied in the Draft Articles now under discussion in Geneva, insofar as they could be put into effect by constitutional legislation in advance of the Convention. Mr. Green was authorized by me to comply with the Committee's request and he has submitted a draft of legislation to the Committee. I attach a copy of this draft legislation. Two Articles—5a and 5b—were submitted separately because they embody the principle of the Arms Embargo Resolution, which encountered opposition in the Senate. Should the Committee decide to present this legislation, it might wish to omit these articles, in order to avoid the controversy which arose when the Arms Embargo Resolution was under discussion. Should the Committee decide otherwise, these Articles could be incorporated in the draft legislation. I believe that this draft legislation embodies the wisest and most practical method of dealing with the evils inherent in the manufacture of and traffic in arms.

The Committee has apparently in recent weeks been diverted from its original interest in the supervision of the arms traffic by its interest in neutrality legislation and legislation designed to take the profits out of war. I believe a word from you in support of this draft legislation might serve to concentrate the efforts of the Committee on this subject and to accomplish some tangible result. I suggest, therefore, that you tell the Committee that you have been informed that Mr. Green has, at the Committee's request, presented a draft of legislation to establish some measure of supervision and control of the manufacture of and traffic in arms; that you understand that the Committee now has this legislation under consideration; that this legislation is based upon the same principles as the Draft Articles which are now under discussion in Geneva; that you hope that the Committee may decide to report favorably on legislation of this type; and that if so you are prepared to give the Committee the backing of the Administration in this matter and, if circumstances appear to warrant it, to send an appropriate Message to Congress.

Investigation of Loans Made by the Allied Powers Through American Banks 1914-17. The Committee, in connection with its study of methods to take the profits out of war, is proceeding with the examination of documents in the files of the Guaranty Trust Company of New York pertaining to the dealings between that Bank and the British Government in 1916 and with documents from the files of the Central Hanover Bank of New York in regard to the French loan of April 1, 1917, made by the Central Union Trust Company of New York, predecessor of the Central Hanover Bank. The Committee is proposing to examine several thousand documents in the files of J. P. Morgan and Company, relating to the dealings between the British Government and that Bank in 1914–17. The British and French Ambassadors, acting under instructions of their Governments, have protested against this procedure. Mr. John W. Davis, acting as counsel for two of the Banks, has drawn up a brief, questioning the legal right of the Committee to examine the documents in question. My legal advisers do not believe that the legal arguments of the British and French Governments and of Mr. Davis are well founded. Nevertheless, as there is a question of international comity involved, I approached the Chairman of the Committee and suggested that he refrain from this phase of its proposed investigation. This suggestion was not agreeable to Senator Nye. He agreed, however, that none of the documents in question, the publicity of which might result in embarrassment to the British and French Governments, would be published until they had been referred to me and I had had an opportunity to consult the interested Ambassador in order to ascertain the attitude of his Government. This agreement did not satisfy the Ambassadors who, acting under instructions, object on principle to any examination of the documents by the Committee whether their contents are made public or not.

Waiving the question of the legal right of the Committee in the premises, I recommend that in your conference with the Committee, you urge that it do not proceed with the examination of these documents. The proposed action of the Committee would result in irritating the British and French Governments and it is difficult to conceive that any useful purpose could be served by a study of these documents. It can scarcely be maintained with reason that such a study is a necessary preliminary to the study of legislation for taking profits out of war particularly as the Committee has already prepared its Bill on that subject.

Cordell Hull

Enclosures: 1. The Nye Committee report to the Senate of April 1, 1935.[8]

2. Digest of the Committee's Bill to take the profits out of war.[9]

3. Copy of the Committee's Bill to take the profits out of war.[10]

4. Draft Bill to Control the trade in arms and implements of war prepared in the Department of State.[11]

[PSF:Neutrality:TS]

[1] Date derived from Hull, *Memoirs*, I, 403.

[2] The Nye Munitions Investigating Committee met with Roosevelt on March 19. On March 25 he left Washington for Florida for a cruise on Vincent Astor's yacht *Nourmahal*. He was back in Washington on April 9.

[3] Hull apparently refers to Nye's speech of March 30, 1935, in which he said that the President had suggested that the Nye Committee study the neutrality question and that the committee would make some recommendations soon (New York *Times*, March 31, 1935, p. 26).

[4] This preliminary report is printed in the *Congressional Record*, vol. 79, pp. 4726–4727.

[5] Rep. John J. McSwain introduced H.R. 5529, "To prevent profiteering in time of war and to equalize the burden of war and thus provide for the national defense and promote peace," on Feb. 7, 1935. It was extensively debated, and amended March 27 and April 8; chief objections to it were that it froze prices and wages but made no mention of taxation of excess profits. It was passed April 9 and sent to the Senate where it was referred to the Senate Committee on Foreign Affairs; no further action was taken (*Cong. Rec.*, vol. 79, pp. 4570–4572, 5034–5076, 5152–5155, 5155–5173, 5178–5200, 5245–5246, 5324–5328, 5446).

6 "U.S. Senate Special Committee on Munitions. Summary of Emergency War Time Act," a mimeographed press release issued April 3, 1935. (This and the other enclosures mentioned are present.)

7 According to the White House appointments list Under Secretary of State Phillips talked with Roosevelt on March 21, 1935. Joseph C. Green was in the Division of Western European Affairs of the State Department. Hull's telegram to Davis is printed in *Foreign Relations, 1934*, I, 75; in this he commented on three methods of international control of arms proposed to him by Davis in a telegram of May 27, 1934 (*ibid.*, pp. 73–74).

8 This mimeographed document is entitled simply "Report, April 1, 1935." It begins: "The United States Senate Special Committee Investigating the Munitions Industry, pursuant to Senate Resolution No. 8 (Seventy-fourth Congress, First Session), wishes to make the following preliminary report: . . ."

9 Cited above.

10 "A Bill to provide revenue and facilitate the regulation and control of the economic and industrial structure of the Nation for the successful prosecution of war, and for other purposes," a committee print dated April 2, 1935.

11 A typed copy.

Press Conference, Executive Offices of the White House, April 12, 1935, 4:20 P.M.

[*Excerpt*] Q: Anything on the Governors' Conference today?

The President: We talked about cotton inside and out. I had some figures for them and they are now all in the Cabinet Room, continuing the talk. It is a very difficult problem, one that I have been more or less familiar with ever since I was a small boy, having spent many months of the year around New Bedford, Massachusetts, and being related to half of the people who own cotton mills in New Bedford. I do know something about it. There is one thing I told the Governors and representatives and that is something that is worth publishing. There has been a great deal of—I don't like the word "propaganda," but there have been a great many statements made and figures given out in regard to Japanese competition. For instance, we have had appeals from many chambers of commerce stating that this year, on the basis of present imports, we will import into this country twenty-four million yards of Japanese cloth. Now, when you come down to actual brass tacks, in other words, actual imports, you find a very different story. The figures show that while the imports of Japanese cotton textiles have gone up very much beginning last December—in the Summer they rose from an average previous part of the year five hundred thousand yards a month, they rose to two million two hundred thousand yards; they went up four times in January, they went up to three million three hundred thousand yards and in February to four million eight hundred thousand yards. Now, on the assumption that during the balance of 1935 we continue to import Japanese textiles at the rate of January and February of this year, it will mean an importation of approximately forty-nine million yards. That sounds like an awful lot of cotton. Based on American production for the year 1933, which is about the same as 1934 and 1935, as far as we can guess, that total Japanese importation this year would be seven-tenths of one per cent—seven-tenths of one per cent of the American production.

In other words, all of these increased imports in the last two months, if carried on through the year, will be less than one per cent of American production. That is just for the record, because that is based in part on the only definite figures we have and in part on estimates for the future. We are merely assuming that the Japanese imports will continue at the same rate.[1]

Now, if they should go up very, very materially, that would be a different thing and we would have to cross that bridge when we come to it. Then there are a great many other phases, the difference between the North and South, the newer machinery they have in the South, and we talked about other countries like Brazil who are putting up cotton mills of their own. They are still engaged in discussing all those things in the Cabinet Room.

[President's Press Conferences:T]

[1] Roosevelt's information on cotton importations was apparently derived from a memorandum addressed to him from Assistant Secretary of Commerce John Dickinson, April 12, 1935 (OF 258); it is possible that he had the memorandum before him at the press conference.

Roosevelt to Cordell Hull, Secretary of State

Washington, April 12, 1935

Memorandum for the Secretary of State: If no special Ambassadors are appointed by other countries for King George's Jubilee Ceremonies, we should appoint none either. If we do decide to appoint one, I think that it will be best from every point of view to appoint Bingham.

F.D.R.

[*Notation*:T] Letter from Ambassador Bingham to the President advising that from what he can learn there is no intention on the part of foreign countries to send special representatives to the Jubilee Ceremonies.[1]

[OF 48:CT]

[1] Not present.

William C. Bullitt, Ambassador to the Union of Soviet Socialist Republics, to Roosevelt

On train enroute to Moscow from Warsaw, April 12, 1935

Personal and Confidential

Dear Mr. President: John Cudahy, with whom I have spent the past twenty-four hours in Warsaw, astonished me this morning by saying that he had only one wish in life: to be appointed Minister to Ireland. He is anxious to get out of Poland as he has had more than enough of the physical disorder of Eastern Europe. It occured to me at once that this wish of Cudahy's might be the key to a happy solution of your diplomatic appointment problems.

As the appointment of Tony Biddle to Dublin has not been announced, I assume that the difficulty of obtaining the agrément of the Irish Government to the appointment of a divorced and remarried man proved to be insuperable. I don't want to do anything to stop Tony getting the job and I write you this about Cudahy on the assumption that Dublin for Tony has proved to be impossible.

In my opinion Cudahy would make an admirable Minister to Dublin. He loves to hunt and is a very attractive fellow of the type that the Irish like and his private life is as blameless as the Pope himself could desire. I don't know what you are thinking about doing with Tony Biddle but in the shuffle that would be produced by Cudahy's moving out of Poland you ought to be able to find a satisfactory post for Tony. The man you send to Warsaw must know French and, if possible, should know German and, if you want to get any information from Warsaw, should also be very much of a gentleman and acutely intelligent.

I had a long talk in Berlin night before last with Lipsky, the Polish Ambassador, and one last night with the Under Secretary of Foreign Affairs in Warsaw. I am convinced not only from these conversations but from every other piece of evidence I have been able to get in Paris and elsewhere that there is no secret agreement or alliance between the

Poles and the Germans, and that the basis of Polish policy is and will remain refusal to make any agreement permitting either German or Russian forces to set foot on Polish soil under any circumstances. It is not, however, impossible that Poland might come into some general agreement to withold aid from an aggressor. In Poland the hatred of Russia and fear of the ultimate power of Russia, is greater than the fear and hatred of Germany. The Poles are convinced that so long as Hitler is in power the German drive will be toward annexing to Germany those portions of Europe which are inhabited predominantly by Germans and not toward the acquisition of any Slav territory. That is to say, the Poles expect the German advance to be toward Austria and Bohemia. If the German drive on those territories should result in war, Poland would attempt to stand aside until it could safely rush to the rescue of the victor.

I think I wrote you from Paris that Titulescu claimed that Beck had told him that there was an understanding between Poland and Hungary with regard to Czechoslovakia—to the effect that Poland would not assist Czechoslovakia in case of an Hungarian attack.

I see nothing in Polish policy which requires any more explanation than the above.

Cudahy has traveled from one end of Poland to the other and is very pessimistic about Poland's future. He insists that the Polish oil fields in Galicia will be exhausted in ten years at the present rate of production and foresees complete collapse at the time of the elimination of this resource. He also insists that the Polish Army is extremely deficient in all forms of motorized material and in guns of the larger calibers.

Litvinov passed through Warsaw without stopping last night on his way to Geneva so that I missed him entirely and shall probably have little news to cable you until he returns to Moscow.[1]

If Tony Biddle is out, I hope you will be able to send Cudahy to Dublin. He is exceptionally well-fitted for the post and would be deeply grateful. When he told me that he wanted Dublin, I said that before taking up the matter I should like to know absolutely definitely that there would be no question of his rejecting the post if it should be offered. He replied, "You let the President know that I would almost jump out of my skin with joy if I should get a telegram transferring me from Warsaw to Dublin. I don't even need to be asked."[2]

Good luck and love to you all.

Yours permanently,

Bullitt

[PSF:Russia:TS]

---

[1] In Roosevelt's brief reply of April 26, 1935, he said, "What a shame that you missed Litvinov in Warsaw and could not travel with him in his compartment to Moscow!" (*Personal Letters, 1928–1945*, I, 477).

[2] Biddle was named minister to Norway in July 1935. Cudahy remained as minister to Poland until 1937 when he was appointed minister to the Irish Free State. Alvin M. Owsley, former minister to Rumania, was appointed minister to the Irish Free State in May 1935.

William Phillips, Under Secretary of State, to Marvin H. McIntyre, Assistant Secretary to the President

[Washington] April 13, 1935

My dear Mr. McIntyre: It is anticipated that the Economic Committee of the League of Nations, at its next session to convene at Geneva in April 29, 1935, will make provision for the appointment of a committee of experts giving it broad powers to examine into the possibility of international action to secure greater freedom in the international trade in meat and meat preparations, particularly as regards sanitary regulations, the object being to abolish such regulations and restrictions as are not necessary to safeguard health in the importing countries. Such action by the Economic Committee would be in accordance with a resolution adopted at the International Monetary and Economic Conference, held recently at London.

From information reaching the Department from the American Consulate at Geneva, it is understood that, if this Government is interested in having an American named to this committee of experts, such appointment could without doubt be arranged. The experts appointed, it should be said, will be appointed in their individual capacities and such expenses as they would incur in connection with their appointments would be paid by the League.

The Department of Agriculture, consulted in the matter, has indicated that it would be pleased to see an American appointed to this committee and has suggested as a suitable person for such appointment, Mr. Timothy P. White, representative of the Bureau of Animal Industry in London.

I should appreciate learning as soon as may be possible whether the action proposed would meet with the President's approval.

Sincerely yours, For the Secretary of State,

William Phillips

[OF 184:CT]

Roosevelt to Cordell Hull, Secretary of State

Washington, April 15, 1935

Memorandum for the Secretary of State: What would be the effect of this?[1] Is it perhaps going too far towards official membership in a direct official Committee of the League itself?

F.D.R.

[OF 184:CT]

[1] Above.

Roosevelt to Senator Key Pittman of Nevada

[Washington, April 15, 1935]

Dear Key: I appreciate having the comments and suggestions in your letter of April 10 which I have passed along to Secretary Morgenthau.[1] I was also gratified to read what you said on the floor of the Senate about your satisfaction with the way in which the Treasury Department was carrying out the policy lying back of the London Agreement and the Silver Purchase Act.[2]

Sincerely,

[OF 229:CT]

[1] Pittman noted (OF 229) that the world price of silver was over 65 cents an ounce and listed the factors that led him to believe it would continue until the price reached $1.29 an ounce. He referred to the fact that the government retained half of the bullion offered for coinage as seigniorage and said that this was accepted in good spirit by most of the producers as fair treatment, although many "did not understand why the Government should make a profit off of any producers of any commodity in the United States." Pittman urged that the silver producer now be allowed 75 per cent, with the government retaining only 25 per cent.

[2] On April 11 (*Cong. Rec.*, vol. 79, p. 5403); the views expressed were essentially those of his letter of April 10, cited above. By proclamation 2125, April 24, 1935, the price offered by the government for domestically mined bullion was increased to $1.29 per ounce and the seigniorage reduced to 45 per cent (49 *Stat.* 3445).

Roosevelt to Senator James E. Murray of Montana

[Washington, April 16, 1935]

Dear Senator Murray: Although the proclamation of the Brazilian Agreement is still subject to delay and I am not prepared to state what action will be taken with respect to generalizing the rates reduced under it, I should no longer delay answering the letter you addressed to me March 20 as Chairman, Special Manganese Committee.[1]

The questions raised regarding the extension to other countries of tariff reductions granted in trade agreements have been very carefully considered and the controlling general principles have been set forth in connection with the proclamation of the Trade Agreement with the Belgo-Luxemburg Economic Union April 1.

You asked that the reduced duty provided for under the Brazilian Trade Agreement be withheld from other manganese ore producing countries and that the tonnage of manganese ore to be imported from Brazil be limited by a quota.

The Trade Agreements Act provides that duties proclaimed under it shall apply to articles the produce of all foreign countries, subject, however, to the proviso "That the President may suspend the application to articles the growth, produce, or manufacture of any country because of its discriminatory treatment of American commerce or because of other acts or policies which, in his opinion, tend to defeat the purposes set forth in this Section." Under these legal provisions, the question of generalization of duty reductions to other countries has to be determined by consideration of the treatment which other countries give our trade. Suspension of the application of the reduced duties to the products of any country can be based only on the grounds stated in the proviso.

As to your suggestion regarding an import quota, our trade agreements contain clauses reserving for both countries the possibility of imposing even on articles on which they make tariff reductions, such restrictions as may be necessary in connection with measures for the control of production, market supply, or prices of domestic articles. Of course, however, these reserved rights which might nullify tariff reductions, can be exercised only under specified conditions. They could not be used to discriminate against any country. As an assurance against discrimination the agreements will provide that quotas shall allot to any foreign country a share of imports equivalent to the proportion which that foreign country supplied during a previous representative period.

Under the circumstances affecting manganese ore, I do not see that the suggestion of imposing quota limitations on imports of manganese ore could reasonably be raised with the Brazilian Government. As to the application of Section 3 (e) of the National Industrial Recovery Act, imports of manganese ore, as you know, have regularly supplied 90 percent in value of American consumption.[2]

Sincerely yours,

[*Notation*:T] 4-16-35
[OF 948:CT]

[1] Above.
[2] Drafted by Frederick Livesey, assistant economic adviser to the State Department.

Cordell Hull, Secretary of State, to Roosevelt

[Washington] April 16, 1935

My dear Mr. President: I request your consideration of a recommendation that the Department inform Mr. Trippe,[1] president of Pan American Airways, that the Government desires that invitation be extended to the Japanese to use, for the southern terminal of a line, if the Japanese should wish to establish such, between Japan and a point on the Pan American Airways trans-Pacific line, the facilities which Pan American Airways will establish at Guam.

The origin of this recommendation and pertinent facts and considerations which have led to its being submitted are set forth in the memoranda here attached—from which you will note that both Mr. Trippe and the Navy Department are favorably disposed.

I believe you will share my view that the course suggested would serve a number of useful purposes in connection with our Far Eastern relations. I should be glad to have your approval of it or your comments at your early convenience.[2]

Faithfully yours,

Cordell Hull

[OF 249:CT]

[1] Juan T. Trippe.
[2] Roosevelt returned the memorandum to Hull with a note of April 17: "I think this is a good suggestion and I approve it" (OF 249).

483

Ray Newton, Emily Cooper Johnson, and Grover Clark to Roosevelt

Washington, D.C., April 18, 1935

Dear Mr. President: Following our conversation regarding the Far Eastern situation[1] we would leave the following memorandum:

1. The outstanding danger in the Far East is not what the present Military Government of Japan may do. It is that the Chinese and the other Asiatic peoples, including the Japanese, may become finally convinced that they must develop powerful armed forces as the sole means of securing international respect and fair dealing.

a. The history of Western relations with the East, and of Japan's rise to prominence in world affairs in proportion to the growth of her armed force, has created the presumption throughout Asia that fighting power is the only final national safeguard and foundation of respect.

b. The Chinese, and also the Japanese people, have been watching to see whether the Western nations really were prepared to outlaw war, to insist that peaceful means alone be used in settling international disputes, and to uphold treaty pledges.

c. The United States and the European powers have failed to do anything effective to check Japan's flat violations of Treaty obligations in these last three and a half years. They also have continued to deal with the present Militaristic Government of Japan as though it had remained in complete fulfillment of its treaty pledges.

d. This has gone far to convince the Chinese and the other Asiatic peoples that the world still is fundamentally militaristic. China is militarizing, and the Japanese civilians are giving up opposition to their militarized Government. The inevitable end of this process is a completely disastrous War between East and West.

e. In these circumstances, it is absolutely essential that effective action be taken to maintain the principles that Treaty obligations must be kept, and that force is not to be used as an instrument of national policy.

f. The United States has been the leader in the move looking toward the settlement of disputes by peaceful means or the respect for a nation's rights without reference to the size of that nation's fighting forces. This is particularly so in relation to the Far East, through the Washington Conference Treaties. It is appropriate, therefore, that the United States should take the lead in the move toward reasserting sanctity of treaty obligations. There is practically no doubt that the British Nations would fall in with any move which the United States might make in this direction.

2. The following are suggested as specific steps to be taken in dealing with the Far Eastern Situation.

a. The United States should call a conference of the Signers of the Nine Power Treaty to consider the present situation in the Far East, with a view to adopting such measures as will insure the maintenance of International Treaty obligations and respect for National rights.

(1) An International conference on Naval limitation is scheduled to be held in the near future. The proposed conference on the Far Eastern situation might be held in conjunction with this naval conference, like the Washington Conference of 1921–22, or it might meet separately.

b. The United States should stand firmly on the doctrine of non-recognition of rights or interests secured by means which violate treaty obligations.

c. When the question of the administration of Manchuria comes up, as it must if Japan is held to her treaty obligations, the proposal should be made that this administration be put under an international commission, preferably with American participation, which would have control for a reasonably long period, after which a plebiscite would be taken.

(1) The handling of the Saar Basin furnishes a precedent for such action.

(2) Japan has said she was in Manchuria only to restore order. This would give her an opportunity to withdraw gracefully.

3. In case it becomes necessary or desirable to put pressure on the Japanese Government, the most effective and most humane method would be through the cessation of trade relations with that country rather than through the display or use of armed force.

a. Because of Japan's very great dependence on foreign markets and raw materials, particularly on those of the United States, a cessation of trade would be completely effective as a means of putting such pressure on the present militaristic Japanese Government as might seem necessary.

b. Such measures would be used in case of war. They could be applied in advance of war. If they were, or even if they were seriously threatened, in all probability War would not come.

c. The use of such means would cause losses to American producers and traders. These losses should be met out of the National Treasury, just as the costs of the Army and Navy are so met, if cessation of trade relations were used as a national measure.

Yours respectfully,

Ray Newton
Emily Cooper Johnson
Grover Clark[2]

[OF 66:TS]

[1] From 11:30 A.M. to 12:15 P.M. on April 18, at the White House.
[2] The signers were a committee of the Society of Friends. Clark had been a teacher and newspaper editor and correspondent in China and was at this time visiting professor in modern history at Wellesley.

Breckinridge Long, Ambassador to Italy, to Roosevelt

Rome, April 19, 1935

My dear Chief: The Stresa Conference has cleared up the situation to a considerable extent. Prior to that there was a great deal of anxiety. I think it was more intense in Italy than in any of the other European countries as far as I can judge. Here there was every indication of preparation for and expectancy of military activities. The authorities at Rome even were preparing the civilian population for airplane activities and getting them accustomed to such activity by keeping continually in the air all day and well into the night airplanes which flew low over the city. This went on for about ten days. In Milan and Naples they held gas attack drills, and in every possible way the Administration brought to the attention of the people the possibility of impending military activities.

That has all changed since the Stresa Conference adjourned and not a single airplane has appeared in the sky. Everything has quieted down, and the whole tempo has been altered.

I am sending by this pouch a despatch of comment. It is my No. 1053, and consists of an analysis of the agreements reached at Stresa.[1] There is also another one going, giving a history of it, but that is all history and just for record purposes.[2]

As I see it, they have put a military ring around Germany. In my last conversation with Suvich he indicated the policy of his Government for the present and the future by saying that Germany would not listen to reason and had to be met by a manifestation of force. Suvich is convinced that Germany has been stopped and bottled up and her aggressive disease cured. I am sorry that I do not share that belief. You think I am a pessimist. As a matter of fact I am a realist. I see the situation in Europe as it exists. They are all prepared for war, and they have got to have it. War is the only cure for the malady with which Europe is affected. There are three and a half million men under arms here today. The Assistant Military Attaché has just returned from Milan on a tour of inspection. He was allowed to inspect very little. The factories were closed to him. However, he discovered that the airplane factories were being enlarged so that their production would be ten planes a day instead of one. The automobile manufacturers are engaged in turning out machine guns. The whole manufacturing show is working day and night making military equipment and supplies. The national hatreds, jealousies, ambitions, and their racial, religious, and language differences, with the superstructure now of trade barriers, have got Europe cut up to such an extent that there is no way for them to stay together. Once the psychology of this moment has passed they will revert to the same situation as existed a few months ago, and it will gradually work up again to another high pitch.

Germany is not going to change her characteristics or her nature. She is not going to throw her ambitions to the winds. The ring which has now been put around her will yield in spots in the east and southeast to German diplomacy and will weaken under the strain of fear of Germany, which will lead them to accept something of German leadership rather than French leadership. The French domination is of military and political alliances. The German infusion is of blood and race. It runs all through Poland, Czechoslovakia, Hungary, Jugoslavia, and Austria.

The only cure for it is a war, from which there will emerge a real victor. There are only two Governments in Europe capable of being a real victor. One is Germany, and the other is Russia. I doubt if Russian education and technique is sufficient to establish itself in a dominant position throughout western and central Europe. I believe the German technique, determination, and character is such that it can. I shudder to think of a Russian domination of Europe. While a German domin-ation would be hard and cruel—at least in the beginning—it would be an intensification of a culture which is more akin to ours than would be that of Russia. Further than that, if Germany should be dominant throughout the greater part of Europe, she would act as a bulwark against the westward progress of Russia, and that Government would be confined to Russia and Siberia and would not have its strength tapped in the European struggle and would be a stronger resistance against Japan. With a Russia successful in Europe and spreading westward, her attention would be taken from Japan, and that country would be even more arrogant in the Far East.

Nevertheless, Stresa has calmed the waters for the time being and postponed the evil day.

Incidentally, the Assistant Military Attaché here has been ordered home.[3] His relief will soon arrive, but the new man will not have contacts and will not speak the language. I am writing Bill Phillips and asking if they can possibly postpone Brady's departure for four or five months so that he can break in this new man. I think it almost necessary to have a flying officer here who is actually in touch with the men from whom he can get information, and a new man cannot do it within the space of, conservatively speaking, six months. For the good of the Government's information here I think it ought to be done if it is possible under the War Department regulations, and both Brady and his chief, the Military Attaché, are agreeable.

I am expecting to leave here the latter part of June to pay a visit to Dr. Cary Grayson and will hope to see you the first part of July— provided they don't get near the boiling point here before that.[4]

Affectionately and Respectfully,

Breckinridge Long

[PSF:Italy:TS]

[1] Not present; printed, *Foreign Relations, 1935,* I, 260–265.
[2] Not present.
[3] Capt. Francis M. Brady.
[4] Answered May 8, 1935, below.

Edward M. House to Roosevelt

New York, April 20, 1935

Dear Governor: Your letter of April tenth has given me much food for thought. You make a suggestion that seems practicable.[1]

If the European Powers opposed to Germany could know that you would recognize a blockade, provided it was effective, it would strengthen their purpose to do it. The American people would approve of such action on your part in the event it did not commit us to war. Germany might not submit to such a blockade without retaliation in the form of air raids. If she took such action, war would result.

Such a war need not involve us. You might warn American citizens and shipping to keep out of the war zone. This, in effect, would make the blockading of Germany more complete and strengthen the hands of her enemies.

War is much more probable at present than it has been for several years because of the feeling that Germany intends to re-arm and place herself in a position to become formidable.

Great Britain does not want war, and I doubt if they would send a single soldier to the Continent. Probably they would confine themselves to the air and sea. Canadians with whom I have talked tell me that they and the other Dominions feel the same way. Of course, you know how overwhelmingly the sentiment in this country would be against our participation in another European conflict. However, the press and those Americans now most vociferous against it would be violently in favor of protecting American citizens and property on the high seas.

The nervous tension in Europe has grown perceptibly within the last few weeks, particularly in Poland and other states bordering on Germany. There is a feeling that unless Germany changes her policy, it would be better to have it out now.

One cannot understand the madness of Hitler in going to such extremes as to precipitate a war in which Germany would have such odds against her.

I am glad you are giving the matter such careful thought and I hope if you come to Hyde Park early in May that I may come up for lunch and discuss it with you.

Affectionately yours,

E. M. House

[PPF 222:TS]

[1] In this letter (*Personal Letters, 1928–1945,* I, 472–473), Roosevelt said that if France, Italy, England, and the "Little Entente" decided on positive action against Germany, it would be wiser for them to set up a blockade rather than to attempt invasion. The United States would have to recognize an effective blockade but sanctions could not be recognized without Congressional action.

Martin H. Carmody, Supreme Knight, Knights of Columbus, to Roosevelt

New Haven, Conn., April 22, 1935

Mr. President: The Supreme Board of Directors of the Knights of Columbus at a meeting held in the city of New York, January 12, addressed a resolution to the President of the United States, asking for an investigation of conditions in Mexico, and respectfully requested that Your Excellency receive a committee of that body to consider this subject.[1]

This resolution was referred to the Secretary of State, Mr. Cordell Hull, and the committee of the Supreme Board of Directors was requested to confer with him, which was done.

Since that time conditions in Mexico have grown steadily worse. Thousands of peaceable and defenseless men, women and children of that country are deprived of their personal and religious liberties and are subjected to most distressing indignities and persecutions because of their religious beliefs, yet no answer has been given to the petition of the Knights of Columbus.

Because of this, the Knights of Columbus respectfully renews its request for a conference with the President of the United States on this subject, and as the committee of the Supreme Board of Directors will meet in New York, April 27, it would be greatly appreciated if Your Excellency would receive the committee on April 29, or as soon thereafter as convenient.[2]

With sentiments of profound esteem, I am, Most respectfully yours,

Martin H. Carmody

[OF 28:TS]

[1] See Carmody to Roosevelt, Jan. 13, 1935, above.

[2] An undated reply to this letter, prepared for McIntyre's signature, was not sent (OF 28). The reply stated that the refusal to grant the request for an interview was no reflection on Carmody's organization but was "merely a matter of procedure." A succeeding letter from Carmody to Roosevelt, May 3, 1935 (OF 28), reviewing alleged religious persecutions in Mexico and again asking that the United States protest these persecutions, was referred to the State Department for preparation of reply. A reply was drafted by Assistant Secretary of State Moore but it was apparently not sent (Moore to McIntyre, May 11, 1935, OF 28). This draft reply noted that the State Department had received no complaint from any American citizen resident in Mexico of discrimination in the enforcement of the Mexican laws; there was therefore no ground for any interference with what was an internal matter. On June 23 Carmody wrote again (OF 28), protesting the fact that his organization had not been given an appointment at

the White House and the ignoring of his May 3 letter. An attached memorandum, Roosevelt to Hull, June 26, 1935, reads: "For preparation of reply for my signature as quickly as possible, as I think that speed is essential." The reply sent, July 3, 1935, is printed below.

Roosevelt to Cordell Hull, Secretary of State

Washington, April 23, 1935

Memorandum for the Secretary of State: What do the Swedes want reductions in, in their exports to us?[1]

F.D.R.

[PSF:State:CT]

[1] This note was in reply to Hull's memorandum of April 20, 1935 (PSF: State), asking the President to look over a list of about fifty tariff concessions proposed by the United States to Sweden and proposed by Sweden to the United States. Hull said he would like to review the proposals with Roosevelt so that the agreement could be carried forward before the Swedish parliament adjourned.

Roosevelt to Cordell Hull, Secretary of State

Washington, April 25, 1935

Memorandum for the Secretary of State: I believe it would be an excellent thing if Grenville Emmet could go out to the Dutch East Indies this summer. Let me know what you think about it.[1]

F.D.R.

[OF 858:CT]

[1] Emmet had asked for authorization to make this trip in his letter to Roosevelt of April 1, 1935 (PPF 372).

Roosevelt to Cordell Hull, Secretary of State

Washington, April 26, 1935

Confidential

Memorandum for the Secretary of State: Please, please what do you think I should write to this?[1] I suppose you had better not show this to anyone else. I fear our friend does not and probably cannot realize our objective.

F.D.R.

[PSF:France:TS]

[1] Straus to Roosevelt, April 9, 1935, above.

Cordell Hull, Secretary of State, to Roosevelt

Washington, April 30, 1935

My dear Mr. President: May I suggest that at your convenience you glance at the attached memorandum of a conversation which took place on April 25 between the Chinese Minister, Mr. Sao-Ke Alfred Sze, and myself, in regard to the effects on China of the silver policy of the United States.[1] I am also sending a copy of my memorandum to Mr. Morgenthau.

Faithfully yours,

Cordell Hull

[PSF:China:TS]

[1] Printed in *Foreign Relations, 1935,* III, 576. The minister expressed his government's concern over the effect of the increase of the Treasury's purchase price of silver bullion to $1.29 an ounce and its effect on China's economic and financial situation.

Henry M. Kannee, Assistant to Marvin H. McIntyre, to Roosevelt

Washington, 4/30—2:40 P [1935]

Said Sec. Phillips: "Tomorrow is Germany's national holiday and we have prepared the following message to Hitler:

'I desire to extend my greetings on this national holiday of the German Reich.'

"As you note, this is a cool telegram. Explain to the President that it is cool, and deliberately so. However, he might want to warm it up a bit; he may not want to send any, although it is customary to do so."

K

[*Notation*:AS] No message   FDR
[OF 198:T]

William C. Bullitt, Ambassador to the Union of Soviet Socialist Republics, to Roosevelt

Moscow, May 1, 1935

Personal and Confidential

Dear Mr. President: I have just come back from the May Day parade on the Red Square. It has been a great show with tanks galloping across at 60 miles per hour and new pursuit airplanes at 400 kilometers p.h. Stalin came late and left early due, I was told, to a last minute hitch in the negotiations with the French. It was also noticeable that when he walked the short space from the Kremlin wall to Lenin's tomb he held a handkerchief to his face. He may really, after all, be a bit frightened as indicated in the very confidential despatch I am sending by this pouch which I have asked the Secretary to send over to you.[1]

Physically, Moscow is a pleasanter place than this time last year. The subway has been completed. Blocks of old buildings have been turned into streets and squares, and the paving of the streets has been improved. Emotionally, however, Moscow is by no means so pleasant a place. The terror, always present, has risen to such a pitch that the least of the Muscovites, as well as the greatest, is in fear. Almost no one dares have any contact with foreigners and this is not unbased fear but a proper sense of reality. The chief engineer of the Amo works, now the largest producers of trucks in the world, has just spent eight months in jail because he ventured to call on the Latvian Minister, a very old friend of his. Every single acquaintance, even the most casual, of the Japanese language students in Leningrad, has been exiled. The only real friend of this Embassy, George Andreytchine, whom I asked you to pardon last year, is in the Lyublianka prison awaiting either death or exile. The only decent guide in the Soviet Union who took my cousin, Marshall, and his family around the country last year and is a thoroughly good friend of mine, has been exiled. Everyone who has had any contact with the Japanese Embassy, even down to the tailor, has been exiled. And the three not-too-awful dentists of the town suffered the same fate, leaving members of the American Embassy hanging on to temporary fillings!

It is extraordinarily difficult to preserve a sweet and loving exterior under the circumstances. I can, of course, do nothing to save anyone. In fact, strictly between ourselves, I got a message from Andreytchine, sent grapevine from the Ogpu Lyublianka prison, asking me for God's sake to do nothing to try to save him, if I should, he would certainly be shot.

The Russians still dare to come to my house for large entertainments when there can be no possibility of private conversation. There was a good turnout for the ball I gave on the 23rd of April. Litvinov came with his wife and eldest daughter. It was an astonishingly successful party, thoroughly dignified yet gay. Everyone happy and no one drunk. In fact, if I can believe the letter I got from the British Ambassadress and many verbal messages, it was the best party in Moscow since the revolution. We got a thousand tulips from Helsingfors and forced a lot of birch trees into premature leafage and arranged one end of the dining room as a collective farm with peasant accordion players, dancers, and all sorts of baby things, such as birds, goats, and a couple of infant bears about the size of cats. We also had pleasant lighting effects done by the best theater here and a bit of a cabaret. It was really great fun and the Turkish Ambassador and about twenty others remained until breakfast at eight.

I survived the night with the assistance of a few doses of strychnine, but with the exception of that evening I have been getting to bed at 7:30 P.M. I am all right for work beginning at 7 A.M. but have not yet sufficiently recovered from this bug to go out at all at night. I shall go right on with my regime of twelve hours in bed and plenty of exercise until I have fully recovered. There is nothing to worry about but it is a nuisance.

Do you remember our bet of one red apple or whatever (I have forgotten what) as to the scene of the first outbreak of war? You picked Europe and I picked the Far East. I am beginning to be inclined to think that you will probably turn out to be right as usual. The Austrian situation seems to contain all the elements of a major explosion while the Far Eastern situation is momentarily quiet. The long range outlook everywhere is about as bad as can be and the worst of it is that we can do nothing whatever to stop the march of events. The economic basis of Germany and Japan is such today that neither nation has any future, except a continuously diminishing standard of living, unless it can acquire new sources of raw materials and new markets. The Japanese line is obvious. My guess is that Hitler has decided that the German line of advance shall be down the Danube and not toward the Ukraine, although if he is blocked in his economic domination of Central Europe and the Balkans he will certainly try to turn toward the Ukraine.

I see no way that we can achieve anything by attempting to stop the march of events—horrible as it is—except our own involvement in war and I hope that you will turn a very deaf ear to the songs of the sirens who must be keeping you awake nights with their music. I saw that Stimson had donned the mermaid's tail and there must be a thousand others whose hearts are better than their heads.

There is nothing very gay to report from Moscow except an incident that happened the other day when, on the completion of a tremendous new hospital at Gorki, aviators were sent up to take pictures from the air for propaganda purposes. When they came down and the pictures were developed, the hospital turned out to be the most perfect German swastika! The architect was immediately exiled and new wings are being built feverishly.[2]

I wish I could hear the sound of your voice.

Bless you.

Bill

[PSF:Russia:TS]

[1] Not found.

[2] Answered June 3, 1935 (*Personal Letters, 1928–1945,* I, 480), in a letter devoted mostly to domestic happenings and personal matters.

Roosevelt to Claude A. Swanson, Secretary of the Navy

[Washington] May 3, 1935

Secret

Memorandum for the Secretary of the Navy: I have carefully read your letter of April twenty-second with regard to Philippine bases.[1] A consideration of all the phases of the matter leads me to the conclusion that I should not issue an Executive Order setting aside bases.

I see no reason why you should not, in the utmost confidence, inform your Chief of Operations and the General board that:

(a) In the light of all circumstances if Philippine independence goes through and becomes an accomplished fact in ten years, the United States must not retain a Naval base in the Philippine Islands. From the point of view of Naval strategy alone, I would consider such a base in an independent territory a military-naval liability instead of an asset.

(b) In the event that independence does not go through, so much may happen in the next ten years that no one can foretell whether such a base or bases are advisable or not.

(c) To make a move at this time, pending further knowledge on whether the Washington and London Naval Treaties will be extended or not, an Executive Order of this kind would undoubtedly be regarded by Japan and other nations as contrary to our determined position in favor of extension of the Treaty.

(d) I cannot agree with the military-naval proposal to keep the Manila-Subic Bay Area as a permanent defense area. It is well known that this area could not be defended over a long period of time against an army attacking it from the land side.

(e) The other areas referred to in 2, 3, 4, 5, 6, and 7, I am familiar with but I think it is a fair assumption that they have not been considered in the light of positive and complete information regarding their defensibility from the Naval point of view without the assistance of large Coast Defense and Army assistance.

I should be glad to have a report in regard to the latter point. Such a report should include, of course, the opinion of the joint Army and Navy Board.

In regard to the necessity for this Order at this time, I do not believe that failure to take action before the Constitutional elections in the Philippines this spring will in any way militate against the agreement between us and the Philippine Legislature and President during the ten year self-government period.

F.D.R.

[PSF:Navy:CT]

[1] Recommending that naval reservations be designated in the Philippines before the Islands became independent (PSF:Navy).

Michael W. Straus, Director of Publicity, Public Works Administration, to Stephen T. Early, Assistant Secretary to the President

Washington, D.C., May 8, 1935

Dear Steve: Secretary Ickes asked that this speech be submitted to you.

To save time, I suggest that the only challengeable part of the speech is the last two paragraphs of page 7. You might read these two paragraphs from the point of view of whether or not it is proper for a Cabinet officer to make specific derogatory references to Italian and German institutions, and to say their universities "are now mere bond slaves to a strutting and vain-glorious Nazism which is only a variation of Fascism."[1]

Sincerely yours,

Michael W. Straus

[OF 6:AS]

[1] The speech (present) was prepared for delivery by Ickes at the University of Alabama commencement exercises at University, Alabama, on May 27, 1935. The paragraphs Straus refers to read in part as follows:

"Academic freedom could not long survive under either Fascism or Communism. If you would have proof of this statement, consider the situation today in Italy where the universities are permitted to teach only what the government permits them to teach. Or turn to the universities of Germany, which were formerly among the greatest in the world . . . Ruthlessly deprived of their right to search for the truth and to proclaim it for the benefit of mankind, they are now mere bond slaves to a strutting and vainglorious Nazism which is only a variation of Fascism.

"Nor is the reverse of this picture any more alluring . . . The universities of Italy and of Germany are no more slavish mouthpieces of governments whose acts they may not examine and whose fallacies they may not expose, than are the universities of Russia of the Communistic dictatorship that has regimented not only the lives but the very thoughts of its people."

See Early's reply, May 9, 1935, below.

Roosevelt to Breckinridge Long, Ambassador to Italy

[Washington] May 8, 1935

Dear Breck: I hope you are not right but I fear you are.[1]

I am looking forward to seeing you the end of June or the first part of July, and it looks as though Congress will still be here.

Always sincerely,

[PSF:Italy:T]

[1] See Long's letter of April 19, 1935, above.

Roosevelt to Jesse Isador Straus, Ambassador to France, Paris

[Washington] May 9, 1935

My dear Jesse: I have discussed with Secretary Hull your letter of April 9[1] and am confident that neither he nor the State Department is unsympathetic to the difficulties with which you have been confronted while shaping the Embassy into an efficient and coordinated unit. There is no doubt that these difficulties have been very real, but I do not think the Department is to blame as it is not entirely its own master in determining what expenditures may or may not be made by its missions in the field. As you know, the Director of the Budget and the Comptroller General keep a very close rein on governmental expenditures and often must disallow requests for expenditure of funds, no matter how humble the request may be, because the particular expenditure in question is contrary to some one of the multitudinous rules and regulations which have accumulated over a period of years and which must be applied by those bureaus in making their decisions. What, therefore, may seem at a distance as an unsympathetic or arbitrary action by the Department is in reality the operation of these laws and regulations which in themselves are, for the most part, inflexible and inelastic to interpretation.

In regard to the assignment of personnel to a particular mission, I think you will agree that the Department of State must, of necessity, consider not only the needs of that mission by itself, but also in terms of the needs of the service as a whole. To consult with each chief of mission in connection with the individual assignments which are constantly being made would render the administration of Foreign Service personnel very cumbersome. Changes naturally have to be made periodically for the good of the service, as well as for the good of the individual officers. I feel, therefore, that a chief of mission, as a commander of a naval vessel, must adapt and assimilate the officers assigned to his vessel or office to the best possible use. However, the Foreign Service Board, on its part, has a responsibility similar to the personnel boards of the military branches of the Government and must see that a post is properly staffed to keep the efficiency of the particular unit at its maximum level. I am assured that the Personnel Board of the Department is not unmindful of that responsibility.

I am thoroughly alive to the personal sacrifice which is often placed upon our representatives abroad in carrying out their duties, and I am interested in your presentation of the situation as it exists in Paris. However, salaries must be uniform throughout the entire Service and I cannot see how any rectifications can be made to meet a situation in a particular post until the Congress is prepared to lift the level all along the line. Something can be done through special allowances to alleviate these sacrifices, but when mention is made of expenditure for "entertainment," we have to reckon with the Hill.

I am glad you felt you could write me as you did and, on my part, I want you to know that you will continue to receive every bit of support and cooperation which it is humanly possible to give. We want the Embassy in Paris to be an outstanding organization, combining efficiency in its political representation with economy of administration. When you accepted the ambassadorship to Paris, everyone remarked that this had been a happy selection, as you were just the right person to get the new organization under way and on the right track. I want to reassure you again that no one, chief or subordinate, has it in his mind to hamper you in your work in any way or to tax your patience by petty retaliatory tactics. I realize that we have been unable at this end to give you all the tools which you should have and, consequently, your accomplishments deserve all the more credit.[2]

I saw Marriner several days ago and enjoyed my conversation with him.[3] At that time I expressed to him the assurances which I have written above and gave him to understand that we only wish you luck and every continued success in carrying out your heavy responsibilities.

Sincerely yours,

[PSF:France:CT]

[1] Above.
[2] Certain of Straus's recommendations for the reorganization of the Paris Embassy, chiefly in respect to centralizing office and reporting functions, were approved by Hull (Hull to Roosevelt, June 1, 1935, PSF:France).
[3] J. Theodore Marriner, counselor of embassy, Paris, was at the White House April 26 (PPF 1-0).

William E. Dodd, Ambassador to Germany, to Roosevelt

Berlin, May 9, 1935

Personal

Dear Mr. President: The remark with which you closed your letter of April 16[1] only emphasizes the attitudes of us all here: What can anyone do now to change the fixed drift everywhere towards war? I sometimes wonder if all democratic peoples ought not to withdraw their representatives to countries which flout all democratic principles and talk constantly of the great honor of bearing arms, shooting fellowmen and the necessity of annexing other peoples' territory.

You know how Wilson struggled in Paris to show Europe how foolish such policies are. The United States saved Italy from conquest in 1918, yet Italian statesmen (?) behaved as if they had won the war, and they made annexations which started the movement which now has that country in a hopeless position. That is, Italy is armed and drilled to the last degree. If Mussolini ceases building great warships, stops making bombing planes or sends his million soldiers to their homes (he is adding 500,000 more), he will have an unemployment which would overthrow him—the imaginary Caesar. If he goes on arming and drilling as heretofore, the debt of his government will soon equal what a hundred billion dollars would be to us! The only other procedure is war and that would ruin him and his country, unless England and France came to his aid. This began when the Italians demanded in Paris what they had no right to ask—yet Senator Lodge lined up Italians and Irishmen in Massachusetts in behalf of Italian demands!

The French Ambassador said to me here in the presence of others: "If it had not been for Wilson, we would have annexed all the German territory west of the Rhine; and that would have guaranteed European peace." But I said: "If it had not been for American assistance, the Germans would have annexed all eastern France and Belgium." The conversation was given another turn. And as to England, I have not the slightest doubt that, but for the United States, Wilhelm II would have dictated a worse peace than Versailles in London, and taken possession of all the British fleet. He would have called himself the second William the Conqueror. The one thing for which the United States entered the war was to stop this mediaeval method of settling difficulties among peoples. Wilson said to me on August 15, 1915: "We may have to enter the war to save all Europe from Berlin domination."

But when the peace of 1918 was about to be drawn, our politicians, like Lodge, united resentful German-Americans, Irish enemies of England and Italian imperialists to take from Wilson the power the real Americans voted to give him, and as a result, the Treaty of Versailles took such a form that only a cooperative League of all nations could give any promise of world peace; and the American Senate, for party reasons, rejected the League idea, quoting Washington and Jefferson, whose very existence once depended upon international assistance and whose administrations also depended upon international attitudes.

But the German masses in 1918–20 were ready for cooperation, receiving millions of dollars from Americans to enable them to recover somewhat. But 40 billions of indemnity demanded by France plus the refusal of France to disarm, slowly brought the population back to their faith in militarism, and the Hitler-Göring-Goebbels triumvirate is the result. Practically every young German, including some women, wears a butcher knife at his side. "Blut and Ehre" is printed on the sharp blade. University students and young "gentlemen" in general fight duels as under the old régime. Children at ages of eight to twelve are taught two or three times a week to throw bombs; from twelve to eighteen they practice with rifles; and after that age all are to serve fixed periods in the standing Army—more proud of the opportunity than Italians under Mussolini. No man can doubt the meaning of this; and anybody who resists or so much as talks pacifism or democracy is imprisoned, sometimes sadly beaten up. So Hitler is another Mussolini, also another Stalin.

And Germany, now encircled, as was to have been expected, has an increasing standing Army and more than a million young men excellently trained in all except the handling of up-to-date guns. She has an amazing barracks and drill ground equipment, air fields of the most up-to-date character and underground storage arrangements in all strategic areas. How many thousands of competent pilots one cannot say; but reports say twice as many always as could be used at any one time. The manufacture of arms and tanks and poison gases goes on day and night. There is a national debt, half of it short-term floating, of about 40 billion marks, about half as heavy, according to resources, as that of Italy. Two years from now Germany will have a population of 67,000,000 increasing faster than the populations of both France and England, and the completest military machine in the world. Last night, talking to an Admiral of the Navy, I said: "In rather short time you will have by far the greatest Army in Europe, abundant supplies of weapons, a debt about as burdensome as that of Italy (about which he had been speaking) and increasing unemployment. What will you do?" He said: "Go to war." That is what Dr. Schacht said six months ago to me. The Chancellor always says to such inquiries: "Peace, peace, always." At the same time we know that he is placing police all over the de-militarized Rhine zone, police who have been well drilled. There is an assembly of Ausland-Germans called to meet at Königsberg in June. In the call it was stated that all the country along the Baltic coast "ought to be ours, and we urge attendance of Germans all the way to the Black Sea"; report of this in our last pouch. I can see no other objective than conquest. Why should we and other representatives of foreign countries be urged to attend movies here which make Napoleon I a great hero and repeat the idea: "Er is der Fuehrer des ganzen Europas," with hearty applause from audiences? One needs not to give further proof, though I know there is a wing of the Reichswehr whose leaders are very fearful lest some blunder precipitate the issue too soon.

Everything I have noticed here tends to show that Germany and Japan have some entente. The new Ambassador has several times betrayed evidence in that direction to me. The Japanese Naval Attaché was here about two weeks for conferences late April and early May. He is almost an understudy of Goering; and the fastest submarines ever made are now building at Wilhelmshaven. Once a break occurs in the Baltic or Austrian areas, I shall look for a break in the Far East. It is not insignificant that three weeks ago Tokyo and Berlin Foreign Offices opened long-distance conversations. While I do not think the Chancellor will wish to make a war before May 1937 or '38, I believe I am right in saying that it is a fixed purpose. Such is the view of every leading diplomat here.

You say: "What can one do?" I can only rehearse some of the false moves we have made. All Europe was prostrate 1918–20. The Americans had fought simply to end war, and Americans were then due 11 billions public and several other billions private debts. Wilson had made definite constitutional commitments. All the leading Republicans over the preceding decades had supported the World Court at the Hague—all Europe, except Germany, favorable. Leading Republicans had agitated for a world league to enforce peace. Under Wilson, most Democrats had come to the same view, and the Europeans, in spite of their animosities, accepted the League of Nations constitution. Wilson also urged lower tariffs in order to avoid economic depression and to enable Europe to pay her debts. No one who knows our history or European behavior over the last three decades can doubt that Wilson's policy was the one promise of a better era.

The Senate minority defeated the League idea; Congress (under minority business pressure) raised tariffs to heights never before contemplated; and our people lost their loans to the outside world and then made other loans to help get exports over tariff walls—and lost those too. And hence we have the existing status, the worst known to all history—and everybody returning to the mediaeval folly of 1914, including ourselves. If anybody wishes to get the true picture of Senate conduct in 1918–20, D. F. Fleming in the *United States and the League of Nations* gives it.[2] Nobody has replied to this able book or tried to refute any part of it.

Since our country is so deeply involved and has made such terrible blunders, I would endeavor in some way to retrace our steps. If we had entered the League in 1919, Mussolini and Hitler would not be in existence today; if we had realized the meaning of freer commerce, our billions would not have been lost; and the wider commerce and partial payment of debts would have saved us half of the depression—the other half being due to Europe and false industrial policy long followed.

This is my appraisal of things. Whether it is too late for so great a people to exert decisive influence I cannot say; but I believe if English-speaking peoples cooperated, without imperialistic practices anywhere, we could save modern civilization another world war.

Sincerely yours,

William E. Dodd

[PSF:Germany:TS]

[1] Printed in *Personal Letters, 1928–1945,* I, 475. Roosevelt concluded this letter by saying he was much concerned over the results of the Stresa Conference and that he felt helpless "to render any particular service to immediate or permanent peace at this time."

[2] Denna Frank Fleming, *The United States and the League of Nations, 1918–1920* (New York and London: Putnam, 1932).

Cordell Hull, Secretary of State, to Roosevelt

[Washington] May 9, 1935

My dear Mr. President: A bill (H.R. 7373) has been introduced by Representative Tonry on April 9, 1935, the purpose of which is to admit whale oil to this country without the payment thereon of the taxes imposed under Section 602 of the Revenue Act of 1934.[1]

In conversation and in memoranda you asked me to investigate the effect which such repeal would have upon the safety of an R.F.C. loan to an American whaling company and upon employment conditions in the American whaling fleet.

First, I find that the R.F.C. loan is only $175,000, which in any event is not, in my opinion, of sufficient consequence to be allowed to affect a broad question of commercial policy. I believe the facts will indicate that there is no immediate or close competition on account of the different marketing localities.

Secondly, as to employment for the Americans engaged in the whaling industry, the crews of the fourteen American vessels engaged in whaling are estimated at two hundred persons. They are supposed to operate in the Arctic Ocean, while the Norwegian fleets operate in the Antarctic Ocean. This evident lack of any real American industry is insufficient [ground] upon which to turn down a mutually profitable trading arrangement on a substantial scale between this country and Norway.

I enclose a brief memorandum epitomizing my investigations of these points.

I enclose a further single page memorandum summarizing and bringing up to date the memorandum submitted with my letter of January 29, 1935.[2]

I find many good reasons for giving support to the Tonry Bill, but I should like to have your approval before doing so. It is possible that, if you approve, you may prefer to communicate directly with the Chairman of the Ways and Means Committee of the House of Representatives.

Faithfully yours,

Cordell Hull

[OF 61-W:CT]

[1] Rep. Richard J. Tonry's bill was referred to the Committee of Ways and Means but was not reported although supported by both the State and Agriculture departments (*Cong. Rec.,* vol. 79, p. 5356; McIntyre to Phillips, Aug. 22, 1935, OF 61-W; with this letter is a copy of the committee print). A State Department memorandum of Aug. 28, 1935, sent to McIntyre by Assistant Secretary of State Carr in a letter of Aug. 31, 1935 (OF 61-W), stated that it would be "very desirable" to have the 3 cents per pound tax removed: "This tax has remained the stumbling block in our negotiations with Norway, since a 50 percent reduction of the tax is not sufficient to permit entry of whale oil into this country, and it is an item of leading importance for Norway." Tonry introduced a similar bill the next year but it also was not reported (*Cong. Rec.,* vol. 80, p. 4363). The Agriculture Department urged passage in the interest of American lard and cotton seed oil producers: with free entry for denatured whale oil (made inedible at point of entry), the amount available for edible use in Europe would be reduced.

[2] Hull enclosed two one-page memoranda, both undated: "Memorandum/American Whaling Fleet," and "Memorandum/Norwegian Whale Oil—A Summary." His letter of January 29 is cited in Roosevelt's letter to him of Jan. 30, 1935, above. See Roosevelt to Wallace, May 14, 1935, below.

Claude A. Swanson, Secretary of the Navy, to Roosevelt

Washington, May 9, 1935

Confidential

My dear Mr. President: The enclosed information seems of such import as to warrant letting you know about it at once.

Very sincerely yours,

Claude A. Swanson

[PSF:Navy:TS]

[*Enclosure*] Captain W. D. Puleston, Office of Naval Intelligence, to Claude A. Swanson

Washington, May 8, 1935

Confidential

Memorandum for the Secretary of the Navy: Subject: Conversation with Captain Yamaguchi,[1] I.J.N., Japanese Naval Attaché.

1. On Friday night, 3 May, 1935, I had a long conversation with Captain Yamaguchi, in which we discussed various phases of the Far Eastern situation. During the course of this conversation, he stated that his Government would probably be willing to accept the five to three ratio provided the United States would abandon all its bases in the Far East.

2. Captain Yamaguchi made a special arrangement to see me and I think his proposal represents the present views of the Japanese Admiralty.

W. D. Puleston

[PSF:Navy:TS]

[1] Capt. Tamon Yamaguchi.

Stephen T. Early, Assistant Secretary to the President, to Michael Straus, Director of Publicity, Public Works Administration

[Washington] May 9, 1935

Dear Mike: With reference to the draft of the Secretary's speech for delivery by him at the University of Alabama commencement exercises on May twenty-seventh.[1]

I had considerable doubt concerning the propriety of his references to the foreign countries. Confidentially, I asked the President to read this portion of the address.

It is the President's request that the references to the foreign countries be entirely eliminated. I am sure the Secretary, upon deliberation, will agree that this is the wise thing to do.

Very sincerely yours,

Stephen T. Early

[OF 6:CT]

[1] See Straus to Early, May 8, 1935, above.

Press Conference, Executive Offices of the White House, May 10, 1935, 4:05 P.M.

[*Excerpt*] Q: Mr. President, maybe this will be a story. There is a lot of lamentation to the effect that foreign trade has become a thing of the past and that our exports are drying up. Could you discuss that for background, that general subject of the prospects of international commerce?

The President: A terrific subject.

Q: Fifty well-chosen words. (Laughter)

The President: A few well-chosen words about to be repeated to the House. I think our imports are up and that our exports are up over last year. I think so. And I think last year they were up over 1933. In other words, my general impression is that there is a general betterment in foreign trade, not only our own but almost all over the world. Foreign trade is better as a world proposition, including our own, than it was last year.

I don't know what else we can develop very well, unless we go into all kinds of theories about tariff agreements and so forth. And there are a few things we have done; for instance, we are shipping potatoes out of Maine to Cuba, which we never did before.

Q: Mr. President, have you finished with that subject?

The President: I don't think there is anything else I can say.

[President's Press Conferences:T]

Robert W. Bingham, Ambassador to Great Britain, to Roosevelt

[London] May 10, 1935

Dear Mr. President: Wide-spread publicity was given here to the statements of certain officers before the House Committee on Military Affairs outlining the plans for the seizure of British Islands and air bases contra Canada. The statement caused wide-spread discussion and resentment here. Your statement, however, on the subject, cleared up the whole situation entirely and restored our relations with the British government and the British people to the proper friendly basis.[1]

Sincerely yours,

Robert W. Bingham

[PSF:Great Britain:TS]

[1] Publication of testimony given in executive session before the House Military Affairs Committee to the effect that the Army proposed construction of a large air base near the Canadian border aroused consternation and resentment in some areas of Canadian public opinion (though not in upper official circles). Roosevelt regarded the incident serious enough to write to Secretary of War Dern and to John McSwain, chairman of the House committee, to say that the testimony did not represent Administration policy, and to reaffirm the long tradition of Canadian-United States peaceful relations (both dated April 29, 1935, OF 25). Publication of the two letters in the New York *Times* of May 1, 1935, together with Dern's reply, of the same date (pp. 1, 8), labeling the testimony as personal, restored calm.

The letters cited are also printed in *Public Papers*, IV, 141–143. The hearings in which the testimony was printed are House Military Affairs Committee, *Air Defense Bases, to Authorize Selection, Construction, Installation, and Modification of Permanent Stations and Depots for Army Air Corps, and Frontier Air-Defense Bases Generally, Hearings, 74th Cong., 1st sess., on H.R. 6621 and H.R. 4130, Feb. 11–13, 1935* (Washington, 1935).

Roosevelt commented on the incident at his May 3, 1935, press conference: "It is closed so far as notice to every Government official, the Army, the Navy and civilians and otherwise, so far as every Government official in this country is concerned, that we are certainly going to do nothing to arm ourselves in any form, either offensively or defensively, against Canada."

Roosevelt to Henry A. Wallace, Secretary of Agriculture

Washington, May 14, 1935

Memorandum for the Secretary of Agriculture: In view of the fact that animal and vegetable fats are to some degree affected by whale oil, will you let me have your thoughts on this from the Secretary of State?[1]

F.D.R.

[OF 61-W:CT]

[1] May 9, 1935, above. Wallace replied May 27, 1935 (OF 61-W), that the view of the Agriculture Department was that repeal of the excise tax on whale oil would probably be little felt by domestic agriculture "and would be definitely beneficial to some branches." Roosevelt thereupon wrote to Hull, May 31, 1935 (OF 61-W): "In view of this very complete study and the memorandum from the Department of Agriculture, I agree with your letter of May ninth."

Press Conference, Executive Offices of the White House, May 15, 1935, 10:45 A.M.

[*Excerpt*] Q: Any reaction from abroad on the talk made the other day by Secretary Morgenthau on stabilization?[1]

The President: Nothing, Stevie.[2] I saw the dispatches from the embassies yesterday afternoon and there was nothing in them yet. I suppose they will begin to come in pretty soon.

Q: Have you talked with Johnston[3] about the world cotton agreement?

The President: He is coming in to see me today at 12:00 o'clock. I have not seen him yet.

Q: Is there anything you can tell us further about stabilization—supplementing what Morgenthau said?

The President: No; I think that covered it pretty well. I do not know of anything else . . .

Q: Have you decided what you are to do about Pan-American air-mail rates?

The President: No; talked about it some more yesterday; no decision made yet.

[President's Press Conferences:T]

[1] In a radio speech from Washington on May 13, Morgenthau said that the United States was now willing to join with other nations in achieving currency stabilization. The speech is printed in the New York *Times,* May 14, 1935, p. 13.

[2] F. M. Stephenson of the Associated Press.

[3] Oscar Johnston was manager of the cotton pool in the Agricultural Adjustment Administration.

Roosevelt to Louis Lipsky, Chairman, American Palestine Campaign of the Jewish Agency for Palestine, New York

[Washington, May 21, 1935]

My dear Mr. Lipsky: In response to your letter of May 9, 1935,[1] I am glad of the opportunity to send you a word of congratulation upon the celebration of the fifteenth anniversary of the Palestine Foundation Fund, the organization which the Jews of the world have formed to assist in the establishment in Palestine of a National Home for the Jewish people. Certainly without the help which the Fund has rendered it would not have been possible for the Jewish agency and the Jewish people to have accomplished the results which have been achieved in the Holy Land. You may well be proud of the part which American Jews have played in this work and of the share which they have contributed toward the Fund.

I wish you and your co-workers every success in your forthcoming celebration.

Sincerely yours,

[*Notation*:A] 5/21/35
[PPF 601:CT]

[1] Lipsky said that a message from the President "would be an historic occasion marking in high relief the moral support which America has given to the great social reconstruction project embodied in the rebuilding of the Jewish Homeland in Palestine" (PPF 601). Early first asked Under Secretary of State Phillips if the message should be sent; Phillips sent the draft here printed (Early to Phillips, May 10, 1935, PPF 601).

Roosevelt to Edward Tuck, Paris

[Washington] May 22, 1935

My dear Mr. Tuck: I am grateful to you for sending me the extract from Mr. Erskine's letter to the London *Financial Times.*[1] This states my thought exactly. There is no question in my mind that practically all of the opposition to our silver purchases comes from the very small fringe who live in the Treaty ports of China and care little about the main bulk of the population.

Very sincerely yours,

[PPF 2537:CT]

---

[1] The enclosure (accompanied only by Tuck's card on which he had written May 8) was a typed copy of a letter to the *Financial Times* of April 30, 1935, written by James M. Erskine (PPF 2537). Erskine said that the rise in the price of silver had helped the mass of the Chinese because it had increased the value of their savings. He pointed out that the latest rise had been accompanied by a sharp rise in the price of rice in Rangoon and also that there was a sustained and growing Chinese demand for Australian wheat. The outcry against the Administration's silver policy, he said, came solely from Chinese banker and other minority interests. Tuck, a writer on financial affairs and a retired banker, lived in Paris. See Roosevelt to Tuck, July 10, 1935, below.

Sumner Welles, Assistant Secretary of State, to Roosevelt

Washington, May 22, 1935

My dear Mr. President: In accordance with your request I am transmitting herewith a memorandum outlining the general problems which you might desire to have Mr. Peek take up with the Italian, Turkish, and Balkan Governments should you determine to send him on the economic mission of which we spoke on Monday.

While you stated that you were not inclined to consider his extending his mission to Russia, and I assume that this is due to the present status of pending negotiations between the two countries, there are, of course, many trade matters that Mr. Peek might profitably take up with the Russian Government.

Believe me, Faithfully yours,

Sumner Welles

[PSF:Agriculture:TS]

[*Enclosure*] Sumner Welles to Roosevelt

May 22, 1935

Italy. The present drastic system of control of imports established by the Italian Government has worked havoc with the trade of the

United States with Italy. In 1933 Italy purchased nearly twice as much from the United States as it sold here. Under the new system of control which requires balancing of trade accounts between Italy and other countries American trade has necessarily been cut approximately in half. For instance, the percentage of 1934 imports of key American products permitted entry in 1935 into Italy under the control system is: wheat, 0; tobacco, 0; lard, 20%; cotton, 25%; iron, 30%, machinery, 25%; motor vehicles, 25%. As a result of representations made by us certain of these percentages have been very slightly increased.

With the fourteen countries with which Italy has general clearing agreements the Italian Government has established 100% quotas on the ground that clearing agreements have the tendency of balancing the commercial exchanges of both parties to such agreements. This operates further to restrict imports from the United States inasmuch as there is, of course, no clearing agreement between the United States and Italy.

In the discussion of the negotiation of a trade agreement between Italy and the United States, Italy has been informed that the United States will not sign any agreement (a) which does not envisage increased exports from the United States to Italy, and (b) whereby the amount of American exports to Italy will depend upon the amount of Italian exports to the United States. This Government has taken the position that the allotment of quotas or exchange to the United States should be based upon a criterion such as the share of Italian imports enjoyed by American trade during a representative period rather than upon the amount of American purchases of Italian goods. Although the Italian Government has indicated that it sees no reason why negotiations for a trade agreement should not continue, indicating acquiescence with our point of view, it is probable that this policy is directed towards postponing retaliatory action by the United States through non-generalization of concessions.

In view of this situation it would be highly interesting for this government if as an emergency measure barter agreements could be negotiated with the Italian Government. The United States is in a position to furnish essential raw materials such as cotton, copper, petroleum, lard, and wheat which it is believed Italy would import provided she could arrange for an equivalent amount of exports.

There should be further secured a commitment that foreign exchange will be furnished immediately to importers who have been granted import permits within quota limits. Under present conditions foreign exchange is not available immediately. The delay varies from a few days to a few months, depending on the volume of export exchange available. The fact that Italian exports to the United States comprise 9% of the total exports while American exports to Italy comprise only 2% of our total exports might carry weight in a favorable sense with the Italian Government.

Information should be obtained from the Italian Government as to their foreign trade control plan. This presumably would necessitate a discussion of monetary stabilization since the Italian system of control of imports and exports was adopted primarily for monetary reasons.

The Balkans and Turkey. The 1926–30 average of the trade between the United States and Yugoslavia, Bulgaria, and Albania including exports and imports totaled less than $5,000,000 per annum. There should be opportunities for trade expansion in this area.

The 1926–1930 average of the trade between the United States and Greece, Rumania, and Turkey totaled approximately $67,000,000 per annum. The adoption by these countries of quota systems and exchange regulations has resulted in a great reduction in the total of this trade. The figure for 1933 was approximately $20,000,000. There should be real opportunities for increasing our exports to these three countries.

Our greatest loss has been with reference to wheat purchases by Greece. Prior to 1933 we supplied Greece with about 50% of its foreign wheat, in this instance chiefly hard red winter wheat. While there is at the present time no exportable surplus of this wheat, it may be desirable to discuss with the Greek authorities the possibilities of reopening this market in the event that we are again in the position to export hard winter wheat.

With Rumania our exports have always outweighed our imports. In 1934 we exported $5,440,000 worth of goods to that country and only purchased Rumanian goods in the amount of $160,000. On March 1, 1935, this Government was informed by the Government of Rumania that in view of "the difficulties of Rumanian foreign trade and the deficit in the Rumanian trade balance with the United States, the Rumanian Ministry of Industries and Commerce has found itself obliged to suspend authorization for the importation of American merchandise pending the conclusion of an agreement safeguarding the interests of both parties." This Government has suggested in reply that in view of the exchange of notes of August 20, 1930, according mutual unconditional most-favored-nation treatment in the matter of prohibitions and restrictions of exports and imports, the Rumanian Government would no doubt wish to review the decision referred to, and the Rumanian Government on

April 20 last stated that the decision quoted merely constituted a declaration of principle and that in practice American imports were being
admitted in quantities substantially equal to those of a year ago. This
situation, however, is obviously unsatisfactory and some more advantageous solution should be negotiated.

[PSF:Agriculture:T]

Roosevelt to the Right Reverend John F. Noll, Bishop of Fort Wayne, Indiana

[Washington] May 23, 1935

My dear Bishop Noll: You will understand, I am sure, that the
pressure of official duties has prevented me from acknowledging earlier
your note of May thirteenth.[1]

I thank you for writing to me. The subject on which you write is one
that deals, of course, in its measure, with international affairs. I need
not repeat here my devotion to the vital American principle of religious
freedom. As we ourselves are devoted to it, so we naturally wish it would
be accepted as a principle by all the governments of the world.

The conduct of international affairs with the ofttimes complicated
issues they involve rests, as you know, in a special, immediate way with
the Executive Department of our Government.

The matter of your letter, and the thousands of petitions and protests
which have been forwarded to us, inspired by our common love of
religious liberty for all peoples, have received and will continue to receive
our earnest, thoughtful attention.

I will do all that lies within the province of my office as Chief Executive to promote the principle of the freedom of conscience and the
exercise of religious liberty.

Very sincerely yours,

[PPF 2406:CT]

[1] Noll had said (PPF 2406) that the Catholic hierarchy, as such, had declined to
endorse the Borah resolution, the Knights of Columbus petition, and other petitions
urging the United States to take diplomatic action in protest against the alleged
persecution of the Catholic Church by the Mexican government, principally to give
the President "an opportunity to do something with less embarassment." He intimated,
however, that it might "be difficult to keep the Catholics quiet" if the hierarchy were

completely ignored. Noll suggested that a strong statement by the President "on the general principles of the rights of all people to religious liberty, in belief and practice, would be a help to oppressed people throughout the world, especially in Russia, Mexico, and Germany." Such a statement might also end the criticism that the President had "a little sympathy for Communism."

The Borah resolution was submitted Jan. 31, 1935, and referred to the Senate Committee on Foreign Relations; it was not reported (*Cong. Rec.*, vol. 79, p. 1298). It is printed *ibid.* This reply was apparently drafted by the Rev. John J. Burke, general secretary of the National Catholic Welfare Conference, according to Burke's letter to McIntyre of May 20, 1935, PPF 2406. Burke was frequently consulted by the Administration on Catholic Church matters and in the Wilson Administration had advised Daniels on the selection of Catholic chaplains for the Navy (OF 28; Daniels to Roosevelt, Oct. 13, 1933, PSF: Mexico). His name appears in another connection at this time. On May 27 Basil O'Connor, Roosevelt's former law partner, telephoned McIntyre to say that "a party" had come to his house the previous evening to urge that the President see Bishop Molloy to talk over the Catholic situation in Mexico and that he also see Judge Manton (McIntyre to Roosevelt, May 27, 1935, OF 28). Thomas E. Molloy was Bishop of Brooklyn; Martin T. Manton was judge of the United States Circuit Court of Appeals. Attached to McIntyre's note is one from Roosevelt to McIntyre, May 29, 1935: "Memo for Mac: Will you talk this over with Father Burke?" See Welles to Roosevelt, June 25, 1935, below.

William Phillips, Under Secretary of State, to Roosevelt

Washington, May 23, 1935

Dear Mr. President: Referring to our conversation this morning[1] with regard to the "open letter" sent to the people of Japan from a number of religious leaders in the United States protesting against the American naval maneuvers, I enclose a copy of the text of this "open letter," together with a paraphrase of a telegram from Mr. Grew, under date of May 3rd, on this same subject. Mr. Grew's telegram also refers to another message, more or less of the same character, from American missionaries resident in Japan, which, however, is of lesser interest.[2]

Faithfully yours,

William Phillips

[PSF:Japan:TS]

[1] At the White House, from 11:30 to 11:45.

[2] Grew said that the open letter had been published only in the *Japan Advertiser,* the *Japan Times,* and the *Yomiuri* and it had as yet aroused no editorial comment. Public reaction had been negative. The Easter Sunday (April 21) appeal of American missionaries in Japan to their fellow Christians in the United States had been obscured by the news of the earthquake in Formosa.

[*Enclosure*] Harry Emerson Fosdick and Others to the People of Japan

(On May 1, 1935, the following letter was received from Mr. Harold E. Fey, Secretary of the American Fellowship of Reconciliation, 2929 Broadway, New York, by W. Axling and T. D. Walser. In April fifteen persons sent the letter to 500 of the religious leaders of the USA for signature. It will be released in the USA on May 3rd, the day the naval maneuvers begin and Mr. Fey requested W. Axling and T. D. Walser to give the letter publicity in Japan on the same day.)

[New York, May 3, 1935]

An Open Letter to the People of Japan: In the name of peace we greet you, our brothers and sisters in Japan. For eighty-one years our two nations have maintained friendly relations. During this time each country has developed in parallel growth the strength and wealth of modern statehood. The broad expanse of the Pacific Ocean has become a highway on which the mighty commerce between yourselves and us is carried without danger. The great germinal ideas of our basic world culture move freely between the two nations. Through the miracles of modern communication the years have united our two peoples more firmly in the bonds of universal brotherhood.

We write this letter of good will at this time because this cherished bond might be menaced by a plan announced by our government which we regard as highly unimaginative and mistaken. We refer to the decision of the Navy Department of the United States to hold maneuvers of a large fleet in the North Pacific during the month of May. While these maneuvers may have been ordered simply as part of the routine idea of naval men to exercise the fleet from time to time in such ways as will promote its technical efficiency, we are strongly opposed to this move because no matter how honestly meant to be without offense to any other nation such maneuvers will hardly escape misinterpretation by sensation-mongers and individuals in each nation who are in a position to profit from the creation of fear and suspicion. We desire to convey to you, therefore, the knowledge that many thousands of our citizens, especially those who constitute the membership of our churches and synagogues, have protested against the holding of these maneuvers. Great meetings have been and are being held, officials have been visited and thousands of letters and telegrams of protest have been sent. Multitudes of our people, whether connected with the institutions of religion or not,

515

oppose these maneuvers and join us in spirit as we convey to you our assurances of continued and undiminished friendship.

In the spirit of equality and brotherhood we therefore ask you to unite with us in redoubling our efforts to maintain our historic friendship and in opposing every effort that is likely to lead to mistrust between our peoples. Together let us move forward in peace and justice to greater service to humanity, weaving the broad seaways of the mighty Pacific into unbreakable bonds of unity in the world community.[1]

Sincerely yours,

Harry Emerson Fosdick	John Haynes Holmes
W. Russell Bowie	S. Parkes Cadman
Sherwood Eddy	Allen Knight Chalmers
Paul Jones	Francis M. McConnell
Edmund B. Chaffee	Rufus M. Jones
Kirby Page	Ernest Fremont Tittle
John Nevin Sayre	Harold E. Fey
E. Raymond Wilson	

[PSF:Japan:T:Copy]

[1] See Roosevelt to Fey, May 29, 1935, below.

Raymond Moley to Marguerite LeHand, Private Secretary to the President

New York, May 23, 1935

Dear Missy: Will you please hand this letter and attached pamphlet to the President? He may have read the essay, but I think he will be interested in Beard's comments and underscoring of the text.

With best regards, I am, Cordially yours,

RM

[PPF 743:TS]

[*Enclosure*] Charles A. Beard to Raymond Moley

New Milford, Conn., May 18 [1935]

Dear Moley: As I have often said to you, I consider the foreign implications of our domestic policy and the hazards of a futile and idiotic war in the Far Pacific more important than old age pensions and all the rest of it. Next year is a crucial year in our history and here is a pamphlet by a naval officer that contains more sound sense on the sea power than all of Mahan's tomes.[1] I wish you would read it, comment on it in *Today,* and send this marked copy to President Roosevelt.

Cordially yours,

Charles A. Beard

[PPF 743:CT]

[1] Beard enclosed an article, "Beyond the Naval Treaties," by Lt. Com. Melvin F. Talbot, from the *United States Naval Institute Proceedings* (April 1935), pp. 465–474. Talbot argued that the Washington and London treaties had failed to halt the armaments race and that the United States should rely on overwhelming defense in its own hemisphere.

Roosevelt to Russell C. Clark, New York

[Washington] May 24, 1935

Personal

Dear Russell: Many thanks for that interesting letter of yours. I had not even heard of the existence of that bill before you wrote me.[1]

Affectionately,

[OF 931:CT]

[1] Clark, a cousin of Roosevelt, wrote May 10, 1935 (OF 931), in opposition to a bill introduced April 23, 1935, by Rep. Sam D. McReynolds, H.R. 7675, "To provide for the national defense by encouraging the domestic production of tin, and by decreasing the dependence of the United States upon foreign nations for a supply of the same." Clark said the bill would not accomplish its professed objectives and would simply be an expensive subsidy to domestic tin producers. "A further effect of this Bill would be to disrupt and affront long established foreign trade connections and impose another penalty on our exports by further cutting down the ability of foreigners to buy primarily American products." The bill, referred April 23, 1935, to the House Committee on Ways and Means, was not reported (*Cong. Rec.,* vol. 79, p. 6257).

Roosevelt to Francis B. Sayre, Assistant Secretary of State

Washington, May 24, 1935

Memorandum for Assistant Secretary Sayre: "Potatoes is Potatoes!" I cannot approve any reduction in the tariff on them. This need not be embarrassing because this decision applies only to potatoes—I know my potatoes![1]

F.D.R.

[OF 61-P:T]

[1] This memorandum refers to Sayre's letter to McIntyre of May 3, 1935 (OF 61-P). Sayre said the State Department had received several letters asking for confirmation of a report that the President had said there would be no reduction in the tariff on potatoes under the Canadian trade agreement. He also said that he doubted that the President had made any such statements; he would know that such promises would "invite all kinds of pressure from lobbyists."

Roosevelt to Samuel R. Fuller, Jr., President, American Bemberg Corporation, New York

[Washington] May 27, 1935

Dear Sam: Many thanks for that mighty nice note of yours. I really believe that the Bonus Message has accomplished some permanent good.

If you are going abroad soon, I wish you would run down and see me before you go because there are some special matters for which I should like to have you keep your eyes open.[1]

Always sincerely,

[PPF 2616:CT]

[1] In his note of May 23, 1935 (PPF 2616), Fuller congratulated Roosevelt on his message to Congress of May 22; he also said that he still made semi-annual business trips to Germany, the Netherlands, and England and he offered his services to the President. See Roosevelt to Dodd, June 26, 1935, below.

Roosevelt to Nathan Ottinger, New York

[Washington] May 28, 1935

My dear Mr. Ottinger: I have given consideration to your letter of May eighth,[1] relating to the restrictions of Public Resolution 53, 73rd Congress, upon the return to German nationals of property seized by the Alien Property Custodian under the Trading with the Enemy Act of October sixth, 1917. You state that the effect of the Resolution is to confiscate private property in time of peace, and that the Resolution is incompatible with the assurance given by the Secretary of State on February eighth, 1917, relating to private rights of aliens, and with the terms of the Settlement of War Claims Act of 1928. You further urge that the embargo is contrary to the best interests internationally of our Government.

Public Resolution 53 provides in terms for a postponement of all payments, conveyances, transfers or deliveries of money or property under the Trading with the Enemy Act, as amended, or the Settlement of War Claims Act of 1928, as amended, and the reservation of all such money and property and the income thereof "so long as Germany is in arrears in any payment of principal or interest" under the debt-funding agreement between Germany and the United States dated June twenty-third, 1930. The act, you will note, provides not for a confiscation but for a postponement of return. It was apparently the intent of the Congress that the time of the resumption of returns and payments should rest primarily with the discretion of the German Government in regularizing its position under the debt-funding agreement of 1930.

The press statement of February 8, 1917 discloses no assurance given for the benefit of nationals of prospective enemy countries. Nor does it appear that any action has been taken inconsistent with rights accorded our Government under the Treaty of Berlin for the protection and security of American nationals having claims against the German Government.[2]

Very sincerely yours,

[OF 77:CT]

[1] OF 77. Ottinger was an attorney representing claimants of property of German nationals seized by the United States in World War I.

[2] Drafted by the Attorney General. With the draft is a copy of a long letter from Secretary of State Hull to Senator Harrison, May 27, 1935, also drafted by the Attorney General and also bearing on the question raised by Ottinger. Ottinger wrote again on the same subject on July 1, 1935; Roosevelt replied that his views on Public Resolution 53 had not changed since his former letter (the one here printed).

Cordell Hull, Secretary of State, to Roosevelt

[Washington] May 28, 1935

My dear Mr. President: I feel that the time has come when you should give serious consideration to the advisability of formally recognizing the Administration of Edwin Barclay, President of Liberia.

You will recall that a friendly inquiry into Liberia's internal conditions in 1930 carried out by the League of Nations with the cooperation of the United States, resulted in promises of specific reforms by Mr. King who was President of the Republic at the time.[1] Shortly thereafter President King resigned in favor of Edwin Barclay, who became Acting President of the Republic in December 1930. Mr. Barclay failed to give satisfactory assurances with respect to the reforms which this Government considered essential to Liberia's economic and social well-being, and formal recognition of Mr. Barclay's Administration was and has since been withheld. Similarly, the British Government has not recognized the Barclay Administration. The United States cooperated with the League of Nations in drawing up a Plan of Assistance to Liberia embodying a number of reforms. This Plan, however, was rejected by Liberia and subsequently withdrawn by the League. Later on President Barclay drew up his own plan of reform which embodied many of the essential recommendations of the League experts. President Barclay is putting his plan into execution and I have been gratified to note that progress has already been achieved. I have also been gratified to observe that the difficulties which have arisen as a result of Liberia's financial default have been successfully removed.

I consider that President Barclay and the Liberian Government are now faithfully endeavoring to carry out their plan for Liberia's rehabilitation and I am in favor of lending the further impetus to their efforts which the resumption of official relations will provide. The Liberian Congress is meeting this week, and according to all reports, will repeal certain confiscatory legislation against which we have been protesting. Just as soon as this step has been taken (though until then our decision should remain confidential), I hope that you will authorize me to instruct the American Chargé d'Affaires ad interim at Monrovia to extend in your name official recognition of President Barclay's Administration.

I was hoping that the British Government which has helpfully cooperated with us in our efforts to bring about the present improved conditions in Liberia would accord simultaneous recognition, but the British continue to feel that a final settlement of certain outstanding difficulties between the Monrovians and the Kru tribes should be reached as a condition precedent by them to recognition. While we regret the absence of a final settlement of the Kru question, nevertheless we continue to feel that this problem is only one part of a larger problem; that President Barclay's reform plan provides for the reorganization of native administration under a foreign specialist who can take up the

Kru question first; that there is no outstanding urgency in the matter as all is quiet in that area. Finally, we are convinced that a continuation of non-recognition can no longer serve a useful purpose; on the contrary, due to the psychology of the Liberians, we believe that further non-recognition would raise an insurmountable barrier which would prevent us from assisting in the formation and operation of President Barclay's plans.[2]

Faithfully yours,

Cordell Hull

[OF 476:CT]

[1] Charles D. King was forced to resign as president as a result of an investigation by the League of Nations of forced labor and slavery in Liberia.
[2] Answered below.

Roosevelt to Cordell Hull, Secretary of State

Washington, May 29, 1935

Memorandum for the Secretary of State: I entirely approve your suggestion[1] that the United States formally recognize the Administration of Edwin Barclay, President of Liberia, and that the American Chargé d'Affaires at Monrovia be instructed to extend recognition.

Please let me know whether you think it advisable for us to send a Minister?

I also approve your recommendation that Mr. Charles I. McCaskey be designated as Financial Adviser to the Liberian Government, subject to the approval of the President of Liberia.[2]

F.D.R.

[OF 476:CT]

[1] Above. Barclay's administration was recognized June 11, 1935.
[2] Hull made this recommendation in a second letter of May 28 (OF 476).

Press Conference, Executive Offices of the White House, May 29, 1935, 4 P.M.

[Excerpt] Q: (Mr. Young) Can you tell us anything about your talk with Governor Harrison?[1]

The President: No, that talk was about the French situation.

Q: Any conclusions?

The President: That you will have to ask the Treasury Department about. That is one of those things I cannot talk about.

Q: During the past few days both Stanley Baldwin and Anthony Eden have expressed the desire of the British for closer cooperation with us in the maintenance of world peace. Can you tell us whether or not that desire is reciprocated on our part?

The President: Yes. (Laughter)

Q: Without equivocation?

The President: Yes, without equivocation, we are in favor of world peace.

Q: Having progressed that far, can we induce you to elucidate on Baldwin's dream that some day the navies and general manpower and resources of the United States and Great Britain might be used jointly in the maintenance of world peace?

The President: Isn't that rather a warlike statement? Jointly against whom?

Q: Just as a guarantee of world peace (laughter), against anyone that attempts to break the peace.

The President: I think that sounds awfully belligerent.

[President's Press Conferences:T]

[1] The questioner was John Russell Young of the Washington *Evening Star*. George L. Harrison, governor of the Federal Reserve Bank of New York, had conferred with Roosevelt that morning (PPF 1-0).

Roosevelt to Harold E. Fey, Secretary, American Fellowship of Reconciliation, New York

[Washington] May 29, 1935

My dear Mr. Fey: I have received from Japan a letter sent by you for publication in Japan under date of May 3rd, 1935.[1] I understand that this letter, sent by fifteen religious leaders in this country, was also signed by five hundred other persons.

Will you be good enough, for my information, to let me know whether this is true?[2]

Very sincerely yours,

[PSF:Japan:CT]

[1] Enclosed in Phillips to Roosevelt, May 23, 1935, above.
[2] No reply has been found.

Roosevelt to Claude A. Swanson, Secretary of the Navy

Washington, May 30, 1935

Confidential

Memorandum for the Secretary of the Navy: I am greatly interested in the reports of the recent expedition to Baker, Howland and Jarvis Islands. Keep me in touch with the progress of the men landed on these Islands.

I am inclined to think in view of general conditions, that we should maintain this colonization for at least a year, even though it means sending a ship every three months to replace personnel.

You might speak to me about this and, in the meantime, will you consult State Department and the Department of Commerce.[1]

F.D.R.

[OF 6-V:CT]

[1] The secret occupation of these small islands in the central Pacific was completed by the United States on April 2, 1935; a small party of soldiers and civilians made up the landing personnel. They were instructed to collect information about the islands and to clear areas for landing fields. In the event knowledge of the occupation should leak out, it was arranged that the Post Office Department would announce that it had to do with the planning of an air mail service for the Pacific (Rex Martin, assistant director of Air Commerce, to Roosevelt, Hull, Swanson, and Roper, April 8, 1935; Swanson to Roosevelt, May 23, 1935, sending copies of the logs of the landing parties, OF 6-V). On Feb. 18, 1936, Hull recommended that the islands be placed under one of the departments by executive order (Hull to Roosevelt, Feb. 18, 1936, OF 6-V); see Roosevelt's reply, Feb. 19, 1936, below.

Roosevelt to Langbourne M. Williams, Jr., President, Freeport Texas Company, New York

[Washington, May 31, 1935]

My dear Mr. Williams: I have received your letter of April 25, 1935,[1] in regard to the extension of the reduction of the duty on manganese ore, as provided for in the trade agreement signed on February 2, 1935, with Brazil, to other manganese-exporting countries. I am glad to have this expression of your views in regard to this matter.

I can assure you that the national defense aspects of this matter were thoughtfully considered before the reduction of the duty on manganese ore was included in the Brazilian agreement. Full consideration also was given prior to the conclusion of that agreement to the probable effects of the extension of the reduction of duty, sooner or later, to all other foreign countries.

With reference to your suggestion that the case of manganese is a special one and that, therefore, the reduction of duty might be withheld from countries other than Brazil, I invite your attention to the fact that the Trade Agreements Act provides specifically that any duty proclaimed under a trade agreement with any foreign country other than Cuba shall be applied to the like article of all foreign countries except those which discriminate against American trade or take actions or pursue policies tending to defeat the purposes of the Act.

You will, I am sure, appreciate the practical importance to American export trade as a whole of the widest possible application of the principle of no discrimination. This policy has long been pursued by this Government and is reflected in the Trade Agreements Act.

The question of whether a particular country merits the enjoyment of our reductions of duty in connection with trade agreements cannot be decided arbitrarily nor on the basis of the probable effects of the generalization of a particular reduction of duty. A special inter-departmental committee has been studying and will continue to study carefully the nature of the treatment accorded by foreign countries to American commerce. The question of withholding our reduced rates from any country must be decided on the basis laid down in the Trade Agreements Act.

I am hopeful that your company, by means of efficient production methods and with the advantage of duty-free entry into the United States, will not be as seriously affected as you anticipate.

Sincerely yours,

[Notation:A] 5/31/35
[OF 61-M:CT]

[1] Williams' letter was sent to the State Department for preparation of reply and apparently was not returned to the White House.

Robert W. Bingham, Ambassador to Great Britain, to Roosevelt

[London] June 1, 1935

Dear Mr. President: At a recent function at Buckingham Palace, the King sent for me and told me that he wanted to tell me how greatly he appreciated your personal letter to him,[1] and that he was happy to feel that you and he were friends, and both striving to maintain peace in the world, and to lead the British and American peoples along the pathway of progress and prosperity. There is no question about the spontaneous enthusiasm displayed by all classes of people here towards the King and Queen during the Jubilee celebrations. It was more than a tribute to the head of the state because it was an expression as well of gratitude and affection to a friend who had wisely and conscientiously and ably served them all.

Sincerely yours,

Robert W. Bingham

[PSF:Great Britain:TS]

[1] Roosevelt had sent a cable to King George on May 6, 1935, congratulating him on the twenty-fifth anniversary of his accession. In Hull's note to Roosevelt of May 1, 1935 (OF 48), sending the draft of the telegram, he suggested that the President also send a personal letter. Presumably this is the letter here referred to although no copy of it has been found and it was not made public.

William C. Bullitt, Ambassador to the Union of Soviet Socialist Republics, to Roosevelt

Moscow, June 3, 1935

Personal and Confidential

Dear Mr. President: Now that I have returned to the status which Queen Victoria used to refer to as that of a "common Duke," I think I ought to give you an account of my experiences during my elevation to the rank of your Special Representative.

To get to Pilsudski's funeral on time was not easy.[1] I received the Secretary's telegram Thursday morning (May 16) and had to be in the church in Warsaw at nine on Friday morning and there were no regular trains or planes available. I got a plane and flew from Moscow to Minsk, noting with stupefaction the improvement in conditions throughout White Russia. The fields were extraordinarily well-planted and there were hundreds of new apple orchards beautifully tended, each tree with its trunk neatly whitewashed. Minsk, the traditional garbage heap of the Jewish pale, was clean and contained one enormous Government office building which would not have been out of place in Washington. The reports that my plane had a crash in Minsk were a pure invention.[2]

The flight was as easy and comfortable as could be. I then crossed the frontier by train and the Poles had waiting for me Pilsudski's private car which they hooked on to a train that got to Warsaw an hour before the ceremonies began.

The Polish Government was obviously delighted that you should have sent a Special Representative (only Crosby,[3] our Chargé d'Affaires seemed somewhat miffed), and went out of its way to place me at the top of the procession by using a pleasant twist of the French diplomatic alphabet. I was the representative of "Amerique, Etats-Unis de," and not "Etats-Unis de Amerique." That put me for all the ceremonies next to Goering who, as representative of "Allemagne," had place No. 1.

Goering swept into the Warsaw cathedral late as if he were a German tenor playing Siegfried. He has the usual German tenor proportions. He is at least a yard across the bottom as the crow flies! In an attempt to get his shoulders out as far as his hips he wears two inches of padding extending each one. It is useless. The shoulders just won't go that far. He is nearly a yard from rear to umbilicus, and as he is not even as tall as I am and encases himself in a glove-tight uniform, the effect is novel. He must carry with him a personal beauty attendant as his fingers, which are almost as thick as they are short, carry long-pointed, carefully enamelled nails and his pink complexion shows every sign of daily attention. His eyes pop wildly as if he were either suffering from a glandular derangement or still taking cocaine. His lips are as thin as those of an infant. When he was 250 pounds lighter he must have been a blond beauty of the most unpleasant sort. He is really the most appalling representative of a nation that I have ever laid eyes on. He made me feel that the Germans will achieve nothing but a series of national disasters until they cease to take the *Niebelungenlied* seriously.

Goering stole the show from the moment he entered the cathedral, and it became not Pilsudski's funeral but Goering's great first-act entrance. Throughout the march from the cathedral to the aviation field— three hours in a drizzling rain—I walked behind the young Siegfried who struck poses everytime a camera appeared.

The crowds that lined the streets were impressive. They were absolutely silent and did not even stir. At the field the troops marched past the coffin to the beat of a drum. The silence was more impressive than any music. That night we took the train from Cracow and the next day the march was repeated, ending at the Wawel, the old hill castle of the Polish kings. The Catholic Church did itself proud by putting on a really beautiful service. It was rather long, however, and Goering went to sleep.

Afterward, President Moscicki[4] held a reception for the representatives of the various nations and asked me to thank you personally for having sent a Special Representative for the occasion. The next day I had luncheon at the Potocki's[5] with Petain.[6] He and Laval[7] had been treated throughout as if they were unwelcome cousins from the country and Laval was sore; but the old man was in great form. He is seventy-nine but after luncheon he kept a crowd of about thirty persons in screams of laughter for a half hour with an account of his attempts to avoid ice water on his visit to the United States during prohibition.

As Vienna is only two and one-half hours by plane from Cracow, I thought I might as well fly down and consult a decent doctor and did so. My last Cracow view was of a regiment turned out to do the honors as I got into the plane.

The visit to Vienna was a colossal success. Professor Luger[8] spotted the difficulty immediately. It appears that the streptococcus is now entirely out of my body but that it took with it about one-half the sugar in my blood. The result was that my blood pressure when I reached Vienna was exactly one hundred, that of a new-born babe! Hence the exhaustion.

It is difficult to believe, but four days of sunlight and plenty of chocolate in Vienna raised my blood pressure from 100 to 130 and I returned to Warsaw feeling quite alive.

When I was in Vienna I saw Schuschnigg[9] and Berger-Waldenegg,[10] the Foreign Minister, and scores of Austrians whom I have known for years. Messersmith arrived just before I did and I had a number of long talks with him. The most interesting conversation I had was with an old friend of mine who for some years has been one of the secret leaders of the Austrian Nazis. He confirmed everything which I gathered from our own representatives and all the Viennese with whom I talked.

No one in Austria really likes the present Government. Schuschnigg is a colorless, bloodless, young man who resembles a tight-lipped young priest in civilian clothing. He wears a gold cross hanging from one button hole and the old Greek sign for Jesus Christ in the other. On a small table just in front of his desk stands a large crucifix with a silver Christ and two candles. He is the representative of the Catholic Church and does nothing without consulting Cardinal Innitzer. That means that he will do nothing especially foolish but also that he can not catch the imagination of a nation in the twentieth century.

Berger-Waldenegg, the Foreign Minister, is an orderly bureaucrat who reminded me of Burian,[11] the first Austrian Foreign Minister I ever saw at that desk in the Ballhaus.

In addition to the support of the Catholic Church the Government has the support of the Jews of Vienna, including the bankers who are scared to death of a Nazi Government. Moreover, the remnants of the Christian-Socialist Party which used to control all the farmers of the country gives a lukewarm support.

Starhemberg[12] doesn't like Schuschnigg much but is not inclined to clash with him immediately. Starhemberg, it appears, has not been taking his politics too seriously lately and has been devoting his larger energies to a series of charming young ladies. Schuschnigg is frankly a monarchist. I asked him when he thought the Emperor would return and he replied that the matter had not yet come up in serious form, that it might be twenty years, that it might be in ten years, and it might be in one. Starhemberg is not too anxious to have the Hapsburgs return. An old friend of mine told me that he had been talking with Starhemberg on this subject a few days before my arrival and Starhemberg had said, "Why should I or Austria want to have the nouveau riche Hapsburgs back again? My people were good enough to defend Austria for centuries before the Hapsburgs were ever heard of." The spirit of the Philadelphia Club is also international.

The financial situation in Austria has improved out of all reason and the general economic situation is improving. The Nazi boss whom I have known so well in the past that I feel able to vouch for the sincerity of the statement, stated that he did not anticipate any Nazi putsch this summer or for a "very long time thereafter." He said that all the public leaders of the Nazis were either in jail or beyond the frontiers, that all the Nazi centers had been smashed, that Hitler was sending few funds, only enough to keep together small nuclei, and that the Government at the moment had all the cannons and machine guns, the decisive factors. Temporarily, therefore, the Austrian structure seems secure although it would collapse at a moment's notice if any of the supporting beams should be withdrawn. If Mussolini withdraws his support, it will surely go. If Starhemberg should get really angry with Schuschnigg there would of course, be a collapse, but if the present planks in the structure hang together there is no chance of the Government being overthrown by a Nazi explosion. I was much surprised to reach this conclusion as all the news I had received here and in Warsaw had led me to believe that the position of the Austrian Government was threatened by internal Nazi explosion. Incidentally, Messersmith holds the same opinion that I do and he is no fool.

When I returned to Warsaw I had lunch alone with Beck[13] and his wife. The lady, who is a charmer, left us immediately after the meal and we had a good talk. From Beck and from many other persons in Poland I got the following bits of information: Before Pilsudski's death it had been arranged that as soon as the new constitution, which gives dictatorial powers to the President, should take effect, Moscicki, who is now President, should resign and be replaced by one of Pilsudski's chief assistants. Pilsudski had not indicated which one he would choose but the general opinion was that it would be General Rydz-Smigly,[14] now Inspector General of the Polish Army. I was told on good authority that just before Pilsudski's funeral, Rydz-Smigly went to Moscicki and asked him how soon he intended to resign and Moscicki replied that he would be glad to consider the question of his resignation at the end of his presidential term, to wit: in 1940! Moscicki is a savant and has some knowledge of economic matters but is a mild old gentleman—about the last man that one should pick as a dictator. The question agitating everyone in Warsaw is whether Rydz-Smigly and the generals, Beck and the colonels, Prystor and the politicians, will attempt to overthrow Moscicki and start a battle royal for the dictatorship. My own guess is that nothing of the kind will happen for some time at least. The Poles are sincere patriots and unless Moscicki should collapse physically or make some big mistakes, I think that Beck, Rydz-Smigly, and the rest will be content to work under and through him. Beck assured me that this would happen and so did many others.

I am more convinced than ever that there is no secret agreement between Poland and Germany. The Polish Army is definitely anti-German and I can not find in Beck a trace of real pro-Germanism. His whole policy is based on the determination never to allow the foot of a German or Russian soldier to be placed on Polish soil and never to permit airplanes of either power to fly over Polish territory. That is not pro-Germanism but plain common sense.

I said this to Litvinov when we travelled together from Warsaw to Moscow. (Incidentally, our late guest in Washington was most affable and invited me to join him in his private car for the trip, which I did.) Litvinov replied that while he agreed that there was no written agreement between Poland and Germany he believed that Beck's unwillingness to enter into a pact of mutual assistance with the Soviet Union was based on the hope that within the next few years Japan would attack the Soviet Union and that Poland would then be able to annex sections of the Ukraine and also would participate in a joint German-Hungarian-Polish demolition of Czechoslovakia. That seems to me pure Bolshevik propaganda. As Litvinov and I were in the same car we talked for many hours about everything in heaven and earth and were finally reduced to playing a Russian card game, the central feature of which is a cork in the middle of the table which one tries to slap before one's opponent.

Litvinov is a quick slapper.

I wish I could transfer myself to Washington by radio for an evening of talk with you. A volume of typewriting would be needed to cover all I have to tell you. And I would like to hear your voice again.[15]

Good luck and every good wish.

Yours always,

Bill

[PSF:Russia:TS]

[1] Josef Pilsudski had died May 12.
[2] See New York *Times,* May 17, 1935, p. 13.
[3] Sheldon L. Crosby, counsellor of embassy at Warsaw since 1932.
[4] Ignacy Mościcky was president from 1926 to 1939.
[5] Jerzy Potocki, Polish ambassador to the U.S.S.R., was sent to Washington as ambassador in 1936.
[6] Marshal Henri Phillippe Pétain.
[7] Pierre Laval, French Minister of Foreign Affairs.
[8] Dr. Alfred P. Luger.
[9] Kurt von Schuschnigg, Chancellor of Austria.
[10] Egon Berger-Waldenegg.
[11] Presumably Count Stephan von Burián von Rajecz, Austrian Foreign Minister in 1918.
[12] Ernst Ruediger von Starhemberg, Austrian vice-chancellor.
[13] Josef Beck, Polish Minister of Foreign Affairs.
[14] Edward Rydz-Smigly became marshal of Poland after Pilsudski's death.
[15] Roosevelt's reply of June 21, 1935, is printed in *Personal Letters, 1928–1945,* I, 488–489.

Roosevelt to Geoffrey Francis Taylor Colby, Nairobi, Kenya

Hyde Park, N.Y., June 11, 1935

Dear Franny: I am glad to hear about your interesting trips and I hope that some day I shall have a chance to see east and northeast Africa.

I envy you your trip to Abyssinia, and of course we all hope that there will not be serious trouble there. Write me some time again and tell me about it.[1]

Always sincerely,

[PPF 1511:CT]

[1] Major Geoffrey Francis Taylor Colby, in the British colonial service in Nigeria, had talked with Roosevelt at the White House on Feb. 1, 1934 (PPF 1-0). He wrote from Nairobi in Kenya, May 10, 1935 (PPF 1511), that he found the situation in Ethiopia "critical and interesting," and thought that its occupation by a European power with a surplus population would be of great advantage to the occupying nation. He wrote again Aug. 28, 1935 (PPF 1511), that the Ethiopian War had created no unrest among the natives of Central Africa, who disliked the Ethiopians and were indifferent to the Italian invasion.

Jesse Isidor Straus, Ambassador to France, to Roosevelt

Paris, June 11, 1935

Personal

My dear Mr. President: Many thanks for your letter of May 9th.[1] I hope that you understand that I did not write you from caprice or irritation, but solely for what I believe to be the good of the service at this particular post, the only one, of course, about which I know anything. I understand that some of the difficulties of the State Department are the result of Congressional action and consequent restrictions imposed upon the Director of the Budget and the Comptroller General; but I had hoped that in calling your attention and that of the Secretary to some of the cumbersome rules and regulations, Congress might be induced to see fit to adapt the laws to changed conditions, and even conceivably discriminate, where discrimination would seem wise, between this post and others at which conditions are doubtless different.

In the meantime, Mr. James C. Dunn, who is to become the Chief of the Division of Western European Affairs, has been here, and I have had several long conferences with him. I am sure that he realizes some of the difficulties under which we here labor and have hopes that he may be able to have some changes effected.

I am glad to hear that Mr. Marriner was able to have a talk with you. He will be back tomorrow.[2]

I have applied for home leave, to sail from here on July 18th, and shall spend my holiday at Mount Kisco and shall visit the State Department when and if the Secretary or the Undersecretary want me. I also hope that you may have time to receive me either at Washington or at Hyde Park, at whichever place you may be, during August or September.

According to all reports, conditions at home are gradually changing for the better. Confidence is returning and your courageous policies are bearing results.[3]

Very sincerely yours,

Jesse Isidor Straus

[PSF:France:TS]

[1] Above.
[2] J. Theodore Marriner, counselor of embassy in Paris.
[3] Answered June 20, 1935, below.

Press Conference, on the Presidential Train En Route from West Point to Washington, June 12, 1935, 3:00 P.M.

[*Excerpt*] Q: Mr. President, there have been several stories in the papers about Admiral Yates Stirling on Sunday, in which he suggested that the rest of the world should gang up on Russia. I understand that the State Department said he was speaking only for himself and not for them.[1]

The President: I have not seen the story—you will have to make this off the record. I talked to Brown (the Naval Aide to the President)[2] this morning and Brown said that several letters had come in and had been referred to the Navy Department, also that somebody over there had read the story and said that he (Admiral Stirling) did not say that at all.

My impression is that it was just that he said that if certain things happened, such and such other things might result in Europe. I have not read the story, so I do not know.

Q: You won't make any comment at all on it?

The President: No, because we do not know yet what we are talking about.

[President's Press Conferences:T]

[1] Stirling, commandant of the Brooklyn Navy Yard, in a syndicated article in the Washington *Herald* of June 9, 1935, proposed that the anti-communist nations concert military measures against Russia; this brought forth numerous protests from anti-war groups and from members of Congress. At his press conference of June 14, 1935, Roosevelt was asked if he was taking any action on the incident; he replied that the Navy Department would make a statement soon (President's Press Conferences). In a letter to Representative Carl Vinson, chairman of the House Naval Affairs Committee,

dated June 14, 1935, and released to the newspapers the next day, Secretary of the Navy Swanson said that Stirling's article represented his private views and not those of the Navy (New York *Times,* June 15, 1935, p. 5).

[2] Capt. Wilson Brown. (Words in parentheses, here and below, were added by the White House reporter.)

Grenville T. Emmet, Minister to The Netherlands, to Roosevelt

The Hague, Netherlands, June 15, 1935

Dear Mr. President: Thank you for your letter of the other day giving me the reaction of the State Department to my going out to the Dutch East Indies as a part of the work of this post.[1] I regret the Department's decision but I understand their position perfectly and acquiesce whole-heartedly in their ruling. Perhaps some day, while I am here, they may want me to go and, if so, I will learn a lot that will be of benefit to the United States and its Minister to the Netherlands.

I have just got back from a trip to Czechoslovakia which Pauline and I took by motor, driving ourselves. I spent four days in Prague and saw considerable of the Butler Wrights,[2] which was a great pleasure. He is most enthusiastic about his post and is very popular with everyone. After all the pessimism over the condition of the beautiful old palace which houses the American Legation, it has now been put in excellent order, arranged attractively by the Wrights, and does the U.S.A. great credit. I was much interested in the political questions affecting Czechoslovakia but they differ so radically from those affecting this country that it is difficult to grasp them in a few days. In Czechoslovakia there are several millions of Germans whereas here there are probably not more than a hundred thousand all told, and in Czechoslovakia the counteracting influences of Austria as well as Hungary are playing strong whereas here they do not exist or are negligible.

My work here continues interesting and busy. The political situation of this country is certainly not static and at the moment it seems to me there is considerable likelihood of political changes arising directly or indirectly from the issue of devaluation, which is coming more and more to the front as a political question. As I have frequently advised the Department and I think told you, this country has had hard sledding and gone through hard times as a result of following a policy of deflation rather than devaluation. However, the banking situation here is so strong and the pillars of the arch which was built to bridge over or avoid devaluation are so sturdy in the shape of men like Colijn[3] and Trip,[4] that purely as a practical question it has up to the present seemed likely that the Government could continue on the present gold standard for a considerable time. However, the devaluation influence as opposed to the deflation influence has increased considerably, and it now begins to look as though the whole currency and financial policy of the Government might come into the open in Parliament on the passage of the Economy Bill, which is now pending and which will begin to be debated about July 1st. Recently there have been two resignations from the Cabinet, one by Minister of Education Marchant who gave as his reason that he had adopted the Roman Catholic faith and could no longer represent the Independent Democratic Party; and the other resignation by Mr. Steenberghe, the Minister of Economic Affairs, who was a prominent member of the Catholic Party and who gave as the reason of his resignation that he was not in sympathy with the Government's policy of deflation as opposed to devaluation. It seems to me not unlikely that further defections will occur among the Government ranks and the opinion is expressed on many sides that the Government may not be able to pass the Economy Bill without considerable amendment. If the Government should be defeated on the Economy Bill, it might easily lead to a change of Government. Altogether it is an interesting situation to observe and follow.

Mrs. Ruth Bryan Owen, United States Minister to Denmark, is coming to spend the week-end with us and we are giving her a dinner party tomorrow night. I met her last winter at the White House one afternoon when I stopped in to have tea with Eleanor and Mrs. Owen and I arranged then that she would come and see us this spring.

Last month we entertained the delegates to the Federation of American Women's clubs in Europe which met here, as well as the delegation of American Garden Lovers who came over to see the tulips and attend the Flower Show. One day we had a buffet luncheon for one hundred and fifty persons at the Legation and a few days later an afternoon tea and reception for over two hundred, so that for a short time Pauline and I were kept very busy attending to the social side of our visiting compatriots.

I hope you are well and are standing the terrific strain of your life in Washington. I know how tremendous is the pressure under which you live and I hope you are able to get some relaxation from time to time.

I am sure it is gratifying to you to see the way the country is responding to the N.R.A. decision and that it is obviously the wish of the rank and file of the people that the principles which the N.R.A. embodies be perpetuated.

With best wishes, believe me to be, Faithfully yours,

Grenville T. Emmet

[PSF:Netherlands:TS]

[1] May 2, 1935 (*Personal Letters, 1928–1945,* I, 478). The State Department recommended against Emmet's proposed trip on the ground that, coming so soon after the Japanese denunciation of the Washington Naval Treaty, it would cause concern in the Far East.
[2] Minister to Czechoslovakia.
[3] Hendrik Colijn, Prime Minister.
[4] Leonardus Trip, president of the Bank for International Settlements.

Roosevelt to Cordell Hull, Secretary of State

[Washington] June 20, 1935

My dear Mr. Secretary: In order that constant effective consideration may be given the development of American air transport lines in foreign territories, I feel it desirable to create an Interdepartmental Committee to be composed of high officials of the Department of State, the Treasury Department, the Post Office Department, and the Department of Commerce for the purpose of making observations and gathering information pertaining to civil international aviation in all its phases and submitting such recommendations as may seem called for.

I will thank you to designate such an official of your Department to serve on the suggested committee.

Similar letters have been sent to the Secretary of the Treasury, the Postmaster General, and the Secretary of Commerce.[1]

Very sincerely yours,

[OF 249-C:CT]

[1] This subject was discussed with the President at the White House on June 14, 1935, at an hour-long conference attended by Assistant Secretary of State Moore and by Hull. Moore's memorandum of the conference, June 15, 1935 (with this letter), noted the State Department's position, that the government "should keep up with the development

of International Aviation, so that the entire field may not largely be taken over by foreign governments," and that to this end it would be well for the President to create "a committee of observation" to keep up with events and to make recommendations. Moore had handed the President a draft executive order to set up such a committee, but he decided simply so to instruct the departments, and had Forster, White House executive clerk, draft the letter here printed (Roosevelt to Forster, June 16, 1935, OF 249-C).

Creation of the Interdepartmental Committee on Civil International Aviation was announced in a White House press release of July 2, 1935 (OF 249-C): its purpose was to assist in the development of American transport lines in foreign countries. Members of the committee were Assistant Secretary of State R. Walton Moore, Assistant Secretary of the Treasury Stephen B. Gibbons, Second Assistant Postmaster General Harllee Branch, and Assistant Secretary of Commerce John M. Johnson.

Roosevelt to Jesse Isidor Straus, Ambassador to France, Paris

[Washington] June 20, 1935

Dear Jesse: It is good to know that you are coming back for a little holiday.[1] I hear that your health is vastly improved, for which I am thankful.

I do not know yet when Congress will adjourn but when you arrive I shall probably still be in Washington. Do run down any time at your convenience.

As ever yours,

[PSF:France:CT]

[1] This note is in reply to Straus's letter of June 11, 1935, above.

Sumner Welles, Assistant Secretary of State, to Roosevelt

Washington, June 25, 1935

My dear Mr. President: In the belief that the information contained in it will be of interest to you, I am enclosing herewith a memorandum of a conversation I had this morning with the Mexican Ambassador. I think you will wish to read it before you talk with the House delegation which may come to see you with regard to the resolution on the Mexican religious question.[1]

I had, this afternoon, a long talk with Father Burke[2] and told him of the information the Mexican Ambassador had given me with regard to the religious situation. I also suggested that it might be useful to him to see Father Serié before he left Washington.[3] Father Burke seemed to be decidedly encouraged by the information I gave him and said to me that he would recommend to the Vatican that if a solution of the religious question could be reached between the Mexican Government and the Mexican bishops, or any one of them, it would be by far the wiser policy for the Vatican to further this move. He has apparently abandoned his insistence that an Italian Nuncio be appointed.

Father Burke also told me that Cardinal Hayes had recently expressed to him his keen regret that you had not seen fit to intervene in the matter of religious freedom in Mexico, and that in order to correct this misapprehension on the Cardinal's part, Father Burke had written him a confidential letter in which he told the Cardinal of all that you had done and of the abiding interest which you had in the solution of this problem.[4] He told me that he had this morning received a reply from the Cardinal saying that he regretted his misapprehension of the facts and expressing his appreciation of your attitude. Father Burke deprecated, in the strongest terms, the most recent letter addressed to you by the Knights of Columbus[5] and told me that he would do everything within his power to be of help in preventing any further outbursts of this character.

Faithfully yours,

Sumner Welles

[PSF:Mexico:TS]

[1] A House delegation of 250 members presented a petition to the President on July 16, 1935, asking that the government investigate conditions in Mexico with respect to rights of worship of United States nationals. With the petition is a memorandum, also submitted by the congressmen, which pointed out that more than two-thirds of the petitioners were either Protestants or Jews (OF 146-A). Roosevelt did not commit himself on the request but issued a statement that he was "in entire sympathy with all people who make it clear that the American people and the Government believe in freedom of religious worship not only in the United States, but also in other nations." The petition and the President's statement are printed in the New York *Times,* July 17, 1935, p. 1; the statement is also printed in *Public Papers,* IV, 305.

[2] John J. Burke, general secretary of the National Catholic Welfare Conference.

[3] Serié is identified in Welles's memorandum, below.

[4] Patrick Cardinal Hayes frequently exchanged friendly letters of greeting with President Roosevelt but no mention of the Mexican religious issue has been found in their correspondence.

[5] Martin H. Carmody, supreme knight, Knights of Columbus, had written to Roosevelt on May 3 and June 23 (OF 28), demanding an audience for his group. Presumably the former letter is meant here though it is not impossible that Burke may have been informed of the later one as soon as it was received.

[*Enclosure*] Memorandum by Sumner Welles

June 25, 1935

Conversation. The Mexican Ambassador, who returned to Washington yesterday after a month's absence in Mexico, came in to see me this morning. Dr. Castillo Nájera told me in some detail of his conferences with President Cárdenas, with General Calles, and with Dr. Portes Gil, until recently Foreign Secretary in the Cárdenas cabinet and now newly elected President of the National Revolutionary Party.

The Ambassador said that General Calles was, at least temporarily and probably definitely, out of the Mexican political picture. He had spent the day with Calles at the latter's house in Cuernavaca on June 11, the day before General Calles's sensational statements criticising the Cárdenas Government were made public. Calles had stated that he desired to make it clear that he believed the course of the Government was wrong and that he refused to accept any responsibility for the policy pursued. He told the Ambassador that he would go to his ranch for a couple of months to await developments and that if no crisis ensued, he would leave the Republic and would remain abroad, probably in Europe. He further said that he would not return to Mexico unless he were called upon to return by the Government of Mexico. The Ambassador said that he found General Calles more vehement against the Catholic Church and more opposed to any arrangement between the Mexican Government and the Catholic Church than at any time in the past.

The Ambassador said that he had discussed the religious question at great length upon several occasions with Portes Gil and once with President Cárdenas. The only commitment that Cárdenas made with regard to religious policy was that he would favor the reopening of the churches and the right to worship in accordance with state laws provided "the political situation made it possible."

Portes Gil, the Ambassador says, has more influence with Cárdenas at the present time than any other member of the National Revolutionary Party. According to the Ambassador, the former desires a reasonable solution of the religious question and is a firm believer in a policy of moderation. As an evidence of this, the Ambassador reports that the replacement as Secretary of Agriculture of Señor Garrido Canabal of Tabasco, the most rabid anti-Catholic in Mexican public life, by Governor Cedillo[1] of San Luis Potosí, nationally known for the favor he has shown the Catholic Church during the heat of the persecution, was due to the influence exerted by Dr. Portes Gil. The Ambassador claims that this is the first concrete evidence of the desire of the Cárdenas Government to adopt a liberal policy towards the Mexican Catholics. The Ambassador was further told on the long distance telephone this morning by Dr. Portes Gil that the churches are now being reopened in the State of Colima and that the churches will also be reopened in the near future in the State of Querétaro. In Mexico City with the full knowledge of the Government many more priests are officiating than are permitted under law. There are no restrictions being placed upon orderly demonstrations by Catholics. It is the intention of the Mexican Government gradually to further this policy in all of the Mexican states although in the State of Sonora where Calles's son, Rodolfo Calles will continue as Governor until the end of next month no change will probably take place until late in the summer. In the State of Tabasco where Garrido Canabal is still in control a considerably longer period will elapse before anything approaching the right to worship can be obtained.

The Ambassador gave me clearly to understand that Portes Gil favored the appointment by the Vatican of Archbishop Diaz[2] as Papal Nuncio in the place of Monsignor Ruiz y Flores now a refugee in San Antonio, Texas, and that if this appointment were made it would probably be possible to work out some satisfactory agreement regarding the right of Catholic priests to officiate in Mexico. I understood that there had been already an exchange of views between Archbishop Diaz and Portes Gil. (Statements published this afternoon by the Universal Service quoting Archbishop Diaz as saying that the moment now seemed propitious for the reaching of an understanding between church and state would seem to confirm this.)

The Ambassador told me that Portes Gil had further said to him that an understanding would be possible provided that an understanding were reached between Mexicans but that if foreign pressure was brought to bear, either from Rome, through the Catholic Church in the United States, or through the Church in any other country, an understanding would be delayed if not rendered impossible.

The Ambassador believes that the political situation in Mexico will be determined before September 1, next. He feels that with the probable removal of General Calles from the scene the danger now will lie in the possibility that the extreme radical groups formerly opposed to Calles will consolidate and either oppose the Cárdenas Government or force it to travel along an extreme radical road. He classified General Cárdenas as a man of integrity and of honest intentions but without experience and as "extremely ingenuous in politics." He gave me clearly to understand that Cárdenas for the time being at least would be guided by the new group within the National Revolutionary power which has seized control. He maintains that the elimination of General Calles of whom he is personally fond is a good thing for Mexico inasmuch as the situation during recent years amounted practically to a dictatorship and that if the dictator had been assassinated or had suddenly died Mexico would probably have been plunged again into civil war.

I told the Ambassador that I appreciated very deeply the very frank statement he had made to me of his trip to Mexico and of conditions as he saw them. I said that, of course, as the President had stated to him, the distress caused many of our American citizens by the condition of Catholics in Mexico created a very serious problem for us here; that I was delighted to hear of the more moderate policy undertaken by his Government with regard to the Church and that I trusted that an improvement in conditions would make it possible for the Mexican Government rapidly to undertake an even more moderate policy.

I asked the Ambassador if he did not now feel authorized to have a confidential conversation with Father Burke and I again told him that in order to avoid publicity I would be very glad to invite them to my own house for such a conversation. The Ambassador said, however, that he would prefer not to see Father Burke at this time and gave as his particular reason for objecting to such an interview the fact that Mr. Montavon,[3] Father Burke's secretary, had published a few years ago some pamphlets in which he attacked the Mexican Government very violently.

The Ambassador said, however, that he had talked yesterday with Father Serié, a Salesian father of Argentine birth who has spent most of his life in Rome and who has recently visited Mexico ostensibly to study leprosy in Mexico. Father Serié is now on his way back to Rome and told the Ambassador that he undoubtedly would be called to the Vatican to give an account of his trip to Mexico and that he would take the opportunity of indicating his urgent hope that the Vatican would select Archbishop Diaz as the new Nuncio in Mexico. The Ambassador is quite sure that the recent visit of Father Serié to Mexico was by instruction of the Vatican and that the Holy See will undoubtedly be guided by the recommendations which Father Serié may make.

[PSF:Mexico:T]

[1] Saturnino Cedillo.
[2] Pascual Díaz.
[3] William F. Montavon.

540

Roosevelt to the State Department

Washington, June 26, 1935

Memorandum for the State Department: Will you send a line to the Ambassador that my old friend—Samuel R. Fuller, Jr.—is going to Berlin and to show him every courtesy, especially in regard to assistance in meeting the German officials?[1]

F.D.R.

[*Notation*:A:FDR] File   Hold till further notice.
[PSF:Germany:CT]

[1] See below.

Roosevelt to William E. Dodd, Ambassador to Germany, Berlin

[Washington] June 26, 1935

My dear Ambassador Dodd: A very old friend of mine, who was closely associated with me in the Navy Department days—Samuel R. Fuller, Jr.—is going to Berlin, and I hope much that he will have an opportunity to have a talk with Herr Schacht and, if possible, with the Chancellor himself. I should, of course, not be brought into it in any way, but he has seen both of them once and I shall be glad to have his new reactions if he can see them once more.[1]

Always sincerely,

[PSF:Germany:CT]

[1] An attached note in Roosevelt's hand reads: "Dodd—When Fuller gets to Berlin I hope he can see Hitler, Schacht, etc." Dodd mentions a visit from Fuller and his wife in his *Diary*, p. 267.

Roosevelt to Morris Rothenberg, President, Zionist Organization of America, New York

[Washington] June 26, 1935

My dear Mr. Rothenberg: I should be appreciative if you would convey my greetings and best wishes to the thirty-eighth Annual Convention of the Zionist Organization of America which I understand will commence its sessions in Atlantic City on June thirtieth. It is hardly necessary for me to reiterate the interest with which I have followed the work that the Organization is doing toward assisting in the establishment in Palestine of a National Home for the Jewish People.

The solution of the numerous pressing problems with which the Convention is faced will be made easier, I am sure, by a realization of the progress which has been made in Palestine. To this progress the Zionist Organization of America has contributed both spiritually and financially in a large measure and the Jews in the United States may well feel proud of the part they have played in the rebirth and upbuilding of the Holy Land.[1]

Very sincerely yours,

[PPF 601:CT]

[1] Rothenberg, in his letter to Roosevelt of June 17, 1935 (PPF 601), asking for a message to the convention, said that his previous expressions of sympathy with the aims of the Zionist movement had been a matter of deep gratification to the membership and to Jews of the world generally. Early asked Hull for a draft of reply, if he thought a reply proper (Early to Hull, June 19, 1935, PPF 601). Phillips returned a draft (the letter here printed) with the comment that he had found that similar messages had been sent on previous occasions (Phillips to Early, June 25, 1935, PPF 601).

William E. Dodd, Ambassador to Germany, to Roosevelt

[Berlin] June 27, 1935

Dear Mr. President: Permit me to introduce my friend Mr. Karl von Wieg[and] whose work you know and whose personal relations with many European leaders will enable him to give you valuable information. Mr. von Wiegand has been in Berlin a great part of his time during the last twenty five years.[1]

With congratulations on what you have done these last months.

Yours Sincerely,

William E. Dodd

[PSF:Germany:AS]

[1] Dodd had not known Von Wiegand, for twenty-five years Berlin correspondent of the Hearst papers, before going to Germany as ambassador. At their first meeting in the summer of 1933, Dodd noted in his *Diary* (p. 19) that Von Wiegand impressed him "most favorably" and the two became friends at once.

542

Robert W. Bingham, Ambassador to Great Britain, to Roosevelt

[London] June 28, 1935

Dear Mr. President: I think you will be interested to know that the speech which the Prince of Wales recently made at a meeting of the British Legion, in which he suggested an exchange of visits between German and British veterans and forgetting the past, was not only not suggested by the government, but, on the contrary, I am reliably informed the government addressed a strongly-worded communication of protest to him on the subject.

The British are tending more and more to the view that they must improve their relations with us. The situation in Europe itself is bad enough, though not so bad as it has been, but the Far East situation is so ominous that they are beginning to realize it is to their interest to cultivate better relations with us. This may be at the bottom of reports that Ramsay MacDonald is contemplating a visit to the United States in order to have a conference with you. You may already have information on this subject which has not reached us. So far, we have no official confirmation of these reports.

At the rate at which their minds are moving, it seems probable to me that they will make some proposals to us within the next few months, although probably not until after their general election. Meanwhile, I can only repeat what I have said to you before, that I am convinced we should leave them entirely alone until they are ready to come to us.

Their naval agreement with Germany may have been desirable from their standpoint, although the clause permitting Germany to build up to 100% of British submarine strength whenever Germany thought it desirable to do so, has been severely criticized by many influential people here. In addition, the method pursued, apart from the agreement itself, has undoubtedly aroused bitter resentment in France, and I think in Italy as well, because, after the Stresa meeting, both the French and the Italians claimed the naval conferences between the British and the Germans were to be merely exploratory and that they were not informed of an actual agreement until it was an accomplished fact. The position taken by the Government, however, is that France missed several opportunities for an agreement with Germany on a much better basis than they finally had to submit to, which they think was a mistake, and they felt they had a chance of an agreement with Germany which they could not afford to let pass, as the French had done.

Many influential people here, though, feel that no agreement with Germany is worth anything, because they do not believe Germany will keep any promise. I believe the whole purpose of the government now is to try to keep everything as quiet as possible until after their general election. Although some time ago the tide was running strongly against the present national government, I think that has turned, and indications now are that the present government will be returned. If and when this happens I think they are likely to reach out towards us, but, in the absence of some event which cannot now be foreseen, I doubt if we can accomplish anything on stabilization or otherwise until after the election.

It goes without saying that I shall be glad to communicate my views on the whole subject to you, either in writing or in person, whenever you think it desirable to do so.[1]

Sincerely yours,

Robert W. Bingham

[PSF:Great Britain:TS]

[1] Answered July 11, 1935, below.

Cordell Hull, Secretary of State, to Roosevelt

Washington, July 1, 1935

My dear Mr. President: At the meeting of the National Emergency Council on December 11, 1934, it was decided that all requests for recommendations for legislation involving immediate or prospective appropriations should be cleared through the Bureau of the Budget and that all other requests or recommendations for legislation should be cleared through the National Emergency Council for your approval before submission to Congress. It is understood that this applies equally to reports requested by Committees of Congress with respect to measures initiated by the legislative branch of the Government. The purpose of the decision was, insofar as it involved the National Emergency Council, to coordinate the views of the executive departments affected by proposed legislation and bring them into conformity with Administration policy.

With respect to one class of questions, namely, that of commercial and trade problems, the procedure described is having an effect which was not foreseen and which is likely to result in inability to have critical comment reach the appropriate committee of Congress considering a pending bill until too late to be of effect.

Within this field of commercial and trade problems affecting exports and imports you have already set up an Interdepartmental Committee known as the Executive Committee on Commercial Policy for the purpose of coordinating the views of the several Government departments. You will recall that in your letter of November 11, 1933, establishing the Executive Committee on Commercial Policy, you instructed the various heads of the departments and agencies as follows:

I have, therefore, decided to designate one officer in the Department of State to carry the primary responsibility of supervising the international commercial policy of this Government into a coherent whole. Hereafter may I ask that you give the necessary instructions in your Department that before any acts are taken under legislation or otherwise which directly affect the export and import trade in this country, this official should be consulted concerning the action and his approval secured.

It is my idea that this official should be the chairman of an Executive Committee for the coordination of commercial policy and the negotiation of commercial treaties and trade agreements, and that in his decisions he would be very largely carrying out the judgment of the Committee. Upon this Committee your Department will be represented.

Executive Order No. 6656, dated March 27, 1935, reaffirms the functions of this Committee to be "for the purpose of coordinating the commercial policy of the United States." The Commercial Policy Committee thus set up is functioning actively and well.

In view of the fact that legislation relating to foreign trade, tariff rates, export subsidies, and the like, is of great importance and must be dealt with speedily and without delay if effective results are to be had, that every effort should be made to integrate such legislation into our general commercial policy, and that you have already directed the Executive Committee on Commercial Policy to coordinate the views of the several departments and to decide questions of policy concerning foreign trade, it has occurred to me that in the interest of expedition you might be willing to exempt from the requirement of clearing through the National Emergency Council all requests or recommendations for legislation relating to our foreign trade or commercial policy. Such an exemption would be predicated upon the assumption that such matters are currently considered in the weekly meetings of the Executive Committee on Commercial Policy in which the views of the several departments interested are fully coordinated.

This suggestion is made solely with a view to expediting the consideration and clearing of reports on legislation in the important field of commercial policy and avoiding what would seem to be an unnecessary duplication of effort and delay which result from having the interested departments in effect consulted a second time through the medium of the National Emergency Council.

I have taken the occasion informally to consult the National Emergency Council and am informed that no objection whatever is seen by it to the exemption suggested. This could readily be accomplished, if you should approve, by the promulgation by the Executive Director of a notice similar to the draft enclosed.[1]

Faithfully yours,

(s) Cordell Hull

[OF 20:T:Copy]

[1] The draft reads: "Nothing in the letter of instructions of December 13, 1934, in reference to the clearing of proposed legislation, or reports thereon to Committees of Congress, shall be construed to include matters which have already been considered by the Executive Committee on Commercial Policy." See reply of July 3, 1935, below.

Roosevelt to Claude A. Swanson, Secretary of the Navy

Washington, July 2, 1935

Confidential

Memorandum for the Secretary of the Navy: Referring to your confidential letter of June twenty-ninth,[1] relating to 1937 new construction program, I entirely approve of the replacement policy relating to destroyers and submarines. However, in regard to the battleship, I think it important that nothing be said in regard to this for a few months to come—until we are more clear in regard to the Naval Treaty.

This does not mean that work on designs for this battleship should be held up but there should be no publicity of any kind.

F.D.R.

[PSF:Navy:T]

[1] Swanson had requested Roosevelt's approval of a naval building program that included one 35,000-ton battleship, twelve 1,500-ton destroyers, and six 1,350-ton submarines (PSF:Navy).

Roosevelt to Cordell Hull, Secretary of State

Washington, July 3, 1935

Memorandum for the Secretary of State: I have your letter of July first[1] in regard to exempting foreign trade matters from reference to the National Emergency Council for clearance purposes; also, that in the future this work of clearance between Departments be handled by the Interdepartmental Committee on Commercial Policy.

I approve of your suggestions and am sending your letter, with a copy of this note, to the Executive Director and the Acting Director of the Budget.

F.D.R.

[OF 20:T]

[1] Above.

Roosevelt to William Phillips, Under Secretary of State

Washington, July 3, 1935

Memorandum for the Under Secretary of State: This is an extremely interesting dispatch from Kirk but it goes so far beyond any of his previous dispatches that I think we can well say that we now have a good picture of the feeling in Italy whereas before we cabled for it, we had no picture at all.[1] If we got dispatches like this one regularly from all our European Embassies it would be useful.

Also, I am wondering if we should not cable to Kirk to be sure to have the Consuls throughout Italy report to him individual incidents within their jurisdiction and also the state of popular feeling at regular intervals.

F.D.R.

[OF 447:CT]

[1] Alexander Kirk, counselor of embassy at Rome, to Hull, July 2, 1935 (*Foreign Relations, 1935,* I, 610–611). He quoted Chambrun, the French ambassador, as saying that France's interest in the Italo-Ethiopian conflict was governed by three factors: her desire for peace, her support of the League, and her friendship for Italy. French interests in East Africa had been safeguarded by the Laval-Mussolini talks; now everything depended on England and her willingness to help find a solution.

Roosevelt to Martin H. Carmody, Supreme Knight, Knights of Columbus, New Haven, Connecticut

[Washington] July 3, 1935

My dear Mr. Carmody: The delay in replying to your communication of June twenty-third and to your earlier communication requesting that I grant an interview to a committee from your Board of Directors[1] has not been due to any lack of interest on my part in the subject mentioned, but rather to the demands upon my time by pressing public business.

I shall be very glad to see you and your associates any day next week if you still care to discuss the matter with me.[2]

Very sincerely yours,

[OF 28:CT]

[1] May 3 and June 23, 1935 (OF 28); see Welles to Roosevelt, June 25, 1935, above, n. 4.

[2] Drafted by Hull, who said he had consulted Farley on what should be said (Hull to Roosevelt, June 29, 1935, OF 28). A delegation of the Knights of Columbus, headed by Carmody and D. J. Callahan, treasurer of the society, discussed the Mexican situation with Roosevelt on July 8 at the White House for over an hour. It was reported in the press that the group had requested that the United States take the same course with respect to religious persecution in Mexico that it had taken in like situations in other countries (New York *Times*, July 9, 1935, p. 6). See Roosevelt to Carmody, Nov. 13, 1935, below.

Roosevelt to Senator Carter Glass of Virginia

[Washington] July 3, 1935

Dear Carter: Your friend, Parker Willis,[1] said in the *Agence Économic* on July first:

Semi-official declarations reiterated on the part of members of the Government according to which no new measure regarding devaluation is planned are received with some skepticism even though there have been no proofs that such projects are under study at the moment. The invitation to Sir Frederick Leith-Ross to include Washington in his itinerary for the purpose of discussing the question of stabilization is considered a great concession on the part of the Administration which until now has shown itself inclined to insist that the first step be taken by Great Britain. It may, however, be remarked that this invitation comes from the Secretary of State who represents the conservative element in the Cabinet and not from the Secretary of the Treasury whose opinions are nearest in accord with the President. In fact a growing opposition of viewpoints is evident within the Cabinet on this whole question. Many people are now inclined to believe that in case an agreement on stabilization were to be signed this might include lowering the dollar value to the 50 cent level, a measure for which the new legislation on the gold clause perhaps constitutes preparation.

Quite aside from the false and alarmist implications of what he says about devaluation, you are doubtless aware that no invitation has been extended to Sir Frederick Leith-Ross to include Washington in his itinerary.

The Secretary of State was asked at a press conference whether if Sir Frederick Leith-Ross proceeded to China by way of the United States he would see him, and he answered properly and courteously that, of course, on this voyage if he should come to Washington, we should all be glad to see him.[2]

Always sincerely,

[PPF 687:CT]

[1] Henry Parker Willis (1874–1937), an economist, was editor of the *New York Journal of Commerce* from 1919 to 1931 and was at this time American representative of the Paris *Agence Économique*.
[2] Answered below.

Senator Carter Glass of Virginia to Roosevelt

Washington, D.C., July 4, 1935

Strictly Personal

My dear Franklin: Responding to yours of July 3rd,[1] if you will authorize me to say to Dr. Willis that the administration thinks such cables as that quoted by you are misleading and distasteful and calculated to do harm, I will be glad to remonstrate with Dr. Willis about contributions of this kind to the foreign press; otherwise I would have no basis for what might seem to Dr. Willis an impertinence on my part. He and I have never been such intimate friends as to warrant my intervention in such matters without a specific reason.

In this connection, permit me again to assure you that I know nothing whatsoever about the matters concerning which Dr. Willis writes and have had no communication with him, direct or indirect, upon any subject for two years, beyond the invitation extended to him, along with various other political economists, to testify before the Banking and Currency Committee. Moreover I desire to say that, aside from the open testimony given by him, I have never opened my lips to Dr. Willis nor has he opened his lips to me on the subject of the pending banking legislation. I have not needed his advice or that of any other political economist on anything proposed or done in the sub-committee of which I am chairman or the full committee to which our report was made. Thirty-four years of intimate contact with the problem has given me a fair understanding of banking legislation.

I am thus specific in order to have you dismiss from your mind any thought that I am, in any sense, responsible in the remotest way for anything said or done by Dr. Willis. My interest in banking legislation has been exclusively dictated by a concern for all the business interests and the welfare of the people of the country; and I could wish that you would believe this.[2]

Sincerely yours,

Carter Glass

[PPF 687:TS]

[1] Above.

[2] Roosevelt wrote again to Glass on July 6, 1935 (*Personal Letters, 1928–1945,* I, 491–492). He said he had sent the quotation because he thought Glass leaned heavily on Willis' advice. Willis, the President said, was one of those Americans who were appendages on the international bankers of London, Paris, Shanghai, and other foreign cities. This international group considered the United States fair game for them and the Americans who played with them had been fooled.

Thomas J. Watson, President, International Business Machines Corporation, to Roosevelt

Berlin, July 6, 1935

Dear Mr. President: I am prompted to write you this letter as a result of my observations and interviews with the representatives of thirty-nine nations at the Congress of the International Chamber of Commerce in Paris. I have also visited England and Germany, and I have been especially impressed with the activity of the European nations in improving trade relations with each other and with South America and with other outside countries.

Yesterday I had luncheon with Dr. Schacht and a small group of

German financial and industrial leaders. During the conversation Dr. Schacht informed me that last year they purchased only one fourth as much cotton from the United States as in the previous year, and that he was now engaged in closing contracts with Brazil for the coming year. All of the people with whom I have talked on the subject of trade relations are very much impressed with Secretary Hull's efforts to improve same, and I hope he will have an increased support from all of our political, financial and industrial organizations.

I would like to cite my own business as an example of the effect the present trade barriers have had on the American payroll. Up until a few years ago we supplied our foreign trade entirely from our American factories, but now in order to protect our interests abroad it has been necessary for us to establish factories in England, France, Germany and Italy, and we are now employing more than one thousand people in our German factory alone.

When we realize that the United States with six percent of the world's population manufactures fifty percent of all the goods manufactured, it convinces me that we should increase our efforts towards restoring and increasing our foreign trade.

I am attaching copy of a speech which I made at the Congress of the International Chamber of Commerce covering my thoughts on some of the things which I believe will assist in restoring world trade.[1]

With best wishes, I remain, Very respectfully yours,

Thos J. Watson

[OF 614-A:TS]

[1] This speech by Watson on June 26 as head of the American delegation was a plea for the removal of barriers to international trade, the stabilization of currencies, and the settlement of the debt question. The American delegation had proposed that there be immediate consultation by governments on international stabilization and this motion, contrary to expectations, was adopted by the Congress (New York *Times,* June 27, 1935, p. 31).

Roosevelt to Representative William L. Fiesinger of Ohio

[Washington, July 9, 1935]

My dear Mr. Fiesinger: I have received your letter of June 21, 1935,[1] concerning the fishing industry in connection with the proposed reciprocal trade agreement with Canada, in which you state that it is your opinion that any reduction in duty on fish or fish products would seriously injure the domestic fishing industry.

I have been informed that in connection with the proposed trade agreement with Canada representatives of the domestic fishing industry have submitted their views, together with much valuable information, to the Committee for Reciprocity Information, which was created pursuant to Section 4 of the Trade Agreements Act of June 12, 1934, and was designated by me to receive the views of persons interested in proposed trade agreements. These statements have been and are being given the most careful and sympathetic study. I can assure you that full account will be taken also of the views expressed in your letter before any decision is made regarding the duty on fish and fish products.

As you know, the trade agreements program was designed for the purpose of expanding foreign markets for the products of the United States. The Administration is exerting every effort to accomplish this purpose with the least possible disturbance to tariff-protected domestic industries.[2]

Sincerely yours,

[*Notation*:A] 7/9/35
[OF 61-F:CT]

[1] Fiesinger, whose district included Sandusky, an important fishing port on Lake Erie, said that lowering duties on fish would "possibly ruin a large percentage of the industry, throw men out of work, and lower the wages of our fishermen in order to compete with Canadian fishermen" (OF 61-F).
[2] Drafted in the State Department.

Roosevelt to Ira Nelson Morris, Paris

[Washington] July 10, 1935

My dear Mr. Morris: I hope much that as soon as you get back you will come and see me and tell me of your observations in Europe. We all realize the seriousness of the times and the sudden changes which are occurring, and I shall be very glad to have your latest slant on things.[1]

With my sincere regards, Very sincerely yours,

[PPF 1479:CT]

[1] Morris, minister to Sweden from 1914 to 1923, wrote June 30, 1935 (PPF 1479), volunteering to observe conditions in Europe and give his reactions.

Roosevelt to Edward Tuck, Paris

[Washington] July 10, 1935

Personal

Dear Mr. Tuck: It is good to know that you feel as I do about some of these International Congresses of what you so well call "financial Solons."[1] There is a kind of accepted jargon which they all speak, following the lead of professional international bankers. You prove this by mentioning that silver was not even spoken of at the recent Paris meeting.

Meanwhile, I am pursuing what might be called "the even tenor of my ways." During the recent flurry of selling among silver speculators, we acquired a very large amount and the average of our purchases during the past year is high. We are pursuing the policy in good faith.

With my sincere regards, Faithfully yours,

[PPF 2537:CT]

[1] Tuck, a retired banker and writer on finance, had written to Roosevelt on July 2, 1935 (PPF 2537). He referred to the pronouncement of the International Chamber of Commerce at its recent meeting in Paris that world prosperity depended upon a stabilization of currencies on an international gold basis. He noted that the Chamber had completely ignored the present policy of Congress and the President "of restoring silver to its historic place established by the founders of our Government as the companion of gold."

Roosevelt to Robert W. Bingham, Ambassador to Great Britain, London

[Washington] July 11, 1935

Dear Bob: I am delighted to have your interesting letter of June twenty-eighth.[1] I agree with you that the British will probably not do much conversing with us until after their general election and that they are beginning to realize that a greater friendliness to us would not hurt them.

Many years ago I came to the reluctant conclusion that it is a mistake to make advances to the British Government; practical results can be accomplished only when they make the advances themselves. They are a funny people and, though always polite, can be counted on when things are going well with them to show a national selfishness towards other nations which makes mutual helpfulness very difficult to accomplish. Their average conception of mutuality differs from mine.

Let me tell you a secret which is not to go beyond your own ears. Sir Josiah Stamp wrote Morgenthau and suggested that, as Leith-Ross will pass through Toronto on his way to China in August, Morgenthau should proceed to the border incognito and have a conference with Leith-Ross—informally, unofficially and wholly secret! I could not help remember that Leith-Ross is merely a financial adviser to the Chancellor of the Exchequer and that Morgenthau is the Secretary of the Treasury of the United States. I could not help wondering what Neville Chamberlain would say if George Harrison of the Federal Reserve Bank in New York were to write Chamberlain that George Haas, a financial adviser in our Treasury Department, was going to Belgium this summer and suggesting that Neville Chamberlain run over to Belgium to see George Haas! Can you imagine the expression on Neville Chamberlain's face? That is the kind of stupid thing that our British friends sometimes try to perpetrate on their American cousins!

I fear me that the British have, in the German Naval agreement, let themselves in for real resentment on the Continent, and also for much trouble to themselves in the days to come. I cannot forget that Germany's new Naval program, just announced, shows a number of submarines and other ships practically completed. In other words, Germany began to violate her Treaty obligations from two to three years ago. What is to prevent Germany from violating this new agreement and calmly announcing the violation after she has doubled her new allowance of submarines, cruisers, etc., etc.?

Most highly confidential—will you try to keep your ear open for any suggestions that England and Germany have agreed on certain other important points not connected with or included in the Naval announcement?

A very wise old bird tells me that a number of important world forces, including the British, would much like to involve us in some way—any way—in the world's critical problems.[2]

As ever yours,

[PSF:Great Britain:CT]

[1] Above.
[2] See Roosevelt to Bingham, Nov. 23, 1935, below.

Roosevelt to Cordell Hull, Secretary of State, Henry Morgenthau, Jr., Secretary of the Treasury, and Henry A. Wallace, Secretary of Agriculture

Washington, July 11, 1935

Memorandum . . . : Would you be good enough to speak with Senator Smith of South Carolina in regard to his proposed Foreign Trade Insurance bill and let me have a memo on it?[1]

F.D.R.

[OF 614-A:CT]

[1] See Roosevelt to Peek, July 17, 1935, below.

Judge Martin T. Manton, United States Circuit Court of Appeals, to Roosevelt

New York City, July 11, 1935

My dear Mr. President: Bishop Spellman of Boston saw the Apostolic Delegate yesterday, as I suggested on Monday last that he would. He advised Bishop Spellman of Fr. Burke having heretofore represented him in the negotiations with reference to the religious controversy in Mexico, and suggested that Fr. Burke continue. Bishop Spellman, of course, will acquiesce in this direction.

If I can be of any service in trying to bring about peace in this controversy, either here or in Mexico, please command me at any time.[1]

With kind personal regards, I remain, Sincerely yours,

Martin T. Manton

[OF 146-A:TS]

[1] An attached memorandum, Roosevelt to Welles, July 13, 1935, reads: "I have no objection to your showing this to Father Burke. Please let me have it back."

Roosevelt to Josephus Daniels, Ambassador to Mexico

[Washington] July 12, 1935

Dear Chief: I have put off writing to you from time to time but I am sure you know we were all thinking of you and Mrs. Daniels after we heard of that bomb explosion in your garden. Your whole conduct was grand.[1]

The general situation is, I well realize, confusing and difficult to forecast in regard to future events. I have had a talk with the Knights of Columbus people and with a number of others who wish to "resolve," start conferences, etc., etc. I think they see the danger to Catholics and to future relations if we Yankees start telling the Mexicans what to do.[2]

I have been having a busy time, as you know, and the Congress got a bit obstreperous but they are going along better this week.

As ever yours,

[PPF 86:CT]

[1] A small bomb had been thrown into the garden of the American Embassy. It did no harm and Daniels ascribed the act to persons who "wished merely to create a sensation or a fear" (Daniels to Roosevelt, June 25, 1935, PPF 86).

[2] See Daniels to Roosevelt, July 23, 1935, below.

William C. Bullitt, Ambassador to the Union of Soviet Socialist Republics, to Roosevelt

Moscow, July 15, 1935

Personal and Confidential

Dear Mr. President: This letter should reach you before the issue raised by the impending congress of the Third International in Moscow becomes acute. As I cannot have a talk with you, I am going to bore you by writing you what I would say if I were with you in the White House.

I am engaged in attempting to keep the congress off the subject of the U.S.A. by exuding gloom and expressing my personal opinion that the congress may produce the severance of diplomatic relations. I think I shall be successful in reducing somewhat the activities of the congress with respect to the United States but have almost no hope that I can forestall violation, at least technical, of the last article of Litvinov's propaganda pledge to you.

Some people in Washington will doubtless want to break relations even if the violation is merely technical; but I can hear you roar with laughter over the idea of breaking relations on the basis of a mere technical violation of Litvinov's pledge. Indeed, if the Soviet Government should lean over backwards to avoid offending the United States, I suppose that you will wish to ignore the congress altogether. If the violation should be merely technical and if you should feel that we cannot ignore it, I think we should confine our action to an oral protest by me to Litvinov, a simultaneous withdrawal of the exequaturs of the Soviet Consuls in New York and San Francisco and a tightening of our liberal policy of giving visas to the United States to Soviet officials.

If we should take these steps the Soviet Government would retaliate by making the position of this Embassy as difficult as possible and might very well pretend that our reluctance to issue visas makes it impossible for the Soviet Government to carry out its intention to purchase thirty million dollars worth of goods in the United States this year. And I shall probably get no news at all from Litvinov or any communist for some time.

If the violation should be not technical but gross and insulting, I suspect that you will feel obliged to break relations. If we should not, the Soviet Government would be convinced that it could break its pledges with impunity and would feel free to direct actively the American communist movement. The results of a break in relations, I think, would be, (1) Reduction of Soviet purchases in the United States; (2) A long period without relations, since, if we break on the ground that the Soviet Government has not kept its pledges, it will be most difficult later to say that we consider its pledges trustworthy; (3) The loss of an observation post in Moscow; (4) An increased chance that Japan will attack the Soviet Union; (5) A considerable decrease in the prestige of the Soviet Union and a weakening of its present ascending influence.

(Parenthetically, it occurs to me that if we break with the Soviet Union it would be a pleasant gesture to ask the Finns to take charge of our interests here. We could not trust any great power. The Finns have more influence than the Norwegians or the representatives of any other minor power. And they paid their debts.)

If the violation should fall between the two extremes and be neither technical nor gross and insulting (and I think it will fall between the extremes) it will be most difficult to decide what to do.

Whatever we do, we should do promptly—instantaneously, if possible. I think we should avoid at all costs the usual practice of writing a large pontifical note of protest which the Soviet Government will answer by a larger, more pontifical and intensely insulting note. It will probably break the heart of Mr. Ralph Hill,[1] the State Department's leading pundit, who loves to find technical violations and to set them forth in legal phraseology; but I think it is in our national interest that his heart, if necessary, should be broken. We shall get no satisfaction by the notes we write and shall merely become a target for the sort of ripe tomatoes that the Bolsheviks throw with genius.

The internal political reaction in the United States to the Communist congress will also have to be considered. About that I shall know nothing.

If we want to do something short of breaking relations, I believe that our protest should be oral and should be accompanied by various actions. We might cancel the exequaturs of the Soviet consuls in the United States, withdraw our Military Attaché in Moscow, indicate to the Soviet Government that the Soviet Military and Naval Attachés in Washington are no longer welcome, withdraw our Counselor of Embassy in Moscow, practically eliminate the issuing of visas to Soviet officials, and show extreme frigidity all along the line.

The gesture of cancelling consular exequaturs would not be as empty as it might appear. It is the practice not only of the Soviet Government, but also the British Government and the governments of all European countries to run their illegal activities not through their Embassies but through their consulates and our Government could explain that, in view of the Soviet Government's disinclination to respect its pledges with regard to propaganda, we cannot have consular representatives of the Soviet Government at large in the United States.

I hope most heartily that all this may blow over and that our relations may continue. The Soviet Union is quite likely to become involved in war, both in the Far East and in Europe, during the next few years and it seems honestly desirable to have diplomatic representation here.

I apologize for this solemn screed. You will know exactly what to do without advice. In a few minutes I shall write Judge Moore the above solemnities.[2]

Every possible good wish to you all.

Yours affectionately,

William C. Bullitt

[PSF:Russia:TS]

[1] Assistant legal adviser to the State Department.
[2] See Bullitt to Hull, July 19, 1935, in *Foreign Relations, The Soviet Union, 1933–1939*, pp. 224–227ff.

William Phillips, Under Secretary of State, to Roosevelt

Washington, July 16, 1935

My dear Mr. President: The Secretary and Judge Moore attended last week a meeting of the Senate Committee on Foreign Relations at which they pointed out the necessity of caution in proceeding with the enactment of legislation which would affect our neutrality policy, and made specific criticisms of certain provisions of the two neutrality bills which the Committee had reported out and of the third bill which was still pending in the Committee.[1] The Committee thereupon voted to recall the two former bills, to give further consideration to this legislation and to appoint a sub-committee to confer with the Department in regard to the whole subject of neutrality legislation.

I have been informed that a delegation of Senators interested in the enactment of neutrality legislation may call upon you in the near future to request you to express your views upon the subject of neutrality legislation and upon the advisability of the enactment of such legislation at the present session of Congress. A group in the Department has been at work for some time studying possible neutrality legislation and we are prepared, if you so desire, to submit to you a draft of proposed legislation which you might wish to consider before receiving the group of Senators should they call upon you.

The sub-committee appointed by the Committee on Foreign Relations may possibly request me to confer with it on this subject and I would not care to comply with such an invitation until I had received a definite expression of your wishes in the premises.

It is possible that no necessity will arise for immediate discussion of this matter with members of the Senate, but it would appear to be advisable to be prepared in case the necessity should arise. I do not wish to burden you with this problem at this time and I am writing merely as a precaution and to let you know that if you are called upon or if the State Department is called upon to take a definite stand on this matter, I should appreciate it if I could have an opportunity in advance of any meeting with the Senators to discuss the matter fully with you and to receive an expression of your views.[2]

Faithfully yours,

William Phillips

[OF 1561:TS]

[1] On July 10 (New York *Times*, July 11, 1935, p. 14). Senators Gerald P. Nye and Bennett Champ Clark had introduced, on April 9, 1935, two joint resolutions, S.J.R. 99, to regulate the issuance of passports to American citizens in time of war, and S.J.R. 100, to prohibit extension of credits and issuance of foreign loans under certain conditions. On May 7 they introduced S.J.R. 120, to prohibit the export of arms and ammunition and to regulate trade in contraband of war. In introducing this resolution, Clark said that it was designed, with the two previously introduced bills, to "form a

complete plan for American neutrality in the event of war." On June 5, Senator Nye and others introduced S. 2998, to control trade in arms, ammunition, and implements of war. Similar bills had been introduced in the House: H.R. 7125, by Frank L. Kloeb of Ohio, and H.R. 7572, by Louis Ludlow of Indiana (*Cong. Rec.,* vol. 79, pp. 4719, 5286–5287, 5913, 7042, 8666, 9743, 10463, 10997–10998, 11607).

These bills required the President to take certain actions under certain conditions; they were opposed by the White House and the State Department who wanted as much discretion as possible left to the President (Hull, *Memoirs,* I, 397–417). Clark and Nye took the position that policy should be fixed before war broke out; later decisions would be considered unneutral. They urged this argument on the Senate Foreign Relations Committee in a long memorandum of July 10, 1935, in support of the resolutions they had introduced (Moore papers). The State Department finally drafted its own neutrality bill and offered it to the Senate Committee on July 31 (Phillips to Pittman, July 31, 1935, *ibid.*) This bill, which would have given the President discretion in invoking an arms embargo and in applying the other measures proposed, was rejected by the committee (Hull, *Memoirs,* I, 411). The Department then made an attempt to draft a resolution applicable only to the Italo-Ethiopian conflict that would be acceptable to both the Senate Foreign Relations Committee and the President; see Memorandum by R. Walton Moore, Aug. 16, 1935, below.

[2] An attached note, Roosevelt to McIntyre, July 17, 1935, reads: "Will you keep this in mind in case I get a call from the Senators and tell Bill Phillips we will let him know beforehand?"

Roosevelt to Gerrit Forbes, Boston

[Washington] July 16, 1935

Dear Gerrit: I do wish I could tell you something definite about Abyssinia because I know of your excellent knowledge of Africa and how useful you could be. At the present time, however, we have just sent some people to strengthen our representation at Addis Ababa and as matters now stand, we believe we have adequate personnel there.

It is very hard to tell what will happen in the next few weeks but I have talked with Bill Phillips and told him of your proffer of service. I shall certainly bear it in mind in case the situation develops to a point where we need to take further steps.

I do wish I could get to Naushon to see you all. Give my love to the family.[1]

Always sincerely,

[PPF 2722:CT]

[1] Forbes, a cousin and Harvard classmate of Roosevelt, had written July 5 (PPF 2722) to ask for an appointment to Addis Ababa. He said he had just returned from a 6,000-mile trip through Africa and was well acquainted with the country. Under Secretary of State Phillips suggested this reply. Naushon is one of the Elizabeth Islands off the Massachusetts coast; Forbes had a summer place there.

George N. Peek, Special Adviser to the President on Foreign Trade, to Roosevelt

Washington, July 16, 1935

Dear Mr. President: I submit herewith for your signature a draft of an Executive Order terminating the Office of Special Adviser to the President on Foreign Trade.[1] In view of Executive Order No. 7076, of June 15, 1935, continuing all agencies created under Title I of the National Industrial Recovery Act, this action is necessary to give formal effect to the decision which we discussed some weeks ago.

In reviewing the work of this office, certain comments seem appropriate. At the time I undertook the duties of Special Adviser, I indicated the necessity of setting up a national bookkeeping record of the movement of visible and invisible accounts comprising our international balance. Accordingly intensive studies were initiated in the Office of the Special Adviser, in cooperation with the Department of Commerce. The results of these basic studies were presented to you in three letters dated respectively May 23, 1934, August 30, 1934, and April 30, 1935,[2] which were subsequently made public at your direction. Arrangements now have been made to have these studies carried forward, country by country, in the Department of Commerce and to have quarterly statements of our balance of international payments issued by that Department. The establishment and expansion of this system of national bookkeeping appears to me to be an important step forward and to afford an indispensable guide to the Government and to the public in our commercial and financial dealings with foreign nations.

As these studies progressed I was forced inescapably to the conclusion that our general depression and the financial collapse of 1931–1932 were traceable in very large measure to the commercial and financial policies pursued by the three post-war administrations in their relations with foreign nations. The effect was to permit a draining off of our liquid resources by foreign nations. These policies rendered us vulnerable to the economic shocks which eventually overwhelmed us.

This conclusion in turn led me to make to you two recommendations of major importance designed to correct the condition to which I refer.

First, was the creation of a permanent foreign trade board to coordinate the various foreign trade activities of the Government under unified direction and to deal comprehensively with our foreign commercial and financial activities. The creation of such an agency appears to me vital if we are to develop adequate foreign trade policies and to administer them effectively. It is my hope that legislation to this end may be introduced in Congress for action at its next session. In this connection I inclose a tentative draft of the form which such legislation might appropriately take as a possible basis for Congressional discussion.[3]

Second, I have recommended that we abandon the unconditional most-favored-nation policy adopted under the Harding administration and return to the traditional American policy of extending conditional most-favored-nation treatment only on a quid pro quo basis.

My objections to the unconditional most-favored-nation policy are two-fold. In the first place, its use involves the progressive destruction of our bargaining power at a time when the conditions in international trade require that we retain the maximum freedom of action and bargaining power if our nationals are to compete on equal terms with the nationals of other countries in the markets of the world. In the second place, the result of the generalization of concessions under the unconditional most-favored-nation policy is to effect a general reduction of our tariff in return for scattered concessions from a limited number of nations. The limited safeguards surrounding the trade agreements already made leave the country apprehensive of what may happen next. The declaration of policy of the Reciprocal Trade Agreements Act does not suggest that Congress in passing it intended to delegate power to effect a general tariff reduction or appreciated that the authority conveyed might be used for that purpose. I believe that a low tariff policy is not an appropriate one for us at a time when our internal economic balance is in process of readjustment and when unemployment figures remain at their present level. I think that before we attempt general tariff reduction there should be a clear indication of policy from Congress on the subject.

In renewing my recommendations I feel that I have completed the special task which you asked me to undertake eighteen months ago. The work of the Special Adviser's Office has been completed, and its recommendations are in your hands. The Export-Import Banks have been reorganized and are in a position to continue their activities. It therefore seems an appropriate moment for me to renew my previous request to be relieved and to tender my formal resignation as Special Adviser and as Trustee of the Export-Import Banks, to take effect immediately. I am submitting my resignation as President of the Banks to the Board of Trustees at its next meeting.

My fundamental reason for taking this step is that I feel increasingly out of sympathy with the foreign trade policies now being pursued. I believe that national recovery will be impossible so long as these policies are continued.

I cannot express too highly my appreciation of the personal courtesies and consideration which you invariably have shown me. You have my very best wishes for success in the task of recovery that lies before you.[4]

Sincerely yours,

George N. Peek

[PSF:Agriculture:TS]

[1] The draft (present) provided for the termination of the office on Aug. 15, 1935. It was not issued.

[2] The May 23 and August 30 letters are printed above; the April 30 letter is not in the Roosevelt papers.

[3] Not present.

[4] Roosevelt replied July 17, 1935, asking Peek to reconsider his decision to resign (*Personal Letters, 1928–1945*, I, 494–495). He sent copies of the letters exchanged to Jesse Jones, head of the Reconstruction Finance Corporation, with a letter of July 18, 1935 (*ibid.*, pp. 493–494), in which he asked Jones to tell Peek that he was "silly and stupid about the general Foreign Trade policy," because the amount involved in the special trade agreements was so small in relation to total exports and imports that it was captious to make an issue of it. See below.

Roosevelt to George N. Peek, Special Adviser to the President on Foreign Trade

[Washington] July 17, 1935

Memorandum for Honorable George Peek: I wish you would give some thought to this proposal of Senator Ed Smith and let me have your general thought on the subject.

Please let me have the papers back.

F.D.R.

[OF 614-A:CT]

[*Enclosure 1*] Memorandum by Senator Ellison D. Smith of South Carolina on a Proposed Foreign Trade Insurance Bill

[*undated*]

The world never has functioned normally without long term foreign credits. We have unfortunately abused it in the past. Therefore, being a creditor nation, it is incumbent upon us to constructively restore foreign commercial credits. This is necessary to enable us to hold and improve our national solvency, and will be effective in reducing unemployment.

Gold left by itself to adjust foreign balances has created impediments in the exchange markets which are gradually destroying our foreign trade and commerce, and this is causing chaotic conditions throughout the world. Until world credit conditions are more nearly normal, we should limit ourselves to a policy of long term credit for actual purchases in this country. Therefore, a government emergency credit insurance should be established for the purpose of putting some of our surplus of agricultural and industrial goods into world consumption. Let us not forget that our own consumption has always increased after we have increased our foreign trade. The following are a few facts favoring this suggestion:

1. Unless foreign credits are restored to regain and develop our export markets, so as to carry on foreign trade, then we will have to adopt a deflationary domestic policy. Such a deflationary policy will lead us to isolation, tariff barriers, and radical nationalism, a lower standard of living.

2. Republican leaders, realizing the importance of regaining and developing our foreign trade, are now working on such a program, probably with the intention of making it a leading issue of the next campaign.

3. Although war loans, political debts and foreign bonds are often repudiated and go into default, yet history shows that commercial credits, handled through trade channels, are very seldom repudiated or left unpaid.

4. In connection with the proposed plan of foreign commercial credits: If we will remember during the War, on account of submarine destruction of shipping, War Risk Insurance became practically unobtainable. Commodities and goods were piling up in our country. In order to break this jam, the Government formed a War Risk Insurance Company which underwrote War Risks at reasonable premiums. This reopened the export markets and the surplus of commodities and goods were sold. A somewhat similar situation exists today due to the impracticability of obtaining foreign credits necessary to regain and develop our export markets. It might be mentioned that the War Risk Insurance Company operated at a profit. It might be stated that England has and is now developing foreign trade through long term credit insurance.

5. These foreign commercial credits on a long term or six months revolving credits are now urgently needed until tariff barriers are lowered on a reciprocal basis.

6. A foreign credit insurance company along the plan outlined would

564

be very helpful to the State Department in bringing about a lowering of the tariff barriers on a reciprocal basis. Those nations that would not cooperate in the lowering of tariffs naturally would not be entitled to obtain credit insurance through American exporters and manufacturers.

7. This foreign credit insurance would only be extended to American exporters and manufacturers; therefore, it would in no way conflict with the Johnson Act.

8. As the foreign long term credit insurance would only be extended to American exporters and manufacturers, it would not interfere or disrupt existing business.

9. The foreign credit insurance would promptly make available the credits that are necessary for the restoration of our foreign trade. This would be most helpful in restoring the price level of commodities. It would be of much benefit to our American manufacturers. It would also greatly help the railroads of our country. They have never prospered unless our country was doing a large export business; this because of the long freight haul to and from the ports.

10. As foreign trade develops through this emergency credit insurance company, then confidence in foreign commercial credits and trade will be gradually restored. Credits then will gradually be extended without credit insurance. Therefore, the duration of the foreign credit insurance will be limited and no longer required when confidence in foreign trade and credit has been re-established.

11. The regaining and increasing of our export trade will be most effective in reducing unemployment and Government relief.

12. Re-establishment of foreign trade is the only practical and effective way of collecting the outstanding foreign debts.

Note: Attached is copy of Tentative Plan for the United States Foreign Credit Insurance Company.

[OF 614-A:CT]

[Enclosure 2]

The Tentative Plan

1. United States Foreign Credit Insurance Company to be organized to facilitate the exportation of American commodities and manufactured goods.

2. Capital of company to be $500,000,000 authorized and subscribed, of which $50,000,000 to be paid in.

3. Foreign credit insurance to be extended only to American exporters and manufacturers.

4. It will be required that the business be handled through regular banking and trade channels so as to avoid disruption or interference with regular business.

5. Foreign credit insurance will only be available for exporting to countries willing to cooperate with the United States to develop reciprocal trade.

6. Length of foreign credits will depend upon the commodities, nature of manufactured goods sold, and credit standing. Length of credit to be determined by nature of transaction; should rarely exceed 24 months. Advisable have many credits on six months revolving basis so as loans will be discountable through Federal Reserve.

7. The American exporter or manufacturer will have to furnish the guarantee of the foreign purchaser, the guarantee of a prime foreign bank, or foreign Government. The American exporter or manufacturer will also have to assume part of the risk not exceeding profits realized.

8. The premium will naturally have to be based on the conditions of the sale and nature of the business; the premium to be as reasonable as possible, so as to facilitate exports.

9. For the success of the company, it is, of course, imperative that it be under the proper leadership. It will, therefore, be essential to place in charge of this company a man who has the necessary ability and long practical and successful experience in dealing in foreign commercial credits.

10. Total amount of credit insurance and total amount extended in any one country to be limited within reasonable bounds.

11. The duration of this company would be limited to a period as conditions warrant. Naturally as foreign trade is reestablished, confidence will be restored and the necessity for such credit insurance will gradually disappear.[1]

[OF 614-A:CT]

[1] Answered, Peek to Roosevelt, July 25, 1935, below.

Press Conference, Executive Offices of the White House, July 17, 1935, 10:30 A.M.

[*Excerpt*] Q: Mr. President, have you anything to say with regard to any possible changes in the Administration's foreign trade program?

The President: What program?

Q: Foreign trade program.

The President: What about it, specifically?

Q: There have been a number of things said in Congress because of tariff reduction in recent treaties.

The President: You will have to be more specific than that.

Q: Senator McCarran of Nevada, particularly on the Russian and Brazilian treaties, because of the manganese.

The President: How many people are employed in this country in the manganese industry?

Q: The State Department says 354.

The President: The State Department says 354 and Senator McCarran says three or four thousand.

Of course the general principle, taking manganese, is this: If we were to produce all the manganese we use in steel, in the mills in the country, alloys of various kinds, and keep foreign manganese out, it would mean that the cost of steel for use in building materials, and so forth and so on, would be tremendously increased. It might put a few thousand people to work but the cost to the country would be ten times, twenty times, fifty times more than the earnings of those people who are put to work.

As a matter of fact, the manganese deposits in this country, as we all know since the war days, are pretty slim. They are very small, scattered, and some of them of very, very low grade ore. It seems to be the economic theory that if we import manganese from the outside it will put more, infinitely more people to work in this country than putting a high tariff on manganese. I don't think it will throw 354 workmen out of business but, even if we should, the increased purchasing power of foreign countries would put ten times that number of Americans to work. That is the simple theory on manganese. It will increase employment in this country through the Brazilian Treaty and Russian Agreement without any question at all by giving them a much larger purchasing power . . .

Q: On the foreign trade, again. Senator McCarran has suggested that the Reciprocal Tariff Act be so amended as to prevent the extension of these trade benefits to any countries except those that give us most-favored-nation treatment. Would you care to comment on that?

The President: No, that is a sort of technical subject. These trade agreements do apply to nations who have the most-favored-nation clause in general but, at the same time, in the agreements there is a thirty-day clause which allows us to cancel on any particular article if we find that as a result of the most-favored-nation clause the imports in here amount to something we had not expected.

In other words, you might say, "Dumping." Therefore we can terminate at the end of thirty days. That is the protective clause.

Q: And the Senator's bill, I believe, is to prevent the extension.[1] For example, in an American-Belgian treaty, where we reduce our tariff on cement, the present program contemplates or includes the extension of that cement tariff reduction, not only to Belgium but to all other countries.

The President: It would have that effect.

Q: And the Senator proposes that that be curtailed so it would be extended only to such countries as extend us most-favored-nation treatment.

The President: I do not quite understand that because nations where we have most-favored-nation clauses, they give us, also, most-favored-nation treatment. I do not see exactly how it can be done.

Q: He would include only such nations as do that and, at the present time, those benefits are being extended to Japan and to Mexico and to these other nations with whom we have no most-favored-nation treatment at all.

The President: That is purely a permissive thing. It can be withdrawn in the case of any nation within twenty-four hours' notice.

Q: You would not be in favor, however, of any bill to limit that power?

The President: I do not think it should be because, after all, each case has to stand on its own feet and it is awfully difficult to get any general piece of legislation which would be fair to everybody. The whole theory is that each one has to stand on its own feet and if, as a result, we get unexpected results from other countries, we can change it on the thirty-day clause.

[President's Press Conferences:T]

[1] McCarran had introduced S. 2232, "to terminate certain foreign trade agreements and to terminate the authority to enter into them," on March 12, 1935. It was referred to the Committee on Foreign Relations and was not reported (*Cong. Rec.,* vol. 79, p. 3433).

Rabbi Joseph Konvitz and Rabbi L. Seltzer to Roosevelt

Belmar, New Jersey, July 17, 1935

[*Telegram*] At an executive committee meeting especially held today reports were made of the unspeakable degradations to which the Jews in Germany are subjected and the pains and humiliations they are made to suffer because they hold sacred the traditions of their fathers. Our hearts are full of grief and in this moment of our adversity we turn to you as guardian of human freedom and protector of culture and the institutions of civilization. We respectfully beg you to give audience to a committee of nationally prominent spiritual leaders of orthodox Jewry who will meet with you in Washington at your convenience to petition you as head of our Government and defender of liberties for advice and assistance in this bitter hour of grief for Jews all over the world.

Rabbi Joseph Konvitz
Rabbi L. Seltzer[1]

[OF 198-A:T]

[1] Konvitz was president and Seltzer was secretary of the Union of Orthodox Rabbis of the United States. Their request for an interview was referred to Under Secretary of State Phillips for advice; Phillips recommended that they be received because the German issue was highly important and because Jewish organizations were concentrating their attention on it (Phillips to Roosevelt, July 23, 1935, OF 198-A). An appointment was made for the rabbis to see the President on August 2 but it was later decided to have them talk with Phillips instead (memorandum by McIntyre, July 26, 1935, OF 198-A).

Representative Fred J. Sisson of New York to Roosevelt

Washington, D.C., July 18, 1935

Dear Mr. President: It is a cause of regret and disappointment to many of us in Congress that nothing effective has been done, either at this Session of Congress or during the Seventy-third Congress, to promote the cause of international peace and good-will among nations.

The Vinson Naval Parity Bill[1] (so-called) was passed at the last Session of Congress and all opposition to what many of us believed to be a war-provoking measure was overridden through the argument that this Bill had the approval of the Administration.

Approximately one billion dollars has been appropriated for war at this Session of Congress under the guise of defense, although we are in a securer position—as no one can deny—than any other nation in the world.

We are, and have been for several years, expending more money for preparation for war than any other nation in the world, and with less excuse to do so than any other nation in the world.

Through a desire to follow the leadership of a responsible Administration, even though we disagreed—so far as were informed—with its military and naval policy, many of your loyal supporters, like myself, have "pulled our punches" so to speak, in opposition to these measures.

A gesture was made toward putting us into the World Court. That proposition, I might say in passing, should not be allowed to be defeated by a small minority of the Congress—one more than one-third of the Senate. Congress, by a vote of the majority of each of the branches thereof by a joint resolution, with the approval of the President, has the power to put the United States into the World Court. For this there is ample precedent. Apparently no Administration recommendation to that end is going to be made, but this is going to be allowed to die.

Many of us had hoped that certain real neutrality legislation, showing at least nominally some expression of good-will and freedom from warlike intentions, might be passed at this Session of Congress. Two resolutions directed toward this end, reported favorably by the Senate Foreign Relations Committee, have lately been recalled.[2] It is currently stated that this has been done at the instance of the Department of State. A Bill introduced by Congressman McReynolds, Chairman of the House Committee on Foreign Affairs, it is expected will be reported and passed at this Session of Congress. This is a Bill to implement the treaty for supervision of the international trade in arms and munitions of war ratified by the United States in June, 1935.[3] In other words, it is for the purpose of setting up machinery for licensing the shipments of arms and munitions of war. This, of course, is something that we were bound to do and constitutes no great advance in the way of a declaration of policy. Other neutrality legislation now pending in the House Foreign Affairs Committee is apparently to be stifled again as it is currently reported, at the instance of the Department of State.

The world is in a condition where war is likely almost at any time to break out. Anyone who faces the facts knows the great difficulty, if not impossibility, of keeping this country out of war in the event of a European conflict of any magnitude. This country certainly cannot be kept out unless certain preventive measures with respect to neutrality are agreed upon and stated—and that in advance of and not after the outbreak of war. Anyone in a position of responsibility in this Administration will certainly be guilty and deserving of moral censure who fails to realize and accept such responsibility.

The sentiment in Congress is, as I know, very much in favor of this legislation and it would be passed were it not for the understanding that it does not meet with the approval of the Administration. I also know that the sentiment in the country—certainly throughout New York State—is very strongly for peace and for all preventive measures.

As a follower of Woodrow Wilson and believer in his policies I am greatly disappointed with the record, so far as peace is concerned, of the past two years. I am still assuming that the hopes, aspirations, and ideals for advancing the cause of peace with which we entered into the 1932 campaign, and which I still possess, may be realized during this Administration.

I hope that if I have spoken plainly you will not take offense, but I could not speak otherwise. I should be glad to hear your views if you will let me know. I am speaking, not in my own behalf alone, but of that of a number of other members of Congress.[4]

Sincerely yours,

F. J. Sisson

[OF 1561:TS]

[1] Act approved March 27, 1934 (48 *Stat.* 503–505).
[2] Senate Joint Resolution 99, to regulate the issuance of passports to American citizens in time of war, and S.J.R. 100, to prohibit the extension of credits and foreign loans; see Phillips to Roosevelt, July 16, 1935, above, n. 1.
[3] H.R. 8788; see press conference following.
[4] Answered July 23, 1935, below.

Press Conference, Executive Offices of the White House, July 19, 1935, 4:10 P.M.

[*Excerpt*] Q: The House Foreign Affairs Committee reported out the Arms Export License Bill.[1] Are you hopeful of seeing it go through this session?

The President: I have not heard of it.

Q: That is the bill to license the export of arms.

The President: I do not know all of it.

Q: The Senate Foreign Relations Committee has appointed a sub-committee to confer with the Administration on the formation of a neutrality program?

The President: I think the State Department is going up there on Monday on it.

Q: Could you say anything about the general study and how far it has progressed?

The President: The only way I can comment on that is off the record, if you don't mind, because it relates to foreign matters to a certain extent. The situation is this: We do want and ought to have some additional neutrality legislation but we are faced with a legislative situation at the end of the session. Therefore I said to Bill Phillips this morning—I said, "I am perfectly willing, if we can get an agreement on neutrality legislation, so long as it does not block the adjournment of Congress. In other words, if you can get it through without waste of time after agreement, that is fine. Or, after the major pieces of legislation have been passed, you can bring it up and say to the Congress, 'Do you want to stay here and pass it?'—put that question to them. But no protracted debate on it—we do not want to even suggest that Congress stay for that one sole reason." That is about the situation.

[President's Press Conferences:T]

[1] H.R. 8788, companion bill to S. 2998, introduced by McReynolds on July 9, 1935, was reported but not further acted upon (*Cong. Rec.*, vol. 79, pp. 10906, 11607–11608).

Roosevelt to William G. Bruce, Milwaukee

[Washington] July 20, 1935

My dear Mr. Bruce: I was very genuinely interested in your letter of July 15th with respect to the St. Lawrence Treaty.[1]

Even in the press of these strenuous days I have been giving a great deal of consideration to this question. I do not feel that it would be at all advisable to inject this into the present session, but do agree with you that we should keep it a live issue.

I was much interested in your suggestion of the appointment of a commission and will give it very thoughtful consideration.

I appreciate very much your fine attitude and will count on a continuation of it from you and your associates.[2]

Very sincerely yours,

[OF 66:CT]

[1] Bruce was a former president of the Great Lakes Harbors Association of the United States and Canada, a director of the Great Lakes-St. Lawrence Tidewater Association, and president of the Wisconsin Deep Waterways Commission. In his letter (OF 66), he said ratification of the St. Lawrence Waterway Treaty was still of paramount importance to the people of the Midwest but that they had confidence in the President's judgment on the re-submitting of the treaty to the Senate. He proposed appointment of a commission that would maintain contact with all pro-treaty elements in the interest of ratification.

[2] Drafted by McIntyre. A letter to Roosevelt from H. E. Flack, president of the Northern Federation of Chambers of Commerce of New York State, Potsdam, New York, Aug. 5, 1935 (OF 66), also urging reconsideration of the treaty, was similarly answered.

Roosevelt to Claude A. Swanson, Secretary of the Navy

Washington, July 20, 1935

Confidential

Memorandum for the Secretary of the Navy: Have you seen this confidential dispatch of July eighteenth from Grew?[1] I think we should seriously consider, if there is a pro forma meeting as suggested, at least a formal agreement that every nation will notify every other nation of all ships authorized or laid down for construction.

F.D.R.

[*Notation*:T] Letter from Secretary Phillips enclosing telegram from Ambassador Grew reporting his final conversation with Hirota giving his thought that a naval conference would have to be held before the end of the year, but that it could be a purely pro forma meeting and could adjourn for a year or two in the hope that meanwhile some satisfactory arrangement could be evolved.

[PSF:London Naval Conference:T]

[1] Not present; presumably not returned to the White House.

Harold L. Ickes, Secretary of the Interior, to Roosevelt

Washington, July 22, 1935

My dear Mr. President: In a letter of May 7, The Helium Company of Louisville, Kentucky, has expressed through its Vice President, Mr. James T. Howington, the desire to export from the United States to the

Institute of Aeronautical Policy, Tokyo, Japan, seven million cubic feet of helium during 1935 and 1936, and thereafter at the rate of 300,000 cubic feet per month. A copy of the above mentioned letter is attached.[1]

This matter is brought to your attention in accordance with the provisions of Section 4 of the Act of Congress approved March 3, 1927 (44 *Stat.*, 1387) and the Executive Order dated February 22, 1934, transferring the Bureau of Mines.

The Acting Secretary of War, in a letter of June 19, recommends against such exportation as follows:

> Helium is a military asset which gives to this country an advantage over all others.
>
> Even though it is to be used for a commercial airship, such a craft is perfectly capable of being used for military reconnaissance as well as being used by this foreign nation as a rival to our aerial commerce.

The Secretary of the Navy, in a letter of May 31, addressed to the Secretary of State, recommends against such exportation and sets out the Navy Department's position in the matter as follows:

> Helium is a military asset which gives this country an advantage over all others if we continue to monopolize its possession. To give our commercial competitors the advantage of using helium in the future development of commercial lighter-than-air transportation is considered inadvisable.
>
> For the above reasons the Navy Department cannot approve the request of The Helium Company to export commercially produced helium.

I do not favor this request and therefore concur in the objections of the Acting Secretary of War and the Secretary of the Navy to granting permission to The Helium Company to export this large quantity of helium to Japan.

Sincerely yours,

(Sgd.) Harold L. Ickes

The White House

Permission is denied the Helium Company of Louisville, Kentucky, to export from the United States to the Institute of Aeronautical Policy, Tokyo, Japan, seven million cubic feet of helium during 1935 and 1936, and thereafter at the rate of 300,000 cubic feet per month. Franklin D. Roosevelt (7/23/35)[2]

[OF 594:CT]

Roosevelt to Frederick H. Allen, New York

[Washington, July 23, 1935]

My dear Mr. Allen: I have received your letter of July 10, 1935, enclosing a letter to me, dated June 25, 1935, from Senator Henri Berenger, President of the Commission on Foreign Affairs of the French Senate, which requested me to sign and return a statute of the Académie Diplomatique Internationale.[1]

I have given the matter careful consideration, as has the Department of State at my request, and I have come to the conclusion that it would not be appropriate for me, acting on behalf of the United States, to accord recognition to the Académie as an international diplomatic institution, as provided in Article 1 of the proposed statute. I could not, moreover, obligate this Government to pay a share of the annual expenses of the Académie, as provided in Article 2 of the statute, in the absence of a prior appropriation from the Congress for that specific purpose. It has therefore been necessary for me to decline Senator Berenger's request.[2]

Very sincerely yours,

[*Notation*:A] 7/23/35
[OF 1107:CT]

[1] The letters are present.
[2] Drafted by the State Department.

Roosevelt to Representative Fred J. Sisson of New York

[Washington] July 23, 1935

Personal

My dear Congressman Sisson: I have your letter of July eighteenth.[1] I do not have to remind you either of my sincere desire for peace or of the many practical steps which have been taken in the past two years

to better our relations with many countries. The Latin American Republics furnish an excellent example.

I had hoped that neutrality legislation would be passed at this session.
The difficulty is that no legislation along this line is on the calendar
of either House.[2] You and I are aware of the legislative situation at this
time—after Congress has been in session for nearly seven months. If such
legislation can still be passed before adjournment, without interminable
debate, it would be very satisfactory to you, to me and to the whole
country. But can that be done, especially in the Senate?[3]

Very sincerely yours,

[*Notation*:T] Letters to Mr. McIntyre 7/19/35 and the President, 7/18/35,
covering the subject of certain neutrality legislation now pending in
Congress—handed to Mr. Green by Mr. Forster 8/10/35.

[OF 1561:CT]

---

[1] Above.

[2] The Nye-Clark legislation was recommitted at the request of Roosevelt and the State
Department; see Hull, *Memoirs,* I, 410.

[3] Answered Aug. 7, 1935, below.

Josephus Daniels, Ambassador to Mexico, to Roosevelt

Mexico, July 23, 1935

Personal

Dear Franklin: I read the statement in the New York *Times*[1] of the
call upon you by a delegation of Congressmen who presented a petition
for an inquiry into the religious situation in Mexico and affirming "the
rights of conscience." I thought the statement you authorized the committee to publish was excellent and I hope it will be satisfactory to the
reasonable people who, like both of us, are disturbed that any country
should limit or deny religious liberty.[2] It may interest you to know that
no mention of the call upon you or of your statement has been printed
in any Mexican paper.

As I have written you, I have unofficially urged General Calles,
President Cárdenas and the Ministers of Foreign Affairs who have been
in office since I have been in Mexico that failure to grant full right to
worship in any part of this republic would cost the country the prestige
which it naturally desired to obtain and hold. General Calles, who was

engaged in defeating the Cristo revolution in 1928, and thinks the priests are still in politics, replied to me that if Mexico's policy caused loss of prestige "we will have to stand it." President Cárdenas, Dr. Puig, Mr. Portes Gil and the present Acting Minister of Foreign Affairs, Mr. Ceniceros,[3] have not been so inflexible and have said there must be no persecution in Mexico and indicated a moderating policy. However, all of them are inflexible as to upholding the law denying any school under the auspices of any religious body. The latest fight of the Catholics was based on opposition to the amendment of the Constitution, ratified by every Mexican state, giving the exclusive control of education to the State, licensing private schools only when they agree to teach "socialistic education" as defined by the Department of Education. There is no hope of changing the educational policy, and the Catholics in Mexico City, where the churches are open as they have been since 1928, are mainly concerned to secure the right to carry on their schools by priests and nuns. This is the big trouble, and I see no way to change it. The Government, backed by the Constitution, holds that education is the exclusive function of government and no school under any church auspices can operate.

My thought has been to quietly convince the authorities that the first thing to do is to permit churches to be opened and priests to officiate in those states where churches are now closed. That is the most important step, and I was glad you confined your statement to "freedom of religious worship."

The lion in the path is that in every stage of the revolution since 1910 the high officials of the Catholic church are said to have been against the Revolutionary Party and its social aims, and have been behind the Cristero and other revolutions looking to the overthrow of the Revolutionary Party. Some of the leaders who are resolved to give the workers a fairer chance regard the clergy as their most dangerous enemies. I think they are making a great mistake, seeing that the Catholic Church, with no wealth or power, could not seriously contest with the Revolutionary Party, even if the hierarchy wished to secure a return of their old dominant influences. But, inasmuch as the Catholic hierarchy in all the past has been dominant and in concert with the Government when the mass of the people was in squalor and in ignorance, it is not easy to convince the Government that this is a new day and that no church ought to be held responsible for past actions.

I hope your wise and moderating influence will calm our Catholic friends in Congress and that there will be no political repercussions that will give trouble next year. I have sought in every unofficial way, and sometimes near-official, to show how deeply you feel about the situation and will continue to do so as occasion offers. My own position is unchanged since my talk with you at the White House.[4]

Affectionately yours,

Josephus Daniels

P.S. In view of the talk about changing the Constitution, you may recall two stories about John Marshall, one of his statements: "The acme of judicial distinction is the ability to look a lawyer in the face for two hours and not hear a damn word he says," and the other the story that the Judges had a sort of club where they ate, the rule being that they not drink anything except when it rained. After the Louisiana Purchase, having a thirst, they decided that though it was not raining on the Atlantic Seaboard, it must be raining on the Mississippi, which had come under their jurisdiction, and the Judges unanimously decided "It is raining" and imbibed.

Certainly he never heard "a damn word" that Jefferson said. It would have been better for the country if he had listened to the sage of Monticello.

I am glad you are "fighting it out on this line if it takes all summer."

[PSF:Mexico:TS]

[1] July 17, 1935, p. 1.
[2] July 16, 1935 (*Public Papers,* IV, 305).
[3] José Angel Ceniceros. Edward Hay, former consul general in Paris, was named Minister for Foreign Affairs on Nov. 30, 1935.
[4] Daniels was in the United States from April 21 to June 16; his White House visit is not noted in the appointments list. See his letter to Roosevelt of Aug. 2, 1935, below.

Press Conference, Executive Offices of the White House, July 24, 1935, 10:40 A.M.

[*Excerpt*] Q: We understand that some of the State Department people were over to see you on neutrality.[1] Can you tell us whether you assured the State Department that the Nye proposal is discretionary rather than mandatory?

The President: It is a terribly long subject. Some should be discretionary and some needn't be.

Q: How about arms embargo?

The President: Well, that is part of the general thing. There are too many ifs and ands in it. It would take me about two hours to go over it.

Q: Nothing definite decided?

The President: No; it is a tremendously big subject . . .

Q: Do you expect anything on the War Profits Bill this session?

The President: I don't know. Probably what I told you last week to the effect that neutrality legislation is a very desirable thing but I didn't want to keep Congress . . .[2]

Q: Is that neutrality answer on the record this time?

The President: You may put it on the record as long as it was printed that same afternoon last week.

[President's Press Conferences:T]

[1] Hull and Phillips talked with Roosevelt on July 22 (PPF 1-0).

[2] This statement was reported generally in the press as Roosevelt's endorsement of "legislation affirming the neutrality status of the United States in the event of conflict between other nations" (New York *Times,* July 25, 1935, p. 1).

Roosevelt to Henry Morgenthau, Jr., Secretary of the Treasury

Washington, July 25, 1935

Memorandum for the Secretary of the Treasury: This strictly confidential summary of forty-seven pages from the State Department is worth your reading if you have not already seen it.[1] I should like to have your slant on it, especially as to whether I should send the State Department any comment or not.

F.D.R.

[*Notation*:CT] Memo., 7/27, "The Interweaving of Political, Economic and Monetary Elements in the Present Position in China."

[OF 20:T]

[1] Not further identified.

Roosevelt to George N. Peek, Special Adviser to the President on Foreign Trade

[Washington, July 25, 1935]

Dear George: I have considered your letter of the 18th very carefully.[1]

I know how very keenly you feel on the subjects discussed and wish that I might be more entirely in agreement with you. As a matter of fact we are probably not as far apart in our views, as I feel the impracticability of accomplishing in a short period, the things that you want to accomplish.

At all events, George, I want the benefit of your services, at least until the management and policies of the Export-Import Bank can be more definitely fixed, and the work you have been doing as Special Adviser definitely adjusted.

As soon as Congress adjourns I want to go West for quite a trip and will hope to discuss these and other matters with you upon my return. Carry on and see me when I get back. Meantime, get a vacation.[2]

Sincerely yours,

[PSF:Agriculture:CT]

[1] July 16, above, is apparently meant.
[2] Answered July 29, 1935, below.

George N. Peek, Special Adviser to the President on Foreign Trade, to Roosevelt

Washington, July 25, 1935

My dear Mr. President: Following receipt of your memorandum of July 17,[1] I have examined Senator Smith's proposal with great care.

I am impressed at once with Senator Smith's evident realization that positive measures by the Government are in order to enable our nationals to trade in world markets on equal terms with the nationals of other countries. The idea of credit insurance has been advanced from a number of sources and for several months past we have examined the question in various forms.

"Credit Insurance" is a very general term. For purposes of analysis it requires close definition.

(a) Insolvency Insurance. In this field is covered the inability of a foreign buyer to pay in the currency of his own country for goods received. There is probably a definite if limited field for this type of insurance. My own feeling is that it can be more appropriately undertaken by private concerns than by the Government, although it is possible that circumstances might warrant Government participation in such insurance, either directly or as a reinsurer. However, to do this legislation would be required empowering some Governmental agency to underwrite such insurance. In my draft of a Foreign Trade Board Bill such authority is contemplated (Section 3, Title II).

(b) Exchange Insurance. When we come into this field, which I think Senator Smith perhaps has in mind, we are on entirely different ground. I do not believe that it is a function of the Government to underwrite the rates of exchange of foreign governments and the transfer of funds from foreign nationals to the United States except under very special circumstances. In the absence of definite agreements with each country as to exchange and the transfer thereof for all or for specific transactions between its nationals and the United States, it would seem to me impracticable for the Government to insure this type of risk. It would amount to underwriting values and the transfer of foreign currencies. In the aggregate this would constitute an enormous risk. I think that it is significant that the important trading nations do not underwrite exchange insurance as such in the absence of definite exchange agreements. As illustrative of practice in international trade, I enclose a memorandum prepared in this office regarding the Export Credit Guarantee Department of the British Board of Trade.[2] You will note that ordinarily the British limit their export credit guarantee insurance to insolvency of the foreign buyer (or state or municipality, as the case may be), except in the case of Germany, where they are covered by the Anglo-German Payments Agreement signed in the autumn of 1934.

(c) War Risk Insurance. Senator Smith in his memorandum refers to this as a successful type of Governmental insurance of shipments in foreign trade. However, the War Risk Insurance Act to which he refers applied only to the insurance of American vessels, passage money, freight and cargoes against the usual marine war risks upon a finding by the Secretary of the Treasury that American shippers or importers were unable to secure adequate war risk insurance on reasonable terms. The Act did not insure payment or the transfer of exchange.

My suggestion would be that if legislation on the subject at this time is considered desirable it be confined to insolvency insurance. Exchange insurance would involve the assumption by this Government of risks against which our present foreign financial and commercial policies do not afford adequate protection.

In accordance with your request the papers in the matter are returned herewith.[3]

Faithfully yours,

George N. Peek

[OF 614-A:TS]

[1] Above.

[2] Present.

[3] Hull, Morgenthau, and Wallace were also asked to comment on Senator Smith's proposal but only Wallace's memorandum is present. Wallace was not in Washington at this time but his assistant, Paul Appleby, sent McIntyre a copy of a memorandum on the Smith plan that Wallace had sent to Chester Davis (Appleby to McIntyre, July 15, 1935; Wallace to Davis, July 9, 1935, OF 614-A). As it stood, Wallace did not like the proposal; if it meant merely renewed lending of large sums to foreign nations to finance American exports, the eventual results might well be as disastrous as the 1930 debacle. If, however, "the rate of the premium charged by the United States Foreign Credit Insurance Company varied up and down according to the degree to which imports (visible and invisible, but excluding foreign bonds, paper promises to pay, and the like) equaled exports (visible and invisible), it might be very useful." What was needed was a "combination governor and traffic light" that would promote exports and imports on a sound basis. He suggested to Davis that he put the idea of a fluctuating premium rate up to Peek. No further reference to Smith's idea has been found.

Press Conference, Executive Offices of the White House, July 26, 1935, 4 P.M.

[*Excerpt*] Q: Mr. President, can you outline what your Administration is doing or planning to do to keep us out of war?

The President: I could do it in an hour and a half. It is a tremendously big subject. Of course there are two main, salient facts: the first is the Good Neighbor policy to keep us friendly with nations, and the other is every effort, through diplomatic agencies, to keep us from getting involved in specific cases that do not concern us. I do not think I can go any further than those two general statements.

Q: And how to keep us in a sufficient state of preparedness so that other nations would not—

The President: Yes, I should say that is a corollary.

Q: Do you consider Ethiopia a specific case that does not concern us?

The President: I should say yes, except world peace and, naturally, the personal feelings of a great many Americans. Americans do, naturally, have personal feelings about those things. That you cannot stop by Government decree . . .[1]

Q: Mr. President, Mr. Grace of the Bethlehem Steel Corporation[2] said in New York yesterday that American producers of steel will not be able to sell steel for relief projects because the differential they get is not high enough. It is only 15%.[3]

The President: Yes, and I also see in the headlines—of course we can talk about the headline fellows all we want here—it said that the foreign steel producer was given a 15% preferential over American steel producers—that was the headline on the story. Isn't that grand?

There is nothing new in it. It is very simple. On Government purchases for a great many years we have been confronted very often with the problem of, "What are you going to do on a Government purchase when some foreign firm comes in with a lower bid?" Well, we had a case this past year—I think I mentioned it about six or eight months ago—on airplane cloth. In that case the Japanese bid was just about half the American bid. There was only one American firm that made airplane cloth and the Jap bid was half of theirs. Of course it meant spending, if we took the American bid, twice as much of public funds as if we took the Jap bid. Of course in that particular case we made an exception to the general rule because we thought that airplane cloth was somewhat in the nature of essential war materials and that we ought to encourage the building up of its manufacture. So we spent twice as much Government money as we would have otherwise and we took the American bid. That was done, frankly, for the purpose of encouraging the manufacture of airplane cloth in the United States.

Now, the general rule laid down some time ago was this: that on proposals for Government materials, take for instance steel, the American manufacturer is protected by a tariff and on steel, depending on what kind of steel it is, it is a fairly high tariff, as we know. That was seen to under various previous administrations, without specifying which, and the steel manufacturers in this country thought that the tariff on steel had been got up high enough to protect them. That tariff on steel, taking it by and large, has not been reduced except on one or two minor parts of steel production. On top of that, there is a general order of the Government that in addition to the tariff, we won't accept a foreign bid unless it is more than 15% less than the American bid. In effect, in other words, we are adding 15% to any existing tariff to protect American manufacturers.

Now, that is the answer to the headline in the paper that I read, and it is a very simple, square, straight proposition. If an American manufacturer is being underbid by 10%, 12%, 14%, or 15% by a foreigner who is able to pay the high tariff and still put in a bid 15% cheaper than the American manufacturer of steel, he still won't get the contract, but when he underbids the American by 15%, then he will get the contract.

Q: There are two points Mr. Grace made, first that this was PWA money, which was designed to stimulate American industry and, secondly, that the Belgians and other foreign producers can sell at more than 15% below Americans.

The President: Is any steel being bought by PWA?

Q: Very little, if any.

The President: When some comes in, talk to me again.

Q: Under the same policy, German steel has come in, and Danish cement, to my knowledge. That developed during the tariff—

The President: How much do you suppose came in?

Q: A Danish ship brought a whole shipload of cement and it all went in.

The President: How much cement do you suppose came in from Denmark and other ports in comparison with what we use?

Q: A great deal of it comes over as ballast.

The President: What percentage?

Q: I do not know.

The President: One or two per cent?

Q: No, more than that.

The President: Are you sure? You had better check.

Q: It was more than two per cent. I do not know what it is now.

The President: I do not believe it is now.

[President's Press Conferences:T]

[1] See statement issued by Roosevelt on Aug. 1, 1935, in *Public Papers,* IV, 315.

[2] Eugene G. Grace had been president of the Bethlehem Steel Corporation since 1916.

[3] Grace referred to an order of the Public Works Administration issued May 25, 1935, to the effect that "a borrower of money must buy foreign material where the value of the order is $10,000 or more and the price is 15 per cent less" (New York *Times,* July 26, 1935, p. 1).

Roosevelt to Fred I. Kent, Governor, Federal Reserve Bank of New York, New York

[Washington] July 26, 1935

Personal

Dear Fred: Many thanks for your interesting letter about China.[1] I wish China were as simple a problem as you indicate. Silver is not the problem of the Chinese past, nor the Chinese present, nor the Chinese future. There are forces there which neither you nor I understand but at least I know that they are almost incomprehensible to us Westerners. Do not let so-called figures or facts lead you to believe that any Western civilization's action can ever affect the people of China very deeply.

Very sincerely yours,

[PPF 744:CT]

[1] Kent, in his letter of July 24, 1935 (PPF 744), referred to a meeting he had had with Roosevelt the week before in which the Chinese silver question was discussed. He said that those who had advised the President that the Chinese masses would not be affected by the rise in the price of silver (because they were unaffected by the bank operations of the metropolitan centers) were wrong. China's banking system reached virtually all parts of the country and the Shanghai money rates were reflected in the prices of the commodities the Chinese bought and sold. When the United States forced up the price of silver "the banks broke down and . . . the business of the people was thrown into chaos." He concluded that the economic stability of China had been seriously impaired.

National Council for Prevention of War to Marvin H. McIntyre, Assistant Secretary to the President

Washington, D.C., July 26, 1935

Dear Mr. McIntyre: A group of men and women representing the civic organizations listed below are seriously concerned about the preservation of American neutrality and desire to see some constructive action taken at this session of Congress. Encouraged by the newspaper reports of the President's awareness of the importance of this legislation, and by the evidences of substantial sentiment among members of Congress, of both parties, and throughout the country, we venture to request an interview with the President, at any time on Monday or Tuesday, July 29th or 30th, in order to submit our views to him and to ask for his support.[1]

The indiscriminate sale of arms and munitions of war, and the making of loans, to belligerent nations and factions has always been a dangerous and dubious procedure. Under the guise of asserting our "neutral rights" the practise has at least twice directly contributed to involving our country in costly foreign wars; and it has become, under modern conditions of warfare and international relationships, incompatible with the preservation of real neutrality and honorable peace.

Since last December, the outbreak of hostilities between Italy and Abyssinia has continuously threatened; and the revival of armament and naval rivalries among the great powers, so lamentable in their historic consequences, has further undermined the foundations of peace which the civilized world regards as the sole compensation for the agonies of the World War. Yet, in the presence of these alarms, the United States has not yet taken a single step to revise those policies which have led to war in the past and to establish its neutrality upon a sounder moral and legal basis. This matter is of the gravest importance.

For many years, ever since the Arms-Traffic Conference of 1925 and the promulgation of the Kellogg Pact, arms-embargo and munitions-control measures have been pending in Congress; and proposals have been made requesting the President to negotiate a multilateral convention, supplementary to the Pact, pledging all its signatories to prohibit the export of arms and munitions of war to states and governments which violate it. We believe that the United States Government, as the principal sponsor of the Pact, ought to lead the world toward making its great promise a reality and that no more effective way of doing so has been suggested than this proposal of pledging all its friends to prohibit the arms-traffic which so directly contributes to nullifying it.

Since March of this year much legislation has been introduced in Congress dealing with this subject in its several phases. On the House calendar, at the present time, with a favorable report from the Committee on Foreign Affairs is the Kloeb Bill designed to make unlawful the advancement of loans or credits by American citizens to foreign governments engaged in armed hostilities.[2] Senator Borah has introduced similar legislation in the Senate. The Senate Munitions Committee has proposed more comprehensive legislation to the same general purpose, in order to prevent commercial activities from contributing to armed conflict, and from profiting by the misfortunes of others.

An important meeting of the Council of the League of Nations has been called to meet next week in Geneva, in order to concert measures for terminating, if possible, the threat to peace in the controversy between Italy and Abyssinia. While our position remains obscure, the

British Government, we rejoice to note, has announced its decision to refuse licenses for the exportation of arms and materials of war to both sides. We should like to see legislation passed in Congress, and Executive action taken immediately, that would place this country squarely behind the position taken by the British Government, and give the League of Nations and the world assurance that the United States not only will not do anything to weaken the efforts of others to prevent war, but will actively assist in curbing the menace of the munitions industries by proclaiming an unequivocal disapproval of any attempts to supply arms and implements of war to nations threatening or precipitating hostilities, as a fundamental national policy consequent upon the Treaty for the Renunciation of War.

Action on the Kloeb Bill could be taken immediately. Congress awaits only word from the President, we think, to ensure its enactment.

The undersigned respectfully renew their request for an interview with the President to press the importance of this legislation and Executive action upon his attention.

Very respectfully,

> Grace M. Sisson
> Jeannette Rankin

Signed: The Women's International League for Peace and Freedom, by Mildred Scott Olmsted, Lois Jameson, Miss Wall, Mrs. Mary Davis

The National Council for Prevention of War, Miss Jeannette Rankin, Miss Seminaris

Oneida County (N.Y.) League of Women Voters, Mrs. F. J. Sisson

The National Council of Jewish Women, Mrs. Koenigsberger

The Women's Christian Temperance Union, Miss Scott

The Peoples' Lobby, Mr. Duncan

The Washington Foreign Policy Committee, Mr. Brent Allinson

American Civil Liberties Union, Mr. Arthur Ballard

Others: Miss Milrod, Miss Borst, Miss Hessler, Mr. Geracci

[OF 1561:TS]

[1] An attached memorandum by Kannee, Aug. 19, 1935, reads: "Mac told them on the phone would appreciate it if they would take it up with Cordell Hull."

[2] H.R. 7125, "to prohibit the making of loans or the extension of credit to the government or national of any government engaged in armed conflict," was introduced by Frank L. Kloeb on March 29, 1935, and reported July 22, 1935 (*Cong. Rec.,* vol. 79, pp. 4719, 11607). No further action was taken.

Roosevelt to William Phillips, Under Secretary of State

Washington, July 27, 1935

Memorandum for the Under Secretary of State: In regard to the Spanish negotiations, I am inclined to go along with the suggestion of a reduction in the duty on cork stoppers. Am I correct in assuming that we grow or manufacture practically no cork in the United States?

In regard, however, to onions—is not this essential commodity grown in almost every county of the United States? Why should it not be considered in the same category as potatoes? I doubt very much the advisability of a further reduction on onions. There is no good reason why we should not grow them here at a reasonable price.[1]

F.D.R.

[OF 422:CT]

[1] Phillips had previously (July 26, 1935, OF 422) recommended to Roosevelt that the United States make further reductions of the import duties on corks and onions as an aid in securing reciprocal tariff benefits, notably on automobile exports. He replied to the letter here printed on August 1 (OF 422), assuring the President that no cork was produced in the United States and that the proposed reduction on the duty on onions would still leave it at 100 per cent ad valorem.

William E. Dodd, Ambassador to Germany, to Roosevelt

[Berlin] July 29, 1935

Dear Mr. President: This may reach you too late to be of any value —though I shall telegraph you before letter's arrival in case of necessity.

Some phases of German situation assume a different aspect from what was supposed to be fixed upon at Stresa and Geneva last April. It was fairly certain May 1 that the encirclement policy of France would be applied. But Hitler's speech of May 21[1] as well as growing British uneasiness led to the unexpected Naval Agreement. This is the first time, I believe, in modern history that England has sided with a threatening imperialist European power, rather than guide a combination of weaker powers against the threatening one: Louis XIV and Napoleon I are best illustrations. I think England's unprecedented attitude is due to the hope that she can moderate Hitler's conduct and still keep on fair terms with France. Of course the English people are more pacifist than ever before.

This is the first and vital phase of the new situation. The second is the Mussolini policy. France agreed in this case to support Italy simply to increase her prestige in the Balkan zone and balance Germany's increasing power. France did not think Italy would actually go to war; but she seems to have misjudged and now the situation is very tense as all the world knows. One may guess events a little better if one knows that Hitler constantly studies Napoleon I and causes Napoleon films to be shown in Germany. The old royalist crowd used to pay similar tribute to Napoleon. At the same time Mussolini writes *The Hundred Days,* a play which shows the French emperor to have been the savior of Europe. So one need not be sure these dictators can be long restrained. But I must add that Hitler and even his moderate supporters, Von Neurath and Schacht, hope and pray that Mussolini will go to war.

If this happens England and France can hardly prevent Hitler from dominating [even annexing parts][2] the Balkan region. His one objective is to expand in this direction. I shall see the Italian Ambassador here as soon as he returns from a "cure" [Rome?] and ascertain the latest moves—if he talks at all.

The Japanese attitude embarrasses Germany a little because the Germans fear it may halt Mussolini whom they wish to eclipse in some way. I am calling Cerruti's[3] attention to this. We have much evidence that Germany and Japan are secretly allied and that any war might bring active co-operation. Never has Germany been more warlike, although "peace" is frequently preached. Our military attaché's reports show how far armaments have gone and that 2,000,000 young Germans are waiting volunteers now—no conscription necessary in some time. They expect to have 8,000,000 trained in few years. It is said now that confiscation of Jewish property is to be resorted to in order to meet urgent expense.

My hope is that England, France [and perhaps the U.S.] can crowd Italy out of Africa through League pressure, that Russia and the leading Balkan states will lend support and thus isolate Japan and Germany again. If not world war—terrible horrors—is fairly certain.

Congratulations on your successes at home, when so many powerful folk have been fighting you. If only the utilities bill could pass as you urged![4]

Yours sincerely,

Wm E. Dodd

[PSF:Germany:AS]

[1] The speech announcing the resumption of conscription.
[2] Brackets, here and below, as in the original.
[3] Vittorio Cerruti, Italian ambassador to Germany, had been named ambassador to Paris early in July but apparently was still in Berlin. He was succeeded by Bernardo Attolico, who had been ambassador in Moscow (New York *Times,* July 6, 1935, p. 4).
[4] Answered briefly Aug. 14, 1933, in *Personal Letters, 1928–1945,* I, 501.

George N. Peek, Special Adviser to the President on Foreign Trade, to Roosevelt

Washington, July 29, 1935

My dear Mr. President: I have your letter of July 25.[1]

In view of your request that I remain at my post for the time being, I shall not now press the matter of my resignation, but will leave it for future events to determine. At the same time I repeat that I think that I have finished the job you asked me to do.

It is true that I am anxious to see certain policies rectified within a brief period. I regard the policies in question as unsound economically and politically. I can not place myself in a position of endorsing them by remaining silent. Delay in revising them simply means a continuation and aggravation of the conditions created by the three preceding administrations. This is a point which political opponents are not likely to overlook.

I appreciate your suggestions as to taking a vacation, and hope to be able to act on it at an early date.

With my best wishes for an enjoyable trip west, I am

Faithfully yours,

George N. Peek

[PSF:Agriculture:TS]

[1] Above.

William Phillips, Under Secretary of State, to Roosevelt

Washington, July 29, 1935

My dear Mr. President: I should be very grateful for your criticism and suggestions of the enclosed draft reply to the letter from the Jewish societies, which I have already spoken to you about. You will note that their letter (which I enclose) refers to Jews, Catholics, Protestants and "liberals of all description" as well as to labor.[1]

We are called upon to protest against the general persecutions. Our reply is so important and so charged with dynamite, from a domestic as well as an international viewpoint, that I do not wish to send any reply without your careful consideration and cordial approval.

In the reply I have not mentioned the Catholics or any other group by name because the Catholics have not approached us and it may well be that they prefer to act through the Pope, who has already spoken.

It is also to be borne in mind that our own position is not altogether perfect, in view of Mayor LaGuardia's recent action against a German citizen in New York and also the flag incident on the *Bremen* resulting in a riot.[2]

It seems to be wise not to go too far in a public statement and yet far enough, and this I have attempted to do.

Faithfully yours,

William Phillips

[PSF:State:TS]

[1] Not present. A memorandum signed by representatives of a number of Jewish organizations was given to Phillips at the State Department on July 26; Phillips replied to this in a letter of July 29, 1935 (both are printed in the New York *Times,* July 27, 1935, p. 2; July 31, 1935, pp. 1–2).

[2] Late on the night of July 26 Communist demonstrators had torn the Nazi flag from the *Bremen* and had thrown it into the Hudson River (*ibid.,* July 27, 1935, p. 1).

Press Conference, Executive Offices of the White House, August 2, 1935, 4:15 P.M.

[*Excerpt*] Q: Some of the radicals recently deported from Cuba called on Phillips of the State Department and demanded Ambassador Caffery's recall on the ground that he had lost the confidence of the American people?

The President: American people or Cuban?

Q: American. Mr. Phillips thought he had the full confidence of both the Cuban and the American people? Do you share in that?

The President: I think that is correct. As a matter of fact, I had an awfully nice talk with Caffery this morning[1] and all the reports about the economic conditions in Cuba are very encouraging. Taking it by and large, the economic conditions in Cuba have picked up almost more than in any other part of the world. That sounds like a very drastic statement but I think it is true. For instance, on the sugar plantations and various other work down there, the wages, three years ago, were down around fifteen and twenty cents a day. They are now up to eighty cents or a dollar a day. The whole complexion of industry and agriculture is infinitely better and has been for a long time.

[President's Press Conferences:T]

[1] With Sumner Welles, at the White House (PPF 1-0).

Josephus Daniels, Ambassador to Mexico, to Roosevelt

Mexico, August 2, 1935

Personal

Dear Franklin: A committee composed of William Franklin Sands (a Catholic who teaches Public Relations at Georgetown University); Dr. Philip Marshall Brown (Protestant) of Princeton, who was Minister to two Central American countries under your Republican predecessors; and Carl Sherman (Hebrew) who was Attorney General of New York when Al Smith was Governor, has been here some weeks.[1] This committee was sent down by the Committee on Religious Rights and Minorities to make a survey of the religious situation in Mexico. I arranged for Mr. Sands (who was at one time in our diplomatic service and stationed here in the last days of Díaz) to see the Acting Minister for Foreign Affairs. He talked with him and other officials of the Mexican Government. The committee was in touch with leading Catholics and others and I gave them all the information I possessed.

They are to make a report to the Committee on Religious Rights and to discuss the Mexican religious situation at a Round Table Conference at Williamstown (Mass.) this month.[2] Dr. Ramón Beteta, a Mexican, has been invited to speak there at the same time. I do not know whether he has accepted.

Their report is not ready, but Mr. Sands, the Catholic member, in a letter to Colonel Callahan[3] stated: "What I want you to know is: That Government officials assured me that Daniels has never let up for a minute stressing the importance of a solution to this religious problem. . . . President Cardenas told Daniels that he could not change the law but there would be no religious persecution."

Yesterday Mr. Edward Reed, Chief of the Mexican Division of the State Department, sent a confidential copy of the rough draft of Mr. Sand's report. Accompanying the draft Mr. Reed sent a confidential memorandum in which he says:

Concerning Mr. Daniels, Mr. Sands expressed the opinion that our Ambassador has been most unjustly maligned. Mexican Foreign Officials told him that Mr. Daniels had gone far beyond what might reasonably have been expected of him in trying to bring about an adjustment of the religious controversy. Mr. Sands was sure that these statements were correct and he wished to do something about the matter in justice to Mr. Daniels. Mr. Daniels, however, had insisted that he keep silent on the subject of his activities unless authorized by the Secretary of State to make a statement in regard to them. Incidentally, Mr. Sands indicated that he was familiar with the purport of Ambassador Daniels' recent conversation on religious matters with President Cardenas.

I do not know what will be the final report of this committee, but I surmise it will stress the deplorable situation in Tabasco, Veracruz and other States where there has been bitter conflict between Catholics and Revolutionary leaders. In the meantime I thought you would like to read the impression of the Catholic member of the committee.[4]

With my affectionate regards, Faithfully yours,

Josephus Daniels

[PSF:Mexico:TS]

[1] Sands, a Foreign Service officer from 1896 to 1910, taught diplomacy and American history at the School of Foreign Service of Georgetown University. Brown had taught international law at Princeton. His last diplomatic post was that of minister to Honduras. Sherman, an attorney, was a member of the governing council of the American Jewish Congress.

[2] The Williamstown Institute of Human Relations was sponsored by the National Conference of Christians and Jews and met from August 26 to 30 (New York *Times,* Aug. 31, 1935, p. 11).

[3] Presumably D. J. Callahan, treasurer of the Knights of Columbus.

[4] In a letter to McIntyre of July 25, 1935 (OF 146-A), Sands said that he and the other members of his committee had had repeated statements from Mexican government officials, in the Foreign Office and elsewhere, that Daniels had consistently tried to bring about a solution of the religious problem. Sands said that there was not the slightest justification for the attacks upon him in the United States, and, as a Catholic, he would have been glad to have so stated publicly but that Daniels had "preferred to let it die."

Representative Fred J. Sisson of New York to Roosevelt

Washington, D.C., August 7, 1935

Dear Mr. President: I have your letter of July 23rd regarding neutrality legislation and thank you for the same.[1] I felt sure that you appreciated the importance of this legislation at this Session of Congress.

I have not replied before this because, together with some others, I have been further investigating the situation with regard to the possibility of passing such legislation at this Session.

You are somewhat mistaken in your statement that no such legislation is on the calendar. The Kloeb Bill is on the calendar; that is to say, it was reported out of the Foreign Affairs Committee and I assume that the usual resolution was passed instructing the Chairman of the Committee to secure a rule and take such steps as are necessary for its passage. It is the opinion of several members of that Committee that such amendments as would be germane to the Kloeb Bill could be added, which would pretty well cover the field of our neutrality policy.

I feel confident that with a little help from the Administration any necessary legislation to this end could be passed through both the House and Senate at this Session; in fact, I am confident that it could be passed were it not for the rather prevalent idea that the State Department and the Administration are opposed to it.

I hope that you will see fit to clarify the situation by dispelling the idea that the Administration is opposed to neutrality legislation at this Session.[2]

Cordially yours,

F. J. Sisson

[OF 156:TS]

[1] Above.
[2] Answered Aug. 13, 1935, below.

William Phillips, Under Secretary of State, to Roosevelt

Washington, August 9, 1935

Dear Mr. President: Referring again to your desire to be kept informed in regard to the health of Italian troops now in East Africa, I beg to enclose for your information a memorandum on the subject which has been prepared for me by our Division of Near Eastern Affairs.[1] It is true that most of the information contained in our despatches is based on rumors and reports, but read together they present a rather definite picture.

I also bring to your attention a telegram just received from our Embassy at Rome, with regard to the same subject. We have yet to hear from our new effort to obtain information from Port Said.[2]

Faithfully yours,

William Phillips

[PSF:Italy:TS]

[1] Aug. 8, 1935, unsigned, consisting of excerpts received from dispatches from Rome between May 3 and July 25, 1935. The gist of these was that there was much illness among the Italian troops in Ethiopia.

[2] Alexander Kirk to Hull, Aug. 8, 1935, on the same subject. At Roosevelt's request, Hull continued to keep him informed on the state of health of the Italian troops (Hull to Roosevelt, Sept. 14, 1935, OF 20).

Jesse Isidor Straus, Ambassador to France, to Roosevelt

Washington, August 9, 1935

Dear Mr. President: I want to report that following your instructions I this morning had a chat with Senator Pittman and gave him an outline of my thoughts as to the possible settlement of France's debt to the United States.

I shall look forward with pleasure to a visit to you at Hyde Park.[1] With kindest regards, I remain, Very sincerely yours,

Jesse Isidor Straus

[OF 280:TS]

[1] Straus had seen Roosevelt at the White House on August 6 and he and Mrs. Straus had lunch with the Roosevelts at Hyde Park on September 19 (PPF 1-0).

Roosevelt to Representative A. Willis Robertson of Virginia

[Washington] August 12, 1935

. My dear Mr. Robertson: This will acknowledge receipt of your letter of July thirty-first, enclosing a telegram from a tobacco firm in Lynchburg, Virginia, in which it is stated that the exports of tobacco from that locality are seriously menaced by the effects of the Silver Purchase Act.[1]

Tobacco produced in the vicinity of Lynchburg, Virginia, is of the fire-cured type. This tobacco has been predominantly exported over a long period, chiefly to Europe. A drastic decline has taken place in the exports of fire-cured tobacco, amounting to more than 50 percent during the last ten years. The development of nationalistic policies by countries formerly importing fire-cured tobacco from the United States, fostered through monopoly control measures and import restrictions, has led to an expansion of foreign tobacco production and a resulting displacement of our tobacco. European consumption of foreign-grown tobacco which competes with our fire-cured types is estimated to have increased from 192 million pounds in 1924 to 297 million pounds in 1932.

However, no part of this decline could in any way be attributed to effects of the Silver Purchase Act, since it took place before the Act became effective. Furthermore, the principal countries involved are not silver-producing or silver-using countries so that the Silver Purchase Act would not affect them. The Silver Purchase Act of 1934 was designed to benefit each of the 48 States as well as the silver-producing States, by adding to the metallic basis of our currency and increasing the level of domestic commodity prices, and by relieving the world demand for gold to increase gold prices of international commodities and improve the purchasing power of our export commodities.

As you know, our Government is now actively engaged in negotiations to establish more favorable trade relations with foreign countries, under the Reciprocal Tariff Act enacted by this Administration, with a view of increasing the export outlets for American products, including tobacco.

Very sincerely yours,

[OF 614-A:CT]

[1] (Act approved June 19, 1934, 48 *Stat.* 1178.) The letter is present (OF 614-A); the telegram is not. Robertson said that he had found that the price on many silver articles had advanced more than 50 per cent; he did not believe that the non-silver-producing states should provide this subsidy to the few silver states.

Thorvald Solberg to Roosevelt

Washington, D.C., August 12, 1935

Dear Mr. President: The one supreme copyright advance desired, is an act of international justice,—a rectification of our unfair treatment of English authors. Only the President of the United States can achieve this, and you have expressed your wish to do it.

On April 19th, by a two-thirds vote, the Senate authorized you to ratify the International Copyright Convention, and thus at once realize the hope entertained by every friend of copyright for more than forty years—our entry into the Copyright Union.

But on the 22d of April this vote was "reconsidered" because of a declared "understanding and agreement" of the various conflicting interests with reference to this particular convention, that the proposed copyright bill should first be enacted before the copyright treaty should be adhered to.

This bargain was not demanded by the true friends of copyright, who were not parties to it, but by the "conflicting interests" who have been in constant contention since 1925, and are apparently willing to forego the one great betterment now possible.

More than four months have been consumed in securing affirmative action by the Senate. What reasonable hope have we that agreement by the House of Representatives can be obtained within the short time now remaining of this session?

Is it not possible for the President to request now a Senate vote for authority to ratify the treaty? Once obtained, he will be at liberty to exercise it at any time that in his judgment is appropriate. Copyright legislation can follow when Congress shall have determined the various controversial matters presented.

Failure to cure the present unfair international copyright situation at this session will be a catastrophe. It will bring about a condition entailing great financial losses both on American and British authors, and will engender a state of ill will that will require half a century of effort to overcome.

May we not count on your personal intervention to eliminate this tragic result and to secure the tremendously important and widely desired advancement urged?[1]

Very sincerely yours

Thorvald Solberg

[OF 699:AS]

[1] The copyright convention had been favorably reported on April 19, 1935, by a subcommittee of the Senate Foreign Relations Committee, of which Senator Duffy was chairman. Pittman, chairman of the main committee, said that the treaty had been under consideration for a long time and asked for favorable action. It was approved by voice vote without debate. (This action is interesting in view of the long history of the question before the Congress: twelve bills and thirteen hearings since 1925.)

Reconsideration of the vote on April 22 (nullification of the action and restoration of the treaty to the Senate executive calendar) was at Duffy's request. He offered no explanation nor was there any comment from either side of the chamber (*Cong. Rec.,* vol. 79, pp. 6027, 6032, 6099). To judge from subsequent debate, however, the action was apparently the result of the protests of certain groups (notably the American Society of Composers, Authors and Publishers, of which the composer section was especially vocal) who feared that ratification of the treaty prior to the enactment of statutory legislation would work against their interests. Thorvald Solberg, who with Robert Underwood Johnson and Raney was leading the pro-treaty contingent, said that "Subsequently Senator Duffy explained that this action was taken because he had agreed with certain copyright interests that the copyright legislation proposed should first be enacted before the treaty was ratified" (Solberg to Roosevelt, Jan. 2, 1936, OF 699). Apparently, no communications, certainly no written exchanges, passed between the White House and either Pittman or Duffy on this rather unusual Senate action.

Senator Duffy thereupon (June 14, 1935) introduced S. 3047, a bill to amend the Copyright Act of 1909 (*Cong. Rec.,* vol. 79, pp. 9257, 12184–12187; for the Senate report, see vol. 80, pp. 1943–1944). When it was debated on June 25, 1935, Duffy described it as an "enabling act" to the copyright treaty, and said there was "a gentleman's understanding" that the treaty would be held on the Senate calendar until S. 3047 could be considered. Senator Wagner, however, said that he had received many protests against the bill and asked that it be passed over; this was done. In the extended debate on the bill on July 31 and on August 1 and 5, it was apparent that those presumed to be benefited by it were divided on its merits, but after extensive amendment it was passed on August 7. In the House it was referred to the Committee on Patents, to which had been previously referred (June 19, 1935) the House companion bill, H.R. 8557 (*Cong. Rec.,* vol. 79, pp. 12181–12191, 12249–12254, 12257–12258, 12475, 12477, 12559–12567, 12904).

Opponents of the measure, including the Screen Writers Guild of the Authors League of America, and individual composers (among them Jerome Kern and George Gershwin), renewed their criticism in telegrams to the President on August 21 and 22. The bill, however, received the support of some groups, among them the American Hotels Association, the Motion Picture Theatre Owners of America, and the National Association of Broadcasters. A printed statement by these organizations, dated July 26, 1935, is in the Roosevelt papers (OF 699). It bears this note: "RF   Will you bring this to me in case the Bill passes? FDR." ("RF" was Rudolph Forster, White House executive clerk.) The House, however, took no action on either its own or the Senate bill. Solberg's letter was briefly acknowledged by McIntyre, Sept. 5, 1935 (OF 699).

Roosevelt to Representative Fred J. Sisson of New York

[Washington] August 13, 1935

Personal

My dear Congressman Sisson: I am in receipt of your letter of August 7, 1935, with further reference to the question of neutrality legislation.[1]

I note your statement that there is an impression prevalent in some quarters that the Department of State and the Administration are opposed to such legislation. I hope that I need not assure you that this impression is entirely without foundation. The Department of State has been studying this subject for some time and for several weeks officers of that Department have been in frequent consultation with a sub-committee of the Senate Committee on Foreign Relations and with the House Committee on Foreign Affairs. Members of the Special Committee of the Senate Investigating the Munitions Industry have been present at the meetings between the sub-committee and officers of the Department of State. In all of these discussions, it has been made clear that the Department of State is in favor of comprehensive and well considered neutrality legislation.

As far as legislation on this subject during the present session of Congress is concerned, I can do little more than repeat what I told you in my letter of July 23.[2] If the Committees of Congress, which are dealing with neutrality legislation, can find it possible to report satisfactory legislation at this session and if such legislation can be passed before adjournment without interminable debate and further lengthening of this already protracted session, the result would be most satisfactory to the Administration and to the whole country. You must realize, however, as well as I the difficulties in the way of the accomplishment of such a program at this time.[3]

Very sincerely yours,

[OF 1561:CT]

[1] Above.
[2] Above.
[3] Drafted in the State Department.

Cordell Hull, Secretary of State, to Roosevelt

Washington, August 13, 1935

My dear Mr. President: With reference to Mr. Peek's report of June 30, 1935, entitled "Foreign Restrictions and Agreements Affecting American Commerce," you inquired recently whether we desired to make any reply.[1]

The report is inaccurate and misleading, and presumably is intended to imply that the policy being pursued by this Government is an unsound and ineffectual one. However, this conclusion is not expressed, and any attempt to refute it would necessitate first a formulation of the policy which Mr. Peek presumably is advocating. It is not believed that any useful purpose would be served by giving his ideas on the subject such publicity. It seems best, therefore, to refrain from public comment until such time as Mr. Peek himself, or others who sympathize with his views indicate what the report is supposed to mean and what conclusions are to be drawn from it.

I may add that a similar, though less complete, compilation of foreign bilateral agreements was prepared by Mr. Peek some time ago and was considered by the Trade Agreements Committee and the Executive Committee on Commercial Policy, and that the results of this consideration were communicated to Mr. Peek. On that occasion it was pointed out that the list included treaties in whose benefits the United States has in fact been sharing; that, of the bilateral agreements in which the United States does not share, some do not affect our trade, some are regional arrangements which we recognize as valid exceptions, and some relate to subjects of new development which our earlier agreements have not been sufficiently broad to cover; and that the remedy lies not in withdrawing to a conditional policy, but in increasing the number and widening the scope of our reciprocal unconditional obligations.

It will be understood that exclusive bilateral agreements largely eliminate triangular and multi-lateral trade and divert commerce from natural to artificial channels. Being generally discriminatory, they provoke retaliation, and, in the end, diminish rather than increase the sum total of world trade. The economic program of this Government, instead of pursuing this narrow and destructive trade policy, points in the opposite direction to an equality of trade opportunities and to the restoration of some twenty billions of dollars' worth of international commerce which under a system of exclusive bilateral agreements would not be possible.

If some country does not thus take the lead another economic collapse, beginning probably in Germany and Italy and resulting in serious repercussions in this and other countries, will be almost certain.

Faithfully yours,

Cordell Hull

[OF 971:TS]

[1] Enclosed in Peek's letter to Roosevelt of July 17, 1935 (OF 614-A).

Memorandum by R. Walton Moore, Assistant Secretary of State

[Washington] August 16, 1935

The attached proposed Joint Resolution, as originally framed, was approved by the Secretary, at whose instance I showed it to the President, who approved it, and at the same time authorized me to say to Senator Pittman that he would be willing to modify it so as to make its provisions mandatory.[1] Then I went to the Capitol and talked with Senator Pittman, who made the modification indicated by his pencil writing. He suggested that he might have it redrafted, but acquiesced in my view that it would be safer for me to take it back to the President and obtain his final approval. I then saw the President again and he said he had changed his mind, and thus the effort to do anything was abandoned. I notified Mr. Lamb,[2] Clerk of the Senate Foreign Relations Committee, and will try to talk to Senator Pittman this morning, and more fully explain what happened.

RWM

[Moore Papers:Neutrality:T]

[1] Moore talked with Roosevelt for over an hour at the White House on the afternoon of August 15 (PPF 1-0). Hull had seen the President in the morning and presumably had at that time received permission to go ahead with the draft of a resolution (PPF 1-0). In his *Memoirs* (I, 411), Hull says that "during the second week in August" he "went to see the President and urged that he request Congress to pass a discretionary-arms embargo resolution" to apply when the Italo-Ethiopian war broke out.

[2] Walter C. Lamb was an assistant clerk; Edward J. Trenwith was clerk.

[*Enclosure*]

[August 15, 1935][1]

Whereas it appears that there is possibility of the outbreak of armed conflict between ~~Italy and~~ Ethiopia *and Italy;*[2] Therefore be it resolved by the Senate and the House of Representatives of the United States of America in Congress assembled, That in case the President finds that such armed conflict is actually in progress, and shall so proclaim, it shall thereafter be unlawful to export any arms, ammunition or implements of war from any place in the United States to *either of* the *said* ~~country or~~ co'ntries ~~designated in his proclamation~~ or to any person, company or association acting in the interest of *either of* such ~~country or~~ countries until *the President shall find that such conflict has terminated and shall so proclaim or* otherwise ordered ~~by the President or~~ by the Congress.

Section 2. Whoever, in violation of any of the provisions of Section one, shall export or attempt to export or cause to be exported, arms, ammunition or implements of war shall, on conviction, be punished by fine not exceeding $10,000, or by imprisonment of not exceeding two years, or both.

Section 3. (a) Any arms, ammunition or implements of war which have been exported or which it has been attempted to export in violation of the provisions of Section one and the property, vessels, or vehicles containing the same shall be subject to seizure and forfeiture in accordance with the provisions of Sections 1 to 8, inclusive, Title 6, Chapter 30 of the Act approved June 15, 1917, 40 *Stat.* 223-225 (Title 22, Sections 238–245, inclusive, U.S.C.)

(b) In the case of the forfeiture of any arms, ammunition, or implements of war by reason of a violation of this Act, no notice of public sale shall be required; no such arms, ammunition or implements of war shall be sold at public sale, but they shall be delivered to the Secretary of War; and the Secretary of War may order such arms, ammunition, or implements of war destroyed or may retain them for the use of the armed forces of the United States.

Section 4. This act shall terminate on the expiration of thirty days following the convening of the next regular session of the Congress.

[*Notation*:AS] Draft prepared 8/19/35   H.M.[3]
[Moore Papers:Neutrality:T]

[1] This supplied date is that of Moore's conference with Roosevelt.

[2] Crossed-out words were crossed out in the original; italicized words indicate words that were added in the process of revising. The revisions in this sentence are in Roosevelt's hand; the others following are in Pittman's hand.

[3] This notation was presumably added when a clean draft was typed and enclosed in Hull's note to Roosevelt of Aug. 19, 1935, below.

Cordell Hull, Secretary of State, to Roosevelt

Washington, August 18, 1935

Memorandum for the President: Whale Oil. The Bill for the repeal of the tax on whale oil, about which I corresponded with you sometime ago and of which you expressed approval, has reached the stage of passing the Senate as an amendment to the Tax Bill (*Congressional Record* of August 15, 1935, pp. 13730–13733.)[1]

I understand that this amendment was discussed last night by the conferees on the Tax Bill and that opposition was heard from some quarters. The conferees will, I understand, discuss this amendment again tomorrow morning.

The opposition appears to come from interests producing edible materials from fish and other sources, who maintain that whale oil would be directly competitive with their products.

I believe that the fears of Mr. Bland of Virginia, who was heard last night at the conference, and others having similar interests, are unfounded. Whale oil has never directly competed with domestic edible products, and American prejudice would undoubtedly prevent its future use for edible purposes. It has been used almost exclusively in soap making and so far as I can learn will continue to be so used.

You will recall that the Secretary of Agriculture in a letter to you dated May 27, 1935[2] stated that, "The repeal of the excise tax on whale oil would probably not be seriously felt by any branch of domestic agriculture and would be definitely beneficial to some branches." Mr. Wallace referred particularly to the loss in foreign markets of our trade in lard. He believes that the diversion of huge quantities of whale oil from our soap kettles to German and other margarine kettles has been instrumental in cutting our exports of lard materially. Moreover, the use of whale oil in Europe for making margarine has so depressed the price of butter there that European butter has surmounted our tariff barrier and reached our markets to the extent of approximately 20,000,000 pounds in the first half of this year in competition with domestic butter. At the conclusion of an exhaustive report to you under cover of the above-mentioned letter, Mr. Wallace says: "Concerning the possible advantages to agriculture from the trade agreement with Norway, which the repeal of the tax would make possible . . . the balance of the argument so far as concerns agriculture probably lies on the side of repealing the tax."

In the event that the feeling persists among producers of edible products that whale oil would compete with them, a certain means of dispelling that fear would lie in amending the amendment to make whale oil tax free only when certified to be imported for inedible purposes. I understand that Senator Metcalf is prepared to make such a proposal.[3]

In view of the conclusions of the Secretary of Agriculture regarding the beneficial effects of this repeal and the practical certainty of pre-

603

venting competition with fishery and other edible products, I feel that those opposing this repeal could safely withdraw.

The pages of the *Congressional Record* which I cited in the first paragraph of this memorandum represent all of the arguments which the interested Executive branches have presented to you and to the Congress.

CH

[OF 61-W:TS]

[1] In the bound edition, vol. 79, pp. 13248–13250.
[2] OF 61-W.
[3] Jesse H. Metcalf of Rhode Island.

Roosevelt to Ray Atherton, Counselor of Embassy, London

[Washington] August 19, 1935

Dear Ray: May I introduce to you Mr. S. R. Fuller, Jr., a very old friend of mine. He has just completed a fine piece of work for the Government in Alaska and has now returned to his private business.

He will be in England shortly and I hope much that you can arrange for him to see the Prime Minister and several others he has in mind.[1]

Always sincerely,

[PPF 2616:CT]

[1] Similar letters were sent by Roosevelt to Dodd in Berlin and Emmet at The Hague.

Roosevelt to Cordell Hull, Secretary of State

Washington, August 19, 1935

Memorandum for the Secretary of State: I have read with great interest the recommendations in regard to the Inter-American Highway and approve the recommended procedure. The Department should proceed to take up the plan with the Republics concerned.[1]

F.D.R.

[*Notation*:T] Copy of let. to the Pres. from Secy. of State, 8/16 (original retained) enclosing communication from Acting Secy. of Agriculture,

7/25, with attached file, re conditions upon which this govt. proposes to cooperate with other interested governments under the pertinent provisions of ERA[2] in constructing bridges along the route of Inter-American highway.[3]

[OF 608:CT]

[1] Under the 1935 Emergency Appropriation Act, in which funds for the highway were provided, the other countries were required to give assurances to the President of their readiness to cooperate in the surveys and construction.
[2] Emergency Relief Administration.
[3] Hull's letter is present (OF 608); the other papers were returned to him.

Cordell Hull, Secretary of State, to Roosevelt

Washington [August 19, 1935][1]

My dear Mr. President: I feel that the time has now come when we should make a vigorous effort to secure the enactment by Congress of the Arms Embargo Resolution in respect to Ethiopia and Italy, which was the subject of discussion last week.[2] To this end, I enclose, for your consideration and, if you approve, your signature, a letter to Senator Pittman transmitting a copy of that Resolution.

I venture to suggest that if you send this letter, you may wish to release it to the press. Public knowledge of the position of the Administration in regard to this matter would, I believe, serve a useful purpose at this time.

Faithfully yours,

Cordell Hull

[PPF 745:TS]

[1] This date is derived from Hull, *Memoirs,* I, 411.
[2] Moore talked with the President at the White House for over an hour on August 15 (PPF 1-0).

[*Enclosure 1*] Roosevelt to Senator Key Pittman of Nevada

Washington, Aug. 19th 1935[1]

My dear Senator Pittman: You will recall the discussions of last week in regard to the advisability of the immediate enactment of a Joint Resolution which would authorize the President, in his discretion, to prohibit the exportation of arms to Ethiopia or to Italy or to both of those countries. After mature consideration in the light of recent developments in the relations between Ethiopia and Italy, I have come to the conclusion that the enactment at this time of such a Joint Resolution conferring this discretionary power upon the President, would assist in the present efforts toward the maintenance of peace and, in the event of the outbreak of hostilities, would serve the best interests of this country.

I enclose a draft of a Joint Resolution. I hope that you may find it possible to expedite its favorable consideration by the Committee on Foreign Relations and its passage by the Senate.

In this connection, I invite your attention to Senate Bill No. 2998, which has already been favorably reported to the Senate by your Committee. I hope that that Bill will be enacted before the end of the present session of Congress. Unless that Bill is enacted, the effective enforcement of this Joint Resolution would be impossible. Furthermore, the enactment of that Bill would lift the veil of secrecy which now shrouds the exports of arms from the United States, and its enactment is necessary in order to enable this Government to carry out its international obligations when the Arms Traffic Convention of 1925, which was ratified on June 21, 1935, becomes effective.

Very sincerely yours,

Franklin D. Roosevelt

Enclosure: Joint Resolution

I hope you will note that as drawn this is only a temporary emergency act to cover the recess period of the Congress. The Act would expire 30 days after Congress reconvenes. FDR[2]

[PPF 745:TS]

[1] The date, signature, and postscript of this letter are in Roosevelt's hand. The letter and resolution were drafted in the State Department and were taken to the White House by Hull (*Memoirs,* I, 411).

[2] This letter was not sent because, although Pittman was willing to introduce the resolution, he would not give it his endorsement (*ibid.* and below).

[*Enclosure 2*]

Whereas it appears that there is possibility of the outbreak of armed conflict between Ethiopia and Italy; Therefore be it resolved by the

Senate and the House of Representatives of the United States of America in Congress assembled. That in case the President finds that such armed conflict is actually in progress, and shall so proclaim, it shall thereafter be unlawful to export any arms, ammunition or implements of war from any place in the United States to the country or countries designated in his proclamation or to any person, company or association acting in the interest of such country or countries until otherwise ordered by the President or by the Congress.

Section 2. Whoever, in violation of any of the provisions of Section one, shall export or attempt to export or cause to be exported, arms, ammunition or implements of war shall, on conviction, be punished by fine not exceeding $10,000, or by imprisonment of not exceeding two years, or both.

Section 3. (a) Any arms, ammunition or implements of war which have been exported or which it has been attempted to export in violation of the provisions of Section one and the property, vessels, or vehicles containing the same shall be subject to seizure and forfeiture in accordance with the provisions of Sections 1 to 8, inclusive, Title 6, Chapter 30 of the Act approved June 15, 1917, 40 *Stat.* 223-225 (Title 22, Sections 238-245, inclusive, U.S.C.)

(b) In the case of the forfeiture of any arms, ammunition, or implements of war by reason of a violation of this Act, no notice of public sale shall be required; no such arms, ammunition or implements of war shall be sold at public sale, but they shall be delivered to the Secretary of War; and the Secretary of War may order such arms, ammunition, or implements of war destroyed or may retain them for the use of the armed forces of the United States.

Section 4. This act shall terminate on the expiration of thirty days following the convening of the next regular session of the Congress.

[PPF 745:T]

Senator Key Pittman of Nevada to Stephen T. Early, Assistant Secretary to the President

[Washington] August 19, 1935

Statement by Senator Pittman to the White House regarding Neutrality Resolutions:[1] This resolution is the same resolution that was brought to me by Mr. R. Walton Moore, Assistant Secretary of State.[2]

I told him at the time that the Committee, with few exceptions, would oppose granting to the President the discretion or power to determine to which of the warring nations arms, ammunition, implements of war, etc., should be exported, and to which it should be lawful to export; in other words, the Committee is almost unanimously opposed to determining in that way the aggressor.

Mr. Moore took that resolution to the President, and he reported that no action would be required at the present time.[3]

I am perfectly willing, and of course I will gladly introduce the resolution as an administration measure. I feel it my duty, however, to the President to state that, in my opinion, the resolution will not receive the approval of the Committee on Foreign Relations, or a majority of the votes of the United States Senate.

The matter was this morning, indirectly, before the Foreign Relations Committee in connection with proposed Neutrality legislation. The Committee has, with the exception of three votes, unanimously decided that any embargo upon the exportation of arms, ammunition, war materials, etc., shall apply equally to both or all of the warring countries.

I will not make any comment when I introduce the resolution, if the President so desires, but I wish to assure him that in my opinion it will not be approved by the Foreign Relations Committee and will not be approved by the United States Senate. I think he is entitled to this information, because I believe that an adverse report by the Foreign Relations Committee and the defeat of the resolution upon the floor of the Senate would do great harm to our foreign policy.

Now, Steve, this is off the record: I have been trying to harmonize things and get away from that fool Munitions Committee.[4] I do not want the Administration put in the position that it is opposed to Neutrality, and I do not want the Committee put in that position. I have prepared a substitute bill for all of these Neutrality resolutions, and it is in the hands of the full committee.[5] I submitted to them the views of the State Department, which are exactly the same as the resolution you just read, that is, that the President be given the power to designate the country at war to which exports might be shipped; and they were unanimously opposed to it. I tell you, Steve, the President is riding for a fall if he insists on designating the aggressor in accordance with the wishes of the League of Nations. He had better have nothing than to get licked, and I assure you that is what he is facing. Once or twice before he did not listen to my advice in regard to the World Court and the St. Lawrence Treaty, which both failed. I told Mr. R. Walton Moore the other day that I would introduce the resolution on behalf of the Administration without commitment personally. And so if he wants this done, I will introduce it, if he wants to take the licking. I will introduce it on behalf of the Administration without comment, but he will be licked as sure as hell.[6]

[PPF 745:T]

[1] This statement was telephoned by Pittman and taken down by Early.
[2] Printed above.
[3] Moore saw the President on August 15 (PPF 1-0).
[4] The Special Committee on Investigation of the Munitions Industry of which Senator Nye was chairman.
[5] See Pittman to Early, Aug. 19, 1935, below, n. 2.
[6] An attached memorandum, undated, by Early, reads: "Please read before luncheon." Following Pittman's refusal to endorse the resolution, a letter to Congressman McReynolds was prepared for the President's signature. This letter, dated August 20, enclosed a copy of the resolution and urged its favorable consideration by the House Committee on Foreign Affairs, which McReynolds headed (PPF 5236). The letter was not signed and is marked "not sent" in Roosevelt's hand.

Senator Key Pittman of Nevada to Stephen T. Early, Assistant Secretary to the President

[Washington] August 19, 1935

Personal

Dear Mr. Early: I herewith enclose you a copy of my memorandum with regard to our conversation over the telephone today.[1] If this is not in accord with your memorandum, would you let me know your corrections?

I have taken these precautions because I consider this the most vitally important matter in connection with foreign relations that has happened this session.

I have said as much as I could over the telephone. I would be pleased, however, to give more details in personal conversation if you desire.[2]

Sincerely,

Key

[PPF 745:TS]

¹ Printed above.

² The day after he wrote this note Pittman introduced S.J.R. 173. This resolution was in lieu of Senate joint resolutions 99, 100, 120, and S. 2998; it provided for "the prohibition of the export of arms, ammunition, and implements of war to belligerent countries; the prohibition of the transportation of arms, ammunition, and implements of war by vessels of the United States for the use of belligerent states; for the registration and licensing of persons engaged in the business of manufacturing, exporting or importing arms, ammunition or implements of war; and restricting travel by American citizens on belligerent ships during war." The resolution was amended by the House to provide for its expiration on Aug. 31, 1935 (*Cong. Rec.* vol. 79, pp. 13795–13797, 13951–13956, 14282, 14365–14372, 14430–14434, 14753; 49 *Stat.* 1081). The resolution gave the President no discretion in applying the law; see Moore to Roosevelt, Aug. 28, 1935, below.

Cordell Hull, Secretary of State, to Roosevelt

[Washington] August 19, 1935

Memorandum for The President: I attach a part of telegram No. 500, from Kirk in Rome, which I think you will find interesting. The balance of the telegram is badly garbled and difficulty is being experienced in decoding.¹

I also enclose a copy of telegram No. 708, from Marriner in Paris, and call your attention to the marked paragraph.²

C. Hull

[PSF:Italy:TS]

¹ The telegram (printed below) is complete; probably this copy was sent later and the imperfect one discarded.

² The second paragraph.

[*Enclosure 1*] Alexander C. Kirk, Counselor of Embassy, Rome, to Cordell Hull

Rome, August 19, 1935

[*Telegram*] Strictly confidential. My 499, August 19, 11 A.M.

Mussolini received me shortly before 11:30 this morning and I left his office at noon. I presented him with a copy of the message contained in your 136, August 18, 1 P.M.,¹ and explained to him that it was a personal and confidential message sent to him by the Secretary of State at the direction of the President which the Department would not give out to the press.

Mussolini read the message carefully. He then asked me to convey to the President and the Secretary his appreciation of the expression of friendliness and of the character of the message. As to the subject matter, however, it was now too late to avoid an armed conflict. Italy, he continued, had mobilized a million men and had spent two billion lire. Two hundred thousand men had already been sent to East Africa and one hundred fifty thousand more were ready to go at any time. Two Black Shirt divisions were being sent out this week and others were to follow. In the face of this preparation and the sacrifices which it implied, any alteration in purpose now would be absolutely disastrous to Italy and would entail consequences from which she would not recover for a century. No nation, and he specifically referred to the United States, could expect that Italy could draw back now and destroy her prestige in incurring the disdain of other countries who would be ready to accuse her of having attempted to bluff or of having engaged in an undertaking which she found she was unable to carry out. Six months ago perhaps some solution might have been found but the opposition of other countries and England in particular, although it had brought the Italian people unanimously to the support of the government, had strengthened the position of the Negus so that now only a military defeat at the hands of Italy could accomplish the ends which Italy had a right to obtain.

Mussolini went on to say that for years Italy had made every effort to cooperate with the Abyssinians to the mutual advantage of both countries. Practically everything that had been done to improve the condition of the Abyssinians and advance their progress along modern lines had been due to the Italians. The treaty of 1928 was intended to declare this policy of amity and to render this collaboration effective. This Treaty, however, had remained entirely ineffective owing to the attitude of the Abyssinians and all efforts to give effect to the purposes of the Treaty were of no avail. Even prior to the construction of the (?) of the road to Assab as an outlet to the sea, for the past few days had met with the opposition of the Abyssinian Government and no progress could be made. It is true, he added, that during that time the influence of the French which during those years was unfriendly towards Italy, was a factor in negativing Italy's efforts at cooperation in Abyssinia but the main difficulty lay in Abyssinia's attitude toward Italy herself. Italy in 1896 had lost the battle of Adowa. That was forty years ago and the circumstances were such that Italy herself need not harbor a necessity for revenge. The Abyssinians, however, regarded Adowa as the triumph of their force over a powerful white nation and this spirit, which had been encouraged by the friendly attitude and support of other European nations, had created a situation in Abyssinia which absolutely precluded the possibility on the part of Italy of safeguarding or developing her legitimate interests. This situation could only be met by a display of force and could only be remedied by inflicting a defeat on the Abyssinians.

The Abyssinians, Mussolini continued, were known to have 450,000 men under arms. Their military plan was to retreat before the Italian advance and then when the Italian lines were extended to launch attacks against those lines in the form of guerilla warfare. The Abyssinians were not taking sufficiently into account the Italian air force which would eliminate the chance of success of these tactics. Mussolini expressed complete confidence in the outcome of this military set up and he intimated that he believed it would be brief. He indicated that following this phase negotiations for a final adjustment would be simple and in this connection he pointed out the success of Italian administration in Eritrea where great progress along modern lines had been made and where no opposition on the part of the natives had ever been encountered. In giving the foregoing account Mussolini took pains to emphasize general attitude so far as envisaging the matter solely from the point of view that the conflict would be confined exclusively to Italy and Abyssinia and had been alluding to the part played by other governments only insofar as they affected the relations between those two countries. If the conflict could be so limited he said no anxiety need be felt as to the consequences. He went on to say, however, that the attitude of England had brought to the fore the possibility that it might not be so confined and in that event he foresaw the gravest consequences to the peace of the world. The conversations at Paris which ended yesterday showed an attitude which gave little indication that there was an unwillingness to admit the Italian viewpoint. The proposals which had been put forward involving concessions in Abyssinia though vague were clear enough to show that they were entirely unacceptable to Italy. England, he said, might profess not to know what Italy really wanted in Abyssinia but she knew very well.

Kirk

[PSF:Italy:M]

[1] No copy has been found in the Roosevelt papers.

[*Enclosure 2*] J. Theodore Marriner, Counselor of Embassy, Paris, to Cordell Hull

Paris, August 19, 1935

[*Telegram*] Strictly confidential. I saw Leger and Eden[1] this morning and communicated orally and in the strictest confidence the nature of the message which Kirk has been instructed to deliver to Mussolini. I informed them that it was not being given to the press and they both agreed that in the present position of affairs this was the wisest means of bringing to Mussolini's attention the solidarity of the world in the interest of peace.

Both Leger and Eden expressed themselves as being extremely grateful for the prompt and effective action of the American Government in this matter and felt that even though the negotiations in Paris had broken down it was not too late for its effects to be felt in Italy.

It was Leger's opinion that with the return of Aloisi to Rome, Mussolini would gain a more accurate impression of the solidarity against him which existed here and what he would have to face in Geneva, where, in accordance with the information which the French have received from Rome, Mussolini still intends to send his representatives on September 4.

Neither Leger nor Eden felt that the failure of conversations here was necessarily the final chapter and that there was still time for Rome to alter its program.

Apparently Mussolini refused even to consider the Anglo-French offer as a basis of discussion. Eden's analysis of the Italian reply was that Mussolini would only be willing to accept through the medium of the League what he would take by force of arms if it were not granted.

Eden said that in his conversation with Laval this morning they both considered that in searching their consciences no efforts had been spared and no means neglected to find a peaceful settlement of the question. In this connection Leger told me that the only benefit that he felt had been derived from the negotiation was a much closer rapprochement and understanding between Great Britain and France. Eden leaves late this afternoon for London and Vansittart for Aix-les-Bains where he will see Baldwin. It is possible that a Cabinet meeting will be called in London for August 22.

Marriner

[PSF:Italy:M]

613

---

[1] Alexis Léger was Secretary General of the French Foreign Ministry. Anthony Eden at this time was Secretary for League of Nations Affairs in the British Cabinet; in December 1935 he was named Secretary of State for Foreign Affairs.

Roosevelt to Cordell Hull, Secretary of State

Washington, August 20, 1935

Confidential

Memorandum for the Secretary of State: In regard to Kirk's meeting with Mussolini, and the latter's remarks:[1]

It would be well in any subsequent note or message by us, either to Italy or to other Nations, to point out that it is never too late to avoid an armed conflict. The mere fact that Italy has mobilized a million men and spent two billion lire does not mean "destruction of her prestige in incurring the disdain of other countries who would be ready to accuse her of having attempted to bluff or of having engaged in an undertaking which she found she was unable to carry out." On the contrary, we could well point out that after all these preparations Italian prestige would be enhanced and not harmed if Italy could take the magnificent position that rather than resort to war, she would cancel the military preparations and submit the whole question to peaceful settlement by arbitration.

In other words, a very strong document can be based on Mussolini's statement by making an appeal to the higher and not the lower ideal.

F.D.R.

[PSF:Italy:CT]

[1] Enclosure 1, above.

Roosevelt to Claude A. Swanson, Secretary of the Navy

[Washington] August 21, 1935

Confidential

My dear Mr. Secretary: In view of the alarming situation which has arisen as a result of the Italo-Ethiopian dispute and after discussing the matter with the Secretary of State, I have become seriously concerned with regard to the well-being of our Legation in Addis Ababa and the maintenance of direct communications between it and this country.

In the event of any outbreak of hostilities it has occurred to me that Addis Ababa would be cut off from all communication with the sea, and the problem of supplying our Legation and of evacuating it if necessary, would, under present circumstances, present a serious problem.

Under these circumstances I would be glad if after the necessary consultation between the Department of State and the French Government, you would arrange to despatch a cruiser or gunboat to Djibouti immediately for the purpose of maintaining communications with our Legation in Addis Ababa. The mission of this vessel would include the maintenance of radio communications with our Legation. The other questions of supplying our Legation in the event of a breakdown of rail facilities with the coast and the evacuation of the Legation staff in the event that circumstances should render this step necessary can be discussed later.

In view of the urgency of the situation I hope that you will let me know if you can put this into effect as soon as possible.[1]

Sincerely yours,

(Sgd.) Franklin D. Roosevelt

[OF 547:CT]

[1] Drafted by Wallace Murray, chief of the Division of Near Eastern Affairs in the State Department. In his letter to Assistant Secretary of State Moore, Aug. 21, 1935, sending the draft, Murray said that communications and railway transportation out of Addis Ababa were in danger of being cut. In addition to the legation staff there were still some American missionaries and newspaper correspondents in the country; although they had been warned to leave, Murray thought there would be serious criticism of the government if it did not take measures for their safety.

Norman Hapgood to Roosevelt

Petersham, Massachusetts, August 22nd, 1935

Confidential

Dear Mr. President: A letter, in the usual succinct style, from Cape Cod, says: "F.D. is making a good fight."[1]

Heartily seconded by me.

Lately I have been thinking much of Woodrow Wilson, always of 1912, but I mean especially of the time from June, 1916, to September, 1919. He has been much laughed at for wishing to make the world safe for democracy. What one-man rule in Italy is now doing to the world supports what Wilson meant. I care more to have you win on the question of the Senate resolution than on any other, at this session. Why are Senators (and others) with virtuous emotions so often somewhat lacking in brains?[2]

Yours sincerely,

Norman Hapgood

[PPF 2278:TS]

[1] Hapgood refers to his friend Justice Brandeis.
[2] Answered Aug. 28, 1935 (*Personal Letters, 1928–1945*, I, 504). Roosevelt said that the Senate resolution had been modified and now took away little executive authority except that relating to the embargo on certain types of arms and munitions.

R. Walton Moore, Assistant Secretary of State, to Roosevelt

Washington, August 23, 1935

Dear Mr. President: This relates to a modified treaty with the German Government, favorably reported by the Senate Committee on Foreign Relations, but yet unacted on by the Senate. Several days ago Senator Pittman told me that he would have action taken, but I fear, unless you should telephone him, the matter might be overlooked.

Enclosed is a memorandum[1] showing the situation, which may be briefly summarized by stating:

(1) Under a notice given our Government by Germany, the entire existing treaty of friendship, commerce and consular rights between the two countries will become ineffective on October 14, 1935, unless meanwhile the modified treaty now on the calendar of the Senate and expected to be approved by Germany should be ratified.

(2) In the absence of any treaty whatever, we would be subjected to such disadvantages as are mentioned on pages 4 and 5 of the enclosure.[2]

Yours very sincerely,

R. Walton Moore

[OF 198:TS]

[1] Not printed.
[2] A new treaty was required because Germany wished to revoke the most-favored-nation clause of the existing treaty. The privileges the State Department wished to retain by

confirmation of the revised treaty included freedom of access to German courts by American officials to oppose arbitrary administrative actions; guarantees against discrimination against American shipping; and the right of American consular officers to communicate directly with German federal, state, and municipal officials without going through Embassy channels. The treaty was approved by the Senate August 24, became effective October 14, and was proclaimed Oct. 25, 1935 (*Cong. Rec.*, vol. 79, p. 14515; 49 *Stat.* 3258).

Roosevelt to Cordell Hull, Secretary of State

[Washington] August 26, 1935

Confidential

Memorandum for the Secretary of State: Every few days I get from Phillips, or Carr, or Welles, or Moore, letters asking my approval of the appointment of official Delegates to attend all kinds of International Congresses. Nearly all of the people so appointed serve without cost to the Government. In almost every case I approve the name suggested without even checking them, for in most cases I have never heard of them. Occasionally, however, we appoint as Delegates people who are definitely unfriendly to our Administration. These people go abroad and run down the American Government.

Do you think there is some way of your getting someone in the State Department, or a new appointee, to handle these cases in the future? I want by no means to confine these appointments to Democrats, but I do think it is only fair that we should confine them to Americans who are friendly to and not hostile to the Government which appoints them, and a check to get this information should be made in every case where we are not positive of the facts.

I "O.K." this list of Geographers, provided you will check them in accordance with the above.

F.D.R.

[*Notation*:T] Let. from the Secy. of State, 8/24, submitting list of names of those eligible for membership on Natl. Committee of Pan American Institute of Geography & History, to meet in Wash. some time in Oct.[1]

[*Notation*:T] Ink notation on first page "CH OK FDR"

[OF 1738:CT]

[1] This letter was returned to Hull.

Josephus Daniels, Ambassador to Mexico, to Roosevelt

México, August 26, 1935

Confidential

Dear Franklin: You know I have been concerned lest the attitude of some Catholics in the United States, feeling that their coreligionists were persecuted in Mexico, would seek to organize opposition to you in the next election. The fact that Borah introduced the resolution calling for investigation, and they believe the administration is not in sympathy with it, has caused severe criticism by some of the clergy in the United States and also on the part of some members of the Knights of Columbus. The recent speech of Al Smith at a meeting of the Knights of Columbus at New York, in which he condemned religious persecution, saying that it was more terrible in Mexico than in Germany, added to my apprehension.

A few days ago Frank Tannenbaum, who has spent much time here and written several books that pleased the liberals and revolutionists here, came in to see me. He said he had been so disturbed because of a fear that attempts would be made to organize the Catholics to oppose you in 1936, that he had stopped off here on his way to South America to see some of his old friends in the hope of inducing them to permit freedom of worship in every State in Mexico. He thinks reactionaries would provide funds for such organizations. He said he felt impelled to his course here because of his deep interest in the approval of the New Deal next year and because of his desire to see Mexico liberal in religion as well as in agrarian and other progressive policies.

This morning he came to see me—said he had just come from an hour's conversation with President Cárdenas and detailed what had been said. I asked him to make me a memorandum of the talk. He dictated the enclosed, which I am enclosing for your eye alone. It may assuage a delicate situation and Mr. Tannenbaum feels that it will. Of course I have spoken of this to nobody else.

Faithfully yours,

Josephus Daniels

[PSF:Mexico:TS]

[Enclosure] Memorandum of Conversation between
Mr. Frank Tannenbaum and President Lázaro Cárdenas

(Dictated to a stenographer at the Embassy, at the request of Ambassador Daniels)

I have been interested in Mexico since 1922 and have written two books about it, which have been well received by the Mexican Government and people, and have been translated into Spanish, with the result that I have a great many friends in Mexico in important positions.

I am on my way to South America for a period of six months, but felt, because of the agitation in the United States against Mexico on account of the religious issue, that I had a matter of personal conscience to perform. I have been so closely in sympathy with the Mexican Government's efforts for social reform that I felt it incumbent upon me to at least discuss the possible repercussions of their contemporary religious policy, not only upon themselves but upon the entire range of liberal opinion in the United States, and indirectly its possible effect upon the politics of the United States, and by implication the effect of such a change of American opinion on the Mexican-American relations and general continental policy. I have talked to a number of friends here about it, trying to make them see that religious persecution in Mexico tended to crystallize Catholic opinion in the United States, not merely against Mexico but against everybody in the United States who directly or indirectly was friendly to Mexico, carrying with it possibilities of serious political consequence.

This morning I had an hour's talk with President Lázaro Cárdenas, arranged by him through mutual friends. I found him a completely sincere and intelligent human being. Fortunately he had read my books about Mexico and so our conversation was completely informal and completely friendly despite the fact that I had never met him before.

I said to him in substance that it was very difficult for Mexico to maintain before American public opinion a position of liberality and progressiveness as long as it was possible to say that there were places in Mexico where it was impossible for pious and innocent persons to go to church and pray to God according to their consciences; that this single fact made it impossible for the friends of Mexico to counteract the unkindly propaganda against Mexico which has developed on account of the religious controversy; that the Catholics in the United States were in a position to make serious political use of Mexico's religious problem, and that Mexico's internal religious policy might in the long run endanger liberalism and liberal politics in the United States, which by implication would have serious consequences for Mexico itself; that I should be glad to cancel my trip to South America and return to the United States if he would permit me to take back a message to the effect that churches would be open in Mexico in all the States within six months; that I understood the difficulties politically of the situation, but that the issue had an international aspect which people in Mexico were not aware of.

In substance he replied, that for various political considerations he could make no definite commitment, but that he would take all I had said into consideration and that he would so conduct the government that these serious grievances would be mitigated to the effect that the Mexican internal religious policy will not be a cause for attack against the liberal policies of the President of the United States.

The conversation was carried on in the very friendliest terms and when I left he said that if ever I saw the President of the United States he would be happy to have me carry a personal and warm greeting of respect and consideration.

Perhaps I need not add that I have done all this on my own account without consultation with anybody and on my own resources, and that I have discussed this matter only with three other people except the President of Mexico and all those are very close to him and important people in the Government, to wit, Francisco J. Mújica, Narciso Bassols, and Emilio Portes Gil.

Mexico, D.F. August 26, 1935.

(Dictated but not revised by Mr. Tannenbaum.)

[PSF: Mexico:T]

Roosevelt to Hugh R. Wilson, Minister to Switzerland, Berne

[Washington] August 26, 1935

Dear Hugh: Many thanks for your note with the quotation from Anthony Eden.[1]

Things look even more serious than they did ten days ago. The

Congress has become tremendously excited in regard to "neutrality to all and shipments to none."

Always sincerely,

[OF 652:CT]

[1] Aug. 13, 1935 (OF 652), in which Wilson quoted from a personal letter he had received from Eden: "We are having a grim time with the Italo-Abyssinian dispute and I am off to Paris for negotiations with the French and Italians some time next week. It looks like being a most difficult business, but I should like you to know how much we appreciated President Roosevelt's recent declaration which was immensely helpful at a critical time." Eden referred to the President's statement of Aug. 1, 1935, expressing the hope that an amicable solution would be found to the dispute (*Public Papers*, IV, 315).

Roosevelt to Cordell Hull, Secretary of State

[Washington] August 27, 1935

Memorandum for the Secretary of State: Before any further commitments are made in regard to the Canadian Trade Agreement relating to cattle, please speak to me about the enclosed.[1]

FDR

[OF 66:TS:Photostat]

[1] A letter from Rep. Harry B. Coffee of Nebraska to Roosevelt, Aug. 26, 1935, protesting proposed tariff reductions on cattle and beef in the pending trade agreement with Canada. He enclosed figures to show that increasing Canadian exports of beef and cattle to the United States were in direct competition with pork. Coffee's letter was acknowledged by Hull in a letter of Sept. 5, 1935 (OF 48B).

Clark M. Eichelberger, Acting President, National Peace Conference, and Others, to Roosevelt

New York, N.Y., August 27, 1935

[*Telegram*] We believe that while the passage of neutrality legislation by the Congress just adjourned represented the wish of public opinion it in no way meant a lessening of public support for the administration foreign policies as expressed by yourself and your representatives at various times. When the National Peace Conference urged that "The neutrality policy of the United States should be revised in order that the risk of entanglement in foreign wars may be reduced and in order that the United States may not obstruct the world community in its efforts to maintain peace" it meant the second half of the sentence as sincerely as the first. Because of the general confusion as to the purpose of the neutrality legislation we believe that it would be helpful if you were to take advantage of the fact that today is the anniversary of the signing of the Kellogg Pact to make a statement at the time you sign the neutrality bill reaffirming your policy that the United States as a signatory of the Kellogg Pact cannot be indifferent to a violation of a treaty to which it is a party. That the neutrality legislation just passed has the advantage of enabling the government to fulfill its determination to refrain from any action tending to defeat such collective effort which states may make to restore peace and that the United States will continue its policy of conferring and cooperating with the League of Nations and urging respect for the Kellogg Pact to which it is a party. We wish your clear voice could call the world's attention to the fact that the outbreak of war now may let loose a train of events that will engulf all of us and destroy our civilization.

Clark M. Eichelberger, Acting President, National Peace Conference and Director, League of Nations Ass'n

Ivan Lee Holt, President, Federal Council of Churches

Michael Francis Doyle, Catholic Association for International Peace

Henry A. Atkinson, Gen. Sec'y, Church Peace Union

Carrie Chapman Catt

Louise Leonard Wright, Chairman, Department of Government and International Cooperation, Nat'l League of Women Voters

Blanche B. Goldman, Chairman, Executive Committee, National Council of Jewish Women

Frederick J. Libby, Executive Secretary, National Council for Prevention of War

Myra Smith, Secretary for International Interests, National Board, Young Women's Christian Association

Clarence E. Pickett, Secretary, American Friends Service Committee

James T. Shotwell

[*Notation*:T] Original telegram sent to State Department. 8/28/35
[OF 1561:M]

Press Conference, Executive Offices of the White House, August 28, 1935, 10:45 A.M.

[*Excerpt*] Q: Mr. President, will you comment on the report that you will sign the neutrality resolution reluctantly?

The President: Well, that is just a—well, I won't characterize it.

Q: Will you sign it today?

The President: I think so. Today or tomorrow.

Q: Will you have a statement on the bill at that time?

The President: I do not think so. As a matter of fact, on the neutrality bill I suppose the easiest way of putting it is this: that it is entirely satisfactory, except that it does not include any power over loans for financing. That did not go through. The question of embargoes as against two belligerents meets the needs of the existing situation. What more can one ask? And, by the time the situation changes, Congress will be back with us, so we are all right.[1]

[President's Press Conferences:T]

[1] Roosevelt signed S.J.R. 173 on Aug. 31, 1935; see his statement of that date, below.

R. Walton Moore, Assistant Secretary of State, to Roosevelt

Washington, August 28, 1935

Dear Mr. President: While the discussion of neutrality is fresh in mind, I have dictated the memorandum herewith enclosed, at which, some time when you are less busy, you may have the opportunity to glance. I believe that it notes many, if not all, of the points that are worth considering.

Yours very sincerely,

R. Walton Moore

[PSF:Neutrality:TS]

[*Enclosure*] Memorandum on Neutrality by
R. Walton Moore, Assistant Secretary of State

August 27, 1935

I suppose that what is meant when we talk about "neutrality," so far as we are concerned, is the importance of some policy or action that will avoid this country being involved in the difficulties and disadvantages of a war to which it is not a party, and that very statement suggests the complexity of the problem.

It is of course clear that the principles of international law now in effect, as illustrated by what occurred during the World War, do not serve to accomplish that purpose, and it seems almost as clear that the present situation is such as to discourage the belief that in the near future the powerful nations can be expected to reach such an agreement as will insure a better status if wars should take place. Accordingly, it is for this country to determine its own course.

Without any legislation whatever on the subject, the position of the United States would be no or little different in the event of another great war from what it was in the last war. Munitions could be shipped to any or all belligerents without any restraint being imposed except that attached to the risk assumed by American and other vessels transporting munitions, and Americans traveling in the war area would be entitled to claim more or less protection by our Government. It is conceivable that it might be wiser to have no important legislation than to enact legislation that would produce greater ills than those that were suffered in the last war.

Recently there has been much thought of legislation. For more than a year the Department of State studied the subject, with the result that it drafted a series of proposals. In the same period, Resolutions containing proposals were introduced in both Houses of Congress.[1] Towards the end of the session of Congress that has just come to a close, the Department of State furnished its draft to the Chairman of the Committee on Foreign Relations of the Senate, and the Committee on Foreign Affairs of the House, and its representatives participated in discussions with the two committees, and a sub-committee of the Senate Committee for several weeks. As a result, the Senate Committee reported a measure in line with the Department's draft, to the extent of prohibiting the transportation to belligerents of munitions on an American vessel during the progress of the war; notifying Americans that they will travel at their own risk on belligerent vessels, and authorizing the President to forbid the entrance into our ports of the submarines of belligerents. In addition, it embodied in the measure the substance of a bill approved by the Department and the President, creating a board to license the shipment of munitions, so far as not prohibited by treaty or law, so as to bring the shipment of all munitions into publicity, which is not now the case. The measure did not follow the Department's draft in forbidding loans being negotiated in this country by a belligerent nation, and in warning a belligerent nation against making use of our flag for deceptive purposes. The most fundamental and vital departure by the Senate Committee from the Department's draft was in respect to the embargo of the shipment of munitions of war to a belligerent nation. The draft proposed that the President should be vested with discretion to apply the embargo not necessarily to all but to any of the belligerents he might designate, whereas the Senate reported a mandatory provision that would have the effect of requiring the embargo to be applied to all the belligerents, without any exception whatever. The measure as reported was adopted by the Senate. It then went to the House, where the Committee on Foreign Affairs had reported a measure retaining all of the Department's suggestions. Finally, the Senate measure was accepted by both Houses amending the Senate Resolution by limiting the mandatory embargo provision to February 29, 1936, when it will expire.

It is clear that the provisions relative to transportation of munitions on American vessels and travel by Americans on belligerent vessels, and the entrance into our ports of belligerent submarines will probably remain in effect hereafter. It is also pretty certain that at the next session of Congress the matter of preventing the negotiation of loans by belligerents in this country will be considered, and in that connection that the matter of credits for trade purposes to belligerents or their nationals will be considered, and that still more important will be the consideration of the crucial question as to whether the embargo of munitions shall be made mandatory or permissive. It is not believed that the loan question will stir any controversy, since it is not a very practical question, in view of the fact that the flotation of loans by other nations, whether in war or in peace, is now to a large extent prohibited by the Johnson Act. But there will be a great deal of controversy as to the expediency of suspending trade between this country and belligerent countries by penalizing credits. The unwisdom of such a step may be illustrated by assuming that Great Britain engages in a war in the Pacific, and that there would be no good reason to prevent a continuance of trade between this country and England across the Atlantic. The unwisdom of the mandatory embargo proposition is illustrated by assuming that a war may occur between two nations, one of which is really fighting our battle and entitled to our assistance, or by assuming that a foreign naval power might make war on a Latin American nation without infringing the Monroe Doctrine, and that the nation attacked would have no means of securing material of war except by overland transportation from the United States, or by assuming that there might be war between Japan and China, and that we would wish to furnish munitions and airplanes to China because of our interest in the protection of the Philippines. It has been and will again be pointed out that no other nation has yet placed itself under a mandate to prevent the exportations of munitions of war, and that it would be highly undesirable for our Government to announce to the world in advance of all that may possibly occur hereafter that we are under such a mandate. It will be urged that this is certainly not a time, when the future is so unpredictable, to tie our hands in advance instead of leaving a discretion to the President, who is primarily responsible for our international affairs.

Beyond the question just mentioned, it would seem, in view of some of the resolutions that have been offered in the Senate, that the effort will be made to prevent Americans, during the progress of a war, from shipping other things than munitions of war, and even from shipping anything that either or any belligerent may elect to nominate contraband. It would seem unthinkable that should two countries engage in war, we will accord to either one of them the right to say to this Government that it shall make no shipments to either belligerent of any of the articles that are commonly exported, whether industrial or agricultural, and in that way subject ourselves absolutely to the will of another nation, whether powerful or insignificant. It may be noted that a resolution introduced in the Senate, and that may be pressed at the next session, goes beyond warning Americans not to travel on belligerent vessels, and warns them not to travel in war zones, although notwithstanding a war zone, which was definable in old days when war vessels were sailing ships, has now become indefinable when warships are of an entirely different character, and bombing planes are in use.

It may be conceded that there can be no objection to disabling American vessels from carrying munitions of war to belligerents and withdrawing the protection of our Government from Americans who choose to travel on belligerent vessels, and preventing belligerent submarines from entering our ports, and it may also be conceded that in preference to maintaining the present policy of allowing shipments of munitions without restraint, the President should be vested with discretion relative to that matter, but it cannot be conceded that mandatory embargo legislation would be desirable, or that ordinary trade should be suspended.

Personally, I doubt whether any legislation in addition to that already enacted, would be effective in safeguarding our neutral rights, and I am driven to the conclusion that nothing would be so effective in that direction as making our navy sufficiently strong to prevent other nations from disregarding those rights. Our geographical location is such that we do not need a large army, but considering the extent of our coast and the magnitude of our trade, it is pretty obvious that our outstanding need is a bigger and better navy. President Wilson, in discussing this matter in an address at St. Louis, Missouri, on February 3, 1916, stated, in speaking of the American Navy:

> But no matter how skilled and capable the officers or devoted the men, they must have ships enough, and we are going to give them ships enough. We have been doing it slowly and leisurely and good-naturedly, as we are accustomed to do everything in times of peace, but now we must get down to business and do it systematically. We must lay down a program and then steadfastly carry it out and complete it. There are no novelties about the programme. All the lines of it are the lines already established, only drawn out to their legitimate conclusion, and drawn out so that they will be completed within a calculable length of time. Do you realize the task of the Navy? Have you ever let your imagination dwell upon the enormous stretch of coast from the Canal to Alaska,—from the Canal to the northern corner of Maine? There is no other navy in the world that has to cover so great an area of defense as the American Navy, and it ought, in my judgment, to be incomparably the most adequate navy in the world.

In conclusion, with reference to legislation pertaining to an embargo on the shipment of arms, it may be said that the argument of those who oppose permissive legislation is that it would afford the President an opportunity to embroil this country in war by applying the embargo to one belligerent and not to its adversary. The answer to this is that discretion vested in the President would give him really no more power then he now has to involve us in war. That power exists because as Commander-in-Chief of the army and navy he can attack and invade some other country and in conducting our foreign relations, he can place our country in such an attitude toward some other country as to make war inevitable. Furthermore, under a very old statute he has authority to not only use the army and navy but call on the militia of the states for the suppression of whatever he regards as an invasion.[2]

[PSF:Neutrality:T]

[1] See Phillips to Roosevelt, July 16, 1935, above.
[2] See Hull to Roosevelt, Aug. 29, 1935, below.

Roosevelt to Senator Josiah W. Bailey of North Carolina

[Washington] August 29, 1935

Dear Josiah: That is a much appreciated letter of yours.[1] I think you are right about the prospective advancement and also that we should capitalize on it. As a matter of fact, the country is coming to realize this also and with the realization there will be less and less attention paid to the silly cries of destruction, radicalism, unconstitutionality, etc.

Frankly, I am much more worried about the world situation than about the domestic. I hope that there will be no explosion before I take my trip on the boat.[2]

In any event, as soon as I get back I do hope you will run up here some day and give me the opportunity to have a good talk with you.

Faithfully yours,

[PPF 2518:CT]

[1] Bailey's letter of August 26 (PPF 2518) was devoted to the evidences of domestic recovery and the coming elections.
[2] Roosevelt's Pacific cruise, October 2–23, 1935.

Cordell Hull, Secretary of State, to Roosevelt

Washington, August 29, 1935

My dear Mr. President: I desire to lay before you a matter requiring an immediate decision in connection with the proposed trade agreement with the Netherlands.

We are seeking to obtain from the Netherlands assurances of nondiscriminatory treatment of American commerce. This involves giving reciprocal assurances to the Netherlands. We are unable to give such assurances with respect to coal because the Revenue Act of 1932 [Section 601 (c) (5)][1] imposes a tax of 10 cents per 100 pounds on coal from countries which export more coal to the United States than they import from it. In order to avoid conflict between the coal tax provisions and our international obligations, the Act provides [Section 601 (a)] that the tax shall be imposed in the above-mentioned circumstances "unless treaty provisions of the United States otherwise provide." This clause probably cannot be held to apply to international obligations in the form of executive agreements such as we are now negotiating with the Netherlands.

Since this problem has arisen previously in connection with the extension of most-favored-nation treatment by executive agreement, we have from time to time given consideration to the advisability of seeking such slight legislative modification of the "saving clause" as would assure its application to executive agreements as well as to treaties. Such modification would enable us to remove the discrimination against the Netherlands by means of the trade agreement. Coal from the majority of coal-exporting countries is already exempt from the tax.

The Netherland negotiators place great importance on having some express commitment that we will recommend appropriate legislation. It is proposed that the following provision be incorporated in the trade agreement:

It is understood that the provisions of this Article [reciprocal most-favored-nation provisions], insofar as they would otherwise relate to duties, fees, charges, or exactions on coal, coke manufactured therefrom, or to coal or coke briquets, shall not apply so long as the law of the United States of America otherwise provides. *It is agreed on the part of the United States that legislation to permit the complete operation of the provisions of this Article with respect to the above-mentioned products will be recommended to the Congress at its next session.* If such law does not permit the complete operation of the provisions of this Article with respect to the above-mentioned products within seven months from the date on which this Agreement enters into force, the Netherland Government shall be free within thirty days after the expiration of the above-mentioned period of seven months to terminate this Agreement in its entirety on thirty days' written notice.

I should appreciate being informed whether the inclusion of the underlined portion of the foregoing provision in the proposed trade agreement meets with your approval.[2]

Faithfully yours,

Cordell Hull

[OF 246:TS]

[1] Brackets and underscoring (shown by italics) are as in the original.
[2] Answered Aug. 31, 1935, below.

Cordell Hull, Secretary of State, to Roosevelt

Washington, August 29, 1935

My dear Mr. President: I am in receipt of Mr. McIntyre's letter of August 24, 1935,[1] requesting me to inform you whether or not I have any objection to

S.J. Res. 173, Joint Resolution providing for the prohibition of the export of arms, ammunition, and implements of war to belligerent countries; the prohibition of the transportation of arms, ammunition, and implements of war by vessels of the United States for the use of belligerent states; for the registration and licensing of persons engaged in the business of manufacturing, exporting, or importing arms, ammunition, or implements of war; and restricting travel by American citizens on belligerent ships during war.

This Joint Resolution was based in part upon tentative suggestions for legislation to modify our neutrality policy which were furnished by the Department to the Senate Committee on Foreign Relations at the request of its Chairman, and in part upon S. 2998—A Bill To control the trade in arms, ammunition, and implements of war—which was drafted by Mr. Green[2] of the Department and has since had the active support of the Department. In combining and redrafting these tentative suggestions and this Bill, the Committee on Foreign Relations modified them in several essential respects. The most important of these modifications are embodied in Sections 1 and 2 of the Joint Resolution.

Section 1 would require the President "upon the outbreak or during the progress of war between or among two or more foreign states" to "proclaim such fact." Thereafter it would be unlawful to export such arms as the President might designate to any of the belligerent states. This provision is, in my opinion, an invasion of the constitutional and traditional power of the Executive to conduct the foreign relations of the United States. It is an attempt to impose upon the Executive by legislative act a fixed and inflexible line of conduct which it must follow, thereby depriving it of a large measure of its discretion in negotiating with foreign powers in circumstances when Executive discretion and flexibility of policy might be essential to the interests of the United States. Furthermore this provision would tend to deprive this Government of a great measure of its influence in promoting and preserving peace. The question of our attitude toward collective action against an aggressor is only one of the many aspects of a much larger question.

Section 2 contains provisions, selected apparently somewhat at random and without due consideration of the importance of the parts which are omitted, drawn from S. 2998, a Bill which in its original form was a carefully considered and well coordinated unit.

Both Sections 1 and 2 contain obscure provisions which it will be difficult to interpret, provisions which are so worded as to make their enforcement unnecessarily complicated and difficult, and provisions of very doubtful constitutionality.

In spite of my very strong and, I believe, well founded objections to this Joint Resolution, I do not feel that I can properly in all the circumstances recommend that you withhold your approval.[3]

Section 1 terminates on February 29, 1936. Section 2 is so manifestly inadequate that it will have to be later amended. I hope that satisfactory legislation to replace these two sections can be enacted at the next session of Congress. I shall at the appropriate time venture to submit, for your consideration, the text of a message on this subject which you may wish to address to the Congress.

If you intend to make a statement to the press in regard to this Joint Resolution you may wish to make some such statement as the following:

I have given my approval to S. J. Res. 173—the neutrality legislation which passed Congress last week.

I have approved this Joint Resolution because it was intended as an expression of the fixed desire of the Government and the people of the United States to avoid any action which might involve us in war. This Joint Resolution may in some degree serve to that end. Section 1 terminates on February 29, 1936. There will be time before that date for Congress to give further and fuller consideration to the subjects dealt with in this Joint Resolution. I hope that Section 1 may be replaced by permanent legislation which will provide for greater flexibility of action in the many unforeseeable situations with which we may be confronted. It is the policy of this Government to avoid being drawn into wars between other nations, but it is equally our policy to exert the influence of this country in cooperation with other governments to maintain and promote peace. It is conceivable that situations may arise in which inflexible provisions of law might have exactly the opposite effect from that which was intended. I hope also that Section 2 may be redrafted along the lines of the Bill to control the trade in arms, ammunition and implements of war, which was favorably reported by the appropriate Committees of both Houses but which failed of enactment. Moreover, when this subject is again considered by Congress, it may well be found that the Joint Resolution may be expanded so as to include provisions dealing with important aspects of our neutrality policy which have not been dealt with in this temporary measure.[4]

If for any reason, you should not deem it advisable to make such a statement, would you or not suggest my giving a similar statement to the press?

The engrossed bill is returned herewith.

Faithfully yours,

Cordell Hull

[*Notation*:A] Approved 8/31/35
[OF 1561:TS]

[1] No copy is present.
[2] Joseph C. Green of the Division of Western European Affairs of the State Department.
[3] Underscored in the original.
[4] See statement issued, below.

Statement by Roosevelt on Approving Senate Joint Resolution 173

[Washington] August 31, 1935

I have given my approval to S. J. Resolution 173—the neutrality legislation which passed the Congress last week.

I have approved this Joint Resolution because it was intended as an expression of the fixed desire of the Government and the people of the United States to avoid any action which might involve us in war. The purpose is wholly excellent, and this Joint Resolution will to a considerable degree serve that end.

It provides for a licensing system for the control of carrying arms, etc., by American vessels, for the control of the use of American waters by foreign submarines; for the restriction of travel by American citizens on vessels of belligerent nations and for the embargo of the export of arms, etc., to both belligerent nations.

The latter section terminates at the end of February, 1936. This Section requires further and more complete consideration between now and that date. Here again the objective is wholly good. It is the policy of this government to avoid being drawn into wars between other nations, but it is a fact that no Congress and no executive can foresee all possible future situations. History is filled with unforeseeable situations that call for some flexibility of action. It is conceivable that situations may arise in which the wholly inflexible provisions of Section I of this Act might have exactly the opposite effect from that which was intended. In other words, the inflexible provisions might drag us into war instead of keeping us out. The policy of the government is definitely committed to the maintenance of peace and the avoidance of any entanglements which would lead us into conflict. At the same time it is the policy of the Government by every peaceful means and without entanglement to cooperate with other similarly minded governments to promote peace.

In several aspects further careful consideration of neutrality needs is most desirable and there can well be an expansion to include provisions dealing with other important aspects of our neutrality policy which have not been dealt with in this temporary measure.[1]

[White House Press Releases:M]

[1] With this statement is a memorandum, Roosevelt to Forster, Aug. 31, 1935: "Ask the Secretary of State if he thinks this memorandum is all right, and to let me know, if possible, before two o'clock this afternoon." On this is written, in Hull's hand, "OK C Hull." The statement is also printed in *Public Papers,* IV, 345–346.

Roosevelt to Cordell Hull, Secretary of State

[Washington, August 31, 1935]

My dear Mr. Secretary: You are hereby authorized in your discretion to make public the payments made by the United States to the League of Nations from the appropriation entitled, "Emergencies Arising in the Diplomatic and Consular Service," as reimbursement of the share of the United States of the extraordinary expenses incurred by the League in connection with conferences held under its auspices and participated in by the United States.[1]

Sincerely yours,

[*Notation*:A] Aug 31/35
[OF 184:CT]

[1] Hull had written to Roosevelt Aug. 29, 1935 (OF 184), concerning a request of A. T. Volwiler, professor of history at Ohio University, that he be furnished with a statement of all contributions made by the United States to the League of Nations. Hull said that all such contributions had been in connection with conferences held under auspices of the League. Payments up to and through the fiscal year 1934 amounted to $69,128.41 of which $35,229.72 was paid from specific appropriations and $33,898.69 from the Foreign Service emergency fund of the State Department. Hull had no objection to furnishing the information wanted but needed the President's authorization. He enclosed a draft authorization, the letter here printed.

Roosevelt to Cordell Hull, Secretary of State

[Washington] August 31, 1935

Memorandum for the Secretary of State: In regard to your memorandum of August 29th,[1] referring to Coal Agreement with the Netherlands, I think we should go rather slowly on this, until you have had a chance to consult with some of the members of the new Bituminous Coal Commission, which will be appointed within the next two weeks.

F.D.R.

[OF 246:CT]

[1] Above.

Representative Fred J. Sisson of New York to Marvin H. McIntyre, Assistant Secretary to the President

Washington, D.C., Aug. 31, 1935

Dear Marvin: I inclose herewith a copy of a letter which I have written to the New York *Herald Tribune* in an attempt to correct the misleading impression conveyed in a news story regarding neutrality legislation and our conference with the President, as appearing in the *Herald Tribune* on Wednesday, August 28th. You are at liberty to use my letter in any way that you see fit.

Sincerely yours,

F. J. Sisson

[OF 1561:TS]

[*Enclosure*] Representative Fred J. Sisson of New York to the New York *Herald Tribune*

Washington, D.C., Aug. 31, 1935

To the New York *Herald Tribune:* My attention has just been called to a special news story which appeared in the *Herald Tribune* on Wednesday, August 28th, under the headlines "Roosevelt Ire Over Neutrality

Act is Revealed. Desk Thumping Challenge to House Group Presages Fight to Re-win Powers." As I left Washington on the day before the appearance of this news story, I did not happen to read this article until yesterday, otherwise, this letter would have been written to you before this.

While frequently disagreeing with the editorial policy of the *Herald Tribune* and the political views expressed in your editorial columns, I have always had respect for the accuracy characterizing your news columns. In this instance, it is apparent that the writer of this news story was misinformed as to the facts regarding the conference between President Roosevelt and the group of nine members of the House of Representatives, including myself, who talked with the President on August 21st regarding Neutrality legislation.[1] While several of the things in this news story are, in substance, correct, yet its general tenor coupled with the headlines are not only so far from the facts but also so unfair to President Roosevelt that I feel obliged to ask you to publish this letter on your editorial page in order that I may, so far as possible, correct the misleading impression conveyed by the article.

In the first place, there was no desk thumping perpetrated by anyone during this conference—either by the President or any of the nine members of Congress who took part in it. The article in one place states that, "Members of the Delegation Say That They Were Permitted To Stand As They Presented the Argument To the President—." This, it seems to me, conveys the impression that the President was discourteous to us. I wish to state, on the contrary, that we were at all times treated with complete courtesy and given the fairest and fullest consideration by the President. I feel some responsibility in this matter because it was I who secured the interview with the President. Through some misunderstanding on the part of the President's secretarial force, a previous attempt to secure an interview made by one of the other members of our delegation had been unsuccessful, through the fact that the matter did not reach the President's personal attention. However, as soon as my efforts to secure an interview did reach the President's attention, our request was promptly granted and an appointment made. When we entered the President's office we were asked to be seated just as, according to my experience and information, members of Congress are always treated in such conferences with President Roosevelt. After we had talked for some considerable length of time and had been given considerably more time than the President is usually able to devote to any one conference, some of us, feeling that the matter had been fully covered and that we had taken all the time that would be proper, arose. The President, however, and one or two other members of the delegation continued talking, and, naturally, some of us continued the conversation while standing for a short time longer. This was all that there was about "being permitted to stand."

As the conference lasted for what I should estimate was nearly an hour, naturally, I could not give a verbatim account of everything that was said, either by the President or by each and every one of the members of our delegation. It is obvious that whoever gave the information to your correspondent did it from memory and that there was no one present who could have given a verbatim report of all that was said.

The high points of the conference were, among others, that we told the President that we were in favor of the Senate Bill on neutrality which had just been reported by the Senate Foreign Relations Committee and was mainly mandatory in its nature,[2] and that we felt sure that this Bill, or some legislation containing in substance its provisions, would pass both the Senate and the House, and that a majority of all parties in the House—Democrats, Republicans, Progressives, etc.—would support it. The President, of course, did not at that time agree with us that the legislation should be mandatory but thought that considerable discretion should be left to the office of the President. This was the point upon which there was the principal difference of opinion. The President said, however, that he had not had an opportunity either to read or study the Senate Bill. As it had only just been made available, it had been, of course, impossible for him to do so. He said that he would read it and study it, and that until he had done so, he would make no commitment. None of us, so far as I know, criticized this very reasonable statement of the President. He maintained his position and we maintained ours. We parted with complete respect for each other. It was the same sort of disagreement that frequently characterizes discussions between honest, right-minded men who see things from different angles. I have always had not only complete respect but the greatest admiration for President Roosevelt as a leader, and my respect for him was increased rather than lessened by his conduct and attitude toward us during this conference. In fairness to him, it should be stated that his position on neutrality legislation is the traditional position of our State Department. While, personally, I do not agree with that position, there is a very strong argument that can be made for it. The fact that the President, together with the State Department, finally agreed with the Senate and the House on the legislation that should be passed is evidence of his reasonableness and that he does not attempt, as he has been unfairly represented by certain newspapers as doing, to coerce Congress. Every strong president has performed the function which the people selected him to perform—of acting as a leader of the American people and performing his duty to recommend, and, if necessary, to strongly recommend necessary legislation.

I am writing this letter because I feel that the news article in your news columns places President Roosevelt in a wrong light and does not give him credit for fairly considering the views of others, and as one who was present at the interview and knows the facts, it is my duty, so far as possible, to correct this impression by stating the essential facts.

In saying this, I have no criticism, either of your paper, which generally, I have admired as stating the facts, or any criticism of your special correspondent who is responsible for this article and whose special news article I have usually admired. However, as he was not present at the interview and must have secured his information from sources such that he is speaking only from hearsay, I know that, in this instance, he is inadvertently conveying an unfair and misleading impression.[3]

Very truly yours,

[OF 1561:CT]

[1] This group is identified in the White House appointments list as "Cong. Kloeb et al." Kloeb (Ohio) was sponsor of H.R. 7125, to bar the making of loans to belligerent governments. The congressmen saw Roosevelt for fifteen minutes on the morning of August 21.

[2] S.J.R. 173.

[3] Acknowledged by McIntyre Sept. 5, 1935 (OF 1561). He said he was sending Sisson's letter to the *Tribune* to Early in case he could make use of it. It is apparently to this meeting that Roosevelt referred in a letter of Sept. 17, 1935, to Edward M. House, in *Personal Letters, 1928–1945,* I, 506–507. He told House that some of the representatives and senators who were suggesting "wild-eyed measures to keep us out of war" were now declaring that House, Robert Lansing, and Walter H. Page forced Wilson into the war. Roosevelt had told them that this point of view was wholly inaccurate.